P9-BHT-451

DATE DUE

DEMCO 38-296

CONTEMPORARY MUSICIANS

Our new fax service makes it easy to advertise your products and services to a sharply defined market. Use it to fax your promotions, press releases and announcements effectively and affordably. Gale's database of over 150,000 fax numbers combined with fast and efficient fax technology is sure to boost your response rates.

 ONLINE

For your convenience, many Gale databases are available through popular online services, including DIALOG, NEXIS (Mead Data Central), Data-Star, Orbit, Questel, OCLC, I/Plus and HRIN.

 CD-ROM

A variety of Gale titles is available on CD-ROM, offering maximum flexibility and powerful search software.

 MAILING AND TELEMARKETING LISTS

If you are conducting a promotional campaign, you'll find Gale's mailing lists to be among the best and most accurate. With more than 25 lists to choose from, you can target your promotion to the specific market you want to reach. Lists are available on Cheshire or pressure-sensitive labels, diskette or magnetic tape.

Explore your options!
Gale databases offered in
a variety of formats

DISKETTE/MAGNETIC TAPE

Many Gale databases are available on diskette or magnetic tape, allowing systemwide access to your most-used information sources through existing computer systems. Data can be delivered on a variety of mediums (DOS formatted diskette, 9-track tape, 8mm data tape) and in industry-standard formats (comma-delimited, tagged, fixed-field). Retrieval software is also available with many of Gale's databases that allows you to search, display, print and download the data.

The information in this Gale
publication is also available in some
or all of the formats described here.
Your Customer Service Representative
will be happy to fill you in.

For information, call

GALE

 **Gale Research Inc.**
1-800-877-GALE

ISSN 1044-2197

R

CONTEMPORARY MUSICIANS

PROFILES OF THE PEOPLE IN MUSIC

JULIA M. RUBINER,
Editor

VOLUME 11
Includes Cumulative Indexes

 **Gale Research Inc.** · *DETROIT* · *WASHINGTON, D.C.* · *LONDON*

Riverside Community College
Library
4800 Magnolia Avenue
Riverside, California 92506

JUN   '94

Ref
ML
197
C741
V. 11

STAFF

Julia M. Rubiner, *Editor*

Nicolet V. Elert, L. Mpho Mabunda, Mary K. Ruby, *Associate Editors*

Marilyn Allen, *Editorial Associate*

Robin Armstrong, Barbara Carlisle Bigelow, Suzanne M. Bourgoin, John Cohassey, Tim Connor, Ed Decker, Robert Dupuis, Mary Scott Dye, Ben Edmonds, Stewart Francke, Simon Glickman, Joan Goldsworthy, Joyce Harrison, Lloyd Hemingway, Kevin Hillstrom, Mary P. LaBlanc, Michael L. LaBlanc, Ondine E. Le Blanc, James M. Manheim, Jonathan Martin, Greg Mazurkiewicz, Diane Moroff, John Morrow, Nicholas S. Patti, Joseph M. Reiner, Joanna Rubiner, Pamela Shelton, Sonya Shelton, Iva Sipal, Jeffrey Taylor, David Waldstein, Elizabeth Wenning, Gillian Wolf, Megan Rubiner Zinn, *Contributing Editors*

Peter M. Gareffa, *Senior Editor, Contemporary Biographies*

Jeanne Gough, *Permissions Manager*
Margaret A. Chamberlain, *Permissions Supervisor (Pictures)*
Pamela A. Hayes, Arlene M. Johnson, Keith Reed, *Permissions Associates*
Susan Brohman, Barbara A. Wallace, *Permissions Assistants*

Mary Beth Trimper, *Production Director*

Cynthia Baldwin, *Art Director*
Barbara J. Yarrow, *Graphic Services Supervisor*
C. J. Jonik, *Desktop Publisher*

Cover illustration by John Kleber

While every effort has been made to ensure the reliability of the information presented in this publication, Gale Research Inc. does not guarantee the accuracy of the data contained herein. Gale accepts no payment for listing; and inclusion in the publication of any organization, agency, institution, publication, service, or individual does not imply endorsement of the editors or publisher. Errors brought to the attention of the publisher and verified to the satisfaction of the publisher will be corrected in future editions.

∞™ This book is printed on acid-free paper that meets the minimum requirements of American National Standard for Information Sciences— Permanence Paper for Printed Library Materials, ANSI Z39.48-1984.

♻ This book is printed on recycled paper that meets Environmental Protection Agency Standards.

This publication is a creative work fully protected by all applicable copyright laws, as well as by misappropriation, trade secret, unfair competition, and other applicable laws. The authors and editors of this work have added value to the underlying factual material herein through one or more of the following: unique and original selection, coordination, expression, arrangement, and classification of the information.

All rights to this publication will be vigorously defended.

Copyright © 1994 by Gale Research Inc.
835 Penobscot Bldg.
Detroit, MI 48226-4094

All rights reserved including the right of reproduction in whole or in part in any form.

Printed in the United States of America
Published simultaneously in the United Kingdom by
Gale Research International Limited (An affiliated company of Gale Research Inc.)

No part of this book may be reproduced in any form without permission in writing from the publisher, except by a reviewer who wishes to quote brief passages or entries in connection with a review written for inclusion in a magazine or newspaper.

ISBN 0-8103-8552-X
ISSN 1044-2197

10 9 8 7 6 5 4 3 2 1

The trademark **ITP** is used under license.

Contents

Introduction

Fills the Information Gap on Today's Musicians

Contemporary Musicians profiles the colorful personalities in the music industry who create or influence the music we hear today. Prior to *Contemporary Musicians,* no quality reference series provided comprehensive information on such a wide range of artists despite keen and ongoing public interest. To find biographical and critical coverage, an information seeker had little choice but to wade through the offerings of the popular press, scan television "infotainment" programs, and search for the occasional published biography or exposé. *Contemporary Musicians* is designed to serve that information seeker, providing in one ongoing source in-depth coverage of the important names on the modern music scene in a format that is both informative and entertaining. Students, researchers, and casual browsers alike can use *Contemporary Musicians* to meet their needs for personal information about music figures; find a selected discography of a musician's recordings; and uncover an insightful essay offering biographical and critical information.

Provides Broad Coverage

Single-volume biographical sources on musicians are limited in scope, often focusing on a handful of performers from a specific musical genre or era. In contrast, *Contemporary Musicians* offers researchers and music devotees a comprehensive, informative, and entertaining alternative. *Contemporary Musicians* is published twice yearly, with each volume providing information on more than 80 musical artists and record-industry luminaries from all the genres that form the broad spectrum of contemporary music—pop, rock, jazz, blues, country, New Age, folk, rhythm and blues, gospel, bluegrass, rap, and reggae, to name a few—as well as selected classical artists who have achieved "crossover" success with the general public. *Contemporary Musicians* will also occasionally include profiles of influential nonperforming members of the music community, including producers, promoters, and record company executives. Additionally, beginning with *Contemporary Musicians 11,* each volume features new profiles of a selection of previous *Contemporary Musicians* listees who remain of interest to today's readers and who have been active enough to require completely revised entries.

Includes Popular Features

In *Contemporary Musicians* you'll find popular features that users value:

- **Easy-to-locate data sections:** Vital personal statistics, chronological career summaries, listings of major awards, and mailing addresses, when available, are prominently displayed in a clearly marked box on the second page of each entry.
- **Biographical/critical essays:** Colorful and informative essays trace each subject's personal and professional life, offer representative examples of critical response to the artist's work, and provide entertaining personal sidelights.
- **Selected discographies:** Each entry provides a comprehensive listing of the artist's major recorded works.
- **Photographs:** Most entries include portraits of the subject profiled.
- **Sources for additional information:** This invaluable feature directs the user to selected books, magazines, and newspapers where more information on listees can be obtained.

Helpful Indexes Make It Easy to Find the Information You Need

Each volume of *Contemporary Musicians* features a cumulative Musicians Index, listing names of individual performers and musical groups, and a cumulative Subject Index, which provides the user with a breakdown by primary musical instruments played and by musical genre.

Available in Electronic Formats

Diskette/Magnetic Tape. *Contemporary Musicians* is available for licensing on magnetic tape or diskette in a fielded format. Either the complete database or a custom selection of entries may be ordered. The database is available for internal data processing and nonpublishing purposes only. For more information, call (800) 877-GALE.

Online. *Contemporary Musicians* is available online through Mead Data Central's NEXIS Service in the NEXIS, PEOPLE and SPORTS Libraries in the GALBIO file.

We Welcome Your Suggestions

The editors welcome your comments and suggestions for enhancing and improving *Contemporary Musicians*. If you would like to suggest subjects for inclusion, please submit these names to the editors. Mail comments or suggestions to:

The Editor
Contemporary Musicians
Gale Research Inc.
835 Penobscot Bldg.
Detroit, MI 48226-4094
Phone: (800) 347-4253
Fax: (313) 961-6599

Photo Credits

PHOTOGRAPHS APPEARING IN *CONTEMPORARY MUSICIANS,* **VOLUME 11, WERE RECEIVED FROM THE FOLLOWING SOURCES:**

Photograph by Randee St. Nicholas, courtesy of RCA Victor/BMG Classics: p. 1; **MICHAEL OCHS ARCHIVES/Venice, CA:** pp. 4, 20, 29, 35, 80, 110, 225, 235, 249; **Courtesy of Elektra Entertainment:** p. 7; **Photograph by Danny Clinch, courtesy of Imago Recording Company:** p. 11; **UPI/Bettmann:** pp. 14, 32, 154; **Photograph by Randee St. Nicholas, courtesy of Gurley & Co., Inc./Liberty Records:** p. 17; **Photograph by Brian Blauser, courtesy of Alligator Records:** p. 23; **AP/Wide World Photos:** pp. 26, 140, 156; **Photograph by Gerry Goodstein, courtesy of Sundance Music:** p. 38; © **Mike Gould/Mimosa Records Production, Inc./ MICHAEL OCHS ARCHIVES/Venice, CA:** p. 41; **Springer/Bettmann Film Archive:** pp. 44, 77; **Photograph by E. J. Camp,** © **1992 Sony Music, courtesy of AGF Entertainment Ltd.:** p. 48; **Photograph by Daniel Hastings,** © **1993 Sony Music, courtesy of Ruffhouse Records:** p. 52; **Photograph by Kim Pieper, courtesy of Mercury Nashville:** p. 56; **The Bettmann Archive:** pp. 60, 182; **Courtesy of Arista Records:** p. 64; © **BMI/MICHAEL OCHS ARCHIVES/Venice, CA:** pp. 67, 198; **Photograph by The Douglas Brothers, courtesy of Mute/Elektra:** p. 70; **Photograph by Charles Miller,** © **1993 Sony Music, courtesy of Columbia Records:** p. 73; **Courtesy of Rap-A-Lot Records:** p. 88; **Photograph by Scott Newton, courtesy of Elektra Nonesuch:** p. 91; **Courtesy of Island Records:** p. 94; **Photograph by Roger Gordy, courtesy of Rhino Records:** p. 98; **Archive Photos/Frank Driggs Collection:** p. 102; **Archive Photos:** pp. 106, 120, 127, 213, 263; **Photograph by Mike Jones,** © **1993 Warner Bros.:** p. 113; **Courtesy of Flyte Tyme Productions:** p. 116; **Courtesy of Tom Jones Enterprises:** p. 123; **Photograph by Michael Miller,** © **1993 Sony Music, courtesy of Ruffhouse Records:** p. 131; **Photograph by Kim Stringfellow,** © **1993 Sony Music, courtesy of Epic Records:** p. 134; **Courtesy of Atlantic Records:** p. 137; **Photograph by Señor McGuire, courtesy of MCA Nashville:** p. 145; **Photograph by Dennis Hopper,** © **1993 The David Geffen Company, courtesy of Geffen Records:** p. 151; **Photograph by John Vella,** © **1993 Sony Music, courtesy of Columbia Records:** p. 158; **UPI/Bettmann Newsphotos:** p. 161; **Photograph by Kristine Larsen, courtesy of Tommy Boy Records:** p. 165; **Photograph by Frank Ockenfels,** © **1993 Sony Music, courtesy of Columbia Records:** p. 169; **Photograph by Donald Christie,** © **1993 Warner Bros., courtesy of Qwest Records:** p. 175; © **Francesco Scavullo, courtesy of Rykodisc:** p. 179; **Photograph by Al Gilbert, F.R.P.S., Toronto, Canada, courtesy of Regal Recordings Limited:** p. 188; © **PolyGram 1993, courtesy of Gee Street Records:** p. 192; **Photograph by Annamaria Di Santo, courtesy of Capitol Records:** p. 195; **Photograph by Andrew MacNaughtan,** © **1993 Interscope Records, Inc.:** p. 201; **Photograph by Dewey Nicks, courtesy of Virgin Records:** p. 205; **Photograph by Anton Corbijn, courtesy of Imago Recording Company:** p. 209; **Photograph by Danny O'Connor/Jean Lannen, courtesy of Forward Records:** p. 215; **Courtesy of Entertainment Services International:** p. 218; **Photograph by Simon Fowler,** © **1992 EMI Records Group, courtesy of Chrysalis Records:** p. 222; **Photograph by Carol Friedman, courtesy of Elektra Entertainment:** p. 228; **Photograph by Timothy White, courtesy of Reunion Records:** p. 232; **Photograph by Ken Sharp, courtesy of Pointblank/Charisma:** p. 238; **Courtesy of Great Pyramid Records:** p. 241; © **1991 Reprise Records:** p. 245; **Courtesy of Shanachie Records:** p. 252; **Photograph by Irene Young, courtesy of Charisma Records:** p. 255; **Courtesy of Abby Hoffer Enterprises:** p. 266; **Photograph by Lorenzo Agius,** © **1993 EMI Records Group, courtesy of Ensign/Chrysalis:** p. 259; **Photograph by Thi Linh Le, courtesy of Gramavision:** p. 270; **Photograph by Randee St. Nicholas, courtesy of Curb/MCA:** p. 274; **Courtesy of Big Life/Mercury:** p. 277; **Photograph by Lynn Goldsmith, courtesy of Private Music:** p. 281.

CONTEMPORARY MUSICIANS

Peter Allen

Stage performer, songwriter

As a songwriter and stage entertainer, Peter Allen sang, danced, wrote, kicked, and leapt his way into the hearts of audiences around the world. A performer in the tradition of Judy Garland and Bette Midler, Peter Allen began singing in his native Australia. Eventually, he toured Southeast Asia, was booked in London, and made it to America, where he starred in sell-out shows at Radio City Music Hall, Carnegie Hall, and on Broadway. As a songwriter, Allen wrote a number of hits for both himself and other singers and received an Academy Award for his work on "Arthur's Theme (The Best That You Can Do)," the title theme for the 1981 hit film *Arthur.* Toward the end of his life, Allen performed continually in New York, Los Angeles, and Sydney, Australia. And while he maintained residences on both coasts of the U.S., his heart remained Down Under; in an interview with Yale Alexander of the *New York Native,* he confided with characteristic warmth, "I do still consider Australia home. In fact, I wrote a song for the Australian Tourist Board. When I go there I can walk down the street and people say 'G'day, Pete!'"

Born Peter Woolnough Allen in Tenterfield, Australia, on February 10, 1944, Allen began his career in the small town where he was raised, Armidale, about 350 miles north of Sydney. He first hit the stage at the age of five as the leader of a school musical-variety holiday show. During the school year, Allen spent his weekends at the local "picture theatre" devouring Hollywood musicals and winning first place in a weekly talent contest. In fact, Allen won the contest so often that the theater hired him to perform professionally on Sunday afternoons.

Picked up Piano in a Half Hour

Allen's mother encouraged his musical leanings from this early age. With his father and uncles off to World War II, Allen was raised primarily by his mother, Marion, with the help of his grandmother and three doting aunts. In their book *Peter Allen,* David Smith and Neal Peters detailed Marion Allen's initial support. She remembered recognizing her son's talent early: "Once, when he was seven years old, we went to visit some friends, and they had a piano. Peter wandered over to it and we hardly took notice of him. Half an hour later we heard a perfect rendition of 'Put Another Nickel in the Nickelodeon' (a popular song of the time). He just played it! With two hands! He knew how to sing every popular song of the day, and somehow he was able to play them by ear. When this happened I thought 'Well, I must get him to a piano.'" Piano and dance lessons

For the Record. . .

Born Peter Woolnough Allen, February 10, 1944, in Tenterfield, Australia; died of AIDS, June 18, 1992, in San Diego, CA; son of Dick and Marion Allen; married Liza Minelli (a singer and actress), 1967 (divorced, 1973).

Played piano in hotels and bars, Armidale, Australia, 1955; with Chris Bell, formed the Allen Brothers, 1958; appeared on *Australian Bandstand*, c. 1959; toured Southeast Asia, 1960-64; "discovered" by singer Judy Garland, 1964; toured Europe and U.S. as opening act for Garland, 1964; toured U.S., late 1960s; solo performer in clubs, New York City, 1970-1992; performed in one-man Broadway show *Up in One*, 1979; performed at Radio City Music Hall, Sydney Opera House, and throughout the U.S., 1980s; appeared in Broadway show *Legs Diamond*, 1988. Songwriter, 1970-92; songs included "I Go to Rio," "Quiet Please, There's a Lady Onstage," "I Honestly Love You," and "Don't Cry Out Loud"; also cowriter of "Arthur's Theme (The Best That You Can Do)," 1981.

Awards: Academy Award (with Burt Bacharach, Carole Bayer Sager, and Christopher Cross), 1981, for "Arthur's Theme (The Best That You Can Do)," from film *Arthur*.

followed, and by age 11, Allen was playing piano alongside his dance instructor at a local hotel and bar in Armidale.

The deaths of two relatives propelled Allen and his mother out of Armidale when Allen was 13; first his grandmother died, which left the boy with "a habit of wringing his hands that lasted for a couple of years," according to Marion Allen, as quoted by Smith and Peters in *Peter Allen*. Then Allen's father, who had become a violent alcoholic since returning from World War II, shot himself. Ostracized in Armidale, the adolescent Allen and his mother left town.

Relocated in Lismore, another small town in eastern Australia, Allen was swept off his feet by the rock and roll touring show of pianist-singers Little Richard and Jerry Lee Lewis. Soon Allen was traveling to beach towns and performing whenever he could; finally, he withdrew his money from the bank and hopped a bus to an audition in "Surfer's Paradise," a stretch of beach on Australia's east coast. In a loose imitation of Little Richard, Allen wore enormous white cricket shoes, which he kicked up onto his upright piano and then off his feet into the audience after each show. Through the course of his regular gigs in Surfer's Paradise, Allen met Chris Bell, who would become his partner.

"Discovered" by Judy Garland

At 14 Allen appeared with Bell on *Australian Bandstand,* one of the most popular Australian television shows of the time. The two then embarked on a three-year tour of Southeast Asia, where they were "discovered" by the famous American singer and film star Judy Garland. Allen and Bell had been playing at the Hong Kong Hilton in 1964 when Garland caught their act. Allen and Bell, by then dubbed the Allen Brothers, played with Garland in Tokyo; immediately thereafter, Garland invited the two to be her opening act at the Palladium in London and later on her U.S. tour.

While touring with Garland, Allen met the singer's daughter, budding star Liza Minelli. The two were engaged in 1964 and married in 1967. But, after touring with Bell and becoming a regular on NBC-TV's *Tonight Show*, Allen began to grow apart from both Minelli and Bell. Based in New York City, he had turned to writing introspective songs toward the end of the '60s, while Minelli was focusing on film roles in Hollywood. In March of 1970, Allen separated from Minelli, dissolved his partnership with Bell, and began a second career as a solo singer and songwriter.

During the early 1970s Allen performed his own material in small New York clubs such as the Bitter End and Reno Sweeney. He recorded two albums, *Peter Allen* and *Tenterfield Saddler,* for the short-lived Metromedia label, then switched to A&M, for which he recorded five records, then to Arista in the early 1980s, and finally to RCA by the '90s. His songs spanning the decade from the early 1970s to the early '80s were his most famous and enduring. Singer Olivia Newton-John's recording of "I Honestly Love You," written by Allen and Jeff Barry, hit the top of the charts in 1974 and stayed there for several weeks.

Solidified Stature With "Arthur's Theme"

It was during this period that Allen began his dual residency, on both coasts of the U.S., maintaining a home in Manhattan and one in Leucadia, California, near San Diego. Beginning in the 1980s Allen achieved success writing songs for films as well. He even won an Academy Award in 1981 for cowriting "Arthur's Theme (The Best That You Can Do)," the theme to the film *Arthur,* which starred Minelli and Dudley Moore.

As the '80s progressed, however, the desire to perform once again seduced Allen back onto the stage. Just before his return to Radio City Music Hall in 1982, Stephen Holden of the *New York Times* recalled Allen's first smash success there, in 1980. Holden wrote: "Mr.

Allen became a Music Hall institution almost two years ago when he made a sensational stage entrance astride a camel, then proceeded to hoof it up with the Rockettes. Not since Bette Midler's *Divine Madness* had a solo performer staged such an uninhibited extravaganza in a major New York house. And its success . . . proved that Mr. Allen had finally arrived as a big-time pop entertainer."

Broadway also beckoned the star songwriter and entertainer. Allen's 1979 one-man show, *Up in One,* mounted at Broadway's Biltmore Theatre, was very popular. During the show, which the *Village Voice* described as "more concert than theatre," Allen created an intimate atmosphere with humorous personal anecdotes. Much of this humor, the *Voice* reported, derived from his play on his admitted sexual ambiguity. He ended each performance, for instance, with a stunt that would become one of his signatures—dressed in Carmen Miranda-like drag complete with fruit-topped headdress, he "[lurched] onstage with a tacky platter of lurid tropical blossoms" and sang "I Go to Rio" to a samba rhythm. Allen's other trademark song in his later performances was a tribute to Judy Garland entitled "Quiet Please, There's a Lady Onstage."

Incorporated Sexuality Into Act

During the early 1980s the question of Allen's sexuality became a hot issue for the press as well as material for his act. He became famous for the line "I'm bi-coastal," which referred ostensibly to his U.S. residences but which also hinted at his sexuality. In their biography *Peter Allen,* Smith and Peters attested, "The double-entendre nature of saying 'bi-coastal' was a funnier, perhaps more daring way to deal with a subject that Peter felt people took all too seriously." Asked in 1991 by the *New York Native's* Yale about the practice of "outing"—revealing a previously closeted gay individual's sexuality—Allen responded, "I was 'out' on stage years before anyone else. . . . But I think 'outing' is limiting. I don't feel like I should be labeled. I don't have to decide that I only want to do things one way."

Allen received what was probably the greatest blow to his career during his second Broadway appearance, in the title role of 1988's *Legs Diamond,* which was a flop; the show lost $3 million after a very brief run. Allen explained the failure to Yale as a matter of poor timing and unlucky circumstances, remarking, "The book was dreadful. The original writer was dying of AIDS and was incapable of making any changes. They brought in [actor-writer] Harvey Fierstein to fix it. Things changed every day. I'd come to rehearsal and my brother was gone. The next day my leading lady was gone. If we

could've gone through the changes out of town, we might have had a chance." Allen deemed the show "the hardest thing I've ever done."

After *Legs* Allen continued to tour the U.S., including prominent stops in Detroit and Chicago, and returned to triumphant applause at Carnegie Hall in 1990. Than, in 1992, the public learned that Allen was suffering from Kaposi's sarcoma, a rare, disfiguring cancer that had become a hallmark of AIDS; leaving his mother and sister in Surfer's Paradise, where he had been enjoying an extended stay, he returned to the States for radiation therapy. Though they had been divorced for nearly two decades, Liza Minelli was at his side. Allen died in San Diego on June 18, 1992. His death, attributed to AIDS, left the entertainment world bereft. Allen's role as a cabaret star, particularly, had helped to define the genre as a contemporary form of theater, and his musical gifts and fun-loving attitude had made him a personal favorite among songwriters, performers, and especially, his beloved audiences.

Selected discography

Peter Allen, Metromedia, 1971.
Tenterfield Saddler, Metromedia, 1972.
The Continental American, A&M, 1974.
Taught by Experts (includes "I Go to Rio"), A&M, 1977.
It Is Time for Peter Allen (live), A&M, 1977.
I Could Have Been a Sailor, A&M, 1978.
Bi-coastal, A&M, 1980.
Legs Diamond, RCA, 1989.
Making Every Moment Count, RCA/BMG, 1990.

Also recorded, as part of the Allen Brothers, *Chris and Peter Allen's Album #1; Not the Boy Next Door,* Arista; and *Peter Allen— Captured Live at Carnegie Hall.*

Sources

Books

Smith, David, and Neal Peters, *Peter Allen: "Between the Moon and New York City,"* Delilah Communications, 1983.

Periodicals

Chicago Tribune, July 16, 1989.
New York Native, September 16, 1991.
New York Times, September 18, 1977; September 24, 1982; June 19, 1992.
People, July 6, 1992.
Village Voice, June 4, 1979.

—*Nicholas Patti*

Herb Alpert

Trumpeter, composer, producer, record company executive

Trumpeter Herb Alpert was messing around in the makeshift recording studio in his garage one day in 1962 when he happened on something interesting; he discovered that he could add a new dimension to his sound by recording a second trumpet part directly on top of the original, a process known as overdubbing. When the two parts were combined slightly out of synchronization, another effect was produced, which he called a "Spanish flair."

At 25, Alpert was already a Los Angeles music industry veteran with a track record of peaks and valleys. Among the former was a songwriting collaboration with friend Lou Adler and seminal soul singer Sam Cooke that had produced several chart entries, among them the oft-covered "Wonderful World." With Adler, Alpert had also produced and managed Jan & Dean in their pre-surf-music days, which had yielded a Top Ten hit in "Baby Talk." Having recently dissolved his partnership with Adler, Alpert was wondering what his next move should be.

The answer came to him a couple of months later in Tijuana, Mexico, during his first visit to a bullfight. Soaking up the atmosphere, he suddenly realized how to utilize that "Spanish flair." He recorded the thunderous chants of the bullfight crowd and, back in his garage studio, he added them to his "flaired" recording of a friend's instrumental composition called "Twinkle Star," which he then retitled "The Lonely Bull."

In October of 1962, Alpert and his partner Jerry Moss put up $200 to press copies of the song, which was credited to the Tijuana Brass featuring Herb Alpert. A&M Records (for Alpert & Moss), with a home address of Alpert's garage, was thus in business. And what business—by the following February, "The Lonely Bull" had muscled its way into the Top Ten and had sold close to a million copies.

Outsold the Beatles

The sound Alpert devised—an easy-to-digest blend of mariachi bounce, Dixieland charm, and the barest hint of rock rhythms—was dubbed "Ameriachi," and it caught on immediately. "The Tijuana Brass," opined *Time,* "is basically just a good old-fashioned melody band that makes no pretensions toward the new. No soul-searching Thelonious Monk stuff, no revolutionary developments—just pleasant music that is as universal in its way as Bob Hope is in his."

The clearest explanation of the appeal of the Tijuana Brass in a world then being swept by Beatlemania came from an unlikely music critic; "Best live entertain-

For the Record. . .

Born March 31, 1937, in Los Angeles, CA; married Lani Hall (a former singer), c. 1968.

Began trumpet study, c. 1944; actor, 1956-58; formed partnership with record producer Lou Adler, 1958; wrote with singer Sam Cooke, 1958; became staff producer for Dore Records, 1959; with Adler, produced and managed Jan & Dean, 1959-62; recorded as vocalist Dore Alpert for RCA, 1960; formed A&M Records with business partner Jerry Moss and released first single, "The Lonely Bull," 1962; recorded 32 albums as solo artist and with Tijuana Brass, 1963-93; co-owner and executive, A&M Records, 1962-89; founded Herb Alpert Foundation, c. 1985; co-owner and executive, Rondor Records, 1993—. *Military service:* U.S. Army.

Awards: Numerous gold and platinum records. Seven Grammy awards, including record of the year, 1965, and best non-jazz instrumental, 1965, for "A Taste of Honey"; best non-jazz instrumental, 1966, for "What Now My Love"; and best pop instrumental performance, 1979, for "Rise."

Addresses: *Office*—Rondor Music, 360 North La Cienega Blvd., Los Angeles, CA 90048.

ment I've seen in years," enthused former Postmaster General J. Edward Day to *Newsweek* after catching the Alpert group's command performance at the 1966 White House Correspondents Dinner. "I wish there were more like them and fewer of those weird and kooky groups."

Alpert reached out to this older, more traditional—and at the time largely disenfranchised—pop audience with a relentless schedule of concert dates and television appearances. It worked. The Top Ten hit "A Taste of Honey" propelled three Tijuana Brass albums onto the charts simultaneously in 1965, but Alpert topped even that the following year; in April of 1966, his fifth album, *Going Places,* resided at Number One, while the four discs previously released crowded the rest of the Top Twenty. Herb Alpert and the Tijuana Brass had five of the Top Twenty albums—and were outselling the Beatles.

But Alpert did not fare especially well during the dawn of the psychedelic era. He charted nine singles in 1966 and 1967, but none even approached the Top Ten. Then he teamed with superproducer Burt Bacharach to record a rare vocal effort called "This Guy's in Love With You." Alpert had been signed briefly to RCA

Records as a vocalist in 1960—it was there, in fact, that he'd first met Jerry Moss—but all the Tijuana Brass records had been trumpet-driven instrumentals.

Vocal "Comeback"

Something about Alpert's soft, reticent voice suited the song and struck a sympathetic chord with listeners everywhere. "This Guy" shot to Number One and became one of the biggest records of 1968. Perhaps even more remarkably, the record represented a number of firsts for three artists already at the pinnacle of the recording industry: it was the first Number One single for Alpert and his first million-selling single, and it was the first Number One for producer Bacharach, as well as the first Number One for the distinguished songwriting team of Bacharach and Hal David. According to a *Time* profile, Alpert grossed $30 million in 1968 and paid his Tijuana Brass sidemen base salaries of $100,000 each. Both were considered astronomical sums in the economic context of the day. Alpert's "comeback" had taken him to a whole new level.

A&M Records, meanwhile, had become a thriving concern. Fewer than five years after launching their business out of Alpert's garage, Alpert and Moss acquired and moved their operation onto the old Charlie Chaplin movie studio lot near the corner of Sunset and La Brea in Hollywood. Their roles would blur somewhat over the years, but Moss generally handled distribution and sales while Alpert looked after the creative side.

Initially the label was stocked with close musical relatives of the Tijuana Brass such as the Baja Marimba Band and Sergio Mendes & Brasil '66. The success of these acts in addition to Alpert's phenomenal sales enabled him and Moss to make A&M whatever kind of company they chose. They took this opportunity seriously, and A&M grew into not only the most successful independent record label of all time, but also one of the most respected.

Michael Goldberg of *Rolling Stone* called A&M "a company that became known as one of the classiest in the business . . . where music really did come first. It was a company known for its commitment to its artists." Over the years A&M developed multi-platinum careers for acts like the Carpenters, Cat Stevens, Carole King, Captain and Tennille, Peter Frampton, Quincy Jones, Bryan Adams, the Police, Amy Grant, Sting, and Janet Jackson. But the real strength of A&M was in its diversity; it welcomed and nurtured left-field talent like Joe Cocker, Procol Harum, Captain Beefheart, the Flying Burrito Brothers, the Tubes, Joe Jackson, Suzanne

Vega, John Hiatt, and the Neville Brothers, to name but a few.

Renaissance Man

Even as he presided over the mushrooming of his company, Alpert maintained a sporadic recording career of his own. In 1978 he released a highly regarded album collaboration with South African trumpeter Hugh Masakela. The following year his disco-inflected single "Rise" rose all the way to Number One, sold a million copies, and won the 1979 Grammy Award for best pop instrumental performance. In 1987 Alpert enlisted the help of hot dance producers Jimmy Jam and Terry Lewis to concoct the Top Ten hit "Diamonds," which also featured a guest vocal by Janet Jackson.

Somehow Alpert also found the time to branch out into other fields. A talented painter, he began showing his quarter century of work publicly in 1989. That same year, he introduced a fragrance for women called Listen. Since the mid-1980s he has directed the activities of the Herb Alpert Foundation, the charitable works of which benefit worthy music, education, and humanitarian projects throughout the country.

After 27 years of running their company as an independent entity, Alpert and Moss sold A&M to the PolyGram Corporation in June of 1989. By that time their little operation had grown to include recording studios, a thriving song publishing arm, the bustling Chaplin Soundstage, and a successful film and television production company. Retaining only the publishing company Rondor Music, the partners sold everything else to PolyGram for close to half a billion dollars.

In June of 1993 Alpert and Moss departed the management posts they had retained at A&M/PolyGram. By the fall of that year, Rondor Music was well on its way to spinning off a full-fledged label. Herb Alpert had come a long, long way from the garage.

Selected discography

On A&M Records

The Lonely Bull, 1962.

Herb Alpert's Tijuana Brass, Volume 2, 1964.
Whipped Cream & Other Delights (includes "A Taste Of Honey"), 1965.
Going Places, 1965.
What Now My Love, 1966.
S.R.O., 1966.
Sounds Like, 1967.
Herb Alpert's Ninth, 1967.
The Beat of the Brass (includes "This Guy's in Love With You"), 1968.
Warm, 1969.
Greatest Hits, 1970.
Solid Brass, 1972.
Coney Island, 1975.
Herb Alpert/Hugh Masakela, 1978.
Rise, 1979.
Magic Man, 1981.
Fandango, 1982.
Bullish, 1984.
Keep Your Eye on Me (includes "Diamonds"), 1987.
My Abstract Heart, 1989.
North on South St., 1991.
Midnight Sun, 1992.

Sources

Billboard, May 1, 1993.
Daily Variety, August 3, 1988; April 26, 1993; June 21, 1993.
Down Beat, September 1991; October 1992; February 1993.
Forbes, October 31, 1988.
Newsweek, April 25, 1966; August 5, 1968.
People, October 24, 1988.
Rolling Stone, May 16, 1991; August 8, 1991.
Time, November 12, 1965; July 19, 1968.

Additional information for this profile was obtained from A&M Records publicity material, 1989, 1991, and 1992.

—Ben Edmonds

Anthrax

Rock band

Cemented by their mutual interest in hardcore punk and heavy metal, comic books and skateboarding, guitarist Scott Ian, bassist Dan Lilker, singer Neil Turbin, guitarist Greg Walls, and drummer Greg D'Angelo in 1981 sparked a blaze that would set the heavy metal/thrash world on fire. Their first step beyond the musical framework of the genre combined the fast and furious pace of hardcore with the slightly more melodic sound of heavy metal. Such stylistic experimentation would later become a habit that would contribute to Anthrax's longevity.

Anthrax toured small-town clubs and rehearsed non-stop during its first two years. In that interim, guitarist Dan Spitz, whose brother David played in Black Sabbath, replaced Walls, and drummer Charlie Benante replaced D'Angelo. Benante became the band's primary songwriter, occasional guitarist, and art director. Then, in 1983, after getting managers Jon and Martha Zazula to listen to their demo, they signed with Megaforce Records and released the single "Soldiers of Metal."

For the Record. . .

Members include **Frank Bello** (born July 9, 1965; replaced **Dan Lilker,** 1984), bass; **Charlie Benante** (replaced **Greg D'Angelo,** early 1980s), drums; **John Bush** (replaced **Joey Belladonna** [born October 30, in Oswego, NY; replaced **Neil Turbin,** 1984], 1992), vocals; **Scott Ian** (born Scott Ian Rosenfeld), guitar; and **Dan Spitz** (replaced **Greg Walls,** early 1980s), guitar.

Band formed in New York, NY, 1981; signed with Megaforce Records, 1983, and released debut album, *Fistful of Metal,* 1984; signed with Island Records, and released *Spreading the Disease,* 1986; signed with Elektra Entertainment, 1992, and released *Sound of White Noise,* 1993.

Awards: *Sound of White Noise* named best metal album in *Guitar Player's* Readers Poll, 1994.

Addresses: *Record company*—Elektra Entertainment, 345 North Maple Dr., Ste. 123, Beverly Hills, CA 90210.

They continued to tour small venues, performing with fellow thrashers Metallica and Manowar.

Anthrax struggled with touring, recording, and promotion for three years before they released their first album, *Fistful of Metal,* in 1984 on Megaforce in the U.S. and Music for Nations in Europe. The album attracted a small following, who generally believed they had discovered the fastest metal music ever heard.

Benante and guitarist Ian also used those lean years to develop a concurrent splinter group, Stormtroopers of Death (SOD), an even faster hardcore outfit marked by a hearty sense of humor. SOD also released its debut, *Speak English or Die,* in 1984.

Enter Belladonna

Also that year, bass player Lilker decided to part ways with Anthrax, later going on to join thrash combo Nuclear Assault. Roadie Frank Bello took over for Lilker. And in August, while the group was in the studio working on the follow-up to *Fistful of Metal,* Ian fired singer Neil Turbin. Joey Belladonna stepped into the vocal slot, giving a new range, style, and polish to Anthrax's sound.

With the new lineup in place, Anthrax finished recording the five-song EP *Armed and Dangerous* in 1985. The mini-album included a cover of punk heroes the Sex Pistols' "God Save the Queen." The set earned Anthrax the interest of Island Records, which signed

the band and put them to work with producer Carl Canedy on their second full-length album, *Spreading the Disease.*

Reaching Number 113 on *Billboard's* pop chart, *Spreading the Disease,* spurred on by the single "Madhouse," spread Anthrax's popularity across the world the following year; in 1986 the band played their first U.K. show at London's Hammersmith Palais. They went on to tour Europe and Scandinavia with up-and-coming headbangers Metallica.

The band left their New York City dwellings behind to record their next album in Miami and the Bahamas with producer Eddie Kramer. Anthrax released *Among the Living* in May of 1987. Lyrics included topics ranging from American Indians to comic-book character Judge Dredd. The disc hit the U.S. charts at Number 62 and the U.K. charts at 18, then earned the band their first gold album. Three singles nurtured *Among the Living's* success—"I Am the Law," "Indians," and the heavy metal/rap hybrid "I'm the Man."

Hip-Hop Change-up

"I'm the Man" was a leap beyond the musical boundaries of heavy metal. Though Anthrax had enjoyed a glancing relationship with hip-hop for some time, the stylistic synthesis was a daring move. Soon the band's ascent in the rock world paralleled the revival of the comic-book heroes depicted in their lyrics.

Anthrax had finally hit the surface of worldwide visibility, but they refused to let go of their heavy metal designation in spite of the borders they continued to cross. "We're a heavy metal band, that's what we are," Ian told *Melody Maker.* "We just don't like people to think we're a heavy metal band like all those other bands. We want people to take notice of the fact that we're different."

Their identity firmly entrenched, Anthrax ventured further down the road toward mass success in 1988 with the release of another, three-song EP, *I'm the Man.* They recorded the set at a show in Dallas in 1987; it eventually went double platinum. Later in the year, the band released their next record, *State of Euphoria.* The title suggested the condition of fans as they left an Anthrax performance.

Euphoria included "Make Me Laugh," a tirade against television evangelism; a cover of the French rock band Trust's "Antisocial"; "Now It's Dark," inspired by the David Lynch film *Blue Velvet;* and "Misery Loves Company," penned in response to the Stephen King novel *Misery.*

Aside from the pantheon of popular culture, the band focused on social and political upheaval, while still managing to maintain the comic appeal they had begun to develop earlier. Ian outlined his personal agenda for social renewal to *Melody Maker,* venturing, "I think there should be a limited number of zombies in circulation, so that people could give vent to their frustrations by beating them up with bats. I think that could be socially useful."

In an effort to prevent exhaustion and their own frustrations, Anthrax took a three-month vacation from recording, touring, and each other to regain their creative energies—the first in three years. Then, just as they began their next project, a major setback hit the band: in January of 1990, Anthrax narrowly escaped injury in a serious fire at their studio. The bandmembers formed a human chain to try to save their equipment, but the conflagration ultimately caused more than $100,000 worth of damage to Anthrax's gear and destroyed the entire studio.

Regrouped After Fire

Picking up the pieces, the band moved their recording sessions to Los Angeles in late February to finish the work they'd begun on the new album. *Persistence of Time* hit the street in 1990. The Salvador Dali painting "Persistence of Memory" had inspired Charlie Benante's cover design for the album. *Persistence of Time* would be nominated for a Grammy Award in the best heavy metal performance category in 1991. In the meantime, Anthrax hit the road supporting heavy metal giants Iron Maiden on their "No Prayer on the Road" tour.

Their next step beyond the heavy metal norm was taken a year later and gained the band recognition, admiration, and a whole lot of press; Anthrax released yet another, so-called EP—despite its ten-song length— of covers and B-sides called *The Attack of The Killer B's.* The disc included covers of Kiss's "Parasite," Trust's "Sects," and Discharge's "Protest and Survive." But the most notable offering was "Bring the Noise," by rebel rappers Public Enemy. Public Enemy's Chuck D joined Anthrax in the studio and later onstage, contributing his trademark commanding vocals. *Billboard* declared the union "a stroke of brilliance," and reported, "The combination of hip-hop grooves, turntable scratching and crunching guitar riffs and rolling drums is mind blowing."

Anthrax then left Island to sign a multimillion-dollar contract with the Elektra label. Almost before the ink on the deal was dry, the band canned singer Joey Bella-donna, citing "creative differences," and a year later hired singer John Bush, formerly of the heavy metal band Armored Saint.

The Bush Administration

"It was frightening to replace a frontman," Benante told *RIP* magazine. "It was frightening to risk sitting there for a year, not being able to get anyone. It was frightening to have done it after signing this big contract with Elektra. But, that makes it all the more worth it. If we'd stayed in one place, I doubt I'd still be in this band. I doubt there'd even be a band! Then, again, we've never been afraid to try out different things, though we never seem to get credit. Like, we wore shorts and thermals in the past, and now that's accepted fashion. But when we did it, people hated us for it!"

Anthrax released *Sound of White Noise,* their first record with their new singer, in 1993. Their sound was markedly transformed by Bush's vocals and writing. "For us, it's a big deal to make a record where you don't know what you're getting," Ian said in a 1993 Elektra press biography. "These tracks are completely different from each other, yet it's all Anthrax. It shows the types of music and ideas that we're into."

The set included "Potter's Field," about abortion, "Only" and "A Thousand Points of Hate," about interpersonal relations, and "Black Lodge," inspired by another David Lynch work, the television series *Twin Peaks.* In fact, *Twin Peaks* composer Angelo Badalamenti made a guest appearance on the song. "It's just different enough to remind you that within the circumscribed parameters of thrash etiquette, Anthrax has always taken chances," *Rolling Stone* said of the album. "And, how many bands in any genre have successfully reinvented themselves a decade into their career? In that sense, *Sound of White Noise* is a powerful comeback from a group that never went away."

After more than ten grueling years of thrashing across the world, Anthrax insisted that their endurance comes from the faith of their fans. "We're following the Iron Maiden path," guitarist Spitz declared in *Screamer.* "We don't rely on radioplay or videos or album sales. We rely on touring and word-of-mouth. We play what we like to play and write what we like to write. We don't have to change for anybody. That's why the kids believe in us." Nonetheless, with a darkly compelling video of *Black Lodge,* by award-winning director Mark Pellington, dominating MTV's *Headbanger's Ball* in the fall of 1993, it seemed clear that Anthrax was poised to move well beyond their diehard core of believers.

Selected discography

Fistful of Metal, Megaforce, 1984.
Armed and Dangerous (EP; includes "God Save the Queen"), Megaforce, 1985.
Spreading the Disease (includes "Madhouse"), Island, 1986.
Among the Living (includes "I Am the Law," "Indians," and "I'm the Man"), Island, 1987.
I'm the Man (EP), Island, 1988.
State of Euphoria (includes "Make Me Laugh," "Antisocial," "Now It's Dark," and "Misery Loves Company"), Island, 1988.
Persistence of Time, Island, 1990.
Attack of the Killer B's (EP; includes "Parasite," "Sects," "Protest and Survive," and "Bring the Noise"), Island, 1991.
Sound of White Noise (includes "Potter's Field," "Only," "A Thousand Points of Hate," and "Black Lodge"), Elektra, 1993.

Sources

Books

Rees, Dafydd, and Luke Crampton, *Rock Movers & Shakers*, ABC/CLIO, 1991.

Periodicals

Billboard, May 29, 1993.
Circus, December 31, 1988.
Guitar Player, July 1993.
Hit Parader, September 1993.
Melody Maker, November 28, 1987; September 17, 1988; February 11, 1989; February 10, 1990; August 18, 1990; August 25, 1990; June 22, 1991; December 21, 1991.
Metro Times (Detroit), July 7, 1993.
Modern Drummer, June 1993.
Pulse!, July 1993; September 1993.
RIP, August 1993.
Rolling Stone, May 13, 1993; June 24, 1993.
Screamer, November 1988; April 1990; September 1990.
Spin, July 1993.

Additional information for this profile was obtained from Elektra Records press materials, 1993.

—Sonya Shelton

Basehead

Rock/rap group

Basehead tends to be classified as a rap or hip-hop act, but its mixture of rock, rap, and soul is too eclectic to pin down definitively. The group is the brainchild of singer-songwriter-guitarist Michael Ivey, whose wide-ranging musical influences seem as noteworthy as his trademark low-energy delivery and low-tech recording principles. Labeled a "pop visionary" by *USA Today,* Ivey has defied popular trends by celebrating inebriation and offering no easy answers to the political and emotional conundrums he explores. "His songs express a stoned, alienated, horny cynicism," observed Dimitri Ehrlich in *Pulse!,* "a viewpoint that is as unconventional as it is unerringly confident."

Ivey came of age in relatively comfortable surroundings; the son of medical professionals, he was raised in East Liberty, Pennsylvania, a suburb of Pittsburgh. He spent his teenage years listening to records by rockers like Led Zeppelin and Jimi Hendrix, smoking pot, and playing guitar; an avid comic book fan, he dreamed for a time of being an illustrator and did not, in general, impress those around him as one destined for greatness. He formed a band with drummer Brian Hendrix (no relation to Jimi) while the two were in high school in Pittsburgh in 1984. They played cover versions of songs by R&B/rock maverick Prince, never really finding a solid band identity.

Ivey graduated from high school—to the surprise of some who knew him—and headed off for the challenge of Howard University in Washington, D.C., one of the most respected of the nation's traditionally black institutions. "I just wanted to start getting some shit from a black perspective," Ivey told *Request.* "It was cool to be around a lot of different types of people, from burnouts to Young Republicans who were just interested in a nice cushy job, kind of like every other school around."

Recorded *Toys* on the Fly

At Howard, Ivey majored in film production. When he didn't have to catch a film class, however, he made his way to a 16-track recording studio in Maryland. There, with the assistance of Brian Hendrix and assorted others, he began recording the songs that would make up Basehead's debut album, *Play With Toys.* Still, Ivey did not have an overall vision of the music he wanted to record. "When I made it, I didn't say, 'I want to mix this with that,'" he claimed in an interview with *Spin.* "I just wanted to come up with something I liked." *Toys* mixed funky grooves with spare, psychedelic guitar, some turntable scratching and, of course, Ivey's sleepy, nearly affectless vocalizing. "It's kinda weird the way the record was made," he noted. "I didn't want it to be *that*

For the Record. . .

Group features **Michael Ivey** (born c. 1968 in East Liberty, PA; son of medical professionals; attended Howard University), vocals, guitar, bass, keyboards, and drum programs; various touring and recording members include Bill Conway, bass; Marco Delmar, guitar; Bob DeWald, bass, engineering; Bruce "Cool Aid" Gardner, drums; Clarence "Citizen Cope" Greenwood, turntables (joined group, 1992); Brian Hendrix, drums; Paul "DJ Unique" Howard, turntables (left group, 1992); and Keith Lofton, guitar.

Ivey formed band with Hendrix, Pittsburgh, PA, 1984; formed Basehead; released debut album, *Play With Toys,* Emigre Records, 1991; signed with Imago Records, 1992, and released *Not in Kansas Anymore,* 1993.

Addresses: *Record company*—Imago Recording Company, 152 West 57th St., New York, NY 10019.

laid-back. I did the whole thing myself, and it's still in the formative thing, and it was my first time in the studio, and stuff."

Basehead shopped its tape to a number of labels—including the well-known rap/hip-hop purveyor Tommy Boy—but found that most record companies considered the group's eclecticism commercially risky. Ivey settled at last on the small independent label Emigre; the label's founder-president, Rudy Vanderlans, told *Pulse!* that he was drawn to the "incredibly honest and revealing sound" of the singing on Basehead's recordings. He was also stunned by the business acumen displayed during contract negotiations by the normally reserved Ivey, who minored in business at Howard. *Play With Toys* cost about $4,000 to record—less than the amount spent by most bands on a single song—and was mastered by Ivey, who again defied conventional wisdom by insisting that as the maker of the music, he knew best how it should be mixed.

Critical Hit

Play With Toys appeared with little promotional hype in 1991. The album dismantled stereotypes and skewered holy cows from beginning to end: "Intro" commenced with Ivey and company masquerading as a country-western group called Jethro and the Graham Crackers performing a lazy rendition of James Brown's funk classic "Sex Machine." The album also featured "Not Over You," in which Ivey laments a doomed relationship and his friend attempts to console him by finding something upbeat on the radio—only to come across one heartbreak hit after another. "Ode to My Favorite Beer" is perhaps the direst drinking song of all time, and the album's title track contemplated the fate of kids with access to hard drugs and guns. But Ivey leavened his languor and moodiness with considerable humor, much of it at his own expense.

Almost immediately, critics and a circle of fans created a buzz about *Play With Toys.* "Every once in a great while, a recording comes out of thin air, without the fanfare of hype, and simply blows our socks off," raved *New Music Report* of the album, which it deemed "the find of the year." Ted Friedman of *Details* noted, "Ivey's fragile melodies and quavering vocals create a quiet sadness that's never been heard in rap before; the result is one of the bleakest expressions of African-American angst since Sly and the Family Stone's *There's a Riot Goin' On.*" Esteemed rock scribe Greil Marcus, writing for the *Village Voice,* detected something historic in Basehead's experimentalism: "This is hip-hop wiping the rules of identity off the chalkboard and loading up a new program. For me, that's the best that pop music can offer."

New Label; Assured Follow-up

In 1992 Basehead was signed by the more-major label Imago, which re-released *Play With Toys* that year. Ivey went on the road with Hendrix, guitarist Keith Lofton, bassist Bill Conway, and DJ Clarence "Citizen Cop" Greenwood, who replaced Paul "DJ Unique" Howard and quipped that he was the group's token white. Basehead toured with rap pranksters the Beastie Boys and appeared on the second stage of the traveling Lollapalooza festival. Late in 1992 they played a series of European dates with alternative rappers the Disposable Heroes of Hiphoprisy. Meanwhile, Ivey had returned to the studio, shouldering most of the work on the sophomore Basehead album himself; Hendrix played drums and the rest of the touring group made sporadic appearances.

The second record, *Not in Kansas Anymore,* featured a slightly more robust sound, an angrier and more politicized—if still stoned—singer-narrator, and tighter instrumentation. Overall, it appeared a more finished version of the approach taken on *Play With Toys.* Ivey noted in an interview with *Request* that he could've done a high-tech, ultra-produced recording but didn't "because, one, everyone would expect me to do it, and two, I did it the way I did it the first time because I wanted to. Even though I did use a small studio, I could've made it slicker-sounding and used more effects. You try not to pay attention, but of course, you're conscious that it can never be like the first album again. When that was done, nobody was watchin', and nobody thought—or at least I didn't think—it would get released the way it was. It was basically, like, 'Well, you ain't in Kansas anymore, Mike.'"

Complicated Identity

Kansas addressed racism bluntly in songs like "Brown Kisses Pt. One," "Greener Pastures," and "Brown Kisses Pt. Two," collegiate pressures and relief from them on "I Need a Joint," and the vicissitudes of romance in the quaintly titled "Do You Wanna F— (or What?)." As Eric Weisbard of *Spin* noted, "Ivey's lyrics aren't subtle at all," but the subtlety lay elsewhere. "It's his identity that's complicated." The song "Split Personality" seemed to validate this interpretation.

Dimitri Ehrlich of *Pulse!,* reviewing *Not in Kansas Anymore,* ventured, "This isn't the kind of record that will greatly expand [Ivey's] audience—there's no catchy hooks or courtesy nods to commercialism—but the record proves that the low-key charm of his debut was no quirk. He can do it again, and he has." *Spin's* Weisbard lavished greater praise on the album: "Basehead never stops unfurling in its complexity and ability to hold your undivided attention for an album at a time. It has precious few peers." *Rolling Stone,* for its part, found the record a true alternative to ubiquitous industry-approved alternative pop and, joining other astute music publications, hazarded, "*Not in Kansas Anymore* taps you, sometimes pinches you hard, asking you to question the fundamentals of musical genre, of where black people fit in besides on the R&B and rap charts."

Of his band's elusive sound, Ivey told *Pulse!* that his record confounds the trend in pop music toward "instant gratification," adding, "I like things that are a little more subtle and complex. As a listener, I like records where you have to work a little harder to get it, because it's more gratifying when you've put some effort into it." Though "effort" usually occupies a fairly low place on the list of things record companies ask of consumers, Ivey has thus far remained content to follow his idiosyncratic muse. "If I tried to find a niche I might have more commercial success," he admitted in an Imago press release. "But I'd prefer to be true to myself and have self-respect."

Selected discography

Play With Toys (includes "Intro," "Not Over You," and "Ode to My Favorite Beer"), Emigre, 1991, Imago, 1992.
Not in Kansas Anymore (includes "Brown Kisses Pt. One," "Greener Pastures," "Brown Kisses Pt. Two," "Do You Wanna F— [or What?]," and "Split Personality"), Imago, 1993.

Sources

Details, April 1992.
Interview, July 1992.
Musician, July 1992; May 1993.
New Music Report, June 28, 1991.
Option, September 1991.
Pulse!, July 1991; October 1991; April 1993; May 1993.
Request, April 1993.
Rolling Stone, May 13, 1993.
Seconds, November 1992.
Spin, April 1992; April 1993.
USA Today, July 8, 1992.
Village Voice, January 21, 1992.

Additional information for this profile was obtained from an Imago Recording Company press release, 1993.

—Simon Glickman

Art Blakey

Drummer, bandleader

Art Blakey's death in 1990 brought to a close a remarkable and multifaceted career; not only was he one of the most influential jazz drummers of his day, but he was also something of a father figure to dozens of aspiring jazz musicians. His group the Jazz Messengers, which he led for nearly 35 years, served as an incubator for talents as diverse as trumpeter Wynton Marsalis and pianist Keith Jarrett. The vast catalog of recordings he left behind documents the development of his trendsetting drumming style, and perhaps more significantly, the evolving sound of his ensemble, which, though its membership was continually in flux, always maintained Blakey's mandate to create first-rate jazz that would, as he remarked in an interview in *The Black Perspective in Music,* "wash away the dust of everyday life."

Blakey was born on October 11, 1919, in Pittsburgh, a city that has produced many other jazz notables, including pianists Earl Hines, Mary Lou Williams, and Errol Garner. As a youngster, Blakey worked in the steel mills dotting the outskirts of Pittsburgh; in the evenings he played piano at local clubs. After hearing the immensely gifted Garner play at one such venue, Blakey decided his talents would best be served on the drums. By the time he was 15 he was leading his own band and listening closely to the work of many of the great swing-era drummers, including Chick Webb, Kaiser Marshall, and Sid Catlett.

Blakey played briefly with the Fletcher Henderson Orchestra in 1939, then joined Mary Lou Williams's group at Kelly's Stable, a club in New York City. After rejoining Henderson for a year and leading his own band in Boston, Blakey was hired by singer Billy Eckstine to play in his orchestra, a group that included several bebop luminaries—trumpeters Dizzy Gillespie, Miles Davis, and Fats Navarro and saxophonists Dexter Gordon and Charlie Parker.

In 1947 Blakey participated in several recordings with pianist Thelonious Monk; the sessions produced timeless early versions of some of Monk's tunes, including "'Round Midnight," "Well, You Needn't," and "Ruby, My Dear." Monk had taken Blakey under his wing when the drummer first arrived in New York from Pittsburgh and had introduced him to the competitive club scene there. As Blakey told *Down Beat's* Zan Stewart of Monk, "He was my best friend. . . . If it hadn't been for him, I'm not so sure I would have been me. I learned so much playing with him, being with him." The many recordings the two musicians made together are, in fact, testaments to the musical and personal empathy between them.

In 1948 Blakey traveled to West Africa to pursue a long-standing interest in world religions. For a year he stud-

For the Record. . .

Born October 11, 1919, in Pittsburgh, PA; died of lung cancer, October 16, 1990, in New York City; married four times; 12 children (five adopted), including Art Blakey, Jr. (deceased).

Worked in steel mills and played piano in nightclubs; switched to drums; became full-time bandleader, c. 1934; member of Fletcher Henderson Orchestra, 1939; joined Mary Lou Williams's band, 1942; member of Henderson Orchestra, 1943-44; led band in Boston; member of Billy Eckstine's Orchestra, 1944-47; recorded with pianist Thelonious Monk, 1947; lived in West Africa, exploring African religion; performed and did radio broadcasts with saxophonist Charlie Parker, trumpeters Miles Davis and Clifford Brown, and pianist Horace Silver, early 1950s; Blakey and Silver formed Jazz Messengers with trumpeter Kenny Dorham, saxophonist Hank Mobley, and bassist Doug Watkins, 1955; leader of Jazz Messengers, 1956-90; toured world with Giants of Jazz, 1971-72.

Selected awards: *Down Beat* New Star Award, 1953; (with Jazz Messengers) Grammy Award for best jazz instrumental performance—group, 1984, for *New York Scene;* honorary doctorate, Berklee College of Music, 1987; Northsea Festival Charlie Parker Award, 1989.

ied Islamic religion and culture, eventually taking the Islamic name Abdullah Ibn Buhaina—from which comes his nickname, "Bu." Although Blakey denied that this trip influenced his music, he did adopt several African drumming techniques after his sojourn, including rapping on the side of the drum and changing drum pitch with his elbow.

After his return to the U.S., in 1949, Blakey continued his association with many of the great early bebop musicians, occasionally performing and doing radio broadcasts with Charlie Parker and Miles Davis. Then, in 1955, Blakey and pianist Horace Silver formed the first incarnation of the Jazz Messengers, with Kenny Dorham on trumpet, Hank Mobley on tenor saxophone, and Doug Watkins on bass. Blakey would lead this group, with varying personnel, for the rest of his life. The diverse Messengers groups recorded prolifically and toured widely, visiting Japan alone at least 47 times.

From 1971 to 1972 Blakey toured the world with a group called the Giants of Jazz, which included Dizzy Gillespie, Thelonious Monk, trombonist Kai Winding, saxophonist Sonny Stitt, and bassist Al McKibbon. In 1984, one of the latter-day Messengers groups recorded *New York Scene,* which won a Grammy Award. During his later years, Blakey was almost completely deaf and played drums by feeling vibrations. Nonetheless, he continued to perform until he was incapacitated by illness during the summer of 1990. Blakey died of cancer in October of that year.

As a drummer, Blakey helped elevate his instrument from the mainly accompanimental role it had occupied in the swing bands of the 1930s and '40s. He sustained such a continuous interaction with the other soloing instruments that, as Mark Gridley commented in his book *Jazz Styles,* "for him to solo was almost anticlimactic." Blakey's distinctive use of the high-hat cymbal and the press roll (a brief and tightly controlled roll on the snare drum) were two influential and instantly recognizable elements of a style notable for both its complexity and direct appeal. As Herb Nolan described it in *Down Beat,* "Blakey developed a driving, emotional style filled with so many levels of sound [that] there is the illusion of great rhythmic waves washing over and through the music. He offers strength, delicacy and soul all mixed into a style that is impossible to mistake for any other drummer."

As a bandleader and discoverer of new talent, Blakey continued a jazz tradition begun by his early employer Fletcher Henderson, who in the 1920s helped launch the careers of musicians such as saxophonist Coleman Hawkins and trumpeter Rex Stewart. The list of musicians who played in the various Jazz Messengers ensembles reads like a Who's Who of Jazz: trumpeters Freddie Hubbard and Terence Blanchard, saxophonists Branford Marsalis, Wayne Shorter, and Jackie McLean, trombonist Curtis Fuller, and pianists Bobby Timmons and Cedar Walton are just a few alumni of the group.

Blakey maintained a "revolving door" policy with the Messengers; whenever he felt a member of his group was ready to make it on his own, he would encourage him to do so. As he told *Down Beat's* Stewart, "I look for the new guys, and I just give them a place to hone their art and they grow. They do it themselves. I just give them a chance. All they need is a little guidance, a little direction, and they're gone. When they get big enough I let them go and get their own thing."

Blakey may not have believed in hoarding talent to make himself look good, but he still benefitted from his "paternal" role. He freely admitted to David H. Rosenthal of *The Black Perspective in Music,* "My imagination is much better by my being around young people." Indeed, the presence of young talent in his group not only provided jazz listeners with an ongoing series of new stars; it also continually revitalized Blakey's own playing.

Selected discography

Art Blakey Quartet: A Night in Birdland, Blue Note, 1954.
Art Blakey: Orgy in Rhythm, Blue Note, 1957.
Art Blakey and the Afro-Drum Ensemble: The African Beat, Blue Note, 1962.
Dr. Jeckyle, Evidence, 1991.
Hard Champion, Evidence, 1992.
New Year's Eve at Sweet Basil, Evidence, 1992.
Jazz Message, Impulse.

With the Jazz Messengers

At the Cafe Bohemia, Vols. 1 and 2, Blue Note, 1955.
Art Blakey and the Jazz Messengers With Thelonious Monk, Atlantic, 1957.
Midnight Session (recorded c. 1957), Savoy.
Moanin', Blue Note, 1958, reissued, LRC, 1992.
A Night in Tunisia, Blue Note, 1960.
Meet You at the Jazz Corner of the World, Vols. 1 and 2, 1960.
The Big Beat, Blue Note, 1960.
Buhaina's Delight, Blue Note, 1961, reissued, 1992.
Mosaic, Blue Note, 1961, reissued, 1987.
The Freedom Rider, Blue Note, 1961.
Witch Doctor, Blue Note, 1961.
Caravan, Riverside, 1962.
Free for All, Blue Note, 1964.
Anthenagin, Prestige, 1973.
Straight Ahead, Concord Jazz, 1981.
New York Scene, Concord Jazz, 1984.
One for All, Λ&M, 1990.
Reflections in Blue, Gowi (Netherlands), 1992.
The History of Art Blakey and the Jazz Messengers, reissued, Blue Note, 1992.

The Complete Blue Note Recordings of Art Blakey's 1960 Jazz Messengers, Mosaic, 1992.
Art Blakey and the Jazz Messengers Paris 1958, Bluebird, 1992.
In Sweden, Evidence, 1993.

Contributor to numerous albums, including *Together!—The Legendary Big Band,* Spotlite, 1945; *Thelonious Monk: Genius of Modern Music,* Blue Note, 1947-52; *Miles Davis All-Stars, Vols. 1 and 2,* Blue Note, 1953; *Horace Silver and the Jazz Messengers,* Blue Note, 1954-55; *Herbie Nichols: The Third World,* Blue Note, 1955; *Leeway,* Blue Note, 1960; *The Giants of Jazz,* Atlantic, 1971; and *All Star Bags,* Blue Note.

Sources

Books

Goldberg, Joe, *Jazz Masters of the '50s,* Da Capo, 1965.
Gridley, Mark C., *Jazz Styles: History and Analysis,* Prentice Hall, 1988.

Periodicals

Black Perspective in Music, Fall 1986.
Cadence, July 1981; September 1981.
Down Beat, March 25, 1976; November 1979; July 1985; December 1988; August 1990; January 1991; December 1992.
Jazz Journal International, December 1990.
Musician, February 1991; November 1992.

—Jeffrey Taylor

Suzy Bogguss

Singer

The youngest of her family by eight years, Suzy Bogguss didn't mind growing up a latchkey kid in the small midwestern farming community of Aledo, Illinois, explaining in *Country Sounds* that she "had a lot of freedom and there was really nothing to be afraid of." This sense of independence was later expressed in the singer's recording of "Letting Go," about a college-bound daughter and her mother adjusting to changes in their relationship, which also prefigured an even more dramatic move Bogguss made; after graduating from Illinois State University with a degree in metalsmithing, she left to make her living out west, singing on the road.

She scheduled and promoted her own gigs and soon built up a following in bars, coffeehouses, and on college campuses in Colorado, Wyoming, and Montana. Though she lived out of her van, she was quick to tell the *New Country Music Encyclopedia,* "I wasn't really a rebel. I was just adventurous. My mom always knew where I was . . . sort of." Much of that time she was on stage, strumming her Taylor guitar and delivering songs in a clear soprano that *Country Music*'s Michael Bane reported "has echoes of Linda Ronstadt, echoes of Kitty Wells, and a little touch of Billie Holiday."

In 1985, Bogguss moved to Nashville, where she quickly got jobs singing at a restaurant and on demo tapes. She soon became a headliner at the Dollywood amusement park and was discovered there by Liberty Records (then Capitol Records) and signed to a singles deal in 1986. Her first hit was a cover version of the 1953 Patsy Montana classic "I Want To Be a Cowboy's Sweetheart," which reflected her own penchant for the "western" in country western. In fact, on a trip to California to visit her grandparents when she was 12, Bogguss had met their good friend Roy Rogers, who, the singer said in the *New Country Music Encyclopedia,* "had a real profound influence on me."

In 1987 Bogguss recorded her first album, *Somewhere Between,* which featured liner notes by legendary country guitarist Chet Atkins praising her voice and garnered her the Academy of Country Music's best new female vocalist award in 1988. 1987 also marked her marriage to Doug Crider, whom she had met when she performed a song of his called "Hopeless Romantic"; he helps engineer her albums and continues to provide her with songs.

Bogguss's second album, *Moment of Truth,* was released to tepid sales in 1989. *Stereo Review*'s Alanna Nash noted that it lacked the grit of her debut. This was perhaps due to the influence of Liberty's new label head and the record's co-producer, Jimmy Bowen, and to what has been termed "tasteful production" by some, but was derided as "faux Reba McEntire Vegas

For the Record. . .

Born December 30, 1956, in Aledo, IL; married Doug Crider (a songwriter and engineer), 1987. *Education:* Degree in metalsmithing from Illinois State University.

Performed throughout the West, early 1980s; performed at Dollywood amusement park, Pigeon Forge, TN, c. 1986; signed with Liberty Records (then Capitol), 1986, and released single "I Want To Be a Cowboy's Sweetheart"; released album *Somewhere Between,* 1987; co-hosted TNN/*Music City News* Country Awards, appeared on *The Women of Country,* CBS-TV, and toured with Dwight Yoakam, all 1993. Designed jewelry for sale at concerts; marketed own line of clothing in venture with Baguda Wear.

Awards: Named best new female vocalist by Academy of Country Music, 1988; (with Lee Greenwood) Grammy Award nomination, 1991, for "Hopelessly Yours"; Country Music Association Horizon Award, 1992; gold records for *Aces* and *Voices in the Wind.*

Addresses: *Record company*—Liberty Records, 3322 West End Ave., 11th Floor, Nashville, TN 37203.

arrangements" by Bane in a review of a later album. Bogguss's own explanation for the album's poor showing was that she hadn't asserted herself enough in the recording studio. She told Sandy Lovejoy of *KNIX Country Spirit,* "Maybe I wasn't hungry."

Indeed, other profitable ventures were occupying her time—designing jewelry to sell while she was on the road and putting together deals to market her own line of clothing in partnership with California-based Baguda Wear. Or maybe Bogguss was just avoiding confrontation. She had established a reputation for being easygoing in the studio, admitting to Lovejoy, "It has always been a part of my character to try to make a lot of people happy. I mean, I was the homecoming queen!" After all, her desire to please *had* helped her in the early days when, as an unknown, she was forced to keep her varied audiences happy.

Ultimately, Bogguss's strength and self-reliance enabled her to pressure Bowen to locate first-rate material for her third album, *Aces.* She also came up "with the unusual technique of recording in a large room in the studio instead of a small booth," according to David Zimmerman in *USA Today.* Bogguss revealed of the new method, "It gives my voice a real big sound. I never felt comfortable singing in a booth, and now I sing like I'm onstage." Her redoubled efforts paid off; *Aces* went gold about the same time that Bogguss won the 1992

Horizon Award from the Country Music Association. In fact, she had been so confident that the album would do well that she booked studio time for her next project, *Voices in the Wind,* before completing *Aces.* In the meantime, she had been nominated for a 1991 Grammy Award for her duet with country stalwart Lee Greenwood, "Hopelessly Yours," which resulted from the time she had spent opening for Greenwood, Alabama, and Clint Black, before her record sales began to pick up again.

The success of *Voices in the Wind* confirmed that Bogguss had arrived; it too went gold in short order. Bogguss's video of the Nanci Griffith song "Outbound Plane" received considerable airplay and exposed the singer to a wider audience, who were captivated by her torch-like delivery and intelligent selection of songs. Bogguss continues to present the best of a variety of songwriters, concerned less with focus than depth and versatility. Songs like John Hiatt's irresistible "Drive South," from her 1993 release *Something up My Sleeve,* harkened back to the vibrancy of her earlier work.

In 1993 Bogguss appeared on *The Tonight Show* and *Live With Regis and Kathie Lee.* And she performed "Take It to the Limit" for a Walden Woods benefit album of Eagles covers and the swing tune "Old Fashioned Love" for a Bob Wills tribute album. Also in 1993—something of a breakthrough year for Bogguss—she honored her mentor, Patsy Montana, on the CBS television special *The Women of Country* and co-hosted the TNN/*Music City News* Country Awards with Ricky Van Shelton and George Jones. As if this weren't enough to keep her busy, she also mounted a sold-out national tour with Dwight Yoakam. Bogguss seemed to be relishing the exposure, telling Margie McGraw in *Country Sounds,* "When I'm 65 or 70 years old and sitting on my porch, I'm not gonna be sitting there going 'Remember when Boyd lost his bike?' I'm gonna be remembering when I was in Brazil, playing at a rodeo in front of 65,000 people."

Selected discography

Somewhere Between, Liberty, 1987.
Moment of Truth, Liberty, 1989.
Aces, Liberty, 1991.
Voices in the Wind (includes "Outbound Plane"), Liberty, 1992.
Something up My Sleeve (includes "Drive South"), Liberty, 1993.
(Contributor) "Take It to the Limit," *Common Thread: The Songs of the Eagles,* Giant, 1993.
(Contributor) "Old Fashioned Love," *Asleep at the Wheel: A Tribute to the Music of Bob Wills and the Texas Playboys,* Liberty, 1993.

Sources

Books

Richards, Tad, and Melvin B, Shestock, *The New Country Music Encyclopedia,* Simon & Schuster, 1993.

Periodicals

Billboard, June 19, 1993.
CMA Close-Up, November/December 1992.
Country Music, November/December 1992; January/February 1993; November/December 1993.
Country Sounds, March 1993.
Entertainment Weekly, September 24, 1993.

First for Women, April 5, 1993.
Hollywood Reporter, December 9, 1992.
KNIX Country Spirit, February 1993.
Music City News, November 1992.
Nashville Banner, February 2, 1993.
New York Times, December 6, 1992.
Stereo Review, March 1991.
Tennessean (Nashville) March 14, 1992.
USA Today, November 4, 1992.

Additional information for this profile was obtained from a Liberty Records press biography, 1993.

—John Morrow

Boston

Rock band

From the very beginning the success story of Boston did not follow the typical pattern for rock bands. The unprecedented sales of their first, self-titled album—which sold more copies than any previous debut album—made Boston seem like an overnight sensation, but the material on *Boston* resulted from six years of work in the basement recording studio of Toledo, Ohio-born Tom Scholz. Scholz, an MIT graduate who had been working as a product designer for Polaroid, was also, in his spare time, a songwriter, keyboardist, and producer. The driving force behind Boston, he has became known for a perfectionism that has resulted in unusually long gaps between Boston albums, a tendency that flies in the face of conventional recording industry wisdom. In spite of the elapsed time between albums, though, each Boston disc has become a platinum seller, demonstrating the enduring popularity of a sound that Jay Cocks described in *Time* as "heavy-metal music with easy-listening inflections, rock fierce enough for the FM stations, flighty enough to fit right into Top 40 AM radio."

For the Record. . .

Original members included **Brad Delp** (born June 12, 1951, in Boston, MA), guitar, vocals; **Barry Goudreau** (born November 29, 1951, in Swampscott, MA), guitar; **John "Sib" Hashian** (born August 17, 1949, in Boston), drums; **Tom Scholz** (born March 10, 1947 in Toledo, OH; B.S. and M.S in mechanical engineering, Massachusetts Institute of Technology), guitar, keyboards, production; and **Fran Sheehan** (born March 26, 1949, in Swampscott), bass.

Later members included **Doug Huffman**, drums; **Jim Masdea**, drums, keyboards; **Gary Phil**, guitar; and **C. David Sikes**, bass.

Scholz recorded demos in Boston home studio, early 1970s; band lineup solidified, 1976; signed with Epic Records and released first album, *Boston*, 1976; signed with MCA Records and released *Third Stage*, 1986.

Awards: Multiplatinum award for *Boston;* platinum awards for *Don't Look Back* and *Third Stage*.

Addresses: *Management*—SR&D Management, 1560 Trapelo Rd., Waltham, MA 02154.

Scholz's early life did not suggest rock stardom. The only member of Boston not from that city, Scholz spent his youth earning good grades, playing center on the high school basketball team, and listening to rock music. After high school, he moved to the Boston area to attend the rigorous and highly regarded Massachusetts Institute of Technology. Although he spent some of his time there playing piano in local bands, he concentrated primarily on his studies, eventually earning both a bachelor's and master's degree in mechanical engineering. He took a job with Polaroid after graduation, but his interest in playing and recording music continued to grow, leading him to answer an ad for a keyboard player that had been placed by a local band that included Barry Goudreau, who would play guitar in Boston's original lineup.

It was not long before Scholz became the leader of the band. Besides playing keyboards, he quickly became proficient on guitar, inspired by the sound of the power chords he had first heard listening to seminal rock bands Cream and Led Zeppelin. Soon he was writing songs for the band and lending their music the sound that would later become Boston's trademark. Along with Goudreau, Scholz recruited vocalist Brad Delp and together they honed the group's material, not by going the usual route of playing live gigs at local clubs, however, but by spending their nights playing in the basement recording studio that Scholz had built with his earnings from Polaroid. Much of the material for the first Boston album came from these sessions. In fact, the first version of "More Than a Feeling" was recorded on Scholz's equipment in 1971, five years before the song would become a Top Five hit.

Evidently intrigued by the sophisticated demo tapes produced on Scholz's home gear, Epic record executives nonetheless wanted to see a performance before tendering Scholz's group a recording contract. Drummer Sib Hashian and bassist Fran Sheehan joined the band at this point, 1976. After the audition, Epic signed the band and sent them to California to re-record their material. Scholz explained to Charles Young of *Rolling Stone* why Epic wanted the songs re-recorded: "They're afraid to release an album unless it has a producer they know. We finished it in California in a regular studio, but I still did most of the producing." Once the record was completed, the band was officially dubbed Boston after its home base.

Epic's caution seemed pointless once the album was released. It debuted in *Record World's* charts at Number 46, a remarkably high position for an unknown band, and it kept climbing until it became the best selling debut album ever (a distinction it maintained until the release of pop diva Whitney Houston's first album almost a decade later). *Boston* hit the Number Three position and by 1994 had sold over 11 million copies. The record spawned the smash singles "More Than a Feeling," which went to Number Five, "Long Time," and "Peace of Mind." The disc peaked at Number 11 in the U.K.

Naturally, Epic wanted more material, so the band went back to the basement, which was now even better outfitted—thanks to Boston's success. But after six years of work on the first album, Scholz was not about to rush the next one. Epic kept announcing release dates, but Scholz kept holding onto the material. Finally, in September of 1978, *Don't Look Back* was released.

The second album also topped the U.S. charts, reached Number Nine in the U.K., and the title track became a Number Four hit. In November the band played two sell-out shows at Boston Garden, its first appearance in the city that bears its name. Despite the band's continued popularity, Scholz was not satisfied with the second record as he considered it largely unfinished. He vowed not bow to record company pressure in the future and put his money where his mouth was, suing Epic to extract himself from a contract that called for five albums in ten years. In retaliation, the record company withheld the band's royalties and obtained an injunction preventing them from recording material for any other label. That did not prevent Boston from working on new songs, however, though Goudreau and Hashian had left during the early 1980s to pursue solo careers. Scholz, Delp, and drummer Jim Masdea, who had played some with the band in the early 1970s, continued to record in the basement.

In order to earn money during the prolonged legal battles, Scholz drew on his training as an engineer; already the inventor of various devices to enhance the output of the electric guitar, he set up Scholz Research & Design, Inc. The company's most successful product was the Rockman, a portable amplifier that boasted the sound of a full-sized one. Scholz received 3,000 orders for the Rockman before the first one had even been produced. With the income from his company, Scholz managed to keep Boston recording.

Although the legal dispute was not wholly resolved, the injunction against Boston was lifted in 1985, and the band signed with MCA. Featuring a lineup of Scholz, Delp, Masdea, Gary Phil on guitar, C. David Sikes on bass, and Doug Huffman on drums, the band finally released their third album, *Third Stage*, in the fall of 1986. The wait apparently had not dampened the appetite of Boston's fans. *Third Stage* topped the charts for four weeks and became the first album to achieve gold status in the then-novel compact disc format. The single "Amanda" also clobbered the charts.

Still, continued success did not turn Scholz into a stereotypical rock star. He explained to Michael A. Lerner of *Newsweek* that the title *Third Stage* referred to the phase in life that follows childhood and adulthood and revealed, "What I'm really interested in is not how all this can change my life, but how I can use the money to change things I care about."

Indeed, Scholz's life appears not to have changed much because of Boston's success. Still living in the same house that he bought while working for Polaroid, Scholz and Boston continue to record in the underground studio. Although they have not released an album since *Third Stage,* the wait has not been due to the legal difficulties that had earlier held up that album—a jury decided in Scholz's favor in 1990. Rather, Boston's long silence has resulted from Scholz's legendary perfectionism. Meanwhile, fans of the band from Beantown must satisfy themselves with their records and the enduring popularity of the group's hits on classic rock radio.

Selected discography

Boston, Epic, 1976.
Don't Look Back, Epic, 1978.
Third Stage, MCA, 1986, reissued, Mobile Fidelity, 1993.
Walk On, MCA, 1994.

Sources

Books

Rees, Dafydd, and Luke Crampton, *Rock Movers & Shakers,* ABC-CLIO, 1991.
Stambler, Irwin, *The Encyclopedia of Pop, Rock & Soul,* St. Martin's, 1989.

Periodicals

Newsweek, December 1, 1986.
Rolling Stone, December 2, 1976; June 18, 1987; August 13, 1987; October 6, 1988.
Time, September 25, 1978.

—Lloyd Hemingway

Clarence "Gatemouth" Brown

Singer, guitarist

Clarence "Gatemouth" Brown is unquestionably a master of the blues, yet he objects strenuously to being called a bluesman. "I'm a *musician*," he insisted to *Guitar Player* interviewer Jas Obrecht, "not some dirty low-down bluesman. I play American and world music, Texas-style. I play a part of the past with the present and just a taste of the future." His refusal to limit himself may be the key to Brown's ability to produce fresh sounds even after more than a half century of touring and recording. In addition to traditional blues, his music encompasses zydeco, country and Texas blues, jazz, rhythm and blues, bluegrass, and swing; and it has been named a major influence on musicians as diverse as Albert Collins, Roy Buchanan, Guitar Slim, and Frank Zappa.

Growing up in east Texas, Brown's first and most important influence was his father, a Cajun singer who accompanied himself on accordion, banjo, fiddle, and mandolin. By the age of five, "Gatemouth"—so nick-named because of his big voice—had learned to play guitar, and within a few more years he had mastered the fiddle, piano, harmonica, and drums as well. He loved his father's lively music, along with that of swing bandleader and pianist Count Basie and proto-rhythm and bluesman Louis Jordan, but, he told Obrecht, "When I was a kid, I listened to very little blues because it made me feel sick inside. It just made me feel physically sick. . . . I wouldn't listen to that stuff. I didn't like it. It made me see disastrous things facing me."

By the time he was in his late teens, however, Brown had become attracted to the sophisticated electric blues of T-Bone Walker. He had been working as the "Singing Drummer" for a group called the Brown Skin Models, but he soon adopted the guitar as his primary instrument in imitation of his idol, Walker. Brown's big break came when he was 23 years old. Don Robey, owner of the most prestigious black nightclub in Texas, invited him to Houston. T-Bone Walker was playing Robey's club, the Bronze Peacock, but a serious ulcer forced him off the stage one night in the middle of a performance. Brown stepped in and "started playing every hot blues and boogie riff he knew," reported Geoffrey Himes in *Down Beat*. "By the end of the night, the whooping audience was stuffing money into his shirt and pants."

Robey negotiated a recording contract for Brown with Aladdin Records, a Los Angeles-based company, but before long he decided to form his own label, Peacock Records, with Gatemouth as his foundation artist. He signed the young musician to a 20-year contract. Their long association was beneficial to both Robey and Brown, but it also had its negative aspects. Between 1947 and 1960, Brown recorded more than 50 sides for

For the Record. . .

Born April 18, 1924, in Vinton, LA; raised in Orange, TX; son of Clarence Brown (a railroad worker and musician) and Virginia Frank; wives included Geraldine Paris, Mary Durbin, and Yvonne Ramsey; two children.

Learned to play guitar, 1929, violin, 1934; worked on father's ranch, Orange, TX, 1930s; drummer for Brown Skin Models, early 1940s; recorded for Aladdin Records, late 1940s, Peacock Records, 1947-1964; recorded for Cue, Cinderella, Pam, Chess, and Heritage labels, mid-late 1960s, for French labels Black and Blue, Barclay, and Blue Star, 1970s, for Rounder Records, early 1980s, and for Alligator Records, 1990s; appeared at Montreux Jazz Festival, 1973, Newport Jazz Festival, 1973, New Orleans Jazz and Heritage Festival, 1974, 1976-77, and Monterey Jazz Festival; toured for U.S. Department of State in Africa, 1976. Worked as deputy sheriff, Farmington (San Juan County), New Mexico, mid-1970s. *Military service:* Served with Army Corps of Engineers, 1946.

Awards: Several Handy Blues awards; Grammy Award, 1982, for *Alright Again.*

Addresses: *Record company/management*—Alligator Records & Artist Management, Inc., Box 60234, Chicago, IL 60660.

Peacock; some, including "Dirty Work at the Cross-roads," "Okie Dokie Stomp," and "Ain't That Dandy," became national hits and remain in the musician's repertoire today. Brown appreciated the exposure Robey won for him but chafed at his employer's lack of vision. Instead of letting his star play the jazz, country, and Cajun music he loved, Robey insisted that Brown record nothing but blues. Furthermore, Robey took credit for many of Brown's compositions, listing them under his own name or the pseudonym "D. Malone."

In 1964, Brown broke his ties with Robey and went to Europe, where he recorded for several French labels and performed at many prestigious music festivals and clubs. Returning to the United States, he was finally able to secure arrangements that would allow him to define his own music. While he has remained largely unknown to mainstream America, he commands the respect of the music world, which has honored him with several Handy Blues awards and a Grammy.

Though many young players look to him for inspiration, Brown carefully guards the secrets of his technique. He told *Guitar Player's* Obrecht: "People ask, 'How do you do that?' I say, 'Magic.' When they say, 'Show me how to

do that,' I say, 'I show no one nothing.' Years ago when I was playing along with my father, I said, 'Dad, how you do this?' He said, 'I'm not going to show you anything.' I said, 'How shall I learn?' He said, 'Pay attention.' It's as simple as that." He is more forthcoming, however, in urging musicians to rediscover dynamics. "Everything is so high volume," he complained to Obrecht. "Why play something so loud where it's going to tear you up inside? I've seen guys that was so loud, my stomach was hurting!"

Brown is unabashed in dispensing general advice to young musicians, counseling them to live a humble, clean, and affirmative life. He speaks out strongly against all drugs except marijuana, which, he told Obrecht, "don't really harm no one. Manmade chemicals—that's what's killing them. Alcohol is killing us. Whiskey is the most deadly drug on earth; it killed my third brother [James "Widemouth" Brown, who died in 1971]. . . . Alcohol is one of the most *devastating* drugs there is. You get too many drinks and run out there and kill everybody, including yourself."

To *Down Beat's* Himes, Brown lamented the ignorance of aspiring blues players who "go off stage and read about blues people who died of drugs and alcohol, so they figure they have to live that same kind of life. The blues should be a healing music. That's why people don't get into my band unless they're willing to play positive music. That means being disciplined, free of alcohol and drugs, and not too much womanizing. When you're on the bandstand working, that's all you're doing. You don't come into my band expecting to be a star. You learn to back off and give everybody a chance."

Asked by Himes about the secret to his longevity and creativity, Brown replied, "It's a big world, and I try to look at all kinds of music; I even try to look at a lot of things beyond music—at kids, millionaires, the frustrations of the world. People ask me what I did to survive so long, and I say, 'I grew like a child.' I refused to do the same thing and kept growing and changing."

Selected discography

Clarence "Gatemouth" Brown Sings Louis Jordan, Black and Blue, 1974.
Gate's on the Heat, Barclay, 1975.
Down South in Bayou Country, Barclay, 1975.
Bogalusa Boogie Man, Barclay, 1976.
(With Roy Clark) *Makin' Music,* MCA, 1979.
San Antonio Ballbuster, Charly, 1979.
Alright Again, Rounder, 1982.
No Looking Back, Alligator, 1992.

Also recorded *The Nashville Session, 1965*, Chess; *Blackjack*, Music Is Medicine; *One More Mile*, Rounder; *The Original Peacock Recordings*, Rounder; *Texas Swing*, Rounder; *Real Life*, Rounder; *Pressure Cooker*, Alligator; and *Standing My Ground*, Alligator.

Sources

Blues Unlimited (U.K.), June 1972.

Down Beat, May 1990; April 1992.
Guitar Player, March 1993.
High Fidelity, May 1988.
Journal of American Folklore, July/September 1989.
Living Blues, Summer 1972.
Pulse!, June 1992.
Spin, August 1992.

—Joan Goldsworthy

Peabo Bryson

Singer, songwriter, producer

"King of the Balladeers" Peabo Bryson can't imagine ever having trouble writing a new love song. "There are no two relationships that are the same," the R&B crooner told William Hanson of the *Detroit Free Press*. "There are no two days in a relationship that are the same. Love and relationships—that's an inexhaustible subject matter." And Bryson seems an inexhaustible source of those love songs; he's been writing, producing, singing, and wooing his audiences with them since 1975.

Delving into his influences, Bryson, who was born in 1951 in Greenville, South Carolina, told Larry McKeithan of *Essence,* "I think the sensitivity in my songs stems from my early childhood. I was raised by women—my grandmother, until she died, and my mother. My grandmother was a woman who lived and loved with incredible passion." Bryson spent much of his childhood on his grandfather's farm in Maudlin, South Carolina. "I have two sisters and a brother, but I'm the oldest male in the family, so I was taught to work—hard. . . . Man I could slop hogs and pick cotton with the best of them," he recalled in *Ebony*. "Hard work is no stranger to me," he pointed out to Hanson, "I like [it]."

Bryson's family not only instilled in him his work ethic, but a love for music as well. "My mother was a serious music lover," he told McKeithan. "Whenever there was somebody great in town, she'd drag us along to catch them. I guess I saw most of the greats of that period—Sam Cooke, Little Richard and even Billie Holiday. Sam Cooke was a great influence on me. His voice had a pure quality—good wholesome from-the-heart music. I think folks should be exposed to that."

Music, in fact, offered Bryson a way out of problems at home and trouble in school. "School was horrible . . . for me—some really bad people in the school system," he told Hanson. "It was a strange kind of prejudice, blacks being resentful of other blacks who had ambition." That ambition drove Bryson to pursue music as a career early on. Singing backup for Al Freeman and the Upsetters, a local Greenville group, marked Bryson's professional debut, at age 14. It was Freeman's difficulty in pronouncing Bryson's French West Indian name, Peapo, that led Bryson to change its spelling. Two years later he left home to tour the now-famous Southern "chitlin' circuit" with another local band, Mose Dillard and the Textile Display.

First Break at Bang

Bryson's first break came during a recording session at Atlanta's Bang Records. Although Bang wasn't sold for long on Dillard's band, the young backup singer caught

For the Record. . .

Born Peapo Bryson (given name changed to Peabo c. 1965) in 1951 in Greenville, SC; mother's name is Marie; children: Linda.

Backup singer for Al Freeman and the Upsetters, c. 1965-1967, and for Mose Dillard and the Textile Display, c. 1967-70; writer, producer, and arranger for Bang Records, c. 1970-1976; released debut album, *Peabo,* Bang, 1976; signed with Capitol Records and released *Reaching for the Sky,* 1977; signed with Elektra Records, c. 1983; signed with Columbia Records, 1990.

Selected awards: (With Celine Dion) Grammy Award for best pop performance by a duo or group, 1992, for "Beauty and the Beast."

Addresses: *Home*—Atlanta, GA. *Record company*—Columbia Records, 51 West 52nd St., New York, NY 10019.

the ear of the label's then-general manager, Eddie Biscoe. Biscoe signed Bryson to a contract as a writer, producer, and arranger and encouraged Bryson to perform his own songs. For several years Bryson worked with hometown bands and wrote and produced for Bang. In 1976 he launched his own recording career with a song called "Underground Music" on the Bang label. His first album, *Peabo,* followed shortly thereafter. Although only a regional success, Bryson turned heads at Capitol Records. Contracts were signed in 1977.

His first release for Capitol, *Reaching for the Sky,* coproduced with Richard Evans, was a commercial success and included the hits "Reaching for the Sky" and "Feel the Fire." His second album for the label, *Crosswinds,* surpassed the first in sales and also featured two hit singles, "I'm So Into You" and the title track. "With 'I'm So Into You' certifying his popularity among black audiences," wrote Mark Kirkeby of *Rolling Stone,* "Bryson's jump from backing vocalist to singer/songwriter, from local acclaim to the big time, was complete."

"With youthful good looks and a relaxed, almost conversational vocal style," Kirkeby continued, "Bryson is unabashedly a romantic balladeer, wooing female listeners much as his R&B idols did in the fifties, but in a reverent, wholesome way, without the earthy sensuality of a Teddy Pendergrass." Wholesome maybe, but Bryson has had trouble quashing the "ladies' man" image that his albums project. Several of the women to whom Bryson has proposed marriage during his career

have turned him down for the security of someone lesser-known. "Competition is not something women look forward to. I can't convince women that they're the only one," he lamented in *Jet.* A curious on-again-off-again engagement to Juanita Leonard—boxing champ Sugar Ray Leonard's former wife—have added to Bryson's romantic distress.

Fruitful Collaborations

Although he has not seemed to find the ideal romantic situation, Bryson has enjoyed superb working relationships with women. A tour with Natalie Cole resulted in the album *We're the Best of Friends.* Another strong affinity grew out of Bryson's touring and recording work with Roberta Flack. Reviewing one of their collaborations, *Born to Love,* for *Stereo Review,* Phyl Garland reported, "The album's quality is established immediately with the opening selection, 'Tonight, I Celebrate My Love,' a fine ballad that has the appeal of a sure hit as well. Bryson steps into the spotlight alone on the title track, his own "Born to Love," which should solidify his position as one of today's more gifted writers and performers of intimate music. This is a flawlessly assembled album of contemporary rhythm-and-blues crafted to appeal to mainstream musical tastes without betraying the artists' roots. Sweeter sounds are not easy to come by."

With each move in his career, applause for Bryson has become louder. *New York Times* music critic Jon Pareles called Bryson the "Pavarotti of soul singers," elaborating, "He has a cherubic presence, plenty of wholesome romantic appeal and a pure, booming tenor voice. When he appeared in the late 1970s, Mr. Bryson would simply stand there and belt, but he has become more of a showman." Still, Pareles did go on to note, "While Mr. Bryson is an undeniable success, he tends to overpower his songs in concert. [They] would be even more romantic if he let them breathe."

Inevitably, criticism has also come Bryson's way; *New York Times* contributor Peter Watrous was less than enthusiastic about the singer's performance style. "Mr. Bryson is a ballad crooner, a would-be matinee idol," wrote Watrous, "who works hard to look like he's not working at all. He sang with a buttery soft voice, and for the first half of his concert everything he did—walk around calmly, unbutton his jacket—projected an image of effortlessness that's fine for the radio or a video, but falls short of what's expected by an audience at a concert. . . . By the end of the show, even though Mr. Bryson had turned up the heat a bit, the audience left without asking for an encore."

Crossover Hits

If he hasn't always hit home in concert, however, Bryson has usually struck grand slams with his albums. In June of 1984 he released his first album for the Elektra label, titled *Straight From the Heart,* which included the song "If Ever You're in My Arms Again." His duets with Natalie Cole—"What You Won't Do for Love"—and Roberta Flack—"Tonight, I Celebrate My Love," a Top 15 pop smash—had earned Bryson the tag "King of Balladeers," and with "If Ever You're in My Arms Again," which landed in the Number 10 spot on the pop charts, he scored another crossover hit and solidified his mainstream audience. Both "Tonight" and "If" went to Number One on the adult contemporary charts. After four albums for Elektra, including the critically acclaimed *Take No Prisoners* set, Bryson returned to Capitol for 1989's *All My Love.* This Top 10 R&B album featured the Number One R&B hit "Show and Tell," a remake of the Al Wilson tune.

In 1990, Bryson signed a recording contract with Columbia Records and, in 1991, released *Can You Stop the Rain. People'*s review of the album assessed, "[Bryson] has consistently offered listening pleasure, even when he parks his talent too close to glibness. March him up the aisle with the right material, however—as this record does—and the result can be a taste of R&B heaven. There's always a nicely tempered dynamic to Bryson's voice," the reviewer went on, "due in part to his intuitive phrasing and his gift for emotional shading. In terms of composition, there's nothing unforgettable on this issue. But it's all as sweet, creamy and hard to put down as a box of fudge." The single "Can You Stop the Rain" won Bryson a 1991 Grammy nomination for best R&B vocal performance by a male, as did "Lost in the Night" in 1992.

That he is frequently pigeonholed as an R&B singer occasionally angers Bryson. He reviles the rigid pop radio programming that tends to leave artists stuck in certain genres, giving them no chance to reach a wider audience. "By virtue of the fact that you're black, you must therefore be an R&B artist," he complained to *Detroit Free Press* contributor Hanson, "and I think that that's prejudicial. It's not an overt kind of racism, it's a racism by omission. If you're a black artist, you're not automatically considered for pop radio."

Despite his fears—and ample testimony of his appeal—Bryson continues to cross over from the R&B charts to the pop charts. A perfect example of this came in 1992, when Bryson's wildly popular duet with Canadian chanteuse Celine Dion, "Beauty and the Beast," garnered Grammy nominations for record of the year and best *pop* performance by a duo or group.

Vindicating the devotion of his fans, Bryson won the award in the latter category.

Selected discography

Peabo, Bang, 1976.

Reaching for the Sky (includes "Reaching for the Sky" and "Feel the Fire"), Capitol, 1977.

Crosswinds (includes "Crosswinds" and "I'm So Into You"), Capitol, 1978.

(With Natalie Cole) *We're the Best of Friends* (includes "What You Won't Do for Love"), Capitol, 1979.

Paradise, Capitol, 1980.

(With Roberta Flack) *Live and More,* Atlantic, 1982.

(With Flack) *Born to Love* (includes "Tonight, I Celebrate My Love" and "Born to Love"), Capitol, 1983.

Straight From the Heart (includes "If Ever You're in My Arms Again"), Elektra, 1984.

Peabo Bryson Collection, Capitol, reissued, 1987.

All My Love (includes "Show and Tell"), Capitol, 1989.

Can You Stop the Rain, Columbia, 1991.

Take No Prisoners, Elektra.

Contributor to *Beauty and Beast,* Disney, 1992; *The King and I,* Phillips, 1993; and (with Flack) *The Christmas Album,* Interscope, 1993.

Sources

American Record Guide, January 1993.

Amsterdam News (New York, NY), January 4, 1992.

Blues & Soul, February 11, 1992.

Chocolate Singles, February 1992.

Detroit Free Press, October 25, 1991; January 8, 1993; February 23, 1993; February 25, 1993.

Ebony, October 1980.

Essence, March 1980.

Jet, June 25, 1984; July 30, 1984; June 10, 1991; July 8, 1991; November 30, 1992.

Los Angeles Magazine, October 1992.

Monday Morning Replay, January 27, 1992.

New York Times, March 30, 1983; March 28, 1988; August 4, 1993.

People, May 27, 1991; February 15, 1993.

Rolling Stone, August 21, 1980.

Stereo Review, December 1983.

Urban Network, January 24, 1992.

Additional information for this profile was obtained from a Columbia Records press release, 1991.

—*Joanna Rubiner*

Kenny Burrell

Guitarist, educator

Kenny Burrell is among the most outstanding guitarists to emerge from the progressive jazz scene following World War II. With a career spanning over 40 years, Burrell's artistry has withstood commercial trends and popular vogues. Distinctive and easily recognizable, his guitar work explores new harmonic possibilities while retaining a strong swing approach. Music critic Lewis McMillan, Jr., described Burrell in *Down Beat* as "a man with a mission," an individual whose "role as a jazz musician was not unlike that of an evangelist."

Known for his musical devotion and versatility, Burrell has won acclaim from musicians and listeners throughout the world. His guitar style is representative of soulful blues, traditional swing, Latin forms, bebop modernism, and classical techniques. His extensive repertoire extends from classical composer Johann Sebastian Bach to maverick jazz pianist Thelonious Monk. Whether on nylon-string acoustic or electric hollow-body guitar, Burrell has advanced his mission to expose audiences to the true essence of jazz.

Born on July 31, 1931, in Detroit, Burrell belonged to a family of talented instrumentalists. His father played banjo, mandolin, and ukulele; his two older brothers, Billy and Donald, were guitarists. At an early age, Burrell's mother, who was a pianist and singer, insisted that the young man receive piano lessons. Despite his mother's urging, Burrell found playing the piano an unpromising venture.

Soon afterward Burrell turned his attention to the saxophone, an instrument that, unfortunately, his parents could not afford. His financial constraints led him to acquire a guitar instead at the age of 12. Under the instruction of his brother, Burrell learned the basics of the fretboard. But it wasn't until his introduction to the recordings of Charlie Christian that Burrell began to take a serious interest in the guitar. The amplified sounds of Christian's smooth horn-like phrasing inspired Burrell to devote himself to the study of his instrument.

At Miller High School in Detroit, Burrell's music advisor, Louis Cabara, furthered the young man's knowledge of composition and theory. Aside from offering first-rate instruction, Cabara furnished valuable advice concerning the philosophical aspects of music. Taken by the sounds of jazz, Burrell, although still underage, began to search for music in downtown nightclubs. One evening he and pianist Tommy Flannagan painted moustaches on their faces to get into an establishment where the legendary saxophonist Charlie "Yardbird" Parker was performing. As Burrell told *Down Beat* contributor Zan Stewart, "Bird was wonderful, and so gracious."

For the Record. . .

Born Kenneth Earl Burrell, July 31, 1931, in Detroit, MI. *Education:* Wayne State University, B.M., 1955; studied classical guitar with Joe Fava.

Began playing guitar c. 1943; founded private musicians collective New World Music Society, early 1950s; made recording debut on Dee Gee Records, 1951; toured with Oscar Peterson Trio, 1955; recorded debut album, Blue Note Records, 1956; studio musician, New York City, recording for Prestige and Savoy labels; played with Benny Goodman Orchestra, 1957-59. Concert performer and seminar participant throughout the U.S. and abroad, including yearly engagement at Baker's Keyboard Lounge in Detroit. Teacher at University of California, Los Angeles, 1971—.

Awards: Winner of *Down Beat* critics and readers polls, 1968-1970.

Addresses: *Office*—Tropix International, 163 Third Ave., #206, New York, NY 10003.

By 1948 Burrell had become a respected member of the thriving Detroit jazz community. His musicianship also impressed nationally known bandleaders Dizzy Gillespie and Illinois Jaquet, both of whom asked him to join their bands on the road. But Burrell's parents discouraged him from leaving Detroit until he had completed his musical education at Wayne State University. During his stint at the university, Burrell founded the New World Music Society, a private musicians collective that included local greats Elvin Jones, Yusef Lateef, Donald Byrd, and Pepper Adams.

A significant boost to Burrell's career came in 1951, when he made his recording debut on Dizzy Gillespie's Detroit-based Dee Gee label. Before earning his bachelor's degree in music from Wayne State, Burrell spent a year and a half studying classical guitar with Joe Fava. These lessons helped him develop a formal fingerstyle technique. Burrell's devotion to jazz, however, overshadowed his interest in classical forms. "I always wanted to change the notes," explained Burrell in *Jazz Journal International.* "Improvisation is the essence of jazz and I have to play the way I feel." After graduating from college in 1955, Burrell spent six months on the road with the Oscar Peterson Trio. A year later, determined to pursue greater career opportunities, Burrell left for New York with Tommy Flannagan.

Within several months of his arrival in New York, Burrell recorded his first LP, for the Blue Note label. As one of Manhattan's most sought-after studio musicians, he appeared on countless sessions for Prestige and Savoy. Between 1957 and 1959 Burrell played with Benny Goodman's band, filling the chair once occupied by his early idol, Charlie Christian. Over the next decade he performed with such jazz giants as John Coltrane, Coleman Hawkins, Thad Jones, and Stanley Turrentine.

In 1965 Burrell collaborated with arranger Gil Evans to record the critically acclaimed *Guitar Forms.* Complemented by Evans's brilliantly orchestrated scores, Burrell demonstrated his ability to perform musical styles ranging from classical and bossa nova to the blues. During this period, Burrell also made several recordings with organist Jimmy Smith, including the classic LPs *Organ Grinder Swing* and *The Sermon.* Since 1971, Burrell has occupied an academic position at the University of California, Los Angeles, teaching "Ellingtonia," a course dedicated to the music of legendary bandleader and composer Duke Ellington. Burrell continues to appear at seminars and concerts in the United States, Europe, and Japan. Each year he returns to Detroit for an always hotly anticipated engagement at Baker's Keyboard Lounge, one of the oldest jazz clubs in the country.

Bluesy bends, horn-like slurs, and tastefully inventive chord patterns are the hallmarks of Burrell's sound. His refined guitar work produces intensity and command without excessive volume. For Burrell, like most great jazzmen, the blues remain essential to his musical approach and sensibility. Ever since he heard the recordings of blues singer Muddy Waters and seminal blues guitarist T-Bone Walker, Burrell has looked to the blues for artistic and spiritual inspiration. "In my case, jazz and blues are inseparable," Burrell commented in *Down Beat.* Jazz guitarists from Grant Green to Pat Metheny have praised Burrell's bluesy sound and versatile musicianship.

Burrell has also been idolized by a legion of modern electric blues guitarists. Texas bluesman Albert Collins admitted that his original ambition was to play jazz in the Burrell style. Jimmy and Stevie Ray Vaughan often cited Burrell as one of their favorite guitarists. In fact, a cover version of Burrell's steamy blues classic "Chitlins Con Carne" appears on Stevie Ray's last LP, *The Sky Is Crying.* With such a widespread following there is little doubt that Burrell will have an enduring impact on guitarists for years to come. A serious and committed musician, Burrell is a performer, arranger, scholar, and above all, one of jazz guitar's greatest practitioners.

Selected discography

Blue Lights, Blue Note, 1958.

Guitar Forms, Verve, 1965.

Listen at Dawn, Muse, 1980.

Bluesin' Around, Columbia, 1983.

(With Rufus Reid) *A La Carte* (recorded in 1983), Muse, 1985.

(With Charlie Parker) *Bird at St. Nicks,* Original Jazz Classics, reissued, 1992.

Sun Up to Sundown, Contemporary, 1992.

Ellington Is Forever Vol. 1, reissued, Fantasy, 1993.

Ellington Is Forever Vol. 2, Fantasy.

Kenny Burrell, Blue Note.

Introducing Kenny Burrell, Blue Note.

The Common Ground, Verve.

Tender Gender, Blue Note.

Moten Swing, Blue Note.

A Night at the Village Vanguard, Argo.

On View at the Five Spot, Blue Note.

'Round Midnight, Fantasy.

Stormy Monday, Fantasy.

All Day All Night Long, Prestige.

Keep on Comin', Elektra.

Back at the Chicken Shack, Blue Note.

Organ Grinder Swing, Blue Note.

The Sermon, Blue Note.

The Essential, Verve.

(With Grover Washington, Jr.) *Togethering,* Blue Note.

(With John Coltrane) *Kenny Burrell/John Coltrane,* Prestige.

(With Coleman Hawkins) *Moonglow,* Prestige.

(With Stanely Turrentine) *Joyride,* Blue Note.

(With Sonny Rollins) *Alfie,* Impulse.

(With Dizzy Gillespie) *Dee Gee Days,* Savoy.

(With Billie Holiday) *Lady in Satin,* Columbia.

(With Jimmy Smith) *Go for Whatcha Know,* Blue Note.

(With Mercer Ellington) *Hot and Bothered,* Doctor Jazz.

(With Jimmy Ramey) *Two Guitars,* Original Jazz.

Sources

Books

Baillet, Whitney, *56 Portraits in Jazz,* Oxford, 1986.

Gillespie, Dizzy, *To Be or Not to Bop,* Doubleday, 1979.

Lyons, Len, and Don Perlo, *Jazz Portraits,* Quill, 1989.

Summerfield, Maurie J., *The Jazz Guitar: Its Evolution and Its Players,* Ashley, 1980.

Periodicals

Down Beat, July 1958; June 1971; June 1972; July 1972; July 1986; September 1993.

Guitar Player, October 1984; July 1986.

Guitar World, September 1990.

Jazz Journal International, November 1978.

Michigan Chronicle, September 1, 1950; June 16, 1955.

Monthly Detroit, September 1984.

Saturday Review, September 1968.

Additional information for this profile was obtained from liner notes by Ira Gitler to *Kenny Burrell,* Blue Note, and by Dan Forte to Stevie Ray Vaughan's *The Sky Is Crying,* Epic, 1991.

—*John Cohassey*

Sammy Cahn

Songwriter, entertainer

Call him irrepressible—Sammy Cahn always had a way with words. As a skinny, bespectacled kid, it kept him out of trouble with his parents and the neighborhood bullies. As an adult, his way with words made him one of the most popular and successful lyricists of all time.

Young Samuel Cohen was not a good student in the classroom, but he studied the theater voraciously; from an early age, he would cut classes to see movies and watch vaudeville shows. One time when he had been at the theater instead of at school, he was spotted by a friend of his mother, who reported Sammy's truancy. He avoided punishment by brazenly lying his way out of the jam.

As a kid, he played the violin. But this was only a hobby until he was 13. At his bar mitzvah, he saw his mother pay the musicians and realized he could make money playing the violin. A year later he joined the small Dixieland orchestra his mother had hired, the Pals of Harmony. The group played local gigs and then began traveling to perform in hotels in Atlantic City and the summer resorts of the Catskills.

Sammy Cohen, who adopted the professional surname Cahn, wrote his first song when he was about 16 years old. As he recalled in his autobiography, *I Should Care,* "It was actually Jackie Osterman at the Academy of Music on 14th Street who inspired my song writing career. . . . In the middle of the act, [Osterman] took a change of pace and said he'd like to sing a song he'd written. It was a fascinating thing for me to be actually looking at a songwriter—in person. . . . Walking home . . . I began to frame a song in my head. By the time I reached home I had actually written a lyric. . . . The song was a piece of idiocy called "Like Niagara Falls, I'm Falling for You—Baby!" But if, as . . . somebody said, a journey of a thousand miles starts with the first step, that was the first step." Soon he teamed up with the pianist from the Pals of Harmony, Saul Chaplin, and a songwriting team was born.

Teamed With Pianist; Sold Songs

The duo of Cahn and Chaplin soon began to have some success at writing specialty numbers for vaudeville acts, but they could not get their songs published. Then one day in 1935, a friend told them that the bandleader Jimmy Lunceford, who was then playing at the Apollo Theater in Harlem, needed a song. They wrote "Rhythm Is Our Business," which was recorded for the Decca label and became a modest hit. They began to write for

For the Record. . .

Born Samuel Cohen, June 18, 1913, in New York, NY; son of Abraham and Elka Riss Cohen; died of congestive heart failure, January 15, 1993, in Los Angeles, CA; married Gloria Delson, 1945 (divorced, 1964); married Virginia "Tita" Basile, 1970; children: Steven, Laurie.

Joined Dixieland group Pals of Harmony as violinist, 1927; wrote first song, c. 1929; with pianist Saul Chaplin, wrote specialty songs for vaudeville acts; wrote songs for big-band singers, including Ella Fitzgerald, mid-1930s; wrote English lyrics to Yiddish song "Bei Mir Bist Du Schön (Means That Your Grand)," 1937; worked for Vitaphone Studios, New York City, late 1930s; split from Chaplin and began working with Jule Styne; worked with Frank Sinatra, early 1940s; worked with various composers; mounted Broadway show *Words and Music,* 1974; toured with show, 1975-early 1990s. President of Songwriters Hall of Fame.

Contributed music to films, including *Lady of Burlesque,* 1943; *Anchors Aweigh,* 1945; *Tonight and Every Night,* 1945; *Wonder Man,* 1945; *The Kid From Brooklyn,* 1946; *Romance on the High Seas,* 1948; *West Point Story,* 1950; *April in Paris,* 1953; *Peter Pan,* 1953; *Three Coins in a Fountain,* 1954; *You're Never Too Young,* 1955; *The Court Jester,* 1956; *All the Way,* 1956; *The Man With the Golden Arm,* 1956; *Serenade,* 1956; *The Joker Is Wild,* 1959; *A Hole in the Head,* 1959; *High Time,* 1960; *A Pocketful of Miracles,* 1961; *Papa's Delicate Condition,* 1963; *Robin and the Seven Hoods,* 1964; *Where Love Has Gone,* 1964; *Thoroughly Modern Millie,* 1967; and *Star,* 1968.

Awards: Academy awards, 1954, for "Three Coins in a Fountain," from *Three Coins in a Fountain;* 1957, for "All the Way," from *The Joker Is Wild;* 1959, for "High Hopes," from *A Hole in the Head;* 1963, for "Call Me Irresponsible," from *Papa's Delicate Condition.* National Cash Box Award, 1959, for "High Hopes." Inducted into Songwriters Hall of Fame, 1972.

other big-band stars like Ella Fitzgerald ("If You Ever Should Leave"), were accepted as members of ASCAP (the American Society of Composers, Authors, and Publishers), and were on their way.

The song that made Cahn and Chaplin famous and rich enough for Cahn to buy his parents a new house was the specialty number "Bei Mir Bist Du Schön (Means That You're Grand)." Cahn heard this Yiddish song at the Apollo Theater and thought an English version would work well. He had trouble selling the idea at first,

but then an as-yet-unknown sister act from the Midwest heard the song. Cahn explained in his autobiography: "One day Lou (Levy) brought the Andrews Sisters, Patty, Maxene, and LaVerne up to our apartment. On the piano was this copy of a song in Yiddish. Patty asked . . . 'How does it go?' I played it for them, and they started to sing right along and to rock with it. 'Gee,' said Patty, 'can we have it?' Cahn penned English lyrics to the song, the Andrew Sisters recorded it, and it shot both Cahn and the Sisters to national fame, eventually selling over one million copies.

During the late 1930s the team of Cahn and Chaplin wrote under contract for New York City's Vitaphone Studios, a subsidiary of Warner Bros. that produced short feature films. The duo wrote songs sung in these films by performers such as Betty Hutton, Bob Hope, and Edgar Bergen. In 1940 Vitaphone Studios closed, and Cahn and Chaplin, still under contract to Warner Bros., moved out to Hollywood. But they had no luck with the western studios, got no commissions, and parted ways.

Film Collaboration With Jule Styne

About the time Cahn was becoming frantic from lack of work, he was asked to write songs with composer Jule Styne. "From the beginning it was fun," he remembered. "He went to the piano and played a complete melody. I listened and said 'Would you play it again, just a bit slower?' He played and I listened. . . . I then said, 'I've heard that song before'—to which he said, bristling, 'What the hell are you, a tune detective?' 'No,' I said, 'that wasn't a criticism, it was a title: "I've Heard That Song Before."'" This song, the first of many Cahn and Styne hits, led to a fruitful series of film collaborations. The duo wrote songs for the films *Anchors Aweigh* (1945), *Tonight and Every Night* (1945), *Wonder Man* (1945), *The Kid From Brooklyn* (1946), *Romance on the High Seas* (1948), and *The West Point Story* (1950). Their songs include "I'll Walk Alone," "I Fall in Love Too Easily," "Saturday Night Is the Loneliest Night in the Week," "As Long as There's Music," "Come Out, Come Out," "Five Minutes More," and "The Things We Did Last Summer."

Cahn wrote many songs specially for certain singers. After he met young Frank Sinatra singing with the Tommy Dorsey Band, he provided Sinatra with a number of songs that became hits and helped to make both men stars. In the early 1940s Sinatra was signed by MGM to appear in the musical *Anchors Aweigh;* he refused to sing unless Cahn wrote the material. In 1954

Cahn and Styne wrote "Three Coins in a Fountain" for Sinatra to sing in the film *Three Coins in a Fountain.* The song garnered Cahn his first Oscar.

During his long career, Cahn worked with many different composers. In 1957 Cahn and composer Jimmy Van Heusen won an Oscar for their song "All the Way," from the movie *The Joker Is Wild;* they won another in 1959 for "High Hopes," from *A Hole in the Head,* and in 1963 they won their third Oscar for the song "Call Me Irresponsible," from the film *Papa's Delicate Condition.* The duo also received Academy Award nominations for their songs "To Love and Be Loved," "Second Time Around," "High Time," "My Kind of Town," "Where Love Has Gone," "Thoroughly Modern Millie," "A Pocketful of Miracles," and "Star." Other Cahn collaborators included Nicholas Brodsky, Sammy Fain, Arthur Schwartz, Sylvia Fine, Vernon Duke, Axel Stordahl, Paul Weston, and Gene de Paul.

Hit on Broadway

In 1974 Sammy Cahn starred in his own Broadway show. Two years earlier he had been asked to put together a show to run as part of a now-legendary series at the 92nd Street YMCA called "Lyrics and Lyricists." The audience loved him. When he finally took the act, titled *Words and Music,* to Broadway, critics raved, and Cahn became the toast of the town. His show ran for nine months on Broadway and almost two decades on tour before declining health put an end to Cahn's performing career.

Cahn died of congestive heart failure on January 15, 1993, at Cedars-Sinai Medial Center in Los Angeles. In 1972 he had been inducted into the Songwriter's Hall of Fame and had later served as its president. He had labored hard to establish a Songwriter's Hall of Fame Museum, and he never lost his love for popular music of any variety. In 1992 he told *Pulse!* that he would love to write songs for contemporary singers like belter Michael Bolton or superstar Madonna. "My opinion of the music of today," he told *Pulse!,* "is simply put: Whatever the number-one song in the world is at this moment, I wish my name were on it."

Selected discography

Walking Happy, Capitol, 1966.
An Evening With Sammy Cahn, DRG, 1978, reissued, 1993.
Frank Sinatra Sings the Songs of Sammy Cahn and Jule Styne, Vintage Jazz Classics, 1993.

Sources

Books

Cahn, Sammy, *I Should Care: The Sammy Cahn Story,* Arbor House, 1974.
Cahn, Sammy, *Sammy Cahn's Rhyming Dictionary,* Warner Bros. Publications Inc., 1983.
Songs With Lyrics by Sammy Cahn, Cahn Music Co., 1982.

Periodicals

Chicago Tribune, January 16, 1993.
Entertainment Weekly, January 29, 1993.
Gentlemen's Quarterly, July 1991.
Facts on File, January 21, 1993.
London Times, January 18, 1993.
Los Angeles Times, July 10, 1990; January 16, 1993.
New York Times, January 16, 1993.
Newsweek, January 25, 1993.
People, February 1, 1993.
Pulse!, April 1992; October 1992.
Time, January 25, 1993.
Variety, January 25, 1993.
Washington Post, July 11, 1990; January 16, 1993.

—*Robin Armstrong*

Maria Callas

Opera singer

Maria Callas, more than most opera singers, had about her an aura that defied explanation—even a decade after her death; she possessed a quality that grabbed audiences quickly and holds them still. And her allure reached outside the traditional audience of opera lovers. She peaked early, though, and began to lose her voice only six years after commencing her performing career, which effectively ended after only a decade. Still, audiences loved her long after her voice was gone, and she will always be mentioned when divas are discussed.

Callas was born in 1923, the year after her parents moved from Greece to New York City. Her mother noticed her musical talent while she was just a child and encouraged her. In 1937 she took her back to Greece, where Maria entered the National Academy in Athens. She thrived at the conservatory and worked extremely hard—she was the first to arrive in the morning and the last to leave at night. She retained her habit of hard work all of her life; even when she was the most famous singer in the cast, she would also be the hardest working. In 1939, Callas started studying with the famous soprano Elvira de Hidalgo, and in 1940, she began singing professionally in Athens as she continued to study.

Callas's first professional engagement involved vocal accompaniment to a performance of Shakespeare's *Merchant of Venice* at the Royal Theater. Throughout the war years she continued to study and sing in concerts and small opera productions. In 1941 she sang Beatrice in von Suppé's *Boccacio* at the Palas Cinema and in 1942, she sang *Tosca* at the summer theater in Klafthmonos Square. After World War II ended, however, she had trouble finding new roles, so she decided to return to New York.

Between 1945 and 1947, Callas studied and auditioned in New York but had few professional opportunities. Finally, she sang for Giovanni Zenatello, artistic director of Verona, Italy's Arena and was contracted to sing *La Giocanda* there. While this performance was not her operatic debut, it was her Italian debut and brought her to the attention of a wide audience. During rehearsals she met Giovanni Battista Meneghini, a wealthy businessman. Greatly taken by the singer, he became her backer, providing financial security for her between jobs. He also became her agent—in actuality if not in formality—and actively pursued roles for her. In 1949 Callas and Meneghini were married.

In the two years preceding her marriage, Callas sang in small houses around Italy in a variety of operas, including *Turandot, La Forza del destino, Tristan und Isolde, Aida,* and *Norma.* With hard work and Meneghini's

For the Record. . .

Born Maria Anna Sofia Cecilia Kalogeropoulos, December 2, 1923, in New York, NY; died September 16, 1977, in Paris; daughter of George and Evangelia Kalogeropoulos; married Giovanni Battista Meneghini, 1949. *Education:* Studied with Elvira de Hidalgo at the Athens Conservatory, beginning in 1939.

Operatic debut, 1941, in *Tosca;* Italian Debut, 1947, Verona; Joined La Scala, Milan, 1951; U.S. debut with Chicago Lyric Opera, 1954, in *Norma;* Metropolitan Opera debut, 1956, in *Norma;* also appeared in *Aida, La Traviata, Don Carlos, Un ballo in maschera, Rigoletto, Anna Bolena, Lucia di Lammermoor, Il Barbiere di Siviglia, Tosca, Turandot, Tristan und Isolde,* and *Die Walküre.*

help, her schedule became filled with performances, and her reputation grew. As one of the most versatile singers of her day, she created a sensation by singing Bellini's *I Puritani* and Wagner's *Walküre*—two very different operas with very different vocal requirements—within a week of each other during the 1948-49 season. In 1949 Callas made one of her most important appearances, on one of the world's greatest stages, singing *Turandot, Norma,* and *Aida* at the Colón opera house in Buenas Aires, Argentina.

By 1950 Callas's career had begun to skyrocket. During the next few years she sang with most of the major opera houses and received rave review. Audiences loved her. The Mexican paper *El Universal* reported, as quoted in *Callas as They Saw Her,* "From her first aria, 'Ritorna vincitor,' the audience was moved. It followed her through the whole aria until the final limpid, brilliant point. . . . The first applause exploded, enthusiastic and prolonged. The audience came to understand that it had found a *rara avos* among singers, one of exceptional qualities that merit calling her . . . a 'soprano assoluta'—such were the ovations."

Callas was fast becoming one of the most loved singers of her day and as such, was making a tremendous impact on the world of opera. Her vocal agility and strength proved perfect for an older repertoire that had not been performed in many years. With Callas in mind, producers were beginning to revive the works of the bel canto composers, including Rossini, Bellini, and Donizetti. Callas's most famous role was as Bellini's *Norma.* She was also capturing the fancy of listeners outside the customary opera audience. In Chicago in 1955, when an extra performance of *Madama Butterfly* starring Callas was scheduled, tickets sold out in fewer than two hours. She had effectively revived the cult of The Diva, which had lacked a goddess since the days of Adelina Patti and Maria Malibrun, whose names Callas would all but eclipse.

In 1953, having gained considerable heft, Callas began a strict diet regimen and over the following two years became quite slim. While critics approved of the results, there were dangers inherent in this program; Callas's best kept getting better, but her voice and her health became increasingly unpredictable. Her acting became more dramatic. But she began to lose both her power and control over her vibrato; her high notes became softer and less consistent. With increasing frequency, she missed performances from ill health, and she began to accept fewer jobs.

By the 1958-59 season, Callas's vocal problems had become so pronounced that she took a long hiatus and after 1959, she performed less and less frequently. During her apex she had sang as many as 50 performances in a year, but after 1959 she sang fewer than 10 a year. Reviews of the performances she did give indicate that while her acting and musicianship remained expressive and accurate, she had little voice left. Harold Schonberg wrote in the *New York Times* in 1964, "When the act was well under way, several things were apparent. This was going to be one of the best-acted *Toscas* in Metropolitan Opera history. . . . Her conception of the role was electrical. Everything at her command was put into striking use. . . . This was supreme acting, unforgettable acting. But now we come to matters vocal, and the story is less pleasant. Miss Callas is operating these days with only the remnants of a voice."

After her few 1965 performances, Callas quit singing altogether. She tried film acting and in 1969 performed in an adaptation of *Medea,* but it was not a success. Callas taught at the Juilliard School during the 1971-72 school year. And in 1973 she began to sing in public again with the tenor Giuseppe di Stefano. They toured in 1973-74, primarily to offset the medical expenses of Stefano's daughter, who was dying of cancer. Despite the deterioration of Callas's voice, her artistry brought audiences in and satisfied them. Schonberg reported, "To the audience, nothing could go wrong. It was understandable that the concert was a representation to them of the singer that was, not the singer who is. And Miss Callas was able, even with her limited resources to give an idea of the kind of temperament and musical understanding that never has deserted her. She looked not a day older than in her last appearance here almost ten years ago, and everybody washed her with oceans of love. She . . . deserved the tribute." The strain of the tour proved immense, however, and Callas did not sing again publicly. She died in 1977.

Today, Callas remains an enigma. Though her voice was never perfect, it could be exquisitely beautiful. Her talent displayed a rare combination of a large voice and great agility. Her acting and musicianship were so expressive that audiences continued to adore her even when her voice had disappeared. She brought to each performance a singular diligence and dynamic intelligence. As David Lowe wrote in *Callas as They Saw Her:* "The interplay between intelligence and instinct, training and talent, often led to phrasing that may haunt the memory forever. . . . The uniqueness of her art, though, lies in how she applied [her] resources to the interpretation of words and music. Indeed, with Callas, it is impossible to divorce the words she sang from the way she sang them."

Selected discography

Donizetti, *Lucia di Lammermoor,* EMI, 1953.
Bellini, *I Puritani,* EMI, 1953.
Mascagni, *Cavalleria Rusticana,* EMI, 1953.
Puccini, *Tosca,* EMI, 1953.
Verdi, *La Traviata,* Cetra, 1953.
Bellini, *Norma,* EMI, 1954.
Leoncavallo, *Pagliacci,* EMI, 1954.
Verdi, *La Forza del Destino,* EMI, 1954, reissued, 1987.
Rossini, *Il Turco in Italia,* EMI, 1954.
Puccini, *Madama Butterfly,* EMI, 1955.
Verdi, *Aida,* EMI, 1955.
Verdi, *Il Trovatore,* EMI, 1956.
Puccini, *La Bohème,* EMI, 1956.
Rossini, *Il Barbiere de Siviglia,* EMI, 1957.
Bellini, *La Sonnambula,* EMI, 1957.
Puccini, *Turandot,* EMI, 1957.
Puccini, *Manon Lescaut,* EMI, 1957.
Cherubini, *Medea,* Mercury, 1957.

Verdi, *La Traviata,* EMI, 1958.
Donizetti, *Lucia di Lammermoor,* EMI, 1959.
Ponchielli, *La Gioconda,* EMI, 1958.
Puccini, *Tosca,* EMI, 1964.
Donizetti, *Lucia di Lammermoor,* Seraphim, 1968.
Verdi, *La Traviata,* Melodram, 1986.
Puccini, *Tosca,* Melodram, 1986.
Various composers, *Maria Callas and Beniamino Gigle: A Samremo,* Suite, 1992.
Rarities, EMI Classics, 1992.
Bellini, *Norma Highlights,* Melodram/Koch, 1993.

Sources

Books

Ardoin, John, *The Callas Legacy,* Scribner's, 1982.
Calla, Evangelia, *My Daughter Maria Callas,* Fleet, 1960.
Jellinek, George, *Callas: Portrait of a Prima Donna,* Arno Press, 1978.
Lowe, David A, *Callas as They Saw Her,* Ungar, 1991.
Meneghini, Giovanni Battista, *My Wife Maria Callas,* Farrar, Strauss, 1982.
Scott, Michael, *Maria Meneghini Callas,* Simon & Schuster, 1991.
Wisneski, Henry, *Maria Callas: The Art Behind the Legend,* Doubleday, 1975.

Periodicals

High Fidelity, February 1983; February 1989.
Musical America, July 1991.
Opera, December 1977.
Opera News, January 1984; September 1987; August 1988.
Opera Quarterly, Summer 1989.
Pulse!, July 1992.

—Robin Armstrong

Tom
Chapin

Singer, songwriter

Tom Chapin's early career may have been overshadowed by that of his more famous brother, singer-songwriter Harry Chapin of "Cat's in the Cradle" and "Taxi" fame, but Tom has made quite a name for himself as an eclectic songwriter and singer nonetheless. By the early 1990s, in fact, his music written especially for children, with its toe-tapping tunes and rich guitar accompaniments, had pleased *parents* so well that they generally think of his later body of work as "family" music rather than "kids" music.

Considering his upbringing, Chapin was destined for a life in the arts. He grew up in New York City's Greenwich Village and Brooklyn Heights in a family that encouraged all the children to develop their creative talents. The senior Chapin, Jim, was a jazz drummer who performed with renowned bandleaders Tommy Dorsey and Woody Herman. One of Tom's grandfathers was a painter, and the other was a philosopher.

When he was 12, Tom and his two brothers, Steve and Harry, fell under the influence of the seminal folk group the Weavers. The Chapin kids formed their own folk trio, calling themselves the Chapins. They played nightclub gigs in New York for a number of years and recorded their first album, *Chapin Music!,* in 1966. The group broke up shortly thereafter, though, so that each brother could pursue his own interests. Meanwhile, Tom had started college in upstate New York, earning a bachelor's degree in history and beginning work on a master's degree. In 1969 he accepted a job working on a documentary on sharks, *Blue Water, White Death.* His various jobs on the film included singing on the soundtrack, which launched his music career.

Songwriter by Default

Between 1971 and 1976 Chapin worked in television, singing and hosting the show *Make a Wish.* He became a songwriter almost by default; his brother Harry had been contracted to write songs for the show but was so busy with his singing career that he was only able to write drafts of the songs, leaving the final versions up to Tom. "It ended up being a great lesson in songwriting," Tom told *Sing Out!* in 1988. "It was a real good experience." So good, in fact, that he realized it was becoming his main focus in life. "By '75-76, I realized: 'This is what I do.' Being a musician, specifically, being a songwriter. . . . No matter how many concerts I do, no matter what other kinds of work I'm pursuing, I feel most righteous when I've written something. That's the real me, that's what gets me up in the morning." During his years in television, Chapin also performed solo concerts, worked with brother Steve in the Chapins, and formed his own band, Mt. Airy, which released a record

For the Record. . .

Born March 13, 1945, in New York, NY; father was a jazz drummer; married wife Bonnie, 1976; children: Abigail, Lily. *Education:* State University College at Plattsburgh, B.A. in history, 1969.

Formed Chapin Brothers, c. 1960; with Chapin Brothers, recorded album *Chapin Music!*, 1969; contributed to soundtrack of documentary *Blue Water, White Death*, 1969; hosted television show *Make a Wish*, 1971-1976; formed band Mt. Airy, early 1970s; appeared in musicals, including *The Night That Made America Famous*, 1975, *Cotton Patch Gospel*, 1981, *Pump Boys and Dinettes*, 1982-83, and *Lies and Legends: The Musical Stories of Harry Chapin*, 1984; arranged music for Off-Broadway show *Cotton Patch Gospel*, 1981; hosted television show *Explorer*, 1986-90; recorded first family album, *Family Tree*, 1988.

Awards: Parents' Choice Award, 1988, for *Family Tree; Moonboat* named notable children's recording, American Library Association, 1980; Harry Chapin Award for Contributions to Humanity, National Association for Campus Activities, 1990; Parents' Choice Award and New York Music Award for best children's album, 1991, for *Mother Earth;* Parents' Choice Award and New York Music Award for best children's album, 1992, for *Billy the Squid;* Parents Prize Award, *Parents Magazine.*

Member: World Hunger Year (board of directors, beginning in 1982); People to People (Rockland County, NY; board of directors, beginning in 1987).

Addresses: *Record company*—Sundance Music, P.O. Box 1663, New York, NY 10011.

in 1973. He recorded his first solo album, *Life Is Like That,* in 1976.

In 1981 Chapin became the arranger for the Off-Broadway musical *Cotton Patch Gospel,* written by his brother Harry. Shortly thereafter, however, Harry was killed in an automobile accident. Tom became determined to keep his brother's musical and social messages alive. He completed work on *Cotton Patch* and saw its successful production. He also became involved in the political organization Harry had founded to fight hunger, World Hunger Year (WHY). He explained to *International Musician* why he started working for WHY: "[Harry] had started a number of things, and [the family] felt very strongly that some of them should continue and we made our own choices as to what we wanted to do. Hunger was one that I had been very

involved in, and Harry and I had done a lot of benefit concerts together for WHY." Tom joined the board of directors of WHY in 1982.

After finishing *Cotton Patch,* Tom continued to work in musical theater for several years. In 1982 and 1983, he starred in *Pump Boys and Dinettes,* first at the Fox Theater in Detroit and later on Broadway. The following year he and brother Steve produced a theatrical tribute to Harry, *Lies and Legends: The Musical Stories of Harry Chapin,* which played Off Broadway. He also actively pursued a songwriting and solo singing career. Chapin recorded solo albums in 1982 and 1986 and began to write music for children, including a series of "Cabbage Patch" songs for Parker Bros., the toy makers who caused a sensation with their Cabbage Patch dolls and who briefly supported a record label. Parker Bros. released Chapin's first children's album, *Cabbage Patch Dreams,* in 1986.

Discovered Need for Children's Music

Chapin enjoyed writing children's songs, but more importantly, he discovered a real need to do so. "Around six years ago," he explained to the *Los Altos Town Crier* in 1992, "I looked around for music for [my daughters], and I realized there's not a lot out there for that age group. Kids [between five and ten] really change a lot— they become more verbal, they learn to get jokes, and I decided I'm going to see if I can write some songs for them." He embarked on a series of children's albums that have won high praise from experts and audiences alike. His first four children's records, marketed as "family" music rather than "children's" in response to Chapin's adult fan base, have all won awards from the American Library Association. Chapin's measure of success, however, is a bit more idiosyncratic. He explained to the *Sun,* "The bottom line is when parents say 'Yours are the tapes we take on long [car] trips.'"

Chapin's music, though firmly rooted in the folk tradition of his idols Pete Seeger and the Weavers, borrows from several types of music. Many of his children's songs rely on the syncopated rhythms of Latin music. And he has written several blues tunes, including "I've got the Blues, Greens, and Reds," from his *Billy the Squid* album. The title track of that album—which features country singer Rosanne Cash and pop-jazz saxophonist Branford Marsalis—is a country tune and the cut "Sore Loser" is a good old-fashioned rock and roll number. Chapin also likes to include at least one piece by a classical composer on each children's album, like his "Ghost of Bleak House," also from *Billy the Squid,* which features music by French composer Charles Gounod. Chapin's folk origins, however, are clearly apparent in his intricate guitar, banjo, and autoharp playing.

Music With a Message

Many of Chapin's songs offer serious messages, but they manage not to be preachy. "Ghost of Bleak House," for instance, praises sharing and making friends in the context of an almost-scary ghost story. His witty "Great Big Words" describes the fun that can be had in learning and reading. Several of his songs, including "Happy Earth Day" and "Bye Bye Dodo," emphasize environmental and conservation concerns; he has even released a concert video titled *This Pretty Planet.*

As with his music, Chapin has come by his social awareness and sense of responsibility through his family, who always encouraged thoughtful activism. In the Chapin household success was never measured by fame and fortune. "It was always 'Great. So you're making a lot of money. So what are you *really* contributing to the world?,'" he told Norm Maves of the *Oregonian.* As a result, Chapin has long contributed in many ways. In addition to his more socially conscious songs, he remains committed to WHY and regularly gives benefit concerts to aid the hungry and homeless. He is active in environmental causes and the anti-nuclear movement as well.

The central theme in all of Chapin's work is his desire to communicate his fundamental belief in the power of the individual. He explained his philosophy to *International Musician:* "If there's an underlying message to my music and my existence, I think it has to do with empowerment . . . the idea that you matter . . . you can make an enormous difference. I think Harry's life showed that—what one man can do in a short amount of time with an enormous amount of energy and not being afraid to try."

Selected discography

Chapin Music!, Riceland Records, 1966.
Mount Airy, Thimble Records, 1973.
Life Is Like That, Sundance Music, 1976.
In the City of Mercy, Sundance Music, 1982.
Cabbage Patch Dreams, Parker Bros., 1986.
Let Me Back Into Your Life, Flying Fish Records, 1986.
Family Tree, Sony Kid's Music, 1988.
Moonboat, Sony Kid's Music, 1989.
Mother Earth, Sundance/A&M, 1990.
Billy the Squid, Sony Kid's Music, 1992.
Family Tree, Sony Kid's Music, 1992.

Sources

Billboard, October 10, 1992.
Entertainment Weekly, May 15, 1992.
Intelligencer Journal (Lancaster, PA), October 8, 1990.
International Musician, April 1987.
Los Altos Town Crier (CA), April 1, 1992.
Oregonian, April 2, 1992.
Publishers Weekly, April 6, 1992; April 19, 1993.
Rolling Stone, March 18, 1982.
Sing Out!, Winter 1988.
Sun (Baltimore, MD), October 24, 1992.
Tampa Tribune (FL), May 11, 1990.
Times-Union (Rochester, NY), January 25, 1990.
TV Guide, April 6, 1992.

Additional information for this profile was obtained from Sundance Music, 1993.

—*Robin Armstrong*

Charlie Christian

Guitarist

From the moment he burst onto New York City's jazz scene with the Benny Goodman Orchestra, Charlie Christian changed forever the way jazz guitar would be played. And although his career—and his life—were brief, Christian's influence on the transformation that jazz underwent through the introduction of bebop remains unquestioned.

Born in Bonham, Texas, northeast of Dallas, in 1916, Christian moved with his family first to Dallas, then, around 1921, to Oklahoma City, Oklahoma. Christian's father, who was blind, earned a living playing guitar and singing, sometimes with his three sons, Clarence (on violin and mandolin), Edward (on string bass), and Charlie, whose earliest guitars often were hand-made from cigar boxes.

Charlie's skills were evident early, and he avidly absorbed the work of the many excellent southwestern blues and jazz players. As family friend, novelist, and essayist Ralph Ellison averred in his *Shadow and Act,* the young guitarist was exposed to a wide variety of musical forms at home and in the Oklahoma City community at large. One of the major stylistic influences on Christian, perhaps as early as 1929 and more extensively in 1931, was the visiting tenor saxophonist Lester Young, whose long, arching solo lines made him a jazz icon.

Until Christian, the jazz guitar had nearly always been relegated to serving as a rhythm instrument, a weaker version of the banjo. Though some excellent acoustic guitar soloists had emerged—Lonnie Johnson, Eddie Lang, George Van Eps, Carl Kress, Dick McDonough, and the legendary Django Reinhardt—the guitar remained a minor solo voice. Early experiments, though, especially those by Eddie Durham, to play a guitar whose sound was amplified—at first mechanically, then electronically—showed some promise. In about 1937 Durham and Christian met, and Durham, a gifted composer and arranger as well, taught Christian what he knew about the amplified guitar. Floyd Smith, guitarist with Andy Kirk, may also have played a part in Christian's amplification of his guitar.

Attention of Hammond Led to Goodman Gig

As he immersed himself in playing, sometimes on bass, Christian joined and often led bands that took him as far as Minneapolis, Wyoming, and North Dakota. Wherever he played, he quickly established a reputation as an exciting, innovative talent, using his pickup-amplified guitar as a horn in conjunction with the saxophone and trumpet and taking extended horn-like solos. When he landed back in Oklahoma City in 1939, pianist-com-

For the Record. . .

Born July 29, 1916, in Bonham, TX; raised in Dallas, TX, and Oklahoma City; died of pneumonia, March 2, 1942, in New York, NY.

Became professional guitarist/bassist, c. 1928; played with father and brothers, then with other territory bands in Texas, Oklahoma, and throughout the Southwest; performed and recorded with Benny Goodman Orchestra, 1939-1942; contributed to the birth of bebop during after-hours gigs, Minton's club, New York City, 1940-41.

Awards: *Metronome* poll winner on instrument, 1939-41; *Down Beat* poll winner, 1941-42.

poser Mary Lou Williams, startled by Christian's artistry, alerted John Hammond. Hammond, benefactor to such jazz stars as singer Billie Holiday and bandleaders Count Basie and Benny Goodman, among others, flew to Oklahoma City enroute to a Goodman recording date in Los Angeles to hear Christian. Hammond found Christian's playing "unbelievable" and convinced a reluctant Goodman to grant the guitarist an audition.

On August 16, 1939, at the Victor Hugo restaurant in Beverly Hills, California, Christian, in full garish regalia, set up his Gibson EH-150 amplifier on Goodman's bandstand, preparatory to auditioning with the quintet. Ever wary, Goodman called for "Rose Boom," thinking the Oklahoma "hick" might not know the tune. Witnesses attested that the group, sparked by Christian's brilliant inventiveness, improvised on the tune for *47 minutes!* According to Bill Simon, in *Jazz Guitarists: An Anthology,* Hammond said he "never saw anyone knocked out as Benny was that night."

Less than a month later, on September 11, 1939, Christian found himself in a New York recording studio with a Lionel Hampton group that included such jazz luminaries as Dizzy Gillespie, Benny Carter, Coleman Hawkins, Ben Webster, Chu Berry, Clyde Hart, Milt Hinton, and Cozy Cole. On October 2nd of that year, Christian cut his first record as a member of the Goodman sextet. His impact was immediate and lasting. Not only was his playing a "must hear" for guitarists, but jazz instrumentalists of every kind were attracted to the mature solos of the friendly, unassuming 23 year old.

Sophisticated Beyond His Years

Indeed, despite his age, Christian's musicianship seemed fully developed: his endless improvised riffs and figures formed the basis for compositions; his

sculpted solo lines were miracles of form; his sense of time was impeccable; his infectious joy at playing seemed boundless; and his playing, evincing as it did such relaxed assurance as well as brilliance, inspired bandmates to personal heights. It may be argued, in fact, that Goodman played his best while Christian was with his band. Among the songs based on Christian's various riffs—but usually co-credited to Goodman and/or writer-arranger Jimmy Mundy-are: "Seven Come Eleven," "Charlie's Idea," "Breakfast Feud," "Solo Flight," and "A Smo-o-o-th One."

In addition to his beautiful, flowing melodic lines—executed at even the fastest tempos—Christian increasingly developed a harmonic structure that intrigued fellow musicians and liberated the approach to solo playing. In *The Swing Era,* Gunther Schuller explained, "Because of Christian's superiority as a solo-line player, his rhythm playing has been much neglected; occasionally one even reads implications that he was not terribly effective in this area. But if proof of Christian's prowess as rhythm guitarist be needed, we can find it abundantly." Christian's skill in this area is documented mainly by four recorded sessions: that first session with Hampton, on which he did not solo; a March, 1940, club session in Minneapolis cut by a local disc jockey; a session on February 5, 1941, with the Edmond Hall Celeste Quartet; and one at Minton's club in May of 1941 that included Thelonious Monk on piano and Kenny Clarke on drums.

Minton's had opened in the Hotel Cecil on Harlem's 118th Street in October of 1940. In an unusual move, Teddy Hill—a musician—was named manager. Hill had led a popular band and knew most of the local *and* visiting musicians. Almost instantly, with Hill acting as benevolent host, Minton's became the after-hours place of choice. It especially attracted the more experimental players, such as Gillespie, Clarke, Monk, and Charlie Parker, and it was here that the ingredients blended—and sometimes clashed—to produce bebop, jazz's direction for decades to come.

Minton's Mix Begat Bebop

Minton's became a second home to Christian. Night after night he held forth on the stand, interacting with all comers but especially with those regulars with whom he created the new musical brew. His Minton's activities would, of course, come after he had completed his day's work with Goodman in the recording studio and/or the Hotel Pennsylvania or other nearby venues, and Christian would usually play continuously until 4 a.m. In fact, Christian logged so many hours at Minton's that

Hill bought an amplifier for him so that he would not have to transport his to Minton's nightly.

Of Christian's contributions to the Minton's scene, *Swing Era* author Schuller wrote: "There can be little doubt that at the time of his death, in 1942, Christian was on the threshold of becoming a major voice, perhaps, had he lived, *the* major voice in shaping the new language of jazz. All the greater the tragedy of his loss, one that has, I believe, not yet been fully fathomed and appreciated." Fortunately, the flavor of these Minton's sessions has been preserved through the acetate recordings of jazz fan and collector Jerry Newman, which were released with the help of writer Bill Simon on Vox records in 1947. Though technically wanting, these extended versions of "Stompin' at the Savoy" and an original, "Charlie's Choice," reveal Christian in full glory, propelling the rhythm and elaborating inventively on several choruses.

But the frenzy of Minton's undoubtedly shortened Christian's life. He was diagnosed with tuberculosis in 1940 and advised to curtail his activities. Christian not only ignored this advice, he accelerated his pace, musically and personally, after Minton's opened and into 1941. Immensely popular, he was often surrounded by admiring women and "friends" who provided him with alcohol and marijuana, even after he was admitted to Seaview Sanitarium on Staten Island around July of 1941. Probably as a result of these extracurricular escapades, the 25-year-old genius contracted pneumonia and died on March 2, 1942.

Christian's legacy is all but unanimously recognized. Two generations of jazz guitarists, admittedly or not, trace their inspiration to him. Most admit it. Herb Ellis, the guitar virtuoso mainstay of the Oscar Peterson trio for many years, was asked by *Guitar Player* magazine for its January, 1992, issue to list "The Solos That Changed Jazz Guitar." His first *five* choices were Christian solos on specific songs; his sixth was "Charlie Christian's other solos with the Benny Goodman Sextet and Orchestra." Simon, writing in *Jazz Guitarists: An Anthology*, deemed Christian one of "a handful of musicians of whom it may be said that they completely revolutionized, then standardized anew the role of their instruments in jazz." And Stan Britt, writing in *The Jazz Guitarists*, contributed: "Christian . . . was to become a

seminal figure in the transition from the swing era to the jazz revolution of the early 1940s called bebop. But initially it was his use of an amplified instrument that in itself was to play an integral role in another revolution—that of the jazz guitar itself." Finally, as Allan Kozinn and coauthors sum up in *The Guitar,* "Christian . . . has been jazz guitar's only authentic figure of genius, responsible for synthesizing the best elements of the instrument's previous history into a seamless, totally original approach of such great melodic-harmonic resourcefulness that it has served as the basis for literally all subsequent developments in the instrument's usage in jazz."

Selected discography

Edmond Hall: Celestial Express, Blue Note, 1941.
Charlie Christian, Vox, 1947.
Solo Flight: The Genius of Charlie Christian, Columbia, 1972.
The Harlem Jazz Scene, 1941, Evidence, 1993.
Lester Young and Charlie Christian: 1939-1940, Jazz Archives.

Sources

Books

Britt, Stan, *The Jazz Guitarists,* Blandford Press, 1984.
Ellison, Ralph, *Shadow and Act,* Vintage, 1972 (originally printed in *Saturday Review,* May 17, 1958).
Feather, Leonard, *The New Edition of the Encyclopedia of Jazz,* Bonanza Books, 1965.
Jazz Guitarists: An Anthology, edited by James Sallis, Quill, 1984.
Kienzle, Rich, *Great Guitarists,* Facts on File, 1985.
Kozinn, Allan; Welding, Pete; Forte, Dan; and Santoro, Gene, *The Guitar: The History, The Music, The Players,* Quill, 1984.
Lyons, Len, and Perlo, Don, *Jazz Portraits,* Quill, 1989.
Rust, Brian, *Jazz Records 1897-1942,* Vol. I, Storyville Publications and Co., Ltd., 1982.
Schuller, Gunther, *The Swing Era: The Development of Jazz, 1930-1945,* Oxford University Press, 1989.

Periodicals

Guitar Player, January 1992.

—*Robert Dupuis*

Eric Clapton

Guitarist, singer, songwriter

At the 1993 Grammy awards ceremony, Eric Clapton barely had a chance to sit down. He received six trophies over the course of the evening for his single "Tears in Heaven" and for the album *Unplugged.* It was something of a valedictory for the veteran musician, who has been a star in the pop music firmament since the mid-1960s and who has weathered an astonishing number of tragedies and hardships—drug addiction, alcoholism, romantic disaster, and the deaths of several loved ones—during his career. Through it all, however, he has maintained a singular grace and a devotion to the emotional truth that music can convey. As B. B. King, a pioneer of electric blues guitar, said of Clapton in *Rolling Stone,* "You know it's the blues when he plays it."

Indeed, Clapton's lifelong musical love has been the blues, and his life has often been the stuff of which the blues are made. Clapton was born illegitimately in Ripley, England, as World War II drew to a close. His mother left him to be raised by his grandparents, Rose and John Clapp, when he was a small child. He was brought up thinking they were his parents—until his real mother returned home when he was nine years old. The family pretended that his mother was his sister, but he soon found out the truth from outside sources. "I went into a kind of . . . shock, which lasted through my teens, really," he told *Musician,* "and started to turn me into the kind of person I am now . . . fairly secretive, and insecure, and madly driven by the ability to impress people or be the best in certain areas."

Caught the Blues

As an adolescent, Eric first heard the sound of blues music from the United States and felt a profound and immediate connection to it. The "shatteringly intimate" voice of Delta bluesman Robert Johnson—as Clapton described it in a *Rolling Stone* interview—and, later, the electric blues of Muddy Waters and others motivated him to pick up the guitar; by his teens he was playing in coffeehouses. He joined groups called the Roosters and Casey Jones and the Engineers before finding his way into the Yardbirds in 1963. That ensemble became a sensation for its guitar-fueled, bluesy rock, but Clapton left the Yardbirds after it became clear that greater success would come from pop hits like "For Your Love" rather than the heavy blues to which he was devoted.

Clapton first attracted real attention as a member of John Mayall's Bluesbreakers. Even then, *Rolling Stone*'s Robert Palmer noted, "he played the blues *authentically,* with a genuinely idiomatic feel." By this time the

For the Record. . .

Born Eric Patrick Clapp, March 30, 1945, in Ripley, Surrey, England; son of Patricia Clapp; raised by grandparents John and Rose Clapp; married Patti Boyd Harrison, March 27, 1979 (divorced, 1988); children: (with model Lori Del Santo) Conor (deceased). *Education:* Attended Kingston College of Art, 1962.

Played with bands the Roosters, Casey and the Engineers, the Yardbirds, John Mayall's Bluesbreakers, Cream, Blind Faith, Delaney and Bonnie and Friends, and Derek and the Dominos, 1963-73; solo artist, 1974—. Appeared in films *Tommy* and *Water.*

Selected awards: Named world's top musician by *Melody Maker,* 1969; *Guitar Player* readers poll, best in rock, 1971-74, overall, 1973, and electric blues, 1975 and 1980-82; Grammy Award for album of the year, 1972, for *The Concert for Bangla Desh,* and 1988, for best historical collection and best liner notes, for *Crossroads;* six Grammy awards, including album of the year and song of the year, 1993, for *Unplugged* and "Tears in Heaven"; multiplatinum album (six million) for *Unplugged,* 1993; numerous gold and platinum records.

Addresses: *Record company*—Reprise Records, 3300 Warner Blvd., Burbank, CA 91510.

guitarist had worshippers—for whom the now-famous London graffito "Clapton is God" formed the only gospel—and they would multiply after he began to perform and record with his next group, the legendary power trio Cream. With bassist-vocalist Jack Bruce and drummer Ginger Baker, Clapton helped take rock in a new direction: Cream fused weighty blues with psychedelic rock and jazzy improvisation. The result, as many critics have observed, laid the groundwork for much of the progressive rock and heavy metal that would follow. Clapton wrote the music for Cream's all-time greatest hit, "Sunshine of Your Love"—inspired by his first attendance at a performance by guitar shaman Jimi Hendrix—and recorded a rollicking live version of Robert Johnson's "Crossroads"; both tracks have become "classic rock" standards. Clapton referred to Cream in a 1985 *Rolling Stone* interview as "three virtuosos, all of us soloing all the time."

Cream disintegrated in 1968; the band's chemistry was intense from the beginning, and substance abuse by all three members rendered that intensity intolerable. Their farewell performance at London's Albert Hall has become a touchstone of rock folklore. The guitarist had in the meantime become close to Beatle George Harri-

son; Clapton co-wrote the late Cream hit "Badge" with him and had played a memorable solo on Harrison's "While My Guitar Gently Weeps" for 1968's *The Beatles,* known colloquially as "The White Album." Clapton's relationship with Harrison, though tempestuous, would be a constant throughout his life. (He would also play live with ex-Beatle John Lennon's Plastic Ono Band). Clapton and Baker joined keyboardist-vocalist Steve Winwood and bassist Rick Grech in forming another supergroup, Blind Faith. That band broke up after an album and a tour, and Clapton was never satisfied with its performance, though songs like "Presence of the Lord" and "Can't Find My Way Home" are widely regarded as classics more than two decades later.

Solo Career and Substance Abuse

Eric Clapton, the guitarist's first solo LP, hit record store shelves in 1970. He recorded the album with his friends from Delaney and Bonnie, the group that had opened for Blind Faith on its tour. Even as he honed his singing and songwriting, however, and publicly declared his commitment to Christianity, Clapton fell under the sway of two very demanding substances: cocaine and heroin. With addiction bearing down on him, Clapton formed another short-lived but powerful group, Derek and the Dominos. The band recorded a passionate double-length album, *Layla and Other Assorted Love Songs;* it featured the superlative guitarist Duane Allman, whose work challenged and inspired Clapton to new heights. "Layla," a driving, anguished rocker about Clapton's unrequited love for Harrison's wife Patti, became one of the enduring anthems of the 1970s. Debilitated by rampant drug abuse and road fatigue, the group disbanded before making another album. Clapton was further devastated by the subsequent deaths of Allman, in a motorcycle accident, and Hendrix, from an overdose of barbituates. The idea of dying this way "didn't bother me," Clapton confessed to *Rolling Stone* years later. "When Jimi died, I cried all day because he'd left me behind."

The early 1970s were especially difficult for Clapton, though he thrilled his fans again with the highly publicized all-star Rainbow Concert, which yielded an album. For the most part he lived a reclusive life; it wasn't until 1974 that he quit heroin and put out a new album, the highly successful *461 Ocean Boulevard.* The record, which featured Clapton's hit version of Bob Marley's "I Shot the Sheriff," set the mood for much of his work during the next decade or so: relaxed and rootsy. Subsequent albums, like 1977's *Slowhand,* suggested Clapton was settling into a comfortable musical middle age; beneath the laid-back surface, however, storm clouds were gathering. Clapton had moved from heroin addiction to alcoholism and would struggle with it for several more years. "Drink is very baffling and cunning," he told *Musician* retrospectively. "It's got a personality of its own."

Clapton married Patti Boyd—who had divorced Harrison some years earlier—in 1979, and the two struggled to make their relationship work for nearly nine years; during much of that time alcoholism was wreaking havoc on Clapton's health. In 1981 he was forced to cancel a tour due to a severe ulcer; as a result he scaled back his drinking and thus improved his musical fortunes. He played a memorable benefit performance with fellow ex-Yardbirds guitarists Jeff Beck and Jimmy Page in 1983 and, over the next few years, released the variously regarded albums *Money and Cigarettes, Behind the Sun*—which contains the hit "Forever Man"— and *August.*

Also during the 1980s, Clapton provided the scores for the *Lethal Weapon* films and the British television film *Edge of Darkness.* Polygram's 1988 release of the four-CD hits package *Crossroads* provided exhaustive evidence of Clapton's massive contribution to rock music; the collection garnered Grammy awards for best historical album and best liner notes. Yet the same period saw what *Entertainment Weekly* called the "sad sight" of Clapton appearing on TV beer commercials, playing his version of "After Midnight"; it scarcely need be added that many found the choice of Clapton as a pitchman for such a product uncomfortably ironic.

In 1988 he and Patti Boyd divorced. By then Clapton had a son, Conor, whose mother was Italian model Lori Del Santo, and had for the most part turned his life around. His 1989 album *Journeyman* was quite successful, and his status as a rock institution was assured. The next couple of years, however, would bring him perhaps the most horrendous blows of all. First, esteemed blues guitarist Stevie Ray Vaughan and Clapton road crew members Colin Smythe and Nigel Browne—all close friends of Clapton's—were killed in a helicopter crash in August of 1990. Vaughan had himself recovered from alcoholism and was in peak form and on his way to major, widespread success at the time of his death. "There was no one better than him on this planet," Clapton noted in a 1991 *Rolling Stone* interview. Yet Eric and his whole crew—with whom Vaughan had been touring—voted to go on with the tour. The next show, he said, was an ordeal, but "it was the best tribute I thought we could make—to carry on and let everybody who was coming to see us know that it was in honor of their memory." Performances at Albert Hall were recorded and released on the 1991 collection *24 Nights.*

Turned Suffering Into Art

Fate dealt Clapton an even more terrible blow a few months later. On March 20, 1991, his son Conor—then four years old—fell 49 stories to his death from a hotel window. "I went blank," he told *Rolling Stone.* "As Lori has observed, I just turned to stone, and I wanted to get away from everybody." With the help of Alcoholics Anonymous meetings and the support of friends like Rolling Stone Keith Richards and Genesis leader Phil Collins, he managed to take a devastating crisis and transform it into art. The song "Tears in Heaven," described by *People* as "his sweet, sorrowful lullaby to Conor" and first recorded for the soundtrack to the film *Rush,* also appeared on *Unplugged,* an album culled from a live acoustic performance on MTV. The set features a delicate rendering of "Layla" as well; both songs became massive hits and pushed *Unplugged* into the Top Ten of the *Billboard* album chart.

Clapton was all over the musical map in 1992 and 1993. He reunited with his old mates from Cream for a blistering reunion set at the banquet commemorating the group's induction into the Rock and Roll Hall of Fame. Despite the power of the performance, he downplayed rumors of a reunion album or tour. He also presided over an intimate night of the blues at his now-traditional Albert Hall concert, disappointing some fans by completely avoiding his hits. *Rolling Stone's* David Sinclair concluded that the guitarist "may be this year's most exalted superstar, but no matter how the trophies stack up, the man still has a mean case of the blues."

The trophies certainly stacked up at the Grammy awards presentation—Clapton won six of the nine statuettes for which he was nominated—and it seemed clear that Grammy voters and fans wanted both to compensate him for his crushing recent experiences and to thank him for a quarter century of memorable music. Clapton's strength and poise in the face of tragedy, noted David Browne of *Entertainment Weekly,* "was optimism incarnate. In a simple unassuming way, it said that if he could get through this mess, then so could we." As Clapton told Palmer of *Rolling Stone,* "I try to look on every day now as being a bonus, really. And I try to make the most of it." He added, "The death of my son, the death of Stevie Ray, taught me that life is very fragile, and that if you are given another twenty-four hours, it's a blessing. That's the best way to look at it."

Selected discography

With the Yardbirds

Sonny Boy Williamson and the Yardbirds, Fontana, 1964.
For Your Love (includes "For Your Love"), Epic, 1965.

With John Mayall's Bluesbreakers

Bluesbreakers, Decca, 1966.

With Cream; on Atco except where noted

Fresh Cream, 1966.
Disraeli Gears (includes "Sunshine of Your Love"), 1967.
Wheels of Fire, 1968.
Goodbye (includes "Badge"), 1969.
Cream Live, 1970.
Cream Live 2 (includes "Crossroads"), 1971.
Strange Brew: The Very Best of Cream, Polygram, 1983.

With Blind Faith

Blind Faith (includes "Presence of the Lord" and "Can't Find My
   Way Home"), Atco, 1969.

With Derek and the Dominos

Layla and Other Assorted Love Songs (includes "Layla"),
   Atco, 1971.
Derek and the Dominos—Live in Concert, RSO, 1973.

Solo albums

Eric Clapton's Rainbow Concert, RSO/Polygram/Polydor, 1973.
461 Ocean Boulevard (includes "I Shot the Sheriff"), RSO/
   Polygram/Polydor, 1974.
There's One in Every Crowd, RSO/Polygram/Polydor, 1975.
E.C. Was Here, RSO/Polygram/Polydor, 1975.
No Reason to Cry, RSO/Polygram/Polydor, 1976.
Slowhand, RSO/Polygram/Polydor, 1977.
Backless, RSO/Polygram/Polydor, 1978.
Just One Night, RSO/Polygram/Polydor, 1980.
Another Ticket, RSO/Polygram/Polydor, 1981.
Time Pieces: The Best of Eric Clapton, RSO/Polygram/Polydor, 1982.
Times Pieces II: Live in the Seventies, RSO/Polygram/Polydor, 1982.
Money and Cigarettes, Warner Bros./Reprise, 1983.

Behind the Sun (includes "Forever Man"), Warner Bros./
   Reprise, 1985.
August, Warner Bros./Reprise, 1986.
Crossroads, Polydor, 1988.
Journeyman, Warner Bros./Reprise, 1989.
24 Nights, Warner Bros./Reprise, 1991.
Unplugged (includes "Tears in Heaven" and "Layla"), Warner
   Bros./Reprise, 1992.

Contributor

The Beatles, "While My Guitar Gently Weeps," *The Beatles,*
   Capitol, 1968.
The Concert for Bangla Desh, 1972; reissued, Capitol, 1991.
The Last Waltz, 1976; reissued, Warner Bros., 1988.
Lethal Weapon (soundtrack), Warner Bros./Reprise, 1987.
Lethal Weapon II (soundtrack), Warner Bros./Reprise, 1990.
Lethal Weapon III (soundtrack), Warner Bros./Reprise, 1992.
Rush (soundtrack; includes "Tears in Heaven"), Warner Bros./
   Reprise, 1992.

Sources

Commonweal, March 13, 1992.
Crawdaddy!, November 1975.
Entertainment Weekly, February 19, 1993.
Guitar Player, July 1985.
Musician, May 1992.
People, March 1, 1993.
Rolling Stone, October 17, 1991; October 15, 1992; April 15,
   1993; April 29, 1993.

Additional information for this profile was obtained from Reprise
Records media information, 1992.

—Simon Glickman

Shawn Colvin

Singer, songwriter, guitarist

During the late 1980s folk-flavored music once again made its way toward the mainstream, through the work of such artists as Suzanne Vega, Tracy Chapman, Nanci Griffith, and the Indigo Girls. Shawn Colvin, after more than a decade in various music scenes, waltzed through the door these performers had opened and was met with critical awe.

Likening her to a host of great vocalists and songwriters—Vega, Joni Mitchell, Rickie Lee Jones, Janis Ian, Emmylou Harris—music critics tended toward hyperbole when they discovered Colvin. "Singing of the athletics of love and the aesthetics of loss (her words not mine), Shawn Colvin is the best thing I've heard since the sliced bread of the Jurassic era," *Melody Maker's* Chris Roberts exclaimed. Indeed, Colvin drew praise for her profound and personal songwriting. According to Martin Johnson of *New York Newsday,* her "songbook is a startlingly articulate chronicle of the pain of adult love," while, as Darryl Morden of the *Hollywood Reporter* noted, there is "a child-wonder in Colvin's writing that balances out her more serious work." She also thrilled critics with her voice, described by the *Hudson Current* as "fragile as antique glass, sultry as smoke," "bouncy," "hypnotic," "supple," and "so soft it's like breathing cotton." And as Peter Howell observed in the *Toronto Star,* "Her voice wraps itself around you, like a favorite song heard on a car radio during a long night ride home."

Colvin was born on January 10, 1956, in Vermillion, South Dakota. As her parents pursued advanced degrees, they transplanted Shawn and her three siblings first to London, Ontario, and then to Carbondale, Illinois. Colvin's parents were both musical; her father played guitar and banjo and loved listening to folk music. Colvin sang in the church choir, particularly enjoying church hymns, and as she told David Keeps of *Harper's Bazaar,* "minor-key Christmas carols."

Colvin was also influenced by rock and pop, particularly the Beatles, Laura Nyro, the Band's Robbie Robertson, and Joni Mitchell. When she was ten she picked up her brother's four-string guitar and learned how to play—by the time she was a teenager she was drawing album covers. "I had a very rich fantasy life," Colvin revealed to Ann Kolson in the *Philadelphia Inquirer.* "I thought I'd be a prodigy. I think I really wanted to be very famous, very young. . . . I knew I was good . . . but nobody got encouraged for stuff like that in South Dakota."

Paid Musical Dues

Colvin began performing as part of a duo while in high school, a time that she described to Timothy White of

For the Record. . .

Born January 10, 1956, in Vermillion, SD; married Simon Tassano (a musician, sound engineer, and tour manager), 1993. *Education:* Southern Illinois University, mid-1970s.

Began performing in folk and rock clubs, Carbondale, IL, mid-1970s; formed Shawn Colvin Band, 1976; performed solo and with various bands in Illinois, Texas, California, and New York, 1976-1983; performed solo in folk clubs, East Coast, 1983-1989; toured Europe with Suzanne Vega, 1987; released independent album *Live Tape,* 1988; signed with Columbia Records, 1988; released *Steady On,* 1989; toured U.S. and abroad, 1989.

Awards: Grammy Award for best contemporary folk recording, 1991, for *Steady On,* and Grammy Award nomination for best pop vocal performance, female, 1994, for "I Don't Know Why"; New York Music awards for best new vocalist, 1988, best debut female vocalist, 1989, for *Steady On,* and best folk artist, 1990.

Addresses: *Record Company*—Columbia Records, 666 Fifth Ave., P.O. Box 4455, New York, NY 10101-4455. *Management*—Ronald Fierstein, AGF Entertainment Ltd., 30 West 21st St., 7th Floor, New York, NY 10010.

Billboard as her "angry high school days," during which she "always felt like an orphan" and had a "pretty self-destructive lifestyle." She graduated a year early and remained in town to attend Southern Illinois University. While in college she played folk and rock in local clubs and soon moved on to music full time. After a turn with her own hard-rock Shawn Colvin Band, she joined the country-swing Dixie Diesels and moved with them to Austin, Texas. Eventually Colvin returned to Carbondale, and after a brief stint back at school, she started performing again.

Colvin's next move took her to California, where for a year and a half she played in small clubs. Then, in 1980, she moved to New York and joined the Buddy Miller Band. When bassist John Leventhal became part of that outfit, he and Colvin bonded over a shared love of the music of roots guitarist Ry Cooder and became involved musically and romantically. Colvin and Leventhal later formed a band that played pop music in the Steely Dan vein. At one point, she was also the only woman in the bluegrass Red Clay Ramblers. These years were not easy on Colvin; as she revealed to Gary Graff of the *Detroit Free Press,* she hit "emotional rock bottom" in the early '80s. But, with the help of Leventhal, she said, "I began to have the courage to say what I really wanted

to in my lyrics." While Colvin and Leventhal's romantic relationship did not last, their musical collaboration did; he would be instrumental in her first major-label albums.

In 1983 Colvin returned to solo work, finding a niche in the enduring folk scene of New York City's Greenwich Village. The Fast Folk music collective discovered her and recorded one of her earliest songs, "I Don't Know Why." Colvin soon built a following in New York and extended it to folk clubs along the East Coast. Her career got a critical boost from Suzanne Vega: Colvin sang back-up on Vega's 1987 hit "Luka," joined Vega on her European tour, and signed with Vega's manager.

By 1988, Colvin had arrived, at least in New York City. That year she was named best new vocalist at the New York Music Awards and released an independently produced cassette titled *Live Tape.* She also signed a recording contract with Columbia Records, which resulted in the release of *Steady On* in 1989. The album included many songs Colvin had written over the years, including some co-written by Leventhal, who also produced the collection. Dark and haunting, *Steady On* gave Colvin the space to address her past wanderings and exorcise some demons.

Won Grammy for Debut

Critics were impressed with the effort. John Leland of *Newsweek* called *Steady On* "a debut album of eye-opening clarity." *Billboard's* White observed, "Colvin mounted a siren-like assault on the sensibilities, enticing with fair words and castle-building imagery, and then delivering concrete disclosures that ran dungeon-deep." A *Sassy* reader gave the album five stars, assessing it as "better than your best religious experience," and gushed, "I can't pick just one song to recommend because they are all just so downright funky!"

Colvin's critics were struck not only by her songwriting, but also by her guitar style. She became known for her unusual tunings and rhythmic playing. The percussive technique is Colvin's way of keeping things lively when she plays for two hours without a band; as she explained to *Guitar Player's* Kevin Ransom, "I don't have the patience to really learn the guitar neck or do a lot of fancy picking or finger work. And, partly because I'm a woman, this rhythmic style seemed like a more gripping way to grab attention and make the songs work." Colvin has also been greatly influenced by guitar virtuoso Richard Thompson, with whom she toured after the release of *Steady On.* "I had to learn a bunch of his songs, which meant learning chord combinations I'd never have thought of," she told Ransom. "His melodies and chord progressions astounded me. Since then, I've wanted to really push myself and take my playing to odd places that it's never been before."

David Hajdu of the *Hollywood Reporter* found Colvin's singing as clever as her guitar work. "She uses dynamics for effect, going from whispers to full-throated belting. But her most effective vocal device is her way of slurring notes and slipping into conversational speech

---

"I haven't sold a zillion records, but these people who come out to see me I think will always be around in some numbers. That's a good place to be. I've got a really, really good job."

---

unexpectedly." Similarly, White noted, "Colvin is an artful yet seemingly effortless vocalist whose prismatic grasp of intonation is married to a serene sense of control." Colvin's colleagues seemed to agree with the music press; in 1991 the artist was awarded a Grammy Award for best contemporary folk recording for *Steady On.*

Following the record's release, Colvin toured the U.S., as well as Canada, Europe, and Australia, performing solo and at folk festivals. Her shows were popular with fans and critics, not only for their quality but for her "easy-going wit and charming stage presence," determined *New York Newsday's* Johnson. She was a guest on *Late Night With David Letterman, The Tonight Show,* and *CBS This Morning,* contributed vocals to a number of friends' recordings and collective albums, recorded a duet with Bruce Hornsby called "Lost Soul," and toured with rock stalwart Neil Young as well as Thompson. It wasn't long before she was ready to return to the studio and record another album. The result was 1992's *Fat City* and a major, headlining tour.

The mood of *Fat City* was a departure for Colvin; when she started on the project, she intended to record an album about accepting her status as a single woman, but, as fate would have it, she fell in love with Richard Thompson's sound man and tour manager, Simon Tassano, and, as she explained in *Rolling Stone,* "It

changed the tone of the songs I'd written and inspired others, songs I didn't know were gonna be written. So the joke was on me, I'm happy to say." Colvin and Tassano would eventually marry, in September of 1993. While John Leventhal co-produced some of the cuts on *Fat City,* the primary producer was Larry Klein, who also played bass on the album. Collaborating with Klein afforded an added bonus—it meant meeting and working with Klein's wife, Joni Mitchell. Colvin recorded *Fat City* in their home studio, and as she told David Wild in *Vogue,* "Meeting Joni was a moment I was waiting for all my life." *Fat City* also included contributions from a wealth of musical luminaries besides Klein and Mitchell: Thompson, Hornsby, Mary-Chapin Carpenter, Booker T. Jones, the Subdudes, Chris Whitley, and Bela Fleck.

Critics raved about *Fat City,* thrilled that Colvin had maintained the momentum of her stunning debut. In *Billboard's* view, the disc "[fulfilled] all the promise of her preceding *Steady On* collection, her deceptively handsome sound concealing a wealth of narrative jolts and surprises." Nashville's *Metro Music Monthly* praised the record's "well-read lyrics with Dylan-esque attention to detail, that shimmery, cool contralto, and a good ear for melody and arrangement"; *The Hudson Current* reveled in the lyric finesse as well, reporting, "Colvin uses words like found objects, stringing them together into collages of imagery."

One of the songs from *Fat City,* Colvin's old standby "I Don't Know Why," quickly became the critics' darling. *Billboard,* the *Chicago Tribune,* and the *Gavin Report* were certain the song would become a classic, the latter calling it "one of the most brilliantly conceived and executed songs of this decade." Reviewer Ben Edmonds, writing in Detroit's *Metro Times,* was a rare dissenting voice: "Sad to say, *Fat City* is somewhat less than the sum of its parts. Most of the songs show flashes of something . . . but none fully press their advantages." Still, even this criticism was qualified, Edmonds conceding, "Most contemporary folk artists would be only too happy to claim *Fat City.* For Shawn Colvin, it's a small sophomore stumble."

Really Good Job

Despite the critical accolades, Colvin was not considered a mainstream pop artist, and her record sales reflected this. As *Vogue's* Wild noted, no specific radio format was targeted, and as such, Colvin failed to reach the wide audience that radio play attracts. *New York Newsday* contributor Johnson observed that her songs had "proven too folk for mainstream and too urbane for country." But, like many contemporary folksingers, Colvin enjoys a strong, dedicated following. "I haven't sold a zillion records, [but] these people who come out to see me I think will always be around in some numbers. That's a good place to be, in my opinion," she remarked in a *Pollstar* profile. "It's a good career to have. I'm not fabulously wealthy and I don't get recognized on the street, but I've got a really, really good job."

With the advantage of hindsight, Colvin was not only happy to be where she was, but glad she had to wait so long to make her mark. Despite her childhood fantasies of "becoming big and famous," she admitted to *Metro Times* contributor Stewart Francke that she finds her lack of notoriety a blessing, reasoning, "I don't have a lot of illusions about what's happening to me now. . . . Bravado is a luxury for the very young. I don't have the early 20s, fearless, immortal vibe anymore." Francke too seemed thankful for her circuitous route to success, venturing, "It's our gain that Colvin . . . knocked around for a lot of years. Because all the ennui, worry, brief rewards and futile aggregations that accompany the maintenance of faith beyond the limelight are now found in her dusky, brave voice."

Selected discography

Live Tape, 1988.
Steady On, Columbia, 1989.
(Contributor) *Acoustic Christmas*, Columbia, 1990.
(Contributor) *Hitchiker Exampler 2*, 1991.
Fat City (includes "I Don't Know Why"), Columbia, 1992.
(Contributor) *Hitchhiker Exampler*, Columbia.

Sources

Books

Harris, Craig, *The New Folk Music*, White Cliffs Media Company, 1991.

Periodicals

Billboard, October 10, 1992; October 31, 1992; December 5, 1992; February 13, 1993; May 29, 1993.
Brum Beat, October 1990.
Chicago Tribune, November 12, 1992.
Detroit Free Press, June 11, 1993.
Gavin Report, January 29, 1993.
Guitar Player, January 1993; October 1993.
Harper's Bazaar, February 1990.
Hollywood Reporter, June 22, 1990; May 28, 1993.
Hudson Current (NY), December 3, 1992.
Los Angeles Daily News, December 12, 1992.
Musician, March 1990.
Melody Maker, July 10, 1993.
Metro Music Monthly (Nashville), December 1992.
Metro Times (Detroit), December 2, 1992; June 9, 1993.
Music Express Magazine, January 1993.
Music Week, April 24, 1993.
Newsweek, November 9, 1992.
New York Daily News, February 19, 1993.
New York Newsday, May 4, 1993.
New Yorker, May 3, 1993.
People, April 9, 1990; February 15, 1993.
Philadelphia Inquirer, November 24, 1992.
Pollstar, April 5, 1993.
Request, January 1993.
Richmond Times Dispatch (VA), May 8, 1993.
Rolling Stone, January 7, 1993; February 4, 1993.
Sassy, December 1990.
Time, January 18, 1993.
Toronto Star, October 31, 1992; November 12, 1992.
USA Today, March 18, 1993.
Vogue, April 1993.

Additional information for this profile was provided by AGF Entertainment Ltd. and obtained from Columbia Records publicity materials.

—*Megan Rubiner Zinn*

Cypress Hill

In the fertile world of rap music—where new artists and groups arrive every day—it isn't that difficult for aspiring rappers to sell a few albums and earn some audience attention, but it can be much harder for them to actually offer something distinctive enough to win national popularity. Cypress Hill succeeded in this task with their first album, not only earning the favor of demanding hardcore hip-hop, or "gangsta rap," fans, but also achieving crossover success with pop music buyers. The group's style has won considerable praise from reviewers, and the trio's mix of ethnic backgrounds—Mexican American, Cuban, and Italian American—has inspired an unusually multicultural audience. Perhaps most distinctive about the band, however, has been their earnest and diligent promotion of marijuana legalization; both on their records and off, they advocate the free use of the drug.

Despite the group's ethnic variety—unusual in a genre dominated by African-American artists and listeners, their background is nonetheless typical for hardcore rap. Lead rapper B-Real, born Louis Freese, hails from

For the Record. . .

M embers include **B-Real** (born Louis Freese c. 1970 in Los Angeles, CA), **DJ Muggs** (born Lawrence Muggerud c. 1970 in Queens, NY), and **Sen Dog** (born Senen Reyes c. 1966 in Cuba).

Group formed in Southgate section of Los Angeles, mid-1980s; began recording together in 1988; produced demo tapes, including *Real Estate,* 1988, and *Light Another,* 1989; signed with Columbia/Ruffhouse, 1989, and released *Cypress Hill,* 1991; toured with Lollapalooza II, 1992.

Awards: Platinum albums for *Cypress Hill,* 1991, and *Black Sunday,* 1993; *Billboard* Music Award for best rap artist, 1991.

Member: NORML (National Organization for the Reform of Marijuana Laws).

Addresses: *Record company*—Columbia Records, 2100 Colorado Ave., Santa Monica, CA 90404.

a Los Angeles neighborhood known as Cypress Hill that typifies the poverty and resultant violence plaguing the inner city. Growing up there, B-Real befriended Senen Reyes, known as Sen Dog on the street, the older brother in a Latino family that had immigrated from Cuba in 1980; Reyes was 14 when he met B-Real. They would eventually form a trio with Lawrence Muggerud, who went by DJ Muggs.

Sen Dog had formed a few groups in the early 1980s after leaving high school. One was DVX, which he started with his younger brother, Mellow Man Ace; B-Real worked with the brothers briefly before the group dissolved. *Pulse!*'s Jon Wiederhorn summarized the friendship that developed between B-Real and Sen Dog, explaining, "They skipped school and smoked pot together. They listened to music and fought in a street gang together." The duo met Muggs in 1986, when he was just beginning to acquire turntable skills, and the three began working together.

DJ Muggs Emerged as Driving Force

Music writers have generally focused on Muggs as the musical force behind the group, cataloguing his early efforts to break into the industry. In 1982, the Italian American moved from Queens, New York, where he lived with an uncle, to live in the Bell Gardens section of Los Angeles with his mother. Soon after arriving in Los Angeles, the teenager began spinning records for a rap group called 7A3; although the group never won

the attention some critics feel they deserved, his experience with 7A3 afforded Muggs the opportunity to cut an album with a major label, Geffen, in 1988. But the label was apparently not experienced enough with rap to produce or market the album properly, and *Coolin' in Cali* faded from view without making an impression.

7A3 dissolved after this disappointment, and Muggs returned to a previous collaboration with B-Real and Sen Dog determined "to flex his own muscle as a freaky-deke producer," according to *Source* contributor Michael Gonzales. Their earlier association had been less serious than Muggs's work with 7A3; they were mainly, as Muggs told Gonzales, "doing house parties and hangin' out gettin' high." Indeed, before Muggs became serious about music, the trio that would become Cypress Hill were primarily involved in the kind of street activity that occupied most young men their in neighborhood: hanging out with friends, or "homies," and negotiating the dangers of gang life. All three have experienced shootings close up, seeing best friends murdered before their eyes; B-Real felt a bullet pass through his lung in 1988. As with most young people in their situation, they had little opportunity for a different life. Music was one of the few outs available.

In 1988 Muggs invited B-Real and Sen Dog to join him in the studio, reserving for himself complete control over the recording. They put their first song, "Real Estate," on tape and followed it with more material in 1989. Several of these songs, such as the single "Light Another," would eventually make it onto the trio's debut album. It was another year, though, before they connected with wily manager Nancy Walker, who won them a contract with Ruffhouse Records, a Columbia subsidiary. At Ruffhouse they hooked up with producer Joe Nicolo, who became "the unofficial fourth member of Cypress Hill," Gonzales reported in *The Source;* Nicolo is credited with nurturing Muggs's DJ talent and production style.

Cypress Hill's self-titled debut album hit record store shelves at the end of 1991, unsupported by extensive advertising or radio airplay; nonetheless, reviewers and listeners greeted it with unexpected enthusiasm. The group dedicated itself to live shows, increasing their exposure as much as possible. Praising the group's "freshness" in his 1991 *Rolling Stone* review, Kevin Powell declared, "*Cypress Hill* unveils an arsenal of sounds ranging from reggae to rock, all firmly rooted in the distinct cultures of Southern California. Rather than capitalize on the violent images prevalent in gangsta rap, this trio spins tales of reality that play down the shock factor; the album is a merger of craft with the commitment to inform." *Spin*'s review further hailed the emergence of something singular, allowing, "The unique

Cypress Hill sound has a place unto itself in the hip-hop realm. It injects heavy doses of funk into your eardrums, giving you a new way to experience hardcore beats and rhymes." Two years later, *Rolling Stone* contributor Dimitri Ehrlich looked back to claim that Cypress Hill had "changed the face of hip-hop."

Potheads

In addition to the quality of Muggs's mixing and B-Real's uncommon rapping—a somewhat unhinged delivery described by several reviewers as "cartoony"—the album boasted something else: the group's unabashed and prevalent endorsement of marijuana use. *Cypress Hill* showcased three songs explicitly about pot, and *Black Sunday* would add more. B-Real explained to *Pulse!*'s Wiederhorn how the group happened on its trademark subject: "When we started out, we didn't plan to be the leaders of any pot legalization thing or nothing. It just sort of happened," explained B-Real. "We were trying to get songs going for our demo, and we didn't know what to write about. One day we was all getting high, and someone goes, 'Yo, Holmes, light another.' And I thought, 'Hey, that's a good idea for a song.' Then after that it became like, 'Shit, I get high every day—I can talk about weed.'"

B-Real and Sen Dog have gone beyond dedicated smoking to dedicated study, schooling themselves in the history of marijuana, as well as in the facts about its many potential uses. *Black Sunday* offers a selection of this information to its buyers in the record's liner notes; members of the group will offer similar information to interviewers. Cypress Hill also became official spokespeople for NORML (the National Organization for the Reform of Marijuana Laws). Finally, the trio has related their support of reefer to the popularity of their music across racial and ethnic divisions. As B-Real told Wiederhorn, "We do our music not to leave anyone out. It's not pro-black, pro-Latin, pro-white, pro-anything. Marijuana is a universal thing and it don't see color."

While the push to legalize marijuana use occupied the group after the release of *Cypress Hill,* it was hardly their only focus. The trio performed regularly, including an opening spot for popular hip-hop act Naughty by Nature. They had their biggest live success as part of the Lollapalooza II music festival in 1992. The band also won considerable public exposure with singles for several movie soundtracks; they contributed to *Juice, White Men Can't Jump,* and *The Last Action Hero* and offered collaborative pieces with Sonic Youth and Pearl Jam to the *Judgment Night* soundtrack. Muggs quickly became a sought-after DJ and producer, lending his talents to a range of rap acts that includes House of Pain, Ice Cube, Yo Yo, and the Beastie Boys.

Black Sunday Broke Records

By the time Cypress Hill's second release, *Black Sunday,* hit the charts in July of 1993, *Cypress Hill* had amply demonstrated its longevity, retaining a consistent position in the *Billboard* Top 200 album chart; it had also long since earned a platinum record. *Black Sunday,* however, not only eclipsed the success of its predecessor, it surpassed the success of every rap album that had come before it. Bursting out of the blocks with the catchy single "Insane in the Brain," it debuted at the top of the pop charts, displaying its crossover power, and sold over 260,000 copies in its first week, hurtling past the record previously set by rapper Ice Cube. Still, not all reviewers loved the album as much as the buying public, some comparing it unfavorably to the debut disc; in *Vibe,* former champion Powell placed it on a list of "disappointing sophomore efforts." Colson Whitehead, however, writing for *Spin,* called *Black Sunday* "a consolidation of power for Cypress Hill, tending more toward perfecting a solid formula than toying with invention." And, as critics had in their reviews of the first album, Whitehead paid special tribute to the DJ, stating, "Muggs has perfected his method, recycling all manner of sonic trash to find the useful artifact."

Signaling the band's musical evolution, a change of tone was noted by many observers on *Black Sunday.* Ehrlich, for one, commented in *Rolling Stone,* "It sounds paranoid, vicious and dark." The writer turned to B-Real for an explanation of that sound: "We just approached this album thinking that any time anybody stays satisfied with what they have, they get lazy and start slipping. . . . So we stayed hungry, stayed in our neighborhoods, and we didn't let the success with the record business go to our heads. It's a little easier making money *legally,* you know, but basically we still go through the same shit. Money can't fix everything, so we just put our frustration into the music, and it came out moody like that."

Selected discography

Cypress Hill (includes "Light Another"), Ruffhouse/Columbia, 1991.
Black Sunday (includes "Insane in the Brain"), Ruffhouse/Columbia, 1993.

Also contributed to soundtracks for films, including *Juice, White Men Can't Jump, The Last Action Hero,* and *Judgment Night.*

Sources

Billboard, August 7, 1993.

Cash Box, August 3, 1991.

Entertainment Weekly, August 6, 1993; August 20, 1993.

L.A. Weekly, June 11, 1993.

Musician, October 1993.

People, August 30, 1993.

Pulse!, October 1993; November 1993.

Request, September 1993.

Rolling Stone, October 3, 1991; May 28, 1992; August 5, 1993; September 16, 1993; November 11, 1993.

Source, July 1993.

Spin, September 1991; August 1993.

Vibe, September 1993.

Additional information for this profile was obtained from Ruffhouse/Columbia, 1993.

—*Ondine E. Le Blanc*

Billy Ray Cyrus

Singer

Loved by fans, loathed by critics, Billy Ray Cyrus rose from obscurity to country music superstardom in 1992 following the release of his debut album, *Some Gave All.* Featuring the monster single "Achy Breaky Heart," the album sold nine million copies worldwide and made Cyrus a household name in over 100 languages. The disc enjoyed the longest tenure ever for a debut record in the Number One spot of *Billboard*'s pop chart—18 weeks—surpassing the mark previously held by the Beatles.

Known far and wide for his ruggedly handsome looks (oft-cited "bad hair" notwithstanding) and swiveling hips, Cyrus has endured a backlash of criticism from detractors who dismiss him as a "flash in the pan." Yet on the heels of a large-scale U.S. and European tour and the release of a second, hugely successful album in 1993, *It Won't Be the Last,* the award-winning Cyrus seemed to have had the last laugh.

Born in 1961 and raised in the small eastern Kentucky town of Flatwoods, Cyrus got his first taste of singing at the age of four in his father's gospel group, the Crownsmen Quartet. His mother also enjoyed music and often played bluegrass piano for young Billy Ray. Cyrus's paternal grandfather was a Pentecostal preacher who instilled a strong sense of religion in the boy. When he was five years old, Cyrus's parents divorced, he and his older brother, Kevin, remaining with their mother in Flatwoods. Both parents later remarried, giving Cyrus half-siblings on both sides of the family.

As a child, Cyrus was quiet, awkward, and sensitive. He later discovered a "wild streak," however, that would eventually serve him well onstage. An interest in sports led him to play high school baseball and football with a passion. It was during this time that he began the weight-lifting regimen that would define his now-famous physique.

One of Cyrus's earliest role models was Cincinnati Reds catcher Johnny Bench, but the young man soon realized that he wasn't cut out to be a professional athlete. Following graduation, he attended Kentucky's Georgetown College, where he played baseball until he dropped out during his junior year.

Inner Voice Urged Him Toward Music Career

Cyrus's early musical influences were country singers Merle Haggard, Johnny Cash, Hank Williams, and Buck Owens, as well as the 1970s rock groups Lynyrd Skynyrd, Bob Seger and the Silver Bullet Band, Led Zeppelin, ZZ Top, and Credence Clearwater Revival. It

For the Record. . .

Born August 25, 1961, in Flatwoods, KY; son of Ronald Ray (a state legislator) and Ruth Ann (Adkins) Cyrus; married Cindy Smith, 1986 (divorced, 1991); married Leticia Finley, 1993; children: (with Kristen Luckey) Christopher Cody; (with Finley) Destiny Hope. *Education:* Attended Georgetown College.

Formed band Sly Dog, 1982; performed with band The Breeze, Los Angeles, c. 1985; became solo artist, 1986; signed with Mercury Records, 1990; released single "Achy Breaky Heart" and album *Some Gave All,* 1992.

Awards: Country Music Association citation for single of the year, for "Achy Breaky Heart"; American Music awards for favorite country single, for "Achy Breaky Heart," and for best new artist; five Grammy Award nominations, including record of the year, for "Achy Breaky Heart," and best new artist; World Music Award for best international new artist of the year; and People's Choice Award, all 1993. Platinum single for "Achy Breaky Heart," 1992; multiplatinum album for *Some Gave All,* 1993, and platinum album for *It Won't Be the Last,* 1994.

Addresses: *Record company*—Mercury Nashville, 66 Music Square W., Nashville, TN 37203.

was in 1982, while attending a Neil Diamond concert, that the 20-year-old Cyrus's intuition told him to pursue music as a career. "I thought I was going crazy for a long time," Cyrus told Marjie McGraw in *Country Music,* "but after many months of listening to the [inner] voice and ignoring it, I finally went and got a guitar and started a band called Sly Dog. I mean, as soon as I got the guitar, the next day we had a band."

Within a year the band was a popular, if unpolished, attraction at nightclubs in Kentucky, Ohio, and West Virginia. Following a fire in 1984 that destroyed Sly Dog's equipment, Cyrus pulled up stakes and headed for Los Angeles. There he gained studio experience playing with a band called The Breeze, but he made his living selling cars. Returning to his old stomping grounds in 1986, Cyrus rebuilt his band and began playing five nights a week at the Ragtime Lounge in Huntington, West Virginia.

In 1986 Cyrus married Cindy Smith, whom he had met while performing at a bar in Ironton, Ohio. Though happy for the first few years, the stress of maintaining different schedules eventually took its toll and the couple divorced in 1991 amid rumors of Cyrus's infidelity. In 1992, in fact, Cyrus admitted to fathering two illegiti-

mate children—conceived after his divorce—and readily accepted his "obligations" to both.

During the mid-1980s, while paying his dues in smoky bars, Cyrus traveled as often as possible to Nashville. With a portfolio of photos, songs, and nightclub credentials in hand, Cyrus searched relentlessly for a recording contract. After nearly five years of rejection, his break came in 1988 when Grand Ole Opry star Del Reeves cut his song "It Ain't Over 'Til It's Over" and introduced Cyrus to manager Jack McFadden. Then, in 1989, Buddy Cannon, the Mercury label's Nashville manager of artist recruitment, saw Cyrus open for Reba McEntire at Louisville's Freedom Hall. By 1990, Cyrus had a contract with Mercury. In 1991 he recorded his debut album, *Some Gave All,* with Sly Dog. The title track was a reference to Vietnam veterans. The album was not released until the following spring.

Benefitted From Canny Marketing

In an incredibly successful—if daring—marketing ploy, Mercury executives created an audience for their handsome singer by releasing the "Achy Breaky Heart" video prior to the single and introducing a popular line dance that soon swept the country. "Heart," a Don Van Tress update of George Jones's 1962 recording "Aching, Breaking Heart," became the most-requested song on country and pop radio—before its release. It went on to sell over a million copies and received the Country Music Association's single of the year award in 1993.

Cyrus immediately began to endure slings and arrows from both music reviewers and his peers, many of whom argued that the single and Cyrus himself were one-hit novelties. Moreover, he was accused of being more pop-oriented than country—more a product of shrewd marketing than genuine talent. Country singer Waylon Jennings compared him to the late '50s pretty-boy teen idol Fabian. And Travis Tritt publicly denounced Cyrus for reducing country music to an "ass wiggling contest," a comment he would later retract. Cyrus fired back during the American Music Awards telecast in early 1993; onstage to accept the award for best new artist, Cyrus borrowed some lyrics from one of Tritt's hit singles, saying, "For those who don't like 'Achy Breaky Heart,' here's a quarter; call someone who cares."

Country superstar Garth Brooks, however, with whom Cyrus battled for space on the music charts during his long reign at the top in 1992, came out in support of Cyrus. As Brooks told Gary Graff of the *Detroit Free*

Press, "I don't think people know how to react to Billy Ray. The worst thing we can do now is what rock 'n' roll did, which is cut itself up into little bits and be real competitive with each other. Billy Ray's success is just as good for country as anyone else's."

A second single from *Some Gave All,* "Could've Been Me," became a Top Five hit on the country charts and made some inroads into shoring up Cyrus's ailing

---

> *"If the bottom drops out tomorrow, two months later you'll find me in some smoky bar in Kentucky or Tennessee or West Virginia, in some corner, making my music."*

---

critical status. A third single, "Wher'm I Gonna Live," — written after Cyrus's ex-wife had thrown his belongings out on their front lawn—also enjoyed heavy airplay and made *Billboard's* Top 10. Two more singles were released but remained further down the charts.

John Morthland, in his *Country Music* review of Cyrus's second album, summarized the singer's image problem following the release of *Some Gave All's* "Achy Breaky Heart," venturing, "I don't think his detractors despise Billy Ray's music so much as they despise what he stands for—the careful grooming, the "dance craze" created to make the record sell, the way every drop of sweat is in place when he does his robotic stage show—but it seems to me that this was all quite inevitable, and if it hadn't been him, it would soon have been someone else."

In February of 1993, Cyrus returned to the studio with Sly Dog to produce the follow-up to *Some Gave All.* The title track from that effort, "It Won't Be the Last," was apparently inspired by Cyrus's broken marriage, but some observers saw it as a bold message to critics. The band spent two months perfecting the album, as opposed to the two *weeks* they had spent recording *Some Gave All.* Released in June of 1993 with great promotional fanfare by Mercury, the disc was certified platinum by mid-September.

Still, critical acclaim continued to elude Cyrus. Billy Altman commented in his *People* review of *It Won't Be the Last,* "Cyrus seems to be making a common mis-

take that rapid-rise performers usually live to regret, namely, believing his own hype. . . . And therein lies his problem. Over the long haul, country music's lifeblood is the union of singer and song, not of beef and cake." *Entertainment Weekly* weighed in with this sentiment: "*It Won't Be the Last* suggests an earnest but generic singer thrust into the big leagues too soon. The songs are a mutant breed of chest-heaving ballads . . . and he-man rock guitars supplied by his band Sly Dog. At least three numbers recycle the kick-up-the-dust riff of 'Achy Breaky Heart.' His song 'Throwin' Stones' is literally a string of cliches. . . . Every so often, though, Cyrus' persona—the sensitive hunk blurting out average-slob sentiments—connects with a good song, and the result nearly makes up for his buffoonery."

Despite the generally negative tone of *his* comments, *Country Music's* Morthland claimed that he intended "neither to praise nor to bury" Cyrus, and charged: "To put it bluntly, Billy Ray doesn't phrase at all; he has no discernible technique, uses none of the fillips with which real singers put their own stamp on their music. In short, the guy's got no personal style whatsoever; he simply mouths the words, and on the louder and faster songs, his producers can either hide or distract from this woeful state of affairs. Favorable comparisons to Elvis—and on 'When I'm Gone,' he's angling for just that—are about as apt as favorable comparisons between weekend adventure hikers and Lewis and Clark." Morthland went on to speculate, "Given today's music-biz politics and economics, I suspect that Billy Ray will come and go just as surely as so many contrived, trend-mongering rockers have done, making a big though short splash, but still offering a little disposable pleasure before disappearing."

Elvis for the '90s

Surprisingly, one of the more enthusiastic reviews of *It Won't Be the Last* came from John Swenson of *Rolling Stone,* who labeled Cyrus "an Elvis for the '90s," maintaining, "Just as Elvis dragged country music kicking and screaming into rock & roll territory, Cyrus signals another generational change. *It Won't Be the Last* completes the transition that high-profile country music has been undergoing in recent years to a sound fashioned out of the conventions of '70s arena-rock bands. This transformation has accelerated so rapidly that Cyrus makes his predecessor, Garth Brooks, sound like Grandpa Jones by comparison."

Ultimately, the context in which Billy Ray Cyrus's career will be judged by musical historians is uncertain. Yet one thing is clear: the heartthrob from Flatwoods, Kentucky, will be remembered for—if nothing else—introducing country music to a broader audience. Many in the industry view him as having kicked down the door to the pop mainstream that Garth Brooks had forced open. Trying to keep his goals in perspective, Cyrus told Graff in a *Country Music* interview: "To look at the achievement of 'Some Gave All' and say I'm going after that, it would be crazy to do that. What I *am* going to do is concentrate on what I've done the last 11 or 12 years—making my music the way I can. If I concentrate on that, the rest will run its course. And even if the bottom drops out tomorrow, two months later you'll find me in some smoky bar in Kentucky or Tennessee or West Virginia, in some corner, making my music."

Selected discography

Some Gave All, Mercury, 1992.
It Won't Be The Last, Mercury, 1993.

Sources

Billboard, June 26, 1993; May 16, 1992.
Country Music, November/December 1993; September/October 1993; November/December 1992.
Cosmopolitan, January 1993.
Detroit Free Press, January 29, 1993; October 9, 1992.
Entertainment Weekly, July 9, 1993.
For Women First, August 9, 1993.
Newsweek, June 22, 1992.
People, September 6, 1993; December 28, 1992; October 5, 1992.
Ladies' Home Journal, May 1993.
Rolling Stone, September 16, 1993; August 6, 1992.
Stereo Review, September 1993.
Time, June 22, 1992.
TV Guide, February 13, 1993.
Tune In, June 1993.

—Mary Scott Dye

Deep Purple

Rock band

The origins of Deep Purple may be traced to a former Searchers vocalist named Chris Curtis. In 1967 Curtis sought band financing from a London textile company boss and an advertising consultant—neither of whom possessed a shred of music business background. With their money, however, a band appeared under the name Roundabout the following year. The group included Jon Lord on keyboards and Ritchie Blackmore on guitar, along with founder Curtis and two others.

By all accounts, Roundabout was terrible. Everyone, save Lord and Blackmore, were immediately replaced—including founder Curtis. Ian Paice now sat behind the drum set, and Roger Glover played bass. The new group, calling itself Deep Purple, modeled themselves on a popular American band of the day called Vanilla Fudge. They debuted in Denmark in April of 1968.

Success took many weeks. In September of 1969 the band's first single, a cover version of the American hit "Hush," reached Number Four on the U.S. singles

For the Record. . .

Members include **Ritchie Blackmore** (born April 14, 1945, in Weston-Super-Marename, Avon, England), guitar; **Ian Gillan** (born August 19, 1945, in Hounslow, London, England), vocals; **Roger Glover** (born November 30, 1954, in Breton, Wales), bass; **Jon Lord** (born June 9, 1941, in Leicester, Leics, England), keyboards; and **Ian Paice** (born June 29, 1948, in Nottingham, Notts, England), drums. **Joe Lynn Turner** replaced Gillan in the early 1990s.

Group formed as Roundabout, 1978; made performance debut in Denmark, 1968; signed with EMI Records in England and Tetragrammaton Records in the U.S.; released first single, "Hush," and first album, *Shades of Deep Purple,* 1969; later recorded for Warner Bros., Metal Blade, and Mercury labels; disbanded, mid-1970s; re-formed, mid-1980s.

Awards: Named world's loudest band by *Guiness Book of World Records,* 1975.

Addresses: *Record company*—Warner Bros., 3300 Warner Blvd., Burbank, CA 91510.

chart. A month later, Deep Purple's first album, *Shades of Deep Purple,* reached Number 24 on the album chart, though it went unnoticed in England. Finally, in December, Purple solidified their status by reviving Neil Diamond's "Kentucky Woman" to the joy of enough statesiders to land a Top 40 hit.

EMI Records signed Deep Purple in England during their first year of prominence, as did comedian Bill Cosby's label Tetragrammaton in the U.S. Despite the first album's success and the rapid issuance of two more discs in 1969, *The Book of Taliesyn* and *Deep Purple,* Cosby's label folded. It was at this time that vocalist Ian Gillan joined the band. Also that year, a performance of keyboardist Lord's work, recorded as *Concerto for Group and Orchestra,* featured Deep Purple ably backed by the Royal Philharmonic Orchestra at London's Albert Hall. With this album, Deep Purple finally appeared on their native charts—at U.K. Number 26. The album managed only Number 149 in the apparently less classically inclined U.S.

Singer Scored First as Jesus

1970 saw the release of *Deep Purple in the Rock* and the momentary departure of Ian Gillan, who left to play the title role in the stage musical *Jesus Christ Super-*

star, to which his impassioned, often screaming, vocals were ideally suited. A studio recording of *Superstar* that appeared later in 1970 landed in the Number One spot on the U.S. album chart, a feat Deep Purple would never accomplish. The band's 1971 offering, *Fireball,* however, hit the top spot in the U.K. for one week.

After a U.S. tour with the Faces, Deep Purple found themselves recording at Switzerland's Montreux Casino. The band was horrified when the place burned down during a set by Frank Zappa's Mothers of Invention. Quickly recovering, though, Purple made art out of life and wrote "Smoke on the Water," a chronicle of the catastrophe. *Machine Head,* the album featuring that song and another hit, "Highway Star," reached the U.S. Top Ten and topped the U.K. charts for three weeks in 1972, perhaps getting an extra push in Britain from a TV advertising campaign. Eventually the album sold over four million copies. A year later, a single version of "Smoke on the Water" was released; it hit U.S. Number Four, sold a million copies, and ensured its residency on "classic rock" radio in the decades to come.

In 1973 *Made in Japan,* which reflected the group's international appeal, began a worldwide chart climb. That year also saw the second departure of Gillan and that of bassist Roger Glover, a mainstay of the band since 1969. Industry scuttlebutt suggested that both left due to disputes with guitarist Blackmore. Gillan began a solo career. Nonetheless, the replacement personnel did not slow the Deep Purple juggernaut; their 1974 album, *Burn,* hit the Top Ten on both sides of the Atlantic.

15 Millon Records Sold by Mid-'70s

In a brief 1974 *New Yorker* article, a Warner Bros. publicity man representing Deep Purple crowed, "Twelve million album units. They sold twelve million album units last year." The flack added that the "Philharmonic thing made them a little classier than some." By this time the band had sold more than 15 million albums total, making them one of the most bankable bands of the early 1970s.

Of course, with success came imitators. In late 1974 an imposter posing as Ritchie Blackmore borrowed a Porsche in Iowa City, Iowa, and totaled it—this after having scammed free meals and shelter from various Deep Purple fans. And who were Purple's fans? A study of rock fans in general, discussed in John Orman's 1984 book *The Politics of Rock,* found that Deep Purple fans responded least well to the name of U.S. president Richard Nixon. On the other hand, these difficult-to-pigeonhole fans were also made most unhappy by the name of feminist Gloria Steinem. Purple fans also topped the study in hours per week spent listening to rock music, reporting an average of 32.5 hours, compared to the relatively paltry 20.2 hours absorbed by Led Zeppelin aficionados.

Much of the unique appeal of Deep Purple's style of rock and roll has been attributed to the "call and response" guitar work of Lord and Blackmore, which *Heavy Metal Thunder* author Phillip Bashe traced to the trading and answering of phrases displayed in the technique of black gospel vocal groups. But one day in 1975 it became clear that Blackmore would no longer call or respond for Deep Purple; he quit the band to form a group called Rainbow with former Elf vocalist Ronnie James Dio (who would go on to replace Ozzy Osbourne in Black Sabbath). Dio shared Blackmore's interest in medieval music, which the two began to explore in their songs.

The Deep Purple album *Come Taste the Band* appeared in early 1976, with Tommy Bolin securing a valuable guitar opportunity in Blackmore's place. But six months later the band called it quits and went their musical ways. Bolin returned to the U.S. to form the Tommy Bolin Band but by year's end had died of a heroin overdose in a Miami motel.

1980s Decline

While various older concert recordings and Deep Purple reissues emerged in the next few years, the band itself was effectively a memory. Attempting to fill the void, Rod Evans, who had been ejected from an early Purple incarnation, began a "bogus" American Deep Purple tour in 1980. Legal action by Blackmore and Glover put the kibosh on that. Blackmore's name was again bandied about in 1980 when rumors began to circulate that, in a truly heavy metal move, he had purchased the house used in the filming of the supernatural thriller *The Amityville Horror.*

During the early 1980s the only Deep Purple alumnus to have much success seemed to be Gillan. His albums *Glory Road* and *Future Shock* hit U.K. Numbers Three and Four, respectively. These years were incredibly prolific for him, his efforts crowned by a Black Sabbath berth in 1983 when he joined that band for their final tour—one that featured three 26-foot-tall replicas of the mystical British ruin Stonehenge. (A similar incidence of stage excess was later parodied in the film *This Is Spinal Tap.*)

Gillan had little time to contemplate his post-Sabbath future; in 1984 Deep Purple reformed for a world tour. Dubbing themselves Deep Purple Mark II, the band

issued *Perfect Strangers.* The record and tour promoting it grossed millions. *Strangers* and the band's 1987 album, *House of Blue Light,* made the U.K. Top Ten and did well in the U.S., too—though controversy ensued on the *House* tour when Blackmore repeatedly refused to play "Smoke on the Water."

In 1989 Gillan once again quit Deep Purple, citing "musical differences." After this exit the singer engaged in a collaboration with Iron Maiden singer Bruce Dickinson. The two later joined other heavy metal performers to record an album benefitting Armenian earthquake victims, the cuts including a version of "Smoke on the Water."

Deep Purple marched into the 1990s with Gillan replacement Joe Lynn Turner. The *Boston Herald* wrote in 1991 that should scientists wish to understand why the dinosaurs disappeared, they need only attend a couple of Deep Purple concerts and observe these former rulers "wallowing in the muck and mire of their past glory." But dinosaurs did not rock. Perhaps if they had, they would still be with us—for, well into their third decade, Deep Purple appears to have staved off extinction.

Selected discography

Shades of Deep Purple, Tetragrammaton, 1968.
The Book of Taliesyn, Tetragrammaton, 1969.
Deep Purple, Tetragrammaton, 1969.
(With the Royal Philharmonic Orchestra) *Concerto for Group and Orchestra,* Warner Bros., 1970.
Machine Head, (includes "Smoke on the Water" and "Highway Star"), Warner Bros., 1972.
Come Taste the Band, Metal Blade, 1976.
Perfect Strangers, Mercury, 1984.
House of Blue Light, Mercury, 1987.
The Battle Rages On, Warner Bros., 1993.

Solo albums by Ian Gillan

Glory Road, Virgin, 1980.
Future Shock, Metal Blade, 1981.

Sources

Books

Bashe, Phillip, *Heavy Metal Thunder,* Doubleday, 1985.
Hardy, Phil, and Dave Laing, *Encyclopedia of Rock,* Schirmer Books, 1988.
Orman, John, *The Politics of Rock,* Nelson-Hall, 1984.
Rees, Dafydd, and Luke Crampton, *Rock Movers & Shakers,* ABC/CLIO, 1991.

The Rolling Stone Encyclopedia of Rock & Roll, edited by Jon Pareles and Patricia Romanowski, Rolling Stone Press/Summit Books, 1983.

Periodicals

Boston Herald, April 15, 1991.
New Yorker, April 15, 1974.

—*Joseph M. Reiner*

Diamond Rio

Country band

In the spring of 1991 Diamond Rio managed the rare feat of reaching the Number One position on *Billboard* magazine's country charts with its very first single, "Meet in the Middle." Since then country radio and record buyers have taken enthusiastically to the group's catchy melodies, perfectly executed three-part harmony singing, and first-rate instrumental work—so smooth that it virtually conceals the formidable skills of the individual players. The group exemplifies the solid, versatile professionalism that contributed to country music's burgeoning national success in the early 1990s.

Country America magazine called the group's eponymous first album "dazzling in its display of instrumental proficiency and exhilarating in its fusion of honky-tonk, bluegrass, mainstream country and other musical influences." Indeed, Diamond Rio made the mix seem effortless. But putting it together required many years of work on the lower rungs of the Nashville music ladder—not to mention six musicians of very different back-

For the Record. . .

Members include **Gene Johnson** (born in Sugar Grove, PA), mandolin, vocals; **Jimmy Olander** (born in Palos Verdes, CA), guitar; **Brian Prout** (born in Troy, NY), drums; **Marty Roe** (born in Lebanon, OH), vocals; **Dan Truman** (born in St. George, UT), keyboards; and **Dana Williams** (born in Dayton, OH), bass, vocals.

As the Grizzly River Boys, then the Tennessee River Boys, band members played together at Opryland amusement park, Nashville, TN, 1984-89; band formed in Nashville, 1989; signed with Arista Records, 1990, and released first album, *Diamond Rio,* 1991.

Awards: Named top vocal group by Academy of Country Music, 1991 and 1992; named vocal group of the year by Country Music Association, 1992; named best group in *Radio and Records* readers poll, 1991 and 1992; two Grammy Award nominations; platinum album for *Diamond Rio,* 1993, and gold album for *Close to the Edge,* 1994.

Addresses: *Record company*—Arista Records, 7 Music Circle N., Nashville, TN 37203; *Management*—International Artist Management, P.O. Box 120261, Nashville, TN 37212; *Booking agent*—William Morris Agency, 2325 Crestmoor Rd., Nashville, TN 37215; *Publicist*—PLA Media, 1303 16th Avenue S., Nashville, TN 37212.

grounds who shared the ability to listen to each other and appreciate each other's varied skills.

During the classic period of country music its practitioners were mostly small-town southerners. But Nashville in the 1990s attracted musicians from all over the United States, many with experience in playing other sorts of music besides country. Diamond Rio lead singer Marty Roe was raised on traditional country music in small-town southern Ohio, while drummer Brian Prout started out playing rock in Troy, New York. Keyboardist Dan Truman studied jazz and classical piano in Utah. Bassist Dana Williams, mandolinist Gene Johnson, and guitarist Jimmy Olander cut their teeth on country and bluegrass. But all shared a desire to rise above the pack. Recalling his lean years on the bluegrass circuit, Johnson told Robyn Flans of *Country Fever,* "I . . . wasn't making enough to raise a family. But I couldn't quit. I knew I shouldn't be doing this. But I had to. It was like a drug."

Opryland Beginnings

Diamond Rio had its beginnings as the Grizzly River Boys, a band employed at Nashville's Opryland amusement park. Vocalist Roe was a member from the early 1980s on, but the current lineup didn't come together until 1989, by which time the group's name had been changed to the Tennessee River Boys. At first, noted Bob Allen of *Country Music,* the band was "hampered by [its] sheer versatility: they could more or less play absolutely anything." Gradually, though, the band members began to size up each other's strengths and work out the distinctive layers of vocal harmony and instrumental detail that would become the group's trademark.

Longtime Restless Heart producer Tim DuBois heard the group's demo tapes and then saw them open for George Jones in concert. He was so impressed that he signed them to Arista Records on the spot, sealing the deal with a handshake. Arista executives asked the group to come up with a more modern-sounding name; they finally settled on Diamond Rio, taking the name from a member of the truck model line that had previously inspired the name of the rock group REO Speedwagon. Roe misspelled "Reo" as "Rio"—but decided to make a virtue out of his mistake. "I like it like that. It has a country-Southwestern flavor," he told the Chicago *Tribune's* Jack Hurst.

Diamond Rio's first album was released early in 1991 and notched both critical and popular successes. Its debut single reached the top of the charts, and three follow-ups, "Mirror, Mirror," "Norma Jean Riley," and "Nowhere Bound," quickly ascended into the Top Five. Vocally and musically the band was at the height of its powers, but also propelling the recording's sales was the singular quality of its songs, several of which blended infectious pop fun with an earnest moral stance (which fit beautifully with the group's gospel-style harmonies) in a manner reminiscent of the Oak Ridge Boys. "Meet in the Middle" and, especially, "Nowhere Bound" were serious songs affirming the value of romantic conciliation, but each was enlivened by the band's toe-tapping instrumental mix.

Popularity Meant Grueling Road Time

Not long before the album's release, though, the band had been reduced to rehearsing in Prout's garage, using a clothes dryer for heat. Their sudden success intensified their touring schedule to a torrid pace of 300 concerts in 22 months. "[Anybody] who's never been through this can never understand the work load that comes with it," Roe told *Country Music.* Also unfamiliar to the hardworking band were the teenage groupies who began to mimic their styles of dress.

Would Diamond Rio ascend to the level of popularity at which fans begin to name their children after band members, as Marty Roe's parents were inspired to by the late Marty Robbins? That question seemed in the balance as the group released its second album, *Close to the Edge,* in the fall of 1992. The first record had generated a juggernaut of praise for the band, which ended up garnering awards from the Country Music Association for vocal group of the year in 1992, as well as the Academy of Country Music's top vocal group award in both 1991 and 1992. Diamond Rio even attracted favorable attention from the alternative-rock-oriented magazine *Spin.* But the trend toward groups in country music, initiated and continually stimulated by the success of the legendary act Alabama, meant a host of strong competitors for Diamond Rio, which by late 1993 had failed to repeat the daunting success of its initial record.

Follow-up Received Mixed Reviews

Close to the Edge nonetheless spawned three singles—"In a Week or Two," "Oh Me, Oh My, Sweet Baby," and "This Romeo Ain't Got Julie Yet"—that cracked the top levels of the country charts. These titles alone reveal Diamond Rio's dependence on what pop songwriters call the "hook"—short, vivid chorus fragments that embed themselves in the listener's memory. The group's instrumental and vocal strength remained undiminished. *Country Music* referred admiringly to Diamond Rio's harmony singing, in which "the closely bunched voices stay in tight formation like sky-show airplanes." The album's critical reception on the whole, however, was mixed. The *Music City News* praised the group's "knack for picking commercial, but appealing songs," opining, "Diamond Rio clearly shows a new country supergroup has arrived." But *Country Music* went on to pan most of the songwriting on the album—supplied largely by hired tunesmiths—and pronounced the set "a fairly conventional outing in these Days of [country superstar] Garth [Brooks]."

The singles from *Close to the Edge* continued as fixtures of country radio for most of 1993, but the album stalled at Number 24 on *Billboard's* country album chart. And though Diamond Rio's future seemed bright enough at the end of the year, it also seemed to depend on whether or not the group could succeed in honing a unique message, a deeply-felt vision that it could convey to listeners. Among country groups, few besides Alabama, with its elaborately produced imaginings of the rural South, has really succeeded in doing that and in remaining at the top of country music for more than a year or two. Still, the skill and commitment revealed in Diamond Rio's early career suggested the potential for an accomplishment of similar magnitude.

Selected discography

Diamond Rio (includes "Meet in the Middle," "Mirror, Mirror," "Norma Jean Riley," and "Nowhere Bound"), Arista, 1991.
Close to the Edge (includes "Oh Me, Oh My, Sweet Baby," "In a Week or Two," and "This Romeo Ain't Got Julie Yet"), Arista, 1992.

Sources

Chicago Tribune, May 26, 1991.
Country America, March 1993.
Country Fever, October 1993.
Country Music, January/February 1993; May/June 1993.
Guitar Player, January 1994.
Music Row, March 8, 1993.
Spin, October 1992.
Tennessean (Nashville), April 3, 1993.

Additional information for this profile was obtained from an International Artist Management press kit, 1993.

—*James M. Manheim*

Thomas A. Dorsey

Composer, songwriter, singer, pianist, music publisher

Thomas A. Dorsey, often called the Father of Gospel Music, migrated from Atlanta to Chicago as a young man, thus exemplifying the experience of many southern blacks of his day. This journey is also critical to an understanding of what Michael W. Harris called "the rise of gospel blues" in his book of that title, which chronicles the role Dorsey's music played in urban churches.

There was a great deal of early resistance to Dorsey's work, partly because it was rooted in the rural southern African-American culture from which the old-line urban churches sought to distance themselves in favor of assimilation. These churches discouraged expressive congregational participation and attempted to incorporate white church traditions in both service and music. In addition, the blues factor of the gospel blues equation had associations with secular venues and activities often discouraged by the church. It is perhaps Dorsey's greatest achievement that he was able to overcome this opposition and thus preserve important aspects of black musical expression as it had existed in both the spiritual and secular realms.

Dorsey, one of five children, was born in Villa Rica, Georgia, but soon moved with his family to Atlanta. His father was a Baptist minister with a flamboyant pulpit style, and his mother played a portable organ and piano wherever the elder Dorsey preached. Young Dorsey was also influenced musically by his mother's brother, an itinerant blues musician, and by her brother-in-law, a teacher who favored shaped note singing—also known as "fasola" (fa-so-la), a rambunctious, 19th-century congregational style propagated by songbooks and popular in the rural South in which four distinct shapes (the diamond, for one) correspond to specific notes on the musical scale. In *The Rise of Gospel Blues* Harris noted, "Other than slave spirituals, the white Protestant hymns and shaped note music, Dorsey describes a type of 'moaning' as the only other style of religious song he recalls." He left school early and was soon hanging around theaters and dance halls. His association with musicians there encouraged him to practice at home on his mother's organ, and by age 12, he claimed that he could play the piano very well. Before long he was earning money playing at private parties and bordellos. In order to improve his skills and identify himself as a professional, he briefly took piano lessons from a teacher associated with Morehouse College, as well as a harmony course at the college itself.

For the Record. . .

Born in 1899 in Villa Rica, GA; died of Alzheimer's disease, January 23, 1993, in Chicago, IL; son of a minister and church organist/pianist; married Nettie Harper, 1925 (died, 1931); married Kathryn Mosely, 1941; children: a daughter and a son. *Education:* Attended Morehouse College; attended Chicago School of Composition and Arranging.

Played for parties and bordellos in Atlanta; became music director of New Hope Baptist Church, Chicago; performed with the Whispering Syncopators, early 1920s; as "Georgia Tom," debuted, with Ma Rainey, at Grand Theater, Chicago, 1924; composed "It's Tight Like That," 1928, and "Precious Lord," 1931; became music director of Pilgrim Baptist Church, Chicago, 1932; with blues singer Sallie Martin, formed National Convention of Gospel Choirs and Choruses, 1932; became minister, 1960s; featured in BBC documentary, 1976; with gospel singer Willie Mae Ford Smith, featured in documentary *Say Amen Somebody,* 1984. Music publisher.

A Migrant Musician

Eventually Dorsey's desire to become a professional musician motivated him to move to Philadelphia, in 1916, but his plans soon changed and he settled in Chicago, then abuzz with both migrant workers and migrant musicians. According to Harris, by then Dorsey's piano style was already somewhat out of vogue. He was, however, able to work, though he remained on the periphery of the music community, held back, Harris observed, by both his lack of technique and repertoire, which prevented him from joining the union, and the sheer size and wealth of the musical community. In order to increase his chances for employment, he enrolled in the Chicago School of Composition and Arranging and thus, for the rest of his life, was able to find work as a composer and arranger. By 1920, Dorsey was prospering, but the demanding schedule of playing at night, working at other jobs during the day, and studying in between led him to the first of two nervous breakdowns; he was so ill that his mother had to go to Chicago to bring him back to Atlanta.

Dorsey returned to Chicago in 1921, and his uncle encouraged him to attend the National Baptist Convention. There he was impressed by the singing of W. M. Nix. As Dorsey related in *The Rise of Gospel Blues:* "My inner-being was thrilled. My soul was a deluge of divine rapture; my emotions were aroused; my heart was inspired to become a great singer and worker in the Kingdom of the Lord—and impress people just as this great singer did that Sunday morning." Dorsey soon began composing sacred songs and took a job as director of music at New Hope Baptist Church on Chicago's South Side, where he described the congregation's singing of spirituals "like down home," noting that the congregants also clapped to his music.

But Dorsey's conversion was fleeting; he was soon playing with the Whispering Syncopators, making a salary commensurate with professional theater musicians. As the popularity of the blues increased in New York and Chicago, especially among non-black audiences, Dorsey was able to adapt his style to the tastes of the day, though singers like Bessie Smith, who embodied the southern tradition, were also popular, especially among black Americans.

In 1924, Dorsey made his debut as "Georgia Tom" with Ma Rainey at the Grand Theater and continued to tour with her, even after he wed in 1925, until he suffered the second of his breakdowns in 1926. The pressures of touring overwhelmed him, and Dorsey considered suicide. His sister-in-law convinced him to attend church, and, while at a service, he had a vision, after which he pledged to work for the Lord. It was not long before he penned his first gospel blues, "If You See My Savior, Tell Him That You Saw Me," which was inspired by the death of a friend.

Doing the Lord's Work

But the Lord's work would not be easy for him. Dorsey's background convinced him that the same experiences that had engendered secular blues should also inform church music. As he said in *The Rise of Gospel Blues:* "If a woman has lost a man, a man has lost a woman, his feeling reacts to the blues; he feels like expressing it. The same thing acts for a gospel song. Now you're not singing blues; you're singing gospel, good news song, singing about the Creator; but it's the same feeling, a grasping of the heart." In a purely musical sense, to Dorsey, the blues was merely a collection of improvisational techniques. Nevertheless, imparting a bluesy feel to a traditional arrangement was shocking to many, though Dorsey was able to vary the effect depending on his audience and their reaction. He was soon making printed copies of his gospel blues, but since he relied on the performer to embellish the music, they did not sell well. Before long he was back to writing and performing secular blues, and in 1928, "It's Tight Like That" became a hit, selling seven million copies.

Although Dorsey claimed to have been thrown out of some of the best churches, Harris observed that the time was right for Dorsey's eventual success; there were increasing numbers of store-front churches that appealed to southern migrants, and there was a booming trade in recorded sermons of the type Dorsey's father might have delivered. Harris even linked the blues soloist to the preacher, as each embodies the yearning of a people and manifests that yearning principally through improvisation. There were also a growing number of influential choirs in Chicago challenging the musical norms of the established churches, though Dorsey was usually more associated with the rise of the solo tradition. Indeed, in the late 1920s, he would begin work with one of the great gospel soloists of all time, Mahalia Jackson. According to Dorsey, she asked him to coach her, and for two months they worked together on technique and repertoire. They would tour together in the 1940s.

"Precious Lord"

In 1931, Dorsey experienced great personal tragedy again: the death in childbirth of both his wife and newborn son devastated him. As he related in the documentary *Say Amen Somebody,* "People tried to tell me things that were soothing to me . . . none of which have ever been soothing from that day to this." Out of that tragedy he wrote the song for which he is best known, "Precious Lord," which has been translated into 50 languages and recorded with success by gospel and secular singers alike, including Elvis Presley, much as Dorsey's "Peace in the Valley" was a hit for Tennessee Ernie Ford and others. In 1932 Dorsey was appointed musical director of Pilgrim Baptist Church in Chicago, a post he held until his retirement in 1983. 1932 was also the year he formed the National Convention of Gospel Choirs and Choruses with blues singer Sallie Martin. Their collaboration would continue over the years as his fame spread, Martin often accompanying him on his tours around the country. She also helped him with his publishing business, which quickly became so successful that people nationwide called any piece of gospel sheet music a "Dorsey."

Dorsey married again in 1941. His career continued to flourish; he would eventually compose over 3,000 songs. Well known within the African-American community, Dorsey nonetheless remained relatively obscure outside of it—though people were singing his songs all over the world—until he became the subject of a BBC documentary in 1976. His appearance with another great gospel singer, Willie Mae Ford Smith, in the documentary *Say Amen Somebody* also afforded him considerable exposure. In that film, after being helped into a room, he addresses a group of people, moving comfortably in and out of song all the while. He was ordained a minister in his sixties, formalizing the union of song and worship; the Pilgrim Baptist Church created the T. A. Dorsey Choir to honor him in 1983. Dorsey died of Alzheimer's disease on January 23, 1993. But he lives on each Sunday as voices rise in praise, singing the gospel across the land.

Selected discography

(As Georgia Tom) *Come on Mama Do That Dance 1931-1940,* Yazoo.
Say Amen Somebody.

Sources

Books

Harris, Michael W., *The Rise of Gospel Blues: The Music of Thomas Andrew Dorsey in the Urban Church,* Oxford University Press, 1992.
We'll Understand It Better By and By: Pioneering African American Gospel Composers, edited by Bernice Johnson Reagon, Smithsonian Institution Press, 1992.

Periodicals

Ann Arbor News, February 24, 1993.
Chicago Tribune, January 25, 1993.
Down Beat, April 1993.
Entertainment Weekly, February 5, 1993.
Jet, February 8, 1993.
Newsweek, February 8, 1993.
New York Times, January 25, 1993.
Time, February 8, 1993.
Village Voice, October 5, 1982.
Washington Post, January 25, 1993; January 31, 1993.

Additional information for this profile was obtained from the documentary *Say Amen Somebody,* produced and directed by George T. Nierenberg, Pacific Arts Video Records, 1984.

—*John Morrow*

Erasure

Contemporary dance duo

The British synth-pop duo Erasure debuted in 1985 to a good deal of attention—well before any of their dance singles became standard tracks in English and American clubs. Vince Clarke, the keyboardist and driving force behind the band, began this new venture on the foundation of a series of previous—and highly successful—bands. Clarke and vocalist Andy Bell generally viewed the media attention surrounding their inception as both a blessing and a curse.

Erasure was born when Clarke advertised for vocalists in the renowned English music journal *Melody Maker* in 1985. He enjoyed the backing of the record label Mute, a result of his success during his brief stays with two important English pop bands: Depeche Mode, from 1980 to 1981, and Yazoo—known as Yaz in the United States—from 1981 to 1983. Consequently, he had the go-ahead from Mute to put together an album featuring ten assorted vocalists. By 1985 it was considered common knowledge that the taciturn Clarke was "difficult." Andy Bell, however, seemed to change all that. Clarke told Paul Strange of *Melody Maker,* "We'd

For the Record. . .

M embers include **Andy Bell** (born April 25, 1965, in Peterborough, England), vocals; and **Vince Clarke** (born July 3, 1960, in Baiseldon, England), keyboards.

Clarke, previously with Depeche Mode, 1980-1981, and Yazoo, 1981-1983, recruited Bell through a print advertisement, 1985; released singles, 1985-86, and album *Wonderland,* 1986, on Mute Records.

Awards: BRIT Award for best British group, 1989; gold Album for *The Innocents,* 1990.

Addresses: *Record company*—Elektra Entertainment, 345 North Maple, Beverly Hills, CA 90210.

auditioned about 40 people and Andy was the 43rd. He was like a breath of fresh air." Clarke settled on just one singer for his new project.

Unlike Clarke, Bell was entirely new to the music industry. In his early twenties in 1985, his singing experience was limited to a church choir in his native Peterborough. His association with Clarke, however, shot him from obscurity to an instant fame—of sorts. In October of that year, Strange underscored the duo's instant credibility when he asked, "Would *MM [Melody Maker]* have dispatched a writer to the depths of Willesden to report on a new synth duo if Vince hadn't been in Depeche or Yazoo? Probably not." In fact, the publicity guaranteed through Clarke's history supported the band through their first year and a half, during which none of their singles broke into the charts. Their debut single, "Who Needs Love Like That?," was, according to Strange, "hardly earth-shattering." This having been the case, Clarke and Bell delayed both the release of their first album and their first large-scale tour; they decided to wait on both until after they had broken through with at least one single.

New Mood for Clarke

Although commercial success was slow in coming, interviewers did report a different kind of success for Erasure in those early years. Kris Kirk noted in *Melody Maker* in 1986, "Five years of monster hits with Depeche Mode, Yazoo and The Assembly may have made Vince Clarke some money, but it never seemed to get him very much happiness." Indeed, Clarke's association with Depeche Mode was brief, and his break with Alison Moyet of Yazoo seemed to leave considerable bitterness in its wake. Even when Erasure was failing to produce a hit, Clarke—as several music journalists

remarked—was declaring uncharacteristic pleasure in his work; he told Kirk, "It is a problem that Erasure aren't getting hits, but I'm really *enjoying* the band. Especially the gigging."

Clarke's relationship with Bell appeared to be the reason for his buoyant mood. The two developed a work style that differed greatly from Clarke's earlier experiences; whereas in the past he would compose music for the band alone and then bring it in for rehearsal, with Bell, Clarke actually began collaborating on his compositions. Bell was also responsible for introducing an element of camp into the band's music and performance that would turn their sound away from the more dour, experimental synth tones of Depeche Mode and Yaz to the dance club beat for which Erasure would eventually become known. The *Maker's* Kirk discovered that this was also new for Clarke, who explained, "I've never experienced pleasure in playing live before. . . . But there's nothing like playing non-stop dance music loud for feeling good. . . . And the other reason it's working for me is that I get on so well with Andy."

The shift to dance music would eventually pay off for Erasure but not until the end of 1986—well after the release of *Wonderland,* their first album, in June of that year. In December, though, the single "Sometimes" shot to the top of the U.K. dance charts, ultimately coming to rest at Number Two. Since they broke that barrier, Erasure's popularity in England has never really wavered. 1987 brought them another hit with "It Doesn't Have To Be" and a Number Six spot for the album *The Circus.* Over the next two years Erasure dominated English airways and dance clubs with "Ship of Fools," "Chains of Love," and "Just a Little Respect"; the 1988 album *The Innocents* claimed first place in the charts immediately on its release.

Even Slower Start in U.S.

Erasure's story in the United States, however, was unfolding a little differently. While *The Circus* took a Number Six chart spot in England as early as April of 1987, it couldn't move past Number 190 in the U.S. even as late as July. Stateside success had to wait for the release of "Chains of Love," which finally brought Clarke and Bell into the Top Thirty in 1988. Writing for *Seventeen* in 1990, Barry Walters described the song as "full of compulsive rhythms and synthetic textures topped by yearning, soulful vocals." Erasure did not break the Top Twenty in the U.S. until March of 1989, when "A Little Respect" peaked at Number Fourteen. By that time, the BRIT Awards had dubbed Erasure best british music group, and singles from *Wild!* brought them even more chart success.

While mainstream audiences in the United States remained ignorant of Erasure, fans in gay clubs were turning "Oh l'Amour" into a classic dance tune as early as 1986. This aside, debate about the band's sluggish rise to popularity in the States has often focused on Bell's refusal to hide his homosexuality. As Clarke explained to Kirk, Erasure had had some difficulty with their American publicity reps over this issue: "It came back to us . . . that people in the [record] company in New York were saying they thought it was really bad that Andy was making it plain he was gay because they were worried it would affect our sales. And yet when we were in San Francisco, Warner Bros. was encouraging us to talk to the biggest U.S. gay paper, the *Advocate*." So while Bell conjectured in *Spin* in 1992, "If I'd never said I was gay, I think Erasure would've taken off years ago in America," Amy Linden could nonetheless describe the twosome in *Entertainment Weekly* as "the techno-pop duo that makes flamboyant gay sensibilities palatable (and marketable) to the Luke Perry posse [of middle-American *Beverly Hills 90210* watchers]."

Bell Vocal About His Sexuality

In 1986 Bell explained his refusal to be closeted to *Melody Maker's* Kirk, saying, "I dont want to go out of my way to talk about it, but I'm not going to pretend I'm not. I won't portray a heterosexual in videos, for example, and we're consciously doing lyrics that can apply to either sex, but I'm not going to bore people rigid with it either." By 1990, however, Bell was more insistent about the political importance of being "out," as he told *Seventeen's* Walters: "I want to be known as a good performer. . . . But it's important to me to take a stance. If you're doing music, you should use it for something and have substance. Being gay and open about it is my substance."

In 1992 Erasure discovered the value of recycling; they released both a collection of their singles and *Abba-esque*, techno cover versions of four disco classics by the monstrously popular 1970s Swedish band Abba. While *Pop! The First Twenty Hits* reintroduced listeners to some of Erasure's neglected early singles, the single releases from *Abba-esque* debuted at Number One on the English dance charts. Kurt Reighley, writing for *Reflex*, was prompted to adulation, enthusing, "If covering another artist's material means plumbing the depths for new meaning, can we honestly expect our heroes to find any substance in this froth? Yes, yes . . . a thousand times, YES!" After the slow start and considerable skepticism of 1985, Erasure had finally reached the point where they could do no wrong.

Selected discography

Wonderland, (includes "Who Needs Love Like That?", "Heavenly Action," and "Oh l'Amour"), Mute/Sire, 1986.
The Circus, (includes "Sometimes" and "It Doesn't Have To Be"), Mute/Sire, 1987.
The Innocents, (includes "Ship of Fools," "Chains of Love," and "A Little Respect"), Mute/Sire, 1988.
Wild!, Mute/Sire, 1989.
Chorus, Mute/Sire, 1991.
Pop! The First Twenty Hits, Mute/Elektra, 1992.
Abba-esque, Mute/Elektra, 1992.

Sources

Books

Rees, Dafydd, and Luke Crampton, *Rock Movers & Shakers*, ABC/CLIO, 1991.

Periodicals

Entertainment Weekly, September 11, 1992.
Keyboard, February 1990.
Melody Maker, October 26, 1985; May 31, 1986.
Reflex, Issue 29.
Rolling Stone, April 19, 1990.
Seventeen, February 1990.
Spin, December 1992.

—*Ondine E. Le Blanc*

fIREHOSE

Rock band

Southern California's fIREHOSE rose from the ashes of the seminal postpunk band the Minutemen; the latter came to an abrupt halt when their influential singer-guitarist, D. Boon, died in a 1985 automobile accident. When bassist Mike Watt and drummer George Hurley decided to start anew with untested Ohio native Ed Crawford in 1986, they did so to carry on the do-it-yourself tradition of punk rock that had inspired them to play music in the first place. In the intervening years, fIREHOSE has established itself as a fixture in the mercurial rock world—"alternative" before it was fashionable and firmly independent even after signing with a major label. According to *Billboard,* the gruff, personable Watt has been elevated to "folk hero" status among record company executives for his keen sense of business in handling the band's affairs. This no-nonsense sensibility surrounds not only the band's logistical values, but its music as well; though the members of fIREHOSE eschew the brevity-at-all-costs ideology of the Minutemen, they strive to "make it econo," as one of their songs declares.

For the Record. . .

Members include **Ed Crawford** (born c. 1964 in Ohio), guitar, vocals; **George Hurley,** drums; and **Mike Watt** (born c. 1958 in Virginia; married Kira Roessler [a musician]), bass, vocals.

Band formed in San Pedro, CA, 1986; released debut album, *Ragin', Full On,* SST Records, 1986; signed with Columbia Records and released *Flyin' the Flannel,* 1991.

Addresses: *Record company*—Columbia Records, 2100 Colorado Ave., Santa Monica, CA 90404; 550 Madison Ave., New York, NY 10022-3211.

The Minutemen came from San Pedro, site of the Los Angeles harbor. The town has never hosted a thriving music scene—L.A.'s clubs are located mostly in Hollywood—but it was where Mike Watt and D. Boon grew up together as best friends. Watt was born in Virginia, but his Navy father moved the family to "Pedro" (as Watt would come to call it) when Mike was nine. In 1978 Watt, Boon, Hurley and a singer formed a group called the Reactionaries; 18 months later the singer had departed and the band's name had been changed to the Minutemen. They began performing wherever they could. "The only gigs we could get were opening for [L.A. punk luminaries] Black Flag," Watt recalled to Steve Peters of *Creem.*

The Minutemen sound wasn't nearly as one-dimensional as the quasi-metallic thrash and "destroy everything" lyrics of most punk; it mixed hard rock, jazzy passages, and a funky groove with terse, cryptic, and usually political messages and in so doing, significantly broadened the palette of independent rock. Their working-class backgrounds both differentiated the Minutemen from their bored, suburban colleagues and gave them more to sing about. Guitarist Greg Ginn, leader of Black Flag, signed the trio to his SST label and for five years, the Minutemen toured and released albums full of honed, evocative, furious compositions that were sometimes no more than 30 seconds long. "The stories we told were little moral plays and stuff, but I don't think that was our trump," Watt told *Option.* "Our trump was personality and fraternity and stuff like that. It sure as hell wasn't foxy looks."

Minutemen Moved Crawford

One particularly enthusiastic convert to their eclectic sound was Ed Crawford. The 21 year old saw the Minutemen play in a small club. "Rarely have I been so moved by a live show," he told *Creem's* Peters. "I got up on top of this damn bar railing, because I wanted to see this. To watch D. Boon up there like that . . . I thought, 'Man, if he can do that, I can do that.' They really inspired me to think about rock in realistic terms." After seeing the band, Crawford—trained on the trumpet—bought his first electric guitar. A few months later, D. Boon died on the road somewhere in the Arizona desert.

Devastated by the loss of his closest friend, Watt was disinclined to do anything—let alone start another band. He hadn't even attended Boon's funeral. "I wouldn't carry D. Boon's casket," he recalled to Peters. "I wouldn't put him in the ground. He was too strong a man. I didn't want to put him to rest." Watt and Hurley tried playing with their friend former Saccharine Trust guitarist Joe Baiza but didn't feel any special musical chemistry. Meanwhile, back in the Midwest, Crawford heard—erroneously—that the surviving Minutemen were auditioning guitarists. He grabbed his guitar and headed for California, determined to find Watt and play with his favorite rhythm section. "I thought, if I have a snowball's chance in hell, I thought it would be because I'm from Ohio and he doesn't know who I am and I've never been in a band," the guitarist recollected to *Option's* Scott Becker. "That's the only thing I have going for me. It was something I couldn't not try."

Crawford was right. Watt told Becker, "This guy kept calling me up, kept calling and calling," and he finally agreed to try him out. "Ed just wanted a chance to go for it. He was influenced by bands like the Police, U2, stuff very foreign to me. He didn't play electric guitar till he saw D. Boon. He knew a lot of our tunes like a hack would, note for note. It was like fate, like D. Boon landed on me out of a tree when I was a kid." Crawford struggled with the guitar, but his sheer determination touched something in Watt. "I knew he must have a powerful hankering to do it," he explained to *Creem.* "So I could really start over, you know what I mean? I knew I'd have a chance." Soon they were a band; taking their name from a Bob Dylan song, they began to play live. Their first gig was in June of 1986. "I remember it distinctly," Crawford joked to Becker. "It was all one big blur."

Recorded for Indie SST

Crawford's melodic, wailing vocals were a far cry from D. Boon's pointed proto-rap talk-singing, and his relatively less-aggressive guitar stylings forced the rhythm section up front. "It was like the tail wagging the dog," Watt told Becker. "Drummers and bass players aren't supposed to [lead] the guitar player. But me and

George are weird players." Watt's inventiveness led to ever more supple, soulful basslines against Hurley's nimble percussion. The first fIREHOSE album, *Ragin', Full On,* released by SST in 1986, begins with Crawford singing the first song Watt wrote for him: "Brave Captain," about an uncertain leader stumbling to marshall his troops. "Consistently interesting, if occasionally tentative, *Ragin', Full-On* should lead to some formidable sequels," opined Jon Young of *Musician.* The band released two more albums for the independent label, *If'n* and *fROMOHIO*—chock full of ringing guitars, angular funk, tricky arrangements, and Watt's cryptic "spiels," or lyrics. *Musician* critic David Gerard felt the former album "was an unusually sharp, concise piece of rock commentary," and the latter "no exception." The band also released an EP for SST called *Sometimes.*

For the most part, fIREHOSE recorded their albums quickly and cheaply; they spent the majority of their time on the road, where the power of their sonic assault could be fully communicated to fans. In 1991 the band made an unexpected move, however—they signed with a major label, Columbia. Though many of their supporters feared a sellout, fIREHOSE quickly dispelled such concerns with their eclectic, loud next set, *Flyin' the Flannel.* It was around this time that "alternative" rock, exemplified by heavy, punk-influenced "grunge" bands like Seattle's Nirvana, lay siege to the charts. One multiplatinum alternative album, 1991's *Blood Sugar Sex Magik,* by longtime L.A. stalwarts the Red Hot Chili Peppers, was, in fact, dedicated to Watt. "Alternative," to the horror of Watt and his cohorts, had become fashionable; the flannel shirts he had bought at thrift shops for years were suddenly being sold in fancy boutiques. "I know all about this grunge," he scoffed to *Option.* "It'll blow over in a year."

Watt a Label Executive's Dream

Watt particularly impressed his new employers with his business savvy. While most bands survive on advances and tour support, sacrificing later profits that the companies "recoup," fIREHOSE never took a penny to go on the road. "Most bands tour to promote records," Watt revealed to *Billboard.* "We make records to promote tours." He further noted in an *Option* interview, "We go out there in the van, and these [record company] guys see the shelf unit and the safe welded to the floor . . . they've never seen this. They're used to signing $10,000-a-week checks to keep bands on the road." fIREHOSE's modus operandi, he added pointedly, is "punk rock"—not just a musical style, but "a way of doing things." Peter Fletcher, a marketing executive at Columbia, expressed to *Billboard* his amazement that "Mike can take care of himself start to finish.

He gives us a tour booked six months in advance, drops the album package on my desk." The company only has to "get the record in stores and they'll do the rest."

1992 saw the release of the *Live Totem Pole EP,* a collection of mostly cover tunes. *Rolling Stone* noted of the outing, "Crawford has grown to be a compelling singer and incisive guitarist" and added, "this rowdy latest chapter will no doubt delight the faithful." Watt took some time to develop a side project, a two-bass and vocals band called Dos that he'd formed with his wife, Kira Roessler, formerly of Black Flag. But fIREHOSE issued another blast with 1993's *Mr. Machinery Operator,* which was produced by Dinosaur Jr. leader J. Mascis. Featuring a bevy of guest players, more of Watt's growling vocals than usual, and a sprawl of ambitious songs, the album nonetheless promised more than it delivered, according to *Rolling Stone's* John Dougan, who called it an "indulgent hodgepodge." Still, Dougan remarked, "Bands this good don't go bad overnight. *Mr. Machinery Operator* isn't a harbinger; it's a misstep."

Whatever the fate of fIREHOSE records with critics, the band has demonstrated its ability to survive adversity through camaraderie and hard work; the ethic of "punk rock" that encouraged the Minutemen to pick up their instruments has helped Watt, Hurley, and Crawford through changing times and the labyrinth of the music business. Ultimately, Watt confided to *Creem,* it's about getting on a stage and performing: "If I'm not shuckin' 'n' jivin' in front of people, I feel like I'm failing miserably."

Selected discography

On SST Records

Ragin', Full On (includes "Brave Captain"), 1986.
If'n, 1987.
Sometimes (EP), 1988.
fROMOHIO, 1989.

On Columbia/Sony

Flyin' the Flannel, 1991.
Live Totem Pole EP, 1992.
Mr. Machinery Operator, 1993.

Sources

Billboard, May 1, 1993.
Creem, July 1987; July 1988; June 1993.
Guitar World, November 1991.
Musician, April 1987; July 1989; September 1989.

Option, November 1986; May 1993.
Rolling Stone, February 6, 1992; May 27, 1993.
Spin, March 1992.

Additional information for this profile was obtained from Columbia Records publicity materials, 1993.

—Simon Glickman

The
Four Tops

R&B/pop vocal group

The Four Tops have been one of the most successful vocal groups to emerge from the pantheon of great singers nurtured at Motown Records. After signing with Motown, they generated 19 Top 40 singles, from 1964 through the early 1980s, and have continued touring steadily into the 1990s. As stated in *The Guinness Encyclopedia of Popular Music,* "The group's immaculate choreography and harmonies have ensured them ongoing success as a live act from the mid-1960s to the present day." The Four Tops are also one of the most stable vocal groups in history, having never changed personnel since forming in 1953.

Levi Stubbles, Renaldo "Obie" Benson, Abdul "Duke" Fakir, and Lawrence Payton all grew up in tough Detroit neighborhoods. They officially became a group after getting a popular reception while singing together at a birthday party. Soon they were harmonizing at graduation parties, church and school functions, and one-night gigs. After becoming attached to a talent agency in 1954, they began doing more serious performances at small supper clubs in Detroit and environs. Mean-

For the Record. . .

Members include **Renaldo "Obie" Benson** (born in 1947 in Detroit, MI); **Abdul "Duke" Fakir** (born December 26, 1935, in Detroit); **Lawrence Payton** (born in 1938 in Detroit); and **Levi Stubbs** (born Levi Stubbles in 1938 in Detroit).

Group formed as the Four Aims in Detroit, 1953; sang backup or as opening act for Brook Benton, Count Basie, Della Reese, and Billy Eckstine, 1950s; changed name to the Four Tops and recorded first single, 1956; recorded for Chess, Red Top, Columbia, and Riverside labels, 1956-1962; toured with Larry Stelle Revue, ending in 1959; signed with Motown Records, 1963, and recorded "Baby I Need Your Loving," 1964; recorded three albums with the Supremes, beginning in 1970; signed with Casablanca Records, 1981; performed in Motown's 25th anniversary television special, 1983; resigned with Motown, c. 1983; signed with Arista Records, 1988.

Awards: Inducted into Rock and Roll Hall of Fame, 1990.

Addresses: *Record company*—Arista Records, 6 West 57th Street, New York, NY 10019.

while, the foursome continued to expand their repertoire of jazz and popular standards.

By the mid-1950s, the group was opening for or backing up such noted jazz and pop performers as Brook Benton, Count Basie, Della Reese, and Billy Eckstine. They changed their name from the Four Aims to the Four Tops in 1956 to avoid being confused with the Ames Brothers, and Stubbles shortened his name to Stubbs. After several years of undistinguished touring, the group recorded "Kiss Me Baby/Could It Be You" for the Chess label, but the song failed to click with the public. The quartet continued to work on vocal arrangements and dance routines and toured with the Larry Stelle Revue through 1959. Another single went nowhere on the charts, but the Tops' riveting harmonies and gliding synchronized dance moves began to attract attention. Legendary talent scout John Hammond signed them to record "Ain't That Love" for his label, Columbia, but sales remained poor.

Lightning Struck at Motown

Finally, after 10 years of relative obscurity, the Four Tops got their big break—they met Berry Gordy, Jr., head of Detroit's Motown Records. Gordy signed the foursome to Workshop, Motown's jazz subsidiary, for an advance of $400 in 1963. Soon the group was enjoying the famed family atmosphere of the company, hobnobbing with the likes of the Temptations, the Supremes, Martha Reeves, and Smokey Robinson and the Miracles.

The Four Tops' early Motown recordings were indeed jazz-oriented, and the group also sang backup for other Motown acts. Their careers shifted into high gear when the legendary Motown songwriter/producer team of Holland-Dozier-Holland saw the group perform at Detroit's 20 Grand Club. Eddie Holland invited them into the studio after the performance to hear him sing a number he thought might be right for them. The moonlighting session paid off, and The Four Tops recorded "Baby I Need Your Loving," their first hit. The song relied heavily on gifted lead Levi Stubbs's tough yet soulful sound, as well as the group's carefully constructed harmonies.

With golden-touch Holland-Dozier-Holland guiding the quartet's career, the Four Tops became one of Motown's most popular acts and as such, churned out a string of hits. Part of their success was due to their ability, nurtured over many years of performing, to switch smoothly from ballads to soul to rock—or even to country. After "I Can't Help Myself" reached Number One in the U.S. in 1965, the group began a tour of the United Kingdom and Europe, where they would become even more popular than in their own country.

Scored Monster Hit With "Reach Out"

The foursome's fame spiked a mighty peak with "Reach Out I'll Be There" in 1966. Featuring an unusual instrumental mix of flutes, oboes, and Arab drums, "Reach Out" soared to the top of the U.S. charts. According to the *Guinness Encyclopedia,* it was "the pinnacle of the traditional Motown style, bringing an almost symphonic arrangement to an R&B love song." *The Harmony Illustrated Encyclopedia of Rock* noted that the song, in fact, "established Motown as [a] force in contemporary music."

In 1967 the Tops demonstrated their versatility with soulful cover versions of hits like the Left Banke's "Walk Away Renee" and Tim Hardin's "If I Were a Carpenter." When Holland-Dozier-Holland left that year to form their own record company after a disagreement with Motown over royalties, it looked as if the group's phenomenal winning streak might end. After their "Greatest Hits" album was released in 1968, the Four Tops began to feel underappreciated as the Motown hierarchy focused increasingly on the more rock-oriented Temptations. Stubbs and company managed some success with Motown producer/writers Frank Wilson, Smokey Robinson, Ivy Hunter, and Johnny Bristol and in 1970, they teamed up with the Supremes for the first of three collaborative albums.

When Berry Gordy, Jr., relocated Motown's main operations to Hollywood, the Four Tops chose to stay behind in Detroit. They signed a new deal with the Dunhill label, thus ending a partnership that had brought them more than 15 Top 40 singles. But the group clearly remained worthy of the hit parade, marching to Number Four with "Ain't No Woman (Like the One I've Got)" in 1973, which became yet another million seller. With Dunhill, the Tops were able to reclaim the style that had made their name in the mid-1960s.

Continued to Crank Out Hits

Appearing ready to settle into the "oldies" nostalgia concert circuit by the end of the 1970s, the Four Tops gained new life after signing with Casablanca Records in 1981. As with the switch to Dunhill, the move proved fortuitous and led to an immediate Number One soul hit, "When She Was My Girl." *The Harmony Encyclopedia* deemed their 1981 album, *Tonight*, "a classy collection of relaxed pop-soul songs that recaptured [a] great deal of the magic of the Tops' great days."

The quartet made two albums for Casablanca before their appearance on the Motown 25th anniversary television special in 1983 set the stage for a renewal of business with Gordy. After resigning with Motown, they toured the U.S. and abroad with the Temptations. Stubbs added to his resume—and demonstrated a flair for acting—when he providing the voice for the man-eating plant Audrey in the film version of the stage musical "The Little Shop of Horrors." Although some of their recordings for Motown during the 1980s were produced by Holland-Dozier-Holland, the renewed collaboration largely failed to capture the old glory. The group defected once again, this time to Arista, where they produced another pair of successful singles.

By 1993 the Four Tops were still performing up to 200 gigs a year, often with the Temptations. By then they had generated a catalog of 36 albums peppered with numerous classic hits. In a review of a 1993 Tops concert, the *New Yorker* called the performance "less of an oldies show than a master class in the golden age of Motor City soul." Clearly, the success and longevity of the Four Tops have earned them a unique niche in R&B history.

Selected discography

Singles

"Baby I Need Your Loving," Motown, 1964.
"I Can't Help Myself," Motown, 1965.
"Reach Out I'll Be There," Motown, 1967.
"Ain't No Woman (Like the One I've Got)," Dunhill, 1973.
"When She Was My Girl," Casablanca, 1981.

Albums

Four Tops Second Album, Tamla/Motown, 1966.
Reach Out, Tamla/Motown, 1967.
Still Waters Run Deep, Tamla/Motown, 1970.
(With the Supremes) *The Magnificent Seven*, Tamla/Motown, 1971.
Main Street People, Dunhill/Probe, 1973.
Tonight, Casablanca, 1981.

Sources

Books

The Guinness Encyclopedia of Popular Music, Vol. II, edited by Colin Larkin, Guinness, 1992.
The Harmony Illustrated Encyclopedia of Rock, Harmony Books, 1988.
Rees, Dafydd, and Luke Crampton, *Rock Movers & Shakers*, ABC/CLIO, 1991.

Periodicals

Billboard, February 28, 1987.
Jet, November 13, 1989; February 5, 1990.
New Yorker, August 1993.
People, March 9, 1987.
Rolling Stone, February 9, 1989; February 20, 1992.
Wilson Library Bulletin, April 1992.

—Ed Decker

George and Ira Gershwin

Composer and lyricist

Brothers George and Ira Gershwin enjoyed a working relationship that Larry Kart of the *Chicago Tribune* likened to "mental telepathy." "When George had many tunes on tap for me" Kart quoted Ira as having said, "and I couldn't recall exactly the start of a particular one I wanted to discuss, I would visualize the vocal line and my forefinger would draw an approximation of its curves in the air. And more often than not he would know the tune I meant." Together they created some of the most popular songs of the 1920s and '30s, songs that would hold a central place in pop music's library throughout the century.

They were unlikely collaborators—George had seemingly unstoppable kinetic energy, whereas Ira, according to composer Arthur Schwartz, as quoted in *Fascinating Rhythm,* was "a hard man to get out of an easy chair." George had the chutzpah to take on the world of popular and concert music with little concern about his lack of formal training. Ira, on the other hand, took on George's often very complicated and inventive music with, in the words of *Encyclopedia of the Musical*

For the Record...

George Gershwin (born Jacob Gershvin, September 26, 1898, in Brooklyn, NY; died of a brain tumor, July 11, 1937, in Beverly Hills, CA; *Education:* Studied music with Charles Hambitzer, Edward Kileny, Rubin Goldmark, Wallingford Riegger, Henry Cowell, and Joseph Schillinger), composer, pianist; **Ira Gershwin** (born Israel Gershvin, December 6, 1896, in New York City; died August 15, 1983, in Beverly Hills, CA; married Leonore Strunsky, September 14, 1926; *Education:* Attended City College of New York), lyricist; sons of Morris (a businessman) and Rose Bruskin Gershwin.

George was music plugger on Tin Pan Alley, 1914-1917; published first song, "When You Want 'Em, You Can't Get 'Em, When You Got 'Em, You Don't Want 'Em," 1916; pianist at Broadway's Century Theater, 1917-1918; composed songs for Harms Publishing, 1918-1919; composed first Broadway score, *La La Lucille,* 1919; first successful concert piece, *The Rhapsody in Blue,* 1924. Ira and George first collaborated on "The Real American Folk Song (Is a Rag)," 1918; Ira scored first show with Vincent Youmans, *Two Little Girls in Blue,* 1921; Gershwins collaborated on first show, *Dangerous Maid,* 1921, and had first hit with *Lady, Be Good!,* 1924. After George's death, Ira wrote lyrics for Broadway shows, including *Lady in the Dark,* 1941, and for films, including *A Star Is Born,* 1954; Ira was author of *Lyrics on Several Occasions* (annotated lyrics), 1959.

Selected awards: Ira, Pulitzer Prize (with George S. Kaufman and Morrie Ryskind), 1932, for *Of Thee I Sing;* George, honorary membership, St. Cecelia Academy in Rome, 1937; together, Academy Award nomination, 1937, for "Let's Call the Whole Thing Off"; Ira (with others) Academy Award nominations, 1944, for "Long Ago and Far Away," and 1954, for "The Man That Got Away;" numerous theaters, musical competitions, and library collections bear the Gershwin name.

Theater author Stanley Green, "agile wit, originality of phrase, and rhyming ingenuity."

Like many of their Tin Pan Alley colleagues, the Gershwins were the children of Eastern European Jewish immigrants. The original family name was Gershovitz, which George and Ira's parents anglicized to Gershvin and which the family later changed to Gershwin. Ira was born first, in New York City on December 6, 1896. Their father, Morris, was a businessman who changed ventures and addresses at a dizzying pace. Ira once reckoned that the family lived in 28 apartments in fewer than 20 years. Morris owned, at various times, restaurants, bakeries, baths, a cigar store, and a pool parlor. When George made his entrance on September 26, 1898, the family had crossed the river into Brooklyn.

In spite of the brothers' remarkable ability to harmonize as adults, as youths, George and Ira led very different lives. Ira was quiet and studious, and he read voraciously. George, conversely, was a rowdy. He hung out on the street, playing sports and getting into trouble. In his books, Ira discovered poetry and light verse; in the streets, George found music.

Piano for Ira Went to George

Standing on a sidewalk in Harlem in 1904, George heard Anton Rubinstein's *Melody in F* on a player piano and loved the sound of it. Six years later, when the Gershwins bought a piano—intending it for Ira—George sat down and immediately began playing. He had been listening to music on the street for years and had played around on the piano at a friend's house. When it became clear that George would be the musician, lessons were arranged with neighborhood teachers.

In 1912 George began to study with Charles Hambitzer, who recognized the youngster's gift immediately. Although George was interested in modern music—particularly jazz—his teacher made sure he learned the classics as well. He took George to classical concerts and introduced him to the music of Frédéric Chopin, Franz Liszt, and Claude Debussy. George also managed to find the jazz he yearned to play—back on the street. As Kart explained in the *Chicago Tribune,* "New York was a hot bed for such swinging black virtuosos as James P. Johnson, Eubie Blake and Willie [The Lion] Smith, and Gershwin learned the Harlem stride-style of piano playing from the men who invented it—being tutored, in particular, by the brilliant Lucky Roberts." George was also influenced by the music he heard downtown, on the Broadway stage. He and Ira went to the theater as often as once a week, and George was inspired by the great songwriters of the period, Irving Berlin and Jerome Kern.

Never one for academics, George dropped out of high school in 1914 to become a song plugger for Jerome H. Remick & Co., a Tin Pan Alley music publisher. Following in the footsteps of Berlin, George promoted the company's music by playing and singing songs for performers. The job was a wonderful introduction to the music business; hearing the works of the best songwriters of the day, George quickly learned what it took to become a great popular songsmith and how to avoid becoming a hack. In his book *American Popular Song* Alec Wilder observed that even with his first song, 1916's "When You Want 'Em, You Can't Get 'Em, When You Got 'Em, You Don't Want 'Em," George showed a "need to break away from the hack writer pattern."

In 1917 George left Remick and was soon working on Broadway as rehearsal pianist for *Miss 1917,* a show by Jerome Kern and Victor Herbert. Afterwards, he continued working at the Century Theater, where the show had opened. By 1918 he had published a smattering of songs, and that year Max Dreyfus, head of Harms Publishing, hired George to compose for his company at $35 a week. Within a year three Broadway shows included his songs, and he had worked as an onstage accompanist for Broadway star Nora Bayes. In May of 1919 *La La Lucille,* for which George had written his first full score, opened on Broadway. Though not a huge success, it ran for 104 performances. Then George turned 21.

Ira Discovered Wordplay Early

Though Ira's aspirations eventually turned toward Broadway as well, his route there was quite different from the one George had taken. Encouraged by the books he read, Ira began writing when he was very young. As early as grammar school he put together humorous newsletters. In high school he found a kindred spirit in future lyricist Yip Harburg, who joined Ira in his publishing ventures. They discovered a shared love for *vers de société*—sophisticated, witty, ironic, satiric, and playful poems and lyrics—and the operettas of W. S. Gilbert and Arthur Sullivan. According to *Fascinating Rhythm* author Deena Rosenberg, Ira and Harburg were especially impressed "that brilliant light verse could work so well in combination with clever, tuneful music."

Ira attended City College of New York, where he continued writing light verse. Eventually, he began to submit one-liners and poems to magazines and newspapers. At that time, newspaper humorists would include in their columns witticisms sent in by readers of the paper. Ira's first such publication was in a 1914 edition of C. L. Edison's *New York Mail* column: "Tramp jokes are bum comedy." After two years of college, Ira dropped out and pursued a variety of jobs. Working at his father's Turkish baths, Ira met British playwright Paul M. Potter, who, according to Rosenberg, advised the budding writer "to learn especially 'your American slang.'" Ira continued to pick up slang in a variety of endeavors, including a stint as the manager of his cousin's touring carnival show. As Rosenberg noted, "He considered himself a 'floating soul,' unsure where he would land."

As he floated, he observed life—the people and city around him—and took notes. Eventually he landed with George in the theater.

Sparked by George's interest, Ira began attending the theater and even reviewed a few shows for a trade paper. He also began to write song lyrics on occasion, some to George's music. Their first full collaboration, in 1918, resulted in "The Real American Folk Song (Is a Rag)," which addressed popular American music's "melting pot." Nora Bayes performed the number in her show. Hearing their work onstage had a profound effect on the Gershwins; with this performance, Ira became, in the words of Rosenberg, "Ira Gershwin, lyricist," and George became determined to compose a show.

But while George moved on to write *La La Lucille,* Ira found other collaborators. George suggested he write a song with Vincent Youmans, a budding composer whose later hits included "Tea for Two." Ira did, and George played the new songs for *Lucille's* producer, Alex Aarons, who signed Ira and Youmans to score his next show, *Two Little Girls in Blue.* Ira did not want to capitalize on George's growing fame and so began his professional career with the pseudonym Arthur Francis—combining the names of the brothers' younger siblings.

During the next few years George and Ira continued to write—but usually not together. While their occasional collaborations showed promise, there were no sparks. In 1921 they collaborated on their first show, *Dangerous Maid,* but it closed on the road. In the meantime, they developed and honed their individual styles. George's career continued on the same trajectory, and he showed no signs of slowing down. His composition "Swanee" was recorded by superstar Al Jolson in 1920; it was George's first popular success. Later, under contract to producer George White, George composed scores for a number of stage shows in New York and London. His scores in the early 1920s included those for *A Dangerous Maid, Our Nell, Sweet Little Devil, The Rainbow, Primrose,* and five installments of the annual revue *George White's Scandals.* As early as 1923, critics began to take notice. In an essay in *Dial,* as reprinted in *Fascinating Rhythm,* critic Gilbert Seldes hailed George as a great talent and a possible successor to the Broadway master, Irving Berlin.

Although George was firmly entrenched in the world of popular music, the classical influence of Hambitzer, his former teacher, was still marked. Furthermore, in 1917, as his professional output increased, he had begun a study of harmony, counterpoint, orchestration, and music form with Edward Kilenyi. He dabbled in classical composition and wrote his first, the *Lullaby* for string quartet, as a harmony exercise for his instructor. He also composed a short opera for *George White's Scandals of 1922* called *Blue Monday,* but it was never included in the show.

Rhapsody in Blue

Because critics and audiences were unaware of George's classical penchant and credentials, they were dazzled when he introduced the *Rhapsody in Blue.* In 1924 band leader Paul Whiteman organized a concert he billed as "An Experiment in Modern Music" and invited George to write a jazz concerto for it. In less than three months he produced the *Rhapsody in Blue.* Whiteman invited classical musicians and music critics to the concert on February 12, 1924, and George's composition was a featured performance. Though the *Rhapsody in Blue* has been criticized by a number of musicians over the years, its debut represented the first time that jazz had found its way into the world of classical music. George wowed the audience and suddenly became very famous.

Critical response was mixed, but the *Rhapsody* garnered a great deal of attention. Many classical critics were mystified by the blending of styles. Some observers, however, were very excited—according to Rosenberg, critic Deems Taylor called Gershwin "the link between the jazz camp and the intellectuals." With decades of hindsight, the *Chicago Tribune's* Kart disagreed: "In retrospect 'Rhapsody' did nothing of the sort—for even though it is a delightfully tuneful piece of light music, it is not really jazzlike." In *Commentary,* William G. Hyland opined, "Gershwin claimed that with the *Rhapsody* he wanted to strike a blow against the stereotype of jazz. But was the *Rhapsody* jazz? In the narrowest sense of the term it was not: there were no improvisations, there were no driving rhythms, and it was not even very 'blue.' It was not the kind of jazz that Louis Armstrong and Jelly Roll Morton were playing. But the spirit of the piece is jazz and owes a lot to the jazz greats of the time." Regardless of critical opinion, in its first decade the *Rhapsody* earned more than a quarter of a million dollars in performances and recordings.

Composing the *Rhapsody in Blue* was instrumental not only in establishing George's reputation in concert music, but in marking the moment that George and Ira were ripe for collaboration. In *Fascinating Rhythm* Rosenberg identified this composition as the catalyst that began the partnership. "Once George had written this consummate fusion of blue-note-dominated melody lines, provocative and novel harmonies, and varied syncopated rhythmic figures, Ira began to find the kind of words that would bring George's distinctive music idiom to life on stage."

The variety of styles and influences that the Gershwins brought to their work created a very distinctive sound that delighted and occasionally mystified critics. They marvelled at George's creativity and daring and often accepted his imperfections as part of the package. "His work is such a personal expression," Charles Schwartz ventured in the *Dictionary of Contemporary Music,* "that even the numerous technical deficiencies in his serious compositions have come to be accepted as part of the Gershwin sound." Rather than staying with one type of music, George blended the strains that wafted through New York, particularly European classical, African-American blues and jazz, and the music of Eastern European Jews. It was, in *Commentary* contributor Hyland's estimation, "the sound of urban America and especially of Manhattan and Broadway."

Extraordinary Ability and Creativity

George was able to be daring and creative in his compositions because he was, in many critics' opinions, a remarkable musician with an instinctive understanding of music. He was a brilliant pianist and excelled in rhythm and harmony. Hyland was especially enthusiastic about this point: "Gershwin's abilities at the piano were truly extraordinary and were the secret of his success as a composer. . . . [He] reveled in rhythm, in part because he played the piano so well." He was also, in Hyland's view, "a superb manipulator of harmony," who understood how to use the newest sounds and "deliberately sought out the most advanced progression of chords."

Also characteristic of George's music was his use of the blues and blue notes. Though not a blues musician, Hyland judged that George "had an unusual feel for the blues." In the *New Grove Dictionary of American Music,* Richard Crawford agreed: "Perhaps the most striking characteristic of Gershwin's melodies is their reliance on blue notes. Sometimes they function as blatant dissonances. . . . At other times they soften the melodic contour with a sinuous grace." Even when critical, scholars of George's music tend to qualify their dissatisfaction with admiration. Typical is composer Arthur Schwartz's assessment of George's longer work, as quoted by Rosenberg: "[The] symphonic pieces contain many structural deficiencies that resulted from Gershwin's rather limited experience in expanding musical materials. However, the tunes in these works are usually so outstanding that they often compensate for other inadequacies."

Most of George's critics agree that his musical style was, in Hyland's words, "helped immeasurably by his brother's witty and sophisticated lyrics." Rosenberg noted that the lyrics of one of their first songs, "Mischa, Jascha, Toscha, Sascha," written in 1919, "give us some early hints of Ira's emerging style, with its whimsy, depth, and unexpected juxtapositions of the sublime and the mundane." Almost exclusively, Ira wrote lyrics after George had composed the music. In doing so, he matched the sophistication, urbanity, and slang-derived quality of George's music and avoided poetic or syrupy lyrics. Crawford quoted Ira on this point: "Since most of [my] lyrics . . . were arrived at by fitting words mosaically to music already composed, any resemblance to actual poetry, living or dead, is highly improbable." In *Poets of Tin Pan Alley* author Philip Furia's opinion, Ira's "most brilliant effects came from finding the ready-made slang phrase to fit every rhythmic turn of his brother's music."

Taking playwright Paul M. Potter's advice, Ira relied heavily on colloquial speech for his lyrics. He used contractions, slurred words, and dropped off letters, as in "'S Wonderful." He also liked to play with clichés and catch phrases—"How Long Has This Been Going On," "Of Thee I Sing,"—twisting their meanings. Furia noted that Ira's favorite subject for lyrics was the excitement of falling in love, but "what really interested him was less the romantic message than the medium of language itself—the vocabulary, idioms, and phrasing of American speech."

Collaboration Began in Earnest

Ira found the perfect words for George's music with producer Alex Aarons's next show. Aarons asked the Gershwins to write the score for a show highlighting a new sister-brother dance team—Fred and Adele Astaire. The result was *Lady, Be Good!,* which opened in December of 1924. The beauty of the brothers' collaboration was evident in the first song they wrote, "The Man I Love," which Aarons used to get financing for the production. The song was eventually dropped but became a huge hit on its own. The numbers that remained in the show—notably "Fascinating Rhythm" and "Oh! Lady, Be Good!"—were no less skillful. "Fascinating Rhythm" included such a complex rhythm that Arthur Schwartz, according to Rosenberg, called Ira's lyrical achievement "a truly phenomenal feat . . . when one considers that . . . [he] was required to be brilliant within the most confining rhythms and accents." The show was a hit with critics and a popular success. It made stars of the Astaires, and the Gershwins became the talk of the musical world.

Through the rest of the 1920s George and Ira wrote hit musicals and made stars of their performers. Singing "Someone to Watch Over Me" in 1926's *Oh, Kay!,*

Gertrude Lawrence became a luminary. Also that year, *Funny Face* brought the Astaires back to rave reviews and produced such hits as "'S Wonderful" and "How Long Has This Been Going On." *Girl Crazy,* which opened in 1930, made celebrities of two of its performers: Ethel Merman, with "I Got Rhythm," and Ginger Rogers, with "Embraceable You" and "But Not for Me."

While George composed musicals with his brother, he did not neglect his other pursuits. Buoyed by the success of the *Rhapsody,* George began to devote more attention to concert music. He continued to study with noted instructors, including Rubin Goldmark, Wallingford Riegger, Henry Cowell, and Joseph Schillinger. In 1925 he composed the *Concerto in F* for piano and orchestra for the New York Symphony Orchestra and introduced the *Preludes* for piano. In 1928, while vacationing in Europe, he composed the tone poem *An American in Paris.* During this sojourn he also met the classical composers Maurice Ravel, Sergei Prokofiev, and Alban Berg. He continued to perform his music in concert halls and tackled conducting as well. George was even commissioned by the Metropolitan Opera to write a "Jewish opera"—*The Dybbuk*—but this never came about.

Despite George's popularity and his brilliant work with Ira, like all Broadway composers, the Gershwins had their share of failures. *Treasure Girl* in 1928 and *Show Girl* in 1929 were both flops, and *East Is West* never made it to the stage. Some of the latter show's songs, however—"I've Got a Crush on You" and "Liza"—became hits when they were showcased in later productions. And one of these failures eventually became a hit. Critics liked *Strike Up the Band,* which was first staged in 1927, but many found the anti-war political satire of George S. Kaufman's script too biting for most audiences. The show closed before reaching Broadway. A few years later, however, Kaufman had colleague Morrie Ryskind tone down the satire; the show's second try, in 1930, was a sucess. George, Ira, Kaufman, and Ryskind followed this with two more presentations, creating a sort of musical political satire trilogy.

Strike Up the Band and the two shows that followed, *Of Thee I Sing* and *Let 'Em Eat Cake,* were very unusual for Broadway musicals of the time. As it was, politically and socially satiric musicals were rare. Furthermore, as Rosenberg noted, "*Of Thee I Sing* is often cited, along with Kern and [Oscar] Hammerstein's *Show Boat,* as a precursor to *Oklahoma!*—one of the rare pre-1943 shows that closely integrated its score into its action. It comments on it, mocks it, deflates it; often, it *is* the action." Ethan Mordden of the *New York Times* agreed, insisting that in *Of Thee I Sing* "the Gershwins constructed a score that sounds like musical comedy but behaves like operetta, all in an air of such insouciant burlesque that the music enriches the satire."

Pulitzer Prize

Of Thee I Sing, which opened in 1931, topped *Strike Up the Band* in popularity and acclaim. It did extremely well at the box office even in the midst of the Depression, and it was the first musical to win a Pulitzer Prize for drama. Its sequel, *Let 'Em Eat Cake,* took on much weightier subjects and was in part a response to the rising power of Adolf Hitler and fears of communism and fascism. Unfortunately, this show was not a hit and ran for only 46 performances.

After their string of satires, the Gershwins embarked on a new musical path. Taking on opera, George composed what *New Grove Dictionary of American Music* contributor Crawford called his "magnum opus," *Porgy and Bess.* The opera was based on DuBose Heyward's *Porgy,* a novel about the black community of "Catfish Row" in Charleston, South Carolina. In 1933 the New York Theater Guild contracted Heyward and the Gershwins to produce a musical; together they created a work that was billed as "an American folk opera."

When it opened in 1935, *Porgy and Bess* received a lackluster response. It ran for only 120 performances and was deemed a financial failure. Critics offered a variety of complaints. "Opera critics have objected to arias that sound too much like Broadway songs and to the score's lack of organic, symphonic integration," Crawford explained. "Black critics have found Gershwin's evocations of their music inauthentic." Rosenberg also noted that critics found the switching of styles within the opera troublesome. Yet, in time, *Porgy and Bess* became considered one of the great compositions, and later stagings were very successful. For George and Ira it was an ideal synthesis. It was, as Rosenberg wrote, "the Gershwins' most thorough and effective mixture of popular and classical elements. Here is . . . a work that consists of the many kinds of music and the diverse rhythms that make up New York, America, and a large part of the human race."

After *Porgy and Bess,* George took a break and went to Mexico. Ira teamed up with Vernon Duke to write songs for the *Ziegfeld Follies of 1936* and had a hit with "I Can't Get Started." In June of 1936, George and Ira signed a contract with RKO film studios and "went Hollywood." They had written there before, when they scored *Delicious* in 1931, but this time around was far more fruitful. They wrote scores for *Shall We Dance, A Damsel in Distress,* and *Goldwyn Follies,* creating a

string of hits: "Let's Call the Whole Thing Off"—nominated for an Academy Award in 1937—"They All Laughed," "They Can't Take That Away From Me," "A Foggy Day," "Nice Work If You Can Get It," "Things Are Looking Up," and "Love Is Here to Stay." In *Fascinating Rhythm* author Rosenberg's opinion, the reason for success was very clear: "At this point, George, thirty-eight, and Ira, forty, were so deeply in tune with each other that in less than a year they produced one standard after another—a concentrated stream of songs written from a more mature sensibility and reflecting the sound and themes of the late thirties. In the twenties, the elements of the Gershwins' love ballads cohere to produce a sense of loneliness and longing; in the thirties, they cohere to produce a sense of tenuous celebration and affirmation of life amid a shifting and unstable world."

Tragedy Ended Partnership

The world was indeed unstable. In 1937, while working on *The Goldwyn Follies,* George began exhibiting strange behavior and symptoms. He stumbled in performance, often lost his coordination, and suffered severe headaches. Many of his friends—and even doctors—believed his condition was emotional, resulting perhaps from the stress of working in Hollywood. Tragically, they were wrong; on July 9th George fell into a coma and two days later died from a too-long-undiagnosed brain tumor that had grown to the size of a grapefruit.

Ira was devastated; he wrote little for three years. He returned to work in 1941 to collaborate with composer Kurt Weill on *Lady in the Dark.* The show was a success and it led to more collaborations with Weill. However, the partnership was cut short when Weill died at age 50. Ira soldiered on, working with a variety of great composers, including Aaron Copland, Harry Warrens, Burton Lane, and Jerome Kern. Ira and Kern's song "Long Ago and Far Away" garnered an Academy Award nomination. His last Broadway show was *Park Avenue,* which he wrote with Arthur Schwartz and which reunited him with George S. Kaufman. Despite this return to Broadway, Ira preferred California to New York and moved there permanently. Ira's last collaborator was Harold Arlen, whose musical style, according to Rosenberg, was very similar to George's. Together they scored *A Star Is Born* in 1952-53, a comeback film for actress Judy Garland. Ira wrote his last songs for the film, including "The Man That Got Away," which, as Rosenberg reported, a *Time* reviewer called "one unforgettable lump in the throat," and for which Ira received another Academy Award nomination.

In spite of the sustained success he enjoyed after George's death, Ira's writing had changed. In *Poets of Tin Pan Alley* author Furia's appraisal, "Although he continued to write lyrics for over twenty years, Ira seldom recaptured the slangy sophistication of the popular songs he had written with his brother." Working with other composers after George's death, Furia found that "his lyrical style shifted away from vernacular ease toward the poetic heights."

Ira spent the last three decades of his life, in Rosenberg's words, as "the guardian, perpetuator, and promoter of all matters Gershwin." He set lyrics to 60 or so of George's tunes that did not have lyrics, many of which were later used in films. He was involved in revivals of their shows, arranged for performances of George's unperformed compositions, and consulted on various films that used their work. He also organized collections of Gershwin documents and recordings for the Library of Congress and collected his own annotated lyrics in *Lyrics on Several Occasions,* published in 1959.

Critics continue to speculate about the Gershwins' work had George not died so young. In *Commentary* contributor Hyland's evaluation, "After *Porgy and Bess* a new [George] Gershwin emerged with more spartan and straightforward lines, less ragged jazz; a greater sense of sadness crept into his final songs. Clearly Gershwin was in a state of transition when he died. He was weary of Hollywood and exasperated with Sam Goldwyn's pressure to write hits 'like Irving Berlin.' Where this transition would have led to no one can say, but it would undoubtedly have been exciting."

Music Endures

Speculation aside, the Gershwins' work has continued to thrill audiences for decades. In the 1980s and '90s three of their scores reappeared on Broadway, in *Crazy for You, My One and Only,* and *Oh, Kay!* New recordings were also released, including a series of scores on Elektra Nonesuch that drew on "long lost" and unpublished material found in 1982 in a Warner Bros. warehouse. And the Gershwins persist in fascinating biographers, who have produced a number of studies of George and Ira and their work as new information and interpretations have come to light. Joan Peyser's 1993 book *The Memory of All That: The Life of George Gershwin* included a number of controversial assertions about George, including the claim that he fathered an illegitimate son and possibly a daughter as well.

"For all their resonance as masters of 20's musical comedy," *New York Times* contributor Mordden observed in 1992, "the Gershwins have proved timeless."

Rosenberg, for her part, offered an explanation for this timelessness: "Well over half a century after Gershwin songs broke over New York, they still retain their power to energize, delight, and illuminate, to disturb and surprise. Their capacity for self-renewal seems inexhaustible; that is why the songs are still among the most widely played and recorded among jazz artists, as well as theater, pop, and classical performers. . . . No matter how witty, sophisticated, and warm the songs, a human vulnerability is always there. The greatest Gershwin songs give us a three-dimensional slice of life, with its ever-shifting moments of doubt, hope, disappointment, and fulfillment—and provide a rich antidote, however brief."

Selected scores

Stage

A Dangerous Maid, 1921.
Lady, Be Good! (includes "Fascinating Rhythm" and "Oh, Lady Be Good!"), 1924.
Tell Me More, 1925.
Tip-toes, 1925.
Oh, Kay! (includes "Someone to Watch Over Me"), 1926.
Strike Up the Band (includes "I've Got a Crush on You,"), 1927, 1930.
Funny Face (includes "'S Wonderful"), 1927.
Rosalie (includes "How Long Has This Been Going On?"), 1928.
Treasure Girl, 1928.
Show Girl (includes "Liza"), 1929.
Girl Crazy (includes "But Not for Me," "Embraceable You," and "I Got Rhythm"), 1930.
Of Thee I Sing (includes "Of Thee I Sing"), 1931.
Pardon My English, 1933.
Let 'Em Eat Cake, 1933.
Porgy and Bess (with DuBose Heyward), 1935.

Film

Delicious, 1931.
Shall We Dance (includes "Let's Call the Whole Thing Off," "They All Laughed," and "They Can't Take That Away From Me"), 1937.
A Damsel in Distress (includes "A Foggy Day," "Things are Looking Up," and "Nice Work If You Can Get It"), 1937.
The Goldwyn Follies (includes "Love Is Here to Stay"), 1938.
The Shocking Miss Pilgrim, 1946.
Kiss Me, Stupid, 1964.

Orchestral works by George Gershwin

Rhapsody in Blue, 1924.
Concerto in F, 1925.
An American in Paris, 1928.
Second Rhapsody for Piano and Orchestra, 1931.
Cuban Overture, 1932.

Catfish Row, 1935-36.

Film scores by Ira Gershwin

The North Star, 1943.
Cover Girl (includes "Long Ago and Far Away"), 1944.
The Barkleys of Broadway, 1949.
Give the Girl a Break, 1953.
The Country Girl, 1954.
A Star Is Born (includes "The Man That Got Away"), 1954.

George Gershwin's stage collaborations with other lyricists include *La La Lucille*, 1919; *George White's Scandals of 1920-1924*; *Our Nell*, 1922; *The Rainbow*, 1923; *Sweet Little Devil*, 1924; *Primrose*, 1924; and *Song of the Flame*, 1925. Ira Gershwin's stage collaborations with other composers include *Two Little Girls in Blue*, 1921; *Ziegfeld Follies of 1936* (includes "I Can't Get Started"); *Lady in the Dark*, 1941; *The Firebrand of Florence*, 1945; and *Park Avenue*, 1946.

Selected discography

Ella Fitzgerald and Louis Armstrong, *Porgy and Bess*, Verve, 1958.
Porgy and Bess, RCA Victor, 1963.
London Symphony Orchestra, *Previn Plays Gershwin*, EMI Angel, 1971.
Fitzgerald, *The George and Ira Gershwin Songbook*, Polygram, 1978.
Marni Nixon Sings Gershwin, Reference Recordings, 1986.
Kiri Te Kanawa, *Kiri Sings Gershwin*, EMI Angel, 1987.
George Gershwin Piano Music, Elektra Nonesuch, 1987.
Michael Feinstein, *Pure Gershwin*, Parnassus Records, 1985, Elektra, 1987.
A Star Is Born, CBS Records, 1988.
Gershwin Songs and Duets, Koch International, 1990.
Bobby Short is K-RA-ZY for Gershwin, Atlantic, 1990.
George and Ira Gershwin: Girl Crazy, Elektra Nonesuch, 1990.
An American in Paris, Original MGM Soundtrack, CBS Records, 1990.
George and Ira Gershwin: Strike Up the Band, Elektra Nonesuch, 1991.
Hollywood Bowl Orchestra, *The Gershwins in Hollywood*, PolyGram Classics and Jazz, 1991.
Crazy for You, Broadway Angel, 1992.

Barbara Hendricks, Katia, and Marielle Labeque, *Gershwin*, Phillips, 1992.
The Authentic George Gershwin, Vol. I, 1918-1925, ASV Digital, 1992.
Wayne Marshall and Andrew Litton, *Rhapsody in Blue*, Virgin Classics, 1992.
The Atlantic Brass Quintet, *By George: Gershwin's Greatest Hits*, MusicMasters, 1993.
Crazy for Gershwin, IMP Classics/Allegro, 1993.
George Gershwin, *Gershwin Plays Gershwin: The Piano Rolls, Realized by Artis Wodehouse*, Elektra Nonesuch, 1993.
Great American Songwriters Vol. I—George and Ira Gershwin, Rhino, 1993.

Sources

Books

Dictionary of Contemporary Music, edited by John Vinton, E. P. Dutton, 1974.
Furia, Philip, *The Poets of Tin Pan Alley*, Oxford University Press, 1990.
Green, Stanley, *Encyclopedia of the Musical Theater*, DaCapo, 1976.
Jablonski, Edward, *Gershwin: A Biography*, Doubleday, 1987.
The New Grove Dictionary of American Music, Volume 2, edited by H. Wiley Hitchcock and Stanley Sadie, Macmillan, 1986.
Peyser, Joan, *The Memory of All That*, Simon & Schuster, 1993.
Rosenberg, Deena, *Fascinating Rhythm: The Collaboration of George and Ira Gershwin*, Dutton, 1991.
Wilder, Alec, *American Popular Song: The Great Innovators, 1900-1950*, Oxford University Press, 1972.

Periodicals

Chicago Tribune, February 15, 1987; April 1, 1990.
Commentary, October 1990.
Down Beat, January 1994.
Entertainment Weekly, April 2, 1993.
New York Times, March 7, 1992; March 17, 1992.
People, June 7, 1993.
Time, January 31, 1994.

—Megan Rubiner Zinn

The Geto Boys

Rap group

Hard-core Houston rappers the Geto Boys inspired an incident in 1990 that smacked of censorship and, consequently, catapulted them to either fame or infamy, depending on one's perspective. In the midst of an effort to broaden the group's market, Geffen Records, a large record label and distribution company that had contracted to release the Geto Boys' first major-label album, backed out—and immediately sparked a public controversy. While hardcore rap is praised by some for its candid depiction of a tense inner-city life created by poverty and racial discrimination, many reviewers and listeners felt that these rappers had gone beyond the line of acceptability. The discussion as a whole fit into a contemporaneous debate about music and censorship that also concerned rap acts 2 Live Crew and Ice Cube.

The name "The Geto Boys" actually refers to a shifting cast of rappers, several of whom have gone on to solo careers since departing the Boys. The group was formed in 1986 at Rap-A-Lot Records, an independent Houston-based label, when owner/producer James Smith decided that he needed an outfit that could express "the street": the experiences with which he had grown up in the slums of Houston's Fifth Ward, what the *Source*'s Adario Strange referred to as "Houston's most notorious war zone." The three original Geto Boys, Jukebox, Raheem, and Sir Rap-A-Lot, had a hit in 1986 with "Car Freaks," their first single. But the group disintegrated before they had a chance to build on that achievement.

Still committed to his vision, Smith decided to try again in 1988. Strange encapsulated the story for *Source* readers in rap terms: "With the goal of vesting the group with a more 'underground flav,' James looked throughout all of Houston to find the illest rhyme slingers to rebuild the Geto Boys." The streets offered up three rappers—Willie D., Scarface, and Bushwick Bill—also known as Willie Dennis, Brad Jordan, and Richard Shaw; backed by the music of DJ Ready Red, this combination scored a hit that far outstripped "Car Freaks." Called "Mind Playing Tricks on Me," the single earned gold and platinum records; that triumph, as well as two popular albums released on Rap-A-Lot in 1988 and 1989, cemented the future of the group, despite continuing personnel changes.

Shifting Lineup

DJ Domination (born Michael Poye) replaced Ready Red in 1991. And even when lead rapper Willie D. decided to devote himself to solo work in 1993, Smith managed to keep the Geto Boys together. He recruited Big Mike—Michael Barnett—from another Rap-A-Lot

For the Record. . .

Members include **Big Mike** (born Michael Barnett; replaced **Willie D.** [Willie Denis; bandmember 1988-93]); **Bushwick Bill** (born Richard Shaw); **DJ Domination** (born Michael Poye; replaced **DJ Ready Red** [bandmember 1988-91]); and **Scarface** (born Brad Jordon). Original members included **Jukebox, Raheem,** and **Sir Rap-A-Lot.**

Group founded by Rap-A-Lot Records owner/producer James Smith, 1986; released single "Car Freaks," 1986; new lineup released single "Mind Playing Tricks on Me," 1988; released two albums on Rap-A-Lot; released *The Geto Boys,* Def American Recordings, 1990; released *We Can't Be Stopped,* Def American, 1991; released *Till Death Do Us Part,* Rap-A-Lot, 1993.

Awards: Gold and platinum records for "Mind Playing Tricks on Me."

Addresses: *Record company*—Rap-A-Lot Records, 5645 Hillcroft, Houston, TX 77036.

outfit, the Convicts. In fact, the give and take of group and solo work had by then been thoroughly worked into the fabric of the Geto Boys, Smith presenting each member with a contract that specified work both with the group and singly. Scarface expressed his support for the group's flexible lineup when he told Strange, "You can't stop this. If it ain't me, Bushwick and Mike, it'll be someone else. But you still can't stop the Geto Boys!" Taking Smith's expansive recording philosphy one step further, Scarface opened his own independent label, Face II Face.

That the Geto Boys have survived in any form is remarkable considering how hard some forces have tried to stop, or at least curtail, their success. By 1990, the Boys were prepared to distribute their major-label debut, on Def American Recordings through Geffen Records. After replacing the original manufacturer, Digital Audio Disc Corporation, which was prompted to pull out in response to the album's lyrics, Def American was forced to look for a new distributor in August of that year, when Geffen decided that it, too, could not handle the product.

That month the *New York Times* quoted a Geffen spokesperson's explanation: "While it is not imperative that lyrical expressions of even our own Geffen artists reflect the personal values of Geffen Records, the extent to which 'The Geto Boys' album glamorizes and possibly endorses violence, racism and misogyny com-

pels us to encourage Def American to select a distributor with a greater affinity for this musical expression." Bushwick Bill told Jon Pareles, the *Times* reporter, "We were just expressing stuff that happens in the ghetto, just being like reporters. We want to make everybody mad enough to look at the ghetto right in their own state, not just to look at the middle-class and the rich areas. There are people who curse worse than me and want to hide it all, but I ain't no hypocrite."

Controversy Over "Mind of a Lunatic"

The song garnering the most attention during this brouhaha was "Mind of a Lunatic," which professed to describe the thoughts and actions of a rapist and murderer, but several critics worried that the narrative too easily crossed over into endorsement. "Assassins" and "Trigga Happy Nigga" similarly described violent attacks on people the narrator encounters, with particularly explicit scenarios reserved for women. In a December, 1990, issue of *Rolling Stone,* a reviewer referred to the "utterly unredeemable . . . snuff-and-rape fantasy 'Mind of a Lunatic'" and criticized the Geto Boys for "mistaking the homicidal misogyny of 'Mind of a Lunatic' and 'Gangster of Love' for justifiably harsh, graphic descriptions of life when you're young, poor and black."

A month earlier, journalist Alan Light had published a longer and more in-depth discussion of the album in *Rolling Stone;* more appreciative of the work than the critic who would review it for the magazine, Light nonetheless argued, "If they want to rap about killing a woman and having sex with the corpse *and* claim that they're not glamorizing violence, the Geto Boys should draw the line between the narrator's voice and the band's own viewpoint a lot more convincingly than they do in 'Lunatic.'" Light did assess the quality of the music as well as its lyrical content and found it impressive, offering, "Of course, even 'Gangster' *sounds* great. [Producer and Def American head] Rick Rubin . . . has crafted roiling, buzzing tracks out of movie dialogue, gunfire and relentlessly funky bass and guitar samples. Rubin's taut, insistent grooves are the perfect setting for the rappers' frenzied street-gang delivery."

A month after Geffen's rejection, *The Geto Boys* was rescued by another major distributor, the Warner-Elektra-Atlantic Records Distribution Network. Aside from ostensibly trumpeting their commitment to free speech, the entities involved in the record's journey to market were also likely to realize quite a good return on their investment. In his August *Times* article, Pareles pointed out that the two Geto Boys albums released on Rap-A-Lot prior to the Def American deal did very well; he noted that the second, *Grip It! On That Other Level,* "is estimated to have sold more than 500,000 copies, an extraordinary number for an independent label." Def American's *The Geto Boys* was actually comprised of old and new songs, eight of which had appeared previously on the earlier albums. But even after overcoming initial obstacles, the record still faced the disfavor of one link in the market chain: some record stores ultimately chose not to stock it.

Critical Applause for Beats, if Not Lyrics

A year after the controversy over *The Geto Boys, We Can't Be Stopped* refueled the fire. *Rolling Stone* critic Rob Tannenbaum acknowledged the validity of violence in a great deal of rap but denied the Geto Boys any such credit, averring, "All gangsta rap is layered with contradictions, but by misdirecting their rage at other blacks, especially women, the Geto Boys confuse their neighbors with their enemies. Only twice, on the album's best songs, do they focus their rage at deserving targets." Tannenbaum further noted, "When their emotions range only from spite to malice, their claim of holding a mirror to a young, black generation is revealed as a lie—the hatred is their own, and it pervades the entire album." But this reviewer did reiterate Light's claim that the quality of the music exceeded that of the lyrics: "Though the rhymes come in old-school couplets that sound simple and old compared with the competition's, DJ Ready Red's beats kick slow and funky, which gives the music its considerable power."

We Can't Be Stopped was plagued by even greater negative publicity when Bushwick Bill ended up in the hospital on May 10, 1991—minus an eye—after he was shot by his girlfriend. Anthony DeCurtis reported in *Rolling Stone* on June 27 that the shooting occurred after a drunken Bushwick Bill had threatened the woman and her son, then "handed her a loaded and cocked .22-caliber derringer and insisted that he wanted to die." No charges were pressed, Bill went home with a glass eye, and the couple made up. (A photograph of the rapper in the hospital later came in handy as album art).

Till Death Do Us Part claimed the Number One spot on *Billboard*'s R&B album chart in the spring of 1993 during its first week of release. Although the album did not incite the controversy of its predecessors, it did manage to coincide with yet more dissenting media attention for the Boys. While attending a panel discussion at a conference of the National Association of Black Journalists, Bushwick Bill offended his listeners so profoundly that approximately 100 of them left the room. Havelock Nelson reported the incident in an August issue of *Billboard*: "He reportedly told the audience that all the women he knew were either bitches or hoes. He then 'cursed out' a woman who asked if he would describe his mother that way. Later, he amended his comments, saying he only meant women he has dated." The incident, of course, created more public criticism—a phenomenon that by then somehow seemed a necessary component of the Geto Boys' existence.

Selected discography

"Car Freaks," Rap-A-Lot, 1986.
"Mind Playing Tricks on Me," Rap-A-Lot, 1988.
Making Trouble, Rap-A-Lot, 1988.
Grip It! On That Other Level, Rap-A-Lot, 1989, reissued, Def American, 1990.
The Geto Boys (includes "Mind of a Lunatic," "Assassins," "Trigga Happy Nigga," and "Gangster of Love"), Def American/Rap-A-Lot, 1990.
We Can't Be Stopped (includes "Mind Playing Tricks on Me"), Def American/Rap-A-Lot, 1990.
Geto Boys Best: Uncut Dope (includes "Assassins," "Mind of a Lunatic," and "Mind Playing Tricks on Me"), Rap-A-Lot, 1992.
Till Death Do Us Part, Rap-A-Lot, 1993.

Sources

Billboard, April 10, 1993; August 14, 1993.
New York Times, August 28, 1990; September 18, 1990.
Rolling Stone, November 15, 1990; December 13, 1990; June 27, 1991; September 5, 1991.
Source, June 1993.
Variety, August 22, 1990.

—Ondine E. Le Blanc

Jimmie Dale Gilmore

Singer, songwriter, guitarist

Jimmie Dale Gilmore was born in the tiny town of Tulia, Texas, where his father played electric guitar in a honky tonk country and western band. But the family moved shortly thereafter to Lubbock—hometown of rock and roll pioneer Buddy Holly—where Gilmore's father went to work as a bacteriologist at the dairy industry plant at Texas Tech University and where the young musician would begin to develop his identity as an artist. In liner notes to *After Awhile,* Gilmore's 1991 release, the singer-songwriter-guitarist mused, "People used to ask us why there was so much music in Lubbock, and we'd say that maybe it was the UFOs that came through in the early fifties." (In fact, there was a famous sighting there in the summer of 1962, which Gilmore claimed to have seen in a 1993 *Pulse!* article.) That bit of whimsy aside, Gilmore noted that in Lubbock he lived in two worlds: "the nightlife element was one, but then a big portion of my associates were creative and academic, studious types." That split, between the smoky-bar scene of country music and the more rarified life of the mind, continues to define Gilmore's life and music.

In a 1993 radio interview with *Fresh Air*'s Terri Gross, Gilmore revealed that country music was almost a religion for his family, and were it not for the influences of folk music and rock and roll in the early 1960s, he may well have become the sort of glitzy country star most often associated with Nashville's Grand Ole Opry. Radio brought the voices of Bob Dylan as well as Elvis Presley and Little Richard to Gilmore's impressionable ears, but it is perhaps more significant to his movement away from pure country music that Gilmore remembers seeing Presley in concert as a boy, in 1955 or '56, though Johnny Cash was the headliner at that show; both performers began as rockabilly stars, but it was Presley who would be more associated with the mature rock style, while Cash would earn a reputation as a country singer, albeit something of a maverick. Still, unlike many of his colleagues, Gilmore never rejected the music of his upbringing, instead serving as a link between rock and folk to his namesake, early country star Jimmie Rodgers, as well as the performers he cites as influences, Hank Williams and Lefty Frizzell.

Fell in Love With Acoustic Guitar

Gilmore took violin lessons as a child and played the trombone in junior high; when he was 16, he picked up the guitar and his father showed him his first chords.

For the Record. . .

Born in 1945 in Tulia, TX; father was a musician and bacteriologist; married Jo Carol Pierce (a singer), (divorced); third wife named Janet. *Education:* Attended Texas Tech University.

Performed locally in Lubbock, TX; with Butch Hancock and Joe Ely, formed band the *Flatlanders,* 1971, and recorded for the Plantation label, 1972; released *Fair and Square,* Hightone, 1988; toured Australia with Hancock, 1990; released *After Awhile,* Elektra/Nonesuch, 1991; signed with Elektra Entertainment.

Addresses: *Record company*—Elektra Entertainment, 345 North Maple Dr., Beverly Hills, CA 90210.

But the elder Gilmore played an electric instrument, for which Gilmore never really developed a feel. Then he discovered and fell in love with the big, acoustic Gibson J-200, which has become something of a trademark for him.

Gilmore, who began to play solo gigs around Lubbock, had been friends with songwriting legend Butch Hancock since 1957. After Hancock and fellow musician Joe Ely heard a record that a hitchhiker named Townes Van Zandt had recorded and passed along to Ely—Van Zandt would later establish a career as one of the finest songwriters ever to have come out of Texas—the three began to play together. Soon the late Buddy Holly's father financed a demo for them. In the meantime, Gilmore was also performing with the Austin Hub City Movers, the first act ever to play the legendary Armadillo Headquarters, located in an old National Guard armory in Austin.

In 1971 Gilmore, Hancock, and Ely formed the Flatlanders, who went on to make a recording in Nashville in 1972 for Shelby Singleton's Plantation label. Unfortunately for Gilmore fans, the album, with the exception of the single "Dallas," had a limited release on the 8-track format only; it remained a collector's item until Rounder Records reissued it in 1990 as *More a Legend Than a Band.* "If the record company had only been a little bit smarter to realize that [the Byrds' countrified] *Sweetheart of the Rodeo* had just happened," Gilmore reasoned in *Request,* "they could have taken the Flatlanders and done something with it. But everything on that album sounded so different from anything being played on country radio." Part of that difference may have resulted from the liberal use of a musical saw throughout the record.

A Product of Austin *and* Nashville

Nonetheless, Gilmore was not bitter about his Nashville experience, maintaining in *Country Music:* "A lot of my friends said I was crazy to go to Nashville at all, you know that big rivalry between Nashville and Texas, but nobody else was interested in even recording us. I don't think there's ever been that much enmity between Nashville and Austin, that's something that just looks good in print. I could just never perceive Nashville as this big ogre, this big enemy, cuz I was always aware that a big portion of my favorite music had come from there."

The Flatlanders soon broke up, and though Ely and Hancock continued their musical careers, Gilmore turned to more spiritual and philosophical pursuits, in which he had become interested when he was a student of Western philosophy at Texas Tech. He eventually became interested in Asian philosophy; after meeting a follower of the guru Maharaji, who had come to the United States at the age of 12 and had a following of several million in India, Gilmore moved from Austin to a spiritual community in Denver, where he lived from 1974 to 1980.

He left, he explained in *Country Music,* because he had reached "the point where I thought I'd gotten what I need out of it. I came to the conclusion that music was my calling, and that not only was there not any contradiction between that stuff and playing music, but also that it really went together. . . . I came to believe I could integrate my life in music with my spiritual life."

Resumed Music Career After Spiritual Sojourn

He returned to Austin and became a fixture on the music scene, playing a free weekly gig at Threadgill's. He recorded two albums with the independent label Hightone, debuting in 1988 with *Fair and Square,* which was produced by Ely. This was followed by *Jimmie Dale Gilmore* in 1989. In 1990, Gilmore toured Australia with Butch Hancock, but it wasn't long before the major labels began calling. Gilmore's major-label debut, the 1991 retrospective *After Awhile,* was a resounding success that garnered him a four-album deal with Elektra. Since then, he has appeared at the Montreux Jazz Festival, on the acclaimed television program *Austin City Limits,* and in a PBS tribute to Jimmie Rodgers. A 1993 *Tonight Show* appearance paired him with pop singer Natalie Merchant.

Though *After Awhile* demonstrated beyond any doubt Gilmore's gifts as a songwriter, he chose to record Hancock's "Just a Wave" for his critically acclaimed

1993 breakthrough outing *Spinning Around the Sun.* With its refrain "You're just a wave/ You're not the water," the song fit well with the spiritual tone of the album. Gilmore also included songs by Elvis Presley and Hank Williams.

Perhaps the most distinctive element of Gilmore's talent is his extraordinary voice. Instantly recognizable, it has been variously described in *Country Music* as "oddly resonant" and "like a hinge that needs a shot of WD-40"; its closest antecedent in country music is probably the voice of Lefty Frizzell. But Gilmore has always been recognized for his versatile guitar prowess as well, his work often reflecting the influence of rhythm and blues when he is not crooning a heartfelt ballad. Though from Gilmore, everything seems heartfelt. As he related to *Fresh Air's* Gross, "I have a good enough ear to sing on key and I can tell if things are out of tune, but I'm not a musician. . . . It's always been more the feeling, the focus and the meaning of the words. And, of course, the melody and the sound has to be there to make that stuff happen, but that's the focus for me." Clearly, music remained a form of meditation for Gilmore.

Selected discography

(With the Flatlanders) *More a Legend than a Band* (includes "Dallas"), reissued, Rounder, 1990.

Fair and Square, High Tone, 1988.
Jimmie Dale Gilmore, High Tone, 1989.
(With Butch Hancock) *Two Roads: Live in Australia,* Caroline, 1990.
After Awhile, Elektra/Nonesuch, 1991.
Spinning Around the Sun (includes "Just a Wave"), Elektra, 1993.

Sources

Country Music, November/December, 1992.
Guitar Player, October 1993.
Metro Times (Detroit), September 29, 1993.
Pulse!, October 1993.
Request, September 1993.
Rolling Stone, October 14, 1993; March 10, 1994.
Spin, July 1992.

Additional information for this profile was obtained from liner notes to *After Awhile,* Elektra/Nonesuch, 1991; an interview conducted by Terri Gross broadcast on the radio program *Fresh Air* August 31, 1993; and an Elektra Entertainment press biography, 1993.

—*John Morrow*

Polly Jean Harvey

Singer, songwriter, guitarist

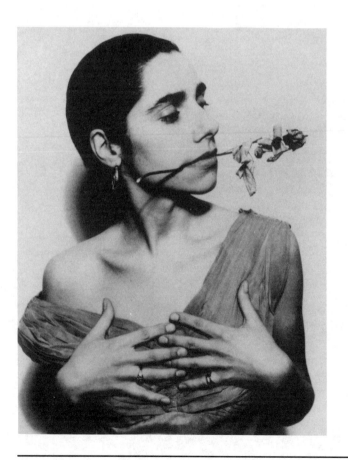

"I don't think I've ever worked on a song and thought, 'Yeah, this is great' while I'm doing it," Polly Jean Harvey, singer-guitarist-songwriter-namesake and focal point of the British rock trio PJ Harvey, told *Musician* magazine's Katherine Dieckmann. "Actually, I've never felt like that. I always think, 'This is so bad, but I've got to finish it because I'll learn so much from doing it.' So I'm never happy." This creative restlessness and ambivalence contrasts sharply with the oceanic praise garnered by PJ Harvey's first two albums, *Dry* and *Rid of Me;* critics almost universally admired the emotional power and inventiveness of Harvey's songs.

Rolling Stone named her best songwriter of 1992, and both she and her group wound up on best-of lists published by the likes of the *Village Voice, USA Today,* the *Los Angeles Times* and the *New York Times;* the British press, often rhapsodic about new talent, exceeded even its own normally high level of adulation in describing the group and, especially, its leader. Yet Harvey has made it clear that insulation from such approval is integral to her survival and continued creativity. In any event, her growth as an artist continued apace in the wake of 1993's *Rid of Me,* even as the trio's future together seemed in doubt.

Her raw songs about gender roles, attraction-repulsion and the power games underlying sex moved many music writers to turn Polly Jean Harvey into a political standard-bearer of one sort or another, something she has manifestly rejected—along with the label "feminist"—in interview after interview. Indeed, an overwhelming amount of press coverage has focused more on her image, looks, and position as a "woman in rock" than on her work. "I don't understand why people have this desire to pinpoint everything," she complained to *Spin.* "It's a desire to control, which isn't necessary. Why not let it speak to you in some way, and not try to interpret it into words all the time."

Loss of control, in fact, is never far away in Harvey's writing; both her lyrics and her music play with the boundaries between self-containment and explosion. As Gene Santoro of the *Nation* remarked, she "has a frightening grasp of the daunting and harrowing complexity beating at the heart of human emotion."

Beefheart, Blues in English Countryside

Her volatility does not come from an urban background. In fact, she was born and raised on a farm in Dorset, England. In addition to their main occupations—her mother's sculpting and her father's work in a quarry—her parents were local music promoters who

---

For the Record. . .

B orn c. 1970 in Yeovil, England.
Signed with Too Pure Records and released single "Dress" and album *Dry*, 1991; signed licensing agreement with Indigo/Island Records, 1992; released first album for Island, *Rid of Me*, 1993.

Awards: Named best songwriter and best new female singer by *Rolling Stone*, 1993, and pop music face of 1993 by *USA Today* and the *Los Angeles Times*.

Addresses: *Record company*—Island Records, 400 Lafayette St., 5th Floor, New York, NY 10003; Polygram Label Group, Worldwide Plaza, 825 8th Ave., New York, NY 10019.

---

exposed young Polly to some of the artists who would influence her most later on: bluesmen Howlin' Wolf and Muddy Waters, rootsy surrealist Captain Beefheart and folk-rock poet Bob Dylan. "My parents have always been enormously interested in music," she told *Pulse!* "It's been my life from the time I was growing up." Of Beefheart she said, "I feel like he's got some sort of divine knowledge," while in an interview circulated by Island Records she praised Dylan as "an incredible songwriter."

"When I was very young, I always had a huge desire to perform," Harvey admitted to *Los Angeles Times* music writer Richard Cromelin. "I had little string puppets and I'd build theaters and I'd get all my family lined up and I'd write plays and perform them. Lots of things like that. I was in a lot of plays at school." During her childhood she hung around with the local boys, and aligned herself with maleness; she wore pants, had short hair, and demanded to be called "Paul." Then disaster—in the form of puberty—struck. "I hated it," she recalled to *Details*. "I started growing breasts and had to wear dresses."

Harvey studied sculpture, like her mother, but while in school she joined up with a band, Automatic Dlamini, playing saxophone and guitar and singing backup. The group toured Europe, but she viewed it largely as a learning experience, and felt disinclined either to sing lead or to showcase her own songs.

After meeting a musician from another band who offered the use of his studio, Polly put together a rhythm section and recorded a number of her own songs. Among them was "Dress," which would appear on her first album. The tape aroused the interest of the British independent record label Too Pure; Harvey got 2,000 pounds—about $3600—to record an album with her band.

Dry

With bassist Stephen Vaughan and drummer Rob Ellis, she laid down the tracks for *Dry*. A bristling, deeply personal set of songs set to propulsive and intricately arranged rock, *Dry* took critics and underground fans by storm. Songs like "Sheela-Na-Gig," in which a crumbling relationship gives way to an image from Celtic iconography of a laughing woman pulling her vulva open, shocked and electrified listeners.

After the group signed an arrangement with Indigo, an independent affiliate of Island Records, the album was released in America to a storm of accolades. As *Request*'s Brian Cullman remarked, "Compared to *Dry*, most '90s releases sound vulgar, careerist, or simply beside the point." William Shaw of *Details* called *Dry* "a primal, irrational, soul-baring album, a mad standoff between desire and revulsion."

Rolling Stone admired the recording's "undeniable electricity," though it noted "not a single angry riff, raw melody or thorny lyric on it would've surprised post-punk trend spotters back in '81. The (big) difference between PJ Harvey and the half-forgotten bands of that period is focus—and competence."

The trio's sound—not "so much stripped-down rock as it is flayed-alive rock," according to *Variety*—also earned much praise. Santoro likened their tumbling rhythms to trailblazers like jazz legend John Coltrane's famous trio and power-rock trio par excellence and (Harvey idols) the Jimi Hendrix Experience; he admired their "fabulous inventiveness" and "precision-tooled interaction."

Harvey was overwhelmed—and a bit chagrined—by the exposure. After moving to London, she suffered what she would later call a nervous breakdown; she retreated to the serenity of her parents' village to recover. "I felt very ill and unworthy of everything that was happening," she said in the *Details* interview, adding, "I didn't know how to have a bath or do anything for myself at all."

Country life suited Harvey and her band. As Ellis remarked to *Spin* reporter Joy Press, "The nice thing about living 'round here is it really is way away from all the people who are interested in PJ Harvey. They're more interested in sheep and cattle around here. And rightly so."

Enter Albini

After the group's 1992 American tour, they began work in Minneapolis on their second album. Harvey asked producer Steve Albini—known for his rough, live-sounding work with bands like the Pixies and Big Black—to capture the band's sound. Despite Albini's reputed misogyny and disdain for the importance of vocals, he and Harvey became good friends. "It wasn't about someone coming in and telling me how to restructure a song or what I should be doing where," Harvey told *Musician*. "Instead, he'd make suggestions, especially when we felt stuck or at a dead end, like 'Why don't you try singing it this way?'"

The hard-edged result of a very brisk process was *Rid of Me*, released by Island in 1993. With songs like "50 Ft. Queenie" and the explosive "Man-Size," Harvey showed her characteristic intensity leavened with greater humor and sophistication. The record also features a driving cover version of Dylan's "Highway 61 Revisited." Santoro of the *Nation* called the album "as visceral and immediate as a stomach pump"; *People* labeled it "a brave, fascinating record that retains the nervous intensity of the first album"; the Detroit *Metro Times* dubbed it "the most intriguing record of the year thus far." *Rolling Stone* admired the album, but qualified its praise by remarking that "its in-your-face dynamics don't leave much room for Harvey to maneuver emotionally."

In the summer of 1993 the band opened for megastars U2 on tour of Great Britain and Europe, but by this time Deborah Frost of *Rolling Stone* reported on "an ever-widening personal gulf" between Harvey and her bandmates. "I'm so frustrated," she told the magazine, describing her intention to get a new group together. "It makes me sad. I wouldn't have got here without them. I needed them back then—badly. But now I don't need them anymore. We all just changed as people."

Harvey insisted in several interviews that she intended to give up the guitar. Her bandmates, meanwhile, claimed that they planned to pursue their own projects. Some tracks recorded for John Peel's radio program in England suggested Harvey's new direction: involving organ and horns, they include her rendition of the Willie Dixon standard "Wang Dang Doodle." She told Frost that these recordings were the "first things I've ever done that make me feel like dancing."

Creative Evolution

Though the precise future of her group had yet to be determined, Harvey seemed, by mid-1993, to be having fun with her music career for the first time. "I'm just allowing myself to enjoy music again and not be so precious or so worried about it or how people are going to take it," she told Frost.

Already established as a force to be reckoned with in rock, she was determined to survive by evolving creatively. "I want to keep experimenting and trying different things, like [rock chameleon] David Bowie," she reflected. "Maybe they won't work, but that's what keeps my interest in music. That's where a lot of musicians fall down—or just stagnate."

In autumn of 1993, with the formation of a new band still in the conceptual stages, Harvey released the musically stark, vocally electrifying *4-Track Demos*. The solo album, a compilation of 14 cuts using demo versions of songs originally recorded for *Rid of Me*, was met with an avalanche of critical acclaim. Critics, long impressed with the singer's artistry within the confines of a group were newly amazed by her solo appeal. *Rolling Stone's* Evelyn McDonnell noted that "the depth, range and conceptual completeness of *Demos* make you wonder why Harvey bothered with such conventions as a band and a producer at all."

Though *4-Track Demos* established Harvey as a self-sufficient musician, her goal remains to assemble a group that will allow her to focus more fully on her dynamic vocals. "The new band will be a five-piece," she told Robert Hilburn of the *Los Angeles Times*. "A couple of guitar players, including one maybe who can double up on playing organ, plus drums. Steve Vaughan will still be on bass. I don't want to play guitar so much live, so that I can concentrate on singing and performing."

Selected discography

Dry (includes "Dress" and "Sheela-Na-Gig"), Indigo/Island, 1992.

Rid of Me (includes "50 Ft. Queenie," "Man-Size," and "Highway 61 Revisited"), Island, 1993.

"Man-Size" (maxi-single; includes "Wang Dang Doodle"), Island, 1993.

4-Track Demos (includes "Reeling," "Goodnight," "Easy," "Legs," and "Ecstasy"), Island, 1993.

Sources

Billboard, August 15, 1992; September 4, 1993.

Details, June 1993.

Detroit Free Press, November 25, 1992.

Los Angeles Times, December 27, 1992; October 31, 1993.

Metro Times (Detroit), May 19, 1993.

Musician, March 1993; May 1993.

Nation, May 24, 1993.

New York Times, May 16, 1993.

People, June 14, 1993.

Pulse!, November 1992; December 1993.

Raygun, May 1993.

Request, December 1992; January 1994.

Rolling Stone, October 1, 1992; December 10, 1992; June 10, 1993; August 19, 1993; November 25, 1993.

Spin, November 1992; May 1993; August 1993; December 1993.

Variety, July 15, 1993.

Additional information for this profile was obtained from Island Records publicity materials, 1993.

—*Simon Glickman*

Richie Havens

Singer, songwriter, guitarist

"**I** really sing songs that move me," Richie Havens remarked to the *Denver Post.* "I make a distinction between me and a lot of my friends. I am not in show business and never was. I'm in the communications business. That's what it's about for me." Best known for his marathon performance at the legendary 1969 rock festival Woodstock, Havens has survived numerous shifts in musical fashion and continued to reach audiences with his rhythmic guitar strumming and husky, impassioned vocals. In addition to numerous recordings on various labels, Havens has been responsible for several ecological education projects, sung jingles on award-winning television commercials, acted in films—and still found time to sculpt. Despite the intensity of his performances, Havens once told *Down Beat,* "Music is not my whole world and I don't think it ever will be."

Havens was born in 1941 and grew up the oldest of eight siblings. In an interview with Joseph D. Younger for *Amtrak Express,* the performer-activist called himself "very fortunate to [have grown] up in Bedford-Stuyvesant [a Brooklyn neighborhood] when everybody lived in Bedford-Stuyvesant. I grew up with Italians, Irish kids with brogues, Poles, Czechoslovakians—everybody. At that time, it was a wonderful melting pot. I grew up with the world." Even so, he told *Down Beat's* Chris Albertson, "I don't think I was ever a Brooklynite," indicating that he eschewed the fighting and crime engaged in by other neighborhood kids. Instead, he became involved in music at a young age, singing with doo-wop groups—always, he noted to Younger, providing "backgrounds, since I was about 12. I never thought I'd end up singing the *words.*" At age 14 he performed with Brooklyn's McCrea Gospel Singers.

Folk Music "a Real Gas"

In his late teens Havens migrated to Greenwich Village where he worked as a portrait artist, roaming the clubs to drum up business. "I made a lot of money until I started singing," he quipped to Albertson. After a couple of years, during which he struggled unsuccessfully to get his music career in motion, Havens discovered folk music, which was then in full flower, and "that was the end," as he described it in a 1968 interview with *Sing Out!* Folk, he said, "gave me the composition of myself, all the things I'd thought about, when I was a kid. All the things I knew were true started happening in folkmusic. It was a real gas." He soon found himself on the grueling schedule of the journeyman musician. "I remember I was working with a trio once at the Bizarre, doing five sets a night," he recalled, "and we were doubling around the corner at the Why Not?. . . . There

For the Record. . .

Born Janurary 21, 1941, in Brooklyn, NY.

Worked as portrait artist; became folksinger, New York City, 1959; released debut album, *A Richie Havens Record,* Douglas Records, 1965; signed with Verve Folkways, 1966, and released *Mixed Bag,* 1967; performed at Monterey Pop Festival, 1967, Woodstock music festival, 1969, and Isle of Wight festival, 1970; signed with A&M, released *The End of the Beginning,* 1976; signed with Elektra and released *Connections,* 1980; released *Simple Things,* RBI, 1987 (reissued on own ELO label); released retrospective *Résumé,* Rhino, 1993; performed at inauguration Earth Ball and Bob Dylan 30th Anniversary Concert, both 1993. Appeared in rock opera *Tommy,* London, 1972, and in films *Greased Lightning, Catch My Soul,* and *Hearts of Fire.* Wrote and recorded commercial jingles. Helped create North Wind Undersea Institute and Natural Guard and worked with Songwriters and Artists for the Earth.

Selected awards: Clio awards for work in McDonald's and cotton industry commercials; gold records for *Alarm Clock* and *The Great Blind Degree,* both 1971, and *Richie Havens on Stage,* 1972.

Addresses: *Record company*—Rhino Records, 10635 Santa Monica Blvd., Los Angeles, CA 90025. *Other*—Songwriters and Artists for the Earth, P.O. Box 7304, Culver City, CA 90233.

we were doing three sets a night, and I was doing three sets at the Fat Black Pussycat by myself! We were doing about ten sets a night . . . for weeks at a time! It was crazy."

When he began playing guitar, Havens told *Frets* magazine, "I didn't have a clue about what I was doing," yet he ascertained that through his "mistakes" he was able "to make personal music." He found it awkward to play guitar with standard figurings because of his outsized hands. As a result, he began using an open D tuning, barring all or most of the strings with his thumb from above and strumming ferociously. "A person looking at him might say he was just flailing about," commented guitar specialist Barry Olivier in *Guitar Player,* "but the way he flailed about was so musical, and it went perfectly with what he was portraying. He's a good example of not having to be a technically perfect guitarist in order to come across."

Although he signed a recording contract with Warner Bros. in 1962, Havens couldn't manage to get a record completed, and his deal lapsed. After releasing a couple of obscure albums in the mid-1960s, he finally signed with Verve Folkways (later Forecast) in 1966; his debut on that label, *Mixed Bag,* followed in short order. It featured such noted Havens fare as the antiwar song "Handsome Johnny," which he co-wrote with actor Lou Gossett, Jr., and his distinctive version of the Bob Dylan classic "Just Like a Woman." His appearance at the 1967 Monterey Pop Festival heightened the singer's visibility. 1968 saw the arrival of his sophomore album for Verve, *Something Else Again,* which was highlighted by such diverse instrumentation as flute and sitar.

Sensation at Woodstock

Havens's performance at Woodstock was scheduled well in advance, but nothing could have prepared him for the circumstances he found there. Because of traffic problems, none of the early acts arrived on time, the concert was nearly three hours late, and Havens was the first performer to appear before the restive throng. "I thought, 'Jeez, they're gonna throw beer cans at me because the concert's late,'" he recollected in *Rolling Stone.* "So I did a little fast talking, a little rap, and then I did a nearly three-hour set, until some of the others [in his band] finally showed up." But it was as an unplanned encore that Havens's most legendary performance came about: "The last thing I did was 'Freedom,' which I made up right there on the spot because I didn't have anything left to sing," he confessed in *Amtrak Express.* "It was an amalgamation of two old hymns, and my feeling of freedom to enjoy what we had. 'Freedom' came from a totally spontaneous place."

In 1971 Havens released the only single that would put him in the Top 20, a soulful rendition of George Harrison's "Here Comes the Sun." For the most part, however, he maintained a loyal following without huge sales. In addition to recording consistently throughout the 1970s, Havens helped establish the North Wind Undersea Institute in New York, an oceanographic installation for young people. He also began acting, starring in such films as *Greased Lightning* and a modern version of Othello called *Catch My Soul,* as well as appearing onstage in the 1972 London debut of Pete Townshend's rock opera *Tommy.* In 1976 he changed record labels, signing with A&M, but the association lasted for only two albums, Havens joining the Elektra roster in 1980. His recorded output in the ensuing decade was fairly slight. He moved to the small label RBI for his 1987 release, *Simple Things;* when RBI folded, he started his own label, ELO, on which the album was reissued. In 1987 he also co-starred with Bob Dylan in the film *Hearts of Fire.*

In the mid-1980s Havens heralded a return to prominence of the style that had made his reputation. "There's a big acoustic renaissance going on," he told *Billboard's* Mike Hennessey, "and the music scene is becoming reminiscent of the late '50s and early '60s." He reminded readers that despite a lack of platinum albums, the old folkies had weathered many a storm. "The record companies say we're not commercial, but we're still working regularly. And I survived five presidents while I was with MGM [Verve's parent company]." Havens's predictions about this "renaissance" may have been a bit premature, but he was correct in declaring that folk would return to the spotlight. Although he continued to work in film and as a commercial-jingle writer and performer, Havens saw the legacy of his career gain renewed recognition as the Woodstock generation began to control the nation's cultural perspective.

Founded Ecological Organization

Havens made the media rounds in 1990 as founder of the Natural Guard, an ecological organization designed to get young people involved in environmental work in their own neighborhoods. He expressed his goal to the *Los Angeles Times:* "to bring up a generation with real information about the environment, for the first time in history." He also received his due for the jingles he had been performing, winning two Clio awards; indeed, his voice became such a winning presence on commercials that an unknown but persistent imitator of his vocal stylings was able to get fairly regular work. In 1991, he released the album *Now*. Lynn Van Matre of the *Chicago Tribune* called it "one of his most appealing efforts in recent years."

The following year, Havens performed "Just Like a Woman" at the 30-year anniversary tribute to Bob Dylan held at Madison Square Garden; a recording of the concert would appear to enthusiastic reviews in 1993. He also played that year at the Earth Ball, an environmentalist inaugural event in honor of President Bill Clinton. Additionally, 1993 was the year in which Havens unveiled a new live album, as well as the Rhino Records career retrospective *Résumé*, which *Entertainment Weekly* called "a concise portrait of a dignified and distinguished artist." Havens's appearance at the 1993 Troubadours of Folk festival inspired *Hollywood Reporter* critic Darryl Morden, who was unimpressed by some of the featured performers, to label the artist's set "an urgently fierce performance" of which "the crowd demanded an encore and got one."

As the 1990s progressed, Havens—entering his fourth decade as a performer, his vigor undiminished—continued in his various activities, expanding the Natural Guard, touring, recording, painting, sculpting, and lecturing. "Some people see me as an idealist," he remarked in the *Chicago Tribune*, "but I know I'm a realist. Positive things are going on all the time. They just don't get the press they deserve." In a later interview with the *Tribune* he noted, "Folk music has never gone away. It's just that as each generation comes of age, they 'discover' the music that is a little deeper from what they have been listening to."

Selected discography

A Richie Havens Record, Douglas Records, 1965.
Electric Havens, Douglas, 1966.
Stonehenge, Stormy Forest, 1970.
The End of the Beginning, A&M, 1976.
Mirage, A&M, 1977.
Connections, Elektra, 1980.
Common Ground, Connection, 1987.
Richie Havens Sings the Beatles and Bob Dylan, 1987.
Simple Things, RBI, 1987.
Now, Solar/Epic, 1991.
Résumé: The Best of Richie Havens, Rhino, 1993.

On Verve

Mixed Bag (includes "Just Like a Woman," "Handsome Johnny," and "Eleanor Rigby"), 1967.
Something Else Again, 1968.
Richard P. Havens, 1969, reissued, 1983.
Alarm Clock (includes "Here Comes the Sun"), 1971.
The Great Blind Degree, 1971.
Richie Havens on Stage, 1972.
Portfolio, 1973.
Mixed Bag II, 1975.

Contributor

"Freedom/Motherless Child," *Woodstock* (soundtrack), Cotillion, 1970.
American Children, Alacazam, 1989.
(With Rockapella) "The Light of the Sun," *Put On Your Green Shoes*, Sony Kids' Music, 1993.
"Just Like a Woman," *Bob Dylan 30th Anniversary Concert*, Columbia, 1993.

Sources

Books

Rees, Dafydd, and Luke Crampton, *Rock Movers & Shakers*, ABC/CLIO, 1991.

Periodicals

Amtrak Express, March 1993.

Billboard, March 23, 1985; December 14, 1990.

Chicago Tribune, February 7, 1985; June 27, 1991; May 16, 1993; June 17, 1993.

Denver Post, May 16, 1993.

Detroit Free Press, January 29, 1993.

Down Beat, February 8, 1968.

Entertainment Weekly, April 30, 1993.

Frets, November 1987.

Guitar Player, December 1974; October 1987.

Hollywood Reporter, June 8, 1993.

Los Angeles Times, August 30, 1990.

Melody Maker, July 9, 1977.

Rolling Stone, August 24, 1989.

Sing Out!, August 1968.

Wall Street Journal, December 26, 1990.

Additional information for this profile was provided by Rhino Records, 1993.

—*Simon Glickman*

Coleman Hawkins

Saxophonist

Listen to recordings of any jazz saxophone player made in the last 50 years and you will be hearing the influence of Coleman Hawkins, the "Father of the Tenor Saxophone." During the early part of his career Hawkins was known simply as the best tenor player in the world; but he now has the rare distinction of being considered a revolutionary, virtuoso performer at a level attained by only a small collection of great jazz musicians. His legacy is a combination of dazzling live performances, a myriad of recordings that remain a vital component of our musical treasury, and innovations and tasteful creativity that continue to inspire musicians and listeners.

As an artist, Hawk's life contained many contradictions. In his younger days he redefined the role of the saxophone with bold and insightful solos, but in later years he hated to listen to his recordings from that period. He helped launch bebop but never fully embraced it and though he was the consummate jazz musician, he did not follow in the degenerative footsteps that led to early death or poverty for so many of his contemporaries. When Hawkins died in 1969, he was remembered at his memorial service by virtually every important jazz musician of the time, as well as a throng of admirers who lined up on the streets outside to pay homage to the great American musician, the man known affectionately as "Bean."

Hawkins was born in 1904 in the small town of St. Joseph, Missouri. His parents both loved music, especially his mother, who was a pianist and organist. When he was five years old, Hawkins began piano lessons and took up the cello, learning classical music, which would provide a foundation for his exploration into more modern music. As John Chilton stated in his book *The Song of the Hawk,* "He was well versed in the classics, as in popular tunes, but his destiny lay in granting form and beauty to the art of improvising jazz." Although Hawkins practiced piano and cello conscientiously, his mother insisted that he demonstrate even more effort and would entice him to play with small rewards. When young Coleman discovered the saxophone, however, he no longer needed enticement—he had found the instrument that would bring him international fame.

Professional Debut at 12

Hawkins landed his first professional gig when he was overheard trying out a new mouthpiece by a musician, who then gave the precocious 12 year old work in local dance bands. When famed blues singer Maime Smith came to Kansas City, Missouri, she hired Coleman to augment her band, the Jazz Hounds. The band was so impressed that they asked the teenager if he would like

For the Record. . .

Born November 21, 1904, in St. Joseph, MO; died May 19, 1969, in New York, NY; mother was a pianist and organist; wives names were Gertrude and Delores; children: Rene (a son), Colette, Mrs. Melvin Wright. *Education:* Attended Washburn College.

Began playing professionally in local dance bands, 1916; performed with Maime Smith and the Jazz Hounds as "Saxophone Boy" and made recording debut, 1922-23; performed with Fletcher Henderson Band, 1923-34; performed and recorded in Europe, 1934-39; formed own band and recorded "Body and Soul," 1939; led own big band at Dave's Swingland, Chicago, 1944; returned to Europe for series of engagements, 1947; played on 52nd St., New York City, late 1940s-early 1950s; continued to record and perform, U.S. and Europe, late 1950s, 1960s.

Awards: Numerous first-place honors in *Esquire* best tenor saxophone poll.

to join them on tour. Garvin Bushell, a reed player with the Hounds, recalled to Chilton that, despite his age, Hawkins was already a complete musician. "His sight reading and musicianship was faultless even at that young age," Bushell said of the young sax player.

Though she had encouraged her talented son to become a professional musician, Hawkins's mother deemed him too young to go out on the road. But when the Jazz Hounds returned two years later, they were still interested in recruiting Hawkins; so, in 1922—with the stipulation that Maime Smith become his legal guardian—Mrs. Hawkins relented, and Hawkins, billed by the Jazz Hounds as "Saxophone Boy," set out on his first long-term touring engagement.

In May of that year he made his recording debut with Smith on "Mean Daddy Blues," on which he was given a prominent role. Hawk learned a great deal on the tour and, playing everyday, developed a self-confidence that eventually enabled him to leave the band and set out for New York to play the Harlem cabaret circuit. These were good days for an accomplished musician like Hawkins, and there was no shortage of gigs or challenging after-hours jam sessions.

Eventually Hawkins was discovered by bandleader Fletcher Henderson, who recruited the young man for his big band, one of the most successful outfits of the 1920s. It wasn't long before Hawkins established himself as an exceptional talent, even among the exceptionally talented musicians already in the band. He was

only 20 years old, but he was making good money and was carving out a reputation in and around New York as the king of the sax.

In addition to his playing, Hawkins stood out among his peers—who had nicknamed him "Bean" for the shape of his head—in terms of speech and manner. Always the sophisticate, he now made it a point to be stylishly dressed as well. This did not go unnoticed by the women in his circle, who generally found Hawkins a charming and irresistible companion. And if he were unable to charm some musical colleagues with his quiet personality, his horn playing usually did the job. Evidence of this came when Hawkins had a run-in with a club owner, who demanded that Henderson fire Hawk on the spot. But the band stood by their tenorman and threatened to walk if Hawk were ejected.

In 1924 the Henderson Band was joined by a young trumpet player named Louis Armstrong, who, though he never really got along with Hawkins, provided a musical challenge to the saxophonist, as well as an influence in phrasing and rhythm that Hawk would eventually—though he would be reluctant to acknowledge it—incorporate and expand on. "Armstrong's arrival brought new breadth to Hawkins' musical expressiveness," Chilton remarked, "and, more importantly, streamlined his phrasing."

This dynamic would be repeated; Hawkins later expressed disaffection for his chief rival on the tenor, Lester Young. Although with Armstrong it seemed to be a personal dislike—Hawkins never disparaged the trumpeter's playing—with Young he expressed on more than one occasion an inability to understand Young's popularity.

Thrived in After-Hours Jams

After engagements with the Henderson band, Hawk would regularly head uptown to the Harlem cabarets, where he would sit in on jam sessions and challenge other musicians, preferably other horn players. During these "cutting sessions, Hawk would routinely leave his competitors gasping for air as he carved them up in front of the delighted audience," reported Chilton. "When a young cat came to New York," Chilton quoted Hawkins as having explained in the magazine *Cadence,* "I had to take care of him quick."

Regardless of his undisputed position and popularity at the time, though, Hawkins hated looking back on this early period of his career. In the November, 1946, issue of *Metronome,* he told jazz writer Leonard Feather, "I thought I was playing alright at the time, too, but it sounds awful to me now. I hate to listen to it. I'm ashamed of it." In fact, Hawkins lamented in an interview with English journalist Mark Gardner, printed in liner notes to the Spotlight album *Disorder at the Border: The Coleman Hawkins Quintet,* that despite electrifying live shows, the Fletcher Henderson Band never recorded well. "I never understood why that band could never record," Hawk told Gardner. "Yet in person it was the most stompin', pushinest band I ever heard."

In 1934, after 11 years with Henderson, Hawkins left and went on a five-year sojourn to Europe, an experience so rewarding that he enthusiastically looked forward to returning in later years. He was originally

---

"When a young cat came to New York, I had to take care of him quick."

---

scheduled to play only in England, but his dates there were so successful that he was quickly signed for a year-long European tour. In a 1962 issue of *Down Beat,* Hawkins recalled his first international exposure: "It was my first experience of an audience in Europe. And it was a huge stage. Just to walk out there was something. And then I was very well received."

After his work in England, Hawkins traveled to Scandinavia and the Continent, where he received consistent praise and adulation from audiences and reviewers alike. During his stay he developed lasting friendships, as well as an expanding admiration for the art, theater, and larger culture of Europe. He may have remained abroad longer, but the gathering of political storm clouds prompted his departure—and triumphant return to the States.

News of Hawkins's conquest of Europe quickly reached the U.S. and when he resumed his place on the New York jazz scene, it was not as a sideman, but as a leader; he formed a nine-piece band and took up residency at Kelly's Stable, from which his outfit received a recording deal.

On October 11, 1939, Hawk took his band into the studio and came away with one of the most famous records in the history of jazz. According to many jazz musicians of the time, the day after "Body and Soul" was released, "everyone" was talking about it. Hawk's

solo on the tune was a lilting, dynamic, and incomparable work of art never before even suggested, and it would change the way solos were conceived and executed from that day on. As Chilton stated, "[With "Body and Soul"] Coleman Hawkins achieved the apotheosis of his entire career, creating a solo that remains the most perfectly achieved and executed example of jazz tenor-sax playing ever recorded." In 1957 pianist Teddy Wilson told *Down Beat* that it was "the best solo record I ever heard in jazz." Hawk's "Body and Soul" was also a huge popular success. "It's funny how it became such a classic," Hawk told *Down Beat* in 1955. "It's the first and only record I ever heard of, that all the squares dig as well as the jazz people . . . I wasn't making a melody for the squares. I played it like I play everything else, and yet they went for it." Indeed, Hawkins played simply and from the heart, and the recording blazed a trail of new opportunities in jazz for creative expression. It would become not only his trademark, but a trademark for all of jazz as well.

By this time the big band era was at its height, and Hawkins, buoyed by the success of "Body and Soul," began an engagement at New York City's Savoy. But Hawk was never an aggressive or well-organized businessman; as a result, his band never reached the wild popularity of Duke Ellington and Count Basie's. After the Savoy engagement ended, Hawk found gigs becoming more scarce. In 1944 he went to Chicago to headline a big band at Dave's Swingland. While in Chicago he made some recordings for the Apollo label that have since been hailed, according to Chilton, "as the first recordings of Bebop." In *Down Beat* in 1962, Hawkins explained his relationship to bebop and two of its pioneers—saxophonist Charlie Parker and trumpeter Dizzy Gillespie: "Charlie Parker and Dizzy were getting started, but they needed help. What they were doing was 'far out' to a lot of people, but it was just music to me."

Resisted Pigeonholing

Despite repeated efforts by critics and fans to associate musicians with a style or "school," Hawkins never felt comfortable being pigeonholed into any single category, including bebop. As much as jazz was his medium, he remained passionately devoted to classical music, playing it at home—mainly on the piano—and maintaining a formidable collection of classical music and opera. He particularly enjoyed the work of Johann Sebastian Bach and would often cite it as an example of true musical genius. He rarely bought jazz records, preferring instead to revel in the vitality of live performances.

By 1947 the once-thriving 52nd Street scene in New York was beginning its decline and Hawk, finding gigs less available, packed up and left for Paris, where he was received warmly by those who had remembered him from his prewar visits. For the next several years Hawk divided his time between Europe and the States, often playing with Jazz at the Philharmonic, which featured many jazz legends, among whom Hawk was always a headliner. As was his way, during this period Hawkins often found time to sit in on recording sessions; his recorded output is indeed extensive.

Whether playing live or in the studio, Hawkins was popular not only with the public, but with that more demanding group, his fellow musicians, who always respected the master. Many musicians, regardless of their instrument, had listened to "Body and Soul" over and over until they had memorized Bean's solo, and they continued to listen to his flowing and lyrical tenor for new gems that they could employ. "Bean," said saxophonist Sonny Stitt in *Down Beat*, "set the stage for all of us." In a conversation with *Song of the Hawk* author Chilton, pianist Roland Hanna expressed his admiration for Hawk's musicianship, revealing, "I always felt he had perfect pitch because he could play anything he heard instantly. He was the complete musician; he could improvise at any tempo, in any key, and he could read anything."

Hawk explained his own theories on solos and improvisation in *Down Beat:* "I think a solo should tell a story, but to most people that's as much a matter of shape as what the story is about. Romanticism and sorrow and greed—they can all be put into music." To be sure, throughout his life, Coleman Hawkins told many stories with his flowing and lyrical style. To this day, jazz musicians around the world have been telling and retelling those stories.

Selected discography

Body and Soul, RCA, 1939.
In Concert With Roy Eldridge and Billie Holiday, Phoenix Jazz, 1944, reissued, 1975.
Disorder at the Border: The Coleman Hawkins Quintet, Spotlight, 1952.
Soul, Prestige, 1958.
The Hawk in Holland, GNP Crescendo, 1968.
The Complete Coleman Hawkins: Vol. I, reissued, RCA, 1976.
At Ease With Coleman Hawkins (recorded in 1960), Moodsville, reissued, Fantasy/OJC, 1985.
The Genius of Coleman Hawkins (recorded in 1957), Verve, 1986.
Body and Soul (recorded 1939-56), Bluebird, 1986.
The Complete Coleman Hawkins on Keynote (recorded in 1944), Mercury, 1987.

Coleman Hawkins and Confreres, Verve, 1988.
Hawk Eyes (recorded in 1959), Prestige, reissued, Fantasy/OJC, 1988.
In a Mellow Tone (recorded 1958-62), reissued, Fantasy/OJC, 1988.
Coleman Hawkins: Hollywood Stampede (recorded 1945-57), Capitol, 1989.
Jazz Tones (recorded in 1954), EPM, 1989.
Thanks for the Memory (recorded 1937-38 and 1944), EPM, 1989.
Night Hawk (recorded in 1960), Swingville, reissued, Fantasy/OJC, 1990.
Desafinado (recorded in 1962), MCA/Impulse, 1990.
Wrapped Tight (recorded in 1965), reissued, GRP/Impulse, 1991.
1926/40, EPM, 1991.
1929-1934, Classics, 1991.
Dali (recorded in 1956, 1962), Stash, 1991.
April in Paris Featuring Body and Soul, Bluebird, 1992.
Bean and the Boys, Fresh Sound, 1992.
(With Roy Eldridge and Johnny Hodges) *Hawkins!Eldridge! Hodges!Alive! At the Village Gate*, Verve, 1992.
Jam Session in Swingville, Prestige, 1992.
The Hawk Relaxes (recorded in 1961), Moodsville, reissued, Fantasy/OJC, 1992.
Rainbow Mist (recorded in 1944), Delmark, 1992.
Loverman (recorded 1958-64), Esoldun, 1993.
Body and Soul Revisited, Decca Jazz, 1993.
Bean and the Boys, Fantasy, 1993.
The Hawk in Paris, reissued, Bluebird/RCA, 1993.
Loverman Live 1958/'64, ROIR, 1994.

Sources

Books

Chilton, John, *The Song of the Hawk: The Life and Recordings of Coleman Hawkins*, University of Michigan Press, 1990.

Periodicals

Down Beat, January 12, 1955; October 31, 1957; February 1, 1962; November 21, 1974.
Metronome, November 1946.
New York Times, May 20, 1960.

Additional information for this profile was obtained from an interview with Mark Gardner that appears in liner notes to *Disorder at the Border: The Coleman Hawkins Quintet*, Spotlight, 1952; and liner notes by Daniel Nevers to *The Complete Coleman Hawkins: Vol. I*, RCA, 1976.

—David Waldstein

Lena Horne

Singer, actress, activist

"**S**he is one of the incomparable performers of our time," Richard Watts, Jr., wrote of Lena Horne in the *New York Post* in 1957. This assessment continued to hold true decades later: Lena Horne, the beautiful, elegant, and talented singer and actress has indeed become a legend. Horne encountered adversity throughout her career—first from her family, who disapproved of her choice of occupation, then from white audiences and managers, who were uncomfortable with her assertiveness, and even from other African-American performers, who felt threatened by her refusal to accept stereotypical roles. But her strong senses of identity, justice, and dignity forced her to struggle against these obstacles—and allowed her to triumph.

Lena Mary Calhoun Horne was born on June 30, 1917, in the Bedford-Stuyvesant neighborhood of Brooklyn, New York, to Edwin "Teddy" Horne and his wife, Edna. Horne's parents separated by the time she was three years old, and she lived for several years with her paternal grandparents, Cora Calhoun and Edwin Horne. Her early life was nomadic. Horne's mother, who was a fairly unsuccessful stage performer, took the young Lena on the road with her, and they lived in various parts of the South before returning to Horne's grandparents' home in Brooklyn in 1931. After her grandparents died, Horne was sent to live with her mother's friend Laura Rollock. Shortly thereafter, her mother married Miguel "Mike" Rodriguez, and Horne moved in with them.

Horne had early ambitions to be a performer—against the wishes of her family, who believed she should aspire to greater heights. The Hornes were an established middle-class family, with several members holding college degrees and distinguished positions in organizations such as the National Association for the Advancement of Colored People (NAACP) and the Urban League. Nevertheless, Horne persisted in her dreams of stardom and in 1933, she began her first professional engagement, at the Cotton Club, the famed Harlem nightclub. She sang in the chorus and though only 16 years old held her own among the older and more experienced cast members. She soon left high school to devote herself to her stage career.

Performed in New York and Hollywood

In 1934 Horne landed a small role in an all-black Broadway show called *Dance With Your Gods*. The next year, she left the Cotton Club and began performing as a featured singer with Noble Sissle's Society

For the Record. . .

Born Lena Mary Calhoun Horne, June 30, 1917, in Brooklyn, NY; daughter of Edwin ("Teddy"; a banker) and Edna (an actress) Horne; married Louis Jones, 1937 (divorced, 1944); married Leonard George ("Lennie") Hayton, 1947 (died, 1971); children: (first marriage) Gail, Edwin ("Teddy"; deceased).

Began singing at Cotton Club, New York City, 1933; appeared in Broadway musical *Dance With Your Gods,* 1934; featured singer with Noble Sissle's Society Orchestra, 1935-37, and Charlie Barnet Orchestra, 1940-41; appeared in musical *Blackbirds of 1939,* 1939, and at Café Society Downtown, 1941; featured performer at Little Troc nightclub, Hollywood, 1942; appeared in films, including *The Duke Is Tops,* 1938, *Panama Hattie,* 1942, *Stormy Weather,* 1943, *Cabin in the Sky,* 1943, *Death of a Gunfighter,* 1969, *The Wiz,* 1978, and *That's Entertainment III,* 1993; signed recording contract with RCA Victor, 1956; featured in Broadway musical *Jamaica,* 1957-59; appeared on television programs, 1950s-'80s, including *The Ed Sullivan Show, The Perry Como Show,* and *The Cosby Show;* starred on Broadway in *Lena Horne: The Lady and Her Music,* 1981-82.

Selected awards: Tony Award, 1981; Drama Desk Award, 1981; Actors Equity Paul Robeson Award, 1982; Dance Theater of Harlem Emergence Award, 1982; Handel Medallion, 1982; NAACP Spingarn Medal, 1983; Kennedy Center Honor for lifetime contribution to the arts, 1984; *Essence* Award, 1993; *Ebony* Lifetime Achievement Award; two Grammy awards.

Member: NAACP; Hollywood Independent Citizens Committee of the Arts, Sciences, and Professions (HICCASP); Delta Sigma Theta (honorary member).

Addresses: *Office*—5950 Canoga Ave., #200, Woodland Hills, CA 91367.

Orchestra under the name "Helena Horne," which Sissle thought more glamorous than "Lena." In 1937 Horne quit her tour with the Sissle Orchestra to marry Louis Jones, a friend of her father, and live with him in Pittsburgh, Pennsylvania. During this short and troubled marriage, Horne went to Hollywood to appear in an all-black film called *The Duke Is Tops.* In 1939 she won a role in the musical revue *Blackbirds of 1939,* which would be performed at the Hudson Theatre in New York City; but it ran for only eight nights. By this time, she had had two children, Gail and Edwin ("Teddy").

Horne left Jones in 1940, took a job as a singer with Charlie Barnet's band, and went out on the road. She was the only black member of the Barnet ensemble, and the kind of racial discrimination she encountered from audiences, hotel managers, and others was so unsettling that she decided to quit the band. In 1941, she began performing at the Café Society Downtown, a club in New York City that catered to intellectuals and social activists, both black and white.

At the Café Society, Horne learned about black history, politics, and culture and developed a new appreciation for her heritage. She rekindled her acquaintance with singer Paul Robeson, whom she had known when she was a child. In her autobiography *In Person: Lena Horne,* she explained that through her conversations with Robeson, she realized, "We [African Americans] were going forward, and that knowledge gave me a strength and a sense of unity. Yes, we were going forward, and it was up to me to learn more about us and to join actively in our struggle." From this point on, Horne became a significant voice in the struggle for equality and justice for blacks in America.

Horne moved to California in the summer of 1941 after getting an offer to appear at an as-yet-unbuilt club on the Sunset Strip in Hollywood called the Trocadero. Although plans for the Trocadero fell through, another, smaller club, the Little Troc, opened in February of 1942, and Horne was featured there. Also in 1942, Horne signed a seven-year contract with MGM—the first black woman since 1915 to sign a term contract with a film studio. "They didn't quite know what to do with me," she told Leonard Maltin of *Entertainment Tonight* regarding the studio's resulting dilemma: she wasn't dark-skinned enough to star with many of the black actors of the day, and her roles in white films were limited since Hollywood wasn't ready to depict interracial relationships on screen. Her first film under contract was *Panama Hattie,* a 1942 version of Cole Porter's Broadway musical in which she had a small singing role and appeared in only one scene.

Draped Around a Marble Column

Several of Horne's roles in subsequent films were similar. James Haskins, in his book *Lena: A Personal and Professional Biography of Lena Horne,* noted, "The image of Lena, always elegantly gowned, singing while draped around a marble column in a lavishly produced musical sequence, would become virtually standardized. Only her ability to appear enigmatic prevented her from being completely exploited in these stock sequences; she managed to carry them off with a dignity that, coupled with her aloof and detached delivery, enhanced both her mystery and her audience appeal." The sad footnote to this is that Horne's scenes were purposely constructed so that they could be easily excised when the films were shown to white audiences in the South.

Horne appeared in the all-black musicals *Cabin in the Sky* and *Stormy Weather,* both released in 1943, but she refused to take any role that she felt would be demeaning to her as a woman of color. This led to an uproar among the black Hollywood "extras" who represented what Horne's daughter, in her book *The Hornes: An American Family,* called "a kind of stock company of stereotypes." These actors felt threatened by Horne and accused her of being a tool of the NAACP. In her defense, Horne wrote in her 1965 autobiography *Lena:* "I was only trying to see if I could avoid in my career some of the traps they had been forced into."

During World War II, Horne went on USO tours along the West Coast and throughout the South. She appeared on the Armed Forces Radio Service programs *Jubilee, G.I. Journal,* and *Command Performances* and helped First Lady Eleanor Roosevelt press for antilynching legislation. After the war Horne worked on behalf of Japanese Americans who faced discrimination because Japan had been an enemy of the United States.

In the fall of 1947, Horne went to Europe with Lennie Hayton, a white musician she had met in Hollywood. They were married in December—in Paris, because interracial marriages were against the law in California. Back in Hollywood, she appeared in more film musicals, among them *Till the Clouds Roll By* in 1946, *Words and Music* in 1948, and *The Duchess of Idaho* in 1950.

Blacklisted

In the early 1950s, Horne, along with many of her colleagues, was a victim of the anti-Communist "witch hunts" that successfully blacklisted performers who were thought to have ties to Communist organizations or activities. The blacklisting hurt Horne's career and kept her from appearing on radio and television. By the mid-1950s, though, Horne was cleared of these charges. In 1956, in fact, she signed a recording contract with RCA Victor. Some of her albums included *Stormy Weather, Lena Horne at the Coconut Grove,* and *Lena Horne at the Waldorf-Astoria.* The latter became the top-selling recording by a female artist in RCA's history. In 1957 Horne was featured in *Jamaica,* a Broadway musical with an all-black cast. The show had a successful run and did not close until the spring of 1959.

Horne was actively involved in the civil rights movement of the 1960s, participating in the March on Wash-ington in 1963, performing at rallies in the South and elsewhere, and working on behalf of the National Council for Negro Women. This period also saw her appear on various television programs, including several performances on the popular Ed Sullivan and Perry Como variety shows and in her own special, *Lena in Concert,* which aired in 1969. Also in 1969 she appeared in a nonsinging role in the western *Death of a Gunfighter.*

The 1970s began tragically for Horne: her son, Teddy, died of kidney disease in 1970, her father died the same year, and Lennie Hayton died of a heart attack in 1971. Still, these years also offered a variety of opportunities for Horne to perform. She appeared on Broadway with Tony Bennett in 1974 in a show called *Tony and Lena* and was featured in several television commercials. In 1978, she played the role of Glinda the Good Witch in the film version of *The Wiz,* the all-black musical based on *The Wizard of Oz.*

Horne launched a "farewell tour" in the summer of 1980, but her greatest success of the decade was still ahead of her—her one-woman show, *Lena Horne: The Lady and Her Music,* which opened in May of 1981 at Broadway's Nederlander Theatre. The production ran for two years and was a tremendous success—so much so that Horne was given a special Tony Award for her performance. She also received a Drama Desk Award and a special citation from the New York Drama Critics' Circle. The soundtrack to the show, produced by Quincy Jones, won two Grammy awards. In *Lena: A Personal and Professional Biography,* Haskins reported that the show was "not only the longest-running one-woman show in the history of Broadway but the standard against which every future one-person show would be measured." Horne herself, in an article she wrote for *Ebony* magazine in 1990, described the show as "the most rewarding event in my entire career."

In the 1990s, Horne cut back on performing, but she continued to be a favorite of audiences throughout the world. Still, some observers consider her most important role that of catalyst in the elevation of the status of African Americans in the performing arts. Despite the strides she's made, Horne has often lamented the sluggishness of progress in Hollywood; if given the chance to do it all again, she told music writer Leonard Feather in *Modern Maturity,* "I'd be a schoolteacher."

Selected discography

(With the Lennie Layton Orchestra) *Lena Goes Latin* (recorded in 1963), DRG, 1987.
(With Sammy Davis, Jr., and Joe Williams) *The Men in My Life,* Three Cherries, 1989.
Stormy Weather: The Legendary Lena, 1941-1958, Bluebird, 1990.

Lena Horne, Royal Collection, 1992.
At Long Last Lena, RCA, 1992.
Greatest Hits, CSI, 1992.
Best of Lena Horne, Curb, 1993.
Stormy Weather, RCA Victor.
Lena Horne at the Coconut Grove, RCA Victor.
Lena Horne at the Waldorf-Astoria, RCA Victor.

Sources

Books

Buckley, Gail Lumet, *The Hornes: An American Family,* Knopf, 1986.
Haskins, James, and Kathleen Benson, *Lena: A Personal and Professional Biography of Lena Horne,* Stein & Day, 1984.
Horne, Lena, as told to Helen Arstein and Carlton Moss, *In Person: Lena Horne,* Greenberg, 1950.
Horne, Lena, and Richard Schickel, *Lena,* Doubleday, 1965.
Many Shades of Black, edited by Stanton L. Wormley and Lewis H. Fenderson, William & Co., 1969.

Periodicals

Ebony, May 1980; November 1990.
Entertainment Weekly, July 9, 1993.
Modern Maturity, February/March 1993.
New York Post, November 1, 1957.
New York Times, May 4, 1981.

Additional information for this profile was obtained from an interview with Leonard Maltin broadcast on *Entertainment Tonight,* ABC-TV, March 22, 1993.

—*Joyce Harrison*

Son House

Singer, guitarist

Two young blues enthusiasts found him in 1964 in a third-floor walk-up in Rochester, New York—a thousand miles from the Mississippi Delta and with no guitar. The duo returned more prepared the next day, then waited patiently as alcohol helped the old man's hands remember how to work the bottleneck along the strings. Son House, the legendary Delta blues singer and the man who had given lessons to blues legends Robert Johnson and Muddy Waters, was back in the blues.

House was born on the Mississippi River Delta, on a plantation between the towns of Lyon and Clarksdale. The Delta, formed by the Big Muddy's deposits of silt, is a flat belt of fertile land that has been used for farming since the eighteenth century. Before the Civil War and the abolition of slavery in 1865, Delta plantation owners had been major purchasers of human labor. After they received their freedom, the displaced former slaves maintained their musical and storytelling traditions, spirituality, endurance, and humor—all of which found a voice through the blues.

Still, the music that emerged from these common beginnings was not embraced by all blacks; the Delta blues belonged to the poorest and most illiterate. It grew to sophistication on street corners and in the rowdy and often dangerous drinking places called juke joints. The performers were usually drifters who could find work anywhere during harvest time. But the most popular became local stars—and often infamous. In *Deep Blues,* blues scholar Robert Palmer explained: "Blues was so disreputable that even its staunchest devotees frequently found it prudent to disown it. If you asked a black preacher, schoolteacher, small landowner, or faithful churchgoer what kind of people played and listened to the blues, they would tell you, 'cornfield niggers.'" The church and the blues were not supposed to mix. This was an ethical dilemma that haunted Son House all of his life.

By the age of 15 House was giving sermons. By 20, he was the pastor of a Baptist church near Lyon. And though he was passionate about religion, House never committed to a career in the church. He rambled from job to job, picking cotton, gathering tree moss, always looking for the least strain. Though his father, Eddie House, Sr., and his uncles had their own horn band, Son House never viewed music as a professional option. In *Guitar Player,* he revealed, "Now, just to tell the truth by it . . . I didn't believe in no blues. I was too

For the Record. . .

Born Eddie (some sources say Eugene) James House, Jr., March 21, c. 1902, near Clarksdale, MS; died on October 19, 1988, in Detroit, MI; son of Eddie House, Sr. (a horn player); married Carrie Martin, c. 1926; married Evie McGown, 1934; children: Beatrice, Sally.

Began as preacher in Mississippi and Louisiana, c. 1917; gathered and bailed tree moss for mattress stuffing, 1916-early 1920s; pastor of Baptist church near Lyon, MS, 1922; worked at Commonwealth Steel Plant, East St. Louis, MO, 1922-23; worked on horse farm in Louisiana, c. 1925; began playing guitar and working as hired musician, Mississippi, 1926; began performing with Charley Patton and Willie Brown, 1929; recorded "My Black Mama" and "Preachin' the Blues," Paramount, 1930; made recordings for Library of Congress, 1941-42; worked for New York Central Railroad as rivet heater in boxcar assembly, Rochester, NY, 1943; porter on Empire State Express, c. 1945-late 1950s; retired as musician, 1960; coaxed out of retirement and signed with Columbia Records, 1964; recorded and performed, 1964-76.

churchy. . . . Just putting your hands on an old guitar, why, looked like that was sin."

By 1926, after a romance had taken him to Louisiana, House had returned to Lyon and was considering going back to the church. Around that time, while doing some rambling and drinking, House had seen a local bluesman named Willie Wilson play bottleneck guitar. He was dazzled. "This boy," House remembered in *Guitar Player,* "had a thing on his finger like a small medicine bottle, and he was zinging it, you know." He recalled, "'Sounds good!' I said. 'Jesus, I like that! I believe I want to play one of them things.'" With a dollar and a half, House went out and bought himself a battered guitar. Wilson taught him how to tune by ear, another player, James McCoy, gave him lessons, and the rest he picked up on his own.

But House's distinctive Delta blues style was not simply a product of McCoy's influence, or the recordings of blues great Charley Patton, or even the sliding guitar style of another model, Rubin Lacy; the church, in fact, had a hand in it, too. In *Deep Blues,* Palmer noted, "[House's] instrument became a congregation, responding to his gravelly exhortation with clipped, percussive bass rhythms and the ecstatic whine of the slider in the treble. . . . It was stark, gripping, kinetic music that demanded to be danced to and would have left few listeners unmoved." Indeed, Son House was preaching the blues.

In those days the Delta was Mississippi's wild west; hard times, heavy drinking, and a gun in the possession of almost every man was a lethal combination. In 1928, House was sent to a state penal farm for shooting and killing a man at a drunken house party near Clarksdale. House had pleaded self-defense. After serving two years, he was released and ordered not to return to Clarksdale. He headed north. In Lula, he met his hero, Charley Patton, and the two became as close as brothers. House, Patton, and a local bluesman named Willie Brown teamed up for gigs and enjoyed some small-time success. In 1930, representatives of Paramount Records ventured to Lula to invite Patton to Wisconsin for a recording session. Patton brought along Son House, Willie Brown, and blues singer and piano player Louise Johnson. The resultant recordings have become classics, and Son House's "My Black Mama" and "Preachin' the Blues" are considered masterpieces of Delta blues singing.

Patton died in 1933. House married, earned a meager living driving a tractor, and continued playing with Brown. Along the way, House taught his classic "My Black Mama" riff to future blues titans Robert Johnson and Muddy Waters. In 1942, House recorded "Walking Blues," "Special Rider Blues," "The Pony Blues," and "The Jinx Blues" for the Library of Congress. Then, in 1943, he left the Delta for good. Unlike Muddy Waters, who made his way to Chicago in search of fame and fortune, House's chief motivation in leaving the Delta was to escape the drudgery of life in Mississippi. Alone again, he took the train to Rochester, New York, and landed himself a job with the train line. When Willie Brown died in 1952, House told *Guitar Player,* "I said, 'Well, sir, all my boys are gone.' That was when I stopped playing. I don't even know what I did with the guitar." House abandoned the blues and joined the Amen Baptist Church.

After he was located by a pair of blues devotees and coaxed out of retirement in 1964, House signed with Columbia Records and resurrected his signature tunes. He performed at blues festivals and colleges, and concerts took him all the way to Europe. Through all the acclaim, he remained a soft-spoken, modest man who depended on the bottle to calm his nerves. By 1976, deteriorating health forced his retirement. Son House moved to Detroit to be with family and died in his sleep on October, 19, 1988. With his passing went the last of the great original Mississippi Delta blues singers.

Selected discography

Singles; on Paramount, 1930

"My Black Mama."
"Preachin' the Blues."
"Dry Spell Blues Part II."
"Mississippi County Farm Blues."
"Walkin' Blues."

Compilations

Delta Blues: The Original Library of Congress Sessions From Field Recordings, Library of Congress, 1941-42, reissued, Biograph, 1991.
Father of the Delta Blues: The Complete 1965 Recordings, Columbia/Legacy, 1992.

Son House in Concert (recorded in 1965), Kicking Mule.
Library of Congress Sessions, Folklyric.

Sources

Books

Palmer, Robert, Deep Blues, Penguin, 1982.

Periodicals

Guitar Player, August 1992.
Newsweek, July 13, 1964; June 28, 1965.
New York Times, December 12, 1969.
Rolling Stone, December 27, 1969.

—Iva Sipal

James Ingram

Singer, songwriter, keyboardist

The music of James Ingram may be familiar to mainstream audiences, but his name most likely does not prompt recognition among listeners. After more than 20 years in the pop music industry, Ingram's voice has been heard on radio and in films, his songs and performances have been nominated for many Grammy awards, and his musicianship has backed up several Top Twenty artists. Yet the popularity of his collaborative work has overshadowed that of his solo output; he is, consequently, what one might call a musician's musician: well known and respected among his colleagues, but less visible to the public.

Ingram was born on February 16, sometime in the early 1950s—he is notoriously reluctant to reveal his age. His musical biography, however, begins in the early 1970s, when he immersed himself in that decade's enthusiasm for soul and funk. Skilled in an array of instruments, including piano, synthesizer, drums, bass, and guitar, Ingram decided to relocate to Los Angeles when his band, Revelation Funk, returned to their hometown of Akron, Ohio, after a brief stint on the West Coast. Ingram described those first years in Los Angeles to Billboard's David Nathan, explaining simply, "I had a lot of doors slammed in my face." 1973 offered him his first real opportunity, as keyboardist for Leon Hayward, the RCA artist and producer who would become known for his hit single "Don't Push It Don't Force It," which featured Ingram's piano work.

The association with Hayward afforded Ingram a brief relationship with an RCA executive who wanted to sign him as a solo artist. Ingram cut three songs with RCA before the executive who had championed him left the label. RCA summarily dropped Ingram—paying him for the work, but never releasing any of the cuts. After this disappointment, Ingram struggled to get by. Several years passed before he made the first significant contact of his career—that of legendary pianist-singer Ray Charles. Through his work with a musician named Joel Webster, Ingram developed a connection to Charles's label, Tangerine Records, and eventually met Charles himself. When Charles scored a hit in 1977 with the single "I Can See Clearly Now," Ingram could be heard backing him up on organ.

Hooked Up With Quincy Jones

Perhaps the most momentous step in Ingram's career occurred, however, when he entered the orbit of acclaimed producer Quincy Jones. Ingram met Jones in Charles's studio but first impressed him some time later, when the producer had an opportunity to hear

For the Record. . .

Born February 16th, early 1950s, in Akron, OH; married wife Debbie, c. 1974; six children.

As a child, taught himself to play piano, synthesizer, drums, bass, and guitar; member of band Revelation Funk, Akron, until 1973; played keyboards for Leon Hayward, c. 1973; recorded three singles for RCA; began working with pianist-singer Ray Charles, late 1970s; began working with producer Quincy Jones; appeared on Jones's album *The Dude*, 1981; as solo artist, released *It's Your Night*, 1983; recorded with numerous artists; released *Never Felt So Good*, 1986; switched from Qwest label to Warner Bros., 1987, and released *It's Real*, 1989, and *Always You*, 1993.

Awards: Grammy awards for best R&B male vocal, 1981, for "One Hundred Ways," and for best R&B performance by a duo or group, 1984, for "Yah Mo Be There"; gold album for *It's Your Night*, 1983.

Addresses: *Record company*—Warner Bros. Records, 3300 Warner Blvd., Burbank, CA 91505-4694.

Ingram's voice on some demo tapes. The tapes were actually intended for a music publishing company, ATV Music, and were supposed to sell Jones the songs, not the singer. Ingram described the scenario to Nathan: "I was singing demos for a publishing company . . . at $50 a song and doing two or three a day. I must have done that for three or four months. Quincy was listening to some of their songs for *The Dude* album and he heard 'Just Once.' He wanted to know who the singer was on the demo and he got my number . . . and called me at home."

In 1981 *The Dude* introduced listeners to Ingram's voice—and Ingram to the taste of success. After hearing the demo, Jones signed the singer to record vocals for three of the tracks on the record: "Just Once," "One Hundred Ways," and "The Dude." The first of these reached Number Seventeen on the pop charts but since the album was credited to Quincy Jones, many listeners assumed the rich, emotive voice they heard belonged to Jones. This odd, peripheral fame persisted despite Ingram's performance of "Just Once" at the 1982 Grammy Awards presentation. He was nominated for three awards that year: best new artist, best pop male vocal, and best R&B male vocal. He won in the third category for his performance on "One Hundred Ways." Several critics, and Ingram himself, have noted the singularity of this achievement; indeed, it is highly unusual for a vocalist to win a Grammy without having a single album to his or her credit.

Ingram followed the success of his work on *The Dude* with a 1983 duet with singer Patti Austin. The single, "Baby, Come to Me," registered some chart movement but had no explosive impact—until it appeared as a theme on the television soap opera *General Hospital*, after which the song rose to the top of the charts. Also in 1983, moviegoers became more familiar with Ingram's voice when he recorded "How Do You Keep the Music Playing" for the movie *Best Friends;* audiences once again had the opportunity to put a face with the voice when Ingram performed the song at the Academy Awards.

As useful as this kind of exposure may have been, in 1983 Ingram's real energies were devoted to recording his first solo album, which Quincy Jones produced. *It's Your Night* reached record stores in November and quickly earned a gold record. Reviewing the album for *Stereo Review*, music critic Phyl Garland noted that Jones had "given Ingram a very classy treatment. The rich arrangements feature far more sophisticated and imaginative instrumentals than are usual for an album of love songs and dance music. But Ingram's resonant voice is fluid enough to handle everything." Decent sales and some critical acclaim, however, were not enough to take *It's Your Night* to the top of the U.S. charts, though it rose to the Number 25 spot on the British charts by April of 1984. Still, just prior to this chart action, Ingram had attained greater fame—in conjunction with another artist; when pop superstar Michael Jackson released his chart-busting *Thriller* album in 1983, one of the songs that hit the Top Ten, "P.Y.T (Pretty Young Thing)," was a Quincy Jones/James Ingram collaboration.

In 1984, however, Ingram gained some ground with one of the singles from *It's Your Night:* "Yah Mo Be There," recorded with former Doobie Brothers vocalist Michael McDonald, hit the U.S. Top 20. The song fared even better in the United Kingdom and would earn Ingram a second Grammy—the 1984 award for best R&B performance by a duo or group. Unfortunately, it was another two years before Ingram released his second album, *Never Felt So Good;* and it did not earn the kind of critical attention that *It's Your Night* had.

Soon enough, though, Ingram would again achieve recognition for work he did outside of his solo career; he had a second hit in 1984, with Kenny Rogers and Kim Carnes, with the Number 15 single "What About Me?" And he offered a soulful turn to the phenomenally successful charity single "We Are the World" in 1985. Similarly, a tear-jerking 1987 duet with pop vocalist

Linda Ronstadt, "Somewhere Out There," from Steven Spielberg's animated *An American Tail,* landed Ingram at Number Two. The song went on to win song of the year honors at the Grammys that year—the event's most coveted prize. (The duet would also garner an Oscar nomination, with Ingram and Ronstadt performing it at the awards ceremony.) "Better Way," from *Beverly Hills Cop II,* further showcased Ingram's voice—just not on *his* records.

Finally, Number One on His Own

After working again with Patti Austin in 1988 on her album *The Real Me,* Ingram rededicated himself to his solo career. The previous year, he had made a break from Quincy Jones and his Qwest label, moving to Warner Bros. in order to work with producer Thom Bell. That association culminated in Ingram's first Number One—and a solo hit at that; "I Don't Have the Heart," from the 1989 album *It's Real,* rose to the top of the charts in 1990. Eager to capitalize on Ingram's momentum, Warner Bros. released a compilation album in 1991; *The Power of Great Music* featured songs Ingram had recorded largely during the 1980s. In 1993 Ingram debuted a second album of originals for Warners, the ballad-oriented *Always You,* which featured vocals that, in the words of an *Upscale* reviewer, "run the gamut from falsetto to some soulful groans, to that world famous Ingram howl." Nonetheless, Ingram had kept his hand in the lucrative soundtrack game, contributing "Where Did My Heart Go" to the hit movie *City Slickers* in 1991.

Aside from his many achievements in music, Ingram has also established a reputation for his commitment to charity work and family. In the mid-1970s, he married his wife Debbie, a friend since grade school. She has assisted him in his work since 1986. The couple have six children, the sixth born in 1993. Ingram's devotion to family life has also influenced his charitable impulses; a 1993 issue of *Billboard* noted that a cut from *Always You,* "Sing for the Children,"—particularly notable for the appearance of the Boys Choir of Harlem—will become the theme song for the Children's Defense Fund, augmenting Ingram's role as the organization's spokesperson.

Selected discography

Singles

(With Patti Austin) "Baby, Come to Me," Qwest, 1983.
"How Do You Keep the Music Playing?," 1983.
(With Kim Carnes and Kenny Rogers) "What About Me?," 1984.
(Contributor) "We Are the World," 1985.
"Better Way," 1987.
(With Linda Ronstadt) "Somewhere Out There," MCA, 1987.
"Where Did My Heart Go?," Varèse Sarabande, 1991.

Albums

(Contributor) Quincy Jones, *The Dude* (includes "Just Once," "One Hundred Ways," and "The Dude"), Qwest, 1981.
It's Your Night (includes "Yah Mo Be There"), Qwest, 1983.
Never Felt So Good, Qwest, 1986.
It's Real (includes "I Don't Have the Heart"), Warner Bros., 1989.
Jones, *Back on the Block,* Qwest, 1989.
The Power of Great Music, Warner Bros., 1991.
Always You (includes "Sing for the Children"), Warner Bros., 1993.
(With Dolly Parton) "The Day I Fall in Love," *Beethoven's 2nd* (soundtrack), Columbia, 1993.

Sources

Books

Rees, Dafydd, and Luke Crampton, *Rock Movers & Shakers,* ABC/CLIO, 1991.

Periodicals

Billboard, November 2, 1991; May 8, 1993.
Melody Maker, July 15, 1989.
Musician, October 1989.
People, August 21, 1989.
Stereo Review, May 1984.
Upscale, October 1993.
Village Voice, September 30, 1986.

Additional information for this profile was obtained from Warner Bros. Records, 1993.

—*Ondine E. Le Blanc*

Jimmy Jam and Terry Lewis

Producers, songwriters, record company executives

When *Elle* music writer Steven Daly said that Janet Jackson's 1986 album *Control* "changed the face of pop radio," he was perhaps saying less about Jackson than about the production team of Jimmy Jam and Terry Lewis. Daly explained, "Their unholy alliance with the youngest daughter of a dysfunctional show-biz family would turn the beat around, setting black music back on its proper course to chart domination." In ten years, Jam and Lewis, now based at their Flyte Tyme Productions in Minneapolis, have written and/or produced over 40 singles and albums that have sold in excess of 500,000 to one million units, as well as an expanse of top hits on the R&B, dance, and pop music charts. *Rolling Stone's* Michael Goldberg aptly described them as "*auteur* producers whose body of work has a musical and thematic unity that transcends the work of the individual artists they produce."

Jam and Lewis both grew up in Minneapolis, though Lewis was not born there. Born in Omaha, Nebraska, on November 24, 1956, Lewis moved to the city with his family in the early 1960s. Jam, born James Harris III, on June 6, 1959, met Lewis while the two were high school students. They did not meet in class, however, but while attending an Upward Bound program for urban youth on the University of Minnesota campus. According to their Flyte Tyme publicity literature, the precise locus of the meeting was "over a piano." The initial encounter, nonetheless, did not blossom into a career option until some years later; in the meantime, Lewis was pursuing a high school athletic career that won him a football scholarship to Notre Dame University, and Jam was earning his nickname spinning records for dancers at Minneapolis clubs.

Made Flyte Tyme in Minneapolis

Lewis was forced to forgo college when a knee injury cut short his athletic potential during his senior year of high school, which compelled him to seriously consider a career in music. Lewis had formed and played bass in a band called Flyte Tyme that, in the mid-1970s, shared the funk spotlight with another homegrown Minneapolis superstar, Prince. The Lewis-Jam musical connection blossomed in the late 1970s when Lewis invited his friend to play keyboards for his band; they would begin regularly writing songs together early in 1981. Around this time, Prince began exercising his entrepreneurial reach by essentially buying Flyte Tyme and replacing vocalist Alexander O'Neal with his friend and protegé Morris Day. Firmly in control, Prince dubbed the band The Time and began shaping them into a professional outfit.

For the Record. . .

Team consists of **Jimmy Jam** (born June 6, 1959, in Minneapolis, MN) and **Terry Lewis** (born James Harris III, November 24, 1956, in Omaha, NE; married Karyn White [a singer]).

Duo met while high school students, Minneapolis, mid-1970s; Lewis formed, and played bass for, funk band Flyte Tyme, mid-1970s, and recruited Jam, on keyboards, late 1970s; formalized songwriting partnership, 1981; members of band The Time, 1981-83; formed production company Flyte Tyme Productions, 1982; wrote and produced tracks for other bands, including Klymaxx and the S.O.S. Band, 1983-86; produced Janet Jackson's debut album, *Control,* and albums for the Human League, the Force M.D.'s, and Robert Palmer, 1986; in joint venture with A&M Records, formed Perspective Records, 1991, and produced Sounds of Blackness debut album, *The Evolution of Gospel;* through Perspective, began management of promotion and marketing of A&M R&B roster, 1993.

Awards: American Music Award for best R&B single, 1986, for Janet Jackson's "Nasty"; Grammy Award for producers of the year, 1986; American Society of Composers, Authors, and Publishers (ASCAP) Writers of the Year awards and R&B Writers of the Year awards, 1987-93; ASCAP Golden Note Award, 1993; NAACP Heritage Award for Lifetime Achievement; Minnesota Dr. Martin Luther King Day Humanitarian Award; numerous gold and platinum singles and albums.

Addresses: *Production company*—Flyte Tyme Productions, 4100 West 76th St., Edina, MN 55435.

Although Jam and Lewis, the primary songwriters for the band at that time, were dissatisfied with their lack of independence under Prince's stewardship, they realized the benefits of the arrangement. Goldberg allowed that "they became professionals while playing in the Time," and he quoted Jam as having recalled, "Prince was going to call the shots. We weren't going to get paid a lot of money, but we were going to learn. We were not going to make a bunch of mistakes Prince had made." Jam further mused that, in the long run, "You came away from that experience definitely having the work ethic. You believe in yourself."

Jam and Lewis vented their creative frustrations by writing songs for other musicians and occasionally producing the tracks. By the time they incorporated their musical and production skills in 1982 with the creation of Flyte Tyme Productions, they had begun traveling to various cities around the country, renting time in recording studios. It was just such a travel engagement that ended their relationship with Prince. Between Time gigs in 1983, Jam and Lewis flew to Atlanta to produce "Just Be Good to Me," a song they had written for the S.O.S. Band. A freak blizzard in Georgia forced them to miss a Time concert in San Antonio, Texas. Prince, widely known for his no-nonsense managerial style, told them to either devote their energy to the band or leave; they left.

Conquered Market With *Control*

Over the next few years, Jam and Lewis developed their talents and built their business as both songwriters and producers. Following their break from The Time in 1983—and the timely success of "Just Be Good to Me" for the S.O.S. Band—Jam and Lewis turned out a string of triumphs, including a hit with Cherrelle's "I Didn't Mean to Turn You On." Jam told *Rolling Stone's* Goldberg how Prince's ultimatum had changed their lives, revealing, "That was the first time that we got serious about producing. . . . Up to that time it was just fun. 'Hey, let's write some songs. Ha-ha, this is fun.' All of a sudden, it's like . . . 'this is how I'm going to make my living now.'" By 1984, they had bought their own studio, also named Flyte Tyme Productions, and had set up full-time operations in Minneapolis.

1986 proved to be the turning point for Flyte Tyme, largely, but not entirely, due to the success of Janet Jackson's debut album, *Control.* Their work with Jackson exemplified the team's production ethic, demonstrating how they manage to realize the potential of musicians whose careers are at a crossroads. Jackson lived in the shadow of her superstar brother, Michael, and had received little attention despite years of work in television and music. Jam and Lewis approached the singer with a concept, designing songs specifically for her image and crafting an album to fill an apparent void in the music scene of the moment.

Jam disclosed to *Elle's* Daly, "With *Control* we tried to make a very street-edged R&B record with a lot of attitude. . . . We just set out to make as black an album as we could." Goldberg noted that after Jam and Lewis brought Jackson to Minneapolis to record, they "were doing their kind of research, gathering the raw material from which they would fashion a batch of semibiographical hit songs . . . that revealed a shockingly emancipated Janet Jackson and subsequently transformed her into the major new superstar of 1986." Of their approach to the songwriting, Jam said, "All we ever try to do is bring out the personality. Janet was like a stick of dynamite.

We lit the fuse." The ensuing explosion produced a multiplatinum album and five Top Ten pop hits, among them the memorable "Control," "Nasty," "What Have You Done for Me Lately," and "When I Think of You."

Broadened Reach

From the landmark of *Control,* Jam and Lewis have focused on expanding their production facilities. Their potential grew markedly as their influence shifted from a black music market to the pop arena, which allowed them to introduce more and more black musicians to greater success and marketability. The Top Ten status of a 1986 single, "Tender Love," with the Force M.D.'s had marked Flyte Tyme's initial transition from the R&B charts to the pop charts, closely anticipating the tremendous crossover success of *Control.* 1986 also saw the production of Top Ten hits with "Human," by the Human League, and a cover version of Cherrelle's "I Didn't Mean to Turn You On" by Robert Palmer. The resounding coup of 1986 demanded industry attention for Jam and Lewis, including the 1986 Grammy for producers of the year. By 1989 the duo were able to reflect their change in status with a change in venue, trading the original Minneapolis studio for a multimillion-dollar, cutting-edge complex outside of the city.

Post-Jackson, Jam and Lewis found themselves free to pick and choose the artists with whom they would work; they received calls from the likes of megastars Aretha Franklin and Whitney Houston. But they continued, despite their movement into a mainstream market that allowed them freedom from the limits imposed on "black" producers in a segregated industry, to champion African-American musicians who weren't quite realizing their musical and business potential. Lewis told Daly, "We've been offered people who've sold millions of records . . . but if we don't feel we can bring something to the party, then we don't take it. . . . It's not that we don't love these people and their work—that's exactly why we won't touch it."

Jam and Lewis brought precisely this philosophy to the record label, Perspective Records, that they created in a joint venture with A&M Records in 1991. Their first recording was an indisputable success, not simply because of positive reviews and sales, but also because Jam and Lewis—characteristically—were able to create mainstream popularity for an unlikely client: a 40-member gospel choir called Sounds of Blackness. Their debut album, *The Evolution of Gospel,* garnered the Grammy for best gospel album by a choir or chorus and landed three singles on the R&B charts. Perspec-

tive's second release, Mint Condition's *Meant to Be Mint,* put this young band in the Number One R&B spot with the single "Breakin' My Heart (Pretty Brown Eyes)." Perspective continued to market new bands, including Lo-Key?, and turned the soundtrack for the Daman Wayans film *Mo' Money* into a platinum record. In 1993 A&M extended its deal with Perspective through a significant infusion of cash and manpower, and it was announced that Perspective would be charged with promotion and marketing of A&M's R&B roster—quite the vote of confidence for Jam and Lewis.

Over the years the dynamic duo—almost as well known for their signature dark suits, fedoras, and shades as for their remarkable skills—have maintained their partnership with Jackson, possibly the one superstar in their roster. *Janet Jackson's Rhythm Nation 1814* built on the success of *Control,* making its mark in 1989 with five Number One assaults on the R&B chart and six Top Five landings on the pop chart. Ms. Jackson's 1993 offering, *janet.,* debuted at Number One on the pop charts and remained there for six weeks; by this time, the lead single from the album, the gently grooving "That's the Way Love Goes," had been prominent on both the pop and R&B charts for almost a month. The record, in fact, seemed unstoppable, spawning two more hits, "If" and "Again," as Jackson's world tour headed off into 1994. Similarly, the momentum of Jam and Lewis's Flyte Tyme showed no signs of letting up.

Selected discography

As producers

The Time, *The Time,* Warner Bros., 1981.

The Time, *What Time Is It?,* Warner Bros., 1982.

Klymaxx, *Girls Will Be Girls,* Solar, 1982.

The S.O.S. Band, *On the Rise* (includes "Just Be Good to Me"), Tabu/Epic, 1983.

Klymaxx, *Meeting in the Ladies' Room,* Constellation/MCA, 1984.

The S.O.S. Band, *Just the Way You Like It,* Tabu/Epic, 1984.

Change, *Change of Heart,* RFC/Atlantic, 1984.

Thelma Houston, *Qualifying Heat,* MCA, 1984.

Cherrelle, *Fragile* (includes "I Didn't Mean to Turn You On"), Tabu/Epic, 1984.

Cherrelle, *High Priority,* Tabu/Epic, 1985.

Alexander O'Neal, *Alexander O'Neal,* Tabu/Epic, 1985.

Force M.D.'s, "Tender Love" (12" single), Warner Bros., 1985.

The Human League, *Crash* (includes "Human"), A&M, 1986.

Robert Palmer, *Riptide* (includes "I Didn't Mean to Turn You On"), Island, 1986.

Janet Jackson, *Control* (includes "Nasty," "Control," "What Have You Done for Me Lately," and "When I Think of You"), A&M, 1986.

The S.O.S. Band, *Sands of Time,* Tabu/Epic, 1986.

O'Neal, *Hearsay,* Tabu/Epic, 1987.

Herb Alpert, *Keep Your Eyes on Me,* A&M, 1987.

Cherrelle, *Affair,* Tabu/Epic, 1988.

New Edition, *Heart Break,* MCA, 1988.

O'Neal, *All Mixed Up,* Tabu/Epic, 1989.

Jackson, *Janet Jackson's Rhythm Nation 1814,* A&M, 1989.

O'Neal, *All True Man,* Tabu/Epic, 1991.

Karyn White, *Ritual of Love,* Warner Bros., 1991.

Sounds of Blackness, *The Evolution of Gospel,* Perspective/A&M, 1991.

Mint Condition, *Meant to Be Mint* (includes "Breakin' My Heart [Pretty Brown Eyes]"), Perspective/A&M, 1991.

Mo' Money (soundtrack), Perspective/A&M, 1992.

Jackson, *janet.* (includes "That's the Way Love Goes," "If," and "Again"), Virgin, 1993.

Sources

Billboard, October 23, 1993.

Ebony, July 1987.

Elle, March 1993.

High Fidelity, September 1986.

Jet, May 24, 1993.

Musician, September 1992.

People, June 29, 1992.

Rolling Stone, April 23, 1987.

—*Ondine E. Le Blanc*

Harry James

Trumpeter, bandleader

Called "a major figure of the swing era" by John S. Wilson in the *New York Times,* Harry James struck a resounding chord with the public of the late 1930s and remained a popular bandleader for over 40 years. He built a reputation as one of the hottest trumpet players in the nation, then skyrocketed to fame after forming his own band and offering listeners a mix of romantic ballads and fast-paced jazz numbers. *The New Grove Dictionary of American Music* called him "a fine jazz improviser, possessing a verve that enhanced many small and large band recordings."

James grew up "on the road" with the Mighty Haag Circus, of which his father, Everette James, was director and star trumpet player. His mother was the trapeze artist, and she reportedly kept performing her high-wire routines until a month before Harry was born. Harry demonstrated his musical talent at an early age and was eagerly trained by his father. The young James played drums by age four, mastered the trumpet by eight, played solos by ten, led the second band for the Christy Brothers Circus at 12, and won a state contest for trumpet playing in Texas at 14. As a teenager he began performing in bands around Beaumont, Texas, where his family had settled. After failing an audition for "champagne" bandleader Lawrence Welk, he was hired in 1935 by Ben Pollack, who had heard James play in Dallas. Before long the lanky Texan with the southern drawl was recording jumping boogie-woogie numbers with the top musicians of the day, including Buster Bailey and Johnny Hodges.

"King of Swing" Benny Goodman found out about James through his brother, Irving, and hired him to play in what was then the most popular swing band in the country. James's sizzling horn became known nationwide as he played alongside such greats as Gene Krupa on drums, Ziggy Elman on trumpet, Teddy Wilson on piano, and Lionel Hampton on vibes. His contribution was a key element of the success of such rocking tunes as "Sing Sing Sing," "One O'Clock Jump," and "Life Goes to a Party." Perhaps most notable about James at the time was the sheer force of his playing. "In his early years James was a brashly exciting player, attacking solos and abetting ensembles with a rich tone and what was at times an overwhelmingly powerful sound," described the *Guinness Encyclopedia of Popular Music.*

In the late 1930s James reportedly took a $40,000 loan from Goodman to start his own band. The fledgling outfit struggled, however, and lost money in its early years. That all changed in May of 1941, though, when James recorded a cover version of "You Made Me Love You," a hit for Judy Garland that he had especially liked. The tender ballad was a smash, with the flames of

---

For the Record. . .

Born Harry Haag James, March 15, 1916, in Albany, GA; died of lymphatic cancer, July 5, 1983, in Las Vegas, NE; son of Everette (a trumpeter and circus director) and Mabel (a trapeze artist) James; married Louise Tobin (a singer), May 4, 1935 (divorced, 1943); married Betty Grable (an actress), July 5, 1943 (divorced, 1965); married Joan Boyd; children: (first marriage) Harry, Timothy; (second marriage) Victoria, Jessica; (third marriage) Michael.

Mastered the drums, c. 1920, and the trumpet, c. 1924; led second band for Christy Brothers Circus, c. 1928; worked as contortionist and led band in father's circus, 1920s; won state contest for trumpet playing, Texas, 1930; performed with bands, Beaumont, TX, early 1930s; member of Ben Pollack band, 1935-1937; member of Benny Goodman orchestra, 1937-1939; formed own band, 1939; recorded "You Made Me Love You," 1941; appeared on weekly musical radio program, 1940s; recorded series of million-selling records, 1940s; featured singers Frank Sinatra, Dick Haymes, Helen Forrest, and Kitty Kallen in his band; played and recorded with Teddy Wilson, Buster Bailey, Johnny Hodges, Corky Corcoran, Buddy Rich, Willie Smith, among other musicians; recorded charts by Ernie Wilkins and Neal Hefti, 1950s; appeared in films, including *Hollywood Hotel,* 1937, *Springtime in the Rockies,* 1942, *Two Girls and a Sailor,* 1944, and *The Benny Goodman Story,* 1955.

---

listener approval fanned by extensive play on the popular *Make-Believe Ballroom* radio program on WNEW in New York City. From there James went on to seal his popularity with a repertoire of easy-listening tunes and swinging instrumentals, shifting with ease from blues and boogie-woogie to Viennese waltzes. Many of his songs, such as "I Cried for You" and "I Don't Want to Walk Without You," addressed the sadness of separation caused by World War II. Churning out hits like "I Had the Craziest Dream," "Ciribiribin," "I've Heard That Song Before," and "Velvet Moon," the Harry James Band scored a series of million-selling discs. At one point the band was actually held responsible for a shortage of shellac, which was rationed during the war, as so much of it was required to press James's records.

By 1943 James was grossing well over $40,000 a week and was at the top of a number of bandleader popularity polls. Key to his rise in fame was a move away from pure jazz. Although James irritated his hard-core jazz fans with what they considered lightweight trumpet

solos on recordings of "The Flight of the Bumble Bee" and "The Carnival of Venice," Wilson attested in the *New York Times* that his "success as a band leader only came when he added to his repertory romantic ballads played with warm emotion and a vibrato so broad that at times it seemed almost comic."

America swooned at a celebrity match seemingly made in heaven when James wed leggy actress Betty Grable in July of 1943. Grable was the designated favorite pinup of G.I.s overseas, and the marriage prompted new lyrics to an old song, which resulted in the ditty "I Want a Girl Just Like the Girl That Married Harry James." The Grable connection further enhanced James's image, and he also appeared in a few of his wife's movies for Twentieth Century Fox. Further aiding his band's prominence during its wartime heyday was James's ability to recruit top-drawer singers. At his microphone during the 1940s were legendary vocalists Dick Haymes, Helen Forrest, and Kitty Kallen. James had even discovered Frank Sinatra in the late 1930s, but Sinatra had left his band to sing for Tommy Dorsey.

When the Big Band sound began to fade toward the end of the 1940s and many of the swing orchestras folded, James was among the few to keep his band going. He settled in Las Vegas but also toured abroad, bringing his entire entourage of 21 with him wherever he went. He continued to attract great performers, among them saxophonist Willie Smith, who had played in the Jimmie Lunceford band, and Juan Tizol, one-time trombonist for Duke Ellington. Other greats sharing the stage with James over the years included trumpet player Nick Buono and drummers Buddy Rich, Sonny Payne, and Louie Bellson.

James served as technical adviser and played the trumpet parts for actor Kirk Douglas in the 1950 Warner Bros. film "Young Man with a Horn." In the mid-1950s, he reassessed his career and turned toward more serious musical pursuits, assembling a group to play charts by Ernie Wilkins and Neal Hefti. The *Guinness Encyclopedia* called this particular James crew "one of the outstanding big bands." Still, it has been suggested that the bandleader's skills on the trumpet may have been best demonstrated outside of the big-band format. *The Oxford Companion to Popular Music* allowed that James "was sometimes inclined to over-emphasize his technique in the big-band context and was at his best in his occasional small group recordings."

James continued to perform throughout the 1960s and 1970s, shuttling between long-term gigs at major hotels and casinos. He also developed a stable of racing horses. Some considered the music of James's later career among his best, tapping as it did the best of both serious jazz and popular music and leaving behind the indulgence of earlier years. Touring to the end, James gave his last performance on June 26, 1983, in Los Angeles—little more than a week before his death. He is remembered by many as the wizard whose horn could blast listeners into a jitterbugging frenzy with one song, then soothe their souls with the next.

Selected discography

(With Benny Goodman) *Jazz Concert No. 2,* Columbia, 1937-1938.
Harry James and His Great Vocalists, Sony, 1976.
Harry James and Les Brown, Ranwood, 1985.
On the Air, Vol. II (recorded 1942-45), Aircheck, 1986.
Big Band Recordings, Hindsight, 1987.
Harry James Plays the Songs That Sold a Million (recorded in 1946 and 1954), reissued, Columbia, 1988.
Best of the Big Bands, Columbia, 1990.
Best of Harry James and His Orchestra, Curb/Cema, 1990.
Young and Swinging (recorded 1936-39), Zeta, 1992.
Young Man With a Horn (soundtrack), Sony Music Special Products.

Sources

Books

The Guinness Encyclopedia of Popular Music, Vol. II, edited by Colin Larkin, Guinness, 1992.
The New Grove Dictionary of American Music, Vol. II, edited by H. Wiley Hitchcock and Stanley Sadie, Macmillan, 1986.
The Oxford Companion to Popular Music, edited by Peter Gammond, Oxford University Press, 1991.

Periodicals

Life, May 10, 1943.
New York Times, July 6, 1983.
Stereo Review, June 1992.
Time, September 28, 1942.

—*Ed Decker*

Tom
Jones

Singer

At age 29 Tom Jones couldn't imagine being a man over 50—he said it was all downhill from there. Yet today, a few years past that feared age, he's just getting his second wind. In recent years Jones has gone from singing in front of sold-out crowds of middle-aged, underwear-tossing matrons to singing in front of sold-out crowds of fist-waving, funkily clad youths. Why the resurgence of this 50-something Welshman who first gained popularity before some of his new fans were even born? Perhaps because he's never lost his unique vocal power or his charismatic stage presence. And it doesn't hurt that he's never fought the changing times.

Born Thomas Jones Woodward in Pontypridd, South Wales, Great Britain, on June 7, 1940, Jones started singing at an early age. His mother had him performing for shillings at the village store at the tender age of three and, later, singing American hits like "Ghost Riders in the Sky" and "Mule Train" for the local women's guild. At home he would ask his mother to pull the drapes and announce him as he sang on his "stage" in the sitting room. Determined not to end up a coal miner like his father, Jones left school at 15 and held a host of laborer's jobs while singing nights in the tough, working-class pubs in town. He married Malinda ("Linda") Trenchard when they were both 16 and she was pregnant with their only child, Mark.

As a teen Jones fancied himself a "Teddy Boy," dressing in the aggressive and affected style of that rough British youth subculture (not unlike the 1950s "greaser" phenomenon in the U.S.). This identification and his struggle to escape his environment created the rugged, macho image that typifies Jones to this day. The hip swivel that "Tiger Tom" developed in those early years and the sheer emotion with which he sings set him on the road to sex-symbol status. In the beginning, however, this persona made for a muddled perception by both audiences and record companies.

Struck Gold With "It's Not Unusual"

In 1964, when Welsh songwriter and manager Gordon Mills came across Jones in a local nightclub, he could tell within a few moments that this man had potential. "The first few bars were all I needed to hear, they convinced me that here was a voice that could make him the greatest singer in the world," Mills was quoted as saying in a 1993 Tom Jones Enterprises press biography. Mills urged Jones to join him in London and promptly shortened Thomas Jones Woodward to Tom Jones in order to capitalize on the then-current film adaptation of Henry Fielding's *Tom Jones,* a hit starring Albert Finney; the name change helped to foster the

For the Record. . .

Born Thomas Jones Woodward, June 7, 1940, in Pontypridd, South Wales, Great Britain; son of Thomas (a coal miner) and Freda Jones; married Malinda Trenchard, c. 1956; children: Mark.

Worked variously as bricklayer's helper, builder's laborer, glove cutter, paper miller, door-to-door vacuum salesman, road construction worker, and hod carrier, among other jobs, c. 1955-64; sang in local pubs as Tommy Scott, the Twisting Vocalist; Tiger Tom, the Twisting Vocalist; and Tommy Scott and the Senators, c. 1955-64; "discovered" by manager Gordon Mills, 1964; signed by Decca label, 1964; released first album, *Along Came Jones,* 1965. Host of variety show in England and U.S., *This Is Tom Jones,* ABC, 1969-71; host of *Tom Jones: The Right Time,* VH-1, 1993. Signed with Interscope Records, 1993.

Addresses: *Office*—Tom Jones Enterprises, Ste. 205, 10100 Santa Monica Blvd., Los Angeles, CA 90067.

same sexy image that the fictional Jones's lusty personality suggested. But record company executives did not know what to make of this newly created Tom Jones. He was too old and he sang too well. His sound was raucous and overwhelmingly powerful, and his performance style was deemed too forward and sexual. At that time record companies were looking for groups of long-haired boys—not solo big-voiced men.

Mills and Jones persisted, and, within a year, Jones had recorded Mills's driving "It's Not Unusual," landed a recording contract with Decca, sold three million copies of the song, and watched it rise to Number One in 13 countries. But Jones's somewhat intimidating, sweating, sexy image again threw him off track. "A lot of the younger girls have said they're frightened of me," he confessed to *New York Times Magazine* contributor Anthony Carthew. Then, in November of 1966, during a post-"Unusual" slump, Mills made the discovery that would relaunch Jones's career: the kids weren't the real market—it was the adults. Armed with this insight, Mills stuck Jones in a tux, added slightly more mature songs to the singer's repertoire, and by Christmas, "Green, Green Grass of Home" was at the top of the charts, signaling the beginning of a panty-waving saga.

Once critics got past the skin-tight pants and romantic, coal-mining background, they tended to agree that Tom Jones had one phenomenal singing voice. "Mr. Jones is both a showman and, all things considered, an unusually good singer," wrote *New York Times* contributor John S. Wilson. Mark Shivas, also of the *Times,*

called Jones's gift "a big, throaty, sexy sound that wallops the studio wall with a satisfying thud." *Time,* in fact, reported that "when Jones growls through a song in a black, bluesy style, the emotion seems to come more from the throat than the heart." And Betty Baer of *Look* assessed, "Tom's musical style is the confessional moan, the raw gut feeling associated with the American soul sound."

Influenced by Rhythm and Blues

It's not surprising, then, that Jones's early influences included blues and R&B greats like Solomon Burke, Little Richard, Jackie Wilson, and Brook Benton. Jerry Lee Lewis's music planted the seed of rock and roll in Jones's heart. These musicians so impressed themselves on Jones's style that many listeners thought he was black. "There was this disk jockey," Jones told Shivas, "who was amazed because I was white and said I should keep my face off the record sleeves because otherwise I'd lose the colored audience I'd built up and the sales would drop. But of course I didn't. I was christened 'our blue-eyed soul brother,' which I liked. It was a fantastic compliment." Even Elvis Presley thought Jones was black when he heard "What's New Pussycat?" The first thing Presley asked on meeting Jones was "How the hell do you sing like that?" The two became close friends and when "Green, Green Grass of Home" became a hit for Jones, Presley frequently called radio stations to request it. Presley also warmed up his voice with Jones's "Delilah" before his own performances.

By the end of 1970 Jones had sold over 30 million discs worldwide. He continued his success throughout the early 1970s, with hits like "Delilah," "What's New Pussycat?," "Help Yourself," "Never Fall in Love Again," and "Without Love." With superstardom came *This Is Tom Jones,* the hour-long, prime-time British musical variety television show, the American rights to which were acquired by ABC-TV, making Jones the first British entertainer to star in a regularly scheduled American television show. *This Is Tom Jones* was a colossal hit for two seasons and touted a varied and impressive list of guests ranging from musical stars The Who, Ella Fitzgerald, Janis Joplin, and Elvis Presley, to actors Anne Bancroft, Peter Sellers, and Kirk Douglas. Jones's TV garb—velvet tuxedos, shirts open to the waist—not to mention his undulating hips, catapulted him into the realm of love god.

Unfortunately, as Jones did not write his own material, he was dependent on good music finding him. "That stopped happening in the '70s," he admitted to *New*

York Times contributor John Marchese. Instead, he relied on his hits and began a heavy touring schedule with long engagements on the Las Vegas circuit. It was during this period that "the underwear thing," as Jones calls it, began. Never before had the voice and gyrations of an entertainer prompted women to remove their underwear and toss it up on stage, often along with their room keys—or themselves. Mortified husbands were constantly retrieving their lust-struck wives. Although it embarrassed him, Jones could not ignore the invariable panty inundation and eventually worked it into his routine, wiping his brow with a lacy morsel and flinging it back to the proud owner. Until 1987 Jones's professional life continued in this fashion, with newer generations of music fans saying things like "Tom Jones? Oh yeah, he's that underwear guy in Las Vegas." Press coverage of his career all but ceased, and his fans got older. Even the singer's own publicity materials omit nearly 20 years of his life.

Late '80s Renaissance

But in 1987 Jones recorded "A Boy From Nowhere" for a musical called *Matador*. When it hit Number Two on the British charts, Tom Jones was suddenly a name that excited the younger generation. With numerous demands by teens that London dance clubs play "It's Not Unusual," Jones was back. The clincher was the 1988 release of "Kiss," a cover version of the Prince song by British avant-garde techno-pop group The Art of Noise; the cut featured Jones on vocals. Heavy rotation of the video incarnation of "Kiss" on U.S. cable stations MTV and VH1 introduced Jones to an entirely new audience. Requests for him to appear began flowing in, including, in 1991, a benefit for Kurdish refugees broadcast by MTV and the 30th anniversary celebration for Amnesty International. Jones was suddenly working with top young performers from both the U.K. and the U.S.

Strong influences at this time were Jones's son Mark and daughter-in-law Donna. In 1986, after the death of manager Gordon Mills, Mark Woodward became his father's manager, with Donna acting as publicist; this young couple encouraged Jones to sing newer material. Jones's longtime wife, Linda, had always been an encouragement as well, although she has kept a decidedly low profile throughout the years. Jones confessed to *New York Times* contributor Shivas, "She doesn't like to be in the audience watching my hips move around. She knows the effect it has on her and she doesn't want to see it having that effect on other girls too." Jones simply attributes the longevity of his marriage to love. "When you really love one another," he told *Details*

interviewer Anka Radakovich, "you become part of one another."

Jones looks at most everything with that easy-going simplicity. Of his current resurgence in the entertainment business, he said nonchalantly to Rick Marin of *TV Guide,* "If you've been around a long time, you get rediscovered." He never did stop performing, and when everything old became new again, Tom Jones became hip. In 1992, *The Right Time*—six half-hour television segments produced for the national inde-

---

> *Although it embarrassed him, Jones could not ignore the invariable panty inundation and eventually worked it into his routine, wiping his brow with a lacy morsel and flinging it back to the proud owner.*

---

pendent ITV network in the U.K.—had Jones singing and chatting again with pop music's most current acts, including Erasure, Lyle Lovett, Stevie Wonder, and Al Jarreau. When the show aired in February of 1993 on VH1, Jones flew once more into the American spotlight, reestablishing the mark he'd made with "Kiss." This success did not surprise his die-hard fans, like plastics manufacturer Burk Zanft. "I remember when Tom filled Madison Square Garden," Zanft reminisced to *New York Times* contributor Marchese. "He was as big as Michael Jackson back then."

Jones still relies on available material, but his ear is perfectly tuned to what's new. His versatility keeps his singing fresh. "I like all types of music," he told Marin. "But I'm not copying, I put my own sound on it. It's all Tom Jones." He's made British pop group EMF's "Unbelievable" his own—indeed, it has become Jones's '90s theme song, replacing "It's Not Unusual." And the eternal sex appeal? He explained to Marin, "It's the sound of [my] voice. It's a sexy sound. [I] don't have to leap all over the place. Sinatra has always been a sexy singer and he's never really done much gyrating."

Since the U.S. debut of *The Right Time,* Jones has been all over American television. He's played himself on prime-time's *The Fresh Prince of Bel Air* and was even featured on the Fox network's animated hit *The Simpsons.*

Popular comedian/performance artist/actress Sandra Bernhard has said that she felt destined to work with Jones after catching his Las Vegas show and realized her destiny when he made an appearance on her HBO special *Sandra After Dark*. Their "Unbelievable" duet was so risqué that even the crotch-grabbing, hip-rolling Jones was embarrassed. Bernhard didn't seem to notice, though. "He's just such a pro," she recalled to Marin. "And he has never lost his sex appeal."

Today Jones is making friends everywhere he goes. Pop singer Sting is one; Jones was the surprise hit of Sting's 1993 Carnegie Hall concert to benefit his rain forest preservation projects. Afterward, actor Dustin Hoffman told Jones that when he opens his mouth to sing it seems like an animal jumped out. Some of the "lads," as Jones call his new young friends—including Jason Priestly and Luke Perry of Fox's popular *Beverly Hills 90210*—have been known to fly to Las Vegas for performances. Jones has also bonded with ribald interviewer Howard Stern, who often rivals Bernhard in his outrageousness.

Meanwhile Tom Jones is loving it all—the late nights, the parties, the performances. For ten months of the year he tours the U.S. and abroad—tackling everything from pop standards to gospel to country—and taking every opportunity to embrace new songs, new genres, and new fans. "I just wanted to make records," he told Marchese. "New records. I don't want people to say, 'He started to make some noise again and then just faded away.'" In mid-1993 Jones signed a recording contract with Interscope Records. Though he has mellowed somewhat onstage, he still breaks into an occasional grind, sending audiences—men and women of every age—into peals of delight. He mused to Marchese, "I just do what I do. If people think it's hip, well, thank God."

Selected discography

Along Came Jones, Decca, 1965.
What's New Pussycat, Parrot, 1965.
Atomic Jones, Parrot, 1965.
It's Not Unusual, Parrot, 1965.
From the Heart, Decca, 1966.
Green, Green Grass of Home, Decca, 1967.
Funny Familiar Forgotten Feelings, Parrot, 1967.
13 Smash Hits, Decca, 1967.
Tom Jones Live at the Talk of the Town, Parrot, 1967.
Delilah, Decca, 1968.
The Tom Jones Fever Zone, Parrot, 1968.
Help Yourself, Decca, 1968.
In Aid of World's Refugees, London, 1969.
Tom Jones Live in Las Vegas, Parrot, 1969.

Tom, Parrot, 1970.
This Is Tom Jones, Parrot, 1970.
I (Who Have Nothing), Parrot, 1970.
Tom Jones Sings She's a Lady, Parrot, 1971.
Tom Jones Live at Caesar's Palace, Parrot, 1971.
Tom Jones Close Up, Parrot, 1972.
Body and Soul of Tom Jones, Parrot, 1973.
Tom Jones' Greatest Hits, Parrot, 1973.
Somethin' Bout You Baby I Like, Parrot, 1974.
Memories Don't Leave Like People Do, Parrot, 1975.
Tom Jones 10th Anniversary Album, Tee Vee, 1975.
The Classic Tom Jones, Epic, 1977.
Say You'll Stay Until Tomorrow, Epic, 1977.
Tom Is Love, Epic, 1977.
What a Night, Epic, 1977.
The Country Side of Tom Jones, Parrot, 1978.
Rescue Me, MCA, 1979.
Do You Take This Man, EMI, 1979.
Darlin', Polygram, 1981.
Country, Polygram, 1982.
Don't Let Our Dreams Die Young, Polygram, 1983.
Love Is on the Radio, Polygram, 1984.
Tender Loving Care, Polygram, 1985.
Matador, Epic/CBS, 1987.
Move Closer, Jive/RCA, 1989.
Carrying a Torch, Chrysalis, 1991.
The Complete Tom Jones, London UK, 1993.
Velvet + Steel = Gold: Tom Jones 1964-69, Deram, 1993.
(Contributor) *The Christmas Album*, Interscope, 1993.

Sources

Coronet, December 1969.
Details, July 1993.
Life, September 18, 1970.
Look, November 4, 1969.
National Observer, July 21, 1969.
Newsweek, January 20, 1969.
New York Post, June 7, 1969.
New York Times, February 8, 1969; March 9, 1969; June 14, 1970; June 15, 1971; March 8, 1974; April 7, 1974; May 17, 1993.
New York Times Magazine, November 14, 1965.
Rolling Stone, May 16, 1991.
Time, July 11, 1969.
TV Guide, January 24, 1970; February 20, 1993.

Additional information for this profile was obtained from a Tom Jones Enterprises press biography, 1993.

—Joanna Rubiner

Louis Jordan

Bandleader, singer, instrumentalist

At the height of his career in the 1940s, bandleader and alto saxophonist Louis Jordan scored 18 Number One hit records. In the tradition of Louis Armstrong and Fats Waller, Jordan exhibited a brilliant sense of showmanship that, as music critic Leonard Feather explained in his book *The Jazz Years,* brought audiences first-rate entertainment "without any loss of musical integrity." Jordan's jazz-based boogie shuffle rhythms laid the foundation for rhythm and blues, modern electric blues, and rockabilly music. Against the backdrop of house parties, fish frys, and corner grills, Jordan, who was black, performed songs that appealed to millions of black *and* white listeners. Able to "straddle the fence" between these two audiences, Jordan emerged as one of the first successful crossover artists of American popular music.

Born on July 8, 1908, in Brinkley, Arkansas, Jordan was the son of Jim Jordan, a bandleader and music teacher. Under the tutelage of his father, Jordan began studying clarinet at age seven. After spotting a saxophone in a music store window, however, he "ran errands all over Brinkley" until he could raise the money to purchase the instrument. While on summer vacation at the age of 15, Jordan landed his first gig, with Ruby "Tuna Boy" Williams's Belvedere Orchestra, at the Green Gables in Hot Springs, Arkansas. His first professional engagement was with Fat Chappelle's Rabbit Foot Minstrels, playing clarinet and dancing throughout the South. At Arkansas Baptist College in Little Rock, Jordan majored in music and played on the school baseball team. After school he played local dates with Jimmy Pryor's Imperial Serenaders.

On the Road

Moving to Philadelphia in 1930, Jordan worked with trumpeter Charlie Gaines's orchestra and tuba player Jim Winters's band. Two years later, Jordan traveled to New York with Gaines's group, where he took part in a recording session with pianist Clarence Williams's band. In New York he briefly worked with the bands of Kaiser Marshall and drummer Joe Marshall. His most important job, though, came in 1936 when he joined drummer Chick Webb's orchestra—a 13-piece ensemble that featured singer Ella Fitzgerald. A small, "hunchbacked" man whose physical deformity nonetheless failed to hinder his inventive drumming talent, Webb hired Jordan as a singer, sideman, and announcer. In 1937 Jordan recorded his first vocal with Webb's band, a song titled "Gee, But You're Swell." During his stint with Webb, Jordan developed his skills as a frontman. "Louis would go out and just break up the show,"

For the Record. . .

Born Louis Thomas Jordan, July 8, 1908, in Brinkley, AR; died from complications after a heart attack, February 4, 1975, in Los Angeles, CA; buried in Mt. Olive Cemetery, St. Louis, MO; son of Jim Jordan (a bandleader and music instructor); married Felice Ernestine Moore (divorced). *Education:* Attended Arkansas Baptist College.

Began clarinet study with father, c. 1915; switched to saxophone; performed with Ruby Williams's Belvedere Orchestra, Hot Springs, AK, c. 1923; toured with Fat Chappelle's Rabbit Foot Minstrels; performed with Charlie Gaines band, Philadelphia, 1930; performed with Kaiser Marshall and Joe Marshall bands, New York City; as singer, sideman, and announcer, joined Chick Webb Orchestra, 1936; formed Tympany Five (originally Elk's Rendevous Band), 1939; recorded "I'm Gonna Move to the Outskirts of Town," 1942; disbanded Tympany Five to form big band, 1951; left Decca label to sign with Aladdin Records, 1954; continued to record for numerous labels; toured England, 1962, and Far East, 1967-68; performed at Newport Jazz Festival, 1973.

Awards: Inducted into the Rock and Roll Hall of Fame, 1987.

recalled former bandmember Garvin Bushell in his autobiography *Jazz From the Beginning.* "Nobody could follow him."

In the summer of 1938, Jordan left Webb's orchestra to form his own, nine-piece, band; although Jordan enjoyed performing as part of large jazz ensembles, he embarked on a career as a bandleader and more general entertainer. "I wanted to play for the people, for millions, not just a few hep cats," explained Jordan in Arnold Shaw's *Honkers and Shouters.* Billing himself as "Bert Williams," Jordan played shows at the Elk's Rendezvous at 44 Lenox Avenue, in Harlem. His long residency at the club eventually prompted him to name his group the Elk's Rendezvous Band. After playing various club dates on 52nd Street, he booked his band at proms and dances at Yale University and Amherst College. In 1939, this group recorded several sides for the Decca label.

That December, after changing the name of his band to the Tympany Five, Jordan reduced the size of the unit to six members (later it would number seven or eight). Invited to open for the Mills Brothers at the Capitol Theater in Chicago, Jordan played a ten-minute spot during the intermission between the featured performances. In no time, Jordan's energetic stage presence began to draw larger crowds than the headline acts, so

Capitol's management decided to lengthen his performance to half an hour.

But the real turning point in Jordan's career came when he performed at a small "beer joint" called the Fox Head Tavern in Cedar Rapids, Iowa. Distanced from the demanding crowds of Chicago and New York, Jordan found he was freer to experiment with new material. At the Fox Head he assembled a large repertoire of blues and novelty songs. On his return to the Capitol Theater, Jordan became a sensation. In January of 1942 he hit the charts with a rendition of the blues standard "I'm Gonna Move to the Outskirts of Town."

King of the Jukeboxes

From 1942 Jordan was rarely absent from the *Harlem Hit Parade.* Over the following ten years he recorded more than 54 rhythm and blues best-sellers. Material for his band came from a number of black and white songwriters. As Jordan's manager, Berle Adams, told *Honkers and Shouters* author Shaw, "When we found something we liked, an arrangement would be made up, and we'd play it on one-nighters. The songs the public asked for again and again were the songs we recorded." Jordan soon produced a stream of hits, including "What's the Use of Getting Sober (When You're Gonna Get Drunk Again)," "Five Guys Named Moe," and "G.I. Jive," a boogie number intended for the entertainment of troops fighting in World War II.

Aside from the universal appeal of his material, the key to Jordan's success lay in his tight organization and the use of talented arrangers such as pianists Wild Bill Davis and Bill Dogget. Though he exhibited a casual manner, Jordan was a serious bandleader who demanded that his outfit be well dressed and thoroughly rehearsed. In *An Autobiography of Black Jazz,* saxophonist Eddie Johnson described how Jordan's penchant for "neatness" led him to require his band to "look right even down to their shoes." Jordan furnished bandmembers with six or seven uniforms, which displayed a post-zoot-suit style with multicolor designs.

In the mid-1940s, Jordan's Tympany Five drew thousands of listeners to white nightclubs and black theaters. Traveling by car caravan, the band toured constantly, playing shows at venues like Billy Berg's Swing Club in Hollywood, the Oriental Theatre in Chicago, the Apollo in Harlem, and the Paradise Theatre in Detroit. In black movie houses, Jordan's releases were featured in film shorts, many of which became so popular that the regular features often received second billing. Around this time Jordan also appeared in several motion pictures, including *Meet Miss Bobby Socks, Swing*

Parade of 1946, and *Beware,* which was advertised as "the first truly great all-colored musical feature."

After World War II, when the big bands began to disappear, Jordan's small combo continued to find commercial success. "With my little band, I did everything they did with a big band. I made the blues jump," Jordan explained in *Honkers and Shouters.* The band became so popular, in fact, that Jordan toured with such sought-after opening acts as Dinah Washington, Ruth Brown, Sarah Vaughan, and Sister Rosetta Tharpe. Following his 1945 million-seller "Caldonia," Jordan and the Tympany Five continued to score hits, among them "Beware Brother Beware," "Boogie Woogie Blue Plate," "Nobody Here But Us Chickens," and "Open the Door Richard," a song adapted from a black vaudeville comedy routine popularized during the 1930s and '40s. In 1950, Jordan recorded a cover version of "(I'll Be Glad When You're Dead) You Rascal You" with trumpeter-singer Louis Armstrong.

Obscured by the Sound He Helped Create

The following year Jordan changed course, disbanding the Tympany Five and forming a 16-piece big band. But this group did not live up to the sound or favor of the earlier unit. On leaving the Decca label in 1954, Jordan largely lost the steady stream of material, sidemen, and producers that had helped him maintain his national celebrity. Determined to keep up with the burgeoning rhythm and blues market, however, he signed with West Coast-based Aladdin Records. But after failing to score commercially, he moved to RCA's Victor X subsidiary. In the meanwhile, Jordan had recorded for more than a dozen labels in the U.S., including Mercury, Warwick, Tangerine, Pzazz, and Blue Spectrum. Despite his persistence, Jordan faced a new record-buying public dominated by teenagers who demanded rock 'n' roll lyrics, idol images, and heavy back-beat rhythms.

Health problems eventually forced Jordan to retire from one-night stands, which required that he drive hundreds of miles across the country. In 1946 he bought a home in Phoenix, Arizona, where he stayed for 18 years; he moved to Los Angeles in the early 1960s. During this period he devoted his time to playing occasional month-long engagements in Phoenix, Las Vegas, and New York. On a tour of England in 1962, Jordan performed and recorded with the Chris Barbers band. Two years later, he reformed the Tympany Five to appear at show lounges and music festivals. His performances in the Near East in 1967 and 1968 received enthusiastic responses. At the 1973 Newport Jazz Festival, too, crowds gave him a warm reception.

In October of 1974, Jordan suffered a heart attack while performing in Sparks, Nevada. After entering St. Mary's Hospital in Reno, he returned home to Los Angeles, where he died on February 4, 1975. His body was flown to St. Louis for burial at Mt. Olive Cemetery.

In 1987 Jordan was inducted into the Rock and Roll Hall of Fame. Though many had forgotten his contributions to popular music over the intervening years, this honor paid tribute to one of the performers most responsible for the development of rhythm and blues and rock and roll. As trumpeter Dizzy Gillespie related in his autobiography *To Be or Not to Bop,* "Rock n' roll had been with us a long time" and "Louis Jordan had been playing it long before Elvis Presley." Jordan helped shape the careers of rock and roll pioneers Chuck Berry, Fats Domino, Bill Haley, and countless others, though his music would later become obscured by evolving trends. In 1990 Jordan's work was celebrated in the hit stage production *Five Guys Named Moe,* a rollicking look at a man whose "whole theory of life" was to make audiences "smile or laugh." With the many reissues of Jordan's music on compact disc, one need only listen to realize the lasting sincerity of his commitment.

Selected discography

With Chick Webb and His Orchestra

"Gee, But You're Swell," Decca, 1937.

Bing Crosby With Louis Jordan and His Band

"(Yip Yip Hootie) My Baby Said Yes," Decca, 1944.
"Your Socks Don't Match," Decca, 1944.

Louis Jordan's Elk's Rendezvous Band

"Honey in the Bee Ball," Decca, 1939.

Louis Jordan and His Tympany Five

"Do You Call That a Buddy?," Decca, 1940.
"I'm Gonna Move to the Outskirts of Town," Decca, 1942.
"Five Guys Named Moe," Decca, 1943.
"G.I. Jive," Decca, 1944.
"Is You Is or Is You Ain't (My Baby)," Decca, 1944.
"Open the Door Richard," Decca, 1947.
"Saturday Night Fish Fry," Brunswick, 1949.

Other

Louis Jordan's Greatest Hits, 1941-1947, 1980.
Look Out! . . . It's Louis Jordan and the Tympany Five, Charly, 1985.
Just Say Moe! Mo' of the Best of Louis Jordan, Rhino, 1992.
One Guy Named Louis: The Complete Aladdin Sessions, 1992.
Jivin' With Jordan: Louis Jordan and His Tympany Five, Charly.
Somebody Done Hoodooed the Hoodoo Man, Jukebox.

Louis Jordan: Let the Good Times Roll, Bear Family Records.
Five Guys Named Moe: Original Decca Recordings Vol. II.

Sources

Books

Bushell, Garvin, *Jazz From the Beginning: As Told to Mark Tucker,* University of Michigan Press, 1988.

Chilton, John, *Let the Good Times Roll: The Story of Louis Jordan and His Music,* University of Michigan Press, 1994.

Feather, Leonard, *The Jazz Years: Earwitness to an Era,* Quartet Books, 1989.

(With Al Fraser) Gillespie, Dizzy, *To Be or Not to Bop: Memoirs,* Doubleday, 1979.

Rusch, Robert D., *Jazztalk: The Cadence of Interviews,* Lyle Stuart Inc., 1984.

Shaw, Arnold, *Honkers and Shouters: The Golden Years of Rhythm and Blues,* Collier, 1978.

Simon, George T., *The Big Bands,* Schirmer, 1981.

Tosches, Nick, *Unsung Heroes of Rock n' Roll,* Scribner's, 1984.

Travis, Dempsey J., *An Autobiography of Black Jazz,* Urban Research Institute, 1983.

Periodicals

Down Beat, March 27, 1975.
Newsweek, April 20, 1992.
Pulse!, November 1992.
Variety, November 1990.

Additional information for this profile was obtained from liner notes by Peter Grendysa to *Just Say Moe! Mo' of the Best of Louis Jordan,* Rhino Records, 1992.

—*John Cohassey*

Kris Kross

Rap duo

When rappers Kris Kross released their first single, "Jump," in 1992, their main claim to fame was precociousness: Mack Daddy and Daddy Mack were only 12. While youth—and a habit of wearing their clothes backwards—earned them notice, more was required to actually make their first record, *Totally Krossed Out,* a quadruple-platinum smash. Matt Diehl accounted for the twosome's success in *Vibe:* "When Kris Kross first blew up, it wasn't hard to see why. They had all the cuteness required of adolescent rappers, and that backwards-clothing business was a clever marketing touch. But where other juvenile crews like Another Bad Creation subsisted on minimal mike skills, familiar samples, and the novelty value of little kids acting like hardcore roughnecks, Kris Kross could *flow*." *Totally Krossed Out* also won awards and critical acclaim, laying a solid foundation for a follow-up album, which would challenge the rappers to rely more on skills and less on cuteness.

Mack Daddy and Daddy Mack—Mack is street parlance for pimp—are the crisscrossed hip-hop handles

For the Record. . .

Members include **Daddy Mack** (born Chris Smith c. 1979 in Atlanta, GA) and **Mack Daddy** (born Chris Kelly c. 1979 in Atlanta).

"Discovered" in an Atlanta mall c. 1991 by writer-producer Jermaine Dupri; recorded first single, "Jump," 1992; released album *Totally Krossed Out,* Ruffhouse/Columbia, 1992; released *Da Bomb,* Ruffhouse/Columbia, 1993.

Awards: American Music awards, 1992, for favorite new R&B artist and favorite hip-hop artist; Jack the Rapper "Yes You Can" Award for Young Entertainers, 1992; double-platinum single for "Jump" and gold singles for "Warm it Up," 1992, and "Alright," 1993; multiplatinum album for *Totally Krossed Out,* 1992, and gold album for *Da Bomb,* 1993.

Addresses: *Record company*—Ruffhouse/Columbia, 2100 Colorado Ave., Santa Monica, CA 90404.

of Chris Kelly and Chris Smith, respectively, both of whom were born in Atlanta, Georgia, in the late 1970s. The Chrises have been friends since early childhood. They were "discovered" in the early 1990s by an equally precocious producer, Jermaine Dupri, who was only 18 at the time. Dupri was formerly a dancer for rap legends Run-D.M.C. He noticed Chris and Chris in an Atlanta mall, where he was struck by their look, which affected the extreme bagginess of hip-hop culture. Dupri proceeded to turn the pair into a polished rap duo; he would also write and produce all of the music on their first album. When *Totally Krossed Out* was released, in fact, Eric Thurnauer declared in *Details,* "The real star . . . is producer Jermaine Dupri, who provides the infectious swing beats that set the duo apart."

The single "Jump" preceded the album; it was an instant hit, taking the top of the pop charts and eventually going double platinum. Reviewers couldn't seem to extol the virtues of the song enough, several remarking on its power to influence human behavior. Bönz Malone noted in *Spin* that "everytime it's played, the crowd gets savage and starts doing what these kids demand!" When Kris Kross appeared on the comedy series *In Living Color* in March of 1992, a reviewer for *People* reported, "The effect their music had on the *In Living Color* ensemble, causing people more than twice their age to pogo deliriously around the stage. In a 1993 review of Kris Kross's second record, *Da Bomb, People* still waxed enthusiastic over "Jump," recalling how it "pulsed with exuberance and attitude."

The album *Totally Krossed Out* took the Number One spot on *Billboard's* rap and R&B charts; it exceeded the sales of "Jump" and produced a second hit single, "Warm it Up," which earned a gold record. A slew of award nominations followed, resulting in two American Music Awards, including favorite new R&B artist and favorite new hip-hip artist, and the Jack the Rapper "Yes You Can" Award for Young Entertainers. The media went nuts for Kris Kross; they appeared on a range of television shows, including *The Arsenio Hall Show* and the sitcom *A Different World* (and it was almost impossible to turn on MTV without seeing the youngsters jumping around in their video). They mounted *two* tours in 1992, one a spot opening for superstar Michael Jackson in Europe, the other their own circuit in North America. In 1993, they would market their talent and fame to the soft drink Sprite, filming slickly produced television commercials for the company.

In response to their overall package, *People* described the Kris Kross sound as one that "combines hard rap rhythms and textures with bubble-gum pop melodies"; the magazine also predicted the duo's popularity on the charts and with audiences, commenting, "Their best trick is inserting catchily melodic refrains in the middle of their free-stylin' raps. That should help them kross over to pop." Indeed, despite the undeniably teen-oriented melodic content of their work, *Totally Krossed Out* did display a hard edge, according to *Details* writer Thurnauer, who maintained, "On their debut LP, these prodigies steer clear of the playground to trade rhymes about gang life ('A Real Bad Dream'), after-hours escapades ('Party'), and the neighborhood scene ('Lil' Boys in da Hood') with all the stone-cold attitude of M.C.s twice their age." Edge would be what Kris Kross needed more of as they started to grow out of childhood.

Almost inevitably, mixed reviews greeted the release of 1993's *Da Bomb*—though it duly went gold within a few months of its release. The first single, "Alright," climbed as high as Number 15 on several charts, including the Hot 100, R&B, and Rap Singles. The challenge facing *Da Bomb,* also produced and largely written by Dupri, was not simply that the kids were growing up—rendering their marketability as pint-size wonders less compelling—but that their relative youth was inconsistent with the emergence of hard-core or gangsta rap as the dominant rap genre; at fourteen, Daddy Mack and Mack Daddy were getting too mature to be perceived as rap moppets, but at the same time were unable to compete with grown men who gave the gangsta stance unquestionable credibility. *People* echoed other media in noting "One year later, Mack Daddy and Daddy Mack are 14, their once squeaky voices have deepened, and they're not so cute anymore. In fact, *Da*

Bomb isn't so much fun. In an effort to show that they are more than rappers in baggy pants, Kris Kross mimics every identifiable hip-hop style without settling on their own."

Still, the more developed Kris Kross did manage to convince several reviewers, including *Billboard's* Craig Rosen, who averred that *Da Bomb* "does feature a new-found street edge." For his part, *Vibe's* Diehl cautioned that "Kris Kross is ultimately more effective on a cassingle than over the course of a whole CD," but he was able to muster some positive impressions: "Where *Da Bomb* improves greatly on the inconsistent *Totally Krossed Out* is in Kris Kross's ever-growing microphone techniques—check out Mack Daddy's rat-a-tat-tat delivery on the title track." Rap scribe Havelock Nelson remarked in *Rolling Stone,* "They sound threatening, even though their chat is strictly PG." Daddy Mack explained the reason for keeping Kris Kross rhymes PG, despite the harm this would undoubtedly do their gangsta image, stating in *Billboard,* "We understand that kids are going to want to listen to our music. . . . There's not that many groups out right now that kids can listen to that are hard, 'cause they use profanity on their albums. We just want to be a group the kids can listen to." Caught in the crossfire of balancing their young audience's needs and the decidedly adult values of the rap world, Kris Kross soldiered on through the troubling teen years.

Selected discography

Totally Krossed Out (includes "Jump," "A Real Bad Dream," "Party," and "Lil' Boys in da Hood"), Ruffhouse/Columbia, 1992.
Da Bomb (includes "Alright"), Ruffhouse/Columbia, 1993.

Sources

Billboard, August 21, 1993.
Details, July 1992.
Entertainment Weekly, February 12, 1993.
People, May 25, 1992; August 23, 1993.
Rolling Stone, October 14, 1993.
Source, October 1993.
Spin, September 1992.
Vibe, September 1993.

Additional information for this profile was obtained from Ruffhouse/Columbia Records, 1993.

—*Ondine E. Le Blanc*

Cyndi Lauper

Singer, songwriter

After years of performing with bands that never made the big time, singer-songwriter Cyndi Lauper made her solo recording debut with the album *She's So Unusual* late in 1983. Through 1984 and early 1985, singles from her album, including "Girls Just Want to Have Fun" and "Time After Time," consistently stayed on the pop charts, making her the first female recording artist to achieve four hits with a debut album. Her quirky style, coupled with her impressive, four-octave range, endeared Lauper to fans and critics alike and netted her awards ranging from 1985's Grammy for best new artist to a spot as one of *Ms.* magazine's 12 women of the year for 1984.

Lauper was born June 20, 1953, in Brooklyn, New York. Shortly afterwards her family moved to neighboring Queens, where she acquired her trademark accent. When she was five, her parents divorced, and her mother worked long hours as a waitress to provide for her three children. From earliest childhood, Lauper mentally escaped hardship by singing. She confided to Bonnie Allen in *Ms.*, "Even when I talked, I sang. Always. As a kid I knew that all my power as a person came from my voice." Lauper also took a lesson from her mother's gruelling work schedule and vowed to escape the difficult life led by her family and neighbors.

The young singer's education was somewhat erratic, due to being expelled from different Catholic schools, where, Lauper told Kurt Loder in *Rolling Stone,* she was abused by overly strict nuns. After obtaining her high school equivalency degree, she was persuaded by friends and family to enter art school rather than pursue a singing career. Though a talented artist, Lauper did not adapt well to the structured environment of art school, and dropped out of several before returning to her first love, music. She worked odd jobs to support herself, including stints as a kennel attendant and a racehorse walker. During the early 1970s Lauper sang on street corners in Greenwich Village before joining a disco group, Doc West.

Silence of the Jams

Performing in local clubs, relying heavily on covers of popular disco songs, the band was much like any other. Only Lauper's unique vocal renderings set them apart and kept the audience interested. People were particularly impressed with the feisty singer's rendition of Janis Joplin songs. But before long, Lauper tired of the disco scene and decided to move on. She joined up with the rock band Flyer, but was with them just a short time before losing her voice because of severely strained vocal chords.

For the Record. . .

Born June 20, 1953, in Brooklyn, NY; mother was a waitress. *Education:* Attended several colleges to study art.

Worked variously as waitress and racehorse walker; singer with disco group Doc West, beginning in 1974; singer with rock bands Flyer and Blue Angel, 1977-81; solo performer, 1981—; signed with CBS Records, and released *She's So Unusual,* 1983. Appeared in films *Vibes,* 1988, and *Life With Mikey,* 1993.

Awards: Named one of 12 women of the year by *Ms.* magazine, 1984; eight MTV Video Music Award nominations and seven National Academy of Video Arts and Sciences award nominations, 1984; Grammy Award nominations for album of the year, for *She's So Unusual,* record of the year and best female pop vocal performance, for "Girls Just Want to Have Fun," and song of the year, for "Time After Time," all 1985; Grammy Award for best new artist, 1985.

Addresses: *Home*—New York City. *Record Company*—Epic Records, 550 Madison Ave., New York, NY 10022.

When doctors informed her that she would not be able to resume a career in singing, Lauper was undaunted. On the advice of a friend, she sought the help of voice coach Katherine Agresta, an opera singer noted for her work with rock stars. Along with vocal exercises, Agresta stressed the importance of physical health in vocal restoration. By heeding her advice and following a strict regimen, Lauper accomplished the impossible and resumed her singing career.

Striking out on her own, Lauper once again worked the local circuit, performing solo at bars and clubs until meeting up with John Turi. Lauper and Turi collaborated to create Blue Angel, a band described by critics as both "rockabilly" and "new wave." The new group allowed Lauper to spread her musical wings as she enjoyed a level of artistic freedom she had not previously experienced. It was during this time that her singular fashion sense began to emerge.

Lauper was hard to ignore, with her carelessly chopped, multi-colored hair and funky, mismatched wardrobe. But it was her vocal acrobatics that brought her to the attention of rock manager Steve Massarsky. Decidedly underwhelmed with the band itself, Massarsky was impressed enough with the young singer's talent to sign Blue Angel to a recording contract with Polydor Records.

Despite a disappointing lack of sales, Blue Angel's first and only album was received favorably by critics, with most of the praise lavished on Lauper's singing. But in 1981 the band, plagued by in-fighting and artistic differences, called it quits, inciting Massarsky to file a lawsuit against them.

On her own again, Lauper declared bankruptcy and landed a job singing (phonetically) at a Japanese bar, where she met David Wolff, the man who became her manager and fiance. Wolff tirelessly promoted his new client and with the help of his connections, landed the singer a recording contract with CBS Records.

A Style Is Born

She's So Unusual debuted in 1983 and though Lauper wrote few of the songs, she was allowed a great deal of artistic control with the album as well as the accompanying videos. "Girls Just Want to Have Fun" was the first release—a rollicking video romp conceived by Lauper and populated with her family and friends. The song rocketed to the top of the pop charts and became part of MTV's heavy-rotation schedule. Hot on its heels was "Time After Time," a haunting ballad co-written with Eric Bazilian and Rob Hyman of the Hooters. Other hits from the album included "All Through the Night," "She-Bop" and "Money Changes Everything."

With the exception of the title song, Lauper's 1986 follow-up album, *True Colors,* did not meet with the success of the first. "I can't blame anybody but myself," Lauper confessed to Ann Kolson of the *Philadelphia Inquirer.* "I was there, but I wasn't there. My heart wasn't into it. I started to take out all the stuff about myself that made it interesting, thinking it was too weird."

Turning her attention to acting, the singer was cast in a starring role opposite actor Jeff Goldblum in the comedy film *Vibes.* Her character was a zany, psychic beautician. When it was released in 1988, reviews were unkind, but focused on the inadequacies of the script rather than Lauper's acting abilities. She told Fred Goodman in *Rolling Stone:* "That's the last time I'll take a part because of the part, hoping that the script will get better. It never does." Even Lauper's theme song from the film, "There's A Hole In My Heart," released as a single, proved a flop.

Critical Success, Commercial Flop

Lauper's 1989 album, *A Night to Remember,* brought mixed reviews from critics. Some called it her best work ever; others noted a new mellowness to the music and lamented the loss of her earlier, more spirited style. Most, however, heaped extravagant praise on her stunning singing ability. "Vocally, she does everything right on *A Night to Remember,*" claimed *People's* David Hiltbrand. "She's earthy on the winsome rocker 'I Drove All Night,' scintillating on the airier 'Primitive' and sweet on the gentle 'Unconditional Love.'" Jimmy Guterman of *Rolling Stone* noted, "On 'My First Night Without You,' she builds from a whisper to a scream and captures all the nuances in between." Though "I Drove All Night" proved a hit for Lauper, *A Night to Remember* did not match the overwhelming success of *She's So Unusual.*

Following the commercial failure of *A Night to Remember,* Lauper virtually disappeared from the public eye. She ended her longtime relationship with Wolff and spent the better part of two years attempting to get her life in order. She credits the Hooters—old friends and collaborators—with helping her rediscover the healing power of music. But it was actor David Thornton, whom she married in 1991, who gave her the courage to make a comeback.

In 1993, after an absence of four years, Lauper released her fourth album, *Hat Full of Stars.* Her return was celebrated by critics who hailed the album as a milestone in the singer's career. Soliciting the aid of several songwriters (including Bazilian, Hyman and Mary-Chapin Carpenter), Lauper produced her most varied, revealing and poignant work to date, addressing such issues as racism, incest, abortion and wife-battering. Holly George-Warren of *Rolling Stone* described the musical effort as "a fresh sound that mixes 60s soul, 70s funk, 80s pop and 90s hip-hop, as well as bits of folk and ethnic music." Ron Givens of *People* commented on the context of the material: "Lauper brings an enticing mix of literal description and oblique metaphor . . . she sets a scene, makes us care, gives us hope." Lauper also made her directorial debut on two of the album's videos, "Who Let In The Rain" and "Sally's Pigeons."

In addition to recording, Lauper has also kept her acting skills honed. Both she and her husband appeared in Michael J. Fox's 1993 movie *Life With Mikey* and more recently she guest starred on the NBC comedy *Mad About You.* As she told Kolson, "I may not be the biggest artist in the whole friggin' world. Who cares?

I'm able to stand up with pride and dignity and say that this is me and this is my gift to the world."

Selected discography

She's So Unusual (includes "Girls Just Want to Have Fun," "Time After Time," "She-Bop," "All Through the Night," and "Money Changes Everything"), Portrait, 1983.

True Colors (includes "True Colors" and "What's Going On"), Portrait, 1986.

A Night to Remember (includes "I Drove All Night," "Primitive," "Unconditional Love," and "My First Night Without You"), Epic, 1989.

(Contributor) *A Very Special Christmas,* A&M, 1992.

Hat Full of Stars (includes "Lies," "Broken Glass," "Who Let In The Rain," "Sally's Pigeons," and "A Part Hate"), Epic, 1993.

(Contributor) *A Very Special Christmas 2,* A&M, 1993.

Sources

Books

Willis, K. K., Jr., *Cyndi Lauper,* Ballantine, 1984.

Periodicals

Audio, September 1989.
Entertainment Weekly, May 29, 1992; June 18, 1993.
Mademoiselle, November 1988.
Ms., January 1985; August 1988.
Nation, June 30, 1984.
Newsday, June 13, 1993.
Newsweek, March 26, 1984; March 4, 1985.
New York, December 26, 1983.
New York Times, May 28, 1993.
People, September 17, 1984; August 15, 1988; June 19, 1989; December 21, 1992; June 28, 1993; July 26, 1993.
Philadelphia Inquirer, May 30, 1993.
Rolling Stone, May 24, 1984; June 1, 1989; June 15, 1989; November 16, 1989; September 2, 1993.
Time, March 4, 1985.
Village Voice, August 17, 1993.

Additional information for this profile was obtained from Epic Records publicity materials, 1993.

—*Elizabeth Wenning*

Tracy Lawrence

Singer, songwriter

Country singer and songwriter Tracy Lawrence didn't wait until the debut of his first album, *Sticks and Stones,* to make headlines; in May of 1991, the then-23-year-old Lawrence was shot four times during a robbery attempt in the parking lot outside a friend's hotel in Nashville. Both he and a girlfriend from his hometown of Foreman, Arkansas, were held at gunpoint by three men who robbed the couple of their money and the keys to the young woman's car. When the robbers attempted to take the couple to the girl's hotel room, Lawrence decided to fight back. "In my mind, the only reason for taking us to a hotel room was to rape her," he later told Dolly Carlisle of *People.* "They didn't try to hide their faces. They would not have let us live. I decided that if I was going to die, I was going to die fighting." The thieves fled the scene after firing several shots; they were never caught.

Lawrence's bravery cost him four bullet wounds; he was hit in the left hand, the upper right arm, the left hip, and the left knee. The last shot would require surgery and extensive rehabilitation at a Nashville hospital before the singer would be able to walk again. Although doctors had estimated it would be over a year before Lawrence's recovery was complete, they had not counted on the singer's determination to get on with his career—friends were amazed when he was up and about on crutches a week after the shooting.

Lawrence had spent his first two years after graduating from high school studying mass communications and business at Southern Arkansas University. But he left college in 1988 to pursue his dream of a career as a musician. He moved to Louisiana to perform as a singer with a country band that played gigs throughout the South but left for Nashville in the fall of 1990, when he decided that the band's booking schedule was leading him nowhere. "Seems like I was always searching for something, but I was always looking for it outside myself," Lawrence told Bob Millard in *Country Music.* "When I finally came to the realization that the only way to be happy is to be happy with yourself, things started changing for me."

When Lawrence arrived in Music City U.S.A., he was full of self-confidence in the musical talent he had developed over several years as a performer. Although he immediately got a job as an ironworker to keep a roof over his head, within two weeks he had abandoned it in favor of giving a musical career his best shot. At first, Lawrence lived off prize money he won at local singing contests, but these soon gave way to a regular spot on *Live at Libby's,* a radio show broadcast from nearby Daysville, Kentucky, for which he was paid $25.00 a night. In less than a year, Lawrence's vocal ability had landed him a recording contract with Atlantic Records.

For the Record. . .

Born January 27, 1968, in Atlanta, TX; son of Dwayne (stepfather; a banker) and JoAnn Dickens; married Francis Wetherford, 1993. *Education:* Attended Southern Arkansas University, 1986-88.

Sang with Louisiana-based country band, performing throughout the South, 1988-90; worked briefly as ironworker, Nashville, 1990; performed regularly on radio show *Live at Libby's*, Daysville, KT, c. 1990; signed with Atlantic Records, and released debut album, *Sticks and Stones,* 1991.

Awards: Named best new male country artist by *Billboard,* 1991; named top new male vocalist, Academy of Country Music, 1993.

Addresses: *Record company*—Atlantic Records, 75 Rockefeller Plaza, New York, NY 10019.

His recovery from the shooting incident delayed the release of Lawrence's first Atlantic album, *Sticks and Stones,* until October of 1991. But the wait did not seem to affect the album's impact on the country countdown: the title song "just lit up the country hit charts," according to Jack Hurt of the *Chicago Tribune,* as it earned the distinction of having the highest rate of airplay of any new country artist's first single during its initial week of release. The album's three singles, which also included "Today's Lonely Fool" and "Runnin' Behind," hit the Number One spot in quick succession.

The year following the release of his first album found Lawrence spending a great deal of time on the road, working almost 300 concert dates as the opening act for such country superstars as Vince Gill, George Jones, and Shenandoah. Lawrence found this experience invaluable. "When you work with so many great acts, you stop trying to play like a bar band," he noted in an Atlantic Records press release. "You start trying to be an entertainer, and you try to motivate yourself to do the best show you can."

Early on, it became clear that Lawrence's vocal influences were his favorite singers, George Jones and Keith Whitley. But with his second album, 1993's *Alibis,* his vocal range matured, as did his own unique style. "As an artist, I feel like I went through a lot of growth in the past year and I feel like I was able to express that on this second album," Lawrence told Jennifer Fusco-Giacobbe in *Country Song Roundup.* "I think its the fresh new sound that has just a little bit of a young edge to it," he added, describing his own honky tonk brand of "young country." But the long-standing traditions of country music still rang true in Lawrence's work. Geoffrey

Himes reviewed the album for *Country Music,* noting, "*Alibis* is crammed full of hooks built around puns so corny they make you wince before you grin. . . . It wouldn't be nearly as effective . . . if Lawrence didn't deliver the authentic tears-in-the-beer ballad vocal." Himes summed *Alibis* up in a few words: "You might say it's corny; you might say its genius. I say it's both." His opinion was reflected by the listening public, who boosted sales of the album to gold status three weeks after its release. By the summer of 1993, *Alibis* had gone platinum, selling one million copies.

Lawrence co-wrote several of *Alibi's* tracks, including "It only Takes One Bar (To Make a Prison)" and the hit single "Can't Break It to My Heart." He has also used his talent as a songwriter to aid in causes to benefit people less fortunate than himself. When Hurricane Andrew devastated parts of Florida and Louisiana in 1992, leaving thousands of people homeless, Lawrence and several friends composed the song "Give the Fans a Hand." Proceeds from a videotaped performance of the tune by Lawrence and several other musicians went to assist hurricane victims in both states.

Unlike some of his fellow country artists, among them Brooks & Dunn and Reba McEntire, Lawrence doesn't think he'll be crossing over to the pop charts any time soon. "I could cut a rock n' roll song and it'd still be country," he noted in his Atlantic press release. "I've played country too much to be anything else." And Lawrence is confident that his burst onto the country charts was due more to those country roots than to the advance publicity he received from the shooting incident back in 1991. "I knew what I wanted when I first got to town," he stated. "I knew what I wanted and worked very hard to get to where I am at right now. I want to be remembered for why I came here, not for some fluke accident."

The honor of receiving the 1993 Academy of Country Music award for top new male vocalist, as well as his continued popularity among country music listeners, seems to prove that Tracy Lawrence is on the right track. Regarding his future plans, he told Fusco-Giacobbe, "I've worked all my life to achieve what I'm working on now, and I've got a good shot at pursuing my dreams and I want to give it everything I've got."

Selected discography

Sticks and Stones (includes "Sticks and Stones," "Today's Lonely Fool," and "Runnin' Behind"), Atlantic, 1991.
(With Kenny Beard and Hank Cochran) "Give the Fans a Hand," 1992.
Alibis (includes "Can't Break It to My Heart" and "It Only Takes One Bar [To Make a Prison]"), Atlantic, 1993.

Sources

Chicago Tribune, November 1, 1991.
Country Music, July/August 1992; May/June 1993.
Country Song Roundup, September 1993.
Music City News (Nashville, TN), June 1993.
Newsweek, April 19, 1993.
People, February 3, 1992.

Additional information for this profile was obtained from Atlantic
Records press materials, 1993.

—Pamela Shelton

Kurt
Masur

Conductor, music director

There is always a tingle of anticipation when a conductor lifts his arms to signal the start of a concert. That tingle ran particularly high on September 11, 1991, when the raised arms belonged to maestro Kurt Masur, music director of the world-renowned Leipzig Gewandhaus Orchestra, who was making his debut as music director of the equally renowned New York Philharmonic. Masur, who holds these appointments concurrently, is unfazed by the challenge of helming a 107-strong ensemble of notoriously independent musicians in America while also leading a 250-year-old European orchestra that is ruled by tradition; he meets the challenge by simply preserving the unique character and sound of each, at the same time overlaying them with his own meticulous interpretation of the featured composer's work.

This is a difficult balance, but it is by no means the highest hurdle Masur has faced; a far more daunting test came in 1989, when the communist regime of East Germany began to teeter. Realizing that clashes between angry pro-democracy demonstrators and police seemed inevitable, Masur used his influence to persuade Communist Party officials and their opponents to convene at the Gewandhaus for talks. As a result, there was no bloodshed in Leipzig when the Berlin Wall crumbled weeks later. In fact, when the dust settled, many Leipzigers viewed Masur as a good choice for the country's first post-communist president. Ultimately, this would not be the case, as Masur dismissed such a possibility before the issue was decided. "I am a musician, not a politician," he told *Time* magazine's Michael Walsh in 1990. "I make my statements in music."

Chose Not to Become an Electrician

Masur was just seven years old when he learned to use music as a means of self-expression. Spurred on by his parents, he taught himself to play the piano and before long was devouring all types of music so eagerly that he abandoned tentative plans to work as an electrician and aimed instead for a career in music. Breslau's National Music School in what is now Wroclaw, Poland, was the first step to achieving this goal. A well-focused young Masur entered in 1942, proving himself a diligent piano and cello student. Piano studies continued at the Leipzig Conservatory in 1946, along with conducting and composition. Once he had graduated, Masur began the long, arduous climb up the ladder toward the recognition that would permit him to put his interpretive signature on any performance. In 1948, he began as a

For the Record. . .

B orn July 18, 1927, in Brieg, Silesia (later Poland); married Tomoko Sakurai (a Japanese soprano; third wife); children: four. *Education:* Studied piano and cello studies at National Music School, Breslau (now Wroclaw), Poland, 1942-44; attended Hochschule fur Musik, Leipzig, East Germany (now Germany), 1946-48.

Rehearsal conductor at Halle State Theater, Saxony, East Germany, conductor at Erfurt City Theater and Leipzig Opera, and guest conductor with Leipzig and Dresden Radio orchestras, 1951-53; general music director, Dresden Philharmonic Orchestra, 1955-58; music director, Mecklenburg Staatstheater, Schwerin, East Germany, 1958-60; music director, Berlin Komische Oper, 1960-64; guest conductor in Europe, Japan, and South America, 1964-67; chief conductor of Dresden Philharmonic Orchestra, 1967-72; music director of Leipzig Gewandhaus Orchestra, 1970—; music director of New York Philharmonic, 1991—.

Selected awards: National Prize of German Democratic Republic, 1969-70; honorary degrees from University of Leipzig and University of Michigan.

Addresses: *Office*—New York Philharmonic, Avery Fisher Hall, 10 Lincoln Center Plaza, New York, NY 10023-6973.

rehearsal coach at the Halle National Theater in Saxony, progressing, in 1951, to a two-year stint as conductor of the Erfurt City Theater. Next came a term as conductor of the Leipzig Opera, beginning in 1953, while he was guest conducting with the Dresden Radio Orchestra. In 1955 came his first major orchestral appointment, as conductor of the Dresden Philharmonic, which he left in 1958 to become general director of opera at the Mecklenburg State Theater in Schwerin.

By 1960, Masur was an accomplished conductor with an extensive repertoire. As such, he was hand-picked for the post of music director at the prestigious Berlin Komische Oper by Walter Felsenstein, the company's opera director. Working with Felsenstein taught Masur a great deal about shaping his own interpretations. An innovative thinker, Felsenstein was an originator of the "realistic" music theater concept, the principal technique of which involved using music as a way to heighten opera's drama to its fullest extent. Because Felsenstein often re-edited original texts, reconstructing them to make the most of their dramatic potential, Masur learned to analyze and re-analyze every piece of music in order to bring out its deepest meaning. This skill enabled him to move past the technical demands of the composer's work, to the artistic spirit behind it.

Masur enjoyed his work with Felsenstein and was glad to have had the opportunity to add so many works to his repertoire during this time. Nevertheless, by 1964 he had spent 12 years in opera, and he was beginning to long for the variety he could derive only from orchestral work. Guest conducting seemed an ideal next step. Despite the fact that the East German government respected their musicians enough to support 88 orchestras, Masur knew he would have trouble getting a visa when he received an invitation to conduct in Venice, Italy. He defiantly accepted the 1966 engagement anyway, then went to the Ministry of Culture to demand the necessary travel permit. While at first adamant in its refusal, the ministry grudgingly backed down, fearing international repercussions if anything should stop the determined Masur from keeping his Venice appointment.

Continued August History of Leipzig Gewandhaus Orchestra

By 1970, when he took the reins of the Leipzig Gewandhaus Orchestra, Masur's guest engagements had made his musical statements familiar to music lovers all over Europe. Experienced, well versed in the Romantic masters whose works formed the backbone of the Leipzig repertoire, he also understood that Leipzig's was an orchestra that had always relied on tradition. It had been founded in 1743, during the lifetime of Johann Sebastian Bach, and had boasted quasi-professional musicians until 1835, when Felix Mendelssohn marched briskly onto the podium and turned his orchestra into the best in Europe. Then, to assure himself a future supply of reliably expert performers, Mendelssohn founded the Hochschule fur Musik (music school), using members of the orchestra as teachers. This tradition continues to rule the ensemble; fully 85 percent of conservatory students go on to the Leipzig Gewandhaus Orchestra. Masur himself heartily approves of the practice; "[we] don't like to take outsiders, especially strings," he told John Rockwell of the *New York Times Magazine,* "we have our own style."

The Leipzig Gewandhaus Orchestra style, which is lyrical and deeply textured, also owes much to conductor Bruno Walter, who passed on to the members techniques he had learned in Hamburg from the brilliant, difficult Gustav Mahler. Walter turned his orchestra into a national treasure soon after he became its music director in 1928; nonetheless, in 1933 he earned the dubious honor of being the first Jewish musician ejected from Germany by the Nazis. Masur was well acquainted with Walter's work. He especially admired his interpretations of Mozart, which he had first heard on a radio broadcast from West Berlin in 1946. Masur had then proceeded to learn everything he could about Walter's interpretations, which have become a guiding force to him.

In a few years Masur had smoothly incorporated the traditions of both Mendelssohn and Walter into an ensemble that bore his own unmistakable style. By 1974 he was ready to take the orchestra overseas; the

---

Many Leipzigers felt Masur would be a good choice for East Germany's first post-communist president. This would ultimately not be the case; "I am a musician, not a politician," he said. "I make my statements in music."

---

tour included performances in Japan, China, Great Britain, and the United States. Masur also traveled frequently on his own, creating such a sensation with the Cleveland Orchestra that it was still remembered when he returned there in the summer of 1982.

Soon after Masur's arrival in Leipzig, the East German government announced plans for a new Gewandhaus to replace the building that had been flattened by bombs during World War II. While leading the orchestra's usual performances in the Congress Hall down the street, Masur himself supervised every detail of the new building's construction, making sure that the acoustics would be perfect for both recording and live performances. Because of the increasingly exacting acoustical detail afforded by newly sophisticated recording media, he knew that live *and* at-home audience expectations would be extremely high, and he was determined not to disappoint. Concertgoers at the orchestra's first Gewandhaus performance, in 1981, marveled at the sound quality and viewing vantage points of its modern amphitheater design, which places most seating in an elevated circle surrounding the orchestra.

By the 1980s Masur's prestige in the government was considerable. He accepted his status without false modesty, enjoying the recognition of fellow Leipzigers without taking advantage of his elevated position. But in 1989 he was thrust unexpectedly into the political glare cast on the tottering communist regime of East German head of state Erich Honecker. The catalyst was a letter

he received during the summer asking for his help in protecting the rights of street musicians. Intrigued by the unusual request, Masur invited the city's street musicians to the Gewandhaus for a meeting with police and Communist Party authorities. The gathering ended so amicably that he repeated the event later in the year when angry pro-democracy demonstrators seething through Leipzig made him fear the possibility of widespread violence. Incredulous opponents of the regime gaped when Masur's influence coaxed party leaders and members of the secret police to meet with them at the Gewandhaus for informal talks. Weeks later, when the Berlin Wall fell, its toppling did not unleash the slaughter that usually accompanies drastic political change.

Still, not every Leipziger was impressed by Masur's feat; detractors growled that his concern for the city had been purely opportunistic. As evidence, they dug up a tragic 1972 traffic accident, in which Masur's second wife and two young men in an oncoming car had been killed on the autobahn. It had been Masur's influence with the government, the opponents claimed, that had prevented an inquiry or other consequences at the time. Masur met this challenge with his usual calm, pointing out that an inquiry had been unnecessary since he had at once accepted full responsibility for the accident. As it was, Masur's admirers far outnumbered the naysayers. Thus it was unusual but not completely unexpected when the conductor's fans bandied his name about as a hot presidential prospect for the post-Honecker government. He made the point moot, however, dismissing the possibility as ridiculous.

Accepted Philharmonic Post

Leipzig's turmoil did not prevent Masur from keeping up with events on the international music scene. The big news in New York City was the imminent departure of Zubin Mehta, the New York Philharmonic's music director, who was planning to step down at the end of the 1990-1991 season. Newspaper reports detailed the progression of the search for a replacement for the irreplaceable Mehta. Bernard Haitink had been approached but had preferred to stay in his post, as had Sir Colin Davis. Claudio Abbado had considered the position but had turned it down in favor of the Berlin Philharmonic. Masur came under consideration when a survey generated by the members of the New York Philharmonic themselves ranked him top among their guest conductors. Other points in his favor were the rave reviews he had received for his 1989 performances, plus his lucrative recording contracts with Philips and Teldec. Masur accepted the assignment, on condition that it run concurrently with his Leipzig duties. Ever obliging, he even stepped into the post a year early after the sudden death of Leonard Bernstein left several weeks of Philharmonic engagements without a maestro.

Masur found the tenor of the New York Philharmonic completely different from that of the competition-free, tradition-bound Leipzig Gewandhaus Orchestra. Far more independent, with a longstanding reputation for challenging conductors, and deeply conscious of their own artistic excellence, the musicians had been, collectively, a tough nut even for the formidable Bernstein, who often had to beg for their attention.

Deft at administration and unperturbed by artistic temperament, Masur lost no time in showing the New York Philharmonic who was boss. "He needed to let everybody know, 'I'm the man, I'm in charge, you're going to do what I ask,'" tuba player Warren Deck told James Oestreich of the *New York Times*, "And . . . if you didn't do it immediately, it was ugly." Most performers chose to comply and found that rewards were swift. First came a return to the maestro's usual modus operandi, which is a reasonable, partnership approach to each project. Then came initiation into the exquisitely detailed analysis that produces his unique musical statement. The result was summed up by principal oboist Joseph Robinson, who told the *New York Times*, "That concern makes our musical adventures together more rewarding than with most people I've ever worked with."

The proof of the union, one might say, was in the listening. And the listening was great, according to *Stereo Review*'s Richard Freed, who in March of 1992 reviewed Masur's production of the Bruckner Seventh Symphony, recorded live at his debut performance. "It is a noble reading," said Freed, adding, "there is a mellowness new to the Philharmonic, and it does not by any means cancel out brilliance." With Masur at the podium, the future promised much for the New York Philharmonic.

Selected discography

With the Leipzig Gewandhaus Orchestra; on Philips, except where noted

Beethoven: *Symphony No. 9 in D Minor, Op. 125.*
Beethoven: *Nine Symphonies.*
Beethoven: *Triple Concerto in C Major for Violin, Cello and Piano, Op. 56; Two Romances for Violin and Orchestra: in G Major, Op. 40 and in F Major, Op. 50,* Angel.

Brahms: *Complete Symphonies* (includes *Variations on a Theme by Haydn, Op. 56a; Academic Festival Overture, Op. 80; Tragic Overture, Op. 81.*)
Brahms: *Concerto No. 1 in D Minor for Piano, Op. 15.*
Brahms: *Concerto No. 2 in B-flat Major for Piano, Op. 83.*
Brahms: *Concerto in D Major for Violin, Op. 77.*
Brahms: *Concerto in A Minor for Violin and Cello, Op. 102.*
Brahms: *Hungarian Dances Nos. 1-21.*
Brahms: *Serenade No. 1 in D Major, Op. 11.*
Bruch: *Concerti for Violin: No. 1 in G Minor, Op. 26; No. 2 in D Minor, Op. 44.*
Bruch: *Scottish Fantasy, Op. 46; Konzertstuck, Op. 44.*
Bruch: *Symphony No. 2 in F Minor, Op. 36; Swedish Dances, Op. 63.*
Busoni; Nielsen; Reinecke: *Twentieth Century Flute Concerti.*
Dvorak: *Slavonic Dances, Op. 46 and Op. 72; Slavonic Rhapsodies, Nos. 1, 2, 3.*
Liszt: *Six Hungarian Rhapsodies.*
Liszt: *Totentanz; Fantasia on Beethoven's "Ruins of Athens"; Malediction; Hungarian Fantasy,* Angel.
Schubert: *Incidental Music to* Rosamunde, *Op. 26, D. 797.*
Strauss: *Concerti for French Horn: No. 1 in E-flat Major, Op. 11; No. 2 in E-flat Major* (includes *Von Weber—Concertino for Horn and Orchestra in E Minor, Op. 45.*)
Strauss: *Four Last Songs; Songs With Orchestra.*
Strauss: *Songs for Male Voice With Orchestra.*
Vivaldi; Handel; Mozart; Gluch; and others: *18th-Century Bel Canto Music.*

With the New York Philharmonic, except where noted; on Teldec

Beethoven: *Symphony No. 5 in C Minor; Egmont.*
Brahams: *Haydn Variations Symphony No. 2; Academic Festival Overture.*
(With the Leipzig Gewandhaus Orchestra) Bruch: *Violin Concerto No. 1 in G Major.*
Bruckner: *Symphony No. 7.*
Dvorak: *Symphoy No. 9, "From the New World"; Slvavonic Dances.*
Franck: *Symphonie in D; Les Eolides.*
Ives: *Variations on America* (Schuman orchestration).
Mahler: *Symphony No. 1; Wayfarer Songs.*
(With the Leipzig Gewandhaus Orchestra) Mendelssohn: *Elijah, Op. 70; Midsummer Night's Dream; Piano Concerti Nos. 1-2; Symphony Nos. 1, 5; Symphony No. 2; Symphonies Nos. 3 & 4; Violin Concerto in E Minor.*
Mussorgsky: *Pictures at an Exhibition.*
Prokofiev: *Alexander Nevsky; Scythian Suite; Symphony No. 1, "Classical."*
Reger: *Variations & Fugue on a Theme by Mozart.*
Schumann: *Symphonies Nos. 1, 4; Symphonies Nos. 2, 3, "Rhenish."*
Sibelius: *Finlandia; Karelia Suite; Swan of Tuonela; Violin Concerto.*
Tchaikovsky: *Manfred; Piano Concerto No. 2; Francesca da Rimini; Gopak; Romeo & Juliet; Festival Coronation March; Symphony No. 1; Francesca Symphony No. 2; Romeo & Juliet*

Symphony No. 3; Festival Coronation; Gopak Symphony No. 4; Symphony No. 5; Symphony No. 6, "Pathetique."

Sources

Books

Craven, Robert, *Symphony Orchestras of the United States: Selected Profiles,* Greenwood Press, 1986.

Craven, Robert, *Symphony Orchestras of the World: Selected Profiles,* Greenwood Press, 1987.

Ewen, David, *Dictators of the Baton,* Ziff-Davis, 1948.

Holmes, John L., *Conductor on Record,* Greenwood Press, 1982.

Periodicals

Audio, December 1991.

Fanfare, October 1984.

New York Times, April 23, 1990; May 1, 1990; December 18, 1990; May 23, 1993.

New York Times Magazine, September 8, 1991.

Stereo Review, March 1992; May 1992.

Time, July 12, 1993.

—Gillian Wolf

Reba McEntire

Singer, songwriter, actress

Reba McEntire is not one to fall into a musical rut. While she built her reputation on traditional country music, she branched out from these roots soon after earning a few gold records. Since then, her music has blurred the lines between country and mainstream pop, and she has made forays into soul and even rhythm and blues. To McEntire, these distinctions simply don't matter. "Lord knows, I'm country. Given who I am and where I come from, no matter what I do, it will be country," she told Tim Allis and Jane Sanderson in *People.* "I don't sing country songs, I don't sing pop, I sing Reba songs." No matter the material, it is McEntire's remarkable voice that has made her, in the words of *Stereo Review's* Alanna Nash, "arguably the finest female country singer since Patsy Cline," or as *Time* dubbed her, the "velvet-throated diva of country music." McEntire has, according to Bob Allen of *Country Music,* a "frightfully precise and supple high-range vocal power," and in Nash's estimation, she is "a no-frills singer with an uncanny gift for phrasing, a talent for sounding as if she's lived every line, and an Oklahoma accent that's as thick as warmed-over grits."

McEntire was born on March 28, 1955, and raised on a 7,100-acre cattle ranch ten miles outside of Kiowa, Oklahoma. Both her father and grandfather were champion steer ropers, the former a three-time world champion. McEntire's mother was a singer, but unlike the men in the family, did not get a chance to pursue her art professionally. Instead, she taught her children to sing. The McEntire children spent a lot of time on the road, singing and following the rodeo circuit. Reba started her professional career early—at five—performing "Jesus Loves Me" for five cents in a hotel lobby. Throughout school she sang with her siblings, the Singing McEntires, in neighboring towns and at rodeos. In fact, Reba wasn't the only future professional in the group; her sister Susie eventually became a gospel singer. McEntire also honed her skills with the barrel race—a rodeo obstacle course—at which she competed across the country. She attended Southeastern Oklahoma State University, intending to become an elementary school teacher. While studying, she continued to race, ranch, and sing.

"Discovered" at Rodeo

In 1974 McEntire got an unexpected break—singing the national anthem at the National Rodeo Finals. Her performance impressed country music star Red Steagall, who convinced her to record a demo tape. She was understandably apprehensive about the undertaking. But, as she explained to Jess Cagle in *Entertainment Weekly,* she put all fear behind her when her mother

For the Record. . .

Born March 28, 1954, outside Kiowa, OK; daughter of Clark (a cattle rancher and rodeo steer roper) and Jacqueline (a teacher); married Charlie Battles (a rancher), 1976 (divorced, 1987); married Narvel Blackstock (a musician and artist manager), 1989; children: (first marriage) two stepsons; (second marriage) Shelby (son); three stepchildren. *Education:* Degree in elementary education (with minor in music), Southeastern Oklahoma State University, c. 1974.

Sang with siblings in small towns in Oklahoma as the Singing McEntires, 1960s; competed as rodeo barrel racer, 1960s-early 1970s; performed national anthem at National Rodeo Finals, Oklahoma City, OK, 1974; signed with Mercury records, 1975; released debut album, *Reba McEntire*, 1978; signed with MCA, 1983; released *My Kind of Country*, 1984; became producer, 1985; formed management company Starstruck Entertainment, c. 1989; made debut as actress, appearing in film *Tremors*, 1990.

Selected awards: 12 gold albums, seven platinum albums; five Country Music Association awards, nine Academy of Country Music awards, nine American Music awards, three People's Choice awards; six awards from *Music City News*; Grammy Award for best female country vocal performance, 1987, for *My Kind of Country*.

Addresses: *Home*—Nashville, TN. *Record company*—MCA, 1514 South St., Nashville, TN 37212. *Management*—Starstruck Entertainment, P.O. Box 121996, Nashville, TN 37212.

revealed, "What you're fixing to do, I'm living my dreams through you." In 1975 McEntire signed with Mercury Records. She wowed observers at her first recording session. According to *Entertainment Weekly,* "Her clear contralto was so big it nearly blew out the studio transistors." McEntire remembered the event thus: "It was a real pretty ballad, and when I got to the powerful part, I stayed right on the microphone and the needles just disappeared. They asked me to back up."

As her career took off, McEntire married Charlie Battles—another national steer wrestling champion and rancher—who managed her career while they also ran a cattle ranch in Oklahoma. She recorded a few singles, but they didn't go far. Mercury released her first album, *Reba McEntire,* in 1978, but she only had minor hits until she teamed with singer Jacky Ward to record a number of duets. The first of these, "Three Sheets in the Wind"/"I'd Really Love to See You Tonight," reached the Top Twenty. With this boost, solo hits followed"(You Lift Me) Up to Heaven," "Today All Over Again," and a cover version of "Sweet Dreams," a song made classic by Patsy Cline.

But throughout the early 1980s, McEntire could not hit Number One. To *Stereo Review* contributor Nash, the reasons were obvious; executives at Mercury "tried their darndest to obscure McEntire's natural assets," packaging a "genuine country article" as a "city sophisticate." They dressed her in evening gowns, painted her with makeup, and had her try a variety of musical styles, though what she really wanted was to sing traditional country. Her image was so malleable that recognizing McEntire from one project to the next was not easy. In spite of these marketing gaffs, McEntire finally hit the top spot, in 1983, with "I Can't Even Get the Blues" and "You're the First Time I've Thought About Leaving" and pleased critics with the record *Behind the Scenes.*

However, little changed until McEntire took her career into her own hands and in 1983, moved to MCA and began choosing her own material. She soon traded the evening gowns for jeans, cowgirl skirts, and the belt buckle she received for singing the national anthem at the rodeo finals. In 1984 she released the aptly titled *My Kind of Country*. The album was, in the words of *People's* Ralph Novak, "straightforward country." *Billboard* dubbed McEntire "the finest woman country singer since Kitty Wells," and reviewers likened her to her idol, Patsy Cline. *My Kind of Country* produced two Number One hits—"How Blue" and "Somebody Should Leave"—and was McEntire's first gold album. 1984 also brought McEntire her first major award, the Country Music Association's female vocalist of the year nod. The CMA honored her with the same award the following year, as did the Academy of Country Music and Music City News, and *Rolling Stone's* critics put her on their list of Top Five country artists. With 1985's *Have I Got a Deal for You,* McEntire took another giant leap in her career by becoming her own co-producer. The album also boasted the first song she wrote on her own, "Only in My Mind," which *Rolling Stone* deemed a "promising debut."

Cemented Position With *Whoever's in New England*

If there was anyone in country music who hadn't noticed McEntire by 1986, the release of *Whoever's in New England* got their attention. The album earned a 1987 Grammy Award for best female country vocal performance, among other laurels, and a gold album. "There's something about the catch and quaver in McEntire's voice that suggests the purest kind of country sound," Ralph Novak observed in his *People* review of the album. Nash placed McEntire in very good company, allowing, "She has confirmed her place alongside Wynette and Wells as one of the foremost woman singers in the history of country music."

Whoever's in New England cemented McEntire's place in country music—every subsequent album she released went gold. Ironically, the album also marked the beginning of her departure from traditional country music and transition into what *Country Music's* Allen called "Yuppie Country." As her choice of music changed, her audience grew and broadened to include fans outside country music, though the singer did not yet move far enough to alienate traditionalists. *Whoever's in New England* also established McEntire's skills as a video artist when the album's title track video won the Academy of Country Music's award for video of the year and the *Music City News'* award for country music video of the year. By the time she released her next album, *What Am I Gonna Do About You,* it seemed that critics had already begun to take her superiority for granted. Novak dubbed the album "routinely excellent." Though she would soon change her tune, Nash proclaimed McEntire "the only modern female vocalist loyal to the true country tradition."

1987 brought even more changes to McEntire's life and music. She and Battles divorced, and she immediately moved to Nashville, later explaining to Allen, "I had to pack everything in one day and leave. I was totally starting over." Instead of explaining her personal life to her fans, she put the emotions of the broken marriage into her next album, *The Last One to Know.* The result demonstrated that even in the grip of personal turmoil, McEntire could produce stunning music. In *Rolling Stone,* Rob Tannenbaum called the album McEntire's best effort to date. Nash was also pleased; she called *The Last One to Know* "another winner of a record" and found that McEntire "[displayed] even more confidence in her already powerful delivery, nailing her notes with greater clarity, and honing a style that is at once urgent, emotional and forceful."

Beat Madonna

Soon McEntire began to take even more control of her career, her music continuing to move away from traditional country. Some critics were less than thrilled. Nash for one, found little to praise; reviewing McEntire's 1988 album, *Reba,* in *Stereo Review,* she complained, "After years of insisting that she'd stick to hard-core country 'because I have tried the contemporary-type songs, and it's not Reba McEntire—it's just not honest,' McEntire . . . has gone whole-hog pop. Okay, so

maybe that's not so terrible. But her rendition of the soul classic 'Respect' is." Frustrated by the album, Nash called it a "disappointing bore, a waste of an exhilarating voice, and a somewhat disturbing harbinger of the fate of country music's traditionalist movement." Fortunately for McEntire, her rapidly growing audience did not agree; her rendition of "Respect" was a big hit in concert, and in 1988 she was named in a Gallup youth survey as one of teenagers' Top Ten favorite female vocalists—she was the only country singer on the list. Even more outstanding was a 1989 *People* poll in which

> *"Lord knows, I'm country. Given who I am and where I come from, no matter what I do, it will be country. I don't sing country songs, I don't sing pop, I sing Reba songs."*

readers voted her their second-favorite female vocalist—behind Barbra Streisand, but ahead of pop superstars Madonna, Cher, and Whitney Houston.

In 1989 McEntire married her manager, Narvel Blackstock, on a boat in Lake Tahoe, and together they built a business. Dubbed Starstruck Entertainment, it brought together all aspects of McEntire's career—management, booking, publishing, promotion, publicity, accounting, ticket sales, and the administration of her fan club. Eventually, the company would grow to include a horse farm and jet charter service, as well as trucking, construction, and book publishing divisions.

By 1990 McEntire had discarded her leather cowgirl skirts, her fiddles, and her steel guitar. On stage, she donned "sequins, flowing gowns, big hair . . . flashy costume changes, blue lights and synthesizers," according to Allen. Though impressed by McEntire's changes, the *Country Music* scribe was disappointed in her "glitzy, hip, high-tech, and flashily new age" performance. "The show smacks of Las Vegas, intricately choreographed, thoroughly rehearsed, and utterly lacking in warmth or spontaneity. It's as if, sad to say, Reba has gone corporate with her music." Despite such comments, McEntire had no regrets about her transformation; in fact, she was delighted. "I'm happier, more confident—though as you can see I still dress in jeans and denim," she told Allen. "I'm not so dead set on making everyone else happy and pleased. I don't listen to anybody's input as much as I listen to my own gut feeling." And in her view, she had not rejected traditional country. "I want to do what sells . . . I want to do what the majority of the public likes to hear," she explained. "The funny thing of it is . . . they all say they want me to go back to traditional country. But the majority of people obviously don't want to hear me sing traditional, even though I love to sing it and could probably sit and do it all my life."

Rumor Has It, released in 1990, gave McEntire a chance to win back some critical praise. Though Allen found the recording predictable in places, he believed she "still leaves most of the competition in the dust." The album also brought *Stereo Review's* Nash back into McEntire's camp; she called *Rumor* "glorious" and while finding little there for the traditionalist, she noted that McEntire "shines so brilliantly—regaining her good judgment and take-charge attitude, and communicating with everything she has—that she is bound to win over her recent critics. *Rumor Has It* is a powerhouse recording that should put McEntire back on top where she belongs." Indeed, the album went platinum, selling over one million copies.

In 1991—at the top of her career, with a successful corporation and a new baby boy, Shelby—McEntire had the rug pulled out from under her. On March 16th, her tour manager and six members of her band were killed when their plane crashed on Otay Mountain in California. McEntire turned to music to assuage her grief, responding with *For My Broken Heart,* released late in the year. While it did not address the tragedy directly, it was a sorrow-filled work that "explores all measure of suffering," as Nash wrote in *Entertainment Weekly.*

Found Solace From Grief in Music

"*For My Broken Heart* is charged with quiet, restrained emotion. It's a moving reminder of how Reba excels at conveying the complexities of adult feeling and relationships," Michael McCall wrote in *Country Music.* In the same publication, George Fletcher predicted that it would be her career album and assessed, "She wrapped her magnificent voice around a good collection of songs, putting her heart and soul front and center." The disc also demonstrated McEntire's talent at reinterpreting well-known material; singing Vicki Lawrence's hit "The Night the Lights Went Out in Georgia," she made the "campy white-trash" song, as Nash described it, "chilling and believable." In McCall's eyes, *For My Broken Heart* was "an affirmation of music's ability to probe ticklishly complicated topics in a powerful, universal way. It also reaffirms that Reba McEntire is a

remarkable talent." *Heart* sold two million copies in nine months. By then McEntire was responsible for more album sales than any performer ever signed to MCA's Nashville division. Still, success did not mitigate the tragedy. After the crash McEntire would find herself in the middle of a performance, turning to face the band and experiencing the shock all over again. "I expect other faces," she told Mary H. J. Farrell and Sanderson in *People.*

McEntire followed *For My Broken Heart* with *It's Your Call* in 1992, explaining in the album's liner notes that it was the second chapter. *It's Your Call* was another commercial triumph, selling over two million copies within the year. Critical reaction to the record, however, was mixed, many reviewers comparing it unfavorably to *For My Broken Heart.* "The truth is, it isn't nearly as pessimistic as its predecessor—and unfortunately it isn't anywhere as involving," Nash complained in *Entertainment Weekly.* *Country Music's* Fletcher called the first three cuts—the title track, "Straight From You," and "Take It Back"—"superb," but he bemoaned the "generally weaker batch of songs and an over-reliance on similar-type ballads that don't really allow Reba the room to stretch." In *Time,* Christopher John Farley agreed, opining, "*It's Your Call* is marred by unadventurous arrangements . . . she should have been willing to shear away the instrumentation, tasteful as it is, and expose her voice and all the raw hurt it bears."

Nonetheless, McEntire's critics managed to find some praise. Qualifying her comments, Nash wrote, "Yet with even the most mediocre song, McEntire is a commanding performer. Singing 'straighter' these days, without so many vocal frills, she almost succeeds in turning average material into something extraordinary." In *Stereo Review,* Ron Givens concurred, noting, "These smooth-as-butter arrangements could easily be mistaken for TV ads or elevator music if it weren't for that crystalline voice breaking over and over again."

Reviewing *It's Your Call,* Farley also observed, "On this album McEntire adds something special: a sort of time-to-put-myself-first feminism." This was actually not new, but something McEntire had developed for years. Throughout her career she had addressed most of her songs to women, celebrating, commiserating, and empowering. She is also willing to confront head-on the lives of contemporary women, addressing such topics as spousal abuse, in "The Stairs," or the difficulties of returning to school as a parent, in "Is There Life Out There." At her concerts many women have told her that the video for the latter song inspired them to get their degrees. "I do think I've made a conscious effort to record more songs for women," she told Holly Gleason in *Ladies' Home Journal.* "It's about time someone focused on them. I think women are special, and I want to make them realize that."

As if McEntire didn't have enough on her plate, during the late 1980s and early '90s she began building an acting career. Noted for her ability to convey character through her singing, she had developed this skill further in videos. According to a 1993 MCA press release, she enjoys using video to "explore the ambiguities of songs instead of as vehicles for simple retelling" and to create mini-movies. In 1992, *Billboard* reported that her enthusiasm did not thrill executives at Country Music Television, though, who complained to MCA that the video of "Is There Life Out There" was too long and featured too much dialogue. Still, the clip won the Academy of Country Music's video of the year award in 1992, and critics hailed McEntire's efforts. *Billboard's* Edward Morris reported, "Many of her music videos are so finely conceived and executed that they become works of art quite separate and distinct from the songs that inspired them."

McEntire's acting did not stop at videos. In 1989 she appeared on television, co-hosting *Good Morning America*. She followed this with a stab at the big screen, earning kudos for her portrayal of an arsenal-wielding survivalist in the 1990 camp horror film *Tremors*. She then joined fellow country singer Kenny Rogers in television's *The Gambler Returns: The Luck of the Draw* in 1991, starred with Burt Reynolds in the small screen's *The Man From Left Field* in 1993, and returned to theaters, filming *North* with director Rob Reiner.

By the mid-1990s it was abundantly clear that trying to pigeonhole McEntire was an essay in futility. She did not always please all her fans and critics, but she certainly kept them interested. In 1986, Nash made an observation in *Stereo Review* that characterized not only McEntire's music, but her entire career: "One of the great surprises about McEntire is that on first listening to one of her records, you miss about half of what she's doing because there's so much quality stuff happening. . . . But about the third time around, it starts to hit you just how first-rate McEntire's approach is." *Billboard's* Morris agreed that there is much more to McEntire than anyone first thought, venturing, "Few artist are as exciting to us five or 10 years into their careers as they were at the moment we 'discovered' them. With Reba McEntire, it's just the opposite. Certainly, her music was alluring when she made her recording debut . . . but it is infinitely more spellbinding now."

Fired by her love of music and competition, there seemed no course McEntire would not pursue. "I'm very competitive," she told television's *20/20* in 1993, as reported by *Entertainment Weekly*. "I want to beat the boys. I want to beat the girls. I want to beat rock & roll." This seemed quite possible when that year *It's Your Call* reached the Top Ten of the *Billboard 200* pop album chart and her *Greatest Hits Volume 2* debuted on Billboard's chart at Number Eight, peaking at Number Five. In 1985, McEntire had told Nash in a *Stereo Review* interview that she didn't feel she was yet a star. "Naw," she corrected, "I'm still just a twinkle." In 1994, with another feature film in the can, her albums staking their claim on various charts, and Bantam Books forking over a seven-figure advance for an autobiography, "the omnipresent McEntire," as Nash dubbed her in *Entertainment Weekly,* was clearly more than just a twinkle. The only remaining question was just how she would redefine the boundaries of stardom.

Selected discography

Singles; on Mercury

"Three Sheets in the Wind"/"I'd Really Love to See You Tonight," 1979.
"Sweet Dreams," 1979.
"(You Lift Me) Up to Heaven," 1980.
"You're the First Time I Thought About Leaving," 1983.

Albums

Reba McEntire, Mercury, 1978.
Out of a Dream, Mercury, 1979.
Feel the Fire, Mercury, 1980.
Heart to Heart, Mercury, 1981.
Unlimited (includes "I Can't Even Get the Blues"), Mercury, 1982.
Behind the Scenes, Mercury, 1983.
Just a Little Love, MCA, 1984.
My Kind of Country (includes "How Blue" and "Somebody Should Leave"), MCA, 1984.
Have I Got a Deal for You, MCA, 1985.
Whoever's in New England (includes "Whoever's in New England"), MCA, 1986.
What Am I Gonna Do About You, MCA, 1986.
Reba McEntire's Greatest Hits, MCA, 1987.
The Best of Reba McEntire: 1980-1983, Mercury/Polygram, 1987.
The Last One to Know, MCA, 1987.
Merry Christmas to You, MCA, 1987.
Reba (includes "Respect"), MCA, 1988.
Sweet Sixteen, MCA, 1989.
Reba Live!, MCA, 1989.
Rumor Has It, MCA, 1990.
For My Broken Heart (includes "The Night the Lights Went Out in Georgia" and "Is There Life Out There"), MCA, 1991.
It's Your Call (includes "It's Your Call," "Straight From You," and "Take It Back"), MCA, 1992.
Greatest Hits Volume 2, MCA, 1993.
(Contributor) "Since I Fell for You," *Rhythm Country & Blues,* MCA, 1994.

Sources

Books

Bufwack, Mary A., and Robert K. Oermann, *Finding Her Voice: The Saga of Women in Country Music,* Crown, 1993.

Stambler, Irwin, and Grelun Landon, *The Encyclopedia of Folk, Country and Western Music,* St. Martin's, 1983.

Periodicals

Billboard, June 10, 1989; February 1, 1992; May 8, 1993; September 4, 1993.

Country Music, November/December 1990; July/August 1991; January/February 1992; May/June 1992; July/August 1992; November/December 1992; January/February 1993; March/April 1993.

Entertainment Weekly, October 11, 1991; March 20, 1992; December 18, 1992; July 30, 1993, October 8, 1993; October 29, 1993.

High Fidelity, March 1985.

Ladies' Home Journal, November 1988; March 1994.

People, April 23, 1984; December 17, 1984; March 31, 1986; October 27, 1986; June 5, 1989; September 18, 1989; November 4, 1991; July 26, 1993.

Rolling Stone, August 29, 1985; December 3, 1987.

Time, June 19, 1989; January 22, 1990; January 25, 1993.

Recording Industry Association of America News, August 3, 1993.

Stereo Review, March 1984; April 1985; August 1985; July 1986; December 1986; December 1987; August 1988; January 1990; April 1993.

Wabash Plain Dealer (IN), March 18, 1992.

Woman's Day, November 3, 1992.

Additional information for this profile was obtained from liner notes to *It's Your Call,* MCA, 1992, and an MCA press release, 1993.

—*Megan Rubiner Zinn*

Maria McKee

Singer, songwriter

Singer and songwriter Maria McKee enjoys the odd claim to fame of having "broken through" to music celebrity twice—first as lead singer for the rockabilly band Lone Justice, then almost ten years later, as a solo artist. The first breakthrough, in the mid-1980s, occurred virtually overnight and earned Lone Justice what *People* music critic Craig Tomashoff called "a few minutes of fame"; in fact, they were the rage of Los Angeles clubs and airwaves during the summer of 1985. McKee's vocals, in particular, were hailed as the driving force behind the band. When Lone Justice fizzled, McKee attempted to shift gears into solo work; but her first solo album fell short of expectations, and by most accounts, McKee did not return to the path promised by her early work with Lone Justice until 1993, with the release of her second solo set.

McKee's career singing rockabilly and country music was actually not incongruent with her Los Angeles childhood. Born in Hollywood in 1965, McKee developed an early and unusual passion for 1930s Americana, artifacts of an era when country and western still reigned in rural America. This musical direction was influenced by McKee's parents, Jack, a carpenter, and Elizabeth, a painter, both of whom also shared the ownership of a neighborhood bar; by the 1970s they had adopted Baptist doctrine and would not allow rock and roll in their home. In 1985, McKee revealed to *Rolling Stone* interviewer Steve Pond, "My friends used to think I was weird because I was really into the Little Rascals and the 1930s, and my favorite movie stars were people like Joan Blondell." She further explained that she even kept her record player in her closet, maintaining, "I wanted the record to sound like it was old and far away, like a scratchy radio or something. I was really into . . . escaping into this era, this time of life I knew nothing about."

Wowed Guitarist at Drive-in Gig

McKee was also influenced by her half brother, Bryan MacLean, who played guitar with a popular 1960s psychedelic rock band called Love; McKee recalled going to L.A.'s famous Whisky A Go-Go to watch him play—though she was not yet six years old. By 1980 McKee, who would eventually drop out of Beverly Hills High, was devoting her time and talents to performing with local bands, including her brother's. Singing at a rockabilly concert held in the parking lot of a drive-in theater, McKee so impressed a young guitarist in the audience that he called her the next day. Ryan Hedgecock told *People* writer Todd Gold that he "was desperate to put a band together." That phone call would eventually blossom into Lone Justice.

For the Record. . .

Born c. 1965 in Hollywood, CA; daughter of Jack (a carpenter) and Elizabeth (a painter) McKee (parents co-owned a bar).

Began collaboration with guitarist Ryan Hedgecock, 1980; local club gigs as country duo led to formation of band Lone Justice, 1983, which included Marvin Etzioni on bass, Don Heffington on drums, and Tony Gilkyson (joined band c. 1984) on guitar; with Lone Justice, performed locally, 1983-1985; band signed with Geffen Records and released self-titled debut album, 1985; became solo performer and released Maria McKee, 1989.

Addresses: Record company—Geffen Records, 9130 Sunset Blvd., Los Angeles, CA 90069.

McKee recounted to Rolling Stone's Pond how simply the connection began: "Ryan came over to my house with his guitar . . . and we just sat around listening to rockabilly records." The listening gradually evolved into writing and playing together, and that collaboration led to engagements as a country duo at local clubs. McKee and Hedgecock began rather modestly, playing standards, but moved to their own music by 1983, when the duo grew into a band. They found experienced collaborators in bassist Marvin Etzioni and drummer Don Heffington, who had played with country veteran Emmylou Harris. With this line-up, Lone Justice took L.A.'s rockabilly scene by storm. McKee early on demonstrated considerable character and definition in her compositions, which, as Pond described them, "evoked a world of dust-bowl immigrants, migrant workers and skid-row habitués."

Created Sensation With Lone Justice

Pond also captured the band's reception in those first years: "Almost from the start, local critics raved about the group's sparkling mixture of galloping two-beat country music and Rolling Stones-style rawness—and particularly about . . . McKee, who's got striking, down-home good looks, a commanding stage presence, and, above all, a startling voice that captures simultaneously the sweetness of Dolly Parton and the grit of Janis Joplin."

Within a year, the band had added guitarist Tony Gilkyson and had secured a record contract with Geffen, a major rock label. Then, music critic Jon Pareles noted in Mademoiselle, "came the hard part—making an album whose songs were as strong as McKee's stage

presence." But veteran producer Jimmy Iovine seemed equal to the challenge. The eponymous album consolidated the band's local prominence and set a national reputation in motion; in the fall of 1985, Lone Justice hit the road. As Gold noted, praise for the album was "almost unanimous." Writing for Rolling Stone in 1987, Jimmy Guterman recalled that the "debut album revealed an astonishingly mature new band and a blockbuster talent in irrepressible singer and primary songwriter Maria McKee."

Although the band had little trouble living up to the high expectations set for their first album, they ultimately were not able to carry their momentum through to a second. Shelter, released in 1987, met with mixed reviews; the band's lineup and musical format had been changed, and critics and listeners were less sanguine this time around. The band disintegrated soon thereafter. McKee detailed her part in the breakup to Chris Morris of Billboard six years later, stating, "I claim full responsibility for the lack of focus. . . . I was 21 years old, and I had a record company that would give me money to do anything that I wanted. . . . I was just confused, very confused." At the time, however, Geffen had no intention of dismissing their still-promising songbird, and they prepared a solo album, Maria McKee, for release in 1989.

Hiatus in Ireland Preceded Triumphant Return

When the performance of the solo debut repeated the disappointment of Shelter, McKee decided that it was time for a hiatus from the music industry. She moved to Dublin, Ireland, in 1989, providing herself with a different atmosphere for her music. While there, she landed a single on the British charts, "Show Me Heaven," from the soundtrack to the film Days of Thunder. Ultimately, however, she felt the experience hindered rather than helped her, as she later told Morris: "I was flirting with all different kinds of music. I didn't know what I was gonna do. . . . I had written all these weird songs, everything from cabaret music to Kate Bush music." When she returned to Los Angeles to start work on a new album, she decided to put aside the experiments for her tried-and-true country sound.

Back with Geffen, she brought in producer George Drakoulias, who had scored recent successes with the Black Crowes and the Jayhawks. She also brought back Lone Justice mates Etzioni and Heffington. She told Morris, "I moved away, I got homesick, I missed my friends. I missed the music I grew up with, I missed that original celebration that Lone Justice had." And You Gotta Sin to Get Saved did, in fact, recreate much of the excitement that Lone Justice had incited ten years before.

Acclaim for *You Gotta Sin* was essentially universal. *People's* Tomashoff, for one, declared McKee "among the best vocalists and songwriters in the business." Thom Jurek of Detroit's weekly *Metro Times* echoed the enamored accolades of the first Lone Justice reviews; he saved his greatest enthusiasm for the song "My Girlhood Among the Outlaws," exclaiming, "[McKee's] country wail breaks out of itself, burns down the past and becomes a vehicle for transformation and change. Her confession registers not merely as atonement, but as a promise to rise from the ashes with her soul intact." Of the album itself, Jurek pointed out that McKee seemed finally to have reclaimed the potential of her first musical venture: "It reveals a singer exploring her talent (and its limits) in the music that inspired her in the first place. It also exposes a songwriter who has crawled back from the dark edge of an abyss to balance the ecstasies and excesses of language and sound by listening intently to the voice of her muse."

Selected discography

With Lone Justice

Lone Justice, Geffen, 1985.

Shelter, Geffen, 1987.

Solo albums

Maria McKee, Geffen, 1989.
You Gotta Sin to Get Saved (includes "My Girlhood Among the Outlaws"), Geffen, 1993.
(Contributor) "Opelousas (Sweet Relief)," *Sweet Relief: A Benefit for Victoria Williams,* Chaos/Sony, 1993.

Sources

Billboard, July 10, 1993.
Mademoiselle, August 1985.
Metro Times (Detroit), June 30, 1993; September 22, 1993.
Musician, July 1993.
People, September 28, 1985; July 5, 1993.
Rolling Stone, July 4, 1985; February 12, 1987; August 10, 1989; September 30, 1993.
Stereo Review, October 1989.

—*Ondine E. Le Blanc*

Zubin Mehta

Conductor, music director

Zubin Mehta is part of a group of conductors—one that includes Lorin Maazel, Seiji Ozawa, Claudio Abbado, André Previn, and Daniel Barenboim—that succeeded older luminaries such as George Szell, Leonard Bernstein, Georg Solti, and Eugene Ormandy in carrying on the American orchestral tradition while infusing it with freshness and vitality. At a time when ticket sales and subscriptions are down, conductors who can woo audiences—and win admiration from orchestra boards—are as sought after as major league pitchers; Mehta's name appears on nearly every short list made when a new conductor search is launched.

Mehta was born in 1936 in Bombay, India. His father was a violinist and founder of the Bombay Symphony. He attended college with the intention of becoming a doctor, but his plans, perhaps in an instance of predestination, changed; he was quoted as saying in the *New York Times,* "My father used to train every section of his orchestra at home, and so I grew up with the orchestra as an instrument. I didn't have perfect pitch. I preferred playing cricket to practicing the piano. But by the time I was 18, I knew that I had to take up music."

In 1954, Mehta went to Vienna to study at the world-renowned Academy of Music. He took conducting instruction from Hans Swarowsky, a pupil of the composer Richard Strauss, and lessons on double bass from Otto Rühm. Mehta also studied conducting in the late 1950s at the Accademia Chigiana in Siena, Italy, first with Carlo Zecchi and later with Alceo Galliera.

He won first place in the Liverpool International Conductors' Competition in England in 1958; this brought him a one-year assistant conducting position there. By 1961, he had become music director of the Montreal Symphony in Canada, and in 1962, he took on a concurrent appointment with the Los Angeles Philharmonic Orchestra. Mehta turned both ensembles into first-class symphonies, raising ticket sales and visibility.

In 1978, Mehta began an engagement with the New York Philharmonic Orchestra, considered by many the best ensemble of its kind in North America. When he took over the Philharmonic, critics and audiences were thrilled that a dynamic conductor known for his interpretations of late Romantic works would replace the ascetic, hyper-modern Pierre Boulez. "Under Mehta's spell," wrote Hubert Saal in *Newsweek,* "the Philharmonic has been born again."

Nonetheless, within two seasons critics began to carp—testimony, perhaps, to the notoriously fickle nature of symphony audiences and critics—and in 1985, Peter G. Davis remarked in *New York* magazine: "Does anyone care anymore? Mehta has few champions in the

For the Record. . .

Born April 29, 1936, in Bombay, India; son of Mehli Nowrowji (a violinist and conductor) and Tehmina Duruvala Mehta; married Carmen Lasky (divorced); married Nancy Kovack, 1969; children: (first marriage) Merwan (son), Zarina (daughter). *Education:* Attended St. Xavier's College, Bombay; Vienna Academy of Music, beginning in 1954; and Accademia Chigiana, Siena, Italy, late 1950s.

Held conductor posts in Yugoslavia, Belgium, and England, 1950s; music director, Montreal Symphony Orchestra, 1961-67, Los Angeles Philharmonic Orchestra, 1962-78, New York Philharmonic Orchestra, 1978-90, and Israel Philharmonic Orchestra, 1969—, appointed director for life, 1981; appeared as conductor at festivals of Spoleto, Vienna, Prague, Los Angeles, and Salzburg; made regular guest appearances with Vienna and Berlin Philharmonic Orchestras; appeared as conductor with Montreal, Metropolitan, and Covent Garden opera companies. Conducted tenors José Carerras, Placido Domingo, and Luciano Pavarotti in World Cup performance, Los Angeles, 1994.

Awards: First place, Liverpool International Conductors' Competition, 1958; recipient of Padma Bhushan (India), Médaille d'Or Verméil (Paris), and Commandre des Arts et des Lettres (France); honorary degrees from Tel Aviv University, Weizmann Institute of Science, Princeton University, Westminster Choir College, Hebrew University, Jewish Theological Seminary, Brooklyn College, and Colgate University.

Addresses: Office—Israel Philharmonic Orchestra, P.O. Box 11292, 1 Huberman St., 61112 Tel Aviv, Israel.

music press, and even his most vocal detractors, at one time a boisterous crew, have not had much to say recently. . . . Whatever controversy remains is carried on in a gray, listless fashion that reflects the kind of unimaginative programs and uneventful music-making heard too frequently these days in Avery Fisher Hall." When Mehta's second term with the Philharmonic expired in 1990, it was not renewed, and he was replaced by the German conductor Kurt Masur.

Mehta has weathered the rough tide of critical acclaim and rebuff with aplomb, always maintaining his good humor and professionalism. He is generally admired for his conducting technique, which is clear, precise, and without flamboyance, and for his deft handling of the often thorny politics of symphony orchestras—especially the demands of managers and board members. He is so beloved by the Israel Philharmonic, of which he has been music director since 1969, that he was appointed director for life in 1981.

The maestro lives in Israel with his second wife, Nancy Kovack, whom he married in 1969. He has two children from his first marriage—a son, Merwan, and a daughter, Zarina. He has won awards and citations from around the world, including numerous honorary degrees and the prestigious Commandre des Arts et des Lettres from the French government.

Selected discography

(Israel Philharmonic Orchestra) Bartók: *Concerto for Orchestra; Miraculous Mandarin Suite,* Sony Classical, 1990.
(Israel Philharmonic Orchestra; with pianist Radu Lupu) Beethoven: *Concerto No. 1 in C Major for Piano and Orchestra, Op. 15; Concerto No. 2 in B-flat Major for Piano and Orchestra, Op. 19,* London, 1990.
(Vienna Philharmonic Orchestra, with pianist Vladimir Ashkenazy) Beethoven: *Concerto No. 5 in E-flat Major for Piano and Orchestra, Op. 73,* London, 1985.
(New York Philharmonic Orchestra, with New York Choral Artists) Beethoven: *Symphony No. 9 in D Minor, Op. 125,* RCA, 1990.
(New York Philharmonic Orchestra) Mahler: *Symphony No. 1 in D Major,*CBS, 1983.
(New York Philharmonic Orchestra) Strauss: *Ein Heldenleben; final scene of* Salome, CBS, 1989.
(New York Philharmonic Orchestra) Stravinsky: *Petrouchka* (complete ballet), CBS, 1980.
Verdi: *La Traviata,* Philips, 1993.

Sources

Books

Bookspan, Martin, and Ross Yockey, *Zubin: The Zubin Mehta Story,* Harper & Row, 1978.

Periodicals

Los Angeles Times, February 5, 1991.
New York, January 14, 1985; June 10, 1991.
New York Times, November 19, 1978.
Newsweek, December 18, 1978.

—*Joyce Harrison*

Yehudi Menuhin

Violinist, violist, conductor

There are few great musicians whose careers have enjoyed both the productivity and longevity of Yehudi Menuhin's. Indeed, he was a child prodigy in the U.S. in the 1920s, as beloved by audiences as child film star Shirley Temple was in the '30s. But unlike many prodigies, his career has never waned. For decades he has been active not only in music, but also in promoting human rights and international understanding; as such, he is one of the world's most admired, respected, and honored figures.

Menuhin was born in 1916 in New York City to Russian Jewish immigrants who were both teachers. In 1918 the family moved to San Francisco. Because he exhibited a precocious interest in music, Menuhin's parents granted his request for a violin, and he began studying in the San Francisco area, first with Sigmund Anker and then with San Francisco Symphony Orchestra concertmaster Louis Persinger. His first professional appearance came at the age of seven, at Oakland Auditorium in Oakland, California.

Fate smiled on the Menuhins in 1924 when a family friend introduced them to Sidney Ehrman, a San Francisco lawyer and philanthropist. Ehrman was so taken by Yehudi's musical talent, and by that of his sisters Yaltah and Hephzibah, that he volunteered to pay for the family's expenses in order for the children to pursue their musical careers. His generosity allowed the family to go to Europe, where Yehudi studied with the violinist Georges Enesco; the family followed Enesco back to the U.S. in 1927.

It was that year that Menuhin made his Carnegie Hall debut, an appearance that launched him to instant stardom. He was a sensation—a mere boy of ten playing "grown up" concertos by Beethoven and Brahms with a mature understanding of the music that left observers breathless. After a concert he gave in Berlin in 1929, a wild-haired man approached Menuhin, embraced him, and exclaimed: "Now I know there is God in heaven!" The man was Albert Einstein.

During the 1930s Menuhin continued to give concerts, pursued a burgeoning recording career, and went on his first world performing tour, in 1935. During World War II he gave hundreds of concerts for Allied soldiers and relief organizations. He was the first foreign musician to perform in liberated Paris, and he played for prisoners who were awaiting liberation from the Bergen-Belsen concentration camp.

Menuhin's humanity is coupled with a serenity that he attributes largely to his discovery of yoga in the 1950s.

For the Record. . .

B orn April 22, 1916, in New York, NY; son of Moshe and Marutha Sher Menuhin (name originally Mnuchin; both teachers); married Nola Ruby Nicholas, 1938 (divorced); married Diana Gould, 1947; children: (first marriage) Zamira (daughter), Krov Nicholas; (second marriage) Gerard, Jeremy. *Education:* Studied violin with Sigmund Anker and Louis Persinger in California; Georges Enesco in Paris and Romania; and Adolf Busch in Basel, Switzerland.

Made professional debut, Oakland Auditorium, Oakland, CA, c. 1923; gave first recital, Scottish Rite Hall, San Francisco, 1925; (with New York Symphony Orchestra) made debut at Carnegie Hall, New York City, 1927; made first recordings, 1928; (with Bruno Walter and Berlin Philharmonic Orchestra) performed concerto program, Berlin, 1929; mounted first world tour, 1935; gave concerts for Allied troops and relief organizations, 1940s. Author of *Theme and Variations,* 1972, autobiography *Unfinished Journey,* 1977, and (with C. W. Davis) *The Music of Man,* 1980. Founded Yehudi Menuhin School, Surrey, England, 1962. Principal guest conductor, Warsaw Sinfonia, 1982—, English String Orchestra, 1988—. President and associate conductor, Royal Philharmonic, 1982—.

Awards: Nehru Award for Peace and International Understanding (India), Canadian Music Council Gold Medal, Kennedy Center Honor, Brahms Medal, Ordre des Arts et des Lettres (France), Légion d'honneur (France), Croix de Lorraine (France), Order of Merit (Germany); honorary knighthood from Queen Elizabeth II, 1965.

Addresses: *Record company*—Symphonic Music Co. Ltd., 65 Chester Square, London SW1, England.

His playing reflects his personality: it is lucid, straightforward, and earnest, without romantic sweep or emotional pathos. He is an impressive interpreter of such 18th-century composers as Bach and Mozart and is equally at home in the language of the 20th century; in fact, several composers, among them Béla Bartók and William Walton, commissioned works especially for Menuhin.

In 1959 Menuhin took up residence in England, and in 1962, he founded the Yehudi Menuhin School in Surrey, where intensive musical instruction is combined with traditional elementary and high school classes. Carrying on his role as a world citizen, Menuhin has championed jazz and non-Western music, performing with musicians such as Indian sitarist Ravi Shankar and French jazz violinist Stephane Grappelli.

Selected discography

As violinist

(Leipzig Gewandhaus Orchestra, Kurt Masur, conductor) Beethoven: *Violin Concerto in D Major, Op. 61,* Eterna, 1981.
Various composers: *Sir Yehudi Menuhin 75th Birthday Edition,* Angel.
Various composers: *Yehudi Menuhin Plays Popular Violin Concertos,* Angel.
(With Stephane Grappelli) *Jealousy,* Classics for Pleasure.

As conductor

(Royal Philharmonic Orchestra and Brighton Festival Chorus) Beethoven: *Symphony No. 9 in D Minor, Op. 125,* RPO.
(Sinfonia Varsovia) Mozart: *Symphony No. 40 in G Minor, K. 550; Symphony No. 41 in C Major, K. 551,* Virgin Classics.

Sources

Books

Daniels, Robin, *Conversations With Menuhin,* St. Martin's, 1980.
Menuhin, Yehudi, *Theme and Variations,* Stein & Day, 1972.
Menuhin, Yehudi, *Unfinished Journey,* Knopf, 1977.

Periodicals

Commentary, July 1977.
New Yorker, October 8, 1955; October 15, 1955.
New York Times, August 12, 1991.
U.S. News & World Report, April 13, 1987.

—Joyce Harrison

Midnight Oil

Rock band, activists

In 1990 the Australian band Midnight Oil gave a lunchtime performance at the headquarters of Exxon in New York City. Before some 10,000 bewildered onlookers, the quintet offered a typically raucous set to protest the Exxon Valdez oil spill in Alaska. A video documentary of the concert titled "Black Rain Falls" was issued shortly thereafter, with proceeds going to the environmental group Greenpeace.

Midnight Oil has, in fact, combined an acute awareness of political, social, and environmental issues with an aggressive rock sound to create one of the most distinctive voices in current popular music. From the moving depiction of the plight of Australian aborigines featured on the 1987 album *Diesel and Dust,* to the bitter commentary of "My Country," about America's Iran-Contra scandal, found in 1993's *Earth and Sun and Moon,* Midnight Oil's "agit-rock," as *Rolling Stone's* David Fricke once called it, has urged their audience to dance—and think.

For the Record. . .

Members include **Peter Garrett** (received law degree from University of New South Wales), vocals; **Bones Hillman** (born in New Zealand), bass; **Rob Hirst**, drums; **Jim Moginie**, guitar; and **Martin Rotsey**, guitar. Other members have included bass players **Peter Gifford** (left group c. 1988) and **Andrew "Bear" James** (left group 1980).

Band formed in Sidney, Australia, 1976; released self-titled debut on own label, Powderworks, 1978; signed with Columbia Records, 1982, and released *10,9,8,7,6,5,4,3,2,1*; Garrett ran for Australian Senate on Nuclear Disarmament Party ticket, 1984; mounted international tour, c. 1988; performed at Exxon Building, New York City, to protest Exxon Valdez oil spill, 1990; released film documentary, *Black Rain Falls*. Band has worked in suppport of numerous activist organizations including Greenpeace, the Movement Against Uranium, and Save the Whales. Garrett was president of Australia Conservation Foundation, 1991, and is a board member of Greenpeace.

Addresses: *Record company*—Columbia Records, P.O. Box 4450, New York, NY 10101.

The original nucleus of Midnight Oil was made up of drummer Rob Hirst, guitarist-keyboard player Jim Moginie, and bassist Andrew "Bear" James. The three friends began playing together in Sidney in 1971 and by 1972 had founded Farm, a group that performed cover versions of songs by Led Zeppelin, Cream, and Creedence Clearwater Revival. The group gained some media attention by touring Australian coastal resorts during the summer.

A Punky Pub Attack

In 1976 Farm advertised for a lead singer and found one in Peter Garrett, then on leave from law studies. Garrett shaved his head— adding a striking visual element to the group that would become the singer's trademark—and the band toughened up its sound, developing what Fricke called "something akin to the early-seventies Who with a leaner, punkier pub attack." Later that year, guitarist Martin Rotsey rounded out the group and the ensemble changed its name to Midnight Oil.

By 1978, Midnight Oil, under the able guidance of manager Gary Morris, had begun to find a wide audience through explosive live performances at inner-city pubs in Sydney, Melbourne, and Adelaide. Inevitably, the band was approached by record company executives, but in order to maintain control over their music, the bandmembers decided to form their own, independent label, Powderworks, on which the first, self-titled Midnight Oil album was released in June of 1978.

In November of 1978 Midnight Oil began to build a reputation as political activists by playing a concert at Sidney Town Hall to protest Australia's policy on uranium mining. Within a few months, the group was playing benefit concerts for the Save the Whales and Greenpeace organizations, Garrett eventually joining the latter as board member.

For the next several years Midnight Oil continued to record and toured England and the U.S. They received a great deal of press—especially when Garrett decided in 1984 to run for the Australian Senate on the Nuclear Disarmament Party ticket—yet commercial success remained beyond their reach; as drummer Hirst told *Rolling Stone's* Fricke, "We were the best-known band in America never to sell records." It was not until the group began to take a closer look at what was occurring literally in their backyard that Midnight Oil finally exploded onto the international scene.

Chronicled Plight of Aborigines

In July of 1986 the group mounted what it called its "Black Fella White Fella" tour, during which it traveled to some of Australia's most remote aboriginal settlements with the Warumpi Band, itself made up of aboriginal musicians. While performing in these far-flung spots, the group witnessed directly the atrocities that Australia's native people have suffered at the hands of white settlers in over 200 years of colonization; they saw communities devastated by poverty and disease.

Shocked and confounded, the group immediately began writing material for a new album. *Diesel and Dust* was released in August of 1987, and despite the ugliness of its subject matter and angry sound—grippingly captured by Garrett's anguished and commanding vocals—the album became a worldwide success and spawned the group's first hit single beyond their native shores, "Beds Are Burning." The record prompted a major tour of Australia, followed by extensive jaunts through Europe, the U.K., and North America. Although the group had existed for 12 years, audiences all over the world began discovering Midnight Oil for the first time.

Blue Sky Mining, the follow-up to *Diesel and Dust*, featured a change in personnel; Peter Gifford, who had replaced James on bass, was himself replaced by New

Zealander Bones Hillman. The focus of the new record was more expansive; songs like "Blue Sky Mine" and "Stars of Warburton" continued to address topics specifically concerning Australia, but others, such as "Antarctica" and "One Country," took a more global view. Another commercial success, the disc was Midnight Oil's most critically acclaimed effort to date and prompted another round of international touring.

Expanded Activism

In 1991, the members of Midnight Oil took a year off, though they continued to remain politically active, giving a series of outdoor benefit concerts for the homeless and Garrett spending a year as president of the Australian Conservation Foundation. In 1992 the group issued a compilation of live performances called *Scream in Blue,* which Fricke evocatively described as "real guitar nirvana: crisp, catalytic agit-twang, pregnant with steely menace, shivering with skittish vibrato and erupting in enraged screams of ice-pick feedback."

Midnight Oil's tenth studio album, *Earth and Sky and Moon,* retreated from the studio slickness of *Diesel and Dust* and *Blue Sky Mining* in order to recapture the rough-edged sound of the band's early pub days. To record the set, the group rented a small facility near Sidney's international airport—"our own little grunge hole," as Garrett described it to *Billboard*—and relied on spontaneous musicianship rather than hi-tech wizardry. The result was a highly personal collection of what *Billboard's* Melinda Newman called "stripped down, thunderous music."

During their discussions with Newman the fiercely self-reliant group also addressed their 1982 move to the major label Columbia. "Coming over to Columbia was always a big step for us as an independent-minded band," admitted Garrett, "and part of it was predicated on the basis that Oils is Oils; what you see is what you get." The singer continued, explaining, "Our deal works in a different way to how must people's arrangements work in that it has more of our own underwriting and control in it."

Though Midnight Oil has maintained their status as what Garrett somewhat jokingly referred to in *Billboard* as a "terminally serious band appearing at the right places for the right things," they have lightened their image somewhat. Garrett went on to admit, "You can't be 100 percent politically, ideologically, ecologically, musically, spiritually, socially correct. You can only do it on your own level." Even as the group continues to spread its message with conviction, it remains at heart a hard-driving, no-frills rock band.

Selected discography

Midnight Oil, Powderworks, 1978, reissued, Columbia.
Head Injuries, Powderworks, 1979, reissued, Columbia.
Bird Noises (EP), Powderworks, 1980, reissued, Columbia.
Place Without a Postcard, Powderworks, 1981, reissued, Columbia.
10,9,8,7,6,5,4,3,2,1, Columbia, 1982.
Red Sails in the Sunset, Columbia, 1984.
Species Deceases (EP), Columbia, 1985.
Diesel and Dust (includes "Beds Are Burning"), Columbia, 1987.
Blue Sky Mining (includes "Stars of Warburton," "Antarctica," and "One Country"), Columbia, 1989.
(Contributors) "Wharf Rat," *Deadicated,* Arista, 1991.
Scream in Blue, Columbia, 1992.
Earth and Sun and Moon (includes "My Country"), Columbia, 1993.
(Contributors) *Alternative NRG,* Hollywood, 1994.

Sources

Billboard, May 1, 1993.
Detroit Free Press, August 6, 1993.
Entertainment Weekly, May 22, 1992.
Musician, June 1993.
Rolling Stone, July 9, 1992; June 10, 1993; August 19, 1993.
Spin, June 1993.

Additional information for this profile was obtained from Columbia Records press materials, 1993.

—Jeffrey Taylor

Mitch Miller

Producer, music director, conductor, oboist

Many associate Mitch Miller with his pop hit "The Yellow Rose of Texas" or his early 1960s "Sing Along" television programs and records. But Miller established his early reputation as an oboist at the Eastman School of Music in Rochester, New York. He played for noted conductor Leopold Stokowski and made some of the earliest chamber jazz recordings with Alec Wilder.

After playing in the Syracuse and Rochester symphony orchestras, Miller moved to New York City in the 1930s, joining the CBS Symphony Orchestra in 1936. His experience with live recording soon landed him a job as an A&R (Artists & Repertoire) representative at Mercury Records, where his responsibilities included scouting and recruiting talent, matching singers and musicians with suitable material, and making sure their records were produced properly. In this capacity he produced the work of such pop legends as Patti Page and Frankie Laine.

Miller moved to Columbia Records in 1950, taking it from fourth to first place in music industry revenues with singers like Tony Bennett, Rosemary Clooney, and Johnny Mathis. Throughout his early career as a music director, he was known for innovative combinations of singers and songs, in an age when most performers did not write their own material. He was also known for strange—if not downright quirky—orchestrations, using the harpsichord on popular recordings and producing classical recordings without strings for Columbia's Golden Recordings for children.

Though he signed the great gospel singer Mahalia Jackson to Columbia and had great success with jazz musicians like Erroll Garner and Charlie Parker, for whom he produced a record with string accompaniment, as the 1950s progressed, Miller was increasingly viewed as an obstacle to change—he reviled rock and roll. After producing his popular Sing Alongs, he turned to guest conducting, leading various symphonies around the world, including the London Symphony Orchestra.

Classical Upbringing

Much about Miller remained a mystery to the public at large until Ted Fox's two-part interview with him for *Audio* magazine appeared in 1985. Aptly titled "Mitch Miller: A Hidden Classic," it revealed much about Miller's early musical education. His father, a Russian immigrant who worked as a toolmaker and wrought-iron worker, bought the family a piano when Miller was six; Miller and his two older sisters were given weekly lessons. But living in Rochester may have been the key factor in Miller becoming a musician, for George East-

For the Record. . .

Born July 4, 1911, in Rochester, NY; son of a tool maker and wrought-iron worker; married Frances Alexander. *Education:* Graduated (*cum-laude*) from Eastman School of Music, early 1930s.

Played oboe with Syracuse and Rochester symphony orchestras; joined CBS Symphony Orchestra, 1936; worked as producer and A&R rep for Mercury Records; joined staff of Columbia Records, 1950; produced television program *Sing Along With Mitch,* 1960-64; international guest conductor of symphony orchestras.

man, of the Rochester-based firm Eastman Kodak, had endowed the first public school system music program there, donating instruments to the schools provided that they would supply instruction.

When he was 11, Miller heard about the program and applied for an instrument. His friends all got brass instruments, but he was left with the oboe, a difficult woodwind consisting of a long tapered chamber that employs a double reed. In fact, as he stated in the *New Yorker,* Miller didn't even realize at first that the instrument used reeds or that each player must make his or her own. Fortunately, his father made him the tools he needed, though he could not pass on the arcane and jealously guarded secrets of the professional oboist.

At 14 Miller began lessons at the Eastman School of Music, and by 15, he had secured a position with the Syracuse Symphony Orchestra. When he was 18, he attended the Eastman School on a full-time scholarship and eventually managed to graduate *cum-laude* despite his reputation for hijinks. He moved to New York City in 1932, and though the nation was struggling with the Great Depression, he was quickly able to find a steady job with the CBS orchestra. In the meantime, he had gotten married. He was soon making a good living doing additional solo work and landing regular spots with the Andre Kostelanetz and Percy Faith orchestras, as well picking up jobs cantering around the city.

The 1930s allowed Miller to hone his playing, as he constantly moved from classical music, to jazz, to soundtracks for radio shows, like the Orson Welles Mercury Theatre "War of the Worlds" broadcast that fooled much of America into believing that a Martian invasion was in progress. But more important to his later career was his exposure and interest in recording technology. In the days before magnetic tape, recordings were made directly to a master print; it was thus crucial to achieve a balanced sound through rehearsal

and the careful placement of specialized microphones. In *Audio,* Miller revealed that the great music directors "Kostelanetz and Stokowski knew more about sound and microphone technique than almost anyone else, and I was able to learn plenty from them."

Putting on the Hits

Miller didn't consider the move from classical to popular music unusual, noting that his friends at Eastman were constantly listening to the jazz and pop music of Louis Armstrong, Duke Ellington, Ella Fitzgerald, and Bing Crosby. He earned his reputation as a capable producer while still working as a sideman, suggesting that more takes be recorded of rehearsals, so that good performances, particularly by soloists, would not be wasted. It was not long before he was summoned by future Columbia A&R great John Hammond to Keynote Records, which would later become Mercury, to do some classical recordings, one of which won a prize in 1948. Hammond suggested he do some popular records, so Miller went to work with Frankie Laine, Vic Damone, and Patti Page. Miller explained in *Audio* that the producer's job is to get the best out of the artist, maintaining, "Many times the artist doesn't know what his best characteristics are, and you're there to remind them. You can't put in what isn't there, but you can remind them of what they have and they're not using."

Frankie Laine's recorded output is a good example of Miller's work in the 1950s. Miller had an impression of Laine as a blue-collar singer, and looked for material to fit that image. Songs like "Mule Train" connected Laine's listeners to the mythical West that went so far in shaping the country's concept of itself. In fact, Miller made a name for himself by producing pop cover versions of the best country western music of the day; acting on a tip from Atlantic Records co-founder Jerry Wexler, he started listening to country great Hank Williams.

Tony Bennett scored a hit with a Percy Faith arrangement of Williams's "Cold Cold Heart," and soon Miller had an exclusive agreement with Fred and Wesley Rose, Williams's publishers, to place the country star's songs with pop artists. Miller also reversed the country crossover process, choosing the pop tune "A White Sport Coat and a Pink Carnation" for country singer Marty Robbins. Success in this area continued for several years—until country writers started writing expressly to cross over and the songs lost their verve. Miller's now-legendary tenure at Mercury also produced novelty songs like "I Saw Mommy Kissing Santa Claus" and saw unusual pairings such as pop crooner

Dinah Shore backed by bagpipes and singer Burl Ives supported by a Dixieland band.

Miller moved to Columbia Records in 1950, in part because Mercury tried to extract payment from him for shares in the company that he had been promised as condition of his employment there. At Columbia, he continued to nurture pop stars like Johnny Mathis and Rosemary Clooney and made Ray Conniff's career by giving him a chance to produce a new choral sound using voices as instruments.

But perhaps the most important aspect of Miller's early career at Columbia was in studio technique. Monaural tape became available in 1951; Miller commented on the then-new medium in *Audio:* "I used the same technique as before, because with monaural tape you could not remix; even with stereo tape there was no remixing. It wasn't until they had multiple tracks that you could remix. The technique when tape first came in was that you could use a big chunk of something, and you could save some good performances." Before tape, and, Miller claimed, before the breakthrough work of guitarist Les Paul and singer Mary Ford, he helped pioneer the technique of overdubbing—in which recordings on various "tracks" are laid over each other to produce a richer, more interesting effect—with Patti Page and Jack Rail on "Money, Marbles and Chalk."

Developed Image Problem

The Columbia years were also famous for Miller's Monday sessions, in which he opened his doors for anyone with a song to pitch. Though this might have seemed a good way to keep the business fresh and the pipeline filled with material, it also reinforced Miller's status as an all-powerful arbiter of what the public got to hear, a charge he disputed on the grounds that the market ultimately determined his success and popularity, not the other way around. He recorded bandleader Duke Ellington and blues singer Big Bill Broonzy and contributed to the folk craze of the early 1950s by covering Weavers songs like "Tzena, Tzena, Tzena" and "Goodnight Irene," but he was vocally opposed to rock and roll, calling it "musical illiteracy." Steadfast in this view, Miller was accused of being unwilling to change.

Indeed, there was a perception that the success of his Sing Along television shows and records depended on a world that no longer existed; writing about a new Sing Along special in the works for 1981, Dick Hyman suggested the "quaintness" of Miller's specialty in *Contemporary Keyboard,* reporting, "Miller's show was built around a 25-voice male chorus with an orchestral combination of accordion, bass, drums, harmonica, and three guitars doubling on ukulele and banjo, a somewhat folksy mix often featured around campfires, country fairs, and other wholesome American venues."

But Miller told a different story about his opposition to rock and roll in *Audio,* citing his refusal to pay "payola"—monetary inducement to radio personnel to spin a given record—and his aversion to "British-accented youths ripping off black American artists and, because they're white, being accepted by the American audience," valid criticism of the new form echoed by others in the industry. Miller left Columbia in 1961; he continued to work on his weekly NBC television show, *Sing Along With Mitch,* until it was canceled in 1964 in favor of programming targeted toward the increasingly sought-after youth market, though ratings for the show were high.

Since then Miller has been guest-conducting symphony orchestras in the Americas and Europe. In 1989, he earned good notices for a Gershwin program with the London Symphony Orchestra. And according to *Entertainment Weekly,* in 1992, at the age of 83, he made five grueling bus tours for Bill Clinton's presidential campaign.

It was perhaps fitting that Miller ultimately returned to classical music, the pop sensations of the '50s on whom most of his reputation rests having long faded. As a leader of a symphony orchestra, he was able to direct timeless pieces, choosing from the greatest selection of "songs." Aside from his seeming inability to progress with popular tastes, Miller's well-documented ego and aggressive personality may also have influenced the way history has treated him. For many a product of the rock age, it is perhaps easier to hold him up to ridicule—his Sing Along version of John Lennon's "Give Peace a Chance" is included on Rhino Records's *Golden Throats 2*—than it is to recall, as folksinger Pete Seeger did in his book *Where Have All the Flowers Gone,* the time Miller helped lead thousands in that song during the 1970s at a rally to end the Vietnam War. Nonetheless, Miller's importance to the history of the music industry, and to the history of popular music itself, is beyond question.

Selected discography

Holiday Sing-Alongs With Mitch, CBS, 1987.
16 Most Requested Albums, Columbia/Legacy, 1989.
Mitch's Greatest Hits, Columbia, 1989.
Favorite Irish Sing-Alongs, Columbia/Legacy, 1992.
34 All Time Great Sing-Along Selections, Columbia.
Christmas Sing-Along With Mitch, Columbia.

Memories: Sing Along With Mitch Miller, Columbia.

Sources

Books

Seeger, Pete, *Where Have All the Flowers Gone: A Singer's Stories, Songs, Seeds, Robberies,* Sing Out Publications, 1993.

Periodicals

Audio, November 1985; December 1985.
Contemporary Keyboard, April 1981.

Entertainment Weekly, November 20, 1992.
Instrumentalist, January 1989.
Musical Opinion, February 1989.
Music Journal, Number 3, 1961.
Music Quarterly, Number 4, 1990.
New Yorker, June 6, 1953.
Ovation, December 1985.
Symphony, Number 6, 1991.
Variety, September 25, 1985.

—*John Morrow*

Naughty by Nature

Rap group

Since the release of their single "O.P.P." in 1991, the rap group Naughty by Nature has been hailed by their fans and reviewers as the embodiment of the "street"—the day-to-day existence of the inner-city, African-American population that gave birth to rap. Ed Lover, co-host of *Yo! MTV Raps,* described his impression of Treach, lead rapper and unofficial head of the group in *Vibe* magazine: "Treach is the first authentic hip-hopper I've seen in a long time. . . . Yeah, he wants to get his, like everybody else, but there's a sincerity there too. Look at him; you can see that he's had a hard life, and it comes out in his music. His hard-core ain't made-up; it's real." Treach and his Naughty colleagues, DJ Kay Gee and rapper Vinnie, appreciate such compliments and intend to maintain their street credentials. Indeed, despite the double-platinum success of their first two albums, all three have remained in the East Orange, New Jersey, neighborhood where they grew up.

Treach and Vinnie, born Anthony Criss and Vincent Brown, respectively, spent their 1970s childhoods only a few blocks away from one another. Both have credited much of their experience on the street to the difficulties of growing up in poor, single-parent homes. Treach's mother had to work full-time, as a nurse, while she raised her two sons. Partly from her experience, Treach has become a strong proponent of birth control and support for the black family, often expressing his belief that his father's absence contributed to his years on the street.

Hooked Up for High School Talent Show

Although none of the three felt that East Orange High School had much to offer them, it was there that they began rapping. According to *Vibe's* Kevin Powell, "Treach knew he wanted to be a weaver of words—a rapper—since he was in the seventh grade." Treach and Vinnie first collaborated in order to enliven a junior-year health class: whenever the class became unbearably dull, they would break into an improvised rap, Treach rapping and Vinnie providing the beat. Friend Kay Gee, who was a year ahead of Treach and Vinnie in school, in the meantime had been polishing his skills as a DJ. When the senior talent show came up, Kay Gee asked his "homeboys" to perform with him. They walked away with the adulation of their audience.

Up to this point, aside from occasional jobs, the main occupation of the Naughty boys had been hanging around with their neighborhood gang, the 118th Street Posse. That life offered some income, largely from the drug trade or other illegal sources, and plenty of risk: fights, shootings, and jail time. After graduating from high school, Treach briefly held a job at Grand Union

For the Record. . .

M embers include **Kay Gee** (born Kier Gist c. 1970 in East Orange, NJ), turntables; **Treach** (born Anthony Criss c. 1971 in Newark, NJ; son of a nurse), vocals; and **Vinnie** (born Vincent Brown c. 1971 in East Orange), vocals.

Group formed for high school talent show, c. 1987; performed locally as the New Style; recorded album *Independent Leaders*, Bon Ami, 1988; signed with Tommy Boy Records, 1990; released single "O.P.P." and album *Naughty by Nature*, 1991.

Awards: Double-platinum single for "O.P.P.," 1991, and "Hip Hop Hooray," 1993; double-platinum album for *Naughty by Nature*, 1991, and *19NaughtyIII*, 1993; named best new artist of 1991 by the *Source*; American Music award for best new rap group, 1992.

Addresses: *Record company*—Tommy Boy, 902 Broadway, New York, NY 10010.

warehouse, but he was laid off and soon landed in jail. When his mother came to bail him out, she told him not to come home, and he ended up sleeping wherever he could—including on a bench in the park. A few years later, he reflected on that experience to Gavin Edwards of *Details,* saying, "She had to do what she had to do. I wasn't contributing to paying the bills. I ain't gonna freeload."

Motivated by the talent show success, the trio dubbed themselves the New Style and began performing locally. It was a significant change for all three—a bona fide chance to escape the dead end of the ghetto. Powell described the life they could look forward to in East Orange without such an opportunity, writing, "Packed tightly on many of these blocks are legions of young black men drifting somewhere between poverty and death. Each year some of these boy/men graduate from the city's two public high school's—East Orange and Clifford Scott—into a shapeless, unpredictable future."

Hustled to Finance Demo

The New Style's shot at a breakthrough came in 1988, when they released *Independent Leaders* on a small record label called Bon Ami. But neither the label nor the group's manager, Sylvia Robinson, were adequately prepared to produce or market the rappers, and the

album failed to make a mark. Dropped by the label, Treach, Vinnie, and Kay Gee were forced back to the street, but all had developed a new sense of purpose and direction: they wanted to make a strong demo tape to impress producers. Mostly through hustling drugs on the street, they were able to put enough money away within one year. Treach explained to Tom Sinclair of *Spin,* "I did what I had to do on the street so I could get mine and not have to do it no more. . . . We didn't put our money into jewelry or cars or anything like that. We put it into studio time. And, once we got signed, we cut [drug dealing] out completely."

After a name change, Naughty by Nature sent their work to every label that handled hip-hop, including Tommy Boy, one of the more intrepid marketers of rap. But, in that first round of promotion, no one appeared to be interested. By 1990, however, the three young men had secured a recording contract with Tommy Boy. Various accounts have surfaced as to the mechanics of this coup, but all feature Queen Latifah, a major name in rap, and the management company she formed, the Flavor Unit.

Tommy Boy publicity maintains that Naughty by Nature were discovered when Queen Latifah and Shakim Campare, another Flavor Unit staffer, were invited to a party where Naughty by Nature performed. *Vibe's* Powell, however, heard a different version of the discovery from Vinnie: "Kay Gee called Latifah's producer, DJ Mark the 45 King, and he camcordered us performing in his basement. That tape started the buzz." Powell also outlined an incident that seems to corroborate Tommy Boy's account; it involves a fund-raiser at Upsala College that the trio, then still the New Style, put together for themselves and at which Latifah and Campare caught their act. Here the stories converge; Latifah, mightily impressed, signed Naughty by Nature to the Flavor Unit and secured them a deal with Warner Bros. for a debut album that was eventually released under the auspices of Tommy Boy.

Boosted by Queen Latifah

Latifah also engineered Treach's first real exposure to the public. In an article for the *Source,* Adario Strange reported that Treach caused a sensation at the Building, a Manhattan club, when Latifah invited members of the audience to perform. Strange mused, "Who would have guessed that a year later thousands would dress like Treach, braid their hair like him, steal his stage moves, use his rhyme style, and run around in Naughty by Nature underwear?" In 1991 Alan Light recounted a similar story in *Rolling Stone,* though the performance under discussion took place at the Apollo Theater, in December of 1990: "As Latifah delivers an adept human beatbox, Treach stuns the Apollo with a quick-fire precision freestyle, bringing the place to its feet when he wraps up his rhyme with 'my pants always sag 'cause I rap my ass off.'"

The group's debut album, *Naughty by Nature,* hit record stores in 1991; it had been preceded that June by the single "O.P.P." Driven by an irresistible sample of the Jackson Five's "ABC," the song did more than top the charts and sell two million copies; it entered into street slang across the country and inspired a slew of merchandise, including t-shirts and hats, that declared "Down Wit O.P.P." "O.P.P." is basically a sly tribute to cheating on one's lover, with the titular initials generally understood to signify "Other People's" and then penis, or a slang term for female genitalia beginning with the letter P, depending on the singer's sex. Benny Medina, the Warner Bros. executive who offered Naughty by Nature their record contract, told *Vibe's* Powell about the first time he heard "O.P.P.," remembering, "I'd never heard anyone use a Jackson sample before, and with the grooves, the smooth bass line, and melodic structure, it was a totally new sound. I thought we'd have a fairly successful record, but no way did I know it was going to be *the* phrase, *the* rap song of the year." Soon after its release, the album supported by "O.P.P." went double platinum.

Still, instant stardom did not lead to the "fat" life that many associate with success in the music industry—testimony to the principles of the Naughty trio; all three reinvested their profits from the album, pursuing a variety of business ventures under the aegis of the band. Naughty Gear, a line of merchandise renowned for its underwear sporting the band's logo, has taken off under Kay Gee's guidance. They also began their own label, Illtown Records, and management company, 118th Management, in order to widen the market for rap. Kay Gee set up his own production company, 118th Productions, and subsequently produced "Hit Em Hard" for rap greats Run-D.M.C. After participating in the production of Naughty by Nature's videos, Treach began directing clips for other artists, including Apache's popular "Gangsta Bitch." And Naughty by Nature have insisted on reserving positions in their businesses for friends from the neighborhood—especially those finishing prison sentences—since they know firsthand the scarcity of legitimate, decent-paying jobs in the ghetto.

Though avoiding the trappings of wealth, Treach has paid for his mother to return to school and is determined to buy her a house. He explained to Strange the decision not to move into a wealthy neighborhood, reasoning, "We still live in Illtown and we still hang with the same people. We still see the things that go on everyday in the 'hood, so we can't lose touch. It's the same situation as before we came out with the record except we don't have to hustle anymore. We still see things like drugs, murders and police harassment everyday."

When "Hip Hop Hooray," the lead single from *19NaughtyIII,* Naughty by Nature's second album, was released in the spring of 1993, it became a sensation akin to the one "O.P.P." had created two years earlier. The song climbed to the Top Ten of the pop charts and was universally recognized as the hip-hop anthem of the summer. Although it did not have quite the video success of "O.P.P.," which had risen to Number One on *Yo! MTV Raps,* "Hip Hop Hooray" did enjoy the distinction of having been directed by Spike Lee, the filmmaker responsible for *Do the Right Thing* and *Malcolm X.* *19NaughtyIII* was equally as commercially successful as the group's debut, also selling double platinum, but reviewers were somewhat more restrained in their praise. James Bernard of *Entertainment Weekly* applauded Treach and Vinnie's mike skills, allowing, "The bass and drum beats stumble over each other here, pushing both rappers . . . to favor dense, intricate deliveries and tough-guy lyrics," but he criticized the music, carping, "There are some melodies that'll make you hum now but make you scream after hearing them for the umpteenth time."

The shortcomings of that effort notwithstanding, critics for the most part continued their love affair with the group. *Spin's* Sinclair, for example, fondly noted Naughty by Nature's dedication to their music, explaining, "There's a zealousness in NBN's embrace of hip hop as a musical form, a stance, a life-style that eclipses all else. They're lifers." He also highlighted their appeal as ambassadors of another life, writing, "Naughty by Nature are homies with heart, happy to have left behind the world of drug-dealing to bring their message of hope through hip hop to a few more ghetto bastards. They're a bridge between the daisy age and the gangsta era." Powell, finally, awarded Treach the highest praise in his description of a Naughty by Nature performance: "There are no gimmicks, no fancy stage design . . . and no dancers. Treach is just a regular brother from around the way, rippin' the mike and doin' it because he loves his craft. [Treach] *is* hip-hop: in dress, in talk, in spirit."

Selected discography

(As the New Style) *Independent Leaders,* Bon Ami, 1988.
Naughty by Nature (includes "O.P.P."), Tommy Boy, 1991.
19NaughtyIII (includes "Hip Hop Hooray"), Tommy Boy, 1993.

Sources

Details, May 1993.
Entertainment Weekly, March 5, 1993.
Rolling Stone, October 17, 1991; June 10, 1993; August 19, 1993.
Spin, April 1993.
Source, March 1993.
Vibe, Fall 1992.

Additional information for this profile was provided by Tommy Boy Records, 1993.

—Ondine E. Le Blanc

Willie Nelson

Singer, songwriter, guitarist

The long and prolific career of Willie Nelson—not to mention his personal life—has been quite a roller coaster ride, slow moving at the start, then climbing straight to the stars, dipping to a heart-rending low, and finally, running straight and true once more. As Cheryl McCall of *People* wrote, "An instant success after 25 years trying, Willie didn't cut a big-selling album until he was 40." Once Nelson's career took off, however, he became "an inadvertent and unassailable national monument." And his output has been prodigious, numbering well over a hundred albums. In the early 1990s, though, Nelson had to overcome two crushing events—a multimillion-dollar battle with the U.S. Internal Revenue Service and the suicide of his oldest son. But, demonstrating an indomitable spirit, he managed to bounce back in 1993 with a new recording that a number of critics called his best in years, in fact, one of his best ever. "Imagine answering a late-night phone call from a friend who's been in a coma, only to find him lucid, clever, and loving as ever. That's what *Across the Borderline* feels like," noted Burl Gilyard of *Request,* adding, "[it is] an album that embodies the artistry, ambition, and amazing grace of Nelson's '70s breakthroughs."

Nelson was born on April 30, 1933, in Abbott, Texas. The country was mired in the Great Depression and times were rough for the little farming community. When Nelson was six months old, his mother left to find a job and never returned. Nelson and his older sister, Bobbie, were then raised by their paternal grandparents, strict, church-going people. They were also devoted amateur musicians who pushed the children into music and performing, teaching both Nelson and his sister how to play an instrument. Nelson's grandfather, a blacksmith by trade, gave him his first and only training on the guitar. His grandmother taught Bobbie how to play piano. Nelson told Teresa Taylor Von-Frederick of *McCall's* that his grandparents were "his true, and earliest, inspiration."

Although his grandparents raised him and his sister to be "solid Methodists and obedient kids," Nelson related in *Willie: An Autobiography,* he strayed from the straight and narrow early. Drinking and smoking were forbidden, yet, "I can't tell you how many Sundays I would be singing in the choir . . .," he revealed, "and my heart would be sad because I was thinking I was going to fry in hell because I had already drunk beer and smoked."

Nelson worked in the cotton fields after school to help bring in some money for the family. And by the age of 10, he was an accomplished enough musician, along with his sister, to begin playing at local dances. After his grandfather died, Nelson learned songs listening to the

For the Record. . .

Born Willie Hugh Nelson, April 30, 1933, in Abbott, TX; son of Ira (a mechanic) and Myrle (a homemaker) Nelson; raised by paternal grandparents; married Martha Matthews, 1952 (divorced, 1962); married Shirley Collie (a singer), 1963 (divorced, 1971); married Connie Koepke, 1971 (divorced, c. 1989); married Anne-Marie D'Angelo (a makeup artist), 1991; children: (first marriage) Lana, Susie, Billy (deceased); (third marriage) Paula Carlene, Amy; (fourth marriage) Lukas, Jacob. *Education:* Attended Baylor University, c. 1950.

As a child, taught to play guitar by grandfather; performed at local dances with sister; joined John Raycheck polka band, c. 1945; worked as disc jockey, San Antonio, TX, 1953; worked as disc jockey in Fort Worth, TX, and Vancouver, British Columbia, Canada; recorded first single, "No Place for Me," 1957; worked as encyclopedia and vacuum cleaner salesman, taught Sunday School, and performed in local clubs, Ft. Worth; joined Larry Butler band, Houston, 1958; sold first song, "Family Bible," c. 1958; worked as songwriter for Pamper Music, Nashville, beginning c. 1960; played bass with Ray Price's Cherokee Cowboys; recorded and performed with Shirley Collie; performed at dance halls and county fairs, Austin, TX; signed with Atlantic Records, c. 1971, and released *Shotgun Willie,* 1973; signed with Columbia Records, 1974, and released *Red Headed Stranger,* 1975; recorded and toured extensively, 1980s; organized first Farm Aid benefit, 1985. Actor, beginning in 1979. Author (with Bud Shrake) of *Willie: An Autobiography,* Simon & Schuster, 1988. *Military service:* U.S. Air Force, c. 1950.

Selected awards: Numerous Country Music Association and Grammy awards, including CMA entertainer of the year, 1979, and Grammy Award for lifetime achievement, 1989; inducted into Nashville Songwriters Association Hall of Fame, 1973; named top album artist of 1976 by *Billboard;* inducted into Country Music Association Hall of Fame, 1993.

Addresses: *Management*—Mark Rothbaum & Associates, Inc., P.O. Box 2689, Danbury, CT 06813-2689.

radio. "He'd pick up things just like that," sister Bobbie told *People*'s McCall. "His ear is so fantastic, *he* doesn't even know how good he is." When Nelson was in the sixth grade, he got his first professional job, with the John Raycheck Band, an Abbott polka outfit that played the bohemian clubs in the area. Needless to say, Nelson's grandmother was horrified that he was play-

ing in beer joints. But it was undeniable that he could make much more money there than in the cotton fields.

As a teenager, Nelson and his sister played in a band that her husband, Bud Fletcher, put together. Fletcher was able to land steady bookings for the group, and they would play whatever the club owner wanted, Nelson honing his craft and broadening his horizons.

Turbulent Early Years

After graduating from high school Nelson joined the U.S. Air Force. But he received a medical discharge after just nine months because of an earlier back injury. He returned to Abbott and formed a band and again started playing in local clubs. He attended Baylor University but quickly dropped out. He also fell in love and married Martha Matthews—he was 18 years old; she was 16. From the start, they struggled to make ends meet and soon began fighting regularly. "She was a full-blooded Cherokee," Nelson told *People,* "and every night with us was like Custer's last stand. We'd live in one place a month, then pack up and move when the rent would come due." Nelson was making as little as 50 cents a night with his band.

The honky tonks and beer joints that were Nelson's second home were rough, rowdy places where the band had to be shielded from flying bottles by chicken-wire fences. In 1953, Nelson and his wife moved to San Antonio, and he landed a job as a disc jockey. He also continued to play his music at clubs in the evenings. He and Martha went back to Abbott for the birth of their first child, Lana. They then moved to Fort Worth, where Nelson got another disc jockey job.

The family next moved west, and eventually Nelson got a job as a disc jockey in Vancouver, Canada. In 1957, his second child, Susie, was born. Also in 1957, Nelson recorded his first single, "No Place for Me." He produced the record himself and promoted and sold it over the radio. With two children and his wife pregnant with a third, Nelson decided to try a regular job. Moving back to Fort Worth, he became an encyclopedia salesman, then worked as a vacuum cleaner salesman. But he soon went back to performing in clubs. He taught Sunday school for a while, but when the congregation complained about him playing in beer joints, he quit.

Sold First Song for $50

Nelson's third child, son Billy, was born in 1958. The family moved to Houston, and Nelson was invited to join Larry Butler's band. He played with the band six nights a week and had a disc jockey job on Sundays. Since the mid-1950s, Nelson had been writing songs, and he now tried to sell some to help support his family. He sold his first, "Family Bible," for $50 to pay for food and rent. It eventually became a Number One country hit. He then sold another song, "Night Life," for $150. "Night Life" went on to become one of the most-recorded songs ever. Performed by more than 70 artists, it has sold more than 30 million records, though Nelson never made a dime off the royalties. Nelson then moved to Nashville to take his shot at the big time.

In Nashville, musician and songwriter Hank Cochran helped Nelson get a job as a songwriter with Pamper Music. And by 1961, several of Nelson's songs had been recorded by country performers and had become hits. "Hello Walls" was released by Faron Young; "Crazy" was recorded by Patsy Cline (and became a classic); and Billy Walker did "Funny How Time Slips Away." Besides becoming country hits, "Hello Walls" and "Crazy" also made the pop Top 40.

Nelson next joined Ray Price's band, the Cherokee Coyboys, as a bass player. Although he was now collecting royalty checks for his songwriting, plus a salary from the band, Nelson spent his money as fast as he made it. His already stormy marriage deteriorated. He began recording his own songs but did not meet with much success. Nelson then got together with singer Shirley Collie and recorded a couple of songs, "Willingly" and "Touch Me," that became Top 10 hits. Nelson started dating Collie, and when his wife found out, she packed up the kids and left for Las Vegas to get a divorce. Nelson formed a small band with Collie and went on the road. In 1963, Collie filed for divorce from her husband, and she and Nelson married. The couple bought a farm near Nashville, and Nelson's children moved back in with him. Collie then became a housewife, while Nelson went on the road alone. She accepted this arrangement at first but after a while became restless and resentful.

Throughout the 1960s, Nelson's own recordings sold few copies. He had an unusual voice—high and quavering—and he favored uncommon phrasing. His music did not fit the traditional Nashville mold, so it was considered uncommercial and as such, his records were not adequately promoted. Nelson was signed by Nashville record companies primarily for his songwriting talents. "They grudgingly allowed me to sing as long as they could cover up my voice with horns and strings," he stated in his autobiography.

By 1968, Nelson's second marriage was foundering. He then met a woman at one of his concerts named Connie Koepke. He and Koepke soon fell in love. A year later, wife Shirley opened a hospital bill that came in the mail and discovered that Nelson had fathered a child by Koepke. She and Nelson split up, and Koepke and child moved in.

The night before Christmas Eve, 1969, Nelson was at a party when he was told that his house had burned to the ground. When he arrived at the scene of the fire, he rushed into the smoking remains to grab a guitar case containing two pounds of marijuana. He was worried that the authorities would find it and he would go to jail. Nelson has long used marijuana and considers it a medicinal herb, calming and instrumental in containing his tremendous energy. "Most people smoke to get high," a friend remarked to McCall, "Willie smokes to get normal." (Rumor has is that the singer even smoked a joint on the White House roof during the Jimmy Carter era.) But Nelson prohibits his bandmembers from using any other drugs, particularly cocaine. "If you're wired," he has said, "you're fired."

Life Among the Outlaws

With his home devastated and his Nashville recording career going nowhere, Nelson decided to move the family to Texas. He settled in Austin, which was becoming the home of the "outlaws"—country singers like himself who could never quite fit in back in Nashville. These included Waylon Jennings and Kris Kristofferson. Nelson started touring the area's dance halls and county fairs and developed a growing following. In the early 1970s, he began sporting the distinctive look he wears to this day: long hair—often fashioned in two braids— and beard, bandanna headband, jeans, and running shoes.

In April of 1971, Connie Koepke became Nelson's third wife, though he was still married to the fomer Shirley Collie at the time. About six months later, Shirley was granted a divorce. Around this time, Nelson signed a contract with Atlantic Records, which allowed him to use his own band to record. Previously, he had been forced to use studio musicians. He had always objected to this approach, since he felt that by working with him for just a few hours, the studio musicians could not get a true feel for his particular style of music.

In 1973 Nelson released the album *Shotgun Willie;* it outsold all his previous albums combined. Also in 1973, Nelson was inducted into Nashville's Songwriters Hall of Fame, and his first Fourth of July picnic—a rock-style country festival—attracted a crowd of 50,000, including rock and rollers, as well as country fans.

Atlantic dropped its country division in 1974 and Nelson signed with Columbia Records, where he finally enjoyed complete creative control over his recordings. In 1975 he released the album *Red Headed Stranger*,

---

"When I was 15 and thought about a 60-year-old person, I figured they were real old and had one foot in the grave. I really don't feel that way right now. I don't have anything to retire into or for. All I do is make music and play golf, and I wouldn't want to give up either one."

---

which became a major hit; the LP rose to Number One on the country charts and also cracked the Top 40 of the pop charts. A single from *Stranger*, "Blue Eyes Crying in the Rain," became a Top 10 hit and won Nelson his first Grammy Award. At long last, he had become a star.

By 1976 Nelson was selling records like crazy. Seven of his albums appeared on the *Billboard* charts that year. Gold and platinum records were rolling in. Then, in 1978, Nelson tried a new direction, releasing an album of pop standards called *Stardust*. It included such songs as the title track, by Hoagy Carmichael, and "Blue Skies," by Irving Berlin, both remade in Nelson's unique style. The set of covers became a country and pop hit. David Gates of *Newsweek* noted, "The archetypal country outlaw reinvented himself as a singer beyond categories; [*Stardust* has] sold more than 4 million copies."

As *Stardust* demonstrated, even when Nelson sang other people's songs, he would truly make them his own. "Everything he does, he reinterprets," wrote Frank McConnell of *Commonweal*. His versions of pop classics are "a reclamation and rediscovery of songs we thought we had already heard too often." *Request's* Gilyard concurred, maintaining, "Nelson's truest gift is his instinctive genius for interpretation. . . . Singing ballads as effortlessly as he exhales, Nelson can even infuse pure corn . . . with genuine feeling."

In 1979, Nelson ventured into acting, taking a supporting role in the film *Electric Horseman,* which starred

Jane Fonda and Robert Redford. He then costarred in the 1980 movie *Honeysuckle Rose,* which was based loosely on his life. Other films followed, including *Barbarosa* in 1982, as well as television movies, such as 1986's *Stagecoach.*

A song Nelson wrote for *Honeysuckle Rose,* "On the Road Again," reached Number One on the country charts and became a Top 20 pop hit; it also became the singer's unofficial theme song. Nelson continued to release successful singles and albums over the course of the 1980s. He also toured extensively throughout the United States and overseas, regularly spending as many as 250 days a year on the road.

In 1985 Nelson organized the first Farm Aid benefit concert. He had witnessed the plight of the nation's farmers and wanted to do something to assist them. "A farmer told me there had been four suicides in the neighborhood, and I could feel how on edge *he* was. Another said that he'd lost his farm, and his wife had left him, and he couldn't find any other work," Nelson told Ellen Hawkes of *Ladies' Home Journal*. "Well, I know what it's like to feel down, and once I realized how bad the farm crisis was, I had to help." Farm Aid has become a yearly event, featuring a variety of musical performers and earning millions of dollars for farm groups.

By the end of the decade, Nelson's marriage to third wife Connie was breaking up. He next took up with Anne-Marie D'Angelo, a makeup artist he had met while filming one of his movies, and had two more children. They married in 1991. Discussing his marriages, Nelson told *Redbook*, "It's not easy being married to a man like me. It's asking a lot to let your husband run around the world, flirting with pretty girls who flirt back. That's a hard one. It's pretty obvious that entertainers marry and remarry . . . more than anyone else. I think it's because they're away from home so much and the temptations are so great."

The year 1991 began and ended with two shattering personal crises. At the end of 1990, the I.R.S. seized Nelson's properties and possessions to settle a tax debt totaled at $32 million. The agency had disallowed various tax shelters. The figure was later reduced to $16.7 million, but in January of 1991, the I.R.S. held what *Newsweek's* Gates termed a "humiliating" auction of all of Nelson's possessions. Friends and supporters stepped in and tendered bids, purchasing his property and allowing him to remain on the premises until he could buy it back. One friend bought his home, another his Pedernales Country Club and Recording Studio.

Nelson sold an album that year through an 800 number—*Who'll Buy My Memories: The I.R.S. Tapes*—to help pay off the seemingly insurmountable debt. He also toured heavily. Then, on Christmas Day of 1991, Nelson's son Billy was found dead, a suicide by hanging. *People* reported that Billy had suffered alcohol problems and "a history of despondency." He lived mostly off an allowance from his father. "I've never experienced anything so devastating in my life," Nelson admitted to a friend. Reflecting further on his troubles, he told Alanna Nash of *TV Guide,* "I think everything we go through is a test. I don't think we're ever asked to endure anything that we can't endure." Nelson put his faith in the power of positive thinking. "I guess I'm just living in the present," he said to Nash. "So far, more good things have come along, and the more I think that way, the more positive things happen. That's how I keep it together."

Eventually, Nelson's I.R.S. debt was negotiated down to $9 million. By 1993, he had paid off about half and had agreed to a schedule to pay off the rest. More importantly, Nelson released a daring new album in 1993, *Across the Borderline,* that was widely praised by critics. Stephen Holden of *Rolling Stone* reported that the record, produced by pop producer Don Was, "seasons the singer's own brand of austere, hard-chugging country swing with echoes of everything from English art rock to Paul Simon's South African-flavored folk rock. These hybrids are remarkable for their lack of clutter and their ultimate fidelity to Nelson's plain-as-dirt sensibility." Ken Tucker of *Entertainment Weekly* called the disc "shockingly good." He added, "Nelson has now topped [Garth] Brooks in the creation of an album that cuts across the borderline of country into every precinct of pop." Jay Cocks of *Time,* for his part, referred to Nelson's album as a "singular achievement" and remarked that "*Across the Borderline* will fix him for good right where he belongs, among the best of American music." Indeed, duets with pop stars Sinead O'Connor, Bonnie Raitt, and Bob Dylan, as well as songs by Dylan, Paul Simon, and Lyle Lovett ensured the record's success with country *and* pop fans.

That triumphant year Willie Nelson also turned 60—an age he never expected to see as a performer. He told Gary Graff of the *Detroit Free Press* that he originally saw himself retiring at 50 and getting a job as a disc jockey at "some small country station somewhere. Then I'd really enjoy life—ride my horses and play golf." Nelson continued, "When I was 15 and thought about a 60-year-old person, I figured they were real old and had one foot in the grave. I really don't feel that way right now. I feel pretty good, in fact. Besides, I don't

have anything to retire into or for. All I do is make music and play golf, and I wouldn't want to give up either one."

Selected discography

. . . And Then I Wrote, Liberty, 1962.
Here's Willie Nelson, Liberty, 1963.
Country Willie—His Own Songs, RCA, 1965.
Hello Walls, Sunset, 1966, reissued, Pickwick, 1978.
Country Favorites—Willie Nelson Style, RCA, 1966.
Country Music Concert, RCA, 1966.
Make Way for Willie Nelson, RCA, 1967.
The Party's Over, RCA, 1967.
Texas in My Soul, RCA, 1968.
Good Times, RCA, 1968.
My Own Peculiar Way, 1969.
Columbus Stockade Blues, RCA/Camden, 1970.
Both Sides Now, RCA, 1970.
Laying My Burdens Down, RCA, 1970.
Willie Nelson and Family, RCA, 1971.
Yesterday's Wine, RCA, 1971.
The Words Don't Fit the Picture, RCA, 1972.
The Willie Way, RCA, 1972.
Country Winners, RCA/Camden, 1973.
Shotgun Willie, Atlantic, 1973.
The Best of Willie Nelson, United Artists, 1973.
Spotlight on Willie Nelson, RCA/Camden, 1974.
Phases and Stages, 1974, reissued, Atlantic, 1991.
What Can You Do to Me Now, RCA, 1975.
Red Headed Stranger, Columbia, 1975, reissued, 1982.
Country Willie, United Artists, 1975.
(Contributor) *Texas Country,* United Artists, 1976.
Willie Nelson and His Friends, Plantation, 1976.
Columbus Stockade Blues, reissued, Pickwick, 1976.
(Contributor) *The Outlaws,* RCA, 1976.
Willie Nelson Live, RCA, 1976.
The Sound in Your Mind, Columbia, 1976.
The Troublemaker, Columbia, 1976.
Willie/Before His Time, RCA, 1977.
To Lefty From Willie, Columbia, 1977.
There'll Be No Teardrops Tonight, United Artists, 1978, reissued, Liberty, 1984.
Stardust, Columbia, 1978, reissued, 1980.
(With Waylon Jennings) *Waylon and Willie,* RCA, 1978.
Willie and Family Live, Columbia, 1978.
Willie Nelson Sings Kristofferson, Columbia, 1979.
Pretty Paper, Columbia, 1979.
(Contributor) *The Electric Horseman* (soundtrack), Columbia, 1979.
(With Leon Russell) *One for the Road,* Columbia, 1979.
Willie Nelson: Country Superstar, Candelite Music, 1980.
Honeysuckle Rose (soundtrack), Columbia, 1980.
(With Ray Price) *San Antonio Rose,* Columbia, 1980.

Family Bible, MCA/Songbird, 1980.

Danny Davis and Willie Nelson, RCA, 1980.

The Minstrel Man, RCA, 1981.

Once More With Feeling, RCA, 1981.

Somewhere Over the Rainbow, Columbia, 1981.

Willie Nelson's Greatest Hits, Columbia, 1981.

The Best of Willie, RCA, 1982.

(With Jennings) *WW II,* RCA, 1982.

Always on My Mind, Columbia, 1982, reissued, 1983.

(With Merle Haggard) *Poncho & Lefty,* Epic, 1982.

(With Roger Miller) *Old Friends,* Columbia, 1982.

(With Webb Pierce) *In the Jailhouse Now,* Columbia, 1982.

Willie Nelson: The Ghost, Solid Gold Productions, 1982.

The Best of Willie Nelson, Liberty Special Products, 1982.

(With Jennings) *Take It to the Limit,* Columbia, 1983.

Without a Song, Columbia, 1983.

Tougher Than Leather, Columbia, 1983.

On My Way, RCA, 1983.

Bandanna Land, H.S.R.D., 1983.

Don't You Ever Get Tired of Hurting Me, RCA, 1984.

City of New Orleans, Columbia, 1984.

Angel Eyes, Columbia, 1984.

(With Kris Kristofferson) *Music From Songwriter* (soundtrack), Columbia, 1984.

Replay: Willie Nelson, Sierra Records, 1984.

Willie Nelson, RCA, 1985.

Willie, RCA, 1985.

Stardust (Classic Nelson), CBS, 1985.

Half Nelson, CBS, 1985.

Me and Paul, Columbia, 1985.

(With Jennings, Kristofferson, Johnny Cash, and Johnny Rodriguez) *The Highwaymen,* Columbia, 1985.

(With Faron Young) *Funny How Time Slips Away,* Columbia, 1985.

(With Hank Snow) *Brand on My Heart,* Columbia, 1985.

Willie Nelson: A Portrait in Music, Premier Records, 1985.

Mellow Moods of the Vintage Years, 82 Music Co., 1985.

Partners, CBS, 1986.

The Promiseland, CBS, 1986.

Island in the Sea, CBS, 1987.

(With Haggard) *Seashores of Old Mexico,* Epic, 1987.

(With Haggard and George Jones) *Walking the Line,* Epic, 1987.

(With Bobbie Nelson) *I'd Rather Have Jesus,* Arrival, 1987.

What a Wonderful World, Columbia, 1988.

A Horse Called Music, Columbia, 1989.

(With Cash, Jennings, and Kristofferson) *Highwaymen II,* Columbia, 1990.

Born for Trouble, Columbia, 1990.

(With Jennings) *Waylon and Willie: Clean Shirt,* Epic, 1991.

Who'll Buy My Memories?: The IRS Tapes, Columbia, 1991.

Across the Borderline, Columbia, 1993.

(Contributor) *Asleep at the Wheel: A Tribute to the Music of Bob Wills and the Texas Playboys,* Liberty, 1993.

Moonlight Becomes You, Justice Records, 1994.

The Classic, Unreleased Collection, Rhino, 1994.

The Early Years, Scotti Bros., 1994.

Sources

Books

Nelson, Willie, and Sheldrake, Bud, *Willie: An Autobiography,* Simon & Schuster, 1988.

Periodicals

Ann Arbor News (MI), July 5, 1993.

Billboard, October 2, 1993; December 11, 1993.

Commonweal, October 4, 1985.

Country Music, March/April 1993; May/June 1993.

Detroit Free Press, April 16, 1993.

Entertainment Weekly, April 2, 1993.

Guitar Player, November 1993.

Ladies' Home Journal, September 1987.

McCall's, May 1988.

Newsweek, March 22, 1993.

People, September 1, 1980; March 4, 1991; January 13, 1992; June 21, 1993.

Redbook, December 1984.

Request, April 1993.

Rolling Stone, August 28, 1986; March 7, 1991; May 13, 1993.

Time, May 17, 1993.

TV Guide, November 21, 1992.

Vanity Fair, November 1991.

—Greg Mazurkiewicz

New Order

Contemporary dance band

The synthesizer-driven British dance outfit New Order had the birth of a phoenix—it rose from the ashes of an influential new wave band called Joy Division. Joy Division ceased to exist when Ian Curtis—the vocalist and core of the band—took his life on May 18, 1980. As a result, the new venture of surviving members Bernard Albrecht, Peter Hook, and Stephen Morris, New Order, was guaranteed media attention, a decidedly mixed blessing in the midst of overwhelming shock and grief and the doomed reputation foisted on them by their colleague's suicide.

Joy Division was developed gradually, in 1977 and 1978, by four teenage chums from Manchester, England. None were musicians or even terribly interested in music—until they went to a local club one evening in 1976 to hear the notorious punk band the Sex Pistols. The Manchester group was gripped by the musical and cultural revolution they saw happening there, and they were determined to be a part of it. Since none of them had any proficiency with the mechanics of music, they experimented for a while, each trying out a different

For the Record. . .

Members include **Gillian Gilbert** (born January 27, 1961, in Manchester, England), guitar, keyboards; **Peter Hook** (born February 13, 1956, in Manchester), bass; **Stephen Morris** (born October 28, 1957, in Cheshire, England; and **Bernard Sumner** (born Bernard Dicken on January 4, 1956, in Manchester; known as Bernard Albrecht while with Joy Division), vocals, guitar.

Hook, Morris, and Sumner were member of Joy Division; formed New Order, 1980; released single "Ceremony," Factory Records, and album *Movement,* Factory/Qwest, 1981; established reputation as dance band with "Blue Monday," 1983; after 1989, bandmembers pursued solo projects, including Sumner's work with Electronic, Hook's with Revenge, and Gilbert and Morris's as the Other Two; collaborated to produce England's World Cup theme, "World in Motion," 1990, and album *Republic,* Qwest, 1993; headlined England's Reading Festival, 1993.

Awards: BRIT award for best music video, 1987, for "True Faith"; gold record for "World in Motion," 1990.

Addresses: *Record company*—Qwest Records, 3800 Barham Blvd., Ste. 503, Los Angeles, CA 90068.

instrument, except for Curtis, who quickly took charge of vocals and most of the songwriting. It was his hypnotic, hair-raising voice and style—characterized by enigma and raw emotional pain—that gave the band its identity.

Crest of English New Wave

The quartet remained in this embryonic stage, trying on a variety of names and maturing musically until 1978, when they released their first EP, *An Ideal for Living.* This earned them some notice in the Manchester music scene, where they generally fit into the industrial punk flavor of the moment but to which they also offered something unique, a slower, more dense, and somewhat dirge-like sound—one that would, in fact, become the progenitor of the new wave style known as "gothic." In retrospect, author Brian Edge claimed in his musical biography of the band, *New Order and Joy Division,* that they were at the "forefront" of what amounted to a musical "renaissance." It would be another year, however, before their reputation began to match their innovation; the album *Unknown Pleasures,* released in 1979 on Factory Records, catapulted Joy Division to the top of the English new wave scene, which was just becoming commercially viable.

Over the next year, the four young men toured the U.K. and Europe, appeared at music festivals and on English television, and weighed persistent contract offers from major record labels. But, they chose not to defect from Factory Records, the small label that had taken them on when they were still virtually unknown and which allowed them to focus on polishing their music. In May of 1980 they were preparing to leave for their first U.S. tour when Curtis hanged himself. There was no hard-and-fast evidence to explain why someone just emerging into fame and fortune would make this choice, but music writers and friends have since cited general depression fed by marital problems and an increasingly deteriorating epileptic condition as contributing to Curtis's untimely death.

The singer's bandmates never entertained the possibility of continuing Joy Division without him. Chris Heath, a music writer for *Details,* recalled, "In Britain, even before Curtis's suicide, they were considered accessories to his vision. For the remaining three members to continue was equivalent to the Doors without Jim Morrison." Instead, they tried to uncover the essence that remained. Naturally, the May tour scheduled for the United States was canceled, but Albrecht—who had now changed his name to Sumner (though he was born Dicken)—Hook, and Morris were forced to set up new dates for September in order to satisfy contractual obligations. After their return to England in October, they asked Gillian Gilbert to bring her experience on keyboards and guitar to their ensemble. At this point, vocal duties were shared, but Sumner gradually took over the role of singer, also playing guitar. By late December the four were in the studio recording as New Order.

Identity Crisis

The band released several singles and one album over the next few years, attracting attention from the media and the public because of their previous incarnation, but not quite breaking through in their own right. A London show scheduled for the Heaven Club in February of 1981, intended to be a secret, instantly sold out. But New Order's releases of that year, the single "Ceremony" and the album *Movement,* could rise no higher on the U.K. charts than the Number 30 spot. In 1982, "Temptation" inched only to Number 29. The band's showing in the United States was even less remarkable. Part of the problem was that the music still sounded too much like Joy Division, with the same dark intensity but without Curtis's vocals, and therefore couldn't seem to fulfill the immense promise that Curtis's death had derailed.

In 1982, however, New Order happened onto a path that would prove the route to their distinct musical identity; the group invested in a new nightclub in Manchester, the Haçienda Club, which catered to a dance trend growing out of the Puerto Rican and gay dance clubs in New York City. New Order began to move away from the punk roots of Joy Division to embrace this movement, mastering its insistent rhythm and polished, synthesizer-laden melodies. When they released "Blue Monday" in the spring of 1983, they leapt to the vanguard of the new dance beat, claiming the Number 12 spot on U.K. charts and, by that fall, breaking into the U.S. Top Ten. Their virtual obscurity in America vanished overnight, their singles becoming requisite club fare across the Atlantic.

The next album, *Power, Corruption, and Lies,* reached the Number Four spot on the U.K. charts, establishing New Order's importance in the English music market for good. While their releases still tended to jump around the charts in the U.S., their performance became stable in England, where *Lowlife* in 1985 and *Brotherhood* in 1986 held Top Ten positions. Qwest Records, which released the band's work stateside, described their centrality to the English music scene in a 1993 press biography, stating, "By 1987, New Order's Haçienda Club [had] developed the style which would become known as "Manchester"—a mixture of working class soccer fashions, [the drug] Ecstasy, and American house and acid house music." "Blue Monday" garnered over three million in sales worldwide and become the best-selling 12" single ever produced. By the time 1989's *Technique* was released, the band's popularity was such that the record immediately took the Number One position on the British charts.

Became Institution

New Order had somehow become an English institution. They were hired to compose and record themes for British television, including one for televised soccer matches—as important as Monday Night Football in the United States—in 1989. The true laurel from mainstream English culture came in 1990, however, when the band received a commission to create a theme for England's World Cup football squad. The resultant release, "World in Motion," held the top spot on U.K. charts in the spring of 1990 and quickly went gold. Perhaps even more indicative of their importance, though, was the tremendous influence they were clearly having on the nascent "rave" music and its attendant dance-as-ritual subculture.

Despite the band's unshakable popularity in England at this time, internal strife was threatening to tear it apart. First Sumner, then Hook, took time off from New Order to pursue work with separate bands. Sumner's project, formed in 1988 with ex-Smiths guitarist Johnny

---

In May of 1980 they were preparing to leave for their first U.S. tour when Curtis hanged himself.

Marr and called Electronic, was so successful with its 1989 single "Getting Away With It" that the singer was encouraged to take even more time off from New Order. Then the stress of New Order's 1989 American tour wore the bandmembers down, landing Sumner in a Chicago hospital for what he described to *Details* contributor Heath as an "overindulgence of a naughty nature." Hook began moonlighting with Revenge in 1990; finally, in 1992, Morris and Gilbert reinvented themselves as a duo called the Other Two. By this time, the putative sweethearts had already pursued various independent projects, including music for the network series *America's Most Wanted.* By 1992 the band's fans were beginning to suspect that New Order might have actually disintegrated for good.

The spring of 1993, however, saw the release of a new single, "Regret," and a new album, called *Republic,* that did not necessarily guarantee the band's future as an integrated entity, but which did prove that they could still produce music together—music that earned both critical and commercial attention, *Republic* landing at Number 11 in the U.S. and selling 500,000 copies— when they made the effort. Heath described *Republic* as "a record born of compromise between four people bound together by history and habit, which shows the fruitful corners into which compromise can force you." In the June issue of *Spin,* however, Eric Weisbard expressed ambivalence, writing, "I especially like "Chemical" for being the one vigorous use of techno shimmy. Too bad there isn't more like that here—a few less rainy-morning-after ponderances and some stains on its precious aura would have done this legendary band good."

With the long break that preceded *Republic,* it remained unclear what the band would do—if anything— after its release. Heath pursued the question with Sumner and Hook, turning up only uncertain responses: "Will this be the last New Order album? I ask them if they believe, in their heart of hearts, there will be another. Bernard says, 'I'm really enjoying being New Order at this moment, but the honest answer is I don't know.' Peter says, 'I don't know, really.'"

Selected discography

Singles

"Ceremony," Factory Records, 1981.
"Temptation," Factory, 1982.
"Blue Monday," Factory, 1983.
"Confusion," Factory, 1983.
"World in Motion," 1990.

Albums

Movement, Factory/Qwest, 1981.
Power, Corruption, and Lies (includes "Blue Monday"), Factory/Qwest, 1983.
Lowlife, Qwest, 1985.
Brotherhood, Qwest, 1986.
Substance, Qwest, 1987.
Technique, Qwest, 1989.
Republic (includes "Regret" and "Chemistry"), Qwest, 1993.

Sources

Books

Edge, Brian, *New Order and Joy Division: Pleasures and Wayward Distractions,* Omnibus Press, 1988.
Rees, Dafydd, and Luke Crampton, *Rock Movers and Shakers,* ABC/CLIO, 1991.

Periodicals

Billboard, September 4, 1993.
Details, August 1993.
Musician, July 1993.
Rolling Stone, September 15, 1983; June 24, 1993.
Spin, January 1993; June 1993; September 1993.
Time, June 28, 1993.

Additional information for this profile was obtained from Qwest Records publicity materials, 1993.

—Ondine E. Le Blanc

Yoko Ono

Singer, composer, artist

Yoko Ono has been sending shock waves through the worlds of art and music since the early 1960s. Although many think she never would have recorded a note if not for her association with John Lennon, Ono had been a musical performer for 11 years before marrying the late Beatle. By the mid-1990s, many critics had reevaluated her musical history, deeming her songs ahead of their time and influential to such cutting-edge musical entities as Public Enemy, Sonic Youth, and the B-52's. In fact, *Onobox*, a 1992 retrospective of Ono's solo work, received widespread critical acclaim. "That she [Ono] made music of marginal worth is repudiated once and for all by this lavish, illuminating six-CD overview of her remarkable pop life," attested David Fricke in *Rolling Stone.*

Born into a prominent Tokyo banking family in 1933, Yoko Ono—"Ocean Child" in Japanese—was burdened with the high musical expectations of a father who had wanted to be a concert pianist. Inevitably, his plans to create a musical prodigy backfired, leading Ono to dislike "accepted" music. After her family moved to the U.S. in 1951, Ono became fascinated with twelve-tone composers such as Alban Berg while attending Sarah Lawrence College. Her own compositions at school were judged too radical by her music teacher.

In 1957 Ono married composer Toshi Ichiyanagi and moved to a loft in New York City's Greenwich Village. Embracing the avant garde, she began displaying her conceptual art and staging "events" organized by eccentric composer La Monte Young. Young was part of a movement known as Fluxus that attempted to break free from conventional standards of art and music. Ono's creative output was greatly influenced by John Cage, a iconoclastic composer whose work incorporated disorder and randomness. Her first musical performance, in 1961 at the Village Gate in New York, featured mumbled words, laughter, atonal music, and an actor speaking in monotone. Perhaps not surprisingly, Ono's early work was largely ignored, and critics referred to it as little more than screaming or moaning.

After divorcing Ichiyanagi, Ono married avant-garde artist Tony Cox in 1964. The couple made a series of bizarre films in London, including 1967's *Bottoms,* which consisted solely of close-ups of 365 bare backsides. In Paris she met jazz saxophonist Ornette Coleman, who further stimulated her interest in vocal experimentation. Her songs tapped an eclectic blend of inspirations, including Berg's operettas, the Japanese Kabuki singing called *hetai,* Indian and Tibetan vocal techniques, and free jazz. Referring to these antecedents, Kristine McKenna wrote in the *Los Angeles Times,* "Ono synthesized those elements into sound collages that had

For the Record. . .

Born February 18, 1933, in Tokyo, Japan; daughter of Yeisuke (a banker) and Isoko Ono; married Toshi Ichiyanagi (a composer), c. 1957 (divorced, c. 1964); married Tony Cox (an artist and filmmaker), c. 1964 (divorced, c. 1969); married John Lennon (a musician), c. 1969 (died, 1980); children: (second marriage) Kyoko; (third marriage) Sean. *Education:* Attended Sarah Lawrence College.

Member of Fluxus avantgarde movement, 1960s; made stage debut with performance art piece, Village Gate, New York City, 1961; collaborated with composers La Monte Young, John Cage, and Ornette Coleman in art shows and musical performances; author of *Grapefruit,* 1964, and *A Hole to See the Sky Through,* 1971; recording artist; with Cox, made film *Bottoms,* 1967; exhibited conceptual pieces, London, 1968; signed with Apple Records; recorded with John Lennon and the Plastic Ono Band; released *Plastic Ono Band,* 1970.

Awards: Grammy Award for album of the year, 1981, for *Double Fantasy.*

Addresses: *Office*—Studio One, 1 West 72nd St., New York, NY 10023.

no precedent and haven't been matched yet in sheer adventurousness."

Ono met John Lennon in 1968 at a London gallery exhibition of her concept pieces. Eight years Lennon's senior, Ono claimed in a *Rolling Stone* interview that she had never even listened to the Beatles' music before meeting the songwriting legend. The outcry against the ensuing liaison was vicious. Although the strains of fame and a desire for individual expression—not to mention growing antipathy among bandmembers—were already threatening to split up the Fab Four, Ono was blamed for hastening the group's breakup. As quoted in *The Guests Go in to Supper,* Ono recalled, "Our partnership was still great, but mainly our energies were used in fighting the world from splitting us up." Ono and Lennon began collaborating on songs, but the public would not accept her as a legitimate contributor.

Ono signed with Apple Records and continued recording her vocal experimentations. Her 1970 *Plastic Ono Band* set—a sister album to Lennon's identically titled offering of that year—featured the contributions of Lennon, Eric Clapton, Klaus Voorman, and Andy White but was called trash by most critics and reviled by the public. Her follow-up album, *Fly,* demonstrated the

influences of her and Lennon's involvement in primal scream therapy. Indeed, Ono persisted in reshuffling the musical deck, integrating everyday sounds into musical patterns and news events into her lyrics. Many of her songs had a strident feminist outlook.

Reunited after a much publicized split in 1974, during which Lennon went on a drunken binge in Los Angeles, the couple had a son, Sean, who was born in 1975 on his father's birthday. Lennon took over child-rearing responsibilities while Ono managed the family's extensive financial empire. Five years later, the couple went back into the studio and created the widely praised *Double Fantasy* album. Soon after the album's release, in 1980, Lennon was gunned down by a psychotic fan outside the couple's apartment building in New York City. Ono—and the world—was devastated.

Ono has remained active in various musical, film, and artistic pursuits since Lennon's death. A highlight was "Walking on Thin Ice," a 1981 single that earned her a Grammy nomination. In 1984 Ono released the album *Milk and Honey,* which showcased original material as well as previously unreleased offerings by Lennon. She produced a movie (and soundtrack) entitled *Imagine* in 1988, which incorporated outtakes from other film projects, videos, home movies, and new songs.

The impact of Lennon and his top-flight musical associates on Ono's career will always be debated. Jerry Hopkins's unauthorized biography, *Yoko Ono,* painted a picture of Ono as an evil, manipulating dictator who used Lennon to fuel her own rise to fame. But others view the much-vilified Ono as a victim whose own artistic development suffered because she was trapped in Lennon's shadow. She has transcended her scapegoating to forge her own musical path, refusing to be deterred by a lack of acceptance by critics or the public. As Fricke said of Ono in *Rolling Stone,* "Her husband may have punched her ticket into the mainstream, but Mrs. Lennon was nobody's rock & roll fool."

Selected discography

With John Lennon

Unfinished Music No. 1: Two Virgins, Apple, 1968.
Wedding Album, Apple, 1969.
Live Peace in Toronto, Apple, 1969.
Some Time in New York City, Apple, 1972.
Double Fantasy, Geffen, 1980.

Solo albums

Plastic Ono Band, Apple, 1970.
Fly, Apple, 1971.
Approximately Infinite Universe, Apple, 1973.

Feeling the Space, Apple, 1973.
Season of Glass, Geffen, 1981.
Starpeace, Polygram, 1985.
Onobox, Rykodisc, 1992.

Sources

Books

Brown, Peter, and Steven Gaines, *The Love You Make: An Insider's Story of the Beatles,* McGrawHill, 1983.
The Guests Go in to Supper, edited by Melody Sumner, Kathleen Burch, and Michael Sumner, Burning Books, 1986.
Hopkins, Jerry, *Yoko Ono,* Macmillan, 1986.
Hounsome, Terry, *New Rock Record,* Facts on File, 1983.
The Playboy Interviews With John Lennon and Yoko Ono, conducted by David Scheff, edited by G. Barry Golson, Playboy Press, 1980.
Rees, Dafydd, and Luke Crampton, *Rock Movers & Shakers,* ABC/CLIO, 1991.

Seaman, Frederic, *The Last Days of John Lennon: A Personal Memoir,* Birch Lane Press, 1991.

Periodicals

Creem, May 1992.
Entertainment Weekly, March 6, 1992.
Interview, February 1989.
Los Angeles Times, April 11, 1993.
Metro Times (Detroit), September 29, 1993.
Musician, April 1992.
New York Times, March 13, 1994.
Oakland Press (Oakland Co., MI), September 25, 1993.
People, July 23, 1992.
Publishers Weekly, December 19, 1986.
Rolling Stone, March 19, 1992; February 18, 1993.
Spin, September 1992.

Additional information for this profile was obtained from liner notes to *Onobox,* Rykodisc, 1992.

—*Ed Decker*

Patti Page

Singer

In the decade immediately following World War II but preceding the flowering of rock and roll, a set of star vocalists rose to the top of popular music, displacing the big swing bands that listeners and dancers had favored during the war era. This was really the point of origin for the music industry as we know it today: record-label executives wrested the power in the industry from the old publishing firms and carefully cultivated the careers of singing stars, assiduously managing their public images. One of the very biggest of these stars was Patti Page. She provided the vocals for "Tennessee Waltz," one of the most successful popular recordings of all time.

Page was born Clara Ann Fowler in Claremore, Oklahoma, near Tulsa, in 1927. Her father worked for the railroad, and she remembers picking cotton sometimes as a girl, but eventually the family settled in Tulsa. In high school she was drawn to acting and singing, and after graduation, she auditioned for a country-music radio program on Tulsa's KTUL radio. Page was not hired, but did land a job in the station's advertising department. When one of the station's regular vocalists fell ill, Clara Fowler received both her first break and her stage name, for the program on which she substituted was called *Meet Patti Page,* sponsored by the Page Dairy company.

She was given a regular afternoon spot on KTUL, and before long, Jack Rael, described by Page as a band manager but by *Life* magazine as an itinerant saxophonist, heard her singing on the radio and offered his services as manager. Rael devoted himself entirely to Page's career, and the two split her earnings equally. He was still managing Page in the early 1990s.

Moved From Tulsa to Chicago

Page's first national exposure came when she moved to Chicago. After months of hard touring during which, *Life* observed, "she nearly starved, and her contours dwindled from size 16 to size 10," she landed a spot on an ABC network radio show called *The Breakfast Club.* From then on, her rise to stardom was rapid. Though only 20 years old, she was signed by the Mercury record label in 1948. She could not have landed in a situation more congenial to her talents.

Mercury in the late 1940s was the domain of legendary pop producer Mitch Miller. Miller was a technical wizard, partial to the new technique of overdubbing—laying one track over another—that enabled Page to sound like she was harmonizing with herself, but he also saw great potential in the simple structures of the country songs of the period, adapting them for the pop

For the Record. . .

Born Clara Ann Fowler, November 8, 1927, in Claremore, OK; father worked for the railroad; married and divorced twice; children: Kathleen, Daniel (both adopted).

Performed on KTUL radio, Tulsa, OK, early 1940s; joined cast of ABC Radio's *The Breakfast Club*, 1946; signed with Mercury Records, 1948; pioneered overdubbing technique with single "Confess," 1948; recorded "Tennessee Waltz," 1950; host of television programs *The Big Record*, 1957, and *The Patti Page Show*, 1958; recorded for Columbia Records, 1962-mid-1970s, and Nashville label Plantation Records; performed at nightclubs and with symphony orchestras.

Addresses: *Management*—Jack Rael Management, 314 Huntley Dr., Los Angeles, CA 90048. *Booking agent*—Thomas Cassidy, Inc., 366 Horseshoe Dr., Basalt, CO 81621.

market. Page, having grown up in Oklahoma singing country music, was comfortable with country-flavored material, and her recording career took off quickly, buoyed by this fare. Her first hit was the overdubbed "Confess," released in 1948; she also scored with "All My Love" in 1950. Several of the sides she recorded then were notable in that they featured a small jazz band in place of the miniature orchestra characteristic of the age.

By the end of 1950 Page had made her New York nightclub debut and was at work on a Christmas release for Mercury, the now-forgotten single "Boogie Woogie Santa Claus." "Tennessee Waltz," which eventually sold an estimated 7,000,000 copies, started life as the B side of this record; it was rescued from oblivion by intense public demand, which began to build almost as soon as the disc was released.

Cemented Reputation With "Tennessee Waltz"

"Tennessee Waltz" was first recorded by a country band called Pee Wee King and His Golden West Cowboys in 1947; it was composed by King and his lead vocalist, Redd Stewart. It was a minor hit both for King's group and for country vocalist Cowboy Copas. Page and Rael apparently became familiar with the song through a recording by jazz artist Erskine Hawkins, and various people, including Atlantic Records founder Jerry Wexler, have claimed that they brought the song to Page's attention. Whoever may have been responsible, "Tennessee Waltz" fit perfectly with what Page,

Rael, and Miller were trying to accomplish. Its simple country narrative of a girl who loses her sweetheart to her best friend at a dance was ideally suited to Page's dreamy, crooning contralto; Page took naturally to the song's tone of reflective, melancholy reminiscence. The record also represented the biggest commercial success for the overdubbing technique to date.

In the ensuing years, over 500 cover versions of "Tennessee Waltz" appeared, and the song remains an indelible part of American popular culture. Page's career never quite reached such a peak again, but she remained one of the country's most popular singers through most of the 1950s, strongly identified in the public mind with country-tinged pop songs, such as 1950's well-received "Mockin' Bird Hill" and Page's personal favorite, "Old Cape Cod," from 1956. Another million-seller for Page was the novelty pet-shop ode "Doggie in the Window"; a widely enjoyed parody of the tune by the outrageous country comedians Homer and Jethro confirmed its near-universal familiarity.

Throughout the 1950s, Page was a fixture of the television variety-show circuit. In 1957 she was offered her own host slot on *The Big Record,* a rock and roll-oriented musical program. But Page's laid-back style proved ill suited to the brashness of the rock era. *Look* magazine noted that "clinkers popped up in the program and there were changes in the staff" in an attempt to rescue it. But the show did not last; nor did a 1958 successor, *The Patti Page Show.*

From Pop to Country

Page moved from Mercury to Columbia Records in 1962, and her new label gradually began to steer her in the direction of country music, with which she had been nominally associated all along. A series of country LPs in the late 1960s and early 1970s were moderately successful, and as late as 1981, Page cracked the country Top 40, with a single on Nashville's Plantation Records. "A lot of people ask me how it feels to be back," she told Edward Morris of *Billboard* at the time. "And I tell them I've never left—that they've just not been around to see me."

These fans could have found her on the stage of the country's poshest nightclubs. Even in the late 1950s, while her recorded work was greatly in demand, club appearances in New York and Las Vegas consumed much of Page's time and energy, and over the next decades, her appeal to nightclub audiences remained strong. By the early 1980s she had reached another pinnacle of pop-music achievement: appearing with a major symphony orchestra. She performed with the symphonies of Cincinnati and Mexico City, among others.

In the early 1990s Page lived near San Diego. The mother of two children she adopted during one of her two marriages, she still made regular appearances on the nightclub circuit. As a reviewer for *Variety* noted in 1990, "[Perhaps] the most surprising thing about watching and listening to a live Patti Page show is realizing how little her pipes have changed. The head tones are as clear and the chest voice as rich as in the golden Mercury Record days."

Somewhere between a true artist and an occupier of the right place at the right time, Patti Page was without question one of the best-loved singers of the postwar era, credited with fourteen million-selling records during the 1950s. The various reissues and compilations of her work that began to appear on compact disc in the early 1990s suggested that the eclipse in reputation she suffered during the early heyday of rock was undeserved.

Selected discography

16 Most Requested Songs, Columbia Legacy, 1989.
The Patti Page Collection, Volume I (includes "Tennessee Waltz" and "Mockin' Bird Hill"), Mercury, 1991.
The Patti Page Collection, Volume II (includes "Doggie in the Window" and "Old Cape Cod"), Mercury, 1991.
Tennessee Waltz, Intersound, 1992.
The Uncollected Patti Page With Lou Stein's Music '49, Hindsight.
Greatest Hits, Columbia.
Christmas With Patti Page, Mercury.

Sources

Books

Hardy, Phil, and Dave Laing, *The Faber Companion to 20th-Century Popular Music*, Faber, 1990.
Stambler, Irwin, *The Encyclopedia of Popular Music*, St. Martin's, 1965.
Stambler, Irwin, and Grelun Landon, *The Encyclopedia of Folk, Country and Western Music*, St. Martin's, 1983.

Periodicals

Billboard, August 1, 1981.
Life, May 21, 1951.
Look, February 18, 1958.
Musical Quarterly, Fall 1992.
New York Times, July 15, 1988.
Variety, July 11, 1990.

—*James M. Manheim*

Charley Patton

Singer, guitarist

Of all the legendary figures whose names have come down to us from the early years of the Mississippi Delta blues tradition, Charley Patton is generally recognized as the most influential blues artist active in the first decades of the twentieth century. No single individual can be credited with "inventing" the Delta blues style, but Patton was among its half dozen earliest practitioners—recognized by 1910 throughout the Delta area as a rowdy, hard-drinking performer of consummate skill and versatility. Patton's rough voice and earthy lyrics place him securely within the tradition of "downhome" country blues, but his guitar playing and rhythmic dexterity were as advanced as those of any of the numerous later bluesmen who benefitted from his innovations.

Patton's parentage and early life are obscure. He was born around the year 1887 in Edwards, Mississippi, the son of Anney Patton and either her husband, Bill Patton, a preacher, or her lover of many years, Henderson Chatmon, a musician and farmer. Whichever man was his actual father, young Patton spent much of his time with the Chatmon family, many of whose members were talented musicians later to make blues records in the 1920s and 1930s. From Bill Patton, Charley Patton became familiar with the gospel tradition, but it seems clear that his true education in music was provided by the huge Chatmon clan.

For reasons unknown, Patton moved from Edwards to the plantation of Will Dockery around 1897. Dockery's plantation covered many thousands of acres of the Delta's best cotton country, straddling the Mississippi River near the towns of Drew and Cleveland. It was a well-run farming community in which hundreds of black sharecropping families enjoyed a relatively decent standard of living. Music was a daily ingredient of life among black sharecroppers—at work, in church, and especially at the Saturday night parties held in remote parts of the backcountry or at rollicking "juke" joints. These gatherings provided black society with some of its only opportunities for recreation free of white domination or the inhibiting influence of the church; in the words of famed novelist Zora Neale Hurston, as quoted in *Early Downhome Blues,* a juke joint was "a fun house. Where they sing, dance, gamble, love, and compose 'blues' songs incidentally."

Patton was one of the earliest such composers. Along with an older mentor named Henry Sloan, Patton seized on a new form of popular song the basic units of which were 12-bar stanzas of three lyric lines each, the first two identical, the third different but end-rhymed with the others; the subjects of these songs were usually farm life, sexual relations, or poverty. When and where this form originated is not known, but its early develop-

For the Record. . .

Born in 1887 in Edwards, MS; died of heart disease, April 28, 1934, in Indianola, MS; buried in unmarked grave in Holly Ridge, MS; son of Anney (one source says Amy) Patton; father was either Bill Patton (a preacher) or Henderson Chatmon (a musician and farmer); married wife Gertrude, early 1900s; married Minnie Toy, 1908; married Minnie Franklin, early 1920s; married to wife Bertha Lee, 1930-34.

Learned to play guitar and sang with Chatmon family, c. 1890s; moved to Dockery's Plantation, near Drew, MS, c. 1900; "invented"/adopted Delta blues style and performed at parties, taverns, and on streets of Delta region, 1905-1929; recorded with Paramount label, Richmond, IN, and Grafton, WI, 1929-1930; recorded with Vocalion label, New York City, 1934.

ment was concentrated in eastern Texas and the Mississippi Delta, where bandleader W. C. Handy, according to *Early Downhome Blues,* reported hearing blues sung in the streets of Tutwiler, Mississippi, in 1903. It is not beyond the realm of possibility that the "lean, loose-jointed Negro" he heard was the 16-year-old Charley Patton.

For 30 years Patton would remain a fixture in the Delta region, playing his guitar and singing the blues wherever he could make a few dollars. This often meant playing on the street, at picnics, at logging camps deep in the pine forests, or for white audiences at the larger plantations; but above all it meant the Saturday night dance parties of the sharecroppers. Patton was an ideal entertainer for such gatherings: he was not only a musician of genius, but "a clowning man with a guitar," in the words of his probable half-brother Sam Chatmon, as printed in *The Devil's Music,* given to bawdy storytelling and crowd-pleasing tricks like playing "his guitar all between his legs, [carrying] it behind his head, [laying] down on the floor." Patton drank excessively, was querulous, changed women constantly, and treated all of them badly, according to contemporaries such as Son House. He was also noted—and sometimes criticized—for his slurring of lyrics and willingness to throw in lines at random, often without any relation to the rest of the song. When House chided Patton for such sloppiness, as reported in *The Devil's Music,* Patton's response was pragmatic: "Oh, man, all I want to do is get paid for it. What's the difference?" Patton was the kind of rough-and-ready performer who would be designated as "countrified" by a later, more sophisticated generation of bluesmen; but there was

nothing primitive about his musical ability, and Patton's combination of refined skills and "downhome" style lend his recordings a unique historical importance.

Patton's stay at Dockery's plantation ended in 1929 when he was recruited to record for the Paramount label in Richmond, Indiana. Delta blues artists were not frequently recorded before the year 1926—vaudeville blues, featuring female singers backed by large bands, was the standard up to that time—but during the four-year period ended by the Great Depression, hundreds of recordings were made by musicians including Patton, Son House, Blind Lemon Jefferson, and Tommy Johnson, to name but a few. Patton recorded for Paramount three times in 1929 and 1930 and for the Vocalion label in New York City in 1934. All of the sides are now available on compact disc, and they reveal a musician far removed from the "clown" described by Sam Chatmon; as music scribe Robert Palmer wrote in *Rolling Stone,* "Patton's sheer focus and magnetic, almost palpable presence will still jump out of your speakers and grab you by the throat." Patton sang in a burly baritone that was nonetheless amply capable of rendering the pathos of many blues songs. His guitar work—often complex and always rhythmically challenging—was accompanied by a variety of hand and foot percussion. And his recorded output ranges widely in genre, from raw downhome blues to nineteenth-century ballads, show tunes, gospel, and country breakdowns.

Patton moved to the town of Lula after his recording session with Paramount, in 1930, and then to Holly Ridge, both of which are in the same Delta region of Mississippi. He died in 1934 of heart disease, though, like many other early blues musicians, he was widely rumored to have been murdered. Patton's music had a deep and lasting influence on the entire history of Delta blues—the basis of nearly all subsequent blues—including the work of such legends as Robert Johnson, Howlin' Wolf, Johnny Shines, and Muddy Waters. He is also credited by Palmer as one of the earliest progenitors of rock and roll, "an American archetype, the first in a series of hard-living, hard-rocking ramblers" that would eventually include the likes of pianist Jerry Lee Lewis and guitarist Jimi Hendrix. Patton painted an apt self-portrait in his "Elder Green Blues": "I like to fuss and fight/Lord, and get sloppy drunk off a bottle and ball/And walk the streets all night."

Selected discography

King of the Delta Blues: The Music of Charley Patton, Yazoo, 1991.

Founder of the Delta Blues: 1929-1934, Yazoo, 1992.

Sources

Books

Charters, Samuel B., *The Bluesmen: The Story and the Music of the Men Who Made the Blues,* Oak, 1967.

Charters, Samuel B., *The Country Blues,* Rinehart, 1959.

Colt, Stephen, and Wardlow, Gayle, *King of the Delta Blues,* Shanachie, 1988.

Oakley, Giles, *The Devil's Music,* Ariel Books/BBC, 1976.

Titon, Jeff Todd, *Early Downhome Blues,* University of Illinois Press, 1977.

Periodicals

Blues World (U.K.), August 1970.

Guitar Player, August 1992.

78 Quarterly, Autumn 1967.

Rolling Stone, March 5, 1992.

—*Jonathan Martin*

Oscar Peterson

Pianist

Since bursting onto the international music scene in the late 1940s, Oscar Peterson has become one of the most phenomenally successful of all jazz artists. The first Canadian-born jazz pianist to achieve worldwide fame, he is one of the most decorated of contemporary musicians, with seven Grammy awards, ten honorary doctorates, and dozens of prizes and medals. Enjoying perhaps the greatest popularity of any jazz musician of his generation, Peterson's admirers among listeners, critics, and musicians are legion; attested Bob Doerschuk in *Contemporary Keyboard*, "The history of Oscar Peterson is a study in superlatives." And when Patricia O'Haire of the *New York Daily News* bluntly called Peterson "the best the jazz piano has to offer," she echoed the opinions of many of Peterson's fans.

One of the most remarkable features of Peterson's long career has been his ability to capture a huge audience without compromising his artistic integrity. Throughout his life he has remained dedicated to the high standards he set for himself as a youngster—and has never altered them to humor popular taste. Proof of this is found in his somewhat aloof stage persona, for as a performer he is far more concerned with his craft than with his audience; indeed, he once told *Down Beat's* John McDonough, "My audience has nothing to do with anything I do when I'm on stage." And though he may not cater to his public's taste or mood, Peterson demands the utmost respect from his listeners and has been known to walk off a stage when he found an audience noisy or distracting.

A Keeper of Tradition

Peterson has always displayed a reverence for jazz history in his piano style; as Josef Woodward wrote in *Down Beat,* "Few pianists have so adeptly combined technical prowess with tradition-reverent poetry." Part of this tradition is the blues, never far distant while Peterson is performing. As he told Doerschuk, "A jazz phrase to me can't be a jazz phrase without some type of blues feeling to it."

Another of Peterson's ties to tradition is the debt he owes earlier jazz pianists, especially Art Tatum. As a youngster Peterson heard Tatum on records; he was so much in awe of the pianist that, clearly intimidated, he gave up piano for an entire month. His first meeting with Tatum, in the early 1950s, was in fact a terrifying experience; as he told Len Lyons of *Contemporary Keyboard,* "I was totally frightened of this man and his

For the Record. . .

Born August 15, 1925, in Montreal, Quebec, Canada; son of Daniel (a sleeping-car porter) and Kathleen Olivia John Peterson; married Lillie Fraser, 1944 (divorced); married Sandra King, 1966 (divorced 1976); married Charlotte Huber, 1977 (divorced); married wife Kelly, c. 1991; children: (first marriage) Lyn, Sharon, Gay, Oscar Jr., Norman; (third marriage) Joel; (fourth marriage) Celine. *Education:* Studied with Hungarian classical pianist Paul de Marky, beginning c. 1939.

Began piano and trumpet study, c. 1930; won first prize in Montreal radio show competition, 1940; appeared regularly on radio station CKAC, Montreal, early 1940s; toured Canada with Johnny Holmes orchestra, 1942-47; formed first trio, 1947; toured U.S. and Europe with Jazz at the Philharmonic, early 1950s; formed trio, with guitarist Herb Ellis and bassist Ray Brown, 1953; Ellis replaced by drummer Ed Thigpen, 1958; helped establish Advanced School of Contemporary Music, Toronto, 1960; toured widely with own trios, early 1960s; performed as solo artist and toured with Ella Fitzgerald, early 1970s; produced television series *Oscar Peterson Presents*, 1974, and *Oscar Peterson's Piano Party*, 1978; composed film score for *The Silent Partner*, 1978; continued to record and compose, experimented with synthesizers, and collected electronic instruments in home recording studio, Mississauga, Ontario, 1980s-early 1990s. Became chancellor of York University, 1991.

Selected awards: Seven Grammy awards; numerous citations for best jazz pianist from *Contemporary Keyboard, Down Beat,* and *Playboy;* awarded the Order of Canada, officer, 1972, companion, 1984; Genie film award for best film score, 1978, for *The Silent Partner;* officer of the Order of Arts and Letters, France, 1989.

Addresses: *Office*—Regal Recordings, Ltd., 2421 Hammond Rd., Mississauga, Ontario, Canada L5K 1T3.

tremendous talent. It's like a lion; you're scared to death, but it's such a beautiful animal, you want to come up close and hear it roar." The two pianists nonetheless became friends, and one can still hear Peterson's link with his idol in his harmonic inventiveness and radiant virtuosity.

Peterson was born in Montreal in 1925 and was introduced to music by his father, a porter on the Canadian Pacific Railroad. Daniel Peterson, an amateur musician himself, insisted that each of his five children be exposed to music, and he started Oscar on both piano and trumpet at the age of five. However, after Oscar suffered a bout with tuberculosis at age seven, he concentrated on piano alone. A strict disciplinarian, Daniel Peterson would give each of his children assignments before he left for a trip on the railway; as Oscar told his biographer Gene Lees, "My dad would leave and he would give us each a task, pianistically. You had to know this, you had to know that. . . . There were no ifs, ands and buts. Have it together. It was that simple."

Practiced Obsessively

No doubt Oscar derived much of his sense of responsibility and dedication to his art from his father. He began practicing continuously all day long; as he told Lees, "I practiced from nine a.m. to noon, took an hour off for lunch, practiced from one to six in the afternoon, then went to dinner, and went back to the piano about seven-thirty. I'd keep practicing until my mother would come in and drag me away from it so the family could get some sleep." It was in these marathon sessions that Peterson cultivated his technique, a prerequisite to the service of his brilliant musical imagination.

At the age of 14, Peterson took up studies with Hungarian classical pianist Paul de Marky. Peterson fondly recalled the pianist as an open-minded teacher who, unlike many piano teachers of the time, encouraged his pupil's interest in jazz; Peterson told *Contemporary Keyboard's* Doerschuk, "He would have admiration for what I did at times, he would have disdain at other times, but at the end of every lesson I can vividly remember him saying, 'All right. Now play me what you're doing in your jazz things.'" Many years later, at the age of 85, de Marky commented to Lees on Peterson's innate talents, saying, "If you have a natural talent for your fingers and harmony, they can't go wrong if they wanted to."

At about the time that he began studies with de Marky, Peterson won first prize on the Ken Soble amateur radio show, which led to a weekly broadcast on CKAC in Montreal. He also performed in Canada on nationally broadcast programs such as *The Happy Gang* and *The Light Up and Listen Hour*. Then, in 1942, he joined the Johnny Holmes Orchestra, one of Canada's most popular jazz ensembles. As Holmes recalled to Lees, "The amazing thing is that when he came into our band at seventeen, he had a technique I think every bit equivalent to what he has now. But he was a diamond in the rough." Peterson used his time in the band to refine his talents.

In 1947 Peterson formed his first trio, with bassist Ozzie Roberts and drummer Clarence Jones, and brought the group to Montreal's Alberta Lounge. It was here that Peterson first met record producer and concert promoter Norman Granz, who was to have a major impact on his career. In 1944 Granz had begun mounting all-star jazz concerts at Philharmonic Hall in Los Angeles. These concerts—as well as the ensembles showcased by them—became known as "Jazz at the Philharmonic" (J.A.T.P.). Eventually the Jazz at the Philharmonic enterprise began to feature national touring groups, as well as recordings. While in Montreal with one of these J.A.T.P. touring groups, Granz heard Peterson perform and invited him to play in a concert at Carnegie Hall. The pianist's appearance there in 1949 set the stage for an international career.

During the early 1950s Peterson toured regularly with Jazz at the Philharmonic, traveling to 41 cities in North America, as well as Japan, Hong Kong, Australia, and the Philippines. In 1953 Peterson formed what was to become his most famous trio, with Herb Ellis on guitar and Ray Brown on double bass. The group, which performed and recorded together for five years, was a perfect blending of musical personalities, with the artists remarkably attuned to each other and to the effect of the performance as a whole. Peterson biographer Richard Palmer called the ensemble "the finest piano-bass-guitar group ever" and wrote in 1984 that "the drive, sonority, and almost spooky level of communication are as phenomenal now as when the group was playing and recording . . . it was a group based on love; and that still comes across irresistibly from the records twenty-five years on."

Eventually weary of touring, Ellis left the trio in 1958; he was replaced by drummer Ed Thigpen, who remained with the ensemble until 1965. Peterson had settled in Toronto in 1958, and in 1960, along with Brown, Thigpen, trombonist Butch Watanabe, and composer Phil Nimmons, founded that city's Advanced School of Contemporary Music. In addition to offering classes in improvisation, Peterson and his colleagues tried to instill in students a sense of tradition; Peterson explained to Doerschuk, "We found that the awareness among youngsters of what had preceded them in jazz was lacking. In those days people were saying 'Who?' about Miles Davis, believe it or not! So we would go through some of their recordings and say, 'This is what this man did. This is what he meant to the music.'" But Peterson and his fellow educators ultimately found the school demanded too much of their time and abandoned it after three years.

Throughout the 1960s and early 1970s Peterson toured the world, usually with a trio. Beginning in the mid-1970s he also performed with symphony orchestras and in duo settings with such jazz giants as trumpeters Dizzy Gillespie and Clark Terry and guitarist Joe Pass. After about 1972 he began to appear with increasing frequency as a concert soloist, becoming one of the most highly praised of all jazz performers in that demanding setting. Peterson also worked in television, producing his own series in 1974 and 1978, and recorded extensively throughout the 1970s and 1980s, sometimes producing as many as five or six albums a year.

In the late 1980s and early 1990s Peterson curbed his exhausting touring schedule somewhat and focused more on composing. He also developed an interest in electronic instruments. At his home in Mississauga, Canada, he built a large collection of equipment for use as both a mechanical aid in creating film scores and as a way to find a new perspective on some of his musical ideas. As he told *Contemporary Keyboard's* Greg Armbruster, "There are an awful lot of things that are within me that I haven't thought of. I find they tend to come out more when I hear them on an instrument other than the piano; I tend to think a little differently."

Peterson has weathered his share of criticism during his long career. As John McDonough revealed in *Down Beat,* there are those who see his phenomenal virtuosity as "an engineering sleight of hand whipped up to conceal something that's not really there—emotion, substance, content, or whatever jazz is supposed to have." Yet even Peterson's critics admit that the standards of excellence he set as a young man have never been compromised, and certainly, his dedication to his chosen art form has never been questioned.

Selected compositions

Hymn to Freedom, 1962.
Canadiana Suite, 1964.
Jazz Exercises and Pieces, 1965.
Oscar Peterson New Piano Solos, 1965.
The Silent Partner (film score), 1978.
Easter Suite, 1984.
Big North (film score).
Fields of Endless Day.
(With Norman McLaren) *City Lights.*
Begone Dull Care.
A Royal Wedding Suite.

Selected discography

I Got Rhythm, RCA, 1947-49.
Keyboard, Verve, 1950-51.
In Concert, Verve, 1950-55.
Oscar Peterson Quartet, Metronome, 1951.
(Contributor) *The Genius of Lester Young,* Verve, 1952.
At the Stratford Shakespeare Festival, Verve, 1956, reissued, 1992.
At the Concertgebauw, Verve, 1958.
On the Town, Verve, 1958.
The Duke Ellington Songbook, Verve, 1959.
Ben Webster Meets Oscar Peterson, Verve, 1959.
Affinity, Verve, 1962.
Night Train, Verve, 1962.
Canadiana Suite, Mercury, 1964.
Live in Tokyo, Pablo, 1964.
The Oscar Peterson Trio Plus One: Clark Terry, Mercury, 1964.
In Russia, Pablo, 1964.
With Respect to Nat, Limelight, 1965.
The Way I Really Play, MPS/Polydor, 1967.
My Favorite Instrument, MPS/Polydor, 1969.
Tracks, MPS, 1970.
The History of an Artist Volumes I and II, Pablo, 1973-74.
Peterson and Dizzy Gillespie, Pablo, 1974.
Oscar Peterson and Roy Eldridge, Pablo, 1974.
Montreux 1975: Big Six, Pablo, 1975.
A Salle Pleyel, Pablo, 1975.
Night Child, Pablo, 1979.
(With Milt Jackson) *Ain't But a Few of Us Left,* Pablo, 1981.
(With Freddie Hubbard) *Face to Face,* Pablo, 1982.
Oscar Peterson Live!, Pablo, 1986.
Time After Time, Pablo, 1986.
If You Could See Me Now, Pablo, 1987.
(With Herb Ellis and Ray Brown) *Saturday Night at the Blue Note,* Telarc Jazz, reissued, 1990.
The Will to Swing, Verve, 1991.
(With Ellis and Brown) *Last Call at the Blue Note,* Telarc Jazz, reissued, 1992.
(With Ellis and Brown) *Live at the Blue Note,* Telarc Jazz, reissued, 1992.

Exclusively for My Friends, Verve, reissued, 1992.
Essential, Polygram, 1992.
Three Originals, Verve, 1993.
Plays Count Basie, Verve, 1993.
Encore at the Blue Note, TelArc, 1993.
Jazz 'Round Midnight, Verve.

With Jazz at the Philharmonic

Norman Granz Jam Session, Verve, 1952.
One O'Clock Jump, Verve, 1953.
J.A.T.P. Live at the Nichegei Theatre, Pablo, 1953.
Blues in Chicago, 1955, Verve, 1955.
The Exciting Battle, Pablo, 1955.
Return to Happiness, Tokyo, 1983, Pablo, 1983.

Sources

Books

Lees, Gene, *Oscar Peterson: The Will to Swing,* Prima, 1990.
Palmer, Richard, *Oscar Peterson,* Spellmount, 1984.

Periodicals

Contemporary Keyboard, March 1978; September 1978; December 1980; October 1983.
Down Beat, January 1991; December 1991; March 1993.
Experience Trillium, 1992.
Hot House, March 1990.
Jazz Journal International, July 1991; February 1992.
Jazz Times, May 1992.
Los Angeles Times, March 12, 1988.
Maclean's, November 2, 1992.
New York Daily News, March 6, 1990.
Sarasota Herald-Tribune (FL), November 29, 1989.

—Jeffrey Taylor

P.M. Dawn

Rap duo

"**P**.M. Dawn's hefty front man Prince Be has been called everything from an ersatz hippie to a fraud," reported David Browne in *Entertainment Weekly*. The name-calling was prompted by P.M. Dawn's challenge to rap's limited subgenre categorization, which fomented a controversy over the legitimacy of rap that tends toward pop music and away from the hardcore, "gangsta" stance. As early as 1989, Prince Be and his brother DJ Minutemix were using the tools of hip-hop—the standard vocal rhymes and "sampling" of bars from previously recorded songs—to make music that appealed to the largely white pop audience. The debate over this genre-bending would even go beyond argument to erupt into a violent confrontation in 1992.

The brothers who comprise P.M. Dawn actually answer to several names. Even those they initially adopted for the music world, Prince Be and DJ Minutemix, mutated in 1993 with the release of their second disc to become The Nocturnal and J.C. The Eternal, respectively. But in Jersey City, New Jersey, where the two grew up, they were known as Attrell and Jarrett Cordes; Attrell, the older of the two, has generally been the decision-maker in their work together and—as Prince Be—is customarily treated by the press as synonymous with P.M. Dawn.

Prince Be described the brothers' 1970s Jersey City home as a reflection of that blurring of genres that he has incorporated into his music; in August of 1991 he told *Melody Maker*'s Everett True, "I lived sort of between the yuppies and the killers. . . . You could literally walk across the street and get into trouble and walk across the street and get into even bigger trouble. It was right next to this park where all of that stuff would mix up. When you're 14, it's hard to know how to deal with that sort of thing." Be detailed a similar scenario in *Spin,* while also stressing his need for escape from that environment: "Being male . . . being in an urban environment, you know what to expect if you don't have that same point of view. I was easily influenced back then, instead of trying to develop my own identity . . . I had no choice but to follow what everybody else was doing. I saw myself slowly becoming an idiot. So I left."

Musical Upbringing

The most accessible exit route presented itself in the music and spirituality of Attrell and Jarrett's parents' home. They were both exposed to the funk and pop of the 1970s through their stepfather's extensive record collection; five uncles and one aunt were DJs who further exposed the boys to new music. The brothers were also afforded the opportunity to see the music

For the Record. . .

Group consists of **Prince Be** (born Attrell Cordes, early 1970s, in Jersey City, NJ), samples, vocals; and **D.J. Minutemix** (born Jarrett Cordes, early 1970s, in Jersey City), turntables.

Prince Be worked as DJ, mid-1980s, and as security guard at homeless shelter, late 1980s. Group formed c. 1989; released single, "Ode to a Forgetful Mind," Warlock, 1989; released singles in U.K., 1991; released *Of the Heart, of the Soul, and of the Cross: the Utopian Experience*, Gee Street/Island, 1991.

Awards: Platinum record for *Of the Heart, of the Soul, and of the Cross*, 1992, and gold record for *The Bliss Album . . .?*, 1993.

Addresses: *Record company*—Gee Street/Island, 825 Eighth Avenue, New York, NY 10019.

world firsthand, since their stepfather was a musician who played briefly in one of the early incarnations of Kool and the Gang, which was among the most influential funk bands of the 1970s. And there was the church, where both boys and their mother sang in the choir.

Attrell began drawing on the family talent as early as the ninth grade, when he offered himself up as DJ at local parties; he was also starting to compose his own songs at the time. Within a few years, he had determined to make a demo tape of some of those pieces; he managed to put aside $600 from his first job after high school. As a security guard at a homeless shelter, he had time to work on his music while earning the money he needed. By then, he and Jarrett were putting in studio time as P.M. Dawn.

They first approached Tommy Boy, the rap subsidiary of Warner Bros., with their demo but were turned away; they were too much like alternative hip-hoppers De La Soul and not enough like hardcore rap they were told. They managed to issue a debut single, "Ode to a Forgetful Mind," in 1989, on Warlock, an independent label that failed to market them. The debut went unnoticed.

The label that released the single in England, however, managed much better. Gee Street mixed and marketed the song so that it earned considerable attention from music reviewers, and P.M. Dawn found themselves courted not just by Gee Street's head, John Baker, but also by most of the major record labels in England. Soon after Gee Street brought the brothers to London in 1990 to record tracks for an album, the label found itself

facing bankruptcy; the P.M. Dawn contract—the company's chief asset—was offered to the highest bidder. The winner was Island Records, a powerful English label that acquired not only P.M. Dawn, but the entire Gee Street operation along with them.

Singles Hit in U.K.

Before the first Dawn album was released in England, Island issued a few more singles to test the water; the reaction remained warm. A *Melody Maker* review in June of 1991 praised the second release, "A Watcher's Point of View (Don't Cha Think)," reporting, "The gently-plucked acoustic guitars, lilting bassline and supple beats, Sixties vocal harmonies and samples of The Monkees' 'Pleasant Valley Sunday' add up to one of the most delightfully summery hip hop tracks ever recorded." By October, "Paper Doll" had become single of the week, Number Five on the charts, and had earned further praise from the august *Melody Maker,* the paper calling it "one of the lovelier tracks from the most pure-and-simply gorgeous album of the year."

With the release of P.M. Dawn's debut album, *Of the Heart, of the Soul, and of the Cross: the Utopian Experience,* in late 1991, Prince Be and DJ Minutemix were effectively rescued from obscurity. In October, Michael Azerrad of *Rolling Stone* had noted "PM Dawn is the hippest thing in England, and the Cordes brothers are hoping their thing hits big in America." It did: the single "Set Adrift on Memory Bliss" reached the Number One spot on three Billboard charts—pop, R&B, and dance. Part of its charm derived from a sampled bit of the song "True," which was a hit for the British "new romantic" band Spandau Ballet in 1983; this stroke of creative borrowing was a splendid and unusual choice in a hip-hop world saturated with James Brown and P-Funk passages. Within two months, *Of the Heart* sold over 500,000 copies, earning a gold record; platinum came close on its heels. James Hunter praised the album in the *Village Voice,* deeming it "brilliantly conceived, executed and marketed." In *Interview,* Rob Tannenbaum went so far as to compare Prince Be to rock legend Jimi Hendrix. And a writer for *People* noted a few years later that the disc "flowed and undulated—it was something new, hip-hop that ignored the streets and aimed for the heavens."

People also commented, however, on the issue that would create so much conflict for P.M. Dawn in the year between the release of the debut album and that of the follow-up, *The Bliss Album . . .? (Vibrations of Love and Anger and the Ponderance of Life and Existence);* *People's* reviewer remarked that the duo was "embraced by the mainly white rock press as the second (non-threatening) coming of rap." Prince Be respond-ed to charges that his music was too "soft"—that it diluted rap with too much pop music—with his own critiques of the rigidity of hardcore rappers; he was especially skeptical of the violence espoused in the lyrics of such hip-hop stars as Ice-T, Public Enemy, and KRS-One of Boogie Down Productions. Although Prince Be was also careful to tell interviewers how much he admired these rappers, the confrontation escalated until KRS-One actually broke up a P.M. Dawn perform-ance at the Sound Factory in New York City in January of 1992.

Incorporated Genre Controversy in Follow-up

P.M. Dawn also took much of the criticism to heart and thought about the conflicts that had arisen while re-cording the second album. In the *Source,* Prince Be recounted to Brioné Lathrop his disappointment with the attention the debut album had received: "P.M. Dawn got a lot of recognition, we got a lot of critical acclaim, we got a lot of street level acclaim, but we got a lot of flack as well. . . . I looked around and I saw that a lot of the stuff that I read—[black-oriented publica-tions] *Black Beat, Ebony*—I wasn't in those and it looked very weird." Be and Minutemix approached the second album with an eye toward correcting this, at-tempting to appeal more explicitly to inner-city and African-American audiences. Prince Be continued in the *Source,* explaining, "I made it more biased to an urban crowd, because they felt so neglected the first time, and I didn't want to do that. I guess that was through my own stupidity. 'Cause I didn't want them to feel neglected, and they do, so I made it for them and their consumption." He also tried to address the black/white, rap/pop tension explicitly in both music and lyrics. The rapper noted that the song "Plastic," in particular, was intended to resolve conflict: "It's about the idiosyncrasies that exist between hardcore hip-hop fans or artists and alternative hip-hop fans. It's about the tensions that's between the two, it's plastic, it's not real."

"I'd Die Without You," the first single from *The Bliss Album . . .?,* was released as part of the soundtrack to the film *Boomerang.* The soundtrack was a best-seller, and the song became a Number One Hit. When the full album followed, in 1993, *Entertainment Weekly's* Browne declared, "Once again, the duo effortlessly blends disparate elements—balladeering and rapping, sam-ples and live orchestration—into gorgeous wide-screen tableaux of sound." James Hunter, writing for *Rolling Stone,* remarked, "A flowing work filled with chaos and conflict, *The Bliss Album . . .?* will not disappoint." But *People's* reviewer was somewhat disappointed, ven-turing, "While there is no denying Be's talent and melodic pop savvy, he needs something new to say and a new way to say it."

Aside from the conflict over genre, P.M. Dawn suffered another setback in their blissful rise to fame: Prince Be's discovery that he is diabetic. After falling into a three-day coma in December of 1992, he was diagnosed and began treatment. But, as he explained to *Spin's* Danyel Smith, the revelation of the malady put a dent in his self-image. He said, "To top it all off I found out I had diabetes, which automatically made me a human be-ing. Pinned me down as a human being. And I like to think that I'm not. I don't like to think that anyone is a human being." This desire to be more than human reflects the spirituality that often defines P.M. Dawn's music. Prince Be told *Interview's* Tannenbaum that his spirituality "comes from myself. I've read the Bible. I believe in God, I believe in Jesus Christ. I don't really like to be told how to worship God." He elaborated on his name—his original rap handle, by which he is generally known—to the *Source's* Lathrop, saying, "My name is Prince Is, Prince Exist, that's my whole entire thing"; and for *Rolling Stone's* Azerrad, he explicated his band's name, stating simply, "the darkest hour, comes a light."

Selected discography

Of the Heart, of the Soul, and of the Cross: the Utopian Experi-ence (includes "Ode to a Forgetful Mind," "Set Adrift on a Memory Bliss," "Paper Doll," and "A Watcher's Point of View [Don't Cha Think]"), Gee Street/Island, 1991.
The Bliss Album . . .? (Vibrations of Love and Anger and the Ponderance of Life and Existence) (includes "Plastic" and "I'd Die Without You"), Gee Street/Island, 1993.
(Contributors) *Alternative NRG,* Hollywood, 1994.

Sources

Details, August 1993.
Entertainment Weekly, April 2, 1993.
Interview, October 1991.
Melody Maker, June 15, 1991; August 31, 1991; October 5, 1991.
Musician, June 1993.
People, June 7, 1993.
Rolling Stone, October 31, 1991; April 15, 1993.
Spin, July 1993.
Source, June 1993.
Village Voice, December 24, 1991.

Additional information for this profile was obtained from Gee Street/Island Records publicity materials, 1993.

—*Ondine E. Le Blanc*

Poison

Rock band

Poison were forerunners of the glam-rock wave that swept the late 1980s. Starting out in Pennsylvania as Paris, they moved to Los Angeles, changed their name, teased up their hair, and adorned themselves in heavy makeup, all because they wanted people to stop and take notice; eventually, people did.

In the early 1980s singer and bartender Bret Michaels and drummer Rikki Rockett joined forces to form a band called the Spectres in Pittsburgh, Pennsylvania. They then teamed up with licensed cosmotologist and bassist Bobby Dall and guitarist Matt Smith to form Paris. After playing mostly rock cover songs in Pittsburgh-area bars, they set out for Los Angeles in an ambulance Michaels bought for $700. In 1985, Smith was replaced by New York-born guitarist C. C. DeVille, a clinical psychology major known for his guitar work with bands like Lace, the Broken Toys, Screaming Mimi & St. James, Van Gogh's Ear, and Roxx Regime (which later became the Christian rock band Stryper). Thus was formed the lineup that would bring the band its greatest fame.

For the Record. . .

Original members include **Bobby Dall** (born in Florida), bass; **C. C. DeVille** (born Cecil DeVille in Brooklyn, NY; replaced by **Richie Kotzen** [born in 1972 in Birdsboro, PA; replaced by **Blues Saraceno**, 1993], 1992), guitar; **Bret Michaels** (born March 15, 1963, in Pittsburgh, PA), vocals; and **Rikki Rockett** (born in Mechanicsburg, PA), drums.

Band formed in Pittsburgh as Paris, 1983; relocated to Los Angeles, c. 1984; DeVille joined group and band name changed to Poison, 1985; signed with Enigma Records and released *Look What the Cat Dragged In,* 1986.

Addresses: *Management*—HK Management, Inc., 8900 Wilshire Blvd., Ste. 300, Beverly Hills, CA 90211. *Record company*—Capitol Records, 1750 North Vine St., Hollywood, CA 90028.

Poison began to spread their potent dosage up and down Hollywood's Sunset Strip, passing out flyers and making the rounds performing in the famous local clubs. It wasn't long before they were recruited by Enigma Records, a division of Capitol Records. In August of 1986, Poison launched their debut album, *Look What the Cat Dragged In.* It cost only $30,000 to record and became the biggest-selling-album in Enigma's history. With radio hits like "Talk Dirty to Me," "I Want Action," and "I Won't Forget You" and heavy rotation on MTV, their debut earned the band tours with fellow glam rockers Ratt, Cinderella, and Quiet Riot, as well as a coveted slot in the Texxas Jam in Dallas.

Widespread Appeal Despite Criticism

Singer Bret Michaels attributed Poison's success to the universality of the band's songs. He told *Teen Star's Photo Album,* "Poison's music is kind of a soundtrack for everyday life. I'm singing about the things that I know about, and that's honestly how I feel." Nonetheless, after four hit singles and videos and a Top 10 multi-platinum debut album, Poison received largely negative criticism from the press and ridicule from fellow musicians. Their glam image and good-time attitude inspired many to make light of their musical skills. Record sales figures and a growing fan base, however, amply attested to Poison's widespread appeal.

The band quickly followed their first world tour with another foray into the studio. In 1988, they teamed with noted rock producer Tom Werman and released *Open Up and Say . . . Ahh!* Originally titled *Swallow This*

(One), Poison's second set was met by controversy. Some large record chains refused to sell the album because of its cover art, which depicted a female devil with a large, phallic tongue. The offending image was reworked to reveal only the woman's eyes, and the album rocketed in sales and popularity, starting with the first single "Nothin' but a Good Time," followed by "Fallen Angel," the smash ballad "Every Rose Has Its Thorn," and "Your Mama Don't Dance."

After touring with former Van Halen frontman David Lee Roth, the band moved from support status to headlining their own tour in September of 1988, and by December, "Every Rose" had become the second-biggest-selling single of the year.

Critical acclaim and respect continued to allude the band even after their second hit release, and conflict pursued them persistently. Bryn Bridenthal, head of publicity at Geffen Records, slapped a $1.1 million lawsuit on the band for drenching her with drinks and a bucket of ice at a music industry party. Then, Sanctuary Music, Poison's former management company, filed a $45.5 million breach of contract suit against the band. Poison retaliated with charges of mismanagement of funds. Michaels's frequent brawling garnered him further lawsuits in Tallahassee, Atlanta, and Los Angeles.

Poison continued their adherence to the "work hard, play hard" motto, following up with their next album in 1990. Four weeks after its release, *Flesh and Blood* reached Number Two on the U.S. charts and Number Three in the U.K., buoyed by the record's infectious first single, "Unskinny Bop."

Retooled Glam Image

Shedding their big-haired image as they moved into the 1990s, Poison took a more mature approach to their third album. In *Screamer* magazine Michaels explained how *Flesh and Blood* signaled a change in the band: "I think that the same way that we shocked people in the beginning with the look, this one might shock them with the music a little bit. This one's the one that's going to show that there's a little bit of another side to the band." Indeed, maturity, cynicism, and loss tempered Poison's previously carefree, party-atmosphere lyrics—partly due to the death of the band's security guard and close friend James Kimo Maano, for whom they wrote their hit single "Something to Believe In." They also stood by their convictions and seemed to gain a fresh sense of hope with songs like "Ride the Wind" and "(Flesh and Blood) Sacrifice."

After a successful tour and their third multi-platinum album, Poison released *Swallow This Live,* culled from performances on their *Flesh and Blood* tour. But by then, drugs and strife among bandmembers had begun to take their toll. "The loneliest time of my life was when I was at the mixes for the live record," Michaels told *RIP*. "It was one of the few live albums to be totally live and unfixed. When we were doing it, I knew C. C.'s heart wasn't there, wasn't with the band."

By the following year, DeVille had parted ways with Poison, young guitar virtuoso and Pennsylvania native Richie Kotzen stepping in to take his place. After three instrumental releases of his own, Kotzen brought a distinctly new sound to Poison's next record, *Native Tongue*. He told *Guitar Player*, "People have to realize that being in this band, and the music that I'm making, is something that has always existed inside me. I'm being even truer to myself on the Poison record, even though it's not a solo thing."

Sales Declined as Themes Deepened

Released in February of 1993, *Native Tongue* earned Poison somewhat better notices in the rock press, but did not sell as well as their previous efforts. The Los Angeles First A.M.E. Church Choir joined Michaels on vocals for the first single from *Tongue,* "Stand," a song about pride and courage. Another tune, "Stay Alive," captured Michaels's state of mind when he was forced to take bassist Dall to a drug rehabilitation clinic in Florida, and "Strike Up the Band" recalled the band's roots playing clubs in Pittsburgh and Los Angeles.

Poison's 1993 Midwest tour averaged a mere 2,000 seats sold per venue, and sales of *Native Tongue* barely passed the gold status of 500,000. Their new blues-rock, down-and-dirty sound took Poison even further away from their *Look What The Cat Dragged In* beginnings. It seemed as though the band's evolution was lost on the largely fickle rock audience.

During their world tour for *Native Tongue,* struggle and discord struck Poison once again. In July of 1993, the band fired Kotzen because of a personal dispute between him and another bandmember. Poison asked DeVille to fill in for the remainder of the tour, but he declined in favor of focusing on his solo project. Poison finished the tour with Los Angeles-based guitarist Blues Saraceno, their second choice after Kotzen, as DeVille's replacement. Saraceno officially joined the band in late 1993. Meanwhile, Kotzen went on to sign a solo deal with Geffen Records.

The members of Poison have seen their share of ups and downs since the release of their first album in 1986—the sale of more than 15 million records, a total of 10 Top 40 singles, sold-out international tours, the well-publicized departure of C. C. DeVille, and the subsequent exit of Richie Kotzen. And despite often withering notices from critics and some of their peers, they have managed to make a significant, occasionally uplifting mark on the rock 'n' roll world and touch the hearts of millions of fans.

Selected discography

Look What the Cat Dragged In (includes "Talk Dirty to Me," "I Want Action," and "I Won't Forget You"), Enigma/Capitol, 1986.
Open Up and Say . . . Ahh! (includes "Nothin' but a Good Time," "Fallen Angel," "Every Rose Has Its Thorn," and "Your Mama Don't Dance"), Enigma/Capitol, 1988.
Flesh and Blood (includes "Unskinny Bop," "Something to Believe In," "Ride the Wind," and "[Flesh and Blood] Sacrifice"), Enigma/Capitol, 1990.
Swallow This Live, Capitol, 1992.
Native Tongue (includes "Stand," "Stay Alive," and "Strike Up the Band"), Capitol, 1993.

Sources

Books

Rees, Dafydd, and Luke Crampton, *Rock Movers & Shakers,* ABC/CLIO, 1991.

Periodicals

BAM, June 3, 1988.
Circus, September 30, 1987; January 31, 1988; December 31, 1988.
Daily Variety, June 10, 1993; July 26, 1993.
Guitar Player, June 1993.
Hit Parader, September 1993.
Los Angeles Times, July 25, 1993.
Metal Edge, October 1989.
People, August 23, 1993.
RIP, May 1993.
Screamer, May 1988; July 1990.
Teen Star's Photo Album, February 1987.

Additional information for this profile was obtained from HK Management, Inc. press materials, 1993.

—*Sonya Shelton*

Ray Price

Country singer

When Ray Price began recording in the early 1950s, he appeared to be the singularly anointed heir to Hank Williams's honky tonk throne. Yet Price, both innovative and fiercely independent, eventually evolved into the king of a style that came to be called "countrypolitan"—lush, carefully orchestrated, and well removed from the genre's lean and lonesome roots. Price was, in fact, much more than a competent honky tonk singer or country's first major artist to successfully employ intricate arrangements; he was, as music scribe Dave Marsh attested in the liner notes to *The Essential Ray Price: 1951-1962*, "an underrated honky tonk singer, possibly because he became such an exceptional balladeer."

Price was surely among country's most exacting singers. He was also a genius at selecting material, early on recording songs by time-proven stars like Willie Nelson, Kris Kristofferson, Bill Anderson, Mel Tillis, Jim Weatherly, Harlan Howard, and Roger Miller. Price's influence is felt to this day; the "Ray Price beat," a laconic shuffle used on such brilliant '50s honky tonk fare as "Crazy Arms" and "Release Me," is now the first word in country's rhythmic language.

Known as the "Cherokee Cowboy"—he was born in Cherokee County, Texas, on January 12, 1926—Price came to music after considering other vocational options. Though raised in Dallas, Price was introduced to farming, ranching, and animal husbandry while still a boy. He chose to study veterinary science at North Texas Agricultural College in Abilene before his education was interrupted by World War II. After serving with the Marines in the Pacific, Price returned to Abilene in 1946. Ranching would remain of vital interest to him throughout his life.

By 1947 Price was playing guitar and singing with various bands at sundry social functions. In 1948 he suspended his schooling to perform regularly on radio station KRBC's *Hillbilly Circus* in Abilene. Though still intent on ranching someday, in 1949 Price joined the prestigious *Big D Jamboree* in Dallas, sponsored by radio station KRLD. The program was eventually broadcast nationally by CBS, giving Price his initial mass exposure.

With the Nashville scene still in its infancy, Texas was the informal center of country music. One of the hot spots was Jim Beck's recording studio in Dallas, a facility visited consistently by stars such as Lefty Frizzell and Floyd Tillman. Price began hanging around at Beck's and soon became friendly with Frizzell; he hastily contributed a song titled "Give Me More, More, More of Your Kisses" to one of Frizzell's 1950 sessions. After recording some undistinguished sides at Beck's—

For the Record. . .

Born Ray Noble Price, January 12, 1926, in Perryville, TX; divorced first wife, 1968; married wife Jeanie, c. 1982. *Education:* Attended North Texas Agricultural College, 1946.

Played guitar and sang with various bands at social functions, mid-late 1940s; performed on radio shows *Hillbilly Circus,* KRBC, Abilene, TX, 1948, and *Big D Jamboree,* KRLD/CBS, Dallas, beginning in 1950; worked with Hank Williams and the Drifting Cowboys, early 1950s; signed to Bullet label, c. 1950; signed to Columbia Records, 1951; appeared on *Grand Ole Opry,* 1952-64; released single "Talk to Your Heart," 1952; formed Cherokee Cowboys, 1953; recorded gospel album with Anita Kerr Singers, 1974; signed with ABC/Dot, 1974; with Willie Nelson, recorded *San Antonio Rose,* 1980; recorded for various labels; re-signed with Columbia; rancher and sporadic concert performer, 1985—. *Military service:* U.S. Marines, World War II, Pacific Theater.

Addresses: Record company—Columbia Records/Sony Music Entertainment, Inc., 550 Madison Ave., New York, NY 10022-3211.

Price was still hard to separate from his heroes Hank Williams and Moon Mullican—he signed with the small Nashville label Bullet. His first record, "Jealous Lies," went nowhere.

Met Hank

Yet the Bullet recordings brought recognition: on March 15, 1951, Price signed a recording contract with the much larger Columbia label. Now socializing frequently with Frizzell, Price followed the older singer to Beaumont, Texas, where he met Hank Williams in the fall of 1951. Williams took Price under his wing, working shows with him and getting him a coveted spot on the *Grand Ole Opry.* In 1952 Price enjoyed his first hit, "Talk to Your Heart."

For a while Price even lived with Williams, worked with his band the Drifting Cowboys, and filled in for the troubled, self-destructive singer when he was unable to perform. Even after Williams's death, on New Year's Day, 1953, Price continued occasionally to front the Drifting Cowboys. But he longed for a sound closer to the western swing he first heard in east Texas, an exciting, less impassive style.

With that aim, Price formed the Cherokee Cowboys— three fiddles, bass, drums, guitar, piano, and steel guitar. By 1954 he was on his way to a fine collection of country hits. "Release Me" and the defiant "If You Don't Somebody Will" both reached the Top Ten. On March 1, 1956, just as Elvis Presley was shaking country music to its core, Price released the Ralph Mooney-penned "Crazy Arms." In addition to unveiling his trademark shuffle, "Crazy Arms" instituted the now-traditional second harmony on each chorus and the predominance of a single, linear fiddle line.

As Price later told *Country Music's* John Morthland, "The sound they had going at the time in country was a 2-4 sound with a double stop fiddle. I added drums to it and a 4-4 bass and shuffle rhythm and the single string fiddle. I don't know where it came from; it's just what I wanted. Everybody at the session thought it was the funniest thing they ever heard. They just thought it was strange. It was—and it was on the charts for 45 weeks."

Scored With the Innovative "Crazy Arms"

Number One for 20 weeks, "Crazy Arms" is one of country's monumental recordings—as compelling coming across the airwaves as it was in an unlit roadhouse. In what would later seem a gentle irony, Price was then considered *the* hardened country traditionalist, ignoring pop's more sugary sentiments. With the death of Williams and the decline of Frizzell, Price and his rhythmically insistent songs of hurt and disappointment nearly singlehandedly kept the hard country torch aflame in the late 1950s.

Although Price had other hits in 1956, notably "Wasted Words" and "I've Got a New Heartache," country music itself was struggling in the wake of Elvis's rockabilly revolution. Price remained undaunted, refusing to sing rock and roll; indeed, the fiddles and pedal steel were even more prominent in his subsequent recordings. By the end of the '50s, Price's influence had become enormous.

In 1958 Price made a hit of the touching "Curtain in the Window" and Bill Anderson's great story of urban anonymity, "City Lights." A year later he was voted favorite male country vocalist in nearly all of the major music magazines. Price's own 1961 hit composition, "Soft Rain," was inspired by his grandfather's death. And by the early 1960s, the Cherokee Cowboys were a way station for a future who's who of country music: Willie Nelson and Johnny Paycheck played bass; Roger Miller at one point was the drummer; Hank Cochran played guitar; and Buddy Emmons was Price's long-time pedal steel player.

Price became a huge concert attraction and continued to enjoy hit records—Nelson's "Nightlife" was Number One in 1963—but his association with the Grand Ole Opry ended in 1964: he was dropped for not appearing the mandatory 26 weeks on the Opry stage. By the mid-1960s Price would leave Nashville, where he had taken up residence, for Texas, the result of divorce, the death of his father, and a controversial career direction.

Strings and the Countrypolitan Sound

After recording a 1957 gospel album with the Anita Kerr Singers, Price had begun seriously considering the use of orchestrated string arrangements with softer, more poignant material. "That got me on the track that people liked strings, so I began adding strings down through the years to certain songs," Price told Morthland. "I was experimenting, until I did 'Danny Boy.' That's when I went all out, and that's when it all hit the fan."

Truly, it was not until 1964's "Burning Memories" and a 1967 remake of the standard "Danny Boy" that the world would hear the new Ray Price sound; his vocal register lowered and subdued, the fiddles and pedal steel replaced by strings, Price made widely popular countrypolitan music that left longtime hard-country fans disgusted and feeling abandoned. Once considered Hank Williams's hand-picked successor, or at least George Jones's great honky tonk contemporary, Price was now lumped in with more conventional crossover stars like Eddy Arnold.

Still, much of this new Price material was emotionally moving. And it improved. In 1969 Price had major hits with Kris Kristofferson's tender lament, "For the Good Times," and Arnold's "Make the World Go Away." He charted his final Number One in 1973, with "You're the Best Thing That Ever Happened to Me." In 1974, after 23 years, Price left the Columbia label for ABC/Dot.

The late 1970s were uneven for Price, among the highlights a Hank Williams tribute album in 1976 and a Cherokee Cowboys reunion LP in 1977. Price moved to Monument in 1978, the label where Roy Orbison had created his dense, operatic singles. Price recorded some decent material with Monument—"Misty Morning Rain" and "Feet" were both hits. Throughout this period Price was also a highly successful rancher, donating his thoroughbreds to Texas A&M University in 1979.

By 1980 Price found it difficult to obtain a recording contract. Turning to his old sideman Willie Nelson—by then a superstar—Price recorded the superb *San Antonio Rose,* an album of duets. It was a stirring return to his old sound. Hits from that outing included a remake of Patsy Cline's "Faded Love" and "Don't You

Ever Get Tired of Hurting Me." In 1981 Price initiated the "Ray Price Country Starsearch," a contest that called for him to appear at the finals in all 50 states. In 1983 he performed "San Antonio Rose" for the soundtrack to the Clint Eastwood film *Honky Tonk Man;* he also portrayed a member of Bob Wills's legendary band the Texas Playboys.

Since the mid-1980s, Price has largely tended to his ranching concerns; he lives outside of Dallas with his wife, Jeanie. He has recorded pleasant, though uneven, albums with several labels, including Dimension, Viva, Warners, and Step One. After reconciling the mammoth contrasts in his influential career, Price had most recently re-signed with Columbia. Ray Price's long musical purpose has been informed by a stubborn self-reliance that found him updating hard country when it was questioning its own relevance, and then abandoning it altogether when he heard in his head a sound more compelling.

Selected discography

For the Good Times, Columbia, 1970.
(With Willie Nelson) *San Antonio Rose,* Columbia, 1980.
Happens to the Best, Pair, 1986.
The Honky Tonk Years (recorded 1951-1956), Rounder, 1986.
Sometimes a Rose, Step One, 1989, reissued, Columbia, 1992.
The Essential Ray Price: 1951-1962, Columbia Legacy, 1991.
Hits on Monument, Monument, 1991.
Greatest Hits (four volumes), Columbia.
All Time Greatest Hits, Columbia.

Sources

Books

Malone, Bill C., *Country Music U.S.A,* University of Texas Press, 1984.
Stambler, Irwin, and Grelun Landon, *The Encyclopedia of Folk, Country & Western Music,* St. Martin's, 1984.

Periodicals

Country Music, March 1976; September 1977; July 1980.
The Journal of the American Academy for the Preservation of Old Time Country Music, Volume II, Number 5, October 1992.

Additional information for this profile was obtained from liner notes by Dave Marsh to *The Essential Ray Price: 1951-1962,* Columbia Legacy, 1991.

—*Stewart Francke*

Primus

Rock band

The Northern California avant-rock trio Primus provides a shining example for bands who want to succeed on their own terms. Fusing the skittering rhythmic attack of progressive-metal bands like Rush, the groove of funk and hippie rock, and the eccentricity of such experimental artists as Frank Zappa, the Residents, and Captain Beefheart, Primus has followed its own musical calling to large-scale industry success. Fronted by bassist-vocalist Les Claypool, who can produce thousands of bizarre tones on his instrument and almost as many cartoonish characters with his voice, Primus has journeyed from the underground to the headlining spot at the 1993 Lollapalooza music festival, arguably the nation's most important alternative rock tour. Joe Gore of *Guitar Player* cited guitarist Larry "Ler" LaLonde's description of the group's sound as "progressive freak-out music"; Gore also noted what he called "the Primus paradox: if your music is *really* uncommercial, you can sell a ton of records."

Like LaLonde, Claypool grew up in the northern California town of El Sobrante. "I was raised in the land of

For the Record. . .

Members include **Tim "Herb" Alexander** (born c. 1965; joined group 1988), drums; **Les Claypool** (born c. 1964), bass; and **Larry "Ler" LaLonde** (born c. 1969; joined group 1989), guitar. Former members include **Todd Huth** (left group 1989), guitar; and **Jay Lane** (left group 1988), drums.

Band formed in El Sobrante, CA, 1984; released first album, *Suck on This*, on self-administered label Prawn Song, 1989; signed with Caroline Records and released *Frizzle Fry*, 1990; signed with Interscope Records and released *Sailing the Seas of Cheese*, 1991; appeared in film *Bill and Ted's Bogus Journey*, 1991; headlined Lollapalooza festival, 1993.

Awards: Gold albums for *Sailing the Seas of Cheese* and *Pork Soda,* both 1993.

Addresses: *Record company*—Interscope Records, 10900 Wilshire Blvd., Ste. 1230, Los Angeles, CA 90024.

Budweiser," he quipped to *Rolling Stone's* Michael Azerrad. Having been raised in a working-class family—his father and grandfather both worked as mechanics—helped form Claypool's worldview but also sharpened his resolve to escape his hometown's oppressive normalcy. "I would have blasted out one way or another," he insisted. His mother told Azerrad that Les "was a bouncing boy. He used to like to jump in his jumpy chair. I think that's where he got the strength in his legs. I never saw anybody who could jump as well as he did in that jumpy chair."

Cartoons and Fusion

Claypool's mother also remembered that her son "liked to watch TV a lot. I think that's where he got a lot of ideas. He'd sit there on his little tiny plastic motorcycle that he had and watch cartoons." Les acquired his first bass at age 13; "I pulled weeds to pay for it," he told *Guitar Player.* He recalled to *Rolling Stone* that he "sat in front of the television and noodled" after first hearing hard-rock guitarist Ted Nugent.

In the ensuing years, his eclecticism alienated most of the single-minded rock players around him. On the one hand, Claypool worshipped the bassist and leader of Rush—"If it wasn't for Geddy Lee," he has declared, "I probably wouldn't be playing bass"—but also adored funk pioneer Larry Graham, the bottom end of the psychedelic soul-rock band Sly and the Family Stone.

He was equally enamored of jazz and fusion masters like Stanley Clarke. Claypool found a kindred spirit in LaLonde, who joined his art-metal project Blind Illusion. LaLonde—who learned much of his technique at the feet of guitar guru Joe Satriani—also played in a "satanic" metal band called the Possessed as a teenager.

Claypool further honed his chops in "biker bars" as bassist for an R&B cover troupe called the Tommy Crank Band. "It was four sets a night, up to five nights a week—that's how I learned discipline and how to actually groove," he explained to *Guitar Player's* Gore. After that, in 1984, he assembled the first version of Primus—initially called Primate—with guitarist Todd Huth and a drum machine. The group gathered a following over the next few years, and Claypool's do-it-yourself ethic extended to buying a printing press and making T-shirts for his and his friends' bands. Drummer Tim "Herb" Alexander finally stuck, replacing Jay Lane, but the day after Claypool asked Alexander to join the group, Huth quit.

Suck on This

For a moment, Claypool thought his claim to fame would be as the bassist for the up-and-coming (and later superstar) metal group Metallica. Original bassist Cliff Burton had been killed in a bus accident, and as a childhood friend of guitarist Kirk Hammett, Claypool got a chance to audition for the spot; but his affinity for R&B acts like the Isley Brothers scared the headbangers off. Eventually, he recruited LaLonde to take Huth's place in a revamped Primus. The group was two-thirds new, but LaLonde undertook the arduous task of learning all of Huth's parts and then participating in a live recording that became the first Primus album, *Suck on This.* Released in 1989 on the group's own Prawn Song label, it was financed with $3,000 borrowed from Claypool's father. "The three of us had a chemistry that sounded like Primus," the bassist recalled in *Rolling Stone,* "but it was different than before. I was nervous as hell the first show we did, but our original fans accepted us."

Long before LaLonde and Alexander joined the band, Claypool explained to Rolling Stone, the group's fans had begun chanting "You Suck" as an honorific at their shows. "People would follow us around telling us how cool we were, and we'd be like 'Nah, we suck.' It evolved, and then it became good marketing. We'd go down the street, and someone will yell, 'You suck,' and I'll say 'Oh, thank you very much,' which freaks out whoever's with you." Soon "Primus Sucks" appeared on T-shirts and became a *de rigeur* slogan on the Bay Area music scene. The group's sound—which caught the attention of critics during the ascent of metal/funk hybrids like the Red Hot Chili Peppers and Faith No More—began to be categorized as "funk-rock," though Alexander despised funk and Claypool has always protested that real funk doesn't sound anything like his band.

In any event, Claypool's busy, percussive bass lines crisscrossed Alexander's tight beats and allowed LaLonde—whose guitar idols are sainted rock experimentalists Frank Zappa and Jerry Garcia—to explore, rather than merely hold down, the group's songs. Claypool's lyrics tend to be loopy character studies, often sung in voices that critics have frequently compared to cartoon voice-over wizard Mel Blanc. Claypool told *Musician* that he tended at first to write "statement" songs, but ultimately, he revealed, "[I] found that's not me, to preach social ideas as music. I'm putting down observations, and sometimes it may just be crap."

Signed With Major Label

Following the cult success of *Suck on This,* the band signed with noted independent label Caroline Records, which reissued their debut and released the follow-up, 1990's *Frizzle Fry,* produced by Primus's 19-year-old friend Matt Winegar. "The Northern California thrash-funk trio recaptures the anarchic spontaneity of their debut (the high-energy, low-budget *Suck on This*)," opined *Guitar Player,* "but with tighter performances and better production." The review praised the "visceral punch" of LaLonde's "angular lines" and noted that Claypool "hammers out dense but groovy lines that flesh out the bony trio texture." The band toured exhaustively in support of the album and soon landed a deal with a major label, Interscope, a joint venture with Atlantic Records.

In 1991 Claypool and company released *Sailing the Seas of Cheese,* a further refinement of their sound. "In many ways the more metallic, undulating *Frizzle Fry* is a better document of the ugliness and energy that is Primus," reflected *Musician's* Matt Resnicoff, "though *Cheese's* pristine presentation captures its own space in a world where saying something sucks is like a love tap." *Guitar Player* marveled at the group's eclecticism: "These avant-headbangers combine speed metal energy, funkoid groove, and art-rock quirkiness (imagine Metallica, Rush, and the Chili Peppers liquified in a blender)." *Cheese* included the rampaging and irresistible single "Tommy the Cat," which featured a cameo vocal by gravelly voiced singer-songwriter Tom Waits and was selected for the soundtrack to the film *Bill and*

Ted's Bogus Journey, in which Primus briefly appeared. *Cheese* went gold in April of 1993.

Also in 1993—in some sense the band's breakthrough year—Primus received widespread public attention when they were named headliner of the Lollapalooza

> *"If this band could write a melody—or, God forbid, a power ballad—it would rule the entire planet."*
> —Entertainment Weekly

rock festival. This assignment helped their new album, *Pork Soda,* debut at Number Seven on the *Billboard* pop chart, a previously unheard-of feat for such an unconventional band. In a feature on Lollapalooza, *Entertainment Weekly* insisted, "There's no resisting the frenetic danceability" of the trio's "P-Funk meets Captain Beefheart set," adding, "If this band could write a melody—or, God forbid, a power ballad—it would rule the entire planet."

Entertainment Weekly called *Pork Soda* "a musical hiccup—a gnarly, funkadelic mix of metal and art rock highlighted by Claypool's slaphappy bass lines and carnival-barker voice." *Rolling Stone* deemed the album "a weird, whimsical grab bag." *Pork Soda* featured the romps "My Name Is Mud" and "Mr. Krinkle," both of which spawned grotesque, surrealistic videos. Of Primus's Lollapalooza offering, *Entertainment Today* claimed, "They put on a superior show that was remarkably tight and demonstrated they were the right choice for the closing band."

Primus recorded *Pork Soda* at minimal cost by bringing digital recording equipment into their rehearsal space rather than renting studio time. "The quality we got on this record has a lot to do with the sheer quantity of things we could afford to record," Claypool explained to *Guitar Player's* Gore. "Had we gone into an expensive studio and tried to do what we did, this album would have cost hundreds of thousands of dollars. We wouldn't have done nearly so many abstract things." This home studio—known as From the Corn—has afforded Primus the opportunity to record other projects, such as a collaboration among Claypool, Metallica guitarist Hammett, and Faith No More drummer Mike Bordin, as well as records by former Primus guitarist Huth's band Porch and Disposable Heroes of Hiphoprisy guitarist Charlie Hunter's side band. Primus hoped to release some of these recordings on the revamped Prawn Song. In other artistic explorations, Claypool collaborated with Lance Montoya on the whimsical clay sculpture that graces the cover of *Pork Soda.*

With major label support, Primus has emerged as one of the most musically daring acts in rock, yet its bizarre cross-fertilizations flourish in a garden of relative independence. It's the best of both worlds, and Claypool knows it: staying involved in all aspects of his band's work "gives you confidence," he insisted to *Guitar Player,* "and that's the most important thing to have in any aspect of the music business."

Selected discography

Suck on This, Prawn Song, 1989, reissued, Caroline, 1990.
Frizzle Fry, Caroline, 1990.
Sailing the Seas of Cheese (includes "Tommy the Cat"), Interscope, 1991.
(Contributors) "Tommy the Cat," *Bill and Ted's Bogus Journey* (soundtrack), Warner Bros., 1991.

Pork Soda (includes "My Name Is Mud" and "Mr. Krinkle"), Interscope, 1993.

Sources

BAM, June 18, 1993.
Billboard, April 10, 1993.
Entertainment Today, August 13, 1993.
Entertainment Weekly, June 18, 1993; July 18, 1993.
Guitar Player, September 1990; June 1991; August 1991; June 1993.
Musician, November 1991; July 1993.
Oakland Press (Oakland Co., MI), October 17, 1993.
RIP, August 1993.
Rolling Stone, June 13, 1991; October 31, 1991; June 10, 1993; September 2, 1993.
Spin, October 1993.

Additional information for this profile was obtained from Interscope Records press materials, 1993.

—Simon Glickman

Keith Richards

Much has been made of Keith Richards's reputation as rock's ultimate bad boy; his weathered face and checkered past are legendary. As the guitarist and primary musical force behind the Rolling Stones, one of the most influential bands in rock and roll history, Richards may have been less visible than flamboyant frontman Mick Jagger, but he provided an example of cool that other musicians have imitated for decades. In the words of author Mark Leyner, who interviewed Richards for *Spin,* "Any one of a thousand Keith Richards photographs could serve as the defining totemic image of the rock 'n' roll life."

Yet Richards's drug history and onstage demeanor have frequently overshadowed his remarkable focus and seriousness as a musician. Inspired by a variety of roots-based musical forms, primarily the blues, he has helped the Stones branch out continually as a vital creative unit. Since 1988 Richards has released two critically acclaimed solo albums with a versatile back-up band called the X-Pensive Winos; though he long avoided recording apart from the Stones, his work without them indicates he has lost none of his fire. As he noted in one of many candid interviews with *Rolling Stone,* his intention has long been to "grow this music up"—to leave behind the teen appeal and theatricality of rock's past and invest it with maturity and honest feeling.

Richards also demonstrated in the wake of his renewed solo effort that he had reached a state of happy grace in his life. "The impression Richards gives is of someone perfectly content to be who he is and do what he does with no evident regard for external judgments or objections," noted Ira Robbins in *Pulse!* The guitarist confirmed this perception in numerous interviews: "To me, the main thing about living on this planet is to know who the hell you are and be real about it," he told *Rolling Stone.* "That's the reason I'm still alive." Content in his second marriage, the father of several children of various ages, he indicated that he'd put aside the youth-obsessed sentimentalism exemplified by a classic line in "My Generation," a 1960s standard by Stones contemporaries The Who: "Hope I die before I get old." *People* quoted an interview in which Richards declared, "Getting old is a fascinating thing. The older you get, the older you want to get."

From Black and White to Technicolor

Richards was born in 1943 in Dartford, England. His father, Bert, worked in a factory, struggling to feed the family. "We just about made the rent," the guitarist recalled in a *Rolling Stone* interview. "The luxuries were very, very few." Keith knew early on that he didn't have

For the Record. . .

Born December 18, 1943, in Dartford, England; known earlier in his career as Keith Richard; son of Bert Richards (a factory laborer and electrician) and Doris Dupress; married Patti Hansen (a model and actress), December 18, 1983; children: (with Anita Pallenberg) Marlon, Dandelion (later Angela); (with Hansen) Theodora, Alexandra. *Education:* Attended art school in Sidcup, England.

Member of the Rolling Stones, 1962—; solo performer, 1988—. Appeared in and acted as musical director of film *Hail! Hail! Rock 'n' Roll* and produced soundtrack album, 1987.

Awards: With Rolling Stones, inducted into Rock and Roll Hall of Fame, 1989.

Addresses: *Agent*—Raindrop Services, 1776 Broadway, New York, NY 10019. *Record company*—Virgin Records, 338 North Foothill Rd., Beverly Hills, CA 90210-3608.

his father's discipline—"That's the hardest work of all, bein' lazy," he quipped to Kurt Loder in 1987, as quoted in the rock scribe's *Bat Chain Puller*—and he was expelled from the Dartford Technical School for truancy at age 15. He spent some time at art school before discovering the guitar and the blues. Rock and roll was brand new in the late 1950s, and its arrival, Richards told Loder, signaled the advent of "a new era. Totally. It was almost like A.D. and B.C., and 1956 was year 1, you know? The world was black-and-white, and then suddenly it went into living color. Suddenly there was a reason to be around, besides just knowing you were gonna have to work and draggin' your ass to school every day. Suddenly everything went *zoom*—glorious Technicolor."

Richards always understood—and is at pains to explain to contemporary rock fans—that rock and roll derived in large part from the blues, an African-American art form. And the work of black artists in ensuing years, from soul and rhythm and blues to the pioneering rock of Richards's idol, Chuck Berry, would provide basic musical compass points for the guitarist and his band. Richards met Mick Jagger in 1960; the singer was then attending the London School of Economics. They shared a love of R&B and ended up jamming together with a handful of other musicians. The Rolling Stones—named after a song by blues legend Muddy Waters—were formed in 1962 and featured a shifting roster of musicians as they coalesced, though Jagger and Richards were constants. The rhythm section of Bill Wyman and Charlie Watts stabilized the band's sound,

and they released their first single, a Chuck Berry cover, in 1963. Although they were often touted as "London's answer to the Beatles" and at first sported a clean-cut look, the group's gritty, sexually charged sound and attitude offered a unique appeal. Their 1965 single "(I Can't Get No) Satisfaction" was a monster hit that became one of the defining songs of the era. *Newsweek* later called Richards's signature "Satisfaction" guitar riff "five notes that shook the world."

The Stones unleashed a string of hit singles—among them "The Last Time," "Time Is on My Side," "19th Nervous Breakdown" and "Get Off My Cloud"—before the tide of the decade turned to "album-oriented" rock. Late-1960s and early-1970s Stones LPs such as *Beggar's Banquet, Let It Bleed, Sticky Fingers,* and *Exile on Main Street* have become hallmarks of committed, adventuresome rock. The Stones also experienced a tragic watershed of the hippie age: at a 1970 concert at California's Altamont Speedway, members of the Hell's Angels motorcycle club—the band's erstwhile security force—fatally stabbed an unruly fan as the Stones played their hit "Sympathy for the Devil."

Poster Boy for Excess

Richards, during this tumultuous period, became something of a poster boy for excess. While many rockers—including Jagger and the Beatles—championed mysticism and psychedelia, Richards was laying low and shooting up. He admitted to Bryan Appleyard of *Vanity Fair* that during his heroin days in New York, he carried a gun, and he recalled, "I got used to getting shot at." At the same time, however, his notoriety often bestowed a strange immunity upon him; would-be muggers waved him through and "cops [gave him] lifts when [it was] raining." In Toronto in 1977 he was arrested on a serious possession charge and—faced with stringent penalties—agreed to undergo drug treatment and perform at a 1979 charity concert. Rock lore has it that Richards periodically had his blood changed in order to curtail various bouts with addiction.

Living on this particular edge, he told *Spin*'s Leyner, was in part a way of dealing with stardom's distorting effect on one's self-regard: "I've tried to keep my feet on the ground—sometimes almost six feet under—in order not to stay up there in that stratosphere [of fame]. Maybe the whole dope thing was some way of negating that—'cause that put me down in the gutter. One minute I'm operating as a superstar and the next I'm shooting up with some guys on the Lower East Side. I'll never know really what that was all about—just an experiment that went on too long, I guess." Richards explained to Loder in *Rolling Stone* in 1981, "The problem is not how to get off of it, it's how to *stay* off of it." By 1980 Richards's long-term relationship with Anita Pallenberg had come to an end, and in 1983 he would marry actress and model Patti Hansen. Jagger served as best man at their wedding in Mexico; by the time Richards and Hansen had their two daughters, his two children by Pallenberg, Marlon and Dandelion, were in their teens. In 1982, the guitarist was reunited with his father, whom he had not seen in many years; their newfound closeness became another constant in Richards's life.

The Rolling Stones sustained their success through the 1970s—releasing such hit albums as *Goat's Head Soup, It's Only Rock 'N' Roll,* and *Some Girls*—and played in more and more massive arenas. By the 1980s, their tours had become events of elephantine proportions, and though he still felt firmly committed to the band, Richards was keenly aware of the intimacy and directness lost in the fanfare. In 1985 Mick Jagger decided to release a solo album, *She's the Boss,* and he announced in 1986 that he would not tour with the Stones in support of their recent record, *Dirty Work.* Richards and Jagger traded barbs in the press; "To me, twenty-five years of integrity went down the drain with what he did," the guitarist told Anthony DeCurtis in *Rolling Stone.* Speculation about the band's imminent dissolution flew about and were not quelled by Richards's decision to ink a deal with Virgin Records and put out his own solo album.

Birth of the X-Pensive Winos

In addition to assembling a band, Richards served as musical director for Taylor Hackford's *Hail! Hail! Rock 'N' Roll,* a film biography of Chuck Berry. "He's a loner," Richards told DeCurtis of the senior rocker. "That's why I could work with Chuck Berry, because he's very much like Mick." But not working with Mick—or rhythm guitarist Ron Wood or Wyman or Watts—was Richards's imperative for the moment. He decided to collaborate with drummer Steve Jordan, who had played in the World's Most Dangerous Band on television's *Late Night With David Letterman,* and assembled a stellar ensemble that included bassist Charley Drayton, guitarist Waddy Wachtel, and keyboardist Ivan Neville.

An air of mutual admiration and camaraderie pervaded the sessions for *Talk Is Cheap,* the first album by Keith Richards and the X-Pensive Winos. "Every drummer's dream is to play with Keith," Jordan declared in *Newsweek.* "He's the Time Machine, right?" Jordan wasn't referring to a nostalgia trip; Richards's rhythmic accuracy as a guitarist—what musician's call "time"—is legendary. Wachtel confirmed this, adding, "It's due to

his right hand. Magic. When he plays rhythm, it's like a room full of the best drummers in the world." *Talk Is Cheap* featured guest musicians like funk superstars Bootsy Collins and Maceo Parker and soulful vocals from Sarah Dash. Yet Richards's own singing, only an occasional feature on the Stones' records, was the biggest surprise for many listeners and critics. *Guitar Player* rated the album the best by the Rolling Stones—even though Richards was the only Stone on it—in nearly two decades. Richards and his group also released a live album taken from a performance at the Hollywood Palladium in December of 1988.

The Stones reassembled for the hugely successful 1989 album *Steel Wheels,* which spawned a tremendous tour. "The songs just tumbled out," Richards told the *New York Times* of the recording sessions in Barbados. "First, we just screamed and yelled at each other. We needed to clear the air, which, as old mates, we're very good at. Then, when we got into that room and sat down with our guitars, something entirely different took over." That year, the Rolling Stones were inducted into the Rock and Roll Hall of Fame. In a 1992 *Guitar Player* interview, Richards noted that the imbalance produced by frenzied playing and idle downtime had been a root cause of the tension within the group. "And that's what the Stones had to live with from the early '70s until the middle '80s: constant work for a year and a half, and then nothing for two years. And that stopping and starting was fraying. That was the underlying force of what all of that shit was about."

1992 saw the publication of Victor Bockris's largely panned Poseidon Press tome *Keith Richards: The Biography,* which Gene Santoro attacked in *Pulse!* as a collection of "recycled press clips" interlaced with pretentious analysis and pop clichés. More importantly, late in the year Richards released his second solo studio album, *Main Offender.* Once again employing the versatile X-Pensive Winos—who traded instruments during the sessions—Richards explored more emotional territory this time around. *Entertainment Weekly* awarded the album a B+ and closed its review with a cheeky "Your move, Mick." Echoing Guitar Player's assessment of *Talk Is Cheap,* Spin's Leyner called *Main Offender* "the finest 'Rolling Stones' album in years," elaborating, "It's stripped down and full of gorgeous songwriting—sinewy and poignant." *Musician* was a trifle more critical, suggesting that *Main Offender* was "the best mediocre album of the year," perhaps because it conveyed a pleasantly raw feel with no obvious effort: "Exile on Easy Street." For his part, Richards revealed in an interview with *Rolling Stone's* Kim Neely, "This band is very new and fresh for me. In a way it reminds me of working with the Stones in the early days."

The Stones were set to regroup for a new record in 1993, despite the departure of bassist Wyman, which apparently had been in the works for some time. Richards had joked about scaring Wyman into remaining by threatening to replace him with a woman, but this macho gambit presumably failed. Richards told Neely, "I think there's a possibility of another golden period in the Stones somewhere," this projection ostensibly undimmed by Wyman's exit. As to his own future, Richards told *Rolling Stone*'s DeCurtis in 1988, "I played with Muddy Waters six months before he died, and the cat was just as vital as he was in his youth. And he did it until the day he died. To me, that is the important thing. I mean, what am I gonna do now, go for job retraining and learn to be a welder? I'll do this until I drop. I'm committed to it and that's it."

In both his role as a Rolling Stone and as that of a solo artist, Keith Richards has demonstrated that it is possible to "grow up" in rock and maintain the spark and intensity required to keep it fresh. "To me, it's important to prove that this isn't just teenage kids' shit and you should feel embarrassed when you're over forty and still doing it," he remarked to DeCurtis. "That's not necessary. This is a job. It's a man's job, and it's a lifelong job. And if there's a sucker to ever prove it, I hope to be the sucker."

Selected discography

With the Rolling Stones; on ABKCO Records

The Rolling Stones (England's Newest Hitmakers), 1964.
12 X 5, 1964.
The Rolling Stones Now!, 1965.
December's Children, 1965.
Big Hits (High Tide and Green Grass) (includes "[I Can't Get No] Satisfaction," "The Last Time," "Time Is on My Side," "19th Nervous Breakdown," and "Get Off My Cloud"), 1966.
Aftermath, 1966.
Got LIVE If You Want It!, 1966.
Between the Buttons, 1967.
Flowers, 1967.
Their Satanic Majesties Request, 1967.
Beggar's Banquet (includes "Sympathy for the Devil"), 1968.
Through the Past, Darkly (Big Hits, Volume II), 1969.
Let It Bleed, 1969.
Get Yer Ya-Ya's Out, 1970.
Hot Rocks, 1964-1971, 1971.
More Hot Rocks (Big Hits and Fazed Cookies), 1972.
The Rolling Stones Singles Collection: The London Years, 1989.

On Rolling Stones/Columbia Records

Sticky Fingers, 1971.
Exile on Main Street, 1972.
Goat's Head Soup, 1973.
It's Only Rock & Roll, 1974.
Made in the Shade, 1975.
Black and Blue, 1976.
Love You Live, 1977.
Some Girls, 1978.
Emotional Rescue, 1980.
Sucking in the Seventies, 1981.
Tattoo You, 1981.
Still Life, 1982.
Undercover, 1983.
Rewind (1971-1984), 1984.
Dirty Work, 1986.
Steel Wheels, 1989.
25 X 5, 1990.
Flashpoint, 1991.

With the X-Pensive Winos; on Virgin Records

Talk Is Cheap, 1988.
Keith Richards and the X-Pensive Winos Live at the Hollywood Palladium, December 15, 1988, 1988.
Main Offender, 1992.

Sources

Books

Loder, Kurt, *Bat Chain Puller: Rock & Roll in the Age of Celebrity*, St. Martin's, 1990.
The Rolling Stone Interviews: The 1980s, edited by Sid Holt, St. Martin's/Rolling Stone Press, 1989.

Periodicals

Entertainment Weekly, November 6, 1992.
Guitar Player, December 1992; September 1993.
Musician, May 1992; December 1992.
New York Times, June 4, 1989.
Newsweek, October 24, 1988.
People, November 9, 1992.
Pulse!, November 1992.
Rolling Stone, November 26, 1992; February 4, 1993.
Spin, January 1993.
Vanity Fair, December 1992.

—Simon Glickman

Henry Rollins

Singer, songwriter, author, spoken-word performer

Formidable and fiercely independent, recording artist Henry Rollins has earned an array of titles from music reviewers; Chris Mundy, writing for *Rolling Stone* in 1992, called Rollins "punk's poet laureate" and a "primal scream personified." Hobey Echlin applied another label in Detroit's *Metro Times,* terming Rollins "the post-punk generation's prophet of rage." These epithets capture the dual nature of Rollins's reputation: brutal rebelliousness characterizes his work as vocalist for Black Flag and the Rollins Band, two of the hardest hard-core bands in punk history, while Rollins's discipline and thoughtful observations of humankind inform his creative output as an essayist, poet, and spoken-word performer. In both incarnations, Rollins is revered by leaders of the punk and alternative rock camps.

Rollins was born Henry Garfield on February 13, 1961, in Washington, D.C. His childhood was shaped by a barrage of painful experiences, among them his parent's divorce when he was still quite young, his father's abuse and emotional abandonment, unwanted sexual encounters, and the torment of classmates who singled Rollins out for being different. After his parents split up, he lived with his mother, moving from apartment to apartment. One of his few positive memories of that time, according to a self-penned 1992 Imago Recording Company press biography, was of the music that remained a constant in his ever-relocating home: "[My mother] played a lot of records and went to plays and musicals. There was music in the house all the time. . . . I used to take her records into my room and play them until they were all scratched up." He recalled enjoying a range of jazz and Motown before discovering hard rock; finally, in high school, he found the underground world of punk, including the Los Angeles-based hard-core ensemble Black Flag.

Iron and Soul

The anger and isolation that Rollins experienced as a child intensified when he was enrolled in a military academy. In an essay titled "Iron and the Soul" that appeared in *Details* magazine, Rollins characterized his life there, writing, "The humiliation of teachers calling me 'garbage can' and telling me I'd be mowing lawns for a living. And the very real terror of my fellow students. . . . I was skinny and clumsy, and when others would tease me I didn't run home crying, wondering why. I knew all too well. I was there to be antagonized." It was in the midst of this hell, however, that Rollins was introduced to something that would make made him

For the Record. . .

Born Henry Garfield, February 13, 1961, in Washington D.C. *Education:* Spent one semester at college, 1979.

Managed reptile department of pet shop, late 1970s, and ice cream shop, 1979-81. Became singer with band Black Flag, 1981; became spoken-word performer, 1983; formed book publishing (and later mail-order and video) company 2.13.61, 1984; Black Flag disbanded, 1986; formed Rollins Band, 1987; band recorded with independent labels Texas Hotel and QuarterStick, late 1980s; signed with Imago Recording Company, 1991; band released *The End of Silence,* 1992; released spoken-word album *The Boxed Life,* 1993; contributor to *Elle* magazine and commentator for *MTV Sports,* beginning in 1994; appeared in film *The Chase,* 1994; established labels Zero Zero and Now Hear This, 1994.

Addresses: *Office*—2.13.61, P.O. Box 1910, Los Angeles, CA 90078.

feel strong and valuable; an advisor named Mr. Pepperman, "a powerfully built Vietnam veteran," put Rollins on a weight-training program—an intensive discipline that prohibited him from becoming preoccupied with the look of his body or the intimidation that it could inflict on others. "At no time was I to look at myself in the mirror or tell anyone at school what I was doing," he recalled.

The regimen had a powerful effect on Rollins, altering both his physique and his sense of self-esteem. "I saw a body, not just the shell that housed my stomach and my heart," he wrote. "My biceps bulged. My chest had definition. I felt strong. It was the first time I can remember having a sense of myself." Rollins understood that the strength he had acquired could be attributed more fully to his emotional convictions than to his body; he explained, "Muscle mass does not always equal strength. Strength is kindness and sensitivity. Strength is understanding that your power is both physical and emotional. That it comes from the body and the mind. And the heart."

Once he had learned control and dedication from "the iron," Rollins was able to apply his new-found drive to everything else in his life. Describing his adolescence to *Musician* contributor Jon Pareles, Rollins said, "If we were into something, we were living it. . . . Skateboards, 24 hours a day. Bikes. Whatever we were doing. I worked at a pet shop, I ran the reptile department,

inventoried, ordered, did everything. Anything I was into I would just land on and totally take over. I'd want to do 80 hours a day."

Invited to Audition for Black Flag

After graduating from high school in 1979, Rollins became involved in the local hard-core punk scene with the same energy. He tried college, but left after one semester. While working at a friend's ice cream store, where he quickly rose to manager, Rollins would spend his off hours watching the bands that he loved, like D.C.'s punk-reggae hybrid Bad Brains. One night, he drove to New York City to see Black Flag perform—leaving right after his shift at the store and planning to return in time to open up again the next morning. When he requested a song that night, the band let him come up on stage to sing with them, and—in an odd take on the Cinderella story—the members of Black Flag asked Rollins to return for an audition a few days later; they just happened to be looking for a new vocalist.

Rollins began singing with Black Flag in 1981 and would stay with the group until guitarist and nominal leader Greg Ginn dissolved it in 1986. During that time, he became both an integral part of Black Flag's image—though the band had been around since 1976—and developed a solid reputation of his own. Larry Birnbaum captured Rollins's typical stage presence in a 1984 concert review for *Down Beat,* reporting, "The muscular, heavily tattooed Rollins . . . made his entrance, clad only in gym shorts. A charismatic figure a la Iggy Pop, he posed and strutted along the lip of the stage, barking and screeching the lyrics with professional aplomb as he fended off attempts by his adoring fans to pull his pants down."

But touring and recording with the band, though it brought a certain fame, by no means made Rollins's life glamorous. Steve Appleford, a writer for *Cream,* noted that Black Flag spent a lot of time "sleeping in parking lots, in train stations, sometimes even shoplifting food, eating off other people's plates in restaurants and hiding from the police, white power groups, religious zealots and a constant media assault."

After the band's dissolution, Rollins turned immediately to his next project. He contacted guitarist Chris Haskett and, within four months, had produced the record *Hot Animal Machine.* By April of 1987, when Rollins recruited drummer Sim Cain and bassist Andrew Weiss, the Rollins Band was starting to solidify; the group soon added a permanent sound man or "stylist" from Holland, Theo Van Rock. That line-up would remain until 1993, when Weiss departed.

Obsessive About Rollins Band

The Rollins Band began touring and recording in the Rollins style—obsessively—and quickly produced a series of records on independent labels. They blossomed into an underground sensation, followed by Rollins's old fans from the Black Flag era and new admirers from the marginal hard-core audience. Rollins described the band as a "well-kept secret" to *Spin's* Jim Greer, explaining, "In the past, we'd do all these tours and all these records and, you know, the records aren't even in print, the tours never get promoted. We're kind of like this band that doesn't really exist." But that began to change in the summer of 1991, when the the Rollins Band went on tour with the Lollapalooza Festival. Their popularity with festival audiences led to a deal with a major recording label, Imago, and an album that generated a great deal of press attention.

Following the release of *The End of Silence* in 1992, superlative reviews from the most august rock magazines began rolled in. *Rolling Stone's* Mundy couldn't decide whether it was "the heaviest jazz record in history or the most intricate hardcore document to date." Mike Gitter called the Rollins aggregate "one of the hardest, most musically deft rock bands under the sun" in his *Pulse!* review. The band members, and Rollins in particular, suddenly found themselves in demand on television talk shows. The ever-articulate Rollins has appeared on *Up All Night, Alive From Off Center, The Dennis Miller Show,* and *The Arsenio Hall Show.* Following the success of *The End of Silence,* Imago also produced the first major recording of Rollins's spoken-word performances, *The Boxed Life.* Consequently, Rollins's exploding reputation as a rocker was powerfully supplemented by recognition for his talents as a poet, improvisational speaker, and stand-up comedian (fans had long appreciated his wry sense of humor).

Rollins had begun the spoken-word performances—a kind of anti-high-culture version of poetry reading—in 1983; a year later, he was publishing volumes of his own written work. He has described himself as being as consumed with his writing as he is with his music, revealing in *Melody Maker,* "I first started writing in High School, but it was no big deal. I started taking it seriously when I was with Black Flag, partly to pass the time on the tour bus and partly to document the intense swirl of events we were caught up in. I've tried to write constantly since then." Early in 1993 he was juggling five writing projects at once, including a history of Black Flag based on his journals. Aside from the occasional essay printed in *Spin* or *Details,* Rollins has released his written work exclusively through his own publishing company, 2.13.61 (his birth date), which he founded in 1984. "I try to take as little shit as possible from the powers that be," he illuminated in his Imago press biography. "I know that we all have to eat some in life's rich pageant. I figured that I could minimize the intake if I could control the release of my work as much as possible."

Rollins's life almost spun out of control in 1991, when his friend Joe Cole was gunned down outside of Rollins's Los Angeles apartment building in a robbery attempt. He poured his rage and grief into *Now Watch Him Die,* a volume that was published in the summer of 1993. In a *Rolling Stone* interview that year, Rollins told David Fricke: "When your best friend gets murdered five feet away from you, it changes you. I always have that experience now permanently riding on my shoulder. I'm more aware of time, more aware of mortality, and I'm not so precious about life anymore. You're eventually going to die. Use the time wisely because it is running out, but don't freak out about it."

In addition to his work with the Rollins band, his spoken-word performances, and his involvement in 2.13.61, Rollins has managed to devote his considerable energy to other projects as well; he has acted as vocalist for Andrew Weiss's band Wartime, and he established a record label with Rick Rubin, president of American Recordings; the imprint, One Records, will focus on uncovering and rereleasing recordings from the 1970s and 1980s that are currently out of print.

In 1993, bassist Melvin Gibbs joined the Rollins Band; a follow-up release to *The End of Silence* was planned for the spring of 1994. No doubt a tour would follow. Rollins once explained his workaholic drive to Gary Graff of the *Detroit Free Press* as the only way he knows to confront a painful life with defiance and commitment: "I don't want to blow my head off. . . . I don't want to take pharmaceuticals, either. So I lift weights, scream into microphones, hit keys on the typewriter."

Selected writings

Published by 2.13.61

20, 1984.
2.13.61, 1985.
End to End, 1985.
Polio Flesh, 1985.
Works, 1988.
1000 Ways to Die, 1989.
Knife Street, 1989.
Art to Choke Hearts, 1989.
High Adventure in the Great Outdoors (includes *2.13.61, End to End,* and *Polio Flesh*), 1990.
Bang! (includes *1000 Ways to Die* and *Knife Street*), 1990.

One From None, 1991.
Black Coffee Blues, 1992.
See a Grown Man Cry, 1992.
Now Watch Him Die, 1993.

Selected discography

With Black Flag; on SST Records

My War, 1983.
Family Man, 1984.
Slip It In, 1984.
Live '84, 1984.
Loose Nut, 1985.
The Process of Weeding Out, 1985.
In My Head, 1985.
Who's Got the 10, 1986.

With the Rollins Band

Hot Animal Machine, Texas Hotel, 1987.
Drive By Shooting, Texas Hotel Records, 1987.
Life Time, Texas Hotel, 1988.
Do It, Texas Hotel, 1988.
Hard Volume, Texas Hotel, 1989.
Turned On, QuarterStick Records, 1990.
The End of Silence, Imago, 1992.
The Weight, Imago, 1994.

Spoken-word recordings

Short Walk on a Long Pier, Texas Hotel/2.13.61, 1987.

Big Ugly Mouth, Texas Hotel, 1987, reissued, QuarterStick, 1992.
Sweatbox, Texas Hotel, 1989, reissued, QuarterStick, 1992.
Live at McCabe's, QuarterStick, 1992.
Human Butt, QuarterStick/2.13.61, 1992.
Deep Throat, QuarterStick/2.13.61, 1992.
The Boxed Life, Imago, 1993.

Sources

Creem, May 1992.
Details, January 1993; January 1994.
Detriot Free Press, April 17, 1992.
Detroit News, May 1, 1993.
Down Beat, December 1984.
Entertainment Weekly, March 12, 1993.
Los Angeles Daily News, May 31, 1992.
Melody Maker, February 13, 1993.
Metro Times (Detriot), March 3, 1993.
Musician, April 1993.
Pulse!, April 1992.
Rolling Stone, April 16, 1992; March 18, 1993; December 23, 1993.
Spin, May 1992.
TV Guide, September 26, 1992.

Additional information for this profile was obtained from an Imago Recording Company press biography, 1992.

—Ondine E. Le Blanc

Arthur Rubinstein

Pianist

Tremendously popular from the 1930s through the 1970s, Arthur Rubinstein enjoyed a performing and recording career that lasted over 75 years. Yet were it not for RCA's having reissued his recordings in the 1980s, those born past the mid-'60s might never have heard of him. This can be largely attributed to the perception that Rubinstein's pianism was of the Romantic school of the first half of the 20th century, a style that infused music with drama and emotion and one that eventually fell out of favor. Nonetheless, Rubinstein was in a class by himself. He performed most of the repertory popular in mid-century: the music of Chopin—whose work was his specialty—Rachmaninoff, Schumann, and Brahms. But he was also the first performer to champion Spanish music: his interpretations of Manuel de Falla, Isaac Albéniz, and Enrique Granados are of genuine historic importance. And though, indeed, Rubinstein did not demonstrate the intellectual asceticism of some of his successors, neither did he sentimentalize his playing or take liberties with the musical text, as did many of his contemporaries.

Music critic Harold C. Schonberg attested in the *New York Times* in 1964: "Vladimir Horowitz may have a more glittering technique, Rudolf Serkin may have a better way with German music, Rosalyn Tureck more of an affinity for Bach, Sviatoslav Richter for Prokofieff and Scriabin, and Claudio Arrau may have a bigger repertory. But no pianist has put everything together the way Rubinstein has. Others may be superior in specific things, but Rubinstein is the complete pianist."

Rubinstein was born in 1886 in Lodz, Poland, and at the age of eight began studying piano in Berlin. He made his debut in Berlin in 1898 and his official U.S. debut at Carnegie Hall in 1906. Critical notices, though, were discouraging, focusing on his underdeveloped sense of tone and expression. Rubinstein then took four years off from performing, spending the years 1906-10 honing his skills and enjoying life in Paris; the many love affairs he maintained during these years became notorious when he recalled them unabashedly in his 1980 autobiography *My Many Years*.

Rubinstein reemerged in 1910 with a concert in Berlin and spent the next six years touring Europe. During World War I, his facility with language kept him busy as an interpreter at Allied Headquarters in London. He continued to play throughout the Continent, most notably in Spain, where a four-concert agenda in 1916 was drawn out to 120 additional performances. His Cross of Alfonso XII from the Spanish government was one of his most valued possessions.

From then on, Rubinstein's career was devoted to performing and recording, both of which nurtured the

For the Record. . .

Born Artur Rubinstein, April 28, 1886, in Lodz, Poland; became U.S. citizen, 1946; died December 20, 1982, in Geneva, Switzerland; son of Ignace (a factory owner) and Felicia Heyman Rubinstein; married Aniela (Nela) Mlynarski, 1932; children: Eva, Paul, Alina, John. *Education:* Studied piano with Karl Heinrich Barth and music theory and composition with Max Bruch and Robert Kahn, Berlin, beginning c. 1894.

(With Berlin Philharmonic Orchestra) made debut, Berlin, 1898; made first U.S. appearance, Philadelphia, 1906; made official U.S. debut, Carnegie Hall, New York City, 1906; gave concerts in Europe, 1910-16; made numerous recordings, 1928-1976. Recorded piano music for films *I've Always Loved You,* 1946, and *Song of Love, Night Song,* and *Carnegie Hall,* all 1947; appeared in *Of Men and Music,* 1950. Author of autobiographies *My Young Years,* 1973, and *My Many Years,* 1980.

Selected awards: Légion d'honneur (France), Cross of Alfonso XII (Spain), Commander of Arts and Letters (Chile), Order of Santiago (Portugal), Polonia Restituta (Poland), Commander of the Crown and Officer, Order of Leopold I (Belgium); National Academy of Recording Arts and Sciences Lifetime Achievement Award, 1994.

zest for life that was long his callling card. And his great joy in living, in turn, extended to his playing; in a 1966 *Time* profile, he was quoted as saying: "I'm passionately involved in life; I love its change, its color, its movement. To be alive, to be able to speak, to see, to walk, to have houses, music, paintings—it's all a miracle. I have adopted the technique of living life from miracle to miracle. Music is not a hobby, not even a passion with me. Music is me. I feel what people get out of me is this outlook on life, which comes out in my music. My music is the last expression of all that."

Selected discography

Bach: *Chaccone;* Franck: *Prelude, Chorale, and Fugue;* Liszt: *Sonata in B Minor,* RCA.
(With Boston Symphony Orchestra, Erich Leinsdorf, conductor) Beethoven: *Piano Concertos 1-5, Sonata in C-sharp Minor, Op. 27, No. 2 ("Moonlight"),* RCA.
Chopin: *Ballades and Scherzos,* RCA.
Chopin: *Nocturnes,* RCA.
Chopin: *Polonaises,* RCA.
(With Philadelphia Orchestra, Eugene Ormandy, conductor) Falla: *Nights in the Gardens of Spain, Ritual Fire Dance;* Franck: *Symphonic Variations;* Prokofiev: *March;* Saint-Saëns: *Concerto No. 2.,* RCA.
(With Chicago Symphony Orchestra, Fritz Reiner, conductor) Rachmaninoff: *Concerto No. 2; Rhapsody on a Theme of Paganini,* RCA.
Schubert: *"Wanderer" Fantasy; Sonata in B-flat Major; Impromptus,* RCA.
Schumann: *Fantasiestücke, Op. 12; Prophet Bird; Romance, Op. 28 No. 2; Carnaval,* RCA.
Schumann: *Kreisleriana; Fantasy in C, Op. 17,* RCA.

Sources

Books

Rubinstein, Arthur, *My Young Years,* Knopf, 1973.
Rubinstein, Arthur, *My Many Years,* Knopf, 1980.
Schonberg, Harold C., *The Great Pianists: From Mozart to the Present,* Simon & Schuster, 1963.

Periodicals

Life, April 5, 1948.
New Yorker, November 1, 1958.
New York Times, January 26, 1964; December 21, 1982.
Time, February 25, 1966.

—*Joyce Harrison*

Todd Rundgren

Singer, songwriter, composer, producer

Evolving in his musical exploits from British-influenced "mod" rock in the 1960s to high-tech musical databases in the 1990s, Todd Rundgren has been one of the true innovators in pop music. He has experimented relentlessly with different musical styles and the latest studio technology, serving listeners with everything from classic pop rockers to concept albums with operatic overtones. Rundgren's work has been compared to that of artists from all over the musical map. He was also among the first to produce music videos.

After getting his first electric guitar at age 17, Rundgren formed a short-lived band called Woody's Truck Stop. Next he founded the Philadelphia-based The Nazz, with Robert "Stewkey" Antoni on keyboards and vocals, Carson van Osten on bass, and Thom Mooney on drums. The Nazz was heavily influenced in both their music and attire by the "British invasion" groups popular at the time. Three albums generated little response from the public, though the band had a minor hit in 1969 with "Hello It's Me." *The Illustrated Encyclopedia of Rock* ventured that the group did not click because it was "probably too advanced for their period." In 1970 Rundgren decided to pursue a solo path, and his desire for creative control also led him into producing. Among his early production clients were The Band, Jesse Winchester, and the Paul Butterfield Blues Band.

One-Man Studio Band

On his solo albums, Rundgren often sang all the vocals and played all the instruments, putting everything together by overdubbing, or laying one recorded track atop another. He scored a nominal hit with "We Gotta Get You a Woman," from his 1970 release *Runt,* which featured comedian Soupy Sales's sons—Tony on bass and Hunt on drums (the two later going on to record with David Bowie in Tin Machine). According to *High Fidelity,* this album and its follow-up, *Ballad of Todd Rundgren,* "fuse Beatlesesque pop with Todd Rundgren's Philly soul."

It was the 1972 double album *Something/Anything* that was Rundgren's creative breakthrough. Displaying a diversity of musical styles and three sides that were entirely his work—as writer, singer, musician, and producer—the album earned Rundgren a loyal following. *High Fidelity* called it "simply one of the most brilliant albums ever recorded." Rundgren's chameleon-like ability in the studio was acknowledged by *The Illustrated Encyclopedia of Rock,* which reported, "He had seemingly mastered every angle from soul to Beach Boys to the raw daring of a Hendrix." Rundgren also made the Top Ten with a million-selling single

For the Record. . .

Born June 22, 1948, in Upper Darby, PA; children: three.

Formed band The Nazz, 1967; signed with Screen-Gems/Columbia and released *The Nazz*, 1968; became solo recording artist, 1969; signed with Bearsville and released *Runt,* 1969; became producer, 1969; produced albums for Hall & Oates, the Tom Robinson Band, Patti Smith, and Meat Loaf, among others; formed Utopia, 1973; session player for artists including Flint, Johnny Winter, and Hall & Oates; mounted first interactive concert, 1978; wrote software for first color computer-graphics tablet, 1980; began producing music videos, early 1980s; composed scores for television programs, including *Crime Story* and *Pee-wee's Playhouse;* created screen-saving computer graphics program, 1989; released interactive CD *No World Order,* Forward/Philips, 1993.

Addresses: *Record company*—Forward/Rhino Records Inc., 10635 Santa Monica Blvd., Los Angeles, CA 90025.

remake of "Hello It's Me"—the song for which he is still best known to many music fans—in 1973.

Everything seemed fair musical game to Rundgren, from soul to ballads to musical parody. Making it easier for the artist to nurture his talent during these years was Albert Grossman, head of the Bearsville recording label. Grossman was a big fan of Rundgren and allowed him to pursue his creative development with little interference. And willingness to work was never an issue for Rundgren, who recorded 18 albums with Bearsville from 1971 through 1983.

Utopia

The constantly evolving Rundgren became a musical scientist in the studio, always looking for new ways to mix the elements of his trade. He also forged a reputation as a perceptive and witty lyricist. In 1974, Rundgren began alternating his efforts between solo output and his newly formed band Utopia, the longest-running lineup of which featured Rundgren on guitar, Roger Powell on keyboards, Kasim Sulton on bass, and Willie Wilcox on drums.

Although Utopia's early albums irritated some Rundgren fans with their long songs and psychedelic, mystical lyrics, they nonetheless helped him attract a larger rock audience. The group produced high-voltage rock that drew on a variety of pop influences, offering listeners a mixed bag of radically unusual rock (*Ra,* 1977), Beatles imitations (*Deface the Music,* 1980), high-tech synthesizing (*Healing,* 1981), and political consciousness (*Swing to the Right,* 1982). A high point for the band was *Adventures in Utopia,* recorded in 1980, which *High Fidelity* deemed "the best of the streamlined group's efforts."

Despite his steady flow of albums, Rundgren was better known as a producer than a songwriter-performer during most of the 1970s. He captained records by Hall & Oates, the Tom Robinson Band, The Tubes, Patti Smith, and Meat Loaf, among others. Meat Loaf's *Bat Out of Hell,* to which Rundgren also contributed guitar solos, eventually generated worldwide sales of eight million copies, making it one of the most commercially successful albums of all time. A shift away from production came in the early 1980s when Rundgren began focusing on music videos. He set up his own production studio, where he made short videos based on his music, as well of that of other performers, including Japanese synthesizer player Tomita.

Pioneer of the Cutting Edge

Remaining on the cutting edge of the music industry, Rundgren became a pioneer in multimedia productions and interactive music. In a 1978 televised concert in Columbus, Ohio, he allowed members of the audience to vote on what songs should be played. Rundgren is also notable for having produced the first national cablecast of a live rock concert and the first live radio concert broadcast in stereo.

He ultimately took the interactive format to the borders of high technology by exploring how computers could create musical databases for serious composers and discriminating listeners. This exploration reached its fruition in 1993, when Rundgren released *No World Order,* the first interactive musical recording. Requiring special playback hardware called a CD-I player, this three-hour compilation of musical "puzzle pieces" could be played in different combinations and sequences to create a virtually unlimited number of song variations. Listeners could input their preferences as to musical style or mood—and let the CD-I player do the rest. Many in the record industry viewed Rundgren's move as a herald of things to come.

In fact, *No World Order* was just the next step in a continuum; Rundgren has never stopped looking for ways to combine or transform musical styles and production techniques in order to create something new. As he said in *Request,* "I have to come up with something that is completely unconnected to all the standard operating procedures. Otherwise, I'm not doing anything unique." Perhaps *Musician* summed up Rundgren's career most aptly, concluding, "From his rock-god period as front man for The Nazz and Utopia through a solo career as a one-man band, songwriter, producer, [and] software development and video pioneer, Rundgren has remained an icon of innovation."

Selected discography

With The Nazz

Nazz, Screen-Gems/Columbia, 1968.
Nazz Nazz, Screen-Gems/Columbia, 1969.
Nazz III, Screen-Gems/Columbia, 1970.

With Utopia

Todd Rundgren's Utopia, Bearsville, 1974.
Adventures in Utopia, Bearsville, 1980.
Deface the Music, Bearsville, 1980.
Swing to the Right, Bearsville, 1982.
Utopia, Bearsville, 1982.

Solo albums

Runt (includes "We Gotta Get You a Woman"), Bearsville, 1970.
Something/Anything, Bearsville, 1972.
Initiation, Bearsville, 1975.
Faithful, Bearsville, 1976.
Hermit of Mink Hollow, Bearsville/Island, 1978.
Healing, Bearsville, 1981.
No World Order, Forward/Philips, 1993.

As producer

The Band, *Stage Fright*, Capitol, 1970.

Hall & Oats, *War Babies*, Atlantic, 1974.
Meat Loaf, *Bat Out of Hell*, Epic, 1978.
XTC, *Skylarking*, Virgin, 1986.

Sources

Books

The Guinness Encyclopedia of Popular Music, Volume II, edited by Colin Larkin, Guinness, 1992.
The Harmony Illustrated Encyclopedia of Rock, Harmony, 1988.
The Illustrated Encyclopedia of Rock, Harmony, 1977.
The New Grove Dictionary of American Music, Volume IV, edited by H. Wiley Hitchcock and Stanley Sadie, Macmillan, 1986.

Periodicals

Billboard, November 27, 1993.
Down Beat, October 1990.
High Fidelity, April 1988.
Guitar Player, November 1993.
Musician, September 1993.
Pulse!, September 1993.
Request, October 1993.
Spin, February 1993.
Stereo Review, May 1991.
Time, January 17, 1994.

Additional information for this profile was provided by Forward, a division of Rhino Records Inc., 1993.

—*Ed Decker*

Mitch Ryder

Singer, songwriter

*R*olling Stone once called Mitch Ryder the Godfather of Motor City Rock and Roll; other tastemakers dubbed him the King of White Soul and the Master of Blue-Eyed Rhythm and Blues. In 1965, several newspapers quoted Keith Richards of the Rolling Stones roaring, "Mitch has got it!" But, over the years, what he had was nearly destroyed by overwork, mismanagement, and substance abuse. Although decades later he remains a rock legend, Ryder is no longer as recognized as he once was. Nonetheless, he continues to perform, often to rave reviews, write critically acclaimed songs, and thrill his cult audience.

Ryder was born William Levise, Jr., on February 26, 1945, in Detroit, Michigan. As a child, he lived in the suburbs of Detroit, but as he was prone to discipline problems, summers saw him shipped off to live in the city with his grandmother. Ryder told *Goldmine*'s Ken Settle of his early exposure to music there, recollecting, "I really started hearing and buying records. I think the first big one for me was 'A Fool in Love' by Tina Turner." His interest in music grew, and he wrote the school song for his junior high and later worked with a high school band called Tempest. But it wasn't until he earned a Number One rating at a county solo/ensemble festival for his rendition of "Danny Boy" that young Billy Levise's confidence really soared.

A "Baaad Dude" on Detroit R&B Scene

In 1962, a 17-year-old Levise emerged on the burgeoning Detroit rhythm and blues scene. The Village, considered one of *the* soul clubs, featured music that, local lore has it, made the walls bulge and the streets quake. Soul singer and Village star attraction Nathaniel Mayer remembered Levise to Settle as "a baaad dude," elaborating, "It was amazin' because, you know, usually when guys sing with all that soul, first thing you think it's a black dude, then you look up and there's a white dude doin' it. So all of us was shocked." Levise cut "That's the Way It's Gonna Be"/"Fool for You," an R&B single on Reverend James Hendrix's gospel Carrie label, and shortly thereafter began fronting a band known as the Peps. The constant rotation of musicians in that outfit, however, began to drive him crazy—often, no one showed up at all.

One night in early 1964, while Levise was hanging around at the Village waiting for his musicians to arrive, he met another group. It was resolved that they would jam together sometime or have a few beers, but the actual result was Billy Lee and the Rivieras. By that summer, this new band found they'd developed a rather large and fanatical following. Dave Prince, disc jockey at Detroit's WXYZ, heard of the band and began

For the Record. . .

Born William Levise, Jr., February 26, 1945, in Detroit, MI; married twice.

Became professional singer, c. 1962; recorded "That's the Way It's Gonna Be"/"Fool for You," Carrie, c. 1963; singer with the Peps, 1963-1964; singer with Mitch Ryder and the Detroit Wheels (originally Billy Lee and the Rivieras), 1964-1966; signed with New Voice label, 1964; released "Jenny Take a Ride," 1965; became solo performer, 1967; released *The Detroit-Memphis Experiment,* Dot, 1969; singer with Detroit, 1971-1972; singer with Knock Down, Drag Out Band, early 1970s; worked as laborer, Denver, 1972-1977; resumed performing/recording career, 1978.

Addresses: *Agent*—Entertainment Services International, 6400 Pleasant Park Dr., Chanhassen, MN 55317.

booking them to open for Motown acts at the renowned Walled Lake Casino, about 40 miles northwest of Detroit.

After just a few shows, Billy Lee and the Rivieras were headlining, billed above top Motown performers. Prince introduced their music to Bob Crewe, a New York City-based independent record producer and head of his own label—New Voice Records—and management firm. Crewe, who'd had major success with Frankie Valli and the Four Seasons, was eager to see the band after listening to a tape Prince had recorded. Prince arranged for Crewe to see Billy Lee and the Rivieras at a large venue where they were third on the bill of a Dave Clark Five concert. Although the former Levise and company were only scheduled to play a few songs, the frenzied audience kept them onstage for nearly an hour and a half. Crewe was shocked and sold, insisting that the band be in New York City within the week.

As another band had already made a name for themselves as the Rivieras, the Lee ensemble became the Detroit Wheels, and Billy Lee became Mitch Ryder, a moniker lifted from the pages of a 1965 Manhattan phone book; the pairing of "Ryder," a play on "rider," and "wheels" seemed apt.

Stardom With Detroit Wheels

Mitch Ryder and the Detroit Wheels didn't hit big with their new name for nearly a year, but when they did, in December of 1965, they hit hard. When the band combined Chuck Willis's slow burner "C.C. Rider" with the driving rhythm of Little Richard's "Jenny, Jenny" to form "Jenny Take a Ride," the music world took notice.

For the next two years the hits and the fans kept coming. Songs like "Little Latin Lupe Lu," "Break Out," "Takin' All I Can Get," "Devil With a Blue Dress On/ Good Golly Miss Molly," "Sock It to Me, Baby," and "Too Many Fish in the Sea" made indelible marks not only on the rock and pop charts, but on the R&B charts as well. The Wheels' showing on the R&B charts was of particular significance as they were the only white group to come out of Motown at that time; whereas black Motown acts were crossing over to the white pop market, Ryder and his cohorts were crossing from the pop/rock market into R&B, testimony to their reverence for the black art form and the black community's respect for the band.

The "Devil/Molly" cut, from their second LP, *Break-out. . .!!!,* was just one example of Ryder's interpretive genius. Shorty Long's obscure Motown release "Devil With a Blue Dress On," paired with Richard's legendary 1958 screamer "Good Golly Miss Molly," was such hyperkinetic, frenetic fun that as late as 1988, *Rolling Stone* listed it among its 100 best singles of the previous 25 years. Such amalgamations helped create near-hysteria during Wheels concerts and ultimately became one of their trademarks. The medleys ended up on albums largely because the band had been rushed into recording; they hadn't had time to learn anything new and were thus forced to cull the best pieces from their club act.

During the band's second year at the top, a number of people, including Bob Crewe, began slowly working on Ryder to become a solo act, with Las Vegas as their goal; Vegas seemed to be where the big money was. (This was before the tremendous stadium shows that would evetually become commonplace). In May of 1967 Ryder finally gave in and left the Detroit Wheels to don the $2,000 tuxedo of the Las Vegas cabaret singer. "I just wanted to make some big, brassy music," Ryder told *Goldmine's* Settle. On the whole, record buyers found Mitch Ryder singing "You Are My Sunshine" and "Personality/Chantilly Lace" on his *What Now My Love?* album somewhat ridiculous. Finally, Ryder split with Crewe and fled the glitzy folly.

In 1969 he released *The Detroit-Memphis Experiment,* the generally agreed on brilliance of which restored his credibility in the wake of the Vegas material he'd produced with Crewe. But although it was critically acclaimed, *Experiment* sold poorly. In 1971 Ryder formed a seven-man hard rock band that reunited him with Wheels drummer John Badanjek. This outfit was called simply Detroit, as was their only album. According to Settle, "Ryder's personal life was becoming increasingly tortuous, and business dealings were in massive disarray after Crewe purportedly stuck Ryder with horrendous expenses before their partnership dissolved, [but the Detroit album] captured the soulful spirit and metallic drive that was the epitome of urban rock."

Hard Times

By then, Ryder desperately needed to get out of rock. "After I'd quit Detroit," he admitted to Settle, "I really wanted a rest, although I couldn't afford one. I didn't have any money saved up; I wasn't making enough to save any." He performed with a group called the Knock Down, Drag Out Party Band—really a just-for-fun project—that allowed him to keep his hand in the business. But soon, even that became too much, and in 1972, Ryder moved to Denver, and, it seemed, out of music altogether. He reasoned to Settle: "Probably by the time I moved out there I had waited way too long to get off the stage and take a break. . . . I knew I had to be off the stage, but couldn't afford not to. . . . And having to need that money pushed me into a situation where, mentally, I shouldn't have even been onstage. Mentally, it was bad for me and precipitated a whole series of events which led me to Colorado." In time, he was frightened to perform in public. A reliance on tranquilizers followed. "Little things would upset me," Ryder revealed in the *Washington Times*. "When I couldn't control situations, I would refuse to deal with them and would do that by sedating myself."

His sojourn in Denver was certainly a healing period, but Ryder did not swear off drugs and alcohol until 1988. He did not leave music behind during his five years out west, as many have suggested; while working as a laborer by day, he wrote songs at night, eventually rehearsing with new musician friends he'd made. Very slowly, Ryder began to re-enter the music business.

"Finally," *Goldmine* contributor Settle reported, "with a bold, renewed musical vision, Ryder reclaimed his Detroit turf in 1977," and in 1978, on his own Seeds & Stems label, he released the aptly titled *How I Spent My Vacation*. "The pain, desire, and deception that Ryder had weathered in his life and career are achingly apparent," Settle observed. He went on to echo many critics—and countless fans—in his assessment of this record and Ryder's later work: "The fortunate few who heard this LP were treated to a modern music classic. The album is full of twisted images of life's gamblers and losers, infused with the realization that in the end they become one and the same. One cannot deny the icy chill in Ryder's vocals. It is the voice of a man who had lost everything except the power to reclaim. Time and time again on Ryder's subsequent recordings, especially *Naked But Not Dead* and a handful of Euro-

pean releases, the artist proves that he still possesses a potent and relevant voice in the contemporary mainstream. His is an artistry that is unafraid, and quite eager to take commercial chances and [make] artistic advances."

Although Ryder remains a rock hero and cult favorite—actress Winona Ryder borrowed his borrowed surname—and continues to earn critical praise and wield influence among younger artists—particularly heartland rocker John Mellencamp, who produced Ryder's *Never Kick a Sleeping Dog*—he has yet to recapture the glory he enjoyed as frontman for the Detroit Wheels. He continues to write and tour and has begun work on an autobiography that is being co-written by star music scribe David Marsh. When Settle asked what the most nagging misconception about him is, Ryder replied, "I don't think they have any misconceptions about what I am in Europe. In America, I feel that the general public has been denied my presence on a mass level for so long that they don't know me here. So there's really no room for misconceptions. Other than the general public thinking that I may have died. That could be a misconception."

Selected discography

With Mitch Ryder and the Detroit Wheels

Take a Ride, New Voice, 1966.
Breakout. . .!!!, New Voice, 1966.
Sock It to Me, New Voice, 1967.
Greatest Hits, Roulette, 1987.
Rev Up: The Best of Mitch Ryder and the Detroit Wheels, Rhino, 1989.

With Detroit

Detroit, Paramount, 1971, reissued, 1987.

Solo albums

All Mitch Ryder Hits, New Voice, 1967.
All the Heavy Hits, Crewe, 1967.
What Now My Love?, Dyno Voice, 1967.
Mitch Ryder Sings the Hits, New Voice, 1968.
The Detroit-Memphis Experiment, Dot, 1969.
How I Spent My Vacation, Seeds & Stems, 1978.
Naked But Not Dead, Seeds & Stems, 1980.
Look Ma, No Wheels, Quality, 1981.
Never Kick a Sleeping Dog, Riva, 1983.

Contributor

Michigan Rocks, Seeds & Stems, 1977.

Was (Not Was), *Born to Laugh at Tornadoes,* Geffen, 1983.

Sources

Books

Rees, Dafydd, and Luke Crampton, *Rock Movers & Shakers,* ABC/CLIO, 1991.

Periodicals

Ann Arbor News (MI), January 9, 1989.

Arkansas Gazette (Little Rock), January 11, 1989.

Boston Globe, July 8, 1988.

Buffalo News (NY), June 23, 1988.

Cape Cod Times (Hyannis, MA), July 14, 1988.

Detroit Free Press, January 28, 1991; May 15, 1991; May 18, 1991; May 9, 1993.

Goldmine, May 20, 1988.

Rolling Stone, September 8, 1988; February 9, 1989.

Washington Times, July 19, 1988.

—Joanna Rubiner

Buffy Sainte-Marie

Singer, songwriter

One of the most striking voices of the contemporary folk music movement of the 1960s, Buffy Sainte-Marie has enjoyed a career far broader than the "protest singer" category into which she has sometimes been placed. She has written and lectured on native-American affairs, written poetry and screenplays, and composed film scores, as well as writing, recording, and performing songs in styles ranging from folk to rock and from art song to electronic music. But while she has become known for love songs like "Until It's Time for You to Go," Sainte-Marie has never abandoned the social and political concerns that marked her early work. And though she resists the label of "protest song," she admitted to Paul Sexton of *Billboard*, "The only reason I ever became a singer in the first place was because I had something to say."

Buffy Sainte-Marie was born on a Cree Indian reservation in western Canada. She was orphaned when she was only months old and adopted by a family from Massachusetts. Though her adoptive parents were part Indian, she has described the cultural environment in which she grew up as completely white. It was routine at the time to place Indian children in white families. "Many Indian children were effectively kidnapped—it was supposed to be for our own good," she told Diane Turbide of *MacLean's*. It was not until she was in her teens that Sainte-Marie discovered her Cree roots and was reunited with her relatives.

By the time she was in high school, she had taught herself to play the piano and the guitar, using her own unconventional tunings. She had no intention of making a career in music when she began singing in coffeehouses while in college, but an appearance at an open mike night at Greenwich Village's Gaslight Cafe brought her to the attention of critics and record companies. By the end of 1963, she had given up her plans to become a teacher and was being hailed as one of the most promising talents on the New York folk scene. Another Indian folksinger, Patrick Sky, taught her to play the traditional native-American instrument the mouth bow, which became a distinctive part of her sound, along with her unique guitar style and her sometimes strident, sometimes delicate vibrato-rich voice.

Shortly after Sainte-Marie began singing professionally, she came down with pneumonia. Unwilling to give up performing, she took codeine to ease her symptoms. The illness persisted for six months, and she became addicted to the drug, recovering only after a painful withdrawal; she also came close to ruining her voice. She wrote of her addiction in the song "Cod'ine."

That song, as well as two of her best-known compositions, "Now That the Buffalo's Gone" and "The Univer-

For the Record. . .

Born February 20, 1942 (some sources say 1941), in Piapat Reserve, Saskatchewan, Canada; adopted by Albert C. and Winifred (Kendrick) Sainte-Marie; married Dewain Kamaikalani Bugbee, 1967; children: Dakota (son). *Education:* University of Massachusetts, B.A. in Oriental philosophy, 1963; Ph.D. in fine arts.

Began performing in coffeehouses, early 1960s; performed at clubs, concerts, and festivals, 1963—; recording artist, 1964—. Actor in films and television shows, including "The Virginian," "Then Came Bronson," and "Sesame Street"; appeared in cable film *The Broken Chain,* TNT, 1993. Free-lance writer on Indian affairs; associate editor of *The Native Voice,* Vancouver, B.C., Canada. Founder of NIHEWAN Foundation for Native American Scholarships, Native North American Women's Association, and Creative Native, Inc. Author of children's book *Nikosis and the Magic Hat.*

Awards: *Billboard* Award, 1965; named outstanding artist of the year by National Association of FM Broadcasters, 1975; Academy Award for best song, 1982, for "Up Where We Belong" (from film *An Officer and a Gentleman);* Premio Roma Award.

Addresses: *Record company*—Chrysalis, 1290 Avenue of the Americas, New York, NY 10104.

sal Soldier," appeared on her first album, *It's My Way.* In the liner notes, Maynard Solomon remarked on "a hint of blues-inflection, a trace of Indian song, a touch of Parisian chanson, an echo of beat" in her music, which was already much more harmonically and rhythmically adventurous than most folksong.

By 1965 Sainte-Marie's growing popularity had taken her out of the coffeehouse scene and into major concert venues like New York City's Carnegie Hall. She toured Europe as well as the U.S., Canada, and Mexico, gaining a large international following. But the folk boom was fading, so Sainte-Marie, who had never let herself be confined by traditional idioms anyway, began exploring other directions. Still, while others were experimenting with folk-rock, she moved another way, recording her song "Timeless Love" with a string ensemble for her third album, *Little Wheel Spin and Spin.* In that record's notes, Nat Hentoff wrote that Sainte-Marie sang "with so unyielding a sense of self that the listener, once seized, finds concern about categories to be secondary. . . . She *is,* there is no one else like her, and that's what counts. . . . The *personal* thrust of

her bristling expressivity is both a satisfaction and a challenge."

Fire & Fleet & Candlelight moved even more in the direction of art song, including a piece by British composer Benjamin Britten and orchestral arrangements by Peter Schickele. But Sainte-Marie's next effort, *Gonna Be a Country Girl Again,* was recorded in Nashville with country music's top studio players; the follow-up, *Illuminations,* featured hard rock songs like "He's a Keeper of the Fire" and "Better to Find Out for Yourself," blended with electronic music synthesized from Sainte-Marie's voice and guitar.

Though she had won a large following, Sainte-Marie did not score a hit record until the early 1970s. The resurgence of interest in singer-songwriters during that decade, however, finally brought her significant airplay and two hit singles, "She Used to Wanna Be a Ballerina" and "Mister Can't You See." Elvis Presley's version of "Until It's Time for You to Go," from her second album, also put her in the Top Forty. But her mid-'70s albums met with mixed reviews and yielded no hits, and by 1977, Sainte-Marie had stopped recording, though she had by no means retired.

"I quit recording when my son was born," she told Paul Sexton of *Billboard.* "[I] decided to take some time off." Her break from the record business stretched to 15 years, but during that time she appeared semi-regularly on the PBS children's show *Sesame Street* (where, among other things, she sang the alphabet song to her son and explained breast feeding to Big Bird). She also wrote a children's book, earned a Ph.D., gave numerous concerts in support of Indian causes, and co-wrote "Up Where You Belong," which was featured in the film *An Officer and a Gentleman,* and for which she won an Oscar in 1982.

In 1992 Sainte-Marie re-emerged with *Coincidence and Likely Stories,* which Sexton called "a striking, modern, and thoughtful collection of rock'n'roll songs that updates Sainte-Marie's musical image." She produced the album in her home studio using state-of-the-art computer technology. While many of the lyrics addressed familiar themes, the modern pop sound displayed on *Coincidence* was a far cry from the acoustic guitar and mouth-bow of her earliest records. "In lesser hands, the washes of synthesized sounds would be an egregious mistake, but Sainte-Marie has artfully managed to tame the technology and bend it to her needs," wrote Tom Graves in *Rolling Stone.* "The result is eleven songs that have deep thematic resonance and that are among her most appealing work." In compositions about the environment, government corruption, and the oppression of native Americans, as well as in love songs, Sainte-Marie demonstrated that her long leave of absence had diminished neither the intensity nor the inventiveness of her music, nor her ambition to tackle major issues in, as she remarked to *Maclean's* contributor Turbide, "the kind of songs that would make as much sense in ancient Rome as they would today."

Selected discography

It's My Way (includes "Cod'ine," "Now That the Buffalo's Gone," and "The Universal Soldier"), Vanguard, 1964.

Many a Mile (includes "Until It's Time for You to Go"), Vanguard, 1965.

Little Wheel Spin and Spin (includes "Timeless Love"), Vanguard, 1966.

Fire & Fleet & Candlelight, Vanguard, 1967.

I'm Gonna Be a Country Girl Again, Vanguard, 1968.

Illuminations (includes "He's a Keeper of the Fire" and "Better to Find Out for Yourself"), Vanguard, 1970.

The Best of Buffy Sainte-Marie, Vanguard, 1970.

The Best of Buffy Sainte-Marie, Volume II, Vanguard, 1971.

She Used to Wanna Be a Ballerina, Vanguard, 1971.

Moonshot, Vanguard, 1972.

Native North American Child, Vanguard, 1973.

Quiet Places, Vanguard, 1973.

Buffy, MCA, 1974.

Changing Woman, Vanguard, 1975.

Sweet America, ABC, 1976.

(Contributor) *Bread and Roses Festival of Acoustic Music*, Fantasy, 1979.

Spotlight on Buffy Sainte-Marie, Vanguard, 1981.

(Contributor) *Greatest Folksingers of the 'Sixties*, Vanguard, 1987.

Coincidence and Likely Stories, Chrysalis, 1992.

(Contributor) *An Officer and a Gentleman* (soundtrack), Island.

Sources

Books

New Grove Dictionary of American Music, edited by H. Wiley Hitchcock and Stanley Sadie, MacMillan, 1986.

Stambler, Irwin, and Grelun Landon, *Encyclopedia of Folk, Country and Western Music,* St. Martins, 1969.

Tudor, Dean, *Popular Music: An Annotated Guide to Recordings,* Libraries Unlimited, 1983.

Periodicals

Billboard, June 13, 1992.

High Fidelity, August 1974.

Life, December 10, 1965.

Los Angeles Magazine, May 1992.

Maclean's, April 20, 1992.

McCall's, March 1971.

Rolling Stone, April 25, 1974; November 26, 1992.

Stereo Review, September 1974; May 1975; September 1992.

Vogue, May 1969.

Additional information for this profile was obtained from liner notes by Maynard Solomon to *It's My Way,* Vanguard, 1964, and by Nat Hentoff to *Little Wheel Spin and Spin,* Vanguard, 1966, and from Chrysalis Records press materials, 1992.

—*Tim Connor*

The Shirelles

R&B/pop vocal quartet

When four high school friends from New Jersey began singing together informally in the mid-1950s, they had no idea that in a few years they would be making music history. But in 1960, Shirley Alston, Doris Kenner, Beverly Lee, and Addie "Micki" Harris became the first black all-female singing group to land a Number One hit on the pop charts. They would go on to become one of the most successful and influential of early rock's "girl groups." Even in the 1990s, their energetic and instantly recognizable vocals remained imbedded in America's musical consciousness, with their songs frequently heard on "oldies" radio stations and used in films and television to evoke the spirit of the 1960s.

The Shirelles were not the first girl group of the rock era, but they were the first to achieve international success. And they had a durable impact on other musicians. Ronnie Spector, singer with the Ronettes, once stated, according to a press release issued by the Shirelles' 1990s management company, Beverly Productions, "The Shirelles were our idols." Singer Dionne Warwick claimed, "The Shirelles taught me how to move on stage." And said Mary Wilson of the Supremes, "[The Shirelles] definitely made a way for girl groups, because prior to that it was all guys. They showed that it could work." As long after the group's heyday as the early 1990s, modern "girl groups" like En Vogue, Jade, and SWV could be heard echoing the harmonies popularized by the Shirelles.

"Discovered" by Florence Greenberg

The four original Shirelles were from Passaic, New Jersey. They began singing together as the Poquellos, and their first live performances took place at high school talent shows. A fellow classmate, Mary Jane Greenberg, heard the group at one of these shows and convinced them to audition for her mother, Florence, who had recently launched a career in the music business. The quartet auditioned in Florence Greenberg's living room, after which she signed them to a five-year contract with her fledgling Tiara label and took over as their manager.

The Shirelles owed much of their early success to Greenberg's creativity and business savvy. She was a remarkable entrepreneur whose life story has been developed into a Hollywood film, with Bette Midler slated to tackle the leading role. Unsatisfied with her life as a housewife during the 1950s, she entered the music industry with a strong love of music but no formal background and, as she told Bill Forman of the *NARAS Journal,* "took a little office at 1674 Broadway hoping somebody would walk in." Over the years a number of

For the Record. . .

Members include **Shirley Alston** (born June 10, 1941); **Addie "Micki" Harris** (born January 22, 1940; died of a heart attack, June 10, 1982, in Los Angeles); **Doris Kenner** (born August 2, 1941); and **Beverly Lee** (born August 3, 1941).

Group formed as the Poquellos for school talent shows, Passaic, NJ; "discovered" by Florence Greenberg and signed with her Tiara label, 1958; recorded "I Met Him on a Sunday"; signed with Greenberg's Scepter Records, 1959, and recorded "Dedicated to the One I Love" and "Will You Love Me Tomorrow"; scored last chart entry, 1967; recorded and toured on nostalgia circuit; surviving members formed and led separate versions of the Shirelles.

Awards: Three gold records; awards from performance rights society Broadcast Music Inc., U.S.O., Vietnam Veterans of America, and U.S. Army; named best female group in *Billboard* and *Cash Box* for five consecutive years; citation in Congressional Record, 1983, in honor of the group's 25th anniversary.

Addresses: *Management*—Bevi Corp., P.O. Box 100, Clifton, NJ 07011-0100.

future music stars walked in, including songwriters Carole King, Gerry Goffin, Hal David, and Burt Bacharach and performers Dionne Warwick and the Isley Brothers.

After their initial audition, the Poquellos, renamed the Shirelles after Alston's given name, recorded two sides for Greenberg, "I Met Him on a Sunday" and "I Want You To Be My Boyfriend." The single sold well locally, and Greenberg arranged with Decca Records to distribute the record nationally. Released in 1958, "Sunday" would remain on the charts for nearly three months, peaking at Number 50.

Developed Distinctive Sound With Dixon

In 1959, Greenberg formed a new label called Scepter Records; this company would become a major force in the music business, warranting the issue in 1992 of *The Scepter Records Story,* a 65-track retrospective of the label. One of her first accomplishments as head of Scepter was the hiring of gifted producer and songwriter Luther Dixon, who had worked for such nationally known performers as Pat Boone, Perry Como, and Nat "King" Cole. Dixon developed a distinctive sound for the early Shirelles records, in which a solid rhythm and blues beat was complemented by lush string arrangements.

Dixon's first recording with the Shirelles was "Dedicated to the One I Love," a song originally popularized by the Five Royales. The single did well in New York and crested nationally at Number 83; it was a promising start for the new label, but both Dixon and Greenberg knew the Shirelles deserved a wider audience. In the summer of 1960, they released "Tonight's the Night," a catchy number featuring Kenner's heartfelt vocals and an irresistible West Indian beat; the record stayed on the charts for three months and rose to Number 39.

Later in 1960, Dixon heard a demo of a country western song by a young singer-songwriter named Carole King. He was entranced by the tune and took it to the Shirelles. The group initially disliked the song, but after King and her cowriter, Gerry Goffin, reworked it—shortening it and giving it a rock beat—they decided to record it. The transformed "Will You Love Me Tomorrow" brought the Shirelles international fame and cemented the careers of King and Goffin.

Made History With "Will You Love Me Tomorrow"

"Will You Love Me Tomorrow" was one of the true treasures of the early rock era, thanks largely to Alston's moving, almost painfully honest vocal performance. In his book *Girl Groups,* Alan Betrock commented, "Here was a record that you felt—that carried you on effortlessly to totally warm and secure terrain." The public was quick to take the song to its heart; after entering the Top 100 at Number 88 in late 1960, the single climbed steadily, reaching the top spot early the following year. The record also reached Number Four in England and Number Six in Australia and created such a demand for more music from the Shirelles that Greenberg rereleased "Dedicated to the One I Love." It quickly shot up the charts as well and in February of 1961 joined "Will You Love Me Tomorrow" in the Top Ten.

For the next six years the Shirelles continued to bring fame and wealth to both themselves and Greenberg's record company. 1961 saw the release of "Mama Said" and "Baby, It's You," both of which reached the Top Ten, and in 1962, "Soldier Boy" became the group's second Number One record. They toured widely, often with such well-known pop artists as Ray Charles, Dion, and the Coasters, and in 1963 recorded several songs for the soundtrack of the film *It's A Mad, Mad, Mad, Mad, World.* But in 1967, the Shirelles would chart for the last time, with "Last Minute Miracle."

In 1968, Kenner left the group, and Alston, Lee, and Harris carried on as a trio, occasionally making new recordings and performing their old hits on the nostalgia circuit. Then, in the mid-1970s, Kenner returned and the group toured again as a quartet, until Harris's untimely death from a heart attack—suffered during a performance—in June of 1982. But even the loss of one of the original members did not bring an end to the Shirelles; by 1990 there were three separate groups touring under the name, each led by one of the surviving members.

Selected discography

Baby It's You, Scepter, 1962, reissued, Sundazed, 1993.
(With Curtis "King Curtis" Ousley) *The Shirelles & King Curtis Give a Twist Party*, Scepter, 1962, reissued, Sundazed, 1993.
Anthology, 1959-1965, Rhino, 1986.
Greatest Hits, Impact, 1987.
Lost and Found, Impact, 1987.
Greatest Hits, Special, 1991.
Dedicated to You, Pair, 1991.
Golden Classics, Collectables, 1992.
The Scepter Records Story, Capricorn, 1992.

Million Sellers, Laurie, 1993.
Foolish Little Girl, reissued, Sundazed, 1993.
Sing to Trumpets and Strings, Sundazed, 1993.

Sources

Books

Betrock, Alan, *Girl Groups: The Story of a Sound*, Delilah, 1982.
Warner, Jay, *The Billboard Book of American Singing Groups*, Billboard, 1992.

Periodicals

Rolling Stone, October 1992.
NARAS Journal, Fall 1992.

Additional information for this profile was provided by Bevi Corp., 1993.

—Jeffrey Taylor

Nina Simone

Singer, pianist

For more than three decades Nina Simone's remarkable career has been fueled by an unswerving resolve to do things her own way. Noted for her soul-stirring voice and eclectic musical meanderings, Simone's music has often been overshadowed by her controversial politics and dedication to the black power movement of the 1960s. Combining elements of classical, jazz, African folk, blues, gospel, and pop, her music has been exceptionally difficult to categorize and attempts to label her a "jazz singer" have met with Simone's angry accusations of racial pigeon-holing. Though her caustic demeanor and outspoken opinions have left many critics divided, the temperamental diva has always possessed an uncanny ability to connect with her audience.

Critics who have followed Simone's career for the last 30 years offer testimony of her erratic talents. John S. Wilson of the *New York Times* stated in 1960 that Simone "defies easy classification." He found pop, jazz, folk, and theater music in her work, but added that she has a singular talent for slipping in and out of these classifications, and making her music unique. "[By] the time she has finished turning a song this way and that way, poking experimentally into unexpected crannies she finds in it, or suddenly leaping on it and whaling the daylights out of it, the song has lost most of its original coloration and has become, one might say, Simonized."

Five years later, Wilson elaborated on Simone's methodology. He noted "her ability to appear to be playing piano and singing in a very casual manner even within what is obviously a carefully constructed format. . . . She sits at the piano, idly fingering the keys, humming, murmuring, talking and singing a lyric that gradually shapes into a melody that . . . she molds and builds with great deliberation and skill." Though in 1978, Wilson found Simone a somewhat more spontaneous presence. He said of her performance of the song "Everything Must Change," "[It] grew in the classic Simone manner from a mumble and a quaver through an intense, breathy declaration, swelling to a shout that burst into gospel excitement that swept the audience into the performance."

An Eccentric Diva

Wilson articulated the overlap of Simone's personality and musical method. Of a 1979 performance he opined in the *New York Times,* "Miss Simone is still, as she always has been, an angry woman." Sometimes that anger could be harnessed to produce a stunning performance, Wilson explained, but in this particular case,

For the Record. . .

Born Eunice Kathleen Waymon, February 21, 1935, in Tyron, NC; daughter of Mary Kate (a minister) and John Divine (a performer, dry cleaner, barber, and truck driver) Waymon; married Don Ross, 1958 (divorced, 1959); married Andrew Stroud, 1961 (divorced c. 1970); children: (second marriage) Lisa Celeste. *Education:* Studied piano with Muriel Massinovitch, Joyce Carrol, Dr. Carl Friedburg, and Vladimir Sokhaloff; attended Juilliard School of Music, 1950-51.

Accompanied church choir on piano as a child; accompanist at Arlene Smith Studio, Philadelphia, mid-1950s; formed accompanist business; performer at Midtown Bar and Grill, Atlantic City, NJ, 1954; performed at various clubs in Philadelphia, 1956; began performing at supper clubs in New York City and upstate New York; signed with Bethlehem Records, 1957; released *Little Girl Blue,* 1958; signed with Columbia Pictures Records (Colpix), 1959, and released *The Amazing Nina Simone;* performed at New York City Town Hall, 1959; traveled to Nigeria with American Society of African Culture, 1961; signed with Philips Records, 1963, and RCA Records, 1966; made Carnegie Hall Debut, New York City, 1965; played frequently at the Village Gate, New York City; toured widely throughout Europe and the U.S. Author (with Stephen Cleary) of autobiography *I Put a Spell on You,* Pantheon, 1991. Appeared in film *Point of No Return,* 1993.

Addresses: *Record company*—Elektra Entertainment, 75 Rockefeller Plaza, New York, NY 10019.

"her anger was focused on personal annoyances and, instead of stimulating her performance, it tended to stifle it." This is, of course, the entertainer's burden, one which Simone actively publicized and made no effort to hide.

Indeed, sometimes her powerful sense of self-worth and privilege worked very much to her advantage. As Don Shewey described in the *Village Voice* in 1983, "She's not a pop singer, she's a diva, a hopeless eccentric . . . who has so thoroughly co-mingled her odd talent and brooding temperament that she has turned herself into a force of nature, an exotic creature spied so infrequently that every appearance is legendary." That same year, *New York Times* music critic Stephen Holden called Simone "obstreperous and brilliant," venturing, "Rooted in extreme emotional ambivalence, her performances have the aura of sacramental rites, in which a priestess and her flock work to establish a mystical communion."

Over the years critics have praised Simone's innate ability to interpret the work of others. Among her most moving pieces have been songs previously recorded by more mainstream artists. Holden reported, "Repeatedly, Miss Simone took familiar material and recharged it with her ferocious pianism and radically personal interpretations." She turned the ubiquitous "My Way" into "an outspoken feminist anthem," and Gilbert O'Sullivan's "Alone Again (Naturally)" into "an autobiographical epic that recounts the death of her father and its emotional aftermath with an astonishing candor." Don Shewey elaborated that when Simone sings "My Way," "she means every word of it just as much as when she slams the piano on 'Pirate Jenny,' stares down white America with serene implacability, and hisses 'That'll learn ya!'"

Oppression of a Prodigy

Born Eunice Kathleen Waymon in Tyron, North Carolina, Simone displayed an astonishing musical aptitude at a very early age. In her 1991 autobiography, *I Put a Spell on You,* the roots of her anger and frustration are evident as Simone details growing up amid an atmosphere of racism, poverty, and oppression. The Depression-era South provided little encouragement for the young prodigy who, by the age of five, understood Bach to be technically perfect. "When you play Bach's music," she explained, "you have to understand that he's a mathematician and all the notes you play add up to something—they make sense. They always add up to climaxes, like ocean waves getting bigger and bigger until after a while when so many waves have gathered you have a great storm."

For many years Simone aspired to be the first black classical pianist. In the early 1950s she attended the prestigious Juilliard School of Music on a one-year scholarship, but was later denied a scholarship to another academy she had hoped to attend. Philadelphia's Curtis School of Music informed her that she was not talented enough to attend, but Simone has always viewed the rejection as a clear-cut case of racism. It is a snub that has haunted her through the years. In a 1985 statement, the *Minnesota Daily* quoted her recollection of the incident. "I never thought about being black 'til I went up for a scholarship at the Curtis Institute," Simone revealed. "I was too good not to get it, but they turned me down . . . I couldn't get over it (then), I haven't got over it now."

Disillusioned, Simone set aside her dreams of a classical career and began to shape her own unique sound in the bars and nightclubs of Philadelphia and Atlantic City. Because her devoutly religious mother considered pop music "sinful," Eunice Waymon changed her name to Nina Simone in an effort to spare her any embarrassment. Combining a rebellious blend of music and emotion, and using classical piano as her main instrumentation, she built upon that foundation. Drawing from a wide range of musical styles, the songstress began to weave intricate patterns of vocal overlay into her pieces. Simone described her earliest perform-

---

"I never thought about being black 'til I went up for a scholarship. I was too good not to get it, but they turned me down. I couldn't get over it then, I haven't got over it now."

---

ances of the late 1950s, recalling, "I knew hundreds of popular songs and dozens of classical pieces, so what I did was combine them: I arrived prepared with classical pieces, hymns and gospel songs and improvised on those, occasionally slipping in a part from a popular tune."

During the 1960s, the socially conscious musician turned her attention to the civil rights movement, loudly denouncing the treatment of blacks in the U.S. Her untiring devotion to the Black Panthers won the admiration of fellow advocates, including Langston Hughes, James Baldwin, and Lorraine Hansberry. As her music became angrier, acquiring a sharper, more jagged edge, critics struggled to understand the artist as well as her art.

In 1974 John Rockwell maintained in the *New York Times,* "Miss Simone's unwillingness to compromise, artistically, financially or personally, can be seen as heroic—as the firm refusal of an artist, a woman and a black, to bow to forces she feels are threatening her." Some felt personally affronted and expressed anger and resentment. Disappointed by a particular performance in 1971, Mike Jahn lamented in the *New York Times,* "It is easy for Nina Simone to be a magnificent artist. She has been many times. It is just as easy for her to be proud and dignified, in keeping both with the level of her artistry, and with the richness of the culture of which she is so justly proud. Why she chose not to do so

is unfathomable and sad." Such controversy has kept a spotlight on Simone throughout her career.

Though music critics have tended to underplay its significance, Simone highlights the importance of politics in her musical career. She attributes her activism particularly to her friendship with Lorraine Hansberry, the author of the 1958 play *Raisin in the Sun.* The infamous bombing of the 16th Street Baptist Church in Birmingham, Alabama, which killed four school-age girls, inspired Simone's hit "Mississippi Goddamn," as well as a more entrenched commitment to the civil rights struggle. *'Nuff Said!* was recorded two days after the murder of Martin Luther King, Jr., and includes a live set specifically inspired by his death. As far as Simone was concerned, the civil rights movement gave her music something that had been missing until that point—relevance.

The turbulence of the 1960s visited Simone's personal life as a series of setbacks and tragedies took their toll. She was divorcing her second husband, Andrew Stroud, a New York City police detective, when her father, from whom she'd been estranged, passed away after a lingering illness. At about the same time, the I.R.S charged her with non-payment of taxes. Bitter and alienated, Simone began a nomadic life of self-imposed exile. Following her divorce from Stroud she moved to Barbados. In 1974, on the advice of friend Miriam Makeba, she settled in Liberia where she spent two years discovering an unprecedented sense of home and belonging as well as a profound spirituality. Years of subsequent wanderings took her to Switzerland, the U.K., and the south of France, which she now calls home.

A new generation of fans were exposed to Simone's work when Chanel used one of her old songs in a 1987 ad campaign. "My Baby Just Cares for Me," a reworked standard from her first album, became a mega-hit in Europe. Six years later she displayed her acting abilities in *Point of No Return,* a 1993 spy thriller to which Simone was also the main musical contributor.

A Single Woman

After nearly 20 years without a major recording, Simone signed with Elektra Records in 1993 and released *A Single Woman,* produced by Andre Fischer, Grammy-winning producer of Natalie Cole's *Unforgettable.* Although some expressed reservations, most critics welcomed the recalcitrant diva back with open arms. The disc featured a 48-piece string section and offered three cuts inspired by Frank Sinatra, two re-recordings of songs dating from the 1960s, and one Simone original, the persuasive "Marry Me." *Musician's* Kristine McKenna called the album "a classy piece of work" and noted, "It's on 'Just Say I Love Him' that Simone casts her spell most completely. The phrasing, inflection and timbre of her voice absolutely impeccable, she winds her way through its haunting melody like a purring cat."

The kudos and new-found popularity have not in any way mellowed Simone's fiery passion or temperament. She maintains a baffling ambivalence toward her fans, caring little for others' expectations, conforming to no one's standards but her own. Through a long and controversial career she has been intensely dedicated to the pursuit of artistic and political freedom. But to many critics she remains a puzzle. Commenting on the enigmatic musician in *Pulse!,* Norman Weinstein mused, "Who knows what psychological rites of passage Simone passes through in order to work her magic? And who knows what trials she believes her audience must endure in order to be moved by the spirit infusing her music? One thing is certain. She'll put you under her spell with her vision of the heart's gospel truth."

Selected discography

Little Girl Blue, Bethlehem, 1958, resissued, 1993.
Nina Simone and Her Friends, Bethlehem, 1958.
The Amazing Nina Simone, Colpix, 1959.
Nina Simone at Town Hall, Colpix, 1959.
Live at the Village Gate, Colpix, 1960.
Nina Sings Ellington, Colpix, 1962.
'Nuff Said!, RCA, 1968.
Baltimore, CTI, 1978.
Fodder in Her Wings, Carrere, 1982.
Let It Be Me, Verve, 1987.
Don't Let Me Be Misunderstood, Mercury, 1989.
Live, Zeta, 1990.
Nina Simone, Bella Musica, 1990.
The Best of Nina Simone, Sound, 1991.
The Blues, Novus, 1991.
Songs of the Poets: Dylan, Harrison and Simone, Edsel (U.K), 1992.

Nina Simone, Royal Collection, 1992.
Best of, Capitol, 1993.
Broadway-Blues-Ballads, reissued, Verve, 1993.
Something to Live For, Drive, 1993.
A Single Woman, Elektra, 1993.
High Priestess of Soul, Polydor.
I Put a Spell on You, Polydor.
Let It All Out, Polydor.
Pastel Blues, Polydor.
Wild Is the Wind, Polydor.

Sources

Books

Simone, Nina, with Stephen Cleary, *I Put a Spell on You,* Pantheon Books, 1991.

Periodicals

Billboard, May 29, 1993.
Blues & Soul, March 30, 1993.
Coda, October/November 1987.
Details, September 1993.
Emerge, August 1992.
Entertainment Weekly, April 30, 1993.
Melody Maker, July 9, 1988.
Minnesota Daily (University of MN; Minneapolis), April 15, 1993.
Musician, November 1993.
New York Times, October 22, 1960; January 16, 1965; May 11, 1971; October 12, 1971; July 1, 1974; December 12, 1978; February 24, 1979; June 6, 1983; March 11, 1985; August 8, 1993.
Philadelphia Inquirer, April 21, 1993.
Playboy, September 1993.
Pulse!, November 1993.
Request, September 1993.
Rolling Stone, November 11, 1993.
Village Voice, December 18, 1970; June 21, 1983.

Additional information for this profile was obtained from an RCA Records press file, 1968, and an Elektra Entertainment artist biography, 1993.

—*Diane Moroff*

Michael W. Smith

Singer, songwriter, keyboardist

Called a "true Renaissance [man] of contemporary Christian music by *Billboard*," gospel singer Michael W. Smith is quickly gaining popularity with mainstream audiences as well. His beautiful ballads and dance songs featuring a driving rock beat have, in fact, attracted a diverse body of listeners. As one young teen told him at a record store promotion, according to the *Wall Street Journal*, "I don't believe in religion . . . but hey, that's cool. I still like your song."

Smith grew up in a small West Virginia town, singing in the church choir and playing in a few local rock bands. After graduating from high school, he tried college for a couple of years but did not find what he was looking for and returned home. In 1978 he discovered his calling when a Nashville music publisher showed some interest in a few of his songs. He packed his bags and moved to Tennessee.

At first, Smith's move was not all that he'd hoped. "I went off the deep end and got into drugs, which messed me up for a while," he confided to the *Wall Street Journal*. He was using marijuana, LSD, and cocaine until one day in 1979, when he said, "I hit the floor in my apartment face down and cried like a baby for two hours. I got up, said a prayer to God to turn me around and its been different ever since. . . . I regret that I did drugs, but it has helped me relate to others with similar problems due to drugs and low self-esteem."

Penned Hits for Patti and Grant

Indeed, life turned around for Smith—personally and professionally. He met his future wife, Deborah, in Nashville and wrote several songs with her that were so successful that in 1981, Meadowgreen Music hired him as a staff writer. He then proceeded to write several big hits for gospel superstars Sandi Patti and Amy Grant, and in 1982, he began playing keyboards for Grant and touring in her band. After he released his first album, *Michael W. Smith Project,* in 1983, he started opening for Grant with his own act.

Numerous honors have accompanied Smith's growing popular success. In 1983, one of his songs, "How Majestic Is Your Name," was a hit for Patti, received a Dove Award nomination (the gospel music equivalent of the Grammy), and he was himself nominated for a Grammy for best gospel performance for his first album. The following year, he received three Dove nominations and won the Grammy for best gospel performance, for his second album, *Michael W. Smith 2.*

After his sophomore release, Smith began touring on his own, performing his own material. Although he

For the Record. . .

Born Michael Whitaker Smith in 1958 in Kenova, WV; wife's name, Deborah; children: five.

Staff songwriter at Meadowgreen Music, 1981; performed with singer Amy Grant, beginning in 1982; opened for Grant, 1983; became solo performer, c. 1984.

Awards: Grammy Award for best gospel performance, male, 1984, for *Michael W. Smith 2;* Dove awards, 1985, 1987, 1988, 1990, 1991, and 1992; American Music Award for favorite new artist, adult contemporary, 1992; voted one of *People* magazine's 50 Most Beautiful People, 1992; honorary doctorate in music from Alderson-Broadus College, 1992.

Addresses: *Management*—Blanton/Harrell, Inc., 2910 Poston Ave., Nashville, TN 37203.

enjoyed writing songs for and performing with Grant, his own career beckoned. "I've got to start hanging on to some of these good songs," he reasoned in the *Los Angeles Times.* His writing style began to change. "I have a new lyric vision," he revealed to Bob Darden of *Billboard.* "I think I'm aiming more of my writing for kids, young people, teenagers. . . . I think musically it is going to be more rock'n'roll, more on the edge, riskier . . . because that's what the kids are listening to."

Addressed Issues Facing Young People

To be sure, Smith's lyrics soon encompassed secular issues of concern to a younger audience. His third album, *The Big Picture,* included songs like "Wired for Sound," which discusses media brainwashing, "The Last Letter," about teen suicide, and "Old Enough to Know," a depiction of the sexual pressures facing teenagers. Smith's album *i 2 (Eye)* was noted by music critics as something new in gospel music. *Billboard's* Darden expressed his belief that the record "may be the first inspirational album with a legitimate shot at capturing a mainstream audience." Darden's assessment proved prophetic, for this was Smith's first gold record.

Smith was undeniably interested in going mainstream, taking his message to a wider audience, but he knew he had a fine line to tread. "I can't imagine radio playing songs that overtly talk about 'Jesus is the answer,'" he allowed in the *Los Angeles Times,* "but on the other hand, I think there is room on pop radio for songs that are very spiritual." Smith's manager, Michael Blanton,

agreed. "Listeners are tired of being hit over the head with dance and rap in recent years," he told the *Wall Street Journal.* "Now they're looking for melodies that they can sing to and [that] have meaning."

In 1991 Smith got help in his effort to go mainstream when his label, Reunion Records, signed a distribution deal with Geffen Records, one of the hottest rock labels in the business, featuring a roster that includes such supergroups as Guns N' Roses and Aerosmith. Once under Geffen's wing, Smith received dual marketing, with different strategies for the secular market and the more traditional Christian market. The approach worked; both of his Reunion/Geffen efforts, *Go West Young Man* and *Change Your World,* quickly went gold.

While he has been financially and artistically successful, Smith's courting of the pop market has been criticized by some fans as too secular. One fan who was quoted by the *Wall Street Journal* wrote Smith to complain of her worries "that he will throw away his message and lose his ministry to make it in the secular market." A few Christian book stores and radio stations have pulled his material. One bookstore owner told the *Journal,* "Mr. Smith may lose some Christian fans by going this route. He must be willing to pay that price."

Balanced Mainstream and Spiritual Themes

Still, Smith does not feel that he has sacrificed his religious message, and he believes his music has something to offer everyone. As a mainstream pop artist, he told *Billboard,* "I've got an incredible platform—what a great opportunity to help somebody." Certainly, his songs maintain a strong Christian orientation. "When the Evil Goes East, Go West," for instance, from *Go West Young Man,* urges listeners to avoid the dangers of temptation, while "For You" sings the praises of friendship.

Smith told *Billboard* that he has made a conscious effort not to change his message just to appeal to more people. "I had to be careful that I not get swayed into thinking that 'I had a Top Five hit, now we've got to write a pop record. . . .' I had to be careful that that didn't distract me from who I really am." He claims that Geffen did not want him to change his music either. "John Kalodner [of Geffen] just said 'Be yourself, man. Be who you are, continue to do what you do.'" But Smith also admitted to *Billboard,* "I don't feel that all of my songs have to be about God." After all, he told the *Wall Street Journal,* "I'm not an evangelist, I'm a singer."

Whatever the proportions, Smith's mix of the secular and the sacred has flourished. He has been cited by *Keyboard* magazine as a top rock keyboardist, has earned several Grammy nominations and Dove awards, and has hit the top of *Billboard*'s charts. Geffen's Robert Smith characterized Smith's appeal in *Billboard* in 1992, explaining, "With Michael it's really about an honesty of presentation, and he's a sincere, well-meaning, and gifted artist." The fans, an ever-increasing number of which are coming from traditional rock and pop backgrounds, seem to agree.

Selected discography

Michael W. Smith Project, Reunion Records, 1983.
Michael W. Smith 2, Reunion, 1984.
The Big Picture (includes "Wired for Sound," "The Last Letter," and "Old Enough to Know"), Reunion, 1986.
The Live Set, Reunion, 1987.
i 2 (Eye), Reunion, 1988.
Michael W. Smith Christmas, Reunion, 1989.
Go West Young Man (includes "When the Evil Goes East, Go West" and "For You"), Reunion, 1990.

Change Your World, Reunion, 1992.
The First Decade: 1983-1993, Reunion/RCA, 1993.
The Wonder Years, Reunion, 1994.

Sources

Billboard, November 16, 1985; October 29, 1988; September 19, 1992.
Forbes, May 11, 1992.
Keyboard, February 1993.
Los Angeles Times, May 4, 1991; March 29, 1993; June 20, 1993.
Time, September 21, 1992.
Wall Street Journal, September 11, 1991.

Additional information for this profile was provided by the management firm Blanton/Harrell, Inc., 1993.

—*Robin Armstrong*

The Soul Stirrers

Gospel vocal group

Although they are known to the secular world primarily as the vehicle for singer Sam Cooke's rise to R&B prominence, the Soul Stirrers are far more important for creating, or at least defining, the modern gospel quartet sound. Cooke, though brilliant, was a member of the group for just six years of its roughly six-decade existence. And while his influence can't be overstated—Cooke was gospel's first true sex symbol, even transforming it in some ways into a sexual music—his is not by any means the Soul Stirrers' entire story. The group embodies the leap gospel made in a generation's time from the backwoods church to today's urbane show business.

The Soul Stirrers differentiated themselves from their contemporaries—The Five Blind Boys, Pilgrim's Traveler—by boasting immensely talented frontmen. Many years prior to Cooke's tenure with the group, the Soul Stirrers were the first quartet to add a fifth member, which allowed the lead singer to step out and bellow ardent lead lines with the four-part harmonies intact. It was a revolutionary move.

R. H. (Rebert) Harris, Cooke's predecessor and one of the group's earliest members, was gospel's consummate stylist, balancing great emotional range with delicately controlled phrasing. Even to this day Harris remains the model for the modern gospel style. Harris was succeeded by Cooke, who in turn was followed by several excellent vocalists—Johnnie Taylor (later of note for the not-so-sanctified Stax hit "Who's Makin' Love to Your Old Lady While You Were Out Makin' Love?"), Willie Rogers, Richard Miles, and Martin Jacox.

Birth of Modern Gospel

Formed in Trinity, Texas, around 1932 by bass singer J. J. Farley and tenor S. R. (Senior Roy) Crain, the Soul Stirrers were first recorded by Alan Lomax for the Library of Congress in 1936. Lomax remembered their music in *The Gospel Sound* as "the most incredible polyrhythmic stuff you've ever heard."

Harris, then a Texas farm boy, joined the group in 1937. His relaxed, insistent vocal style—greatly influenced by the Blind Lemon Jefferson blues recordings he had heard at home—changed the group's approach from rural jubilee to what would soon be called modern gospel. As their style developed, the Soul Stirrers made full use of their own innovations. Their harmonies were full of rhythmic invention: Farley began employing the two-beat bass line, a technique very important to doo-wop, and later, rock and roll.

For the Record. . .

Founding members include **S. R. (Senior Roy) Crain,** tenor; **J. J. Farley,** bass; **R. H. (Rebert) Harris,** lead vocalist; and **James Medlock,** baritone. Later members include **Keith Barber, Thomas Bruster, Sam Cooke, Julius Cheeks, Paul Foster, Martin Jacox, Bob King** (instrumentalist), **Richard Miles, Jimmy Outler, R. B. Robinson, Willie Rogers, Johnnie Taylor, Leroy Taylor,** and **Faidest Wagoner** (instrumentalist).

Group formed in Trinity, TX, c. 1932; recorded by Alan Lomax for the Library of Congress, 1936; added R. H. Harris, 1937; toured churches and gospel venues, 1938-43; performed on White House lawn for President Franklin D. Roosevelt and British prime minister Winston Churchill, 1944; added fifth member, Paul Foster, 1949; recorded "By and By," 1949; signed to Specialty label, 1950; Harris left group, 1950; added Sam Cooke, 1951; recorded "Peace in the Valley" and "Touch the Hem of His Garment," 1952-53; added instrumentalists Faidest Wagoner and Bob King, 1953; added Julius Cheeks, 1954; Cooke replaced by Johnnie Taylor, 1957; Taylor replaced by Jimmy Outler, 1961; Cooke joined group for anniversary reunion, Chicago, 1962; group continued with changing lineup, anchored only by original member Farley, 1965-70; released *Resting Easy* and *Tribute to Sam Cooke,* 1986.

Addresses: *Record Company*—Specialty Records, c/o Fantasy Inc., Tenth and Parker, Berkeley, CA 94710.

Less than ten years after Lomax's primitive field recordings, the Soul Stirrers performed on the White House lawn for President Franklin D. Roosevelt and British prime minister Winston Churchill. Perhaps most important to their development was that Harris and Crain began composing. Classic gospel material like "By and By," "He's My Rock, My Sword, My Shield," and "I'm Still Living on My Mother's Prayer" were written and recorded by the Soul Stirrers.

Innovated With R&B-Style Instrumental Backing

In 1949, Paul Foster—previously a member of the Golden Echoes—joined the lineup; he would stay until 1963. By the late 1940s, the Soul Stirrers, led by Harris, had pioneered the concept of bringing sophisticated church songs—often with R&B-like instrumental backing—to the contemporary gospel scene. Instrumentalists Faidest Wagoner and Bob King were added, greatly enhancing much of the group's work. Particularly compelling is King's pedal steel guitar part on the haunting "Come and Go to That Land."

But there were other, more tawdry, aspects associated with the gospel group, the wages of popularity one may argue. Frustrated by the amount of moral compromise around him—particularly in regard to sex—Harris quit the Soul Stirrers in 1950. Harris was a happily married man; his wife, Jeanette, sang lead with the great female quartet the Golden Harps. "The singers felt they could do anything they wanted," Harris complained at the time, as quoted in *The Gospel Sound.*

The sad irony in the timing of Harris's departure is that the group had just been signed to Art Rupe's Specialty label. Rupe became interested in the Soul Stirrers at the urging of Pilgrim's Traveler singer J. W. Alexander. Harris, the seminal vocal influence in modern gospel, would only record one session for Specialty. Yet his historical significance would endure: Harris introduced the technique of ad-libbing over the harmony parts, was the first to sing in delayed time (drawing comparisons to jazz), and used the falsetto voice at will. Harris would go on to form the Christland Singers and later the National Quartet Convention. He eventually recorded for Cooke's label SAR as R. H. Harris and the Gospel Paraders.

Enter Sam Cooke

After Harris's somewhat traumatic departure, the Soul Stirrers developed an entirely new sound and image. Baritone singer R. B. Robinson discovered the angelic, 19-year-old Cooke while he was still with the Chicago-based Highway QC's. Cooke joined the Soul Stirrers in January of 1951 and recorded his first Specialty session on March 1, 1951.

In the beginning, Cooke greatly imitated Harris; his cool sensuality was partially the result of his inability to match Harris's technique. Still, Cooke's early recordings, particularly the ebullient "Touch the Hem of His Garment," show him developing his own style. With the matinee-idol-handsome Cooke, the Soul Stirrers jammed churches and auditoriums. Women, even in this religious, pre-Beatles setting, would often faint and scream. Most importantly, the boyish Cooke was able to interest young people in gospel music. Farley recalled to author Peter Guralnick, as quoted in liner notes to *The Soul Stirrers: Jesus Gave Me Water,* "In the old days, young people took seats six rows from the back; the old folks stayed up front. When Sam came on the scene, it reversed itself. The young people took over."

As a gospel singer, Cooke was transcendent. His precise diction and modulated timbre were, in effect, pop vocal techniques employed in the service of sacred song. His two gospel masterpieces, "Wonderful" and "Jesus Wash Away All My Troubles," demonstrated all of the nuances that would characterize his soul success. Indeed, the subtle "Whoa-whoa-ao-o," later used so perfectly in "You Send Me," made its first appearance in "Wonderful."

Cooke's Departure for Pop Stardom

By 1956 Cooke was a gospel singer in name only. The following year, Specialty found itself in debt to house producer Bumps Blackwell for back royalties. In lieu of money, Blackwell asked for the rights to a pop demo that Cooke had cut. Blackwell persuaded Cooke to attempt a career in secular music and released the material—the song, "Lovable," was credited to "Dale Cook" so as not to offend Sam Cooke's gospel following—on his own Keen Records. From 1957 until his death in 1964, Cooke was a superstar. Yet only with the beautiful, gospel-tinged "A Change Is Gonna Come," released posthumously, did Cooke in his pop career match the artistic fervor of his gospel days.

For a time, in the early 1960s, Cooke pondered a return to gospel. For about six weeks he attended Soul Stirrers shows, eventually singing at a 1962 anniversary performance in Chicago. All of the original members attended, and R. H. Harris himself emceed. Cooke was, however, treated with disdain by the audience. Two years later, he was murdered by a motel clerk who thought he was an intruder. Rumors circulated that the killing was a mafia hit, but evidence suggested that Cooke's death was actually the result of a clandestine romantic tryst gone horribly awry.

In the wake of the singer's untimely demise, the Soul Stirrers ground to a halt. Farley, the only original member remaining with the gospel outfit, struggled to keep the group afloat. Other lead singers, even gifted vocalists like Willie Rogers and Martin Jacox, tried to live up to the legacy left by Harris and Cooke. The albums *Rest Easy* and *Tribute to Sam Cooke* were released on Chess in 1986. Versions of the group, albeit with changing lineups, performed into the '90s.

Although his sexuality was largely innocent, Cooke's crossover to pop and his unseemly, violent death greatly defeated the efforts of R. H. Harris. Harris, through the Soul Stirrers' sanctity and innovation, had tried to make a music, in his words, "fit for a King."

Selected discography

The Original Soul Stirrers Featuring Sam Cooke, Specialty, 1959.
Rest Easy, Chess, 1986.
Tribute to Sam Cooke, Chess, 1986.
The Soul Stirrers Featuring R. H. Harris: Shine on Me, Specialty 1991.
The Soul Stirrers Featuring Sam Cooke, Paul Foster, Julius Cheeks: Jesus Gave Me Water, Specialty, 1993.
God Said It, Savoy.
I Can See the Light Shining, Savoy.
I've Got Much to Be Thankful For, Savoy.
She's Gone on Home, Savoy.

Sources

Heilbut, Anthony, *The Gospel Sound: Good News and Bad Times*, Simon & Schuster, 1971, reissued, Limelight, 1992.
Rolling Stone Album Guide, edited by Anthony DeCurtis, James Henke, and Holly George-Warren, Straight Arrow, 1992.
Rolling Stone Record Guide, edited by Dave Marsh, Rolling Stone Press, 1979.

Additional information for this profile was obtained from liner notes by Lee Hildebrand and Opal Nations to *The Soul Stirrers: Jesus Gave Me Water*, Specialty, 1991.

—Stewart Francke

Pops Staples

Singer, songwriter, guitarist

Since his earliest days as a blues musician in rural Mississippi, Pops Staples has used music to bring people together. Although he has enjoyed critical accolades and popular success, he has never lost sight of his most important goal—as he told *Guitar Player*'s Jas Obrecht, "to sing a song that says together we stand and divided we fall." As guitar soloist, singer, and leader of one of the most successful and influential groups in the history of gospel and soul, Staples has enjoyed career enough for several men; yet he has remained vital as a recording and performing artist even as he approaches his 80th year.

By the early 1990s, legions of younger musicians claimed Staples as an inspiration. When he began preparing to record his second solo album, recording stars and fans such as Bonnie Raitt, Jackson Browne, and Ry Cooder all offered to lend a hand. The result was a heartfelt and utterly contemporary statement on the problems of race relations in America, an issue of enduring importance to Staples.

Born in Winona, Mississippi, in 1914, Staples heard some of the country's greatest blues players, including Charley Patton, Dick Bankston, and Howlin' Wolf, when they performed near his home. He bought his first acoustic guitar when he was 15. Although Staples came from a devoutly religious family, one that considered blues playing "sinful," he practiced the style diligently and was soon in demand as a guitarist at house parties and other social functions. This contact with the rich vernacular music of his childhood was woven deeply into his musical personality and would be heard throughout his career, even when he was performing in a strictly religious setting.

Besides developing his talents as an instrumentalist, Staples also began to earn a reputation around his hometown as a member of a gospel group called the Golden Trumpets. Yet the prospect of raising a family in the Depression-era South was a gloomy one, and Staples, now newly married, decided to try his luck in Chicago. He arrived there with his wife in 1935 with only $12 in his pocket and was forced to put his music aside to provide for his children. As he told Obrecht, "My wife was havin' children so fast, I worked about 12 years before I even picked up a guitar again. My wife and I—we did it ourselves—she worked at night and I worked in the day."

As his children became more able to look after themselves, Staples felt the call of a musical career once again, and in 1947 he bought his first electric guitar. In his spare time he began teaching the youngsters to perform songs like "If I Could Hear My Mother Pray

For the Record. . .

Born Roebuck Staples, December 2, 1914, in Winona, MS; children: Cleotha, Yvonne, Mavis, Purvis.

Began playing guitar c. 1929; sang with gospel group the Golden Trumpets; formed group the Staples Singers with daughters Mavis and Cleotha and son Purvis (later replaced by daughter Yvonne), 1947; Staples Singers joined Dr. Martin Luther King's crusade for civil rights, early 1960s; with group, recorded "I'll Take You There," 1972; began solo career, 1985; released *Pops Staples,* IAM/A&M, 1987; toured U.S. and Europe as solo act and with Staples Singers. Appeared in film *True Stories,* 1985, and in stage productions *A Gospel at Colonus* and *Something New for the Holidays,* both 1990.

Awards: (With Staples Singers) Rhythm and Blues Foundation Pioneer Award, 1992.

Addresses: Pointblank/Charisma Records America, Inc., 1790 Broadway, 20th Floor, New York, NY 10019.

Again" and "Do Not Pass Me By" in harmony by assigning each of them a note of a chord he played on his instrument. It was through this informal singing in the home that the Staples Singers—Pops, Cleo, Mavis, and Purvis—was formed.

During the late 1940s the Staples Singers began to find some local exposure in Chicago; then, in 1956, they began their long recording career with a series of discs for the city's United and Vee Jay labels, with Pops's passionate guitar playing as their only accompaniment. They also began to perform at several area churches. Initially, there was considerable resistance to the presence of Pops's blues-drenched guitar at religious services. But once the ministers witnessed the utter conviction with which the group performed, they softened their stance. "We weren't trying to pull off no stunts for money," Staples explained to *Musician's* Obrecht. "We were singing because we love God's word and we love God. The ministers could see that, and they let us come in with the guitar. That was a new thing—the guitar!"

With best-selling records such as "Uncloudy Day," "Stand by Me," and "Swing Low," the Staples Singers became one of the country's most popular gospel ensembles. And with the rise of the civil rights movement in the late 1950s and early 1960s, the group joined many well-known performers, including Aretha Franklin and her family, in supporting Dr. Martin Luther King, Jr.'s call for social change.

In 1968 the Staples Singers signed with the Memphis-based Stax label and developed more of a contemporary soul sound. It was for Stax that the group recorded its most enduring hits, including "Respect Yourself," "Heavy Makes You Happy," and, in 1972, "I'll Take You There," which reached Number One on the pop singles charts that year (and which was sampled almost two decades later to great effect by the rap duo Salt-N-Pepa in their smash "Let's Talk About Sex"). In 1975 the group recorded "Let's Do It Again" for the soundtrack of the Bill Cosby/Sidney Poitier film of the same name; this became their second Number One hit.

The mid-1980s found the Staples Singers touring widely and appearing on radio and television—and Pops Staples beginning to explore the possibility of a solo career. He performed a solo version of "Nobody's Fault But Mine" on a telecast of the 1985 Grammy Awards, and in 1987 released his first solo album, *Pops Staples,* on IAM/A&M Records.

Staples also began developing an interest in acting. He had a small role as a voodoo practitioner in David Byrne's 1985 film *True Stories,* and in 1990 starred in both the Chicago and San Francisco stage productions of *A Gospel at Colonus.* That year Staples also appeared in a Minneapolis production of *Something New for the Holidays.*

As the 1990s began to unfold, Staples showed little sign of slowing down. He toured extensively as a solo artist in 1991, and that year also found him attending the dedication of Pops Staples Park in Drew, Mississippi. In February of 1992, The Staples Singers traveled to New York to accept a Pioneer Award from The Rhythm and Blues Foundation. During the trip the group found time to record two songs with jazz vocalist Abbey Lincoln. After the release of *Peace to the Neighborhood,* his star-studded second solo album, Staples made plans to tour extensively in the U.S. and Europe, both as a solo act and with his family. He also recorded a duet with pop folksinger Michelle Shocked, thereby carrying his abiding message of hope and unity to a generation of younger listeners.

Selected discography

With the Staples Singers

Uncloudy Day, Vee Jay, 1961.
Hammers and Nails, Riverside, 1962.
Amen, Epic, 1965.
Why?, Epic, 1966.
Soul Folk in Action, Stax, 1968.
The Staples Swingers, Stax, 1970.
Bealtitude: Respect Yourself, Stax, 1972.

Be What You Are, Stax, 1973.
Let's Do It Again, Curtom, 1975.
This Time Around, Stax, 1981.
The Best of the Staples Singers, Stax, 1986.
Freedom Highway, Columbia, 1991.
(Contributors, with Marty Stuart) "The Weight," *Rhythm, Country & Blues,* MCA, 1994.

Solo albums

Pops Staples, IAM/A&M, 1987.
Peace to the Neighborhood, Pointblank/Charisma, 1992.

Sources

Books

Shaw, Arnold, *Black Popular Music in America,* Schirmer, 1986.

Heilbut, Anthony, *The Gospel Sound: Good News and Bad Times,* Simon & Schuster, reissued, Limelight, 1992.

Periodicals

Entertainment Weekly, July 10, 1992.
Guitar Player, September 1992.
Metro Times (Detroit), September 16, 1992.
Rolling Stone, August 20, 1992.

Additional information for this profile was obtained from Pointblank/Charisma Records America, Inc., 1992.

—*Jeffrey Taylor*

The Stray Cats

Rockabilly band

What began as a high school dropout, his brother, and some guy on stand-up bass playing next to the pool table in the back of a corner bar, turned into the rockabilly revival of the 1980s. The Stray Cats single-handedly brought back a style of music the heyday of which had ended before the bands' members were toddlers. The resurgence of this early form of rock and roll saw girls borrowing their mothers' poodle skirts and boys slicking back their hair in greasy pompadours, doing the Stray Cat Strut in a James Dean rebel slouch—all because of a guitar, a bass, a snare drum, and a rockin' rockabilly ethic.

The high school dropout was Brian Setzer; the brother and other guy were the first of a constantly rotating roster of musicians that eventually ended with Jim McDonnel, also known as Slim Jim Phantom, and Leon Drucker, calling himself Lee Rocker. Setzer started pestering his parents for a guitar at the age of six—when he discovered the Beatles in their record collection. At 14 he'd begun modeling himself after a picture of rockabilly original Eddie Cochran; he cut his hair

For the Record. . .

Members include **Slim Jim Phantom** (born Jim McDonnel, March 20, 1961, in Brooklyn, NY), drums; **Lee Rocker** (born Leon Drucker in 1961 in New York; son of Stanley Drucker [a clarinetist]), string bass; and **Brian Setzer** (born April 10, 1959, in Massapequa, NY), vocals, guitar.

Band formed as the Tom Cats in Massapequa, NY, c. 1978; signed with Arista/UK, 1980; released single "Runaway Boys," 1980; signed with EMI in U.S. and released *Built for Speed,* 1982; disbanded, 1984; recorded and performed sporadically, late 1980s-early 1990s, while bandmembers pursued solo work.

Selected awards: Platinum records for *Built for Speed* and *Rant 'N Rave With the Stray Cats.*

short, greased it back, and donned T-shirts with rolled-up sleeves, tucked into baggy cuffed pants, and loafers. Phantom also started out with a love of the Beatles, while Rocker's interest in music began more out of rebellion against his years of classical cello instruction. (He is the son of Stanley Drucker, longtime first clarinetist with the New York Philharmonic Orchestra.) What brought the trio together was a dedication to simple, old-fashioned rock and roll.

Rockabilly Roots

Rockabilly was born in 1954, in Sam Phillips's Memphis-based Sun Studios, where Elvis Presley, guitarist Scotty Moore, and bassist Bill Black invented a rocking hillbilly blues. Setzer explained these beginnings to *Guitar Player*'s Jas Obrecht as "basically a country guitarist trying to play rock and roll guitar, which is a mixing of black blues and white country . . . [it] leans towards the hillbilly side of rock and roll." Soon now-legendary performers like Carl Perkins, Johnny Cash, Buddy Holly, Gene Vincent, and Cochran were spreading the rockabilly gospel. But the sound virtually died out by the end of the 1950s. Still, bands like the Beatles and Creedence Clearwater Revival kept the rockabilly spirit going, with others picking it up along the way, because, as *Rolling Stone*'s Kurt Loder put it, "Whenever rock seems played out and ready for pasture, rockabilly is always there to remind a new generation of the music's still-marvelous possibilities."

At 16, calling himself the Rockabilly Rebel, Setzer started singing and playing guitar at "old man" bars on the south shore of Long Island, New York. When he had garnered a small following, he suggested to one of the bar owners that his brother be allowed to play drums for an extra $25. With an acquaintance on bass, this became the first incarnation of the Stray Cats. When Phantom and Rocker started showing up regularly—greased, eager, and versed in drums and bass, respectively—the Stray Cats became a solid threesome, though then they were called the Tom Cats. The stages they played were so small that they couldn't accommodate a complete drum set. Phantom compensated by using just two drums—base and snare—and a cymbal. Standing up behind the drums allowed him to save space and seem more a part of the band; the simple setup stuck and became a Stray Cats trademark.

Hit the Big Time in England

Alas, disco was the rage at the time and folks in their white suits and spandex didn't know what to make of the hard-rockin' hepcats. One night in 1980, while Setzer was moonlighting with the new wave band the Bloodless Pharaohs in a New York City bar, he met Tony Bidgood, a British bartender. Bidgood, a rocker himself, told Setzer that back in England rockabilly had never died. The boys promptly sold all their belongings and moved to London, with Bidgood in tow as manager. Sources vary as to whether the band changed their name before or after the London move, but it was around this time that they became the Stray Cats, spending their days knocking on doors in search of work and sleeping in all-night-movie theaters or in Hyde Park. Once they got their first gig, jobs began to pile up, with record companies falling in line right behind them. Because they "seemed nice," the Cats were signed to the Arista label. Other musicians started to catch their shows, among them the Rolling Stones, Led Zeppelin's Robert Plant, and musician and producer Dave Edmunds. Edmunds took the boys under his wing, worrying that a producer with too modern a sensibility would get his hands on the Cats and dilute their sound.

Having dodged that bullet, the sound demonstrated on their debut, *The Stray Cats,* was pure rockabilly, and Europe ate it up. The first single, "Runaway Boys," broke into the British Top Ten in December of 1980. Two more, "Stray Cat Strut" and "Rock This Town," became hits the next year, and the album leapt into the Top Ten. Concerts on the continent spread the band's fame, and a two-week stint in Japan—where it seemed rockabilly fever had never abated—inspired a reaction not seen since the days of Beatlemania. The Rolling Stones honored the Cats by inviting them to open for a handful of shows during the Stones' 1981 North American tour, exposure from which would make the band a big import seller in the States. In the meantime, the international whirlwind blew the boys to Montserrat, West Indies, to record their second album.

The isolated tropical island, it turned out, did not lend itself to rockabilly recording. The Cats cut *Gonna Ball* as fast as possible just to get out of the Caribbean, which perhaps had something to do with the record's lackluster reception. Still, the trio remained headliners in Europe and in the spring of 1981, flew home for the Stones dates and a small U.S. tour of their own. The big break on their home turf came when the Cats gave a remarkable performance on ABC-TV's short-lived *Fridays*. The ensuing sensation won them a domestic recording contract, with EMI Records, which in turn led to the release of *Built for Speed,* a compilation of songs from their two British albums, plus the title track. "Rock This Town," the Cats' first U.S. single, reached the Top Ten, and the album—spurred on by heavy MTV exposure and an intensive U.S. tour—sold steadily, also landing in the Top Ten; by January of 1983, *Built for Speed* had been on the Billboard charts for 30 weeks and had sold over two million copies.

Abrupt Breakup and Spotty Collaborations

The continued prominence of *Built for Speed* delayed the release of the next U.S. album, *Rant 'N Rave With the Stray Cats,* until May of 1983, but it hit fans with a vengeance, buoyed by the irresistible swing of "Sexy and Seventeen." Reviewers of both U.S. albums seemed to fall into two camps: one skeptically viewing the Stray Cats as decent-enough rockabilly practitioners trying to breath life into a tired cliché, and the other hailing the trio as adherents to a classic form that they had made their own with a clever and original modern approach. Regardless, the Cats were a huge musical force until September of 1984 when, quite suddenly, Brian Setzer pulled the plug.

Rolling Stone's Michael Goldberg asked the guitarist and songwriter why, to which Setzer replied, "When I saw string basses and bowling shirts in the windows at Macy's, I thought, 'Well, it was nice while it lasted.'. . . I didn't think I had anything else to say in that genre. . . . This way people will have a good memory of the Cats." But Goldberg hinted that the breakup had more to do with Setzer's irritation with the rock-star attitudes and lifestyles of his bandmates.

Phantom and Rocker went on to record a couple of rockabilly albums with journeyman guitarist Earl Slick as Phantom, Rocker, and Slick. Setzer released two solo albums, 1986's *Knife Feels Like Justice* and 1988's *Live Nude Guitars,* and portrayed one of his idols,

Eddie Cochran, in the hit film *La Bamba.* He received critical praise for his musicianship and the maturation of his now-varied style, but the pull of rockabilly and a continuing bond to his fellow former Cats would not keep him from his roots for long. In 1986 the Stray Cats reunited for *Rock Therapy,* which they recorded and mixed in a week. They got together again, in 1988, for *Blast Off* and, in 1992, for *Choo Choo Hot Fish,* touring sporadically when they weren't working on an assortment of solo projects.

Although fans seemed happy to see the Cats back after what the boys had begun calling their hiatus, critics were not as positive. In his *Rolling Stone* review of *Blast Off,* Jimmy Guterman echoed others in the rock press, saying, "[This reunion album] reintroduces the Long Island trio as rockabilly revivalists supreme, which both makes sense and stifles the group." After seeing what they could do beyond rockabilly, critics appeared disappointed that the Cats had not developed further stylistically. More than one reviewer suggested that despite their undeniable skill, with nothing new, they risked becoming just a rockabilly version of the 1950s nostalgia group Sha Na Na.

As the 1990s wore on, the Stray Cats continued to tour and record together, sometimes parting for prolonged periods, as was the case when Setzer took on his rockabilly big-band project, The Brian Setzer Orchestra, which resulted in a 1994 release. Perhaps the ultimate answer to the question of their future as an integrated entity could be found in one of their famed rebellious rants, "How long do you wanna live anyway?"

Selected discography

Stray Cats (includes "Runaway Boys," "Stray Cat Strut," and "Rock This Town"), Arista/UK, 1980.
Gonna Ball, Arista/UK, 1981.
Built for Speed, EMI, 1982.
Rant 'N Rave With the Stray Cats (includes "Sexy and Seventeen"), EMI, 1983.
Rock Therapy, 1986.
Blast Off, EMI, 1988.
Rock This Town: Best of the Stray Cats, EMI, 1990.
Choo Choo Hot Fish, Great Pyramid/JRS/BMG, 1992.
Original Cool, Griffin Music, 1993.
Live: Tear It Up, Receiver, 1993.

Solo albums by Brian Setzer

Knife Feels Like Justice, 1986.
Live Nude Guitars, 1988.
Brian Setzer Orchestra, Hollywood Records, 1994.

Sources

BAM, February 11, 1994.

Billboard, August 28, 1982; October 2, 1982; May 19, 1984; June 22, 1985; July 31, 1993.

Creem, January 1983; December 1983.

Guitar Player, September 1983; February 1993; October 1993.

Melody Maker, February 21, 1981; October 3, 1981; November 7, 1981; March 14, 1981; January 2, 1982; May 29, 1982; September 3, 1983; September 10, 1983; October 1, 1983; November 10, 1984; February 4, 1989; March 11, 1989; April 1, 1989; June 23, 1990.

Musician, October 1982; November 1983; January 1985; June 1989.

Pulse!, September 1993; December 1993.

Record, January 1984.

Rolling Stone, September 30, 1982; November 11, 1982; March 3, 1983; October 13, 1983; December 22, 1983; April 10, 1986; September 11, 1986; May 18, 1989.

Trouser Press, April 1982; October 1982; December 1983; February 1984.

Variety, November 4, 1981; October 13, 1982.

Village Voice, August 3, 1982; November 15, 1983.

Additional information for this profile was provided by Levine/Schneider Public Relations, 1992.

—*Joanna Rubiner*

Allen Toussaint

Singer, songwriter, pianist, producer

Allen Toussaint likes to talk about the old days, when, as he related to Don Palmer in a 1986 *Down Beat* article, he and his friends would spend the day in the front two rooms of his parents' shotgun house in New Orleans. Friends like Aaron Neville, Ernie K-Doe, Benny Spellman, and Irma Thomas would socialize and sing popular songs. Or Toussaint would write a song for Neville or Thomas and the others would sing behind him or her as they learned the song. Then they would head down to Cosimo Matassa's J&M Studios, where Toussaint had begun directing sessions for Minuit Records in 1960, singing all the way. Sometimes they would even return to the house afterwards and sing some more.

Not too much has changed since then. J&M Studios closed and was replaced in 1973 by the state-of-the-art Sea-Saint Studios, owned by Toussaint and Marshall Sehorn, a New Orleans record producer since the late '60s. But Toussaint is still writing songs and making records with his friends, who now sometimes hail from outside the Crescent City. He has scored gold records producing and arranging material for Paul Simon and Patti LaBelle, and Paul McCartney, Joe Cocker, and Maria Muldaur have all recorded at Sea-Saint. Toussaint's solo career has been an on-again-off-again affair; nonetheless, he remains one of New Orleans's most important impresarios and in recent years has had success with his work in theater.

Influenced by Professor Longhair

Toussaint started playing piano when he was five or six, though he had only about two months of formal training, "and I don't mean in succession," he noted in *Down Beat*. His sister helped him to read music and soon he was learning Grieg's *piano concerto* from a record, transposing it up a few keys so that his flat piano would be in tune with the recording. He counts New Orleans pianist Professor Longhair as his greatest influence, as does Toussaint's longtime associate Mac "Dr. John" Rebennack. In a 1991 piece in *Cultural Vistas,* Toussaint remembered, "When I heard Professor Longhair, good heavens, [it was] just wonderful. When I heard that [music] it was just a shock to my life because before that things were fairly mild. [Even] boogie woogie, you know, would get there and it would stay there, and everything had a different kind of order, but Professor Longhair [was] wild and untamed." In fact, Toussaint can be seen behind the keyboard in the 1982 documentary *Piano Players Rarely Ever Play Together,* produced by Stevson J. Palfi, which traces the musical lineage passed down from Isidore "Tuts" Washington to Roy "Professor Longhair" Byrd to Toussaint.

For the Record. . .

Born January 14, 1938, in New Orleans, LA; children: three, including Clarence and Alison.

Contributed piano to Fats Domino recordings; toured with Shirley and Lee, 1955; solo recording artist, 1958—; began producing sessions at Minuit Records, 1960; with Marshall Sehorn, founded label Sansu Enterprises, 1965; opened Sea-Saint Studios, 1973; composed music for theater, 1980s; appeared in documentary *Piano Players Rarely Ever Play Together*, 1982; released Warner Bros. retrospective *The Allen Toussaint Collection*, 1991. *Military service:* U.S. Army, 1963-65, served as musician.

Awards: Named "One of the Top 200 Executives of Tomorrow" by *Billboard,* 1976; "Southern Nights" named most performed song of the year by BMI, 1977; Outer Critics Circle Award for best music in an Off-Broadway musical, 1986-87, for *Staggerlee;* gold records for work with other artists.

Addresses: *Booking agent*—New Orleans Entertainment Agency, 3530 Rue Delphine, New Orleans, LA 70131.

Toussaint was performing in clubs like the famous Dew Drop Inn while he was still in his teens. It was at that venue that Dave Bartholomew, the Imperial Records executive who worked on many of pianist-singer Fats Domino's hits, recognized the young player's gift for imitating current musical styles. Toussaint was soon laying down Domino-like piano tracks on songs like "I Want You to Know" and "Little School Girl," onto which Domino would later dub his voice. He also toured briefly in 1955 with Shirley and Lee, but Toussaint soon returned to session work in New Orleans. There, while accompanying scores of singers at a three-day open audition, producers Murray Sporn and Danny Kesler realized Toussaint's talent and arranged for him to cut his own album in just two weeks. In 1958, Toussaint's all-instrumental *The Wild Sounds of New Orleans* was released by RCA and yielded the artist's first hit, "Java," soon remade to great effect by Al Hirt, much as Herb Alpert and the Tijuana Brass would later gain fame with Toussaint's "Whipped Cream," which became the theme for television's popular *Dating Game.*

The Toussaint Sound

Toussaint's most famous production hit with Minuit Records, at which he had become a fixture, was Ernie K-Doe's "Mother-in-law," which hit Number One on the national charts in the summer of 1961. Meanwhile, what came to be known as the "Toussaint Sound" recurred in local hits such as Aaron Neville's "Over You" and Irma Thomas's "It's Raining." Toussaint's output at Minuit was curtailed in 1963, however, when he was inducted into the Army, where he served as a musician for two years. While he was in the service, Minuit was sold to interests outside the New Orleans area and Toussaint's involvement would never be the same. Still, his time at Minuit and his exposure to the musicians there would have a lasting effect on him. As John Broven noted in his book *Rhythm and Blues in New Orleans,* "Toussaint was able to get away from the ensemble riffing sounds of Dave Bartholomew and also the Studio Band, mainly by allowing each instrumentalist a far freer role—at any moment the tenor would stutter through, the trumpet punchily interject, or the baritone moan a deep, bridging phrase. His own brilliant piano and the second line of the regular rhythm section of Chuck Badie and ex-Longhair drummer John Boudreaux provided the solid base."

Aside from their groundbreaking work with Toussaint, these musicians were also important because they formed the A.F.O. Combo, a project that sought not only to play, but to earn royalties instead of flat union wages. With Toussaint shouldering piano duties, the group saw enough success to create some bad blood with others on the New Orleans music scene; but they disbanded after an unsuccessful attempt to move the operation to California.

Formed Sansu, Nurtured Meters

Toussaint continued producing and arranging and started working with Marshall Sehorn in 1965; soon the two founded their own label, Sansu Enterprises. The mid-1960s saw the release of Lee Dorsey's hits "Get Out of My Life Woman," "Working in a Coalmine," and "Holy Cow." But Sansu was also home to the highly influential and now-revered Meters, composed of Art Neville, Leo Nocentelli, George Porter, and Joseph "Zigaboo" Modeliste, who served as the label's house band while also putting out their own string of late '60s hits, including "Sophisticated Cissy," "Cissy Strut," and "Ease Back," which exemplified the best of the modern soul-funk sound. Toussaint told *Audio's* Ted Fox, "The Meters were mostly a percussion group—not percussion instruments, but they played percussively. Everything they played was heavily syncopated. . . . Their songs were a conglomeration of firecrackers going off here, and pops there, explosions here. It was just fire." The Meters backed Dr. John on "Positively" and LaBelle on "Nightbirds"—both major hits that served to renew interest in the New Orleans sound.

In 1970 Toussaint was signed by Sceptor Records and, after a 12-year hiatus, was persuaded to make his second LP, *Toussaint,* for the Tiffany imprint. He then released a string of recordings for Warner Bros. The 1978 album *Motion* displayed less of the New Orleans sound, however, perhaps because it was produced by Atlantic Records co-founder Jerry Wexler, who may have been trying to mold Toussaint the way he had Ray Charles and Aretha Franklin. In 1978, Toussaint again stopped recording his own material. Nevertheless, albums like 1975's *Southern Nights*—which has been called Toussaint's "Sergeant Pepper"— yielded song after song for other artists, including Glen Campbell, the Pointer Sisters, and Little Feat.

The mid- to late '70s was a period of phenomenal success for Toussaint. In 1976, *Billboard* named him "One of the Top 200 Executives of Tomorrow," and in 1977, "Southern Nights" was recognized by the performers' rights society Broadcast Music Inc. (BMI) as "The Most Performed Song of the Year." Campbell's rendition of the song was nominated for a Grammy Award and for song of the year by the Country Music Association. In 1978, the Nashville Songwriters' Association International honored Toussaint's "Creative Genius in Words and Music"—a rare distinction for a practitioner of New Orleans rhythm and blues.

Broadened Horizons to Theater

But, the early 1980s were a slow time for Toussaint; Warner Bros. did not renew its contract with his Sea-Saint studios, for which Toussaint blamed himself. These years nonetheless afforded the artist time to explore theater music, serving as composer-lyricist for the stage production *We Love You, William* and the movie *Black Samson.* The music he wrote and performed in Vernel Bagneris's *Staggerlee* won the Outer Critics Circle Award for best music in an Off-Broadway musical for the season 1986-1987. In 1991, the Broadway musical *High Rollers Social and Pleasure Club*'s short run at the Helen Hayes Theater earned another nomination for Toussaint's efforts from the Outer Critics Circle, as well as a Tony nomination for the show's star, Vivian Reed.

Though Toussaint may not do much touring, he continues to appear in Europe and Japan and remains active in New Orleans, playing at benefits or at the Jazz and Heritage Festival, where, in 1986, his closing performance set an all-time attendance record and where, in 1989, he debuted new songs with a 12-piece big band. That year Toussaint stated in *Musician,* "I'm finding performing fun now. It was tragic at one point. I'd felt my stuff was done in the studio to prepare the way for other folks to do it live. . . . Now I'd like to do even more performing. I've got a different focus when I'm onstage. I let people know that I'm not one of the stars. I'm the guy that wrote the songs, that's all, and here I am." In 1991, Warner Bros./Reprise released *The Allen Toussaint Collection.*

Toussaint spends much of his time at Sea-Saint studios, where his son Clarence serves as his chief engineer and his daughter Alison as his personal assistant. He continues to turn out hits as a new generation, including artists as varied as pianist-singer Bruce Hornsby and hip-hoppers Heavy D and the Boyz, are influenced by the style he pioneered as the chief architect and master of the New Orleans sound.

Selected discography

The Wild Sounds of New Orleans, RCA Victor, 1958.
Toussaint, Tiffany/Sceptor, 1970.
From a Whisper to a Scream, Kent, 1970.
Life, Love, and Faith, Warner Bros./Reprise, 1972.
Southern Nights, Edsel, 1975.
Motion, Warner Bros., 1978.
The Allen Toussaint Collection, Warner Bros./Reprise, 1991.
(Contributor, with Chet Atkins) "Southern Nights," *Rhythm, Country & Blues,* MCA, 1994.
(With Crescent City Gold) *The Ultimate Session,* High Street, 1994.
The Stokes With Allen Toussaint, Bandy.
Bump City, Warner Bros.
(Contributor) *New Orleans Jazz and Heritage Festival 1976,* Island.
(With Kip Hanrahan) *Conjure: Music for the Texts of Ishmael Reed,* American Clave.

Sources

Books

Broven, John, *Rhythm and Blues in New Orleans,* Pelican Publishing Company, 1978.

Periodicals

Audio, November 1987.
Billboard, March 21, 1987.
Cultural Vistas: Louisiana Endowment for the Humanities, Winter 1991.
Down Beat, April 1986; October 1986.
Go Magazine, August 1985.
Living Blues, September/October 1989.
Musician, December 1989.
Spin, August 1992.
Variety, April 1, 1987.

Additional information for this profile was provided by the New Orleans Entertainment Agency, 1992.

—John Morrow

T. Rex

Rock band

irect predecessor of two important trends in the music of the 1970s—glam rock and punk—T. Rex was the manifestation of one highly original musician's personal vision. The core of the band was its singer and lead guitarist, Marc Bolan. Bolan employed a series of percussionists, and other musicians rounded out the band's sound on records and in concert; but T. Rex was essentially a vehicle for Bolan's songwriting and distinctive stage presence.

T. Rex is perhaps best remembered for its single American hit "Bang a Gong (Get It On)," recorded in 1971. But at the peak of their popularity in England, in 1972 and 1973, the band attracted fan adulation rivaled only by that of the Beatles in their prime. And the musicians who would create the rock styles of the future were carefully observing the mix of stage flamboyance, concept-album fantasy, eroticism, frenzied guitar work, and mystical poetry that Bolan concocted.

Bolan was born Mark Feld in London on September 30, 1947 (some sources list his birth date as July 30, 1947,

For the Record. . .

Members include **Marc Bolan** (born Mark Feld, [according to most sources] September 30, 1947, in London, England; married Gloria Jones [second wife; a singer]; died in an automobile accident, September 16, 1977), vocals, guitar; **Steve Currie** (bandmember c. 1971-72; died in 1981), bass; and **Steve Peregrine Took** (born July 28, 1949, in London; replaced by **Micky Finn** [born June 3, 1947], 1970; died in 1980), percussion.

Group formed as Tyrannosaurus Rex in London, 1967 (name shortened to T. Rex, 1970); released albums in U.S. on Blue Thumb label; signed with Reprise Records in U.S., 1970.

created free musical structures that matched the imaginativeness of Bolan's lyrics. Indeed, such early recordings as "Strange Orchestras" and "Deborah" sounded as novel to many in the 1990s as they did when they were first released.

The latter song was a Top 40 hit in Britain, and, with the support of the influential BBC disc jockey John Peel, Tyrannosaurus Rex's albums gained a strong following. But Bolan hoped for wider success. Took left the act and was replaced by Micky Finn in 1970, also the year that the band's name was truncated to T. Rex.

Went Electric

It was at about this time that producer Tony Visconti, who would later team with David Bowie, began to devise a more elaborate and grandiose sound for T. Rex, including the use of a variety of instruments and even occasional string and orchestra arrangements. Bolan reverted to an electric guitar. This caused a small furor among his folk-oriented fans, not unlike the one American folksinger Bob Dylan had experienced in 1965 when he made a similar switch. But as they did in Dylan's case, the changes opened the door to a popular breakthrough.

The new T. Rex sound was displayed at its simplest and most intense on 1971's *Electric Warrior* and its successor, *The Slider,* released the following year. Bolan had discarded fantasy themes in favor of short blues and rock forms that frequently bore erotic content. A series of metaphors likening women to automobiles—"You're built like a car/You got a hubcap/Diamond-star halo," Bolan intoned in "Bang a Gong (Get It On)"—might have seemed ludicrous coming from someone with less vocal authority.

Bolan's lyrics were obscure, seemingly more concerned with the sound of the words than with their meaning. To be sure, we may never know what Bolan intended by "She's got luggage eyes," from 1970's "One Inch Rock." But he had an undeniable gift for simple, alliterative images of great power, like the fragment "You're windy and wild," from "Bang a Gong (Get It On)," or even the bacchanalian refrain that gave the song its title.

or September 30, 1948). As a teenager he was drawn to London's "teddy boy" and "mod" fashion scenes, and he even worked, briefly but apparently successfully, as a fashion model. A penchant for unusual outfits would remain with Bolan throughout his career. On stage he often appeared in the striking combination of black stovepipe hat and V-neck sweater, an image captured on the famous cover of T. Rex's album *The Slider* by photographer and ex-Beatle Ringo Starr.

Hallucinated Band Name

But like many other British young people of his generation, Bolan was also drawn to American rock and roll, and he soon began to aspire to a musical career. He joined a group called John's Children, which had some success before disbanding in 1967. Then Bolan joined with percussionist Steve Peregrine Took to form Tyrannosaurus Rex. He chose the name after experiencing a hallucination in which a dinosaur pictured on a poster on the wall of his room began to move.

The titles of Tyrannosaurus Rex's early albums, released in the U.S. on the Blue Thumb label, offer pointed suggestions of their content; two examples are 1968's *Prophets, Seers & Sages* and the following year's *Unicorn*. Bolan's compositions from this period had a fantastic air inspired by the quasi-medieval writings of C. S. Lewis and J. R. R. Tolkien. But more significant was the duo's unique sound. Possibly due to a finance company repossession of his electric instruments, Bolan favored an acoustic guitar on these recordings; the results fit well with the late-1960s trend toward folk rock. And his vocal style was instantly memorable for its drawing out of long notes into a strangled, rapid vibrato. Took contributed a varied palette of bongo drum sounds, and the two musicians

Pioneered Glam, Embraced by Punks

Certain junctures in these songs were augmented by producer Visconti with backing vocals that mirrored Bolan's singing one octave higher, which created an eerie, gothic atmosphere that greatly influenced so-called glam rockers like David Bowie in the ensuing years. Bowie's early music, described by Scott Isler in the New Rolling Stone Record Guide as "heavy metal with an art-school education," owed much to T. Rex. But the influence of Electric Warrior and The Slider led in another direction as well. Electric Warrior's "Rip Off" featured full-throated screams of barely coherent complaint ("The President's weird/He's got a burgundy beard/It's a rip-off/Such a rip-off") from Bolan, with loud rudimentary guitar accompaniment, frenetic drumming from Finn, and a swirling, abrasively blown saxophone. Offerings of this sort earned T. Rex the respect of musicians in the nascent punk movement. On tour shortly before his death in 1977, Bolan featured a punk band, the Damned, as his opening act.

The effect of all this on youthful English audiences was extraordinary. Michael Thomas of Rolling Stone quoted an English newspaper account as having reported: "Girls, mostly young, went mad. Their eyes glazed in delirium. They danced adulatorily in the aisles. They emitted falsetto shrieks. It was all rather reminiscent of Beatlemania." T. Rex notched a total of 11 Top Ten hits in Britain. "Bang a Gong" reached the same level in America, but despite an extensive television advertising campaign—the first of its kind, on the part of T. Rex's American label, Reprise—the band never really achieved mass success in the U.S., though they did cultivate a die-hard cult following there.

Even in Britain, Bolan's period of real stardom was brief. Ringo Starr directed a 1973 documentary on T. Rex's career called Born to Boogie; but even by that time public attention had shifted elsewhere and the film was a commercial failure. Later T. Rex albums were panned by critics and generally ignored by the public, and Bolan descended into what he described to Rolling Stone as "a twilight world of drugs, booze and kinky sex." He died on September 16, 1977, when a car driven by his second wife, an American soul singer named Gloria Jones, crashed into a tree. Took died in 1980, and Steve Currie, who had played bass on Electric Warrior and The Slider, met his end in 1981.

By the early 1990s there were signs that Bolan's talent and T. Rex's immense historical significance were beginning to receive their proper appreciation. The Power Station released a hit version of "Bang a Gong" in 1985 (arguably that short-lived group's best work), and in 1993, heavy metal superstars Guns 'N' Roses—who began their career with a decidedly glam look—covered 1972's "Buick Mackane," the cutting of which guitarist Slash said finally got the song "out of his system." A boxed-set compilation of the band's recordings was made available, as were individual CD reissues of some of their albums, though the early

Tyrannosaurus Rex folk-rock albums remained mostly unavailable. (Electric Warrior is among the handful of classic rock albums that have remained in print continuously since their date of release.) Perhaps most telling of the band's influence, though, was the emergence in 1993 of the much-hyped British group Suede, which made a splash with an admittedly T. Rex-inspired sound; it seemed the glam movement that Bolan had largely created was on the verge of a full-blown revival.

Selected discography

Prophets, Seers & Sages, Blue Thumb, 1968.
Unicorn, Blue Thumb, 1969.
Electric Warrior (includes "Bang a Gong [Get It On]" and "Rip Off"), Reprise, 1971.
The Slider, Reprise, 1972.
The T. Rex Collection, Relativity, 1991.
20th-Century Boy/The Best of T. Rex, Relativity.
Bolan's Zip Gun, Relativity.
Futuristic Dragon, Relativity.
Zinc Alloy and the Hidden Riders of Tomorrow, Relativity.
BBC Live, Windsong.

Sources

Books

The Guinness Encyclopedia of Popular Music, edited by Colin Larkin, New England Publishers Associates, 1992.
Jahn, Mike, Rock: The Story of Rock From Elvis Presley to the Rolling Stones, Quadrangle, 1973.
Marsh, Dave, and John Swenson, The New Rolling Stone Record Guide, Rolling Stone Press/Random House, 1983.
The Rolling Stone Encyclopedia of Rock & Roll, edited by Jon Pareles and Patricia Romanowski, Rolling Stone Press/Summit Books, 1983.
Stambler, Irwin, Encyclopedia of Pop, Rock & Soul, St. Martin's, 1989.
Ward, Ed, Geoffrey Stokes, and Ken Tucker, Rock of Ages: The Rolling Stone History of Rock & Roll, Rolling Stone Press/Summit Books, 1986.

Periodicals

Rolling Stone, July 23, 1970; September 16, 1971; March 16, 1972; September 26, 1974.

—James M. Manheim

Bunny Wailer

Bunny Wailer, named by *Newsweek* as one of the three most important musicians in world music (along with Nigeria's King Sunny Ade and Brazil's Milton Nascimento), is an enigmatic figure in the world of reggae. During his ten years as a member of the original Wailers, he was acknowledged as a songwriting equal to reggae greats Bob Marley and Peter Tosh and was often described as the finest singer of the trio. Yet when the group disbanded in 1973 and Tosh and Marley went on to world acclaim, Wailer disappeared into the hills of Jamaica. For three years he was scarcely seen or heard from. Rumors proliferated about his ascetic existence and passionate study of the principles of the Rastafarian religion. But when he reemerged to record again, Wailer proved that he had not lost touch with the rhythms that moved the people; his albums were masterful blends of sociopolitical commentary and infectious, danceable melodies. After the untimely deaths of Marley and Tosh, Wailer was looked to as the elder statesman of reggae. He has refused to exploit or even acknowledge that status, however, preferring to remain focused on his own vision of what his life and music should be.

Wailer was born Neville O'Reilly Livingston in Kingston, Jamaica, but spent most of his early childhood in the idyllic rural village of Nine Miles. There he acquired a nickname, "Bunny," and a best friend, Bob Marley. The boys grew up as brothers, their bond growing even tighter when Marley's mother and Wailer's father moved together to Jamaica's largest city, Kingston. Although the ghetto in which they lived, called Trenchtown, was one of the world's poorest and most violent, Wailer perceived it as a magical place. Like Hollywood, it was full of stars and would-be stars. The two boys were no exception. Listening to rhythm and blues on New Orleans radio, they dreamed of making music; they fashioned crude guitars for themselves out of sardine cans, bamboo, and discarded electrical wire. When they met another local youth, Peter Tosh, who owned a real guitar, they happily expanded their duo to a trio. By 1966, their biggest dream had come true—they were offered, and signed, a recording contract.

Wailer, Marley, and Tosh were first known as the Teenagers, then the Wailing Rudeboys, which became the Wailing Wailers, and finally just the Wailers. Somewhere along the way, Bunny adopted the group's name as his own surname. From the start, and through all their various incarnations, the Wailers were a hit in Jamaica. As the music evolved from rollicking ska to rock-steady to reggae, they were always in the forefront. The three members considered themselves equals, alternating leads; Wailer's sweet tenor was featured on a cover version of Bob Dylan's "Like a Rolling Stone," as well as on his own compositions "Dancing Shoes," "Dreamland,"

For the Record. . .

Born Neville O'Reilly Livingston, April 10, 1947, in Kingston, Jamaica; son of Thaddeus Livingston.

With Bob Marley and Peter Tosh, founded group the Wailers (originally known as the Teenagers, then the Wailing Rudeboys, then the Wailing Wailers), mid-1960s; established Solomonic Records, 1972; recorded and performed with the Wailers until 1973; solo artist, 1973—.

Awards: Grammy Award and NAACP Image Award nominations, both 1989, both for *Liberation.*

Addresses: *Record company*—Shanachie Records, 37 East Clinton St., Newton, NJ 07860.

and many others. In fact, he composed some of the group's most enduring tunes, including "One Love," "Who Feels It Knows It," and "Pass It On." Despite their popular success, though, hastily signed contracts meant that the Wailers made almost no money in their early years, and the group broke up briefly at the start of the 1970s when Wailer was imprisoned for possession of marijuana and Marley went to work on an American assembly line.

When they reunited some two years later, Marley was determined to get them a new contract—one that would give them their due. Accordingly, he sought an alliance with Chris Blackwell, a wealthy white Jamaican whose company, Island Records, was the home of many major rock stars. Blackwell signed the group, despite the prevailing wisdom that reggae would never find an audience beyond Jamaica; the sound was considered too primitive, and the growing influence on the music of Rastafarianism—a religion based on the belief that Emperor Haile Selassie I of Ethiopia is the living God who will deliver blacks from oppression and in which the smoking of marijuana is considered a sacrament—was deemed entirely too esoteric for mass consumption. But Blackwell's faith in the Wailers proved justified; with his promotional efforts, the albums *Catch a Fire* and *Burnin'* were enthusiastically received and have since become classics.

But Blackwell was also instrumental in the undoing of the original Wailers, grooming Marley to be the star of the group rather than one of three equals, which was reflected in the renaming of the band—to Bob Marley and the Wailers. This was unacceptable to Tosh, and Wailer had reservations about it as well; moreover, he found the world tours arranged by Blackwell virtually unbearable and longed to return to Jamaica. In 1972 Wailer founded his own label, Solomonic Records, and

cut a few singles; in 1973, he broke entirely with Blackwell and Island, as did Tosh. Marley and Tosh went on to solo success, but Wailer retired to a reclusive life in the country, contemplating all that had happened. His reputation as a mystic with supernatural powers grew from 1973 to 1976, a period in which he recorded no music and was rarely seen.

Then, in 1976, Wailer made a sudden and surprising reappearance. Backed by Marley, Tosh, and the new Wailers band, he released *Blackheart Man* on the Island label. Hailed as a masterpiece, the album's cryptic lyrics solidified Wailer's image as a shaman of sorts, and he continued in his elusive ways; he did not perform in public again until after Marley's death, on May 11, 1981. But his stage comeback was quite spectacular: he organized the 1982 Christmas Day Youth Consciousness Festival in Kingston, featuring himself, Tosh, reggae notables Jimmy Cliff, Marcia Griffiths, Judy Mowatt, and the Wailers band, and performed a stunning three-hour set, the other performers backing him in turn. Just as astonishing was his decision, in 1987, to venture from Jamaica for the first time in 14 years. The occasion was a solo performance at Madison Square Garden to support his *Rootsman Skanking* album. Although the concert was his debut at the stadium—and went virtually unpromoted—Wailer played to a sellout crowd.

Wailer continues to release music and perform, but only when the time seems right to him. The *Liberation* album, for example, was scheduled for release in the late 1980s, but he held it back in favor of the lighter, more dance-oriented *Rule Dance Hall;* when Wailer did unveil *Liberation,* it proved strangely prophetic, foretelling the release from prison of African National Congress leader Nelson Mandela and the fall of the Berlin Wall just months before those events occurred. His seeming gift of clairvoyance aside, Wailer's earthly performances and recorded output—insightful, morally uncompromising, and consistently enjoyable—have demonstrated that his music is rightly hailed as among the best of reggae's past and present.

Selected discography

With Bob Marley and the Wailers; reissued on Tough Gong/Island, 1990, except where noted.

Burnin'.
Catch a Fire.
Confrontation.
Exodus.
Kaya.
Legend (The Best of Bob Marley and the Wailers).
Live.

Natty Dread.
Rastaman Vibration.
Rebel Music.
Survival.
Uprising.
The Never Ending Wailers, Ras, 1994.

Solo albums

Blackheart Man, Island, 1976.
Protest, Island, 1977, reissued, Mango.
Struggle, Solomonic, 1979.
Bunny Wailer Sings the Wailers, Island, 1980, reissued Mango.
In I Father's Groove, Solomonic, 1980.
Rock 'n' Groove, Solomonic, 1981.
Tribute to the Late Hon. Robert Nesta Marley, O.M., Solomonic, 1981, reissued as *Time Will Tell: A Tribute to Bob Marley,* Shanachie, 1990.
Hook, Line and Sinker, Solomonic, 1982.
Roots, Radic, Rockers, Reggae, 1983.
Live, Solomonic, 1986.
Marketplace, 1986, reissued, Shanachie, 1991.
Rootsman Skanking, Shanachie, 1987.
Rule Dance Hall, Shanachie, 1988.

Liberation, Shanachie, 1989.
Gumption, Shanachie, 1990.
(Contributor) *People Get Ready: A Tribute to Curtis Mayfield,* Shanachie, 1993.
Crucial: Roots Classics, Shanachie, 1994.

Sources

Books

Davis, Stephen, *Reggae Bloodlines: In Search of the Music and Culture of Jamaica,* Anchor Press, 1979.
White, Timothy, *Catch a Fire: The Life of Bob Marley,* Holt, 1983.

Periodicals

Down Beat, March 1991; June 1991.
High Fidelity, May 1989.
Rolling Stone, April 20, 1989.
Vibe, March 1994.
Village Voice, December 29, 1987.

—Joan Goldsworthy

Loudon Wainwright III

Singer, songwriter, actor

When Loudon Wainwright III released his first album in 1970, the music press branded him, as it had other young singer-songwriters, "The New Bob Dylan." Two decades later, in "Talking New Bob Dylan," a 1992 tribute to the rock and folk legend, Wainwright suggested that he and the other New Bob Dylans, "your dumb-ass kid brothers," get together at singer and songwriter Bruce Springsteen's house as part of a 12-step program. Wainwright has also been dubbed "the Woody Allen of Folk" and "the Charlie Chaplin of Rock."

Though originally lumped with the many singer-songwriters of the early 1970s, Wainwright's finely tuned wit served to separate him from the pack, and critics eventually stopped looking for comparisons. "[There are] a million amateurs out there who call themselves songwriters, but for my money, [there are] only a few who belong in this guy's league," asserted *City Pages* contributor Jim Walsh. Called "the not-so-sensitive folk singer" by Greg Reibman in *Billboard,* Wainwright built a cult following with funny, biting, and incisive songs about virtually any subject. He is, according to Tom Surowicz of the *Twin Cities Reader,* "a thoroughly compelling master of irony" and in *Rolling Stone* contributor David Browne's words, "our greatest pop satirist."

Wainwright was born in Chapel Hill, North Carolina, in 1946, but grew up in affluent Westchester County, New York, the eldest of the four children of renowned *Life* magazine editor and columnist Loudon Wainwright, Jr. His high school years were spent in Delaware, at the St. Andrews School for Boys, where he began to listen to and play folk music. Wainwright learned to play the guitar in his early teens and performed with a few folk groups at school. He also spent weekends at folk clubs in Philadelphia and saw Bob Dylan "go electric" at the Newport Folk Festival in 1965. Dylan was a big influence musically, as was folksinger and guitarist Ramblin' Jack Elliot. Wainwright went to Carnegie Mellon University in Pittsburgh to study acting and directing but left after a year and a half, dropping out in January of 1967 to head for San Francisco.

"Discovered" in New York City Club

But by 1968, Wainwright was back East, living in Cambridge, Massachusetts. He started writing songs and playing in Boston-area, and occasionally New York City, clubs. It was at New York's Village Gaslight that Milton Kramer, a music publisher, caught Wainwright's act. Kramer quickly became his manager and secured him a recording contract with Atlantic Records in 1969. Wasting little time, Atlantic released Wainwright's first album, *Loudon Wainwright III,* in 1970, followed by *Album II* in 1971.

For the Record. . .

Born Loudon Wainwright III, September 5, 1946, in Chapel Hill, NC; son of Loudon S. Wainwright, Jr., (a columnist and editor of *Life* magazine) and Martha (a yoga instructor); married Kate McGarrigle (a singer), (divorced, 1977); married Suzzy Roche (a singer), (divorced); children: (first marriage) Rufus, Martha; (second marriage) Lucy. *Education:* Attended Carnegie Mellon University, 1965-1967.

Began writing and performing in Boston and New York City, 1968; signed with Atlantic Records, 1969, and released *Loudon Wainwright III,* 1970; signed with CBS Records, and released *Album III,* 1972; signed with Arista Records, c. 1976; signed with Demon Records in England, Rounder in the U.S., and released *Fame and Wealth,* 1982; appeared in films *The Slugger's Wife,* 1985, and *Jacknife,* 1989; performed on stage and television in England, 1980s—.

Awards: Grammy award nominations for best contemporary folk recording, 1986, for *I'm Alright,* and 1987, for *More Love Songs.*

Addresses: *Record Company*—Virgin Records, 338 North Foothill Rd., Beverly Hills, CA 90210. *Management*—Teddy Wainwright, P.O. Box 115, Purdys, NY 10578. *Booking agent*—The Rosebud Agency, P.O. Box 170429, San Francisco, CA 94117.

Wainwright's early work was personal and confessional, and the instrumentation was very spare—usually just the singer and his acoustic guitar. Critics were impressed. Reviewing the first album for *Rolling Stone,* Gary Von Tersch marveled, "Usually artists of Wainwright's obvious genius write and play out their lives and songs on old friends' back porches, in local smoke-stung coffeehouses or on anonymous sidewalks and park benches. Somehow Wainwright found his way onto a record. I just hope it's not a one-shot affair—he's got something to say." Though Stephen Holden, also of *Rolling Stone,* deemed the artist's first two offerings poorly produced, he acknowledged that "the records were wonderful. The crudeness of production, the extremely static nature of the music itself: these at least accentuated the poetry by making it inescapable." Also evident on the early albums was a bitterness that put some listeners off. Looking back a decade later, Steven X. Rea of *High Fidelity* recalled that these first attempts "were not easy records to listen to. The singer-songwriter . . . was certainly clever and cunning, smart and satirical, but the emotions behind his words—sung in a high, bitter whine—were angry, distraught, and dark."

Wainwright's relationship with Atlantic was stormy and the label dropped him after *Album II.* Picked up by CBS Records, he released *Album III* in 1972. This LP was not only a critical success, but a popular one as well, reaching the Top 100. Much of the attention it garnered could be attributed to the comic song "Dead Skunk," which landed in the Top 20. *Album III's* humor, in fact, marked a change in Wainwright's music. As he explained in *Sing Out!,* though he started his career as a fairly serious songwriter, "humor started to leak in after a couple of years, and rather than change what I was doing, I sort of threw gasoline on it, 'cause I enjoyed having people laugh at me—or with me." He told Craig Harris, author of *The New Folk Music,* that he also liked the way his new approach increased record sales, as did CBS, which pushed him to write more funny, commercial songs.

"Completely Freaked"

Wainwright released five more albums during the '70s, all of them sounding very commercial, according to *High Fidelity's* Rea. But the singer was not particularly pleased with his work, even though his core of devotees continued to grow. Songs intended to ensnare a wide audience were not his forte. "Generally my impulse to write has been autobiographical. I never really thought much about writing something for the radio audience at large," he told *Sing Out!* "When I've half-heartedly tried to make radio records, they were failures." By 1976, CBS had dropped him and he had moved to Arista. *Rolling Stone's* David Wild called Wainwright's Arista albums his "least distinguished efforts." Wainwright himself called them his "plane-crash albums." As he explained to the journalist, "When my plane goes down, those records come out again. At that time I was under pressure to have a hit single . . . and I didn't know what the hell I was doing. I was just looking over my shoulder—completely freaked."

Wainwright had also spent the 1970s pursuing his interest in acting. He appeared in three episodes of television's *M*A*S*H* in 1975 and performed Off Broadway in the musical *Pump Boys and Dinettes.* This occupation continued into the '80s, when he appeared in two films—*The Slugger's Wife* in 1985 and *Jacknife* in 1989—and on stage and television in Britain. Also during the '70s, Wainwright married singer Kate McGarrigle of the Canadian folk duo the McGarrigle Sisters, and the couple had two children, Rufus and Martha. But the marriage ended in 1977 and a year later, Arista let him go. "I just wound up at the end of the 70's in a heap," he confessed to Bill Flanagan in *Musician.* He left his manager and his agent, moved to California, and then to England. Except for a live LP released by Radar Records in 1979, Wainwright, who had dutifully unveiled an album every year since 1970, did not produce another until 1982.

In 1980 Wainwright started over, signing with independent record companies—Demon in England and Rounder in the U.S. As he told Flanagan in 1989, he loved the freedom of working with independents, which allowed him to make the music he wanted without the pressure to produce hit singles and big sales. "And slowly, through this decade I've made five albums just trying to somehow figure out how to do work that I feel good about that is related to something real." He began working with British folk and guitar favorite Richard Thompson, who played on his albums and helped produce several, and found a new manager in his sister Teddy. He married Suzzy Roche of the singing sister trio The Roches, and they had a daughter, Lucy, in 1982. The marriage to Roche didn't last either, but it apparently gave Wainwright plenty of new song material.

Returned to Personal Songwriting

In this second phase of his career, Wainwright returned to more personal songwriting. As he mused in "Harry's Wall," from 1988's *Therapy,* "I guess by now you've noticed/ Almost all the songs I write/ Somehow pertain to me." Wainwright also, according to Rea, exhibited a "newfound emotional maturity." Reviewing 1982's *Fame and Wealth,* he asserted, "His first collection of new songs in four years shows a wiser, worldlier set of perceptions." The next album, 1985's *I'm Alright,* was co-produced by Thompson, who, according to *High Fidelity's* Leslie Berman, encouraged Wainwright to concentrate on his "softer side." In doing so, he "[fashioned] a portrait of the artist as a gloomy hopeful fellow; the anger and disdain of so many of his earlier songs is gone. By toning down his negativity, he has discovered a more complicated and effective level of humor." *I'm Alright* was nominated for a Grammy Award for best contemporary folk recording, as was the 1986 followup, *More Love Songs.*

1988 saw Wainwright inching his way back to the major labels; that year's *Therapy* was recorded by Silvertone, another independent, but distributed by RCA. *People's* David Hiltbrand considered *Therapy* an "uneven effort for Wainwright," but *Rolling Stone* contributor Wild felt differently, declaring, "[*Therapy*] reaffirms that [Wainwright] is one of the wittiest and most literate singer-songwriters on the scene." Wainwright's following remained strong in the United States and England, which had become his primary residence. In 1989, England's Edsel Records reissued his first five albums.

Wainwright's faithful were rewarded in 1992 with *History.* Released by Virgin Records, it marked the artist's full return to the majors. Kent Zimmerman of the *Gavin*

"Generally my impulse to write has been autobiographical. I never really thought much about writing something for the radio audience at large. When I've half-heartedly tried to make radio records, they were failures."

Report described *History* as "beautifully played, produced, sung and phrased," and along with the *Twin Cities Reader's* Surowicz and *Entertainment Weekly,* assessed it as one of the best albums of the year. The family-focused record was highly personal—in the words of Wild, an "intimate, painfully honest album, which should be called *Songs for the Whole Dysfunctional Family.*" Less cynically, Dave DiMartino of *Musician* labeled *History* "Wainwright's shining moment of personal introspection."

Throughout his checkered recording career, Wainwright's mainstay has been his live performances—as he acknowledged to *Musician's* Flanagan, saying, "I still more than anything love to play for people." Although *High Fidelity* contributor Berman judged his performances "mannered and predictable," Surowicz identified in Wainwright "a rare honesty, biting wit, moving depth, impish sex appeal, a punk's energy, a star actor's charisma, and a great biographer's gift for detail." His relationship with his audience is at once antagonistic and naked. As Flanagan described, onstage Wainwright is a "hammy extrovert, making faces as he sings, lifting one leg in the air, sticking out his tongue and then—unexpectedly—opening his veins for the audience's inspection."

In spite of his critical acclaim, Wainwright continued to feel the pinch of life on the musical fringe. "It would be bullshitting you to say that I don't want to be more successful. I'm obsessed with success and failure. . . .

And I'm frustrated because I'm on the periphery of the music business," he admitted to Flanagan. In songs like "Harry's Wall" he takes stabs at his minor celebrity, and in "The Home Stretch," from *More Love Songs,* he rails, "But keep lifting your left leg/ And sticking out your tongue/ There's nothing else that you can do/ And you're too old to die young." Still, he conceded to Flanagan that he loves his job. "I'm one of those people who got to do basically what they wanted to do and get paid for it. So I consider myself very fortunate." Four years later, in the liner notes to his much-applauded 1993 live album *Career Moves,* he maintained his optimism, reporting, "In February of this year I did a show at the Royal Festival Hall in London and a few weeks later I was in Orlando, Florida, playing in a blues bar called the Junkyard. Both were good nights."

Through exposure on such venues as National Public Radio and the word of mouth of loyal fans and critics, Wainwright's satire, wit, and sincerity persisted in gracing both concert halls and bars. *City Pages* contributor Walsh suggested why: "Loudon Wainwright III leaves you with something. Something peculiar, something special, something to chew on. And though he says he draws lines as to how much he's willing to reveal about his life, he also writes with an unflinching honesty while others in his same arena cover up with poetry and volume." Wainwright countered, "Well, it could just be my exhibitionist tendencies, too; I don't think we have to turn it into so much of a noble thing." This characteristic deflation only confirmed Holden's *New York Times* explanation of Wainwright's appeal. "A great singing storyteller," the music scribe ventured, "he still projects the slightly scary radarlike vision of a precocious brat who sees through all disguises, including his own, and feels compelled to tattle on everybody."

Selected discography

Loudon Wainwright III, Atlantic, 1970.
Album II, Atlantic, 1971.
Album III (includes "Dead Skunk"), CBS, 1972.
Attempted Mustache, CBS, 1974.
Unrequited, CBS, 1975.
T Shirt, Arista, 1976.
Final Exam, Arista, 1978.

A Live One, Radar, 1979.
Fame and Wealth, Demon/Rounder, 1982.
I'm Alright, Demon/Rounder, 1985.
More Love Songs (includes "The Home Stretch"), Demon/ Rounder, 1986.
Therapy (includes "Harry's Wall"), Silvertone/RCA, 1988.
History (includes "Talking New Bob Dylan"), Virgin, 1992.
Career Moves, Virgin, 1993.

Sources

Books

Harris, Craig, *The New Folk Music,* White Cliffs Media Company, 1991.
The Penguin Encyclopedia of Popular Music, edited by Donald Clarke, Viking, 1989.

Periodicals

Billboard, August 19, 1989; January 9, 1993.
City Pages (Minneapolis/St. Paul), November 25, 1992.
Entertainment Weekly, November 20, 1992; December 25, 1992.
Evening Standard (London), October 5, 1992.
Gavin Report, November 20, 1992.
High Fidelity, June 1983; March 1986; October 1987.
Independent (London), October 13, 1992.
Minneapolis Star and Tribune, November 30, 1992.
Musician, September 1989; February 1993.
Music Paper, November 1993.
New York Times, November 22, 1992.
People, July 3, 1989.
Rolling Stone, October 29, 1970; October 26, 1972; April 23, 1987; October 5, 1989; March 4, 1993.
St. Paul Pioneer Press, October 31, 1993.
Sing Out!, Winter 1993.
Stereo Review, May 1986; April 1993; November 1993.
Twin Cities Reader (Minneapolis/St. Paul), November 25, 1992.
Utne Reader, May/June 1993.
Village Voice, September 28, 1993.

Additional information for this profile was provided by The Rosebud Agency and obtained from liner notes to *Career Moves,* Virgin, 1993.

—*Megan Rubiner Zinn*

Karl Wallinger

Singer, songwriter, instrumentalist

Critic David Hiltbrand, writing for *People,* referred to English rock band World Party as "essentially a platform for . . . Karl Wallinger," and the history of the group bears out that claim. Indeed, Wallinger has managed to put together three successful albums and forge a band identity of sorts all by himself. He has had the occasional help of studio musicians and invited a guest producer to join him on 1993's *Bang!,* but he alone can take credit for World Party's burgeoning popularity.

Born in Prestatyn, northern Wales, on October 19, 1957, Wallinger was the youngest in a middle-class family of six. They lived on the modest means afforded by Wallinger's father's architectural work for the British government. Wallinger was obsessed with music as a child, particularly with the then-reigning lords of rock, the Beatles. In a June, 1990, *Rolling Stone* interview, he told Jeff Giles how, at the age of nine, he tried to recreate the Beatles' revolutionary album *Sgt. Peppers Lonely Hearts Club Band* sound for sound, explaining, "I used to wander around trying to make all those sounds with my mouth. I found that if I waved the album cover in front of my face, it made my voice sound like it was double tracked. And I've got a gap between my teeth, so I could get a really great distorted guitar sound." This revelation also hinted at Wallinger's early interest in and ear for the subtleties of studio recording, which he described to Tony Scherman in *Musician:* "I've always been in love with the studio. . . . The sound, the mystique of the sound, was always totally enthralling. Way before I was 10, I took over the family tape recorder. I'm still accused of breaking it. . . . Then we had a little cassette radio which I even recorded on, I bought a mike and put it in the side, sounded terrible but what the hell, it was the only thing I had." He ultimately progressed from there to the 32-track studio in which he records World Party albums.

Despite Classical Training, Needed to Rock

Wallinger also enjoyed a more formal musical education, starting with piano lessons at the age of nine. A year later, he began on the oboe, playing so well that he eventually sat in with a few orchestras. He also had professional vocal training for a time and often sang with choirs. His musical skill in general and aptitude for the oboe in particular won him a musical scholarship to Charterhouse, an upper-class school with a 300-year history that Scherman referred to as "hallowed." After this education it was expected that Wallinger would attend college and become a classical musician; he resisted, however, later telling Scherman, "I didn't want to teach oboe, I didn't want to join an orchestra and I

For the Record. . .

Born October 19, 1957, in Prestatyn, Wales; son of an architect.

Began piano study, c. 1966, oboe study, c. 1967, and formal vocal training; worked as royalties clerk, then songwriter, for music publisher ATV/Northern Songs, London, c. 1976; joined series of underground rock bands; joined band the Waterboys as keyboardist, 1983; began recording material for first World Party album, 1985; signed with Ensign Records, and released *Private Revolution,* 1986; purchased London studio Seaview Cottage, 1988; collaborated with other musicians, including Dave Catlin-Birch, Chris Sharrock, and producer Steve Lillywhite, and released *Bang!,* 1993; wrote score and provided additional music to film *Reality Bites,* Universal, 1994.

Addresses: *Record company*—EMI Records Group, 8730 Sunset Blvd., Los Angeles, CA 90069.

didn't want to form my own wind quintet. I wanted to rock!"

Wallinger gave rock his first serious try when he was still a teenager, playing local gigs in a band called Pax with Nigel Twist and Dave Sharp, who would later form The Alarm. After school, at age 19, he relocated to London and worked briefly as a royalties clerk at ATV/Northern Songs, a company that published music; the firm promoted him to songwriter within three months, but Wallinger's skills were not yet mature enough to win him success. During occasional stints on unemployment, he took a job as musical director for a West End production of *The Rocky Horror Picture Show.*

Needing to be in the eye of the storm, however, Wallinger put aside such occupations in order to immerse himself in London's late-1970s underground rock scene. His first recording experience was fruitless, as he told *Rolling Stone*'s David Wild in 1987, remembering, "I ended up being discovered by some sort of alcoholic old producer. When he took me to the studio the first time, we got in about nine in the morning, and around eleven, he said, 'Right—time to go down to the pub.'" But Wallinger did manage some useful studio experience with a series of bands, including the opportunity to record an independent-label single with a group called Invisible Body Club.

Wallinger had his first taste of musical mastery with the Waterboys, an English band that eventually became known for a Gaelic-folk-rock sound. Wallinger joined the group in April, 1983, after responding to an ad for a guitarist in *Sounds* magazine; he convinced Mike Scott,

the band's creative and business leader, that he needed a keyboardist as well as a guitarist. The Waterboys were an up-and-coming band when Wallinger joined them, and their reputation expanded considerably with him on board. The 1984 album *A Pagan Place* did well with reviewers and buyers but was greatly eclipsed by 1985's *This Is the Sea,* which peaked at Number 37 on the English pop charts. Although Scott had largely defined the band in 1983, by 1985 the Waterboys' sound bore Wallinger's distinctive mark as well; in fact, he had gradually maneuvered Scott into a more collaborative working arrangement.

Left Waterboys for Solo Pursuits

During the Waterboys' rise to fame, Wallinger was also recording songs on 16-track equipment in his London apartment. Ultimately, he found these efforts more compelling than the work he was doing with Scott's band; he told Wild, "It was just sort of frustrating. . . . On the one hand, I was enjoying doing this stuff with Mike. On the other hand, I knew I had some songs that should get out. At first, I thought of my solo work as running alongside the Waterboys'. But that was impractical; it turns out to be a full-time job." With the support of Nigel Grainge, co-founder of the Ensign label, for which the Waterboys recorded, Wallinger was able to take a stab at a solo career. While still with the Waterboys, he had played some of his homegrown cuts for Grainge, impressing him particularly with a song called "Ship of Fools." Grainge told *Musician*'s Scherman, "I could see he was already a fully realized artist. . . . Karl could have gone solo much earlier."

Late in 1985, Wallinger left the Waterboys. He had already secured a contract with Ensign and a home studio in the English countryside that would allow him to record 16 tracks of virtually self-made music. He began recording in December. Those sessions yielded World Party's first album, *Private Revolution.* The disc fared fairly well, holding the Number 56 spot on the British charts for four weeks and winning Wallinger some media attention. "Ship of Fools," the song that had sold Grainge, was particularly popular on American radio as the lead single from the album.

Certain mainstays of Wallinger's solo reputation were established immediately, including heavy critical attention to his dependence on 1960s and 1970s influences. Right off the bat, he was compared to a slew of earlier musicians, sometimes with hints of derision, but usually quite favorably; not surprisingly, the Beatles were acknowledged as his greatest inspiration, but critics also cited the Rolling Stones, the Beach Boys, and Bob Dylan. When Scherman suggested that the Beatles and Stones echoes appear in World Party's sound "as a sort of sales hook," Wallinger responded, "I'm not going to purge my music of all signs of the Beatles, just to allay some critic's suspicions."

Wallinger's one-man band technique for recording *Private Revolution* laid the second foundation of his reputation; in 1987, he defined World Party for *Rolling Stone's* Wild as "me and whoever's playing with me at any given time. But when I'm playing with people—then all of us playing really are World Party." Although he took a six-member World Party on a short English tour in 1987, much of the music on *Private Revolution,* and later on *Goodbye Jumbo,* were the result of Wallinger's musicianship alone. In 1988 he bought a 32-track London studio called Seaview Cottage that allowed him to play guitar, piano, keyboards, and drums himself as he recorded tracks for *Goodbye Jumbo,* which was released in 1990.

Engaged in Some Collaboration

Beginning that year, though, Wallinger allowed other professionals into his studio. He hired Mike Winder to back him up technically and tackle housekeeping duties at Seaview Cottage. When Wallinger went on a promotional tour for *Goodbye Jumbo,* World Party included Dave Catlin-Birch on bass and guitar and Chris Sharrock on drums; Wallinger would later invite these two to record tracks for his next album, *Bang!* In probably his most fully collaborative move, he would ask noted producer Steve Lillywhite to go over the production of *Bang!* with him; Lillywhite would share production credit with Wallinger for five cuts on the album.

In the meantime, *Goodbye Jumbo* had expanded the reputation that *Private Revolution* had created. The album hit Number 36 in the U.K. and stayed on the charts twice as long as *Private Revolution* had. Listeners seemed especially taken by "Way Down Now" and "Put the Message in the Box," which several critics also deemed the album's greatest strengths. Don McLeese gave *Jumbo* a four-star review in *Rolling Stone,* maintaining, "As it moves from fevered desperation to a romantic, almost dreamy utopianism, *Goodbye Jumbo* displays an ambition as broad as the emotional range of its music." Even where McLeese was critical, compliments emerged. "World Party can't sustain such intensity (what party could?)," the music scribe averred, "but Wallinger's multi-instrumental textures suggest

the freshness of first-take inspiration, and his reedy vocals bristle with immediacy." Scherman called *Goodbye Jumbo* "easily one of 1990's best records."

When *Bang!* was released three years later, a number of reviewers noted the evolution that had occurred in World Party, *Rolling Stone's* David Sprague noticing "a new-found urgency." *Musician's* Scherman, comparing *Bang!* to the previous album, remarked, "*Goodbye Jumbo's* rainbows and bright new days, its cherubs-blowing-trumpets aura, are gone. The new album . . . is richer, a welter of guitars, keyboards, layered rhythm tracks." Wallinger accounted for the generally less optimistic feel of *Bang!* in graphic terms, stating, "There's a point where you question things so much, it leads to auto-destruct. That's what the album's about: bang!— like an earthquake in your head." Asked to comment on the personal experiences that contributed to the new World Party mood, Wallinger stated simply, "They're not things I'd like to talk about." This was typical as he has, over the years, carefully kept his personal life out of the media glare.

The popularity of *Bang!* marked a new phase in Wallinger's career; Scherman reported in the spring of 1993, "His days are speeding up now, filling with video shoots and meetings." Wallinger even ventured that he was beginning to enjoy working with a band and was looking forward to the live performances. His label sent him to the United States in March, where he spent a month giving promotional interviews and making personal appearances. By May, "Is It Like Today?" the lilting first single from *Bang!,* had reached the Number Five spot on *Billboard's* Modern Rock Tracks chart, where it hovered for about a month. At the time, Wallinger, who would soon tour stateside with World Party in support of 10,000 Maniacs, couldn't predict what he would do next, though he did speculate that audiences might see video work come out of his studio at some point in the future.

Selected discography

With the Waterboys

A Pagan Place, Ensign, 1984.
This Is the Sea, Ensign, 1985.

Solo albums

Private Revolution (includes "Ship of Fools"), Ensign/Chrysalis, 1986.
Goodbye Jumbo (includes "Way Down Now" and "Put the Message in the Bottle"), Ensign/Chrysalis, 1990.

Thank You World (EP), Ensign/Chrysalis, 1991.
Bang! (includes "Is It Like Today?"), Ensign/Chrysalis, 1993.

Sources

Billboard, May 8, 1993.
Musician, May 1993.
People, August 6, 1990.
Pulse!, July 1993.
Rolling Stone, January 29, 1987; May 31, 1990; June 28, 1990;
    July 8, 1993.

—*Ondine E. Le Blanc*

Ethel Waters

Singer, actress

Singer and actress Ethel Waters had an extremely difficult childhood. In fact, she opened her autobiography *His Eye Is on the Sparrow* with these words: "I was never a child. I never was coddled, or liked, or understood by my family. I never felt I belonged. I was always an outsider. . . . Nobody brought me up." She was conceived in violence and raised in violence. She had a minimal education at best, dropping out of school early to go to work as a maid. But despite her inauspicious beginnings, Ethel Waters made history, garnering many laurels and many "firsts." She was the first black woman to appear on radio (on April 21, 1922); the first black woman to star on her own at the Palace Theater in New York (in 1925); the first black woman to star in a commercial network radio show (in 1933); the first singer to introduce 50 songs that became hits (in 1933); the first black singer to appear on television (in 1939); and the first black woman to star on Broadway in a dramatic play (also in 1939). She is remembered as much for her fine acting as for her expressive singing—and even more for her spirit.

When Waters's mother, Louise Anderson, a quiet, religious girl, was in her early teens, a local boy named John Waters raped her at knifepoint. Shortly after Waters was born, Anderson married Norman Howard, a railroad worker. Waters went by the name Howard for a few years and used several other names, depending on whom she was living with, but finally settled on her father's name.

Rejected by Mother, Abused by Aunts

Because of the manner in which Waters was conceived, her mother found it hard to accept the child, so the little girl was sent went to live with her grandmother, Sally Anderson, the woman whom Waters would really think of as her mother, and her two aunts, Vi and Ching. Sally Anderson, a domestic worker, moved frequently to find employment and was rarely at home; Waters's aunts usually ignored her, but what attention they paid her was most often physically abusive. Waters was exceptionally bright and enjoyed near-perfect recall; when she was able to attend school, she enjoyed learning. Mostly, though, she grew up on the street.

Waters started cleaning houses professionally when she was about eight. As a teenager, she dropped out of school to work as a substitute maid, dishwasher, and waitress in local hotels and apartment houses. One night in 1917, she sang at a party at a local bar, Jack's Rathskeller. Two vaudeville producers heard her and convinced her to sign on with them. With little regret, she left her job and began her career.

For the Record. . .

Born October 31, 1895, in Chester, PA; died of cancer September 1, 1977, in Chatsworth, CA; daughter of John Weley Waters and Louise Tar Anderson; married Merritt "Buddy" Pernsley c. 1910; married Clyde Edward Matthews c. 1928.

Began work as a maid, c. 1903; worked as substitute maid, dishwasher, and waitress in local hotels and apartment houses; c. 1908-1914; sang and toured vaudeville circuit, 1917-mid-1930s; began recording for Cardinal and Black Swan labels, 1921. Appeared in stage musicals, including *Hello 1919!*, 1919; *Jump Steady*, 1922; *Plantation Revue*, 1925; *Black Bottom*, 1926; *Miss Calico*, 1926-27; *Paris Bound*, 1927; *Ethel Waters Broadway Revue*, 1928; *Rhapsody in Black*, 1930, 1933; *From Broadway Back to Harlem*, 1932; *Stormy Weather*, 1933; *As Thousands Cheer*, 1934; and *Cabin in the Sky*, 1940. Appeared in dramas, including *Mamba's Daughter*, 1939; *Member of the Wedding*, 1950; and *The Voice of Strangers*, 1956. Appeared in films, including *On With the Show*, 1929; *Rufus Jones for President*, 1933; *Cairo*, 1942; *Tales of Manhattan*, 1942; *Stage Door Canteen*, 1943; *Cabin in the Sky*, 1943; *Pinky*, 1949; *Member of the Wedding*, 1953; *The Heart Is a Rebel*, 1956; *The Sound and the Fury*, 1959; and *Harriet Tubman and the Underground Railroad*, 1963. Appeared on television programs, including series *Beulah*, ABC-TV, 1950-51. Author of *His Eye Is on the Sparrow*, Greenwood Press, 1951, and *To Me It's Wonderful*, Harper & Row, 1972.

Awards: Negro Actors Guild Award, 1949, for film *Pinky*; Academy Award nominations, 1949, for *Pinky*, and 1953, for *Member of the Wedding*; New York Drama Critics Award for best actress, 1950, for *Member of the Wedding*; Tamiment Institute Award, 1951, for *His Eye Is on the Sparrow*; St. Genesius Medal from American National Theater and Academy, 1951; U.S. Postal Service commemorative stamp, 1994.

Waters had a sweet voice, but even more attractive was her ability to imbue a song with emotion—when she sang the blues, the audience felt her pain; when she sang humorous songs, they forgot their cares for the moment. She was unusual on the vaudeville circuit because she did not sing the traditional blues in the time-honored style, popularized by the great Bessie Smith; she sang instead in a light, clear voice, not in the customary deep, rough, southern blues way. Waters quickly became a sensation. Within two years, she was appearing on Broadway and touring in musical revues.

In 1921, she began a fruitful recording career, eventually waxing over 250 songs.

The 1920s and '30s kept Waters working hard. She arrived in New York City in 1919 and performed in Harlem nightclubs like her favorite, Edmond Johnson's Cellar. She appeared in musical shows, including *Hello 1919!*, which was her first, and frequently toured with both musicals and vaudeville acts. Until the mid-1920s, she performed exclusively in black shows and clubs for black audiences and had little desire to move to the more lucrative white-audience theater circuit.

Pushed Into "White Time"

But in 1925 her friend and colleague Earl Dancer convinced her to audition for a white Chicago theater, where she ultimately became a great success at a higher salary than she had ever earned. "Dozens of people in show business say they discovered me. This always irritates me," she wrote in *His Eye Is on the Sparrow*. "[Club owner] Edmond's piano player, Lou Henly, was the first one to get me to sing different types of songs. Earl Dancer pushed me into the white time." Whatever her route, Waters had arrived; she was the first black singer to break into the "white time."

Life was better, but far from easy. When Waters performed in the South, she faced deeply entrenched racist attitudes. Once, after she had been seriously hurt in a car accident, she lay neglected in the hospital and almost lost her leg. Another time, she was forced to flee a town minutes before she would have been lynched. Even in some northern locales, blacks did not fare much better. In her autobiography, Waters casually described her working conditions at Chicago's Monogram Theater. "That was the theater," she wrote, "where you had to dress way downstairs with the stoker [heater] and come up to the stage climbing slave-ship stairs. While working there I took sick from the migraine headaches I'd had off and on for years. The air was very bad down there where the stoker was." And yet Waters never grew bitter over the hardships she suffered. Indeed, her autobiography maintains a distinctively matter-of-fact tone; it is both funny and sad, a touching testimony to human survival and dignity.

During the 1930s, film became an important part of Waters's career; in her first motion picture, 1929's *On With the Show*, she sang "Am I Blue," a tune that would later become a hit for her. She also made a few short feature films for Vitaphone studios in New York, including *Rufus Jones for President* (1933) and *Bubbling Over* (1934), all the while continuing to perform in stage and club shows throughout the country and to make records.

Stunned World With Acting Prowess

In 1939 Waters stunned the world when she debuted as a dramatic actress playing Hagar in DuBose Heyward's *Mamba's Daughter*. She longed to play the role after having read the book—before the play had even been written. "Hagar had held me spellbound," she wrote in *His Eye Is on the Sparrow*. "In Hagar was all my mother's shock, bewilderment, and insane rage at being hurt. . . . But Hagar, fighting on in a world that had wounded her so deeply, was more than my mother to me. She was all Negro women lost and lonely in the White man's antagonistic world." Ethel held audiences spellbound with her portrayal of Hagar; at the end of her first performance, she received 17 curtain calls. As had been so with her singing, she was able to touch those in the house with the very essence of her character.

While she was one of the highest-paid performers in New York in the 1930s, inexplicably in the 1940s, Waters had trouble finding work. In 1942 she moved to Los Angeles to appear in the film *Cairo* and stayed on to film *Cabin in the Sky* in 1943. After that, the roles dried up; substantial dramatic parts for black women in films and on stage were almost nonexistent. And when she returned to New York, she found that the nightclub scene was changing and even had trouble finding work as a singer. She hit professional bottom in 1948, working only a few weeks that year.

Then, in 1949, Waters's luck changed. She played Granny in the film *Pinky* and received an Academy Award nomination for her work. A year later, she opened to great critical acclaim in the play *Member of the Wedding*. In 1953, she received another Academy Award nomination, for her work in the film version of *Member*. Although she continued to sing, her acting career received considerably more notice.

Despite her success, by the end of the 1950s, Waters began to question the meaningfulness of her career. She had always been a religious woman, but after seeing the Billy Graham Crusade at Madison Square Garden in New York, she rededicated herself and her talents to the glory of God. She joined the Graham Crusade and toured extensively with it. She continued some secular work all of her life, appearing in *The Sound and the Fury* and *The Heart Is a Rebel* in the late '50s and doing occasional guest spots at clubs and on television, but her main focus was the Crusade. She sang with Graham until cancer overtook her in 1977.

Ethel Waters was a great singer because she was a brilliant actress; she sold everything she sang to the audience, making them feel each emotion as if it were their own. After establishing her singing career, she brought her formidable abilities to the legitimate theater to the highest critical acclaim. In her best work, she played characters like herself, who fought hard against a cruel world. In the last decades of her life, she used the same talents to express her religious devotion. No matter where she performed, no matter what or whether she sang, she touched people with the pain, humor, and above all, the dignity of her spirit.

Selected discography

Ethel Waters on Stage and Screen (1925-40), CBS, 1989.
Cabin in the Sky, Milan Records, 1992.
Ethel Waters 1925-1926, Classic Records, 1992.
Ethel Waters 1926-1929, Classic Records, 1993.
Who Said Blackbirds Are Blue?, Sandy Hook.

Sources

Books

DeKorte, Juliann, *Ethel Waters: Finally Home*, Fleming H. Revell Company, 1978.
Knaack, Twila, *Ethel Waters: I Touched a Sparrow*, Word Books, 1978.
Morehead, Philip D., and Anne MacNeil, *The New American Dictionary of Music*, Dutton, 1991.
Notable Black American Women, Gale, 1992.
The Penguin Encyclopedia of Popular Music, edited by Donald Clarke, Viking/Penguin Inc., 1989.
Slonimsky, Nicolas, *Baker's Biographical Dictionary of Musicians*, Schirmer, 1992.
Southern, Eileen, *Biographical Dictionary of Afro-American and African Musicians*, Greenwood Press, 1982.
Waters, Ethel, *His Eye Is on the Sparrow*, Greenwood Press, 1951, reprinted, 1978.
Waters, Ethel, *To Me It's Wonderful*, Harper & Row, 1972.

Periodicals

American Studies, Fall 1990.
Billboard, April 16, 1988.
Jazz Journal International, December 1988.
Reader's Digest, December 1972.
Variety, January 27, 1988; April 13, 1988.

—Robin Armstrong

Joe Williams

Singer

His name is not as well known to the general public as those of jazz legends Louis Armstrong, Duke Ellington, or Ella Fitzgerald, but Joe Williams is nevertheless counted among the masters of jazz and blues singing; he has, in fact, earned the title "Emperor of the Blues." His singing style, which he developed over a long and consistently successful career, contributed to the success of the great Count Basie Orchestra and influenced the style of many younger singers. Williams has also dabbled in acting, playing the role of Claire Huxtable's father, Grandpa Al, on *The Cosby Show*.

Williams was born Joseph Goreed in the small farming town of Cordele, deep in the heart of Georgia, on December 12, 1918. His father, Willie Goreed, left the family early on, but Williams's mother, Anne Beatrice Gilbert, who was no older than 18 when she had her only child, provided a strong emotional bond until her death in 1968.

Soon after Williams was born, his mother moved them in with his grandparents, who had enough money to support an extended family. During this time, Anne Gilbert was saving for a move to Chicago. Once she had made the move—alone—she began saving the money that she earned cooking for wealthy white Chicagoans so that her family could join her. By the time Williams was four, he, his grandmother, and his aunt had joined his mother in Chicago, where they would live for many years.

Probably most important to Williams's later life was the music scene—fueled largely by African-American musicians—that thrived in Chicago in the early 1920s. Years later, he recalled going to the Vendome Theatre with his mother to hear Louis Armstrong play his trumpet. Chicago also offered a host of radio stations that featured the then-rebellious sounds of jazz, exposing Williams to the stylings of Ellington, Ethel Waters, Cab Calloway, Joe Turner, and many others. By his early teens, the budding vocalist had already taught himself to play piano and had formed a quartet, known as the Jubilee Boys, that sang at church functions.

Cleaned by Day, Sung by Night

During his mid-teens Williams began performing as a vocalist, singing solo at formal events with local bands. The most that he ever took home was five dollars a night, but that was enough to convince his family that he could make a living with his rich baritone; so, at 16, he dropped out of school. After a family conference, the name "Williams" was chosen as a stage name, and Joe began marketing himself in earnest to Chicago clubs and bands. His first job was a kind of compromise—not

For the Record. . .

B orn Joseph Goreed, December 12, 1918, in Cordele, GA; changed surname to Williams, c. 1934; son of Willie Goreed (a farm laborer) and Anne Beatrice Gilbert (a cook); married Wilma Cole, 1942 (divorced, 1946); married Anne Kirksey, 1946 (divorced, c. 1950); married Lemma Reid, 1951 (divorced, 1964); married Jillean Milne Hughes-D'Aeth, 1965; children: (third marriage) Joe, Jr., JoAnn.

Formed, and performed at church functions with, vocal quartet the Jubilee Boys, early 1930s; performed with various bands, Chicago, 1930s; performed with bands of Jimmie Noone, 1938-39, Les Hite, 1939-40, Coleman Hawkins, 1941, Lionel Hampton, 1942-43, Andy Kirk, 1946-47, and Red Saunders, 1951-53; worked briefly as Fuller Cosmetics door-to-door salesman, 1940s; performed and toured with Count Basie Orchestra, 1954-1961; began solo career, 1961; contributed to film soundtracks, including *Jamboree*, 1957, *Cinderfella*, 1960, *The Moonshine War*, 1969, *Sharkey's Machine*, 1981, *City Heat*, and *All of Me*, both 1984. Actor.

Selected awards: New Star Award, 1955; international critics' poll citations for best male vocalist, 1955, 1974-78, 1980, 1981, 1983, 1984, and 1989-91; and readers' poll citation for best male vocalist, 1955, 1956, 1990, and 1991, all from *Down Beat. Rhythm and Blues* plaque for top song for "Every Day (I Have the Blues)," 1956; *Billboard* disc jockeys' poll citation for best male vocalist, 1959; National Academy of Recording Arts and Sciences Governor's Award, 1983; Grammy awards, 1985, for *I Just Want to Sing*, and 1992, for *Ballad and Blues Master; Ebony* Lifetime Achievement Award, 1993.

Addresses: *Agent*—Abby Hoffer Enterprises, 223 East 48th St., New York, NY 10017-1538.

unusual for a young singer—at a club called Kitty Davis's. Hired to clean the bathrooms, Williams was allowed to sing with the band in the evening and keep the tips, which would sometimes amount to $20.

Williams's first real break came in 1938 when clarinet and saxophone master Jimmie Noone invited him to sing with his band. Less than a year later, the young singer was earning a reputation at Chicago dance halls and on a national radio station that broadcast his voice from Massachusetts to California. He toured the Midwest in 1939 and 1940 with the Les Hite band, which accompanied the likes of Armstrong and Fats Waller. A year later, he went on a more extensive tour with the band of saxophonist Coleman Hawkins.

It wasn't long before Williams found himself in the upper reaches of the musical stratosphere; in 1942 jazz great Lionel Hampton hired him to fill in for his regular vocalist, both for the Hampton orchestra's home performances at the Tic Toc Club in Boston and for their cross-country tours. Williams's work with Hampton ended when the band's former singer returned, but by that time Williams was in great demand, his fame particularly burgeoning back in Chicago.

Treated for Depression

Williams's first marriage—to Wilma Cole in 1942—set in motion a pattern of marital difficulties that would plague him until the 1960s. The emotional relationship quickly became painful for both partners, though the union remained legal until 1946. That year, the singer married Anne Kirksey, with whom he also had a brief and unhappy relationship; they separated in 1948 and divorced several years later. It was during his second marriage that Williams experienced a serious bout of depression. Following a breakdown in the spring of 1947, he spent a year in the Elgin State Hospital, where he received now-controversial psychiatric treatments such as electroshock therapy.

His third marriage, to Lemma Reid, survived from 1951 until 1964, and produced Williams's two children, Joe, Jr., and JoAnn. Sadly, this union, too, proved fragile; Reid returned to her mother's home in Cincinnati soon after JoAnn's birth. Then, in 1957, Williams met Englishwoman Jillean Milne Hughes-D'Aeth. Their first meeting, which was very brief, was not followed by an opportunity for a lengthier tryst until two years later, when the Basie band was touring England. Before Williams left Europe, he knew that he was in love. In May of 1960, he and Hughes-D'Aeth moved into a New York apartment together, but it wasn't until January 7, 1965, that they were married, since Reid had not divorced Williams until the fall of 1964. At long last, Williams had forged a relationship that would endure.

In the early 1950s, Chicago disc jockey Daddy-O Daily secured for Williams an chance to sing with the band of one of the most powerful leaders of the era—Count Basie. After his early gigs with Basie, Williams returned to his nascent solo career, but by 1954 Basie wanted him on contract. Williams would remain with the "Basie machine" until 1961, garnering some of the best exposure a blues and jazz singer could have. National tours were interspersed with long spells in a number of America's musical capitals, wherein the band would play at one club for three or four weeks at a time. After 1955, the Basie group stopped every year at the Newport Jazz Festival, one of the biggest events on the jazz calendar. The years 1956, 1957, and 1959 also found the ensemble touring Europe, where the popularity of jazz had skyrocketed.

Cemented Stature With Basie Orchestra

Williams developed his essential repertoire while he was with Basie, including standards such as "Every Day (I Have the Blues)," "Five O'Clock in the Morning," "Roll 'em Pete," "Teach Me Tonight," "My Baby Upsets Me," and "The Comeback." These recordings and many others cemented his popularity, selling in droves and earning heavy airplay on major radio stations across the country. Williams became an important name in the pages of the vaunted jazz journal *Down Beat* as early as 1955, when he won their New Star Award. Also that year, he was cited by the magazine's international critics' poll as best new male singer, as well as by its readers' poll in that category—honors he would continue to accumulate throughout his career. In 1958, his pop standing was second only to Frank Sinatra, and he maintained second place on the rhythm and blues charts as well, right behind pianist-singer Ray Charles.

Despite his tremendous success with Count Basie and company, Williams eventually began to feel that the position was limiting his potential as an artist. By 1960 he was planning the beginning of a solo career that would allow him to pursue a broader range of material in blues, jazz, and pop. Initially, Basie's manager, Willard Alexander, set Williams up with a group of strong musicians and a tour schedule that would take him across the United States for six months. The bookings soon multiplied; Williams was on the road for almost all of 1961. By the late 1960s, he was performing in various locations between 30 and 40 weeks each year. He went on to collaborate with such jazz luminaries as "Cannonball" Adderly, Benny Carter, George Shearing, and Thad Jones, recording over 45 albums.

Williams continued to produce albums and received overwhelmingly positive reviews for both his recordings and his performances. Even after his 70th birthday, in 1988, Williams maintained a hectic schedule of touring and recording. He has been particularly sought after to sing at tributes to his peers, including Sarah Vaughan, Ella Fitzgerald, and Louis Armstrong. As ever, his performances sparked laudatory reviews in magazines and newspapers; the *New Yorker* described a 1986 performance thus: "Williams has an enormous bass-baritone. It is lilting and flexible. It moves swiftly and lightly from a low C to a pure falsetto. It moves through glottal stops and yodels and delicate growls, through arching blue notes and vibratos that barely stir the air."

Williams was, of course, regularly called back to sing at Count Basie "reunions," even after the Count's death, in 1984; just a year earlier, the singer had had his star placed beside Basie's in the "gallery of stars" on Hollywood Boulevard. In 1991 Williams attended his own gala tribute, entitled "For the Love of Joe," which celebrated the contribution that he had made and was still making to music. The next year, he won his second Grammy Award, for the release *Ballad and Blues Master—I Just Want to Sing* having won a Grammy in 1985. As the 1990s rolled along, Williams, his mantle growing ever-cluttered with laurels, persisted in releasing acclaimed records, wowing audiences, tackling the occasional acting role, and conducting workshops for up-and-coming singers—after 50 years, his repertoire and popularity still growing.

Selected discography

Count Basie Swings, Joe Williams Sings (includes "Every Day [I Have the Blues]," "The Comeback," "Teach Me Tonight," and "Roll 'em Pete"), Clef, 1955.
A Man Ain't Supposed to Cry, Roulette, 1957.
Memories Ad-lib, Roulette, 1958.
Joe Williams Sings About You, Roulette, 1959.
A Swingin' Night at Birdland: Joe Williams Live, Roulette, 1962.
Joe Williams at Newport '63, Victor, 1963.
The Heart and the Soul of Joe Williams, Sheba, 1971.
Joe Williams With Love, Temponic, 1972.
Joe Williams Live, Fantasy, 1973.
Big Man, the Legend of John Henry, Fantasy, 1975.
Prez and Joe, GNP/Crescendo, 1979.
Then and Now, Bosco, 1984.
I Just Want to Sing, 1984.
Every Night: Live at Vine St., Verve/PolyGram, 1987.
The Overwhelming Joe Williams, RCA, 1988.
Ballad and Blues Master, Verve/PolyGram, 1992.
Joe Williams: A Song Is Born, VIEW, 1992.
Jump for Joy, Bluebird/RCA, 1993.
Chains of Love, Natasha Imports/Landmark, 1993.
Every Day: The Best of the Verve Years, Verve, 1993.

Sources

Books

Grouse, Leslie, *Everyday: The Story of Joe Williams,* Quartet, 1984.

Periodicals

Entertainment Weekly, November 20, 1992.

Jet, September 9, 1985.

Los Angeles Times, June 14, 1991.

Metro Times (Detroit), September 1, 1993.

New Yorker, October 27, 1986.

New York Times, June 22, 1989; June 27, 1991.

Washington Post, October 16, 1991.

—Ondine E. Le Blanc

Bernie Worrell

Composer, keyboardist, vocalist

"I work by sound and feel," Bernie Worrell told *Keyboard* magazine. "And you must feel it first, baby." As "musical director" of the P-Funk family—an outrageous assemblage of projects that dominated dance music in the 1970s and continues to exercise a huge influence two decades later—Worrell can fairly be designated one of the architects of modern funk. But his work as a solo artist and sideman and his considerable classical training demonstrate that even this designation tends to foreshorten his accomplishments.

"I work by sound and feel," Bernie Worrell told *Keyboard* magazine. "And you must feel it first, baby." As "musical director" of the P-Funk family—an outrageous assemblage of projects that dominated dance music in the 1970s and continues to exercise a huge influence two decades later—Worrell can fairly be designated one of the architects of modern funk. But his work as a solo artist and sideman and his considerable classical training demonstrate that even this designation tends to foreshorten his accomplishments.

Moving from the P-Funk circle to avant-pop gurus Talking Heads and contributing session work to the Rolling Stones, Pretenders, and many others, Worrell has proved himself one of contemporary music's most versatile keyboardists. On his solo albums, he has attempted to reconcile many of his disparate passions, exploring modern classical music, jazz, funk, and hip-hop. Talking Heads leader David Byrne once dubbed Worrell "a genius"; *College Music Journal (CMJ)* referred to him as "perhaps the fullest manifestation of the universe-roving, ever-questing P-Funk work ethic." And *Keyboard* critic Bob Doerschuk summed up Worrell's gifts as a "combination of classically trained chops, street-bred soul, and carefully honed showmanship."

Worrell was born in the mid-1940s in Long Branch, New Jersey. His mother sang in church and introduced him to music. "She could pick out notes on the piano, too," he told Doerschuk, "so I used to go to the keyboard every day and practice a scale she'd taught me. She observed me, and pretty soon she started wondering if maybe there was something there." He had his first lesson with a piano teacher at the tender age of three; at four he gave his first concert. The family moved to the town of Plainfield a few years later, and he continued his studies. By the time he was ten, Worrell had performed with the National Symphony Orchestra in Washington D.C. "It was a child prodigy thing," he recalled. His classical repertoire began with "Schubert Impromptus, a little Bach, Beethoven Sonatas, and a lot of Mozart" and was tempered with a homegrown appreciation of church music. As for rock and roll or rhythm and blues, however, he was in the dark.

"Went Wild," Joined Clinton Mob

Seeing rock idol Elvis Presley on the *Ed Sullivan Show* changed all that: Worrell was suddenly smitten with popular music. It was during this time that he met an ambitious young hairstylist named George Clinton, who sang with a vocal group called the Parliaments and enlisted the 11-year-old Worrell to help him with the technical end of his music. Even so, Worrell continued

For the Record. . .

Born c. 1945 in Long Branch, NJ. *Education:* Attended Juilliard School and New England Conservatory of Music.

Toured with singer Maxine Brown and performed with numerous artists in Boston area, including Tammi Terrell, Freddie Scott, Valerie Holiday, and Chubby and the Turnpikes (later known as Tavares); joined Funkadelic, 1968; performed and recorded with Funkadelic, Parliament, Bootsy's Rubber Band, the George Clinton Band, the Brides of Funkenstein, and other "P-Funk" projects until 1980; released solo debut, *All the Woo in the World,* Arista, 1978; recorded and toured with Talking Heads, 1983-84; recorded and/or performed with numerous artists, including the Pretenders, Keith Richards, Jerry Harrison, the Last Poets, Nona Hendryx, Material, Praxis, Billy Bass, and George Clinton, 1981-93; played with CBS Late Show Orchestra, 1993.

Addresses: *Record company*—Gramavision, 33 Katonah Ave., Katonah, NY 10536. *Publicity*—Patrick Communications, 100-13 Carver Loop, Bronx, NY 10475.

to study classical piano; he was at the famed Juilliard School at age 14. He went on to attend the New England Conservatory of Music. During this period away from familial supervision, he told *Keyboard,* "I went wild. Everything I'd kept inside just busted out." His father's death one semester before he was set to graduate meant the end of his tuition money. But, as *Musician's* Scott Isler remarked, "The conservatory's loss was the nightclubs' gain." Worrell had been backing up R&B acts in the Boston area while attending school, which seemed like easy money since, as he told Isler, "I was able to pick up anything I could hear." Thus, a spot was waiting for him in vocalist Maxine Brown's band after he left the Conservatory.

While on tour with Brown in Bermuda, Worrell got a long-distance call from Clinton. He and his group were at New York's Apollo Theater, the R&B performer's mecca. "The message was: 'Worrell, come on up. We're ready,'" Worrell recalled to *Keyboard.* He joined Clinton in 1968; the civilized soul harmonies of the Parliaments had metamorphosed into the acid-rock-tinged experimentalism of Funkadelic. As critic Mark Jacobson wrote in *Esquire,* nobody had quite seen anything like it: "Wham, there were these impeccably cool black people running around in bed sheets and diapers and less, and they were playing some kind of *rock 'n' roll.* It was more outside than Sly [Stone], raunchier than [Jimi] Hendrix, a big-bottomed, acidic

R&B conjured to the coat-pulling smack of *something new.* The Bomb."

Funkadelic began on Detroit's Westbound label and over the years fashioned a rock hybrid that would transform the psychedelic soul of the late 1960s into a ferocious mind-expanding sound that many credit as a precursor of heavy metal. Worrell's eclecticism pushed the envelope ever further, incorporating classical and jazz lines as well as way-out noises. "His keyboards," wrote Isler, "could be surprisingly ethereal or funky-butt as needed." In 1974 Clinton and company launched the other half of the equation: Parliament, a theatrical, horn-driven troupe that performed booty-shaking anthems with freakishly conceptual lyrics about "motherships" and 'bop guns." It was this group that popularized the phrase "P-Funk"; the "P" stood for "Pure." For "Flash Light," one of the most played—and, later, sampled—dance tracks ever, Worrell concocted a bass line on his minimoog synthesizer, providing what Isler called "an influential funk crossover landmark."

Insurance Man for the Funk

Funkadelic signed to Warner Bros. and in the late 1970s scored some dance-floor hits, notably "One Nation Under a Groove" and "(Not Just) Knee Deep." Parliament continued to sell millions through the decade with its immaculately off-kilter hits and elaborate, science-fiction-themed stage show. Worrell also assisted Clinton and bassist Bootsy Collins in Bootsy's Rubber Band, not to mention such P-Funk offshoots as the Brides of Funkenstein and Parlet. Worrell released his own solo debut in 1978; a single demonstrated that Clinton had reserved a modest but telling moniker for his musical director: "Insurance Man for the Funk." But Worrell left the organization in 1980—partly due to disputes with Clinton that resulted in litigation. Even so, he would later perform with Clinton's group in the wake of the singer/leader's solo hit "Atomic Dog."

In 1981 Worrell was approached by Jerry Harrison of Talking Heads; the seminal alternative rock band had retooled its minimalist avant-pop image and begun to pursue a multi-ethnic, funk-based sound. Worrell joined the group in the studio after first working on Harrison's debut solo album. His contributions to the Heads' 1983 album *Speaking in Tongues* led to his inclusion in the tour that followed, which in turn resulted in both an album and a film called *Stop Making Sense.* "In live performances he can really change the texture of a song, or add another level," Byrne told *Musician.* "We're playing, say, really straight and he'll play along. But then he'll throw in all these little things—chord inversions or whatever—that kind of throw the whole thing into a different perspective for a couple of seconds. Then he whips right back into a straight reading, or does a completely unexpected thing at the end of a song."

Worrell brought his considerable resources to a number of different projects during the 1980s, playing with artists as diverse as the rock band the Pretenders, the spoken-word group the Last Poets, African pop innovator Fela Kuti, and the eclectic shifting-roster band the Golden Palominos, as well as a plethora of activities with bassist-producer Bill Laswell, including Material. He also appeared on the first solo album by Rolling Stones guitarist Keith Richards. In 1990 Worrell released *Funk of Ages* on the Gramavision label; many of his former collaborators, including Bootsy Collins, Richards, Byrne, singer Phoebe Snow, jazz keyboardist Herbie Hancock, and guitarist Vernon Reid lent a hand.

As the 1990s unfolded, it became clear that the legacy of P-Funk was far greater than could have been imagined. The sampling of Parliament-Funkadelic records, many of which were dominated by Worrell's keyboard lines, became an industry unto itself as funk-based rap ruled the charts. Clinton himself returned to the spotlight and by 1993 had released a high-profile new solo album, on which Worrell appeared. Meanwhile, Worrell and bassist Collins joined forces in the avant-garde band Praxis. Worrell also worked briefly with the CBS Late Show Orchestra after talk show host David Letterman changed networks and his musical director, Paul Shaffer, expanded his former World's Most Dangerous Band.

Blacktronic Science a Quantum Leap

Worrell also continued session work, but in 1993 he too had a new solo album out, *Blacktronic Science*, which *USA Today* called an "ambitious, wildly eclectic project." Among the disc's highlights: Worrell accompanying a string section on harpsichord for some original modern chamber music; a greasy jazz trio collaboration with funk sax king Maceo Parker and former Miles Davis drummer Tony Williams; and some state-of-the-art hip-hop with Clinton, Collins, funkateer Gary "Mudbone" Cooper—their first writing with Worrell since his departure from the P-Funk fold—and several rappers. Clearly, *Blacktronic Science* represented a quantum leap in stylistic reach from Worrell's previous solo efforts. "It's like creating a motion picture, only it's musical, because it takes you through different changes, different vibes, different feels," the keyboardist told *Billboard.* "I'm not trying to be trendy or current, but as I see it, making it pure and just doing a 'feel' thing so that it is timeless. I work on emotion."

The album received largely enthusiastic reviews; Tom Moon of *Request* called it "an integrated patchwork of ideas from many styles," noting, "The juxtapositions between simple rap lyrics and florid, far-reaching music become compelling and expansive, embracing Duke Ellington and [rap production wizards] the Bomb Squad in the same breath." *New York Newsday's* Frank Owen praised "Worrell's consistently inventive playing," adding that *Blacktronic Science* "furthers the case, if indeed it still needs to be made, that funk has as much right to be considered a serious musical art form as jazz or the blues." For its part, the *Washington Post* termed the set "one of the best P-Funk albums in several years."

Bernie Worrell had at last come to be recognized as more than merely a great funk player; his compositional versatility, not to mention the range of his chops, was now a matter of public record. He announced his intention to appear on an album paying tribute to Funkadelic guitarist Eddie Hazel, who died in 1993, and possibly to reunite with Clinton and friends for a P-Funk road trip. The "Mothership" tour, Worrell told the *Chicago Tribune,* "is gonna get done, it's just a matter of time." As *Jazz Express* critic Will Montgomery mused, "Who would have thought those guys in space suits would have cast such a long shadow?"

Selected discography

Solo albums

All the Woo in the World (includes "Insurance Man for the Funk"), Arista, 1978.
Funk of Ages, Gramavision, 1990.
Blacktronic Science, Gramavision, 1993.
The Other Side, CMP, 1994.

With Funkadelic

On Westbound

Funkadelic, 1970.
Free Your Mind and Your Ass Will Follow, 1970.
Maggot Brain, 1971.
America Eats Its Young, 1972.
Cosmic Slop, 1973.
Standing on the Verge of Getting It On, 1974.
Let's Take It to the Stage, 1975.
Tales of Kidd Funkadelic, 1976.
Greatest Hits, 1977.
Best of the Early Years, Volume I, 1979.
Music for Your Mother, 1993.

On Warner Bros.

Hardcore Jollies, 1976.

One Nation Under a Groove, 1978.
Uncle Jam Wants You (includes "[Not Just] Knee Deep"), 1979.
The Electric Spanking of War Babies, 1981.

With Parliament; on Casablanca, except where noted

Osmium, Invictus, 1970.
Up for the Down Stroke, 1974.
Chocolate City, 1975.
The Clones of Dr. Funkenstein, 1976.
Funkentelechy vs. the Placebo Syndrome (includes "Flash Light" and "Bop Gun [Endangered Species]"), 1977.
Motor Booty Affair, 1978.
Gloryhallastoopid (Pin the Tail on the Funky), 1979.
Trombipulation, 1981.
The Bomb: Parliament's Greatest Hits, Casablanca/PolyGram, 1984.
Rhenium, Demon/HDH, 1989.
Tear the Roof Off: 1974-1980, Casablanca/Mercury, 1993.
First Thangs, HDH, 1993.

With the P-Funk All-Stars

Urban Dancefloor Guerillas, Uncle Jam/CBS, 1983.
Live at the Beverly Theater in Hollywood, 1983, Westbound/Ace, 1990.

With George Clinton; on Capitol, except where noted

Computer Games (includes "Atomic Dog"), 1982.
You Shouldn't-Nuf Bit Fish, 1983.
Some of My Best Jokes Are Friends, 1985.
Hey Man, Smell My Finger, Paisley Park, 1993.

With Bootsy's Rubber Band; on Warner Bros.

Stretchin' Out, 1976.
Ahh . . . The Name Is Bootsy, Baby!, 1977.
Bootsy? Player of the Year, 1978.

With the Brides of Funkenstein; on Atlantic

Funk or Walk, 1978.
Never Buy Texas From a Cowboy, 1979.

With Parlet; on Casablanca

Pleasure Principle, 1978.
Invasion of the Booty Snatchers, 1979.
Play Me or Trade Me, 1980.

With Talking Heads; on Sire

Speaking in Tongues, 1983.
Stop Making Sense, 1984.

With the Golden Palominos

Visions of Excess, Celluloid, 1985.
A Blast of Silence, Celluloid, 1986.
This Is How It Feels, Restless, 1993.

With Material

The Third Power, Axiom, 1991.
Hallucination Engine, Axiom, 1994.

With Praxis

Transmutation (Mutatis Mutandis), Axiom/Island/PLG, 1992.

Contributor

Jerry Harrison, *The Red and the Black*, Sire, 1981.
Keith Richards, *Talk Is Cheap*, Virgin, 1988.
Syd Straw, *Surprise*, Virgin, 1990.
Billy Bass, *Out of the Dark*, 1993.
Nona Hendryx, *The Heat*, RCA.
Fela Kuti, *Army Arrangement*, Celluloid.
The Last Poets, *Oh My People*, Celluloid.

Sources

Billboard, April 3, 1993; April 17, 1993.
Chicago Tribune, June 25, 1993.
College Music Journal (CMJ), April 23, 1993.
Courier-News (Bridgewater, NJ), August 30, 1993.
Down Beat, September 1990; February 1994.
Esquire, May 1993.
Jazz Express, July 1993.
Keyboard, September 1978; November 1985.
Melody Maker, February 19, 1977.
Musician, January 1985.
New York Newsday, May 23, 1993.
Oakland Tribune, August 18, 1993.
Orlando Sentinel, April 23, 1993.
Pulse!, December 1993.
Request, June 1993.
Source, August 1993.
USA Today, April 20, 1993; May 26, 1993.
Washington Post, May 2, 1993.

Additional information for this profile was obtained from Gramavision promotional materials, 1993.

—*Simon Glickman*

Wynonna

The lead vocalist but very much the silent partner in country music's most successful duo of the 1980s, the Judds, Wynonna Judd found herself on her own, musically and emotionally, when her mother, Naomi, was diagnosed with chronic hepatitis in the fall of 1990. In the process of her transformation into a solo star, Wynonna discovered a new sense of personal independence and at the same time stepped out musically onto country's cutting edge. Indeed, Wynonna's popularity in the first years of her solo career equalled or surpassed the enormous success the Judds had achieved as a duo.

When she shed her last name, billing herself simply as Wynonna, the auburn-haired singer was indulging in something of a family tradition; for both Wynonna and Naomi Judd, remaking themselves has involved renaming themselves. Wynonna was born Christina Claire Ciminella in Ashland, Kentucky, in 1964. When her mother took the biblical name Naomi after her divorce in 1977, thirteen-year-old Christina decided to change her name as well. She got her new moniker from the lyrics to the old swing song "Route 66"—"Flagstaff, Arizona/ Don't forget Wynona." Wynonna's childhood was spent partly in California, but it was in rural Kentucky, cut off from television reception, that she, her sister Ashley, and her mother began to entertain themselves by harmonizing around the kitchen table, trying to duplicate the pure mountain harmonies of Kentucky's classic bluegrass singers. Naomi Judd knew immediately that her daughter was a gifted vocalist.

Shone as Judds Lead Vocalist

The Judds moved to Nashville in 1979, and their rise to country-music stardom has gradually assumed the character of legend. Naomi, by then a registered nurse, found herself treating the daughter of Nashville producer Brent Maher and parlayed the connection into an audition at RCA Records. The Judds won over the assembled RCA staff at first hearing, and the duo went on to rack up a half dozen gold albums and 18 Number One country singles between 1984 and 1990.

Often mistakenly classified as "new traditionalists," the Judds specialized in sentimental songs of love and nostalgia. But there was nothing traditional about Wynonna's singing; it has often been likened to that of blues-rock star Bonnie Raitt, with a low, sometimes growling, intensity equally suited to party songs like "Girls' Night Out" and folkish odes like "John Deere Tractor." Still, despite Wynonna's vocal dominance, it was Naomi who acted as spokesperson, organizer, and general sparkplug for the Judds. Wynonna "seemed to disappear between songs," noted Geoffrey Himes of

For the Record. . .

Born Christina Claire Ciminella, May 30, 1964, in Ashland, KY; changed name, 1977; daughter of Michael and Diana Ciminella (later Naomi Judd, a former nurse and singer).

Lead vocalist of country duo the Judds, 1983-1991; solo artist, 1991—; released *Wynonna*, MCA, 1992.

Selected awards: Four Grammy awards; eight gold albums, two platinum albums.

Addresses: *Record company*—MCA Records, 1514 South St., Nashville, TN 37212. *Management*—Ken Stilts Co., 40 Fiberglass Dr., Mount Juliet, TN 37122.

Country Music magazine. So, when Naomi announced her departure from the group in October of 1990, Wynonna faced the challenge of remaking both her musical and personal selves.

"I went through every possible emotion," Wynonna told Mary Murphy of *TV Guide*. "I felt terrified. I felt frustrated and resentful of the fact that . . . all of a sudden—bam! My mother was gone. I didn't speak to Mama for a month. I had to leave home, you know, pack my bags, just take off. . . . It was the most alone I have ever been in my life, and the most depressed."

Triumph of Solo Debut

Under these conditions, the recording of Wynonna's debut solo album took on something of the character of therapy. "[We'd] sit there for three, four hours just talking about what was going on in her life," recalled revered country producer/executive Tony Brown in an interview with *Request*'s Keith Moerer. The selection of songs was painstaking, and in all *Wynonna* took eight months to record, by some accounts a record for a country album. But after all the work was done, Wynonna Judd emerged as a spectacularly successful solo act. She took a major risk with the first single: "She Is His Only Need" challenged the conventions of country radio with its wandering melody and four-and-a-half-minute length. Her gamble paid off as both single and album shot to the top of *Billboard*'s country charts. The disc even reached the Number Four position on the pop chart. Wynonna, without surname, had become a star in her own right.

"Trying to untangle and [yet] not sever the incredible layers of emotion that Mother and I share," as Wynonna was quoted as saying by Bob Millard in his book *The*

Judds, has had great rewards, bringing the singer a new confidence and even a bit of brashness—once she eyeballed a fan trying to slip out early from one of her concerts and commanded him back to his seat. She enjoys riding Harley-Davidson motorcycles, two of which travel with her on tour in a trailer behind her bus. Perhaps another indication of Wynonna's blossoming independence came when she broke off her engagement to country singer Tony King, telling Moerer, "I had just ended an eight-year relationship with Mom on the road, and I wasn't ready to enter into another partnership."

Wynonna's vocal style remained intact as her solo career matured, but her material, which she has always played an active role in selecting, had changed, her stylistic range expanded. In "I Saw the Light," from *Wynonna,* the title of Hank Williams's country-gospel classic is quoted, but it is expanded into the accusation of a woman who has discovered her lover's unfaithfulness, the song introducing a note of arch cleverness that had not been a part of the more straightforward Judds. Even farther afield, "No One Else on Earth" was one of the first country recordings subjected to the club remix treatment that rapidly gained popularity in 1993. In fact, Wynonna's second album, *Tell Me Why,* released that year, featured an innovative mix of styles well beyond what most other country vocalists would attempt.

Stylistic Development

The album's title track was a middle-of-the-road soft-rock number composed by veteran folk-pop songwriter Karla Bonoff. While on "Rock Bottom," noted *Country Music*'s Himes, Wynonna "invades Travis Tritt territory," southern-rock-style country. "Only Love," the second single from the disc, was a hushed, sophisticated pop love song—complete with a string section and unusual harmonic scheme—the video for which garnered substantial airplay on the CMT cable network. "Father Sun" displayed the splashy, keyboard-heavy rock sound and lyrically indirect religiosity of contemporary Christian music, whereas "I Just Drove By" was straight country and "That Was Yesterday" straight blues. "Girls With Guitars" partook of the combination of rock sound and country lyric wit pioneered by its composer, Mary-Chapin Carpenter. And in yet another stylistic change of course, the third single, a lush, heart-wrenching ballad called "Is It Over Yet," was as welcome to the ears of pop listeners as it was to those of their country counterparts.

Still, producer Brown was well aware of the dangers of moving Wynonna too far away from her country roots. "We have to think about not doing anything that would turn off Judds fans. You have to be smart about it, but at the same time, I didn't feel at any moment that our hands were tied," he explained to Moerer. Wynonna for her part insisted, "I'm always going to be country. I don't ever have any plans not to be country."

The public reacted as favorably to *Tell Me Why* as it had to *Wynonna;* the album sold a million copies within 15 days of its release and climbed rapidly to the Number One position on the country charts. By the end of September, 1993, it had sold over three million copies. On a fall concert jaunt that year with country heartthrob Clint Black—the aptly named "Black and Wy" tour—Wynonna seemed poised to dispel her reputation as a weak concert draw, which she had acquired on her first outings after the nearly interminable Judds farewell tours. Critical reaction to *Tell Me Why* was generally favorable as well, with even the august rock journal *Rolling Stone* approvingly noting that the album was "comfortably packed with more emotions that most mood rings can handle." *Country Music,* however, dissented, opining, "Only three of the 10 songs . . . capture the authoritative singer who stomped her way across our stages last summer."

Truly, *Country Music* held Wynonna to the loftiest standards: in its July/August, 1993, issue, the magazine ascribed to her "the potential to be the greatest female country singer since Patsy Cline." Not yet 30 years old at the time, she was still a developing artist, and there seemed few limits to what she might accomplish. Speculation as to the future aside, Wynonna had already reached an important personal plateau; as she told *TV Guide,* "I can go out in public and people don't say, 'Ooh, there's that girl that tried to make it on her own and didn't.'"

Solo albums

Wynonna (includes "She Is His Only Need" and "I Saw the Light," and "No One Else on Earth"), Curb/MCA, 1992.

Tell Me Why (includes "Only Love," "Rock Bottom," "Father Sun," "I Just Drove By," "That Was Yesterday," "Girls With Guitars," and "Is It Over Yet"), Curb/MCA, 1993.
(Contributor) "Blue Christmas," *The Christmas Album,* Interscope, 1993.

With the Judds

Had a Dream, RCA, 1983.
Why Not Me, RCA, 1984.
Rockin' With the Rhythm, RCA, 1986.
Heartland, RCA, 1987.
Talk About Love, RCA, 1988.
Greatest Hits, RCA, 1988.
River of Time, RCA, 1989.
Love Can Build a Bridge, RCA, 1990.
Greatest Hits, Volume II, RCA, 1991.

Sources

Books

Judd, Naomi, *Love Can Build a Bridge,* Random House, 1993.
Millard, Bob, *The Judds,* St. Martin's Paperbacks/Doubleday, 1992.

Periodicals

Billboard, April 7, 1993.
Country Music, July/August 1993.
Detroit Free Press, May 10, 1993.
Entertainment Weekly, August 1993.
People, May 17, 1993.
Request, September 1993.
Rolling Stone, May 28, 1992; July 8, 1993.
TV Guide, July 3, 1993; September 25, 1993.

—*James M. Manheim*

X

Rock band

One of the most highly regarded groups to emerge from the Los Angeles punk rock scene, X brought a commitment and maturity of vision to a genre best known for its expressions of rage. Fronted by vocalist Exene Cervenka and bassist-vocalist John Doe, both of whom wrote the band's material, X stunned critics and fans alike with their debut album, *Los Angeles,* in 1980. After struggling to carry their music beyond a cult audience for the better part of a decade, the group finally disbanded, pursued solo projects, and then—after the multi-platinum success of such "alternative" rock bands as Nirvana—reunited for a new album and tour in the early 1990s.

John Doe was born in Illinois to a family that moved frequently; they finally settled in Baltimore, where Doe spent his teenage years in local rock bands. Tiring of the city's limited music scene, he moved to Los Angeles in 1976. The following year he was united with guitarist Billy Zoom through an ad in the venerable free-ad newspaper *The Recycler*. Zoom's roots were in rockabilly, and he played tasty, economical leads that

For the Record. . .

Members include **Dave Alvin** (bandmember 1985-87), guitar; **Mick Basher** (bandmember 1977), drums; **D. J. Bonebrake** (born December 8, 1955, in Burbank, CA; married; joined group 1978), drums; **Exene Cervenka** (born Christine Cervenka, February 1, 1956, in Chicago), vocals; **John Doe** (born February 25, 1954, in Decatur, IL; son of librarians), bass, vocals; **Tony Gilkyson** (joined group 1986), guitar; **Billy Zoom** (born February 20, c. 1949, in Illinois; bandmember 1977-85), guitar. Cervenka and Doe were married. Both have remarried and had children.

Group formed in Los Angeles, 1977; released debut single, "Adult Books"/"We're Desperate," Dangerhouse Records, 1978; signed with Slash Records and released debut album, *Los Angeles,* 1980; signed with Elektra Records and released *Under the Big Black Sun,* 1982; signed with Big Life/Mercury Records and released *Hey Zeus!,* 1993. Appeared in films *The Decline of Western Civilization,* 1980, *Urgh! A Music War,* 1981, and *The Unheard Music,* 1985.

Cervenka is the author (with Lydia Lunch) of poetry collection *Adulterers Anonymous,* Grove Press, 1982; Doe and Cervenka released solo records, contributed to film soundtracks, and pursued film roles, among other projects, 1989-92; Bonebrake worked as session player and sideman, late 1980s-1992; Gilkyson played on Cervenka and Alvin solo albums.

Awards: *Wild Gift* named album of the year by *Los Angeles Times, New York Times, Rolling Stone,* and *Time,* among others, 1981; named band of the year in *L.A. Weekly* readers' poll, 1987.

Addresses: *Record company*—Mercury Records, 825 Eighth Ave., New York, NY 10019; 11150 Santa Monica Blvd., Los Angeles, CA 90025.

would last the better part of a decade and ultimately lead to marriage but would not outlast their artistic collaboration. Cervenka—who used "Exene" as an "Xmas"-type abbreviation of her given name, Christine—reworked one of her poems as a song lyric and auditioned for Doe and Zoom's new band. "At the beginning, I wanted to do gospel vocals, all up and down with every word somehow bent," she noted to Chute. "But it seemed that a sort of flat delivery, more like country singing, worked better." While some listeners would consider "sort of flat" an understatement of Cervenka's unusual, sometimes grating vocals—especially when compared to Doe's supple and rich countrified tones—the two's unique harmonies helped to define the group's sound. *Newsweek* later called Cervenka's approach "a keening kind of punk plainsong"; Doe told the magazine he considered it "good and natural."

Drummer Mick Basher initially rounded out the foursome, but Doe and Cervenka were so impressed with D. J. Bonebrake's work with the punk group the Eyes—whose performance they caught at the legendary underground club The Masque—that they persuaded him to leave his group and replace Basher. Bonebrake, the group's only native Angeleno, debuted with X in February of 1978.

Over the next two years, X built a powerful reputation on the local rock scene through relentless gigging. Soon they were, in the words of *Rolling Stone* reporter Chris Morris, "the city's most respected and written-about punk band." Their 1978 single "Adult Books"/"We're Desperate" helped fuel their underground success. The group's sound was nonetheless too radical for the major record labels, which gravitated toward safer-sounding "New Wave" bands. X cast their lot with the fledgling company Slash, a tiny operation run by friends. They achieved a major coup, however, by enticing Ray Manzarek, keyboardist of the legendary L.A. band the Doors, to produce their debut album. Recorded for a mere $10,000 and titled *Los Angeles,* it would make X a musical act of national importance.

fit the emerging punk aesthetic of the period. "John and I had two totally different approaches," Zoom explained to *Rolling Stone's* David Chute. "We influenced each other and turned it into one thing. But we really didn't have a sound until John met Exene in Venice [California]."

From Poetry to Plainsong

That meeting took place at a poetry workshop. Immediately impressed by the Chicago-born Cervenka's writing, Doe asked her out; the two began a romance that

Critical Raves

Rolling Stone's Ken Tucker called *Los Angeles* "a powerful, unsettling work," claiming, "X have already perfected a style that achieves jolting effects through enormously compressed, elliptical imagery held together by succinct, brutally played guitar and drum riffs." Featuring such blistering original tunes as "Johnny Hit and Run Paulene," "Sex and Dying and High Society," and the shattering title song, along with a souped-up cover version of the Doors classic "Soul

Kitchen," *Los Angeles* became one of the most critically celebrated records of the year. The group's sound during that period was captured live in Penelope Spheeris's film *The Decline of Western Civilization.*

In 1981 X aced the sophomore jinx by releasing the compelling *Wild Gift,* which further refined the formula of their debut. The blazing "We're Desperate" became something of a punk anthem, declaring, "We're desperate/ Get used to it." The group also explored more diverse musical territory, even offering a touch of retro-balladry on the anguished "Adult Books." *Wild Gift* made the Top Ten lists of the *New York Times,* the *Los Angeles Times, Rolling Stone,* and *Time* magazine, among others. X's increased popularity enabled them to leave Slash and sign with a major label, Elektra; the move angered friends at Slash and led some of the band's industry-distrusting hardcore fans to accuse them of selling out. Undaunted, the group released *Under the Big Black Sun* in 1982; Parke Puterbaugh declared in his *Rolling Stone* review, "America needs to hear this album." He added that the group "evince a surefootedness, a throttling punch, that's deliriously subversive." In addition to rockers like "The Hungry Wolf," the album contained two songs commemorating the death of Cervenka's sister: "Riding With Mary" and "Come Back to Me."

Attacked Radio Cowardice

X released its second Elektra album, *More Fun in the New World,* the next year; full of political fury aimed in large part at the values of President Ronald Reagan's administration, it also represented a further development of X's sound. Cervenka's lyrics for "I Must Not Think Bad Thoughts" targeted radio cowardice, an issue first explored on "The Unheard Music," from *Los Angeles.* This time out she decried the predominance of modish British pop—"glitter disco synthesizer night school"—and asked, "Will the last American band to get played on the radio/ Please bring the flag?" *More Fun* sold fairly well, though X's predictions about adventurous domestic music's fate on radio would hold true for the rest of the decade. Indeed, *Creem* writer Richard Riegel proclaimed somewhat prophetically in 1984, "We can't have a whole generation grow up who don't realize until 1991 or so that they wish they'd gotten into X way back when."

In 1984 the group released the single "Wild Thing," a manic cover version of the rock classic by the Troggs. Doe and Cervenka recorded a punk/folk/country album for Slash as the Knitters; it was released in 1985, as were *The Unheard Music,* a documentary film about X that was some five years in the making, and the X

album *Ain't Love Grand.* The latter contained the single "Burning House of Love."

Billy Zoom left X after the release of *Ain't Love Grand,* and by the end of 1985 Doe and Cervenka had divorced. They decided to keep working together, however, and in 1986 were joined by guitarists Dave Alvin, known for his work with the Blasters, and ex-Lone Justice member Tony Gilkyson. In addition to their work with the Knitters and other L.A. groups, Doe and Cervenka pursued a variety of projects; Doe began fairly steady work as a film actor, while Cervenka, who had co-written a 1982 book of poetry with Lydia Lunch, became increasingly involved in political activism and toured as a spoken-word performer. She also did some film and television acting. Bonebrake became a popular sideman for local performers.

X released the album *See How We Are* in 1987; it fared poorly both with critics and consumers, despite the inclusion of Dave Alvin's lyrical rocker "4th of July," which seemed destined for radio success. Alvin left the group soon after the album's release. X was named band of the year by readers of *L.A. Weekly,* but its members felt little momentum. They put out a double live album in 1988 and then lapsed into retirement.

Cervenka unveiled two solo albums, one in 1989 and another in 1990. Doe released a solo venture as well in 1990 and continued to act in films, including *Roadside Prophets* and *Pure Country.* X seemed a thing of the past. Then, in 1991, the commercial equivalent of a tornado hit the music industry. Its name was Nirvana, a punk-derived "grunge" trio from Washington that achieved mega-platinum success with *Nevermind,* an album of well-crafted but sonically abrasive songs. Suddenly, major labels, Top 40 radio stations, and MTV were very interested in "alternative" rock and the success of other bands who had felt the influence of groups like X, including Jane's Addiction, the Red Hot Chili Peppers, and Faith No More. This musical climate convinced Doe, Cervenka, and company to reunite. "Radio has changed," Cervenka reflected in 1993 to Gary Davis of the *Los Angeles Reader.*

X signed with Big House, a British-based subsidiary of Mercury Records. Joining first with an English producer, the group ended up recording with Tony Berg, a music-industry veteran who would soon be an Artists & Repertoire executive for the Geffen record company. Working at Berg's house, X recorded tracks that would become their 1993 release, *Hey Zeus!* While in their earlier days Doe and Cervenka had largely collaborated on songs, this time they wrote independently for the most part, offering a kind of song-by-song counterpoint. Doe penned the album's first two singles, "Country at War" and "New Life." As he told the *L.A. Village*

View, "What's different with X these days is that we have an incredible musical history, musical vocabulary, with each other." He added, "The band's friendship stayed intact, so it was a fairly smooth transition coming back together." Both he and Cervenka had had children with other spouses, though any mellowing was not apparent on *Hey Zeus!*

Rolling Stone, in a generally positive review, noted that the group "seems to have come to terms with their postpunk identity." Robert Hilburn of the *Los Angeles Times,* who insisted that "X still has much to tell us," reported, "X's music remains honest, liberating and welcome," though he did feel the record had its shortcomings. *Spin,* meanwhile, panned *Hey Zeus!* as little more than a "commodity," qualifying this critique only by concluding, "When asked 'How's the new X album?,' the correct response is, 'Not as bad as it could've been.'" The band, however, seemed prepared to accept relatively poorer reviews and higher visibility, a marked contrast to its earliest reception. After a tour of southern California "area codes," X planned a series of national shows. When Davis of the *Los Angeles Reader* asked John Doe how it felt to be a "survivor of punk," the bassist replied with characteristic wit, "It's fabulous! It's just like being a non-survivor, except that you're still alive."

Selected discography

"Adult Books"/"We're Desperate," Dangerhouse, 1978.
Los Angeles (includes "Johnny Hit and Run Paulene," "Sex and Dying and High Society," "Los Angeles," "Soul Kitchen," and "The Unheard Music"), Slash, 1980.
(Contributors) "Beyond and Back," "Johnny Hit and Run Paulene," and "We're Desperate," *Decline of Western Civilization* (soundtrack), Slash, 1980.
Wild Gift (includes "We're Desperate" and "Adult Books"), Slash, 1981.
(Contributors) *Urgh! A Music War* (soundtrack), 1981.

On Elektra

Under the Big Black Sun (includes "The Hungry Wolf," "Riding With Mary," and "Come Back to Me"), 1982.
More Fun in the New World (includes "I Must Not Think Bad Thoughts"), 1983.
"Wild Thing," 1984.
Ain't Love Grand (includes "Burning House of Love"), 1985.
See How We Are (includes "Fourth of July"), 1987.
X Live at the Whisky-a-Go-Go on the Fabulous Sunset Strip, 1988.

On Big Life/Mercury

Hey Zeus! (includes "Country at War" and "New Life"), 1993.

The Knitters

Poor Little Critter on the Road, Slash, 1985.

Solo recordings by Exene Cervenka

Old Wives' Tales, Rhino, 1989.
Running Sacred, RNA, 1990.
(Contributor) "Clean Like Tomorrow," *Roadside Prophets* (soundtrack), Fine Line/Vanguard, 1992.
(Contributor) *Tahachapi* (soundtrack), Hemdale, 1993.

Solo recordings by John Doe

Meet John Doe, Geffen, 1990.
(Contributor) "Beer, Gas, Ride Forever," *Roadside Prophets* (soundtrack), 1992.
(Contributor) "I Will Always Love You," *The Bodyguard* (soundtrack), Warner Bros., 1992.

Sources

Books

Stambler, Irwin, *Encyclopedia of Pop, Rock and Soul,* St. Martin's, 1989.

Periodicals

BAM, September 10, 1993.
Billboard, June 5, 1993.
Creem, February 1984.
Factor X, July 1993.
L.A. Village View, September 10, 1993.
Los Angeles Reader, September 3, 1993.
Los Angeles Times, June 6, 1993.
Mademoiselle, January 1983.
Melody Maker, March 17, 1984.
Newsweek, April 19, 1982.
Ray Gun, August 1993.
Rolling Stone, July 10, 1980; August 7, 1980; October 15, 1981; August 19, 1982; September 30, 1982; June 24, 1993; September 2, 1993.
Spin, July 1993.
Venice, July 1993.

Additional information for this profile was provided by Mercury Records publicity materials, 1993.

—*Simon Glickman*

Yanni

Composer, keyboardist

A lot of people think they've never heard Yanni's music. Yet in the early 1990s, the keyboardist's work was heard by more people than perhaps that of any other composer; from commercials to soundtracks to sporting events, this Greek-born synthesizer wiz has been everywhere, establishing a fan base beyond his diehard New Age constituency.

When, in 1972, he left his home in Kalamata, Greece, at age 18, Yanni Chrysomallis had no plans to become a New Age music star. Although music had always been a passion, the study of psychology overrode it. Having read all the works of Sigmund Freud by the time he was 16, Yanni chose to go to the United States to study psychology at the University of Minnesota. Just two years away from a graduate degree, however, it occurred to him that "to have a Ph.D. at 24 and go into practice and have children and do the same thing over and over again—it would drive me crazy," he confessed to *People*. And with that, music took over.

As a child, Yanni had mastered the piano without lessons. He would play for hours trying to re-create the music he'd heard on the radio or at the movies. Having perfect pitch certainly helped. In time he even developed his own system of musical notation, something he still uses. But as a youth, Yanni also found room for sports; he is a former member of the Greek National Swimming Team and broke the national freestyle record at age 14.

After leaving school, Yanni worked as a studio musician, toured for years with the cult rock band Chameleon, and would often spend fifteen-hour days at the keyboard. The distinctive musical style that developed from his hard work and talent urged him toward a solo career. In 1986 Yanni's demo tape caught the ear of Private Music's Peter Bowman; he was convinced that the musician had something special. Later that year, Private Music released Yanni's first solo album, *Optimystique*. From there Yanni went on to very quietly develop a tremendous following.

Doesn't Mind New Age Label

Bowman made the top of the New Age charts his first objective for Yanni. Although he generally categorizes his music as "adult contemporary," Yanni does not object to the New Age designation, as do some contemporary instrumentalists who are lumped into that category. "When I was studying psychology," he told *Keyboard*'s Bob Doerschuk, "I learned that one of the worst things you can do to patients is to label them. If you call someone a neurotic, he'll go into his box and behave like a neurotic. But we have to use labels,

For the Record. . .

B orn Yanni Chrysomallis, November 14, 1954, in Kalamata, Greece; son of a banker. *Education:* B.A. in psychology, University of Minnesota; graduate work.

Studio musician, c. 1978; keyboardist for group Chameleon, early 1980s; became solo artist, 1986; signed with Private Music and released first solo album, *Optimystique,* 1986.

Selected awards: World Music Award, 1993, for best-selling Greek recording artist of the year; numerous gold and platinum records; Grammy Award nomination for best New Age album, 1994, for *In My Time.*

Addresses: *Record Company*—Private Music, 9014 Melrose Ave., Los Angeles, CA 90069.

because they help us to communicate quickly and understand each other. That's why the New Age label doesn't bother me. . . . I want my music to be heard. I want it to affect people. I want to connect with my audience at an intimate level. . . . I don't want anybody to think that you have to be a spacehead to enjoy my music. If I can affect you emotionally and get under your skin, then I'm succeeding."

Indeed, "having an effect" means everything to Yanni. "It is my intention to share my emotions with the listener, but I also want to allow the listener to take this music and make it their own," he stated in a 1993 Private Music press release. "The only way people can fully relate to it and enjoy it is when it means something in their life. . . . Instrumental music, used correctly, is very direct and extremely accurate in describing even the most subtle human emotions. My music does not describe the circumstances, but how the circumstances make you feel. Since the music projects no gender, and there are no lyrics to be interpreted, the listener can personalize it, and in a far more precise way."

In addition to his albums, Yanni has secured a niche in television and is developing a successful film scoring career. "In the old days," he told Doerschuk, "I was so interested in soundtracks that when I saw a movie I loved that had music I didn't love so much, I would take a copy of the film home, recut it, and write a new soundtrack for it. I've done 50 or 60 films that way. Now, finally, I get to do this for real." Yanni has created music for numerous television movies, though his most widely heard television work has probably been in the area of sports. His music has been used on *The Wide World of Sports* and on broadcasts of the Tour de France, the World Figure Skating Championships, the U.S. Open Tennis Championships, the World Series, and the Olym-

pic Games. In 1992, Yanni even composed the theme for the ABC-TV nightly news program *World News Now.* Beyond the small screen, his compositions have appeared in the theatrical release *Heart of Midnight,* and he has collaborated with British entertainment impresario Malcolm McLaren on an award-winning commercial for British Airways, as well as scoring music for a U.S. government film biography of Pope John Paul II.

High-Profile Romance

Having scaled the New Age charts, Private Music made plans to focus on the romance inherent in much of Yanni's work; his relationship with actress Linda Evans has been a boon to this marketing angle. Yanni, who met Evans in 1989, remarked to *People,* "This is not a situation where love is blind and we're walking around on cloud nine. It's that we are on cloud nine and we allow ourselves to be there and to love it." Evans fell in love with the artist's music before meeting the man. When she did meet him, she confessed in *People,* "I looked at him and I had no idea. . . . No idea! If I had known what he had looked like, I never would have had the nerve to call him."

New York Times music critic Stephen Holden described Yanni as "a shrewd showman" and elaborated, "Wearing a mustache and curly locks that fall below his shoulders, and clad in a puffy white shirt, white trousers, and shiny white shoes, he has refined a sensitive swashbuckler look that might be found on the cover of a romance novel. While playing the keyboard, he sometimes dances around, tossing his head back in rapt intensity." Evans, for one, loves it. "Maybe a regular person would just throw up, but I play his music all the time," she admitted in *People.* Evans, whose attitude undoubtedly reflects that of many of Yanni's women fans, hand-picked the songs that would appear on Yanni's *Reflections of Passion* disc.

Reflections was, in fact, a career retrospective of Yanni's most romantic compositions that also included three new selections. The release was part of Private Music's plan to reach a wider audience—one that does not usually buy instrumental music—while maintaining Yanni's already large and loyal New Age following. Evans had quite an assortment from which to choose for *Reflections,* it being the composer's sixth album.

Keyboard's Doerschuk assessed Yanni's earlier albums *Keys to Imagination* and *Out of Silence* as featuring "concise but vividly orchestrated instrumentals. Though they were quickly slotted into New Age bins, their prominent melodies and often propulsive rhythms encouraged listeners to move rather than to meditate." Romance, though, figured strongly in a later album, *In My Time*. Brain Soergel of Pamona, California's *Daily Bulletin* said of that record, "There's too much to like . . . [it is] a masterpiece of mood music, an unabashed Cupid's arrow straight into the heart." Writing shortly after the release of *In My Time,* United Press International's Vernon Scott noted that Yanni's "symphonic style, lilting melodies and such musical basics as harmony and counterpoint . . . trigger responses in listeners of all ages everywhere."

Some dissenters could even see a bright side to Yanni's work. Jim Aikin, in his review of *Reflections of Passion* for *Keyboard,* owned up, "I have a tendency to ignore Yanni because he's so blatantly enthusiastic. And not subtle about it, either. But as this best-of collection demonstrates, when he goes for the emotional jugular he hits it every time. . . . If you've never experienced Yanni and find yourself unaccountably yearning to, *Reflections of Passion* would be a dandy place to start."

Hot Sales, Despite Dissenters

Not everyone, however, has waxed rhapsodic about the artist. *New York Times* contributor Holden described a 1993 Yanni performance thus: "A typical composition has the sound and form of an instrumental theme for a televised sports event, soap opera or newscast divested of melody and padded out to four or five minutes. Playing a battery of electronic instruments, he . . . [inserts] motifs that evoke the hoariest Hollywood clichés of Middle Eastern, Far Eastern and other regional styles. The largely shapeless pieces huff and puff with a galloping energy that suggests an action-movie soundtrack. Although there are meditative moments, the mood is predominantly upbeat, with vigorous rock drums and percussion continually spurring things on and introducing crescendos that go nowhere."

Despite the occasional pan, Yanni has managed to score numerous gold and platinum records. *Reflections of Passion,* for instance, went platinum, topping *Billboard*'s Adult Alternative chart for a record-breaking 47 weeks, landing in the Number One spot on the New Age album chart, and even crossing over to become one of the fastest-rising album's on *Billboard*'s pop album chart. 1992's *Dare to Dream* went gold within two months of its release and was nominated for a Grammy for best New Age album. Yanni also received the 1993 World Music Award for best-selling

Greek recording artist of the year, capping off the summer of that year with his *In My Time* set certifying gold.

Still, even without his impressive record and ticket sales, Yanni would no doubt still reap as much enjoyment from life. He rigorously follows his father's advice to always "taste life like a fruit," and he thrives on his music. "My music heals me," Yanni stated in the Private Music promotional literature. "It is the most valuable and unexpected gift that I get in return for the effort of creating it. That it has a similar impact on the listener is very rewarding."

Selected discography

Optimystique, Private Music, 1986.
Keys to Imagination, Private Music, 1986.
Out of Silence, Private Music, 1987.
Chameleon Days, Private Music, 1988.
Niki Nana, Private Music, 1989.
Reflections of Passion, Private Music, 1990.
In Celebration of Life, Private Music, 1991.
Dare to Dream, Private Music, 1992.
In My Time, Private Music, 1993.
(Contributor) *I Love You Perfect* (soundtrack), Silva America/ Koch, 1993.
Live at the Acropolis, Private Music, 1994.

Sources

Billboard, July 7, 1990; November 24, 1990; April 24, 1993.
Boston Globe, May 11, 1991.
Daily Bulletin (Pomona, CA), April 4, 1993.
Los Angeles Daily News, March 24, 1993.
Keyboard, May 1988; September, 1990.
Hollywood Reporter, June 16, 1992.
New York Times, December 12, 1990; June 11, 1993.
Oakland Press (Oakland Co., MI), March 21, 1993.
People, November 16, 1990.
Performance, February 28, 1992.
Washington Post, May 13, 1991.
United Press International (wire service report) May 7, 1993.
USA Today, March 31, 1993.

Additional information for this profile was provided by Private Music, 1993.

—Joanna Rubiner

Cumulative Indexes

Cumulative Subject Index

Volume numbers appear in **bold.**

Professor Longhair **6**
Raitt, Bonnie **3**
Redding, Otis **5**
Rich, Charlie **3**
Robertson, Robbie **2**
Robillard, Duke **2**
Roomful of Blues **7**
Smith, Bessie **3**
Snow, Phoebe **4**
Taj Mahal **6**
Taylor, Koko **10**
Vaughan, Stevie Ray **1**
Waits, Tom **1**
Walker, T-Bone **5**
Wallace, Sippie **6**
Washington, Dinah **5**
Waters, Ethel **11**
Waters, Muddy **4**
Williams, Joe **11**
Williamson, Sonny Boy **9**
Winter, Johnny **5**
ZZ Top **2**

Cajun/Zydeco
Brown, Clarence "Gatemouth" **11**
Buckwheat Zydeco **6**
Chenier, Clifton **6**
Doucet, Michael **8**
Queen Ida **9**
Richard, Zachary **9**
Rockin' Dopsie **10**
Sonnier, Jo-El **10**

Cello
Casals, Pablo **9**
Gray, Walter
   See Kronos Quartet
Harrell, Lynn **3**
Jeanrenaud, Joan Dutcher
   See Kronos Quartet
Ma, Yo-Yo **2**

Children's Music
Chapin, Tom **11**
Harley, Bill **7**
Lehrer, Tom **7**
Nagler, Eric **8**
Penner, Fred **10**
Raffi **8**
Rosenshontz **9**
Sharon, Lois & Bram **6**

Christian Music
Grant, Amy **7**
King's X **7**
Patti, Sandi **7**
Petra **3**
Smith, Michael W. **11**
Stryper **2**
Waters, Ethel **11**

Clarinet
Adams, John **8**
Dorsey, Jimmy
   See Dorsey Brothers, The
Fountain, Pete **7**
Goodman, Benny **4**
Shaw, Artie **8**

Classical
Anderson, Marian **8**
Arrau, Claudio **1**
Bernstein, Leonard **2**

Boyd, Liona **7**
Bream, Julian **9**
Bronfman, Yefim **6**
Canadian Brass, The **4**
Casals, Pablo **9**
Chang, Sarah **7**
Clayderman, Richard **1**
Copland, Aaron **2**
Davis, Chip **4**
Fiedler, Arthur **6**
Galway, James **3**
Gingold, Josef **6**
Gould, Glenn **9**
Harrell, Lynn **3**
Hendricks, Barbara **10**
Horne, Marilyn **9**
Horowitz, Vladimir **1**
Jarrett, Keith **1**
Kennedy, Nigel **8**
Kissin, Evgeny **6**
Kronos Quartet **5**
Levine, James **8**
Liberace **9**
Ma, Yo-Yo **2**
Marsalis, Wynton **6**
Masur, Kurt **11**
Mehta, Zubin **11**
Menuhin, Yehudi **11**
Midori **7**
Ott, David **2**
Parkening, Christopher **7**
Perahia, Murray **10**
Perlman, Itzhak **2**
Phillips, Harvey **3**
Rampal, Jean-Pierre **6**
Rubinstein, Arthur **11**
Salerno-Sonnenberg, Nadja **3**
Schuman, William **10**
Schickele, Peter **5**
Segovia, Andres **6**
Shankar, Ravi **9**
Stern, Isaac **7**
Takemitsu, Toru **6**
Upshaw, Dawn **9**
von Karajan, Herbert **1**
Wilson, Ransom **5**
Yamashita, Kazuhito **4**
Zukerman, Pinchas **4**

Composers
Adams, John **8**
Allen, Geri **10**
Alpert, Herb **11**
Anka, Paul **2**
Atkins, Chet **5**
Bacharach, Burt **1**
Benson, George **9**
Berlin, Irving **8**
Bernstein, Leonard **2**
Bley, Carla **8**
Brubeck, Dave **8**
Burrell, Kenny **11**
Byrne, David **8**
   Also see Talking Heads
Cage, John **8**
Cale, John **9**
Casals, Pablo **9**
Clarke, Stanley **3**
Coleman, Ornette **5**
Cooder, Ry **2**
Cooney, Rory **6**
Copland, Aaron **2**

Crouch, Andraé **9**
Davis, Chip **4**
Davis, Miles **1**
de Grassi, Alex **6**
Dorsey, Thomas A. **11**
Elfman, Danny **9**
Ellington, Duke **2**
Eno, Brian **8**
Enya **6**
Gillespie, Dizzy **6**
Glass, Philip **1**
Gould, Glenn **9**
Grusin, Dave **7**
Guaraldi, Vince **3**
Hamlisch, Marvin **1**
Hancock, Herbie **8**
Handy, W. C. **7**
Hartke, Stephen **5**
Hunter, Alberta **7**
Jarre, Jean-Michel **2**
Jarrett, Keith **1**
Jones, Quincy **2**
Joplin, Scott **10**
Jordan, Stanley **1**
Kitaro **1**
Lee, Peggy **8**
Lincoln, Abbey **9**
Lloyd Webber, Andrew **6**
Mancini, Henry **1**
Marsalis, Branford **10**
Masekela, Hugh **7**
Menken, Alan **10**
Metheny, Pat **2**
Mingus, Charles **9**
Monk, Meredith **1**
Monk, Thelonious **6**
Morton, Jelly Roll **7**
Nascimento, Milton **6**
Newman, Randy **4**
Ott, David **2**
Parker, Charlie **5**
Peterson, Oscar **11**
Ponty, Jean-Luc **8**
Porter, Cole **10**
Reich, Steve **8**
Reinhardt, Django **7**
Ritenour, Lee **7**
Rollins, Sonny **7**
Satriani, Joe **4**
Schickele, Peter **5**
Schuman, William **10**
Shankar, Ravi **9**
Shaw, Artie **8**
Shorter, Wayne **5**
Solal, Martial **4**
Sondheim, Stephen **8**
Sousa, John Philip **10**
Story, Liz **2**
Summers, Andy **3**
Sun Ra **5**
Takemitsu, Toru **6**
Talbot, John Michael **6**
Taylor, Cecil **9**
Threadgill, Henry **9**
Tyner, McCoy **7**
Washington, Grover Jr. **5**
Williams, John **9**
Winston, George **9**
Winter, Paul **10**
Worrell, Bernie **11**
Yanni **11**
Zimmerman, Udo **5**

Drums
See **Percussion**

Dulcimer
Ritchie, Jean **4**

Fiddle
See **Violin**

Film Scores
Anka, Paul **2**
Bacharach, Burt **1**
Berlin, Irving **8**
Bernstein, Leonard **2**
Byrne, David **8**
    Also see Talking Heads
Cafferty, John
  See Beaver Brown Band, The
Cahn, Sammy **11**
Cliff, Jimmy **8**
Copland, Aaron **2**
Crouch, Andraé **9**
Dolby, Thomas **10**
Donovan **9**
Eddy, Duane **9**
Elfman, Danny **9**
Ellington, Duke **2**
Ferguson, Maynard **7**
Gershwin, George and Ira **11**
Gould, Glenn **9**
Grusin, Dave **7**
Guaraldi, Vince **3**
Hamlisch, Marvin **1**
Hancock, Herbie **8**
Harrison, George **2**
Hayes, Isaac **10**
Hedges, Michael **3**
Jones, Quincy **2**
Knopfler, Mark **3**
Lennon, John **9**
    Also see Beatles, The
Mancini, Henry **1**
Marsalis, Branford **10**
Mayfield, Curtis **8**
McCartney, Paul **4**
    Also see Beatles, The
Menken, Alan **10**
Metheny, Pat **2**
Nascimento, Milton **6**
Nilsson **10**
Peterson, Oscar **11**
Porter, Cole **10**
Richie, Lionel **2**
Robertson, Robbie **2**
Rollins, Sonny **7**
Sager, Carole Bayer **5**
Schickele, Peter **5**
Shankar, Ravi **9**
Taj Mahal **6**
Waits, Tom **1**
Williams, Paul **5**
Willner, Hal **10**
Young, Neil **2**

Flute
Anderson, Ian
  See Jethro Tull
Galway, James **3**
Rampal, Jean-Pierre **6**
Wilson, Ransom **5**

Folk/Traditional
Arnaz, Desi **8**
Baez, Joan **1**
Belafonte, Harry **8**
Blades, Ruben **2**
Brady, Paul **8**
Bragg, Billy **7**
Bulgarian State Female Vocal Choir,
  The **10**
Byrds, The **8**
Carter Family, The **3**
Chapin, Harry **6**
Chapman, Tracy **4**
Cherry, Don **10**
Chieftains, The **7**
Childs, Toni **2**
Clegg, Johnny **8**
Cockburn, Bruce **8**
Cohen, Leonard **3**
Collins, Judy **4**
Colvin, Shawn **11**
Crosby, David **3**
    Also see Byrds, The
Cruz, Celia **10**
de Lucia, Paco **1**
Donovan **9**
Dr. John **7**
Dylan, Bob **3**
Elliot, Cass **5**
Enya **6**
Estefan, Gloria **2**
Feliciano, José **10**
Galway, James **3**
Gilmore, Jimmie Dale **11**
Gipsy Kings, The **8**
Griffith, Nanci **3**
Guthrie, Arlo **6**
Guthrie, Woodie **2**
Harding, John Wesley **6**
Hartford, John **1**
Havens, Richie **11**
Iglesias, Julio **2**
Indigo Girls **3**
Kingston Trio, The **9**
Kuti, Fela **7**
Ladysmith Black Mambazo **1**
Larkin, Patty **9**
Lavin, Christine **6**
Leadbelly **6**
Lightfoot, Gordon **3**
Los Lobos **2**
Makeba, Miriam **8**
Masekela, Hugh **7**
McLean, Don **7**
Mitchell, Joni **2**
Morrison, Van **3**
Nascimento, Milton **6**
N'Dour, Youssou **6**
Near, Holly **1**
Ochs, Phil **7**
O'Connor, Sinead **3**
Odetta **7**
Parsons, Gram **7**
    Also see Byrds, The
Paxton, Tom **5**
Peter, Paul & Mary **4**
Pogues, The **6**
Prine, John **7**
Redpath, Jean **1**
Ritchie, Jean, **4**
Rodgers, Jimmie **3**

Sainte-Marie, Buffy **11**
Santana, Carlos **1**
Seeger, Pete **4**
    Also see Weavers, The
Shankar, Ravi **9**
Simon, Paul **1**
Snow, Pheobe **4**
Sweet Honey in the Rock **1**
Taj Mahal **6**
Thompson, Richard **7**
Tikaram, Tanita **9**
Vega, Suzanne **3**
Wainwright III, Loudon **11**
Watson, Doc **2**
Weavers, The **8**

French Horn
Ohanian, David
  See Canadian Brass, The

Funk
Brown, James **2**
Clinton, George **7**
Collins, Bootsy **8**
Fishbone **7**
Gang of Four **8**
Jackson, Janet **3**
Khan, Chaka **9**
Mayfield, Curtis **8**
Parker, Maceo **7**
Prince **1**
Red Hot Chili Peppers, The **7**
Stone, Sly **8**
Toussaint, Allen **11**
Worrell, Bernie **11**

Fusion
Anderson, Ray **7**
Beck, Jeff **4**
    Also see Yardbirds, The
Clarke, Stanley **3**
Coleman, Ornette **5**
Corea, Chick **6**
Davis, Miles **1**
Fishbone **7**
Hancock, Herbie **8**
Metheny, Pat **2**
O'Connor, Mark **1**
Ponty, Jean-Luc **8**
Reid, Vernon **2**
Ritenour, Lee **7**
Shorter, Wayne **5**
Summers, Andy **3**
Washington, Grover, Jr. **5**

Gospel
Anderson, Marian **8**
Brown, James **2**
Carter Family, The **3**
Charles, Ray **1**
Cleveland, James **1**
Cooke, Sam **1**
    Also see Soul Stirrers, The
Crouch, Andraé **9**
Dorsey, Thomas A. **11**
Ford, Tennessee Ernie **3**
Franklin, Aretha **2**
Green, Al **9**
Houston, Cissy **6**
Jackson, Mahalia **8**
Knight, Gladys **1**

Little Richard **1**
Oak Ridge Boys, The **7**
Pickett, Wilson **10**
Presley, Elvis **1**
Redding, Otis **5**
Robbins, Marty **9**
Smith, Michael W. **11**
Soul Stirrers, The **11**
Staples, Pops **11**
Take 6 **6**
Waters, Ethel **11**
Watson, Doc **2**
Williams, Deniece **1**
Womack, Bobby **5**

Guitar
Ackerman, Will **3**
Allman, Duane
 See Allman Brothers, The
Atkins, Chet **5**
Baxter, Jeff
 See Doobie Brothers, The
Beck, Jeff **4**
 Also see Yardbirds, The
Belew, Adrian **5**
Benson, George **9**
Berry, Chuck **1**
Bettencourt, Nuno
 See Extreme
Betts, Dicky
 See Allman Brothers, The
Boyd, Liona **7**
Bream, Julian **9**
Buck, Peter
 See R.E.M.
Buckingham, Lindsey **8**
 Also see Fleetwood Mac
Burrell, Kenny **11**
Campbell, Glen **2**
Christian, Charlie **11**
Clapton, Eric **11**
 Earlier sketch in CM **1**
 Also see Cream
 Also see Yardbirds, The
Clark, Roy **1**
Cockburn, Bruce **8**
Collins, Albert **4**
Cooder, Ry **2**
Cray, Robert **8**
Daniels, Charlie **6**
de Grassi, Alex **6**
de Lucia, Paco **1**
Dickens, Little Jimmy **7**
Diddley, Bo **3**
Earl, Ronnie **5**
 Also see Roomful of Blues
Eddy, Duane **9**
Edge, The
 See U2
Feliciano, José **10**
Fender, Leo **10**
Flatt, Lester **3**
Ford, Lita **9**
Frampton, Peter **3**
Frehley, Ace
 See Kiss
Fripp, Robert **9**
Garcia, Jerry **4**
George, Lowell
 See Little Feat
Gibbons, Billy
 See ZZ Top

Gilmour, David
 See Pink Floyd
Gill, Vince **7**
Green, Peter
 See Fleetwood Mac
Guy, Buddy **4**
Haley, Bill **6**
Harrison, George **2**
Havens, Richie **11**
Healey, Jeff **4**
Hedges, Michael **3**
Hendrix, Jimi **2**
Hillman, Chris
 See Byrds, The
 Also see Desert Rose Band, The
Hitchcock, Robyn **9**
Holly, Buddy **1**
Hooker, John Lee **1**
Howlin' Wolf **6**
Iommi, Tony
 See Black Sabbath
James, Elmore **8**
Jardine, Al
 See Beach Boys, The
Johnson, Robert **6**
Jones, Brian
 See Rolling Stones, The
Jordan, Stanley **1**
Kantner, Paul
 See Jefferson Airplane
King, Albert **2**
King, B. B. **1**
Klugh, Earl **10**
Knopfler, Mark **3**
Larkin, Patty **9**
Leadbelly **6**
Lennon, John **9**
 Also see Beatles, The
Lindley, David **2**
Lockwood, Robert Jr. **10**
Marr, Johnny
 See Smiths, The
May, Brian
 See Queen
Mayfield, Curtis **8**
McGuinn, Roger
 See Byrds, The
Metheny, Pat **2**
Montgomery, Wes **3**
Nugent, Ted **2**
Owens, Buck **2**
Page, Jimmy **4**
 Also see Led Zeppelin
 Also see Yardbirds, The
Parkening, Christopher **7**
Patton, Charley **11**
Perkins, Carl **9**
Perry, Joe
 See Aerosmith
Petty, Tom **9**
Prince **1**
Raitt, Bonnie **3**
Ray, Amy
 See Indigo Girls
Reid, Vernon **2**
 Also see Living Colour
Reinhardt, Django **7**
Richards, Keith **11**
 Also see Rolling Stones, The
Ritenour, Lee **7**
Robbins, Marty **9**
Robertson, Robbie **2**

Robillard, Duke **2**
Rodgers, Nile **8**
Santana, Carlos **1**
Saliers, Emily
 See Indigo Girls
Satriani, Joe **4**
Scofield, John **7**
Segovia, Andres **6**
Skaggs, Ricky **5**
Slash
 See Guns n' Roses
Springsteen, Bruce **6**
Stewart, Dave
 See Eurythmics
Stills, Stephen **5**
Stuart, Marty **9**
Summers, Andy **3**
Taylor, Mick
 See Rolling Stones, The
Thompson, Richard **7**
Townshend, Pete **1**
Tubb, Ernest **4**
Vai, Steve **5**
Van Halen, Edward
 See Van Halen
Vaughan, Jimmie
 See Fabulous Thunderbirds, The
Vaughan, Stevie Ray **1**
Walker, T-Bone **5**
Walsh, Joe **5**
 Also see Eagles, The
Watson, Doc **2**
Weir, Bob
 See Grateful Dead, The
Wilson, Nancy
 See Heart
Winston, George **9**
Winter, Johnny **5**
Yamashita, Kazuhito **4**
Yarrow, Peter
 See Peter, Paul & Mary
Young, Angus
 See AC/DC
Young, Malcolm
 See AC/DC
Young, Neil **2**
Zappa, Frank **1**

Harmonica
Dylan, Bob **3**
Guthrie, Woodie **2**
Lewis, Huey **9**
Waters, Muddy **4**
Williamson, Sonny Boy **9**
Wilson, Kim
 See Fabulous Thunderbirds, The

Heavy Metal
AC/DC **4**
Aerosmith **3**
Alice in Chains **10**
Anthrax **11**
Black Sabbath **9**
Danzig **7**
Deep Purple **11**
Def Leppard **3**
Faith No More **7**
Fishbone **7**
Ford, Lita **9**
Guns n' Roses **2**
Iron Maiden **10**
Judas Priest **10**

Burnett, Carol **6**
Carter, Nell **7**
Channing, Carol **6**
Chevalier, Maurice **6**
Crawford, Michael **4**
Crosby, Bing **6**
Curry, Tim **3**
Davis, Sammy, Jr. **4**
Garland, Judy **6**
Gershwin, George and Ira **11**
Hamlisch, Marvin **1**
Horne, Lena **11**
Jolson, Al **10**
Laine, Cleo **10**
Lloyd Webber, Andrew **6**
LuPone, Patti **8**
Masekela, Hugh **7**
Menken, Alan **10**
Moore, Melba **7**
Patinkin, Mandy **3**
Peters, Bernadette **7**
Porter, Cole **10**
Robeson, Paul **8**
Rodgers, Richard **9**
Sager, Carole Bayer **5**
Sondheim, Stephen **8**
Waters, Ethel **11**

Opera
Adams, John **8**
Anderson, Marian **8**
Battle, Kathleen **6**
Callas, Maria **11**
Carreras, José **8**
Caruso, Enrico **10**
Cotrubas, Ileana **1**
Domingo, Placido **1**
Gershwin, George and Ira **11**
Hendricks, Barbara **10**
Horne, Marilyn **9**
Norman, Jessye **7**
Pavarotti, Luciano **1**
Price, Leontyne **6**
Sills, Beverly **5**
Te Kanawa, Kiri **2**
Upshaw, Dawn **9**
von Karajan, Herbert **1**
Zimmerman, Udo **5**

Percussion
Baker, Ginger
See Cream
Blakey, Art **11**
Bonham, John
See Led Zeppelin
Burton, Gary **10**
Collins, Phil **2**
Also see Genesis
DeJohnette, Jack **7**
Densmore, John
See Doors, The
Dunbar, Aynsley
See Jefferson Starship
Also See Whitesnake
Fleetwood, Mick
See Fleetwood Mac
Hampton, Lionel **6**
Hart, Mickey
See Grateful Dead, The
Henley, Don **3**
Jones, Elvin
Jones, Kenny
See Who, The

Jones, Spike **5**
Kreutzman, Bill
See Grateful Dead, The
Mason, Nick
See Pink Floyd
Moon, Keith
See Who, The
N'Dour, Youssou **6**
Palmer, Carl
See Emerson, Lake & Palmer/Powell
Peart, Neil
See Rush
Powell, Cozy
See Emerson, Lake & Palmer/Powell
Sheila E. **3**
Starr, Ringo **10**
Also see Beatles, The
Watts, Charlie
See Rolling Stones, The

Piano
Allen, Gerri **10**
Arrau, Claudio **1**
Bacharach, Burt **1**
Basie, Count **2**
Berlin, Irving **8**
Bley, Carla **8**
Bronfman, Yefim **6**
Brubeck, Dave **8**
Bush, Kate **4**
Charles, Ray **1**
Clayderman, Richard **1**
Cleveland, James **1**
Cole, Nat King **3**
Collins, Judy **4**
Collins, Phil **2**
Also see Genesis
Connick, Harry, Jr. **4**
Crouch, Andraé **9**
DeJohnette, Jack **7**
Domino, Fats **2**
Dr. John **7**
Ellington, Duke **2**
Feinstein, Michael **6**
Flack, Roberta **5**
Frey, Glenn **3**
Glass, Philip **1**
Gould, Glenn **9**
Grusin, Dave **7**
Guaraldi, Vince **3**
Hamlisch, Marvin **1**
Hancock, Herbie **8**
Horn, Shirley **7**
Hornsby, Bruce **3**
Horowitz, Vladimir **1**
Jackson, Joe **4**
Jarrett, Keith **1**
Joel, Billy **2**
John, Elton **3**
Joplin, Scott **10**
Kissin, Evgeny **6**
Levine, James **8**
Lewis, Jerry Lee **2**
Liberace **9**
Little Richard **1**
Manilow, Barry **2**
McDonald, Michael
See Doobie Brothers, The
McRae, Carmen **9**
McVie, Christine
See Fleetwood Mac
Milsap, Ronnie **2**

Mingus, Charles **9**
Monk, Thelonious **6**
Morton, Jelly Roll **7**
Newman, Randy **4**
Perahia, Murray **10**
Peterson, Oscar **11**
Professor Longhair **6**
Rich, Charlie **3**
Roberts, Marcus **6**
Rubinstein, Arthur **11**
Russell, Mark **6**
Schickele, Peter **5**
Sedaka, Neil **4**
Solal, Martial **4**
Story, Liz **2**
Taylor, Cecil **9**
Tyner, McCoy **7**
Waits, Tom **1**
Waller, Fats **7**
Winston, George **9**
Winwood, Steve **2**
Wonder, Stevie **2**
Wright, Rick
See Pink Floyd

Piccolo
Galway, James **3**

Pop
Abdul, Paula **3**
Adams, Bryan **2**
Alpert, Herb **11**
Andrews Sisters, The **9**
Armatrading, Joan **4**
Arnold, Eddy **10**
Astley, Rick **5**
Atkins, Chet **5**
Avalon, Frankie **5**
B-52's, The **4**
Bacharach, Burt **1**
Bailey, Pearl **5**
Basia **5**
Beach Boys, The **1**
Beatles, The **2**
Beaver Brown Band, The **3**
Bee Gees, The **3**
Bennett, Tony **2**
Benson, George **9**
Benton, Brook **7**
Blood, Sweat and Tears **7**
BoDeans, The **3**
Bolton, Michael **4**
Boston **11**
Bowie, David **1**
Bragg, Billy **7**
Branigan, Laura **2**
Brickell, Edie **3**
Brooks, Garth **8**
Brown, Bobby **4**
Browne, Jackson **3**
Bryson, Peabo **11**
Buckingham, Lindsey **8**
Also see Fleetwood Mac
Buffett, Jimmy **4**
Campbell, Glen **2**
Carey, Mariah **6**
Carlisle, Belinda **8**
Carnes, Kim **4**
Chapin, Harry **6**
Chapman, Tracy **4**
Charles, Ray **1**
Checker, Chubby **7**

Ross, Diana **1**
Roth, David Lee **1**
 Also see Van Halen
Ruffin, David **6**
Sade **2**
Sager, Carole Bayer **5**
Sainte-Marie, Buffy **11**
Sanborn, David **1**
Seals & Crofts **3**
Seals, Dan **9**
Sedaka, Neil **4**
Sheila E. **3**
Shirelles, The **11**
Siberry, Jane **6**
Simon, Carly **4**
Simon, Paul **1**
Sinatra, Frank **1**
Smiths, The **3**
Snow, Pheobe **4**
Spector, Phil **4**
Springfield, Rick **9**
Springsteen, Bruce **6**
Squeeze **5**
Stansfield, Lisa **9**
Starr, Ringo **10**
Steely Dan **5**
Stevens, Cat **3**
Stewart, Rod **2**
Stills, Stephen **5**
Sting **2**
Streisand, Barbra **2**
Supremes, The **6**
Sweet, Matthew **9**
Talking Heads **1**
Taylor, James **2**
Tears for Fears **6**
Temptations, The **3**
10,000 Maniacs **3**
They Might Be Giants **7**
Three Dog Night **5**
Tiffany **4**
Tikaram, Tanita **9**
Timbuk 3 **3**
Torme, Mel **4**
Townshend, Pete **1**
 Also see Who, The
Turner, Tina **1**
Valli, Frankie **10**
Vandross, Luther **2**
Vega, Suzanne **3**
Walsh, Joe **5**
Warnes, Jennifer **3**
Warwick, Dionne **2**
Was (Not Was) **6**
Washington, Dinah **5**
Watley, Jody **9**
Who, The **3**
Williams, Andy **2**
Williams, Deniece **1**
Williams, Joe **11**
Williams, Lucinda **10**
Williams, Paul **5**
Williams, Vanessa **10**
Wilson, Jackie **3**
Wilson Phillips **5**
Winwood, Steve **2**
Womack, Bobby **5**
Wonder, Stevie **2**
"Weird Al" Yankovic **7**
XTC **10**
Young M.C. **4**
Young, Neil **2**

Producers
Ackerman, Will **3**
Alpert, Herb **11**
Baker, Anita **9**
Bogaert, Jo
 See Technotronic
Browne, Jackson **3**
Cale, John **9**
Clarke, Stanley **3**
Clinton, George **7**
Collins, Phil **2**
Costello, Elvis **2**
Crowell, Rodney **8**
Dixon, Willie **10**
Dolby, Thomas **10**
Dozier, Lamont
 See Holland-Dozier-Holland
Eno, Brian **8**
Ertegun, Ahmet **10**
Fripp, Robert **9**
Grusin, Dave **7**
Holland, Brian
 See Holland-Dozier-Holland
Holland, Eddie
 See Holland-Dozier-Holland
Jam, Jimmy, and Terry Lewis **11**
Jones, Booker T. **8**
Jones, Quincy **2**
Jourgensen, Al
 See Ministry
Lanois, Daniel **8**
Lynne, Jeff **5**
Marley, Rita **10**
Martin, George **6**
Mayfield, Curtis **8**
Miller, Mitch **11**
Prince **1**
Robertson, Robbie **2**
Rodgers, Nile **8**
Rubin, Rick **9**
Rundgren, Todd **11**
Simmons, Russell **7**
Skaggs, Ricky **5**
Spector, Phil **4**
Toussaint, Allen **11**
Vandross, Luther **2**
Willner, Hal **10**
Wilson, Brian
 See Beach Boys, The

Promoters
Clark, Dick **2**
Geldof, Bob **9**
Graham, Bill **10**
Hay, George D. **3**
Simmons, Russell **7**

Ragtime
Joplin, Scott **10**

Rap
Basehead **11**
Beastie Boys, The **8**
Biz Markie **10**
Campbell, Luther **10**
Cherry, Neneh **4**
Cypress Hill **11**
De La Soul **7**
Digital Underground **9**
DJ Jazzy Jeff and the Fresh Prince **5**
EPMD **10**
Eric B. and Rakim **9**

Geto Boys, The **11**
Hammer, M.C. **5**
Heavy D **10**
Ice Cube **10**
Ice-T **7**
Kane, Big Daddy **7**
Kid 'n Play **5**
Kool Moe Dee **9**
Kris Kross **11**
KRS-One **8**
L.L. Cool J. **5**
MC Lyte **8**
MC Serch **10**
Naughty by Nature **11**
N.W.A. **6**
P.M. Dawn **11**
Public Enemy **4**
Queen Latifah **6**
Rubin, Rick **9**
Run-D.M.C. **4**
Salt-N-Pepa **6**
Shanté **10**
Simmons, Russell **7**
Tone-L c **3**
A Tribe Called Quest **8**
Vanilla Ice **6**
Young M.C. **4**
Yo Yo **9**

Record Company Executives
Ackerman, Will **3**
Alpert, Herb **11**
Busby, Jheryl **9**
Davis, Chip **4**
Ertegun, Ahmet **10**
Geffen, David **8**
Gordy, Berry, Jr. **6**
Hammond, John **6**
Harley, Bill **7**
Jam, Jimmy, and Terry Lewis **11**
Marley, Rita **10**
Martin, George **6**
Mayfield, Curtis **8**
Miller, Mitch **11**
Mingus, Charles **9**
Near, Holly **1**
Penner, Fred **10**
Phillips, Sam **5**
Robinson, Smokey **1**
Rubin, Rick **9**
Simmons, Russell **7**
Spector, Phil **4**

Reggae
Cliff, Jimmy **8**
Marley, Bob **3**
Marley, Rita **10**
Marley, Ziggy **3**
Tosh, Peter **3**
UB40 **4**
Wailer, Bunny **11**

Rhythm and Blues/Soul
Abdul, Paula **3**
Baker, Anita **9**
Basehead **11**
Belle, Regina **6**
Berry, Chuck **1**
Blues Brothers, The **3**
Bolton, Michael **4**
Brown, James **2**
Bryson, Peabo **11**

Kiss **5**
Knopfler, Mark **3**
Kravitz, Lenny **5**
Led Zeppelin **1**
Lennon, John **9**
    Also see Beatles, The
Lennon, Julian **2**
Lindley, Dave **2**
Little Feat **4**
Living Colour **7**
Loggins, Kenny **3**
Los Lobos **2**
Lydon, John **9**
    Also see Sex Pistols, The
Lynne, Jeff **5**
Lynyrd Skynyrd **9**
Martin, George **6**
Marx, Richard **3**
MC5, The **9**
McCartney, Paul **4**
    Also see Beatles, The
McKee, Maria **11**
McMurtry, James **10**
Megadeth **9**
Mellencamp, John "Cougar" **2**
Metallica **7**
Midnight Oil **11**
Miller, Steve **2**
Ministry **10**
Morrison, Jim **3**
    Also see Doors, The
Morrison, Van **3**
Mötley Crüe **1**
Motörhead **10**
Mould, Bob **10**
Myles, Alannah **4**
Nelson, Rick **2**
Newman, Randy **4**
Nicks, Stevie **2**
Nirvana **8**
Nugent, Ted **2**
Ocasek, Ric **5**
O'Connor, Sinead **3**
Ono, Yoko **11**
Orbison, Roy **2**
Osbourne, Ozzy **3**
Page, Jimmy **4**
    Also see Led Zeppelin
    Also see Yardbirds, The
Palmer, Robert **2**
Parker, Graham **10**
Parker, Maceo **7**
Parsons, Gram **7**
    Also see Byrds, The
Petty, Tom **9**
Perkins, Carl **9**
Phillips, Sam **5**
Pink Floyd **2**
Plant, Robert **2**
    Also see Led Zeppelin
Pogues, The **6**
Poison **11**
Pop, Iggy **1**
Presley, Elvis **1**
Pretenders, The **8**
Primus **11**
Prince **1**
Prine, John **7**
Queen **6**
Queensr che **8**
Raitt, Bonnie **3**
Ramones, The **9**

Red Hot Chili Peppers, The **7**
Reed, Lou **1**
    Also see Velvet Underground, The
Reid, Vernon **2**
    Also see Living Colour
R.E.M. **5**
Replacements, The **7**
Richards, Keith **11**
    Also see Rolling Stones, The
Robertson, Robbie **2**
Rolling Stones, The **3**
Rollins, Henry **11**
Roth, David Lee **1**
    Also see Van Halen
Rubin, Rick **9**
Rundgren, Todd **11**
Rush **8**
Ryder, Mitch **11**
Satriani, Joe **4**
Sex Pistols, The **5**
Shannon, Del **10**
Shocked, Michelle **4**
Simon, Carly **4**
Simon, Paul **1**
Siouxsie and the Banshees **8**
Slayer **10**
Smith, Patti **1**
Smiths, The **3**
Sonic Youth **9**
Soul Asylum **10**
Soundgarden **6**
Spector, Phil **4**
Spinal Tap **8**
Springsteen, Bruce **6**
Squeeze **5**
Starr, Ringo **10**
Steely Dan **5**
Stevens, Cat **3**
Stewart, Rod **2**
Stills, Stephen **5**
Sting **2**
Stone, Sly **8**
Stray Cats, The **11**
Stryper **2**
Sugarcubes, The **10**
Summers, Andy **3**
T. Rex **11**
Tears for Fears **6**
10,000 Maniacs **3**
Texas Tornados, The **8**
They Might Be Giants **7**
Thompson, Richard **7**
Three Dog Night **5**
Timbuk 3 **3**
Townshend, Pete **1**
    Also see Who, The
Turner, Tina **1**
U2 **2**
Vai, Steve **5**
Valli, Frankie **10**
Van Halen **8**
Vaughan, Stevie Ray **1**
Velvet Underground, The **7**
Wallinger, Karl **11**
Walsh, Joe **5**
    Also see Eagles, The
Whitesnake **5**
Who, The **3**
Winter, Johnny **5**
Winwood, Steve **2**
X **11**
Yardbirds, The **10**

Yes **8**
Young, Neil **2**
Zappa, Frank **1**
Zevon, Warren **9**
ZZ Top **2**

Rock and Roll Pioneers
Berry, Chuck **1**
Clark, Dick **2**
Darin, Bobby **4**
Didley, Bo **3**
Dion **4**
Domino, Fats **2**
Eddy, Duane **9**
Everly Brothers, The **2**
Francis, Connie **10**
Haley, Bill **6**
Hawkins, Screamin' Jay **8**
Holly, Buddy **1**
James, Etta **6**
Jordan, Louis **11**
Lewis, Jerry Lee **2**
Little Richard **1**
Nelson, Rick **2**
Orbison, Roy **2**
Paul, Les **2**
Perkins, Carl **9**
Phillips, Sam **5**
Presley, Elvis **1**
Professor Longhair **6**
Sedaka, Neil **4**
Shannon, Del **10**
Shirelles, The **11**
Spector, Phil **4**
Twitty, Conway **6**
Valli, Frankie **10**
Wilson, Jackie **3**

Saxophone
Carter, Benny **3**
Clemons, Clarence **7**
Coleman, Ornette **5**
Coltrane, John **4**
Dorsey, Jimmy
    See Dorsey Brothers, The
Gordon, Dexter **10**
Hawkins, Coleman **11**
Kirk, Rahsaan Roland **6**
Marsalis, Branford **10**
Morgan, Frank **9**
Parker, Charlie **5**
Parker, Maceo **7**
Rollins, Sonny **7**
Sanborn, David **1**
Shorter, Wayne **5**
Threadgill, Henry **9**
Washington, Grover, Jr. **5**
Winter, Paul **10**

Songwriters
Acuff, Roy **2**
Adams, Bryan **2**
Allen, Peter **11**
Alpert, Herb **11**
Anderson, Ian
    See Jethro Tull
Anderson, John **5**
Anka, Paul **2**
Armatrading, Joan **4**
Atkins, Chet **5**
Bacharach, Burt **1**
Baez, Joan **1**

Cumulative Musicians Index

Volume numbers appear in **bold.**

Beatles, The **2**
  Also see Harrison, George
Beaver Brown Band, The **3**
Beck, Jeff **4**
  Also see Yardbirds, The
Becker, Walter
  See Steely Dan
Bee Gees, The **3**
Beers, Garry Gary
  See INXS
Behler, Chuck
  See Megadeth
Belafonte, Harry **8**
Belew, Adrian **5**
Belfield, Dennis
  See Three Dog Night
Bell, Andy
  See Erasure
Bell, Derek
  See Chieftains, The
Belladonna, Joey
  See Anthrax
Belle, Regina **6**
Bello, Frank
  See Anthrax
Belushi, John
  See Blues Brothers, The
Benante, Charlie
  See Anthrax
Benatar, Pat **8**
Bennett, Tony **2**
Benson, George **9**
Benson, Ray
  See Asleep at the Wheel
Benson, Renaldo "Obie"
  See Four Tops, The
Bentley, John
  See Squeeze
Benton, Brook **7**
Bentyne, Cheryl
  See Manhattan Transfer, The
Berigan, Bunny **2**
Berlin, Irving **8**
Berlin, Steve
  See Los Lobos
Bernstein, Leonard **2**
Berry, Bill
  See R.E.M.
Berry, Chuck **1**
Berry, Robert
  See Emerson, Lake & Palmer/Powell
Best, Pete
  See Beatles, The
Bettencourt, Nuno
  See Extreme
Betts, Dicky
  See Allman Brothers, The
Bevan, Bev
  See Black Sabbath
  Also see Electric Light Orchestra
Big Mike
  See Geto Boys, The
Big Money Odis
  See Digital Underground
Bingham, John
  See Fishbone
Binks, Les
  See Judas Priest
Bird
  See Parker, Charlie
Birdsong, Cindy
  See Supremes, The

Birchfield, Benny
  See Osborne Brothers, The
Biscuits, Chuck
  See Danzig
Biz Markie **10**
Björk
  See Gudmundsdottir, Björk
Black, Clint **5**
Black Crowes, The **7**
Black Sabbath **9**
Blackmore, Ritchie
  See Deep Purple
Blades, Ruben **2**
Blakey, Art **11**
Bley, Carla **8**
Blood, Sweat and Tears **7**
Blues Brothers, The **3**
Blues, Elwood
  See Blues Brothers, The
Blues, "Joliet" Jake
  See Blues Brothers, The
BoDeans, The **3**
Bogaert, Jo
  See Technotronic
Bogguss, Suzy **11**
Bolade, Nitanju
  See Sweet Honey in the Rock
Bolan, Marc
  See T. Rex
Bolton, Michael **4**
Bon Jovi **10**
Bon Jovi, Jon
  See Bon Jovi
Bonebrake, D. J.
  See X
Bonham, John
  See Led Zeppelin
Bono
  See U2
Bonsall, Joe
  See Oak Ridge Boys, The
Bordin, Mike
  See Faith No More
Bostaph, Paul
  See Slayer
Boston **11**
Bottum, Roddy
  See Faith No More
Bouchikhi, Chico
  See Gipsy Kings, The
Bowen, Jimmy
  See Country Gentlemen, The
Bowens, Sir Harry
  See Was (Not Was)
Bowie, David **1**
Boyd, Liona **7**
Brady, Paul **8**
Bragg, Billy **7**
Branigan, Laura **2**
Brantley, Junior
  See Roomful of Blues
B-Real
  See Cypress Hill
Bream, Julian **9**
Brickell, Edie **3**
Bright, Ronnie
  See Coasters, The
Briley, Alex
  See Village People, The
Brooks, Garth **8**
Bronfman, Yefim **6**
Brown, Bobby **4**

Brown, Clarence "Gatemouth" **11**
Brown, James **2**
Brown, Jimmy
  See UB40
Browne, Jackson **3**
  Also see Nitty Gritty Dirt Band, The
Brubeck, Dave **8**
Bruce, Jack
  See Cream
Bruford, Bill
  See Yes
Bruster, Thomas
  See Soul Stirrers, The
Bryant, Elbridge
  See Temptations, The
Bryan, David
  See Bon Jovi
Bryson, Bill
  See Desert Rose Band, The
Bryson, Peabo **11**
Buck, Mike
  See Fabulous Thunderbirds, The
Buck, Peter
  See R.E.M.
Buck, Robert
  See 10,000 Maniacs
Buckingham, Lindsey **8**
  Also see Fleetwood Mac
Buckley, Betty **1**
Buckwheat Zydeco **6**
Budgie
  See Siouxsie and the Banshees
Buffett, Jimmy **4**
Bulgarian State Female Vocal Choir,
  The **10**
Bulgarian State Radio and Television
Female Vocal Choir, The
  See Bulgarian State Female Vocal
  Choir, The
Bumpus, Cornelius
  See Doobie Brothers, The
Bunker, Clive
  See Jethro Tull
Burch, Curtis
  See New Grass Revival, The
Burnett, Carol **6**
Burnette, Billy
  See Fleetwood Mac
Burnham, Hugo
  See Gang of Four
Burns, Bob
  See Lynyrd Skynyrd
Burr, Clive
  See Iron Maiden
Burrell, Kenny **11**
Burton, Cliff
  See Metallica
Burton, Gary **10**
Busby, Jheryl **9**
Bush, John
  See Anthrax
Bush, Kate **4**
Bush, Sam
  See New Grass Revival, The
Bushwick Bill
  See Geto Boys, The
Butler, Terry "Geezer"
  See Black Sabbath
Buzzcocks, The **9**
Byrds, The **8**
Byrne, David **8**
  Also see Talking Heads

Cafferty, John
See Beaver Brown Band, The
Cage, John **8**
Cahn, Sammy **11**
Cale, John **9**
Also see Velvet Underground, The
Calhoun, Will
See Living Colour
Callas, Maria **11**
Calloway Cab **6**
Cameron, Matt
See Soundgarden
Campbell, Ali
See UB40
Campbell, Glen **2**
Campbell, Luther **10**
Campbell, Phil
See Motörhead
Campbell, Robin
See UB40
Canadian Brass, The **4**
Cantrell, Jerry
See Alice in Chains
Captain Beefheart **10**
Carey, Mariah **6**
Carlisle, Belinda **8**
Carlson, Paulette
See Highway 101
Carnes, Kim **4**
Carpenter, Bob
See Nitty Gritty Dirt Band, The
Carpenter, Mary-Chapin **6**
Carr, Eric
See Kiss
Carrack, Paul
See Squeeze
Carreras, José **8**
Carroll, Earl "Speedo"
See Coasters, The
Carruthers, John
See Siouxsie and the Banshees
Carter, Anita
See Carter Family, The
Carter, A. P.
See Carter Family, The
Carter, Benny **3**
Carter, Betty **6**
Carter, Carlene **8**
Carter Family, The **3**
Carter, Helen
See Carter Family, The
Carter, Janette
See Carter Family, The
Carter, Joe
See Carter Family, The
Carter, June **6**
Also see Carter Family, The
Carter, Maybell
See Carter Family, The
Carter, Nell **7**
Carter, Sara
See Carter Family, The
Caruso, Enrico **10**
Casady, Jack
See Jefferson Airplane
Casals, Pablo **9**
Cash, Johnny **1**
Cash, Rosanne **2**
Cates, Ronny
See Petra
Cave, Nick **10**
Cavoukian, Raffi
See Raffi

Cease, Jeff
See Black Crowes, The
Cervenka, Exene
See X
Cetera, Peter
See Chicago
Chambers, Martin
See Pretenders, The
Chambers, Terry
See XTC
Chang, Sarah **7**
Channing, Carol **6**
Chapin, Harry **6**
Chapin, Tom **11**
Chapman, Tony
See Rolling Stones, The
Chapman, Tracy **4**
Chaquico, Craig
See Jefferson Starship
Charles, Ray **1**
Chea, Alvin "Vinnie"
See Take 6
Checker, Chubby **7**
Cheeks, Julius
See Soul Stirrers, The
Chenier, Clifton **6**
Cher **1**
Cherone, Gary
See Extreme
Cherry, Don **10**
Cherry, Neneh **4**
Chevalier, Maurice **6**
Chevron, Phillip
See Pogues, The
Chicago **3**
Chieftains, The **7**
Childs, Toni **2**
Chilton, Alex **10**
Chimes, Terry
See Clash, The
Chopmaster J
See Digital Underground
Christ, John
See Danzig
Christian, Charlie **11**
Christina, Fran
See Fabulous Thunderbirds, The
Also see Roomful of Blues
Chuck D
See Public Enemy
Church, Kevin
See Country Gentlemen, The
Clapton, Eric **11**
Earlier sketch in CM **1**
Also see Cream
Also see Yardbirds, The
Clark, Dick **2**
Clark, Gene
See Byrds, The
Clark, Roy **1**
Clark, Steve
See Def Leppard
Clarke, "Fast" Eddie
See Motörhead
Clarke, Michael
See Byrds, The
Clarke, Stanley **3**
Clarke, Vince
See Depeche Mode
Also see Erasure
Clash, The **4**
Clayderman, Richard **1**

Claypool, Les
See Primus
Clayton, Adam
See U2
Clayton, Sam
See Little Feat
Clayton-Thomas, David
See Blood, Sweat and Tears
Clegg, Johnny **8**
Clemons, Clarence **7**
Cleveland, James **1**
Cliff, Jimmy **8**
Cline, Patsy **5**
Clinton, George **7**
Clooney, Rosemary **9**
Coasters, The **5**
Cobain, Kurt
See Nirvana
Cockburn, Bruce **8**
Cocker, Joe **4**
Coe, David Allan **4**
Cohen, Jeremy
See Turtle Island String Quartet
Cohen, Leonard **3**
Cohen, Porky
See Roomful of Blues
Cole, Lloyd **9**
Cole, Nat King **3**
Cole, Natalie **1**
Coleman, Ornette **5**
Collin, Phil
See Def Leppard
Collins, Albert **4**
Collins, Allen
See Lynyrd Skynyrd
Collins, Bootsy **8**
Collins, Judy **4**
Collins, Phil **2**
Also see Genesis
Collins, William
See Collins, Bootsy
Colomby, Bobby
See Blood, Sweat and Tears
Colt, Johnny
See Black Crowes, The
Coltrane, John **4**
Colvin, Shawn **11**
Conneff, Kevin
See Chieftains, The
Connick, Harry, Jr. **4**
Cooder, Ry **2**
Cook, Jeff
See Alabama
Cook, Paul
See Sex Pistols, The
Cooke, Sam **1**
Also see Soul Stirrers, The
Cooney, Rory **6**
Cooper, Alice **8**
Copland, Aaron **2**
Copley, Al
See Roomful of Blues
Corea, Chick **6**
Cornell, Chris
See Soundgarden
Cornick, Glenn
See Jethro Tull
Costello, Elvis **2**
Cotoia, Robert
See Beaver Brown Band, The
Cotrubas, Ileana **1**
Cougar, John(ny)
See Mellencamp, John "Cougar"

Hay, George D. **3**
Hayes, Isaac **10**
Haynes, Warren
　See Allman Brothers, The
Hays, Lee
　See Weavers, The
Hayward, Richard
　See Little Feat
Headon, Topper
　See Clash, The
Healey, Jeff **4**
Heart **1**
Heavy D **10**
Hedges, Michael **3**
Hellerman, Fred
　See Weavers, The
Helm, Levon
　See Band, The
　　Also see Nitty Gritty Dirt Band, The
Hendricks, Barbara **10**
Hendrix, Jimi **2**
Henley, Don **3**
　Also see Eagles, The
Herman's Hermits **5**
Herndon, Mark
　See Alabama
Herron, Cindy
　See En Vogue
Hetfield, James
　See Metallica
Hewson, Paul
　See U2
Hiatt, John **8**
Hidalgo, David
　See Los Lobos
Highway 101 **4**
Hijbert, Fritz
　See Kraftwerk
Hill, Dusty
　See ZZ Top
Hill, Ian
　See Judas Priest
Hillman, Bones
　See Midnight Oil
Hillman, Chris
　See Byrds, The
　　Also see Desert Rose Band, The
Hirst, Rob
　See Midnight Oil
Hirt, Al **5**
Hitchcock, Robyn **9**
Hodo, David
　See Village People, The
Hoffman, Guy
　See BoDeans, The
Holiday, Billie **6**
Holland, Brian
　See Holland-Dozier-Holland
Holland, Dave
　See Judas Priest
Holland, Eddie
　See Holland-Dozier-Holland
Holland, Julian "Jools"
　See Squeeze
Holland-Dozier-Holland **5**
Holly, Buddy **1**
Honeyman-Scott, James
　See Pretenders, The
Hook, Peter
　See New Order
Hooker, John Lee **1**
Hopwood, Keith
　See Herman's Hermits

Horn, Shirley **7**
Horn, Trevor
　See Yes
Horne, Lena **11**
Horne, Marilyn **9**
Hornsby, Bruce **3**
Horovitz, Adam
　See Beastie Boys, The
Horowitz, Vladimir **1**
Hossack, Michael
　See Doobie Brothers, The
House, Son **11**
Houston, Cissy **6**
Houston, Whitney **8**
Howe, Steve
　See Yes
Howlin' Wolf **6**
Hubbard, Preston
　See Fabulous Thunderbirds, The
　　Also see Roomful of Blues
Hudson, Garth
　See Band, The
Huffman, Doug
　See Boston
Hughes, Glenn
　See Black Sabbath
Hughes, Glenn
　See Village People, The
Hughes, Leon
　See Coasters, The
Hunt, Darryl
　See Pogues, The
Hunter, Alberta **7**
Hunter, Shepherd "Ben"
　See Soundgarden
Hurley, George
　See fIREHOSE
Hutchence, Michael
　See INXS
Huth, Todd
　See Primus
Hütter, Ralf
　See Kraftwerk
Hutton, Danny
　See Three Dog Night
Hyman, Jerry
　See Blood, Sweat and Tears
Hynde, Chrissie
　See Pretenders, The
Ian, Janis **5**
Ian, Scott
　See Anthrax
Ibbotson, Jimmy
　See Nitty Gritty Dirt Band, The
Ice Cube **10**
　Also see N.W.A
Ice-T **7**
Idol, Billy **3**
Iglesias, Julio **2**
Indigo Girls **3**
Inez, Mike
　See Alice in Chains
Ingram, James **11**
INXS **2**
Iommi, Tony
　See Black Sabbath
Iron Maiden **10**
Irons, Jack
　See Red Hot Chili Peppers, The
Isaak, Chris **6**
Isley Brothers, The **8**
Isley, Ernie
　See Isley Brothers, The

Isley, Marvin
　See Isley Brothers, The
Isley, O'Kelly, Jr.
　See Isley Brothers, The
Isley, Ronald
　See Isley Brothers, The
Isley, Rudolph
　See Isley Brothers, The
Ivey, Michael
　See Basehead
Jackson 5, The
　See Jacksons, The
Jackson, Alan **7**
Jackson, Eddie
　See Queensr che
Jackson, Freddie **3**
Jackson, Jackie
　See Jacksons, The
Jackson, Janet **3**
Jackson, Jermaine
　See Jacksons, The
Jackson, Joe **4**
Jackson, Karen
　See Supremes, The
Jackson, Mahalia **8**
Jackson, Marlon
　See Jacksons, The
Jackson, Michael **1**
　Also see Jacksons, The
Jackson, Randy
　See Jacksons, The
Jackson, Tito
　See Jacksons, The
Jacksons, The **7**
Jacox, Martin
　See Soul Stirrers, The
Jagger, Mick **7**
　Also see Rolling Stones, The
Jam, Jimmy
　See Jam, Jimmy, and Terry Lewis
Jam, Jimmy, and Terry Lewis **11**
Jam Master Jay
　See Run-D.M.C.
James, Andrew "Bear"
　See Midnight Oil
James, Cheryl
　See Salt-N-Pepa
James, Doug
　See Roomful of Blues
James, Elmore **8**
James, Etta **6**
James, Harry **11**
James, Rick **2**
Jane's Addiction **6**
Jardine, Al
　See Beach Boys, The
Jarobi
　See A Tribe Called Quest
Jarre, Jean-Michel **2**
Jarreau, Al **1**
Jarrett, Keith **1**
Jasper, Chris
　See Isley Brothers, The
Jay, Miles
　See Village People, The
Jeanrenaud, Joan Dutcher
　See Kronos Quartet
Jefferson Airplane **5**
Jefferson Starship
　See Jefferson Airplane
Jennings, Waylon **4**
Jessie, Young
　See Coasters, The

Lavis, Gilson
  See Squeeze
Lawrence, Tracy **11**
Lawry, John
  See Petra
Lawson, Doyle
  See Country Gentlemen, The
Leadbelly **6**
Leadon, Bernie
  See Eagles, The
    Also see Nitty Gritty Dirt Band, The
Leavell, Chuck
  See Allman Brothers, The
LeBon, Simon
  See Duran Duran
Leckenby, Derek "Lek"
  See Herman's Hermits
Ledbetter, Huddie
  See Leadbelly
Led Zeppelin **1**
Lee, Beverly
  See Shirelles, The
Lee, Brenda **5**
Lee, Geddy
  See Rush
Lee, Peggy **8**
Lee, Sara
  See Gang of Four
Lee, Tommy
  See Mötley Crüe
Leese, Howard
  See Heart
Lehrer, Tom **7**
Lemmy
  See Motörhead
Le Mystère des Voix Bulgares
  See Bulgarian State Female Vocal
  Choir, The
Lennon, John **9**
    Also see Beatles, The
Lennon, Julian **2**
Lennox, Annie
  See Eurythmics
Leonard, Glenn
  See Temptations, The
Lesh, Phil
  See Grateful Dead, The
Levene, Keith
  See Clash, The
Levine, James **8**
Levy, Ron
  See Roomful of Blues
Lewis, Huey **9**
Lewis, Jerry Lee **2**
Lewis, Otis
  See Fabulous Thunderbirds, The
Lewis, Roy
  See Kronos Quartet
Lewis, Terry
  See Jam, Jimmy, and Terry Lewis
Liberace **9**
Lifeson, Alex
  See Rush
Lightfoot, Gordon **3**
Lilienstein, Lois
  See Sharon, Lois & Bram
Lilker, Dan
  See Anthrax
Lincoln, Abbey **9**
Lindley, David **2**
Linnell, John
  See They Might Be Giants

Lipsius, Fred
  See Blood, Sweat and Tears
Little Feat **4**
Little, Keith
  See Country Gentlemen, The
Little Richard **1**
Living Colour **7**
Llanas, Sammy
  See BoDeans, The
L.L. Cool J. **5**
Lloyd Webber, Andrew **6**
Lockwood, Robert Jr. **10**
Loggins, Kenny **3**
Lombardo, Dave
  See Slayer
Lord, Jon
  See Deep Purple
Los Lobos **2**
Los Reyes
  See Gipsy Kings, The
Loughnane, Lee
  See Chicago
Love, Mike
  See Beach Boys, The
Loveless, Patty **5**
Lovett, Lyle **5**
Lowe, Chris
  See Pet Shop Boys
Lowe, Nick **6**
Lozano, Conrad
  See Los Lobos
Lucia, Paco de
  See de Lucia, Paco
Luke
  See Campbell, Luther
Lupo, Pat
  See Beaver Brown Band, The
LuPone, Patti **8**
Lydon, John **9**
    Also see Sex Pistols, The
Lynn, Loretta **2**
Lynne, Jeff **5**
    Also see Electric Light Orchestra
Lynne, Shelby **5**
Lynyrd Skynyrd **9**
Ma, Yo-Yo **2**
MacGowan, Shane
  See Pogues, The
Mack Daddy
  See Kris Kross
Madonna **4**
Magoogan, Wesley
  See English Beat, The
Maher, John
  See Buzzcocks, The
Makeba, Miriam **8**
Malone, Tom
  See Blood, Sweat and Tears
Mancini, Henry **1**
Mandrell, Barbara **4**
Maness, J. D.
  See Desert Rose Band, The
Manhattan Transfer, The **8**
Manilow, Barry **2**
Manuel, Richard
  See Band, The
Manzarek, Ray
  See Doors, The
Marie, Buffy Sainte
  See Sainte-Marie, Buffy
Marini, Lou, Jr.
  See Blood, Sweat and Tears

Marley, Bob **3**
Marley, Rita **10**
Marley, Ziggy **3**
Marr, Johnny
  See Smiths, The
Marriner, Neville
Mars, Chris
  See Replacements, The
Mars, Mick
  See Mötley Crüe
Marsalis, Branford **10**
Marsalis, Wynton **6**
Martin, Barbara
  See Supremes, The
Martin, Christopher
  See Kid 'n Play
Martin, Dean **1**
Martin, George **6**
Martin, Greg
  See Kentucky Headhunters, The
Martin, Jim
  See Faith No More
Martin, Jimmy **5**
    Also See Osborne Brothers, The
Martin, Tony
  See Black Sabbath
Marx, Richard **3**
Mascis, J
  See Dinosaur Jr.
Masdea, Jim
  See Boston
Masekela, Hugh **7**
Maseo, Baby Huey
  See De La Soul
Mason, Nick
  See Pink Floyd
Masse, Laurel
  See Manhattan Transfer, The
Masur, Kurt **11**
Mathis, Johnny **2**
Matlock, Glen
  See Sex Pistols, The
Mattea, Kathy **5**
May, Brian
  See Queen
Mayall, John **7**
Mayfield, Curtis **8**
Mazibuko, Abednigo
  See Ladysmith Black Mambazo
Mazibuko, Albert
  See Ladysmith Black Mambazo
MC5, The **9**
MCA
  See Yaunch, Adam
McBrain, Nicko
  See Iron Maiden
McCarrick, Martin
  See Siouxsie and the Banshees
McCartney, Paul **4**
    Also see Beatles, The
McCarty, Jim
  See Yardbirds, The
MC Clever
  See Digital Underground
McCracken, Chet
  See Doobie Brothers, The
McDaniels, Darryl "D"
  See Run-D.M.C.
McDonald, Barbara Kooyman
  See Timbuk 3
McDonald, Michael
  See Doobie Brothers, The

McDonald, Pat
See Timbuk 3
McDorman, Joe
See Statler Brothers, The
McDowell, Hugh
See Electric Light Orchestra
McEntire, Reba 11
MC Eric
See Technotronic
McEuen, John
See Nitty Gritty Dirt Band, The
McFee, John
See Doobie Brothers, The
McFerrin, Bobby 3
McGeoch, John
See Siouxsie and the Banshees
McGuinn, Jim
See McGuinn, Roger
McGuinn, Roger
See Byrds, The
McIntosh, Robbie
See Pretenders, The
McIntyre, Joe
See New Kids on the Block
McKagan, Duff
See Guns n' Roses
McKay, John
See Siouxsie and the Banshees
McKean, Michael
See St. Hubbins, David
McKee, Maria 11
McKernarn, Ron "Pigpen"
See Grateful Dead, The
McKnight, Claude V. III
See Take 6
McLean, Don 7
McLeod, Rory
See Roomful of Blues
MC Lyte 8
McMeel, Mickey
See Three Dog Night
McMurtry, James 10
McRae, Carmen 9
MC Serch 10
McShane, Ronnie
See Chieftains, The
McVie, Christine
See Fleetwood Mac
McVie, John
See Fleetwood Mac
Mdletshe, Geophrey
See Ladysmith Black Mambazo
Medley, Bill 3
Medlock, James
See Soul Stirrers, The
Megadeth 9
Mehta, Zubin 11
Meisner, Randy
See Eagles, The
Melax, Einar
See Sugarcubes, The
Mellencamp, John "Cougar" 2
Menken, Alan 10
Menuhin, Yehudi 11
Menza, Nick
See Megadeth
Merchant, Natalie
See 10,000 Maniacs
Mercier, Peadar
See Chieftains, The
Mercury, Freddie
See Queen

Metallica 7
Methembu, Russel
See Ladysmith Black Mambazo
Metheny, Pat 2
Meyers, Augie
See Texas Tornados, The
Michael, George 9
Michaels, Bret
See Poison
Midler, Bette 8
Midnight Oil 11
Midori 7
Mike D
See Diamond, Mike
Miles, Richard
See Soul Stirrers, The
Miller, Glenn 6
Miller, Mitch 11
Miller, Rice
See Williamson, Sonny Boy
Miller, Roger 4
Miller, Steve 2
Milli Vanilli 4
Mills, Fred
See Canadian Brass, The
Milsap, Ronnie 2
Mingus, Charles 9
Ministry 10
Miss Kier Kirby
See Lady Miss Kier
Mitchell, John
See Asleep at the Wheel
Mitchell, Joni 2
Mizell, Jay
See Run-D.M.C.
Moginie, Jim
See Midnight Oil
Molloy, Matt
See Chieftains, The
Moloney, Paddy
See Chieftains, The
Money B
See Digital Underground
Monk, Meredith 1
Monk, Thelonious 6
Monkees, The 7
Monroe, Bill 1
Montgomery, Wes 3
Moon, Keith
See Who, The
Moore, Alan
See Judas Priest
Moore, Angelo
See Fishbone
Moore, Melba 7
Moore, Sam
See Sam and Dave
Moore, Thurston
See Sonic Youth
Moraz, Patrick
See Yes
Morgan, Frank 9
Morgan, Lorrie 10
Morley, Pat
See Soul Asylum
Morris, Kenny
See Siouxsie and the Banshees
Morris, Stephen
See New Order
Morrison, Bram
See Sharon, Lois & Bram
Morrison, Jim 3
Also see Doors, The

Morrison, Sterling
See Velvet Underground, The
Morrison, Van 3
Morrissey 10
Also see Smiths, The
Morrissey, Steven Patrick
See Morrissey
Morton, Everett
See English Beat, The
Morton, Jelly Roll 7
Morvan, Fab
See Milli Vanilli
Mosely, Chuck
See Faith No More
Moser, Scott "Cactus"
See Highway 101
Mötley Crüe 1
Motörhead 10
Motta, Danny
See Roomful of Blues
Mould, Bob 10
Moulding, Colin
See XTC
Mueller, Karl
See Soul Asylum
Mullen, Larry
See U2
Murph
See Dinosaur Jr.
Murphy, Dan
See Soul Asylum
Murphey, Michael Martin 9
Murray, Anne 4
Murray, Dave
See Iron Maiden
Mustaine, Dave
See Megadeth
Also see Metallica
Mwelase, Jabulane
See Ladysmith Black Mambazo
Mydland, Brent
See Grateful Dead, The
Myles, Alannah 4
Nagler, Eric 8
Nascimento, Milton 6
Naughty by Nature 11
Navarro, David
See Jane's Addiction
N'Dour, Youssou 6
Near, Holly 1
Neel, Johnny
See Allman Brothers, The
Negron, Chuck
See Three Dog Night
Neil, Vince
See Mötley Crüe
Nelson, Rick 2
Nelson, Willie 11
Earlier sketch in CM 1
Nesmith, Mike
See Monkees, The
Neville, Aaron 5
Also see Neville Brothers, The
Neville, Art
See Neville Brothers, The
Neville Brothers, The 4
Neville, Charles
See Neville Brothers, The
Neville, Cyril
See Neville Brothers, The
New Grass Revival, The 4
New Kids on the Block 3

Newman, Randy **4**
Newmann, Kurt
  See BoDeans, The
New Order **11**
Newton, Wayne **2**
Newton-John, Olivia **8**
Nicholls, Geoff
  See Black Sabbath
Nicks, Stevie **2**
  Also see Fleetwood Mac
Nico
  See Velvet Underground, The
Nilsson **10**
Nilsson, Harry
  See Nilsson
Nirvana **8**
Nitty Gritty Dirt Band, The **6**
Noone, Peter
  See Herman's Hermits
Norica, Sugar Ray
  See Roomful of Blues
Norman, Jessye **7**
Norman, Jimmy
  See Coasters, The
Novoselic, Chris
  See Nirvana
Nugent, Ted **2**
Nunn, Bobby
  See Coasters, The
N.W.A. **6**
Oak Ridge Boys, The **7**
Oakley, Berry
  See Allman Brothers, The
Oates, John
  See Hall & Oates
Ocasek, Ric **5**
Ocean, Billy **4**
Oceans, Lucky
  See Asleep at the Wheel
Ochs, Phil **7**
O'Connell, Chris
  See Asleep at the Wheel
O'Connor, Mark **1**
O'Connor, Sinead **3**
Odetta **7**
O'Donnell, Roger
  See Cure, The
Ohanian, David
  See Canadian Brass, The
Olafsson, Bragi
  See Sugarcubes, The
Olander, Jimmy
  See Diamond Rio
Olson, Jeff
  See Village People, The
Ono, Yoko **11**
Orbison, Roy **2**
O'Riordan, Cait
  See Pogues, The
Örn, Einar
  See Sugarcubes, The
Örnolfsdottir, Margret
  See Sugarcubes, The
Orzabal, Roland
  See Tears for Fears
Osborne, Bob
  See Osborne Brothers, The
Osborne Brothers, The **8**
Osborne, Sonny
  See Osborne Brothers, The
Osbourne, Ozzy **3**
  Also see Black Sabbath

Oslin, K. T. **3**
Osmond, Donny **3**
Ott, David **2**
Outler, Jimmy
  See Soul Stirrers, The
Owen, Randy
  See Alabama
Owens, Buck **2**
Owens, Ricky
  See Temptations, The
Page, Jimmy **4**
  Also see Led Zeppelin
  Also see Yardbirds, The
Page, Patti **11**
Paice, Ian
  See Deep Purple
Palmer, Carl
  See Emerson, Lake & Palmer/Powell
Palmer, David
  See Jethro Tull
Palmer, Robert **2**
Pankow, James
  See Chicago
Parazaider, Walter
  See Chicago
Parkening, Christopher **7**
Parker, Charlie **5**
Parker, Graham **10**
Parker, Kris
  See KRS-One
Parker, Maceo **7**
Parsons, Gene
  See Byrds, The
Parsons, Gram **7**
  Also see Byrds, The
Parsons, Tony
  See Iron Maiden
Parton, Dolly **2**
Partridge, Andy
  See XTC
Pasemaster, Mase
  See De La Soul
Patinkin, Mandy **3**
Patti, Sandi **7**
Patton, Charley **11**
Patton, Mike
  See Faith No More
Paul, Alan
  See Manhattan Transfer, The
Paul, Les **2**
Pavarotti, Luciano **1**
Paxton, Tom **5**
Payne, Bill
  See Little Feat
Payne, Scherrie
  See Supremes, The
Payton, Lawrence
  See Four Tops, The
Pearl, Minnie **3**
Peart, Neil
  See Rush
Pedersen, Herb
  See Desert Rose Band, The
Peduzzi, Larry
  See Roomful of Blues
Pegg, Dave
  See Jethro Tull
Pendergrass, Teddy **3**
Pengilly, Kirk
  See INXS
Penn, Michael **4**
Penner, Fred **10**

Perahia, Murray **10**
Perez, Louie
  See Los Lobos
Perkins, Carl **9**
Perkins, John
  See XTC
Perkins, Steve
  See Jane's Addiction
Perlman, Itzhak **2**
Perry, Doane
  See Jethro Tull
Perry, Joe
  See Aerosmith
Pet Shop Boys **5**
Peter, Paul & Mary **4**
Peters, Bernadette **7**
Peterson, Oscar **11**
Petra **3**
Petty, Tom **9**
Phantom, Slim Jim
  See Stray Cats, The
Phelps, Doug
  See Kentucky Headhunters, The
Phelps, Ricky Lee
  See Kentucky Headhunters, The
Phife
  See A Tribe Called Quest
Phil, Gary
  See Boston
Philips, Anthony
  See Genesis
Phillips, Chynna
  See Wilson Phillips
Phillips, Harvey **3**
Phillips, Sam **5**
Phillips, Simon
  See Judas Priest
Phungula, Inos
  See Ladysmith Black Mambazo
Piaf, Edith **8**
Piccolo, Greg
  See Roomful of Blues
Pickett, Wilson **10**
Pierson, Kate
  See B-52's, The
Pilatus, Rob
  See Milli Vanilli
Pink Floyd **2**
Pinnick, Doug
  See King's X
Pirner, Dave
  See Soul Asylum
Pirroni, Marco
  See Siouxsie and the Banshees
Plant, Robert **2**
  Also see Led Zeppelin
P.M. Dawn **11**
Pogues, The **6**
Poindexter, Buster
  See Johansen, David
Pointer, Anita
  See Pointer Sisters, The
Pointer, Bonnie
  See Pointer Sisters, The
Pointer, June
  See Pointer Sisters, The
Pointer, Ruth
  See Pointer Sisters, The
Pointer Sisters, The **9**
Poison **11**
Poland, Chris
  See Megadeth

Sabo, Dave
  See Bon Jovi
Sade **2**
Sager, Carole Bayer
Sahm, Doug
  See Texas Tornados, The
Sainte-Marie, Buffy **11**
Salerno-Sonnenberg, Nadja **3**
Saliers, Emily
  See Indigo Girls
Salt-N-Pepa **6**
Sam and Dave **8**
Sambora, Richie
  See Bon Jovi
Sampson, Doug
  See Iron Maiden
Samuelson, Gar
  See Megadeth
Samwell-Smith, Paul
  See Yardbirds, The
Sanborn, David **1**
Sanders, Steve
  See Oak Ridge Boys, The
Sanger, David
  See Asleep at the Wheel
Santana, Carlos **1**
Saraceno, Blues
  See Poison
Satriani, Joe **4**
Savage, Rick
  See Def Leppard
Saxa
  See English Beat, The
Scaccia, Mike
  See Ministry
Scarface
  See Geto Boys, The
Schermie, Joe
  See Three Dog Night
Schickele, Peter **5**
Schlitt, John
  See Petra
Schmit, Timothy B.
  See Eagles, The
Schmoovy Schmoove
  See Digital Underground
Schneider, Florian
  See Kraftwerk
Schneider, Fred III
  See B-52's, The
Scholz, Tom
  See Boston
Schuman, William **10**
Schuur, Diane **6**
Scofield, John **7**
Scott, Bon (Ronald Belford)
  See AC/DC
Scruggs, Earl **3**
Seals & Crofts **3**
Seals, Dan **9**
Seals, Jim
  See Seals & Crofts
Sears, Pete
  See Jefferson Starship
Sedaka, Neil **4**
Seeger, Pete **4**
  Also see Weavers, The
Segovia, Andres **6**
Seldom Scene, The **4**
Sen Dog
  See Cypress Hill
Seraphine, Daniel
  See Chicago

Sermon, Erick
  See EPMD
Setzer, Brian
  See Stray Cats, The
Severin, Steven
  See Siouxsie and the Banshees
Severinsen, Doc **1**
Sex Pistols, The **5**
Shabalala, Ben
  See Ladysmith Black Mambazo
Shabalala, Headman
  See Ladysmith Black Mambazo
Shabalala, Jockey
  See Ladysmith Black Mambazo
Shabalala, Joseph
  See Ladysmith Black Mambazo
Shallenberger, James
  See Kronos Quartet
Shane, Bob
  See Kingston Trio, The
Shankar, Ravi **9**
Shannon, Del **10**
Shanté **10**
Shanté, Roxanne
  See Shanté
Sharon, Lois & Bram **6**
Shaw, Artie **8**
Shearer, Harry
  See Smalls, Derek
Sheehan, Fran
  See Boston
Sheila E. **3**
Shelley, Peter
  See Buzzcocks, The
Shelley, Steve
  See Sonic Youth
Sherba, John
  See Kronos Quartet
Sherman, Jack
  See Red Hot Chili Peppers, The
Shirelles, The **11**
Shock G
  See Digital Underground
Shocked, Michelle **4**
Shogren, Dave
  See Doobie Brothers, The
Shontz, Bill
  See Rosenshontz
Shorter, Wayne **5**
Siberry, Jane **6**
Siegal, Janis
  See Manhattan Transfer, The
Sikes, C. David
  See Boston
Sills, Beverly **5**
Silva, Kenny Jo
  See Beaver Brown Band, The
Simmons, Gene
  See Kiss
Simmons, Joe "Run"
  See Run-D.M.C.
Simmons, Patrick
  See Doobie Brothers, The
Simmons, Russell **7**
Simon, Carly **4**
Simon, Paul **1**
Simone, Nina **11**
Simonon, Paul
  See Clash, The
Simpson, Ray
  See Village People, The
Sinatra, Frank **1**

Singer, Eric
  See Black Sabbath
Sioux, Siouxsie
  See Siouxsie and the Banshees
Siouxsie and the Banshees **8**
Sir Rap-A-Lot
  See Geto Boys, The
Sixx, Nikki
  See Mötley Crüe
Skaggs, Ricky **5**
  Also see Country Gentlemen, The
Skillings, Muzz
  See Living Colour
Slash
  See Guns n' Roses
Slayer **10**
Sledd, Dale
  See Osborne Brothers, The
Slick, Grace
  See Jefferson Airplane
Slovak, Hillel
  See Red Hot Chili Peppers, The
Smalls, Derek
  See Spinal Tap
Smith, Adrian
  See Iron Maiden
Smith, Bessie **3**
Smith, Chad
  See Red Hot Chili Peppers, The
Smith, Curt
  See Tears for Fears
Smith, Fred
  See MC5, The
Smith, Garth
  See Buzzcocks, The
Smith, Michael W. **11**
Smith, Parrish
  See EPMD
Smith, Patti **1**
Smith, Robert
  See Cure, The
  Also see Siouxsie and the Banshees
Smith, Smitty
  See Three Dog Night
Smith, Willard
  See DJ Jazzy Jeff and the Fresh Prince
Smiths, The **3**
Sneed, Floyd Chester
  See Three Dog Night
Snow, Don
  See Squeeze
Snow, Phoebe **4**
Solal, Martial **4**
Soloff, Lew
  See Blood, Sweat and Tears
Sondheim, Stephen **8**
Sonic Youth **9**
Sonnenberg, Nadja Salerno
  See Salerno-Sonnenberg, Nadja
Sonnier, Jo-El **10**
Sosa, Mercedes **3**
Soul Asylum **10**
Soul Stirrers, The **11**
Soundgarden **6**
Sousa, John Philip **10**
Spector, Phil **4**
Spence, Skip
  See Jefferson Airplane
Spencer, Jeremy
  See Fleetwood Mac
Spinal Tap **8**
Spitz, Dan
  See Anthrax

Trugoy the Dove
  See De La Soul
Truman, Dan
  See Diamond Rio
Tubb, Ernest **4**
Tubridy, Michael
  See Chieftans, The
Tucker, Moe
  See Velvet Underground, The
Tucker, Tanya **3**
Tufnel, Nigel
  See Spinal Tap
Turbin, Neil
  See Anthrax
Turner, Joe Lynn
  See Deep Purple
Turner, Tina **1**
Turtle Island String Quartet **9**
Twitty, Conway **6**
2Pac
  See Digital Underground
Tyler, Steve
  See Aerosmith
Tyner, McCoy **7**
Tyner, Rob
  See MC5, The
Tyson, Ron
  See Temptations, The
U2 **2**
UB40 **4**
Ulrich, Lars
  See Metallica
Upshaw, Dawn **9**
Vachon, Chris
  See Roomful of Blues
Vai, Steve **5**
  Also see Whitesnake
Valli, Frankie **10**
Vandenburg, Adrian
  See Whitesnake
Vandross, Luther **2**
Van Halen **8**
Van Halen, Alex
  See Van Halen
Van Halen, Edward
  See Van Halen
Vanilla Ice **6**
Van Shelton, Ricky **5**
Van Vliet, Don
  See Captain Beefheart
Van Zant, Johnny
  See Lynyrd Skynyrd
Van Zant, Ronnie
  See Lynyrd Skynyrd
Vaughan, Jimmie
  See Fabulous Thunderbirds, The
Vaughan, Sarah **2**
Vaughan, Stevie Ray **1**
Vega, Suzanne **3**
Velvet Underground, The **7**
Vettese, Peter-John
  See Jethro Tull
Vicious, Sid
  See Sex Pistols, The
  Also see Siouxsie and the Banshees
Village People, The **7**
Vincent, Vinnie
  See Kiss
Vinnie
  See Naughty by Nature
Virtue, Michael
  See UB40

Vito, Rick
  See Fleetwood Mac
Volz, Greg
  See Petra
Von, Eerie
  See Danzig
von Karajan, Herbert **1**
Vox, Bono
  See U2
Wadenius, George
  See Blood, Sweat and Tears
Wagoner, Faidest
  See Soul Stirrers, The
Wahlberg, Donnie
  See New Kids on the Block
Wailer, Bunny **11**
Wainwright III, Loudon **11**
Waits, Tom **1**
Wakeling, David
  See English Beat, The
Wakeman, Rick
  See Yes
Walker, Colin
  See Electric Light Orchestra
Walker, Ebo
  See New Grass Revival, The
Walker, T-Bone **5**
Wallace, Sippie **6**
Waller, Charlie
  See Country Gentlemen, The
Waller, Fats **7**
Wallinger, Karl **11**
Wallis, Larry
  See Motörhead
Walls, Greg
  See Anthrax
Walsh, Joe **5**
  Also see Eagles, The
Ward, Bill
  See Black Sabbath
Warnes, Jennifer **3**
Warren, Mervyn
  See Take 6
Warwick, Dionne **2**
Was, David
  See Was (Not Was)
Was, Don
  See Was (Not Was)
Was (Not Was) **6**
Washington, Dinah **5**
Washington, Grover, Jr. **5**
Waters, Ethel **11**
Waters, Muddy **4**
Waters, Roger
  See Pink Floyd
Watley, Jody **9**
Watson, Doc **2**
Watt, Mike
  See fIREHOSE
Watts, Charlie
  See Rolling Stones, The
Watts, Eugene
  See Canadian Brass, The
Weaver, Louie
  See Petra
Weavers, The **8**
Webber, Andrew Lloyd
  See Lloyd Webber, Andrew
Weir, Bob
  See Grateful Dead, The
Welch, Bob
  See Fleetwood Mac

Wells, Cory
  See Three Dog Night
Wells, Kitty **6**
Welnick, Vince
  See Grateful Dead, The
West, Dottie **8**
Westerberg, Paul
  See Replacements, The
Weymouth, Tina
  See Talking Heads
White, Alan
  See Yes
White, Barry **6**
White, Clarence
  See Byrds, The
Whitesnake **5**
Whitford, Brad
  See Aerosmith
Whitley, Keith **7**
Whitwam, Barry
  See Herman's Hermits
Who, The **3**
Wilder, Alan
  See Depeche Mode
Wilkeson, Leon
  See Lynyrd Skynyrd
Wilkinson, Keith
  See Squeeze
Williams, Andy **2**
Williams, Boris
  See Cure, The
Williams, Cliff
  See AC/DC
Williams, Dana
  See Diamond Rio
Williams, Deniece **1**
Williams, Don **4**
Williams, Hank, Jr. **1**
Williams, Hank, Sr. **4**
Williams, Joe **11**
Williams, John **9**
Williams, Lamar
  See Allman Brothers, The
Williams, Lucinda **10**
Williams, Otis
  See Temptations, The
Williams, Paul
  See Temptations, The
Williams, Paul **5**
Williams, Vanessa **10**
Williamson, Sonny Boy **9**
Willie D.
  See Geto Boys, The
Willis, Larry
  See Blood, Sweat and Tears
Willis, Pete
  See Def Leppard
Willis, Victor
  See Village People, The
Willner, Hal **10**
Wills, Bob **6**
Wilson, Anne
  See Heart
Wilson, Brian
  See Beach Boys, The
Wilson, Carl
  See Beach Boys, The
Wilson, Carnie
  See Wilson Phillips
Wilson, Cindy
  See B-52's, The
Wilson, Dennis
  See Beach Boys, The